WTO AGREEMENT ON SUBSIDIES AND COUNTERVAILING MEASURES

A Commentary

Panels and the WTO Appellate Body have rendered a large number of complex and lengthy rulings on the Agreement on Subsidies and Countervailing Measures. The reasoning behind these rulings is often intimately linked to the underlying facts of a particular case and the methods of litigation adopted by the parties. Without guidance, it is difficult to find and research a specific subsidy issue quickly. This book provides an essential article-by-article commentary on the Agreement and sets out the law as it emerges from this body of rulings, providing the legal basis for further analysis of subsidy disciplines within the realms of economics and political science. It also includes a useful summary of the negotiating history and the links to other WTO Agreements such as GATT 1994. This important reference work will appeal to international trade lawyers, government officials, researchers, students of international trade law, business associations and NGOs.

Wolfgang Müller works in the European Commission (Directorate General for Trade). He leads the policy unit of the Commission's trade remedy services and in this capacity represents the EU in the relevant WTO committees.

WTO AGREEMENT ON SUBSIDIES AND COUNTERVAILING MEASURES

A Commentary

WOLFGANG MÜLLER
Head of Unit, DG Trade H1, European Commission

CAMBRIDGE
UNIVERSITY PRESS

CAMBRIDGE
UNIVERSITY PRESS

University Printing House, Cambridge CB2 8BS, United Kingdom

One Liberty Plaza, 20th Floor, New York, NY 10006, USA

477 Williamstown Road, Port Melbourne, VIC 3207, Australia

4843/24, 2nd Floor, Ansari Road, Daryaganj, Delhi – 110002, India

79 Anson Road, #06-04/06, Singapore 079906

Cambridge University Press is part of the University of Cambridge.

It furthers the University's mission by disseminating knowledge in the pursuit of education, learning, and research at the highest international levels of excellence.

www.cambridge.org
Information on this title: www.cambridge.org/9781108417396
DOI: 10.1017/9781108277549

First published 2017

Printed in the United Kingdom by Clays, St Ives plc

A catalogue record for this publication is available from the British Library.

Library of Congress Cataloging-in-Publication Data
Names: Müller, Wolfgang, 1957 August 29– writer of added commentary.
Title: WTO agreement on subsidies and countervailing measures: a commentary / Wolfgang Müller.
Description: Cambridge [UK]; New York: Cambridge University Press, 2017.
Identifiers: LCCN 2017020805 | ISBN 9781108417396 (hardback)
Subjects: LCSH: Subsidies – Law and legislation. | World Trade Organization. | Antidumping duties – Law and legislation. | Dumping (International trade) – Law and legislation. | Foreign trade regulation. | BISAC: LAW / International.
Classification: LCC K3825 .M85 2017 | DDC 382/.63–dc23
LC record available at https://lccn.loc.gov/2017020805

ISBN 978-1-108-41739-6 Hardback

SYNOPTIC CONTENTS

DETAILED CONTENTS

PREFACE

> A free trade regime that does not reign in or seek to regulate artificial subventions will likely help trigger its own demise.
>
> *Bhagwati* (1988, p. 35)

The WTO *Agreement on Subsidies and Countervailing Measures* (ASCM) was one of the most important achievements of the Uruguay Round of Multilateral Trade Negotiations, and it was a major step in the international regulation of subsidies and anti-subsidy action. With the WTO now comprising more than 160 members including all major economic powers, the ASCM is a truly global charter governing subsidies.

The WTO celebrated its twentieth anniversary in 2015. While rule-making in the WTO proved to be difficult (most notably, the fate of the Doha Development Agenda Negotiations launched in 2001 is uncertain), the WTO's dispute settlement system can clearly be considered a success. After GATT 1994 and the WTO Anti-Dumping Agreement, the ASCM is the WTO agreement that is most frequently referred to in requests for consultations. The largest disputes dealt with by the WTO's dispute settlement mechanism involved subsidies such as the civil aircraft cases that opposed the US and the EU, *US – FSC* and *US – Upland Cotton*. There exists now an important body of rulings adopted by the WTO Dispute Settlement Body that has considerably clarified the ASCM.

This book undertakes to set out comprehensively panel and Appellate Body rulings concerning the ASCM. It is thus meant to be an inventory of the multilateral subsidy disciplines as they have developed over the years. The reasoning developed by panels and the Appellate Body in these rulings is often complex, subtle and intimately linked to the underlying facts and the way the parties litigated their claims. Therefore, the description of the findings normally closely follows the wording employed by panels and the Appellate Body. Moreover, a considerable degree of circumspection is usually warranted when trying to distil more general principles from these rulings.

Subsidies can distort trade, e.g. when they are used as part of the mercantilist toolbox or when they support ailing industries and thus prevent necessary structural changes of the economy. But subsidies can also correct market failures, for instance those linked to climate change. Therefore, it is important that subsidy disciplines target 'bad' subsidies while leaving sufficient policy space to governments to address market failures. This book does not intend to provide an analytical framework for distinguishing 'good' and 'bad' subsidies. Such a task clearly falls into the realm of economics and political science. But by setting out the law as it emerges from this body of rulings, it can serve as a basis for such an analysis.

My former colleagues Steve Gospage and Peter Klein have seen earlier drafts of this book. The text has greatly benefited from their comments and suggestions and the author is very thankful for these contributions. Obviously, all remaining errors are those of the author.

Last but not least, it should be pointed out that the usual disclaimers apply. Any views expressed in this book are personal and cannot be attributed to the European Commission or the EU.

ABBREVIATIONS

ABS	Anti-lock braking system
AD	Anti-dumping
AMS	Aggregated Measurement of Support
AoA	Agreement on Agriculture
APO	Administrative Protective Order
APRG	Advance Payment Refund Guarantee
ASCM	Agreement on Subsidies and Countervailing Measures
BSC	British Steel Corporation
BSES	British Steel Engineering Steels
CASA	Construcciones Aeronáuticas SA
CB	Convertible bonds
CIF	Cost, Insurance, Freight (Incoterm)
CIRR	Commercial Interest Rate Reference under the OECD Arrangement
CKD	Completely knocked-down
CVD	Countervailing duty
DDA	Doha Development Agenda
DOC	Department of Commerce
DRAM	Dynamic Random Access Memory
DSB	Dispute Settlement Body
DSU	Understanding on Rules and Procedures Governing the Settlement of Disputes
EADS	European Aeronautic Defence and Space Company
EBR	Enhanced Bond Requirement
EC	European Communities
EU	European Union
FIT	Feed-In Tariff
FSC	Foreign Sales Corporation
FSC/ETI	Foreign Sales Corporation/Extraterritorial Income
GATS	General Agreement on Trade in Services
GATT 1994	General Agreement on Tariffs and Trade 1994
GDP	Gross Domestic Product

GDR	Global depository receipts
GKN	Guest, Keen and Nettlefields
GOC	Government of China
GOI	Government of India
GOK	Government of Korea
IBK	Industrial Bank of Korea
IMF	International Monetary Fund
IRB	Industrial Revenue Bonds
ITC	International Trade Commission
JIA	Japan's investigating authorities
KDB	Korean Development Bank
KEB	Korea Exchange Bank
KEIC	Korea Export Insurance Corporation
KEXIM	Export-Import Bank of Korea
LA/MSF	Launch Aid/Member State Financing
LCA	Large Commercial Aircraft
LuFo	Luftforschungsprogramm (Aviation Research Programme)
MBB	Messerschmitt Bölkow Blohm GmbH
MOFCOM	Ministry of Commerce of the People's Republic of China
NAFTA	North American Free Trade Agreement
NASA	National Aeronautics and Space Administration
NMDC	National Mineral Development Corporation
PPI	Producers Price Index
PROEX	Programa de Financiamento às Exportações
PSL	Pre shipment loans
R&D	Research & Development
S&D	Special & differential treatment for developing countries
SDF	Steel Development Fund
SOCB	State-owned commercial banks
TDM	Temporary Defensive Mechanism for Shipbuilding
TPC	Technology Partnership Canada
TRIMs	Trade-Related Investment Measures
TRIPS	Trade-Related Aspects of Intellectual Property Rights
UES	United Engineering Steels Limited
UK	United Kingdom
USDOC	United States Department of Commerce
USITC	United States International Trade Commission
WTO	World Trade Organization

TABLE OF CASES

Cases relating to the ASCM. The disputes are listed in chronological order, i.e. by the DS number and thus by the date when the complaining party filed the dispute.

Case	*Also quoted as*
Brazil – Desiccated Coconut	
WT/DS22/R of 17 October 1996, *Brazil – Measures Affecting Desiccated Coconut*	*Brazil – Desiccated Coconut*
WT/DS22/AB/R of 21 February 1997, *Brazil – Measures Affecting Desiccated Coconut*	*Brazil – Desiccated Coconut*
Brazil – Aircraft	
WT/DS46/R of 14 April 1999, *Brazil – Export Financing Programme for Aircraft*	*Brazil – Aircraft*
WT/DS46/AB/R of 2 August 1999, *Brazil – Export Financing Programme for Aircraft*	*Brazil – Aircraft*
WT/DS46/RW of 9 May 2000, *Brazil – Export Financing Programme for Aircraft (Article 21.5, first recourse)*	*Brazil – Aircraft (1st Article 21.5)*
WT/DS46/AB/RW of 21 July 2000, *Brazil – Export Financing Programme for Aircraft (Article 21.5, first recourse)*	*Brazil – Aircraft (1st Article 21.5)*
WT/DS46/RW/2 of 26 July 2001, *Brazil – Export Financing Programme for Aircraft (Article 21.5, second recourse)*	*Brazil – Aircraft (2nd Article 21.5)*
WT/DS46/ARB of 28 August 2000, *Brazil – Export Financing Programme for Aircraft (Arbitration under Articles 22.6 DSU and 4.11 ACSM)*	*Brazil – Aircraft (Arbitration)*

WT/DS108/AB/RW of 14 January 2002, *United States – Tax Treatment for 'Foreign Sales Corporations' (Article 21.5, first recourse)*	*US – FSC (1st Article 21.5)*
WT/DS108/RW of 20 August 2001, *United States – Tax Treatment for 'Foreign Sales Corporations' (Article 21.5, first recourse)*	*US – FSC (1st Article 21.5)*
WT/DS108/ARB of 30 August 2002, *United States – Tax Treatment for 'Foreign Sales Corporations' (Arbitration under Articles 22.6 DSU and 4.11 ASCM)*	*US – FSC (Arbitration)*
WT/DS108/AB/RW2 of 13 February 2006, *United States – Tax Treatment for 'Foreign Sales Corporations' (Article 21.5, second recourse)*	*US – FSC (2nd Article 21.5)*
WT/DS108/RW2 of 30 September 2005, *United States – Tax Treatment for 'Foreign Sales Corporations' (Article 21.5, second recourse)*	*US – FSC (2nd Article 21.5)*
WT/DS108/ARB of 30 August 2002, *United States – Tax Treatment for 'Foreign Sales Corporations' (Arbitration under Articles 22.6 DSU and 4.11 ASCM)*	*US – FSC (Arbitration)*
Australia – Automotive Leather II	
WT/DS126/R of 25 May 1999, *Australia – Subsidies Provided to Producers and Exporters of Automotive Leather*	*Australia – Automotive Leather II*
WT/DS126/RW of 21 January 2000, *Australia – Subsidies Provided to Producers and Exporters of Automotive Leather (Article 21.5)*	*Australia – Automotive Leather II (Article 21.5)*
US – Lead and Bismuth II	
WT/DS138/R of 23 December 1999, *United States – Imposition of Countervailing Duties on Certain Hot-Rolled Lead and Bismuth Carbon Steel Products Originating in the United Kingdom*	*US – Lead and Bismuth II*
WT/DS138/AB/R of 10 May 2000, *United States – Imposition of Countervailing Duties on Certain Hot-Rolled Lead and Bismuth Carbon Steel Products Originating in the United Kingdom*	*US – Lead and Bismuth II*
Canada – Autos	
WT/DS139/R and WT/DS142/R of 11 February 2000, *Canada – Certain Measures Affecting the Automotive Industry*	*Canada – Autos*
WT/DS139/AB/R and WT/DS142/AB/R of 31 May 2000, *Canada – Certain Measures Affecting the Automotive Industry*	*Canada – Autos*

WT/DS139/12 and WT/DS142/12 of 4 October 2000, *Canada – Certain Measures Affecting the Automotive Industry (Arbitration under Article 21(c) of the Understanding on Rules and Procedures Governing the Settlement of Disputes)*	*Canada – Autos*
US – Export Restraints	
WT/DS194/R of 29 June 2001, *United States – Measures Treating Export Restraints as Subsidies*	*US – Export Restraints*
US – Countervailing Measures Concerning Certain Products from the EC	
WT/DS212/R of 31 July 2002, *United States – Countervailing Measures Concerning Certain Products from the European Communities*	*US – Countervailing Measures Concerning Certain Products from the EC*
WT/DS212/AB/R of 9 December 2002, *United States – Countervailing Measures Concerning Certain Products from the European Communities*	*US – Countervailing Measures Concerning Certain Products from the EC*
WT/DS212/RW of 17 August 2005, *United States – Countervailing Measures Concerning Certain Products from the European Communities (Article 21.5)*	*US – Countervailing Measures Concerning Certain Products from the EC (Article 21.5)*
US – Carbon Steel	
WT/DS213/R of 3 July 2002, *United States – Countervailing Duties on Certain Corrosion-Resistant Carbon Steel Flat Products from Germany*	*US – Carbon Steel*
WT/DS213/AB/R of 28 November 2002, *United States – Countervailing Duties on Certain Corrosion-Resistant Carbon Steel Flat Products from Germany*	*US – Carbon Steel*
US – Offset Act (Byrd Amendment)	
WT/DS217/R and WT/DS234/R of 16 September 2002, *United States – Continued Dumping and Subsidy Offset Act of 2000*	*US – Offset Act (Byrd Amendment)*

WT/DS217/AB/R and WT/DS234/AB/R of 16 January 2003, *United States – Continued Dumping and Subsidy Offset Act of 2000*	*US – Offset Act (Byrd Amendment)*
Canada – Aircraft Credits and Guarantees	
WT/DS222/R of 28 January 2002, *Canada – Export Credits and Loan Guarantees for Regional Aircraft*	*Canada – Aircraft Credits and Guarantees*
WT/DS222/ARB of 17 February 2003, *Canada – Export Credits and Loan Guarantees for Regional Aircraft (Arbitration under Articles 22.6 DSU and 4.11 ASCM)*	*Canada – Aircraft Credits and Guarantees (Arbitration)*
US – Softwood Lumber III	
WT/DS236/R of 27 September 2002, *United States – Preliminary Determinations with Respect to Certain Softwood Lumber from Canada*	*US – Softwood Lumber III*
US – Softwood Lumber IV	
WT/DS257/R of 29 August 2003, *United States – Final Countervailing Duty Determination with Respect to Certain Softwood Lumber from Canada*	*US – Softwood Lumber IV*
WT/DS257/AB/R of 19 January 2004, *United States – Final Countervailing Duty Determination with Respect to Certain Softwood Lumber from Canada*	*US – Softwood Lumber IV*
WT/DS257/RW of 1 August 2005, *United States – Final Countervailing Duty Determination with Respect to Certain Softwood Lumber from Canada* (Article 21.5)	*US – Softwood Lumber IV (Article 21.5)*
EC – Export Subsidies on Sugar	
WT/DS265/R, WT/DS266/R and WT/DS283/R of 15 October 2004, *European Communities – Export Subsidies on Sugar*	*EC – Export Subsidies on Sugar*
WT/DS265/AB/R, WT/DS266/AB/R and WT/DS283/AB/R of 28 April 2005, *European Communities – Export Subsidies on Sugar*	*EC – Export Subsidies on Sugar*
US – Upland Cotton	
WT/DS267/R of 8 September 2004, *United States – Subsidies on Upland Cotton*	*US – Upland Cotton*
WT/DS267/AB/R of 3 March 2005, *United States – Subsidies on Upland Cotton*	*US – Upland Cotton*
WT/DS267/RW of 18 December 2007, *United States – Subsidies on Upland Cotton (Article 21.5)*	*US – Upland Cotton (Article 21.5)*

WT/DS267/AB/RW of 16 May 2008, *United States – Subsidies on Upland Cotton (Article 21.5)*	*US – Upland Cotton (Article 21.5)*
WT/DS267/ARB/1 of 31 August 2009, *United States – Subsidies on Upland Cotton (Arbitration under Article 22.6 DSU and 4.11 ASCM)*	*US – Upland Cotton (Arbitration under Articles 22.6 DSU and 4.11 ASCM)*
WT/DS267/ARB/2 of 31 August 2009, *United States – Subsidies on Upland Cotton (Arbitration under Article 22.6 DSU and 7.10 ASCM)*	*US – Upland Cotton (Arbitration under Articles 22.6 DSU and 7.10 ASCM)*
Korea – Commercial Vessels	
WT/DS273/R of 7 March 2005, *Korea – Measures Affecting Trade in Commercial Vessels*	*Korea – Commercial Vessels*
US – Softwood Lumber VI	
WT/DS277/R of 22 March 2004, *United States – Investigation of the International Trade Commission in Softwood Lumber from Canada*	*US – Softwood Lumber VI*
WT/DS277/RW of 15 November 2005, *United States – Investigation of the International Trade Commission in Softwood Lumber from Canada – Recourse to Article 21.5 of the DSU by Canada*	*US – Softwood Lumber VI (Article 21.5)*
WT/DS277/AB/RW of 13 April 2006, *United States – Investigation of the International Trade Commission in Softwood Lumber from Canada – Recourse to Article 21.5 of the DSU by Canada*	*US – Softwood Lumber VI (Article 21.5)*
Mexico – Beef and Rice	
WT/DS295/R of 6 June 2005, *Mexico – Definitive Anti-Dumping Measures on Beef and Rice / Complaint with Respect to Rice*	*Mexico – Beef and Rice*
WT/DS295/AB/R of 29 November 2005, *Mexico – Definitive Anti-Dumping Measures on Beef and Rice / Complaint with Respect to Rice*	*Mexico – Beef and Rice*
US – Countervailing Duty Investigation on DRAMs	
WT/DS296/R of 21 February 2005, *United States – Countervailing Duty Investigation on Dynamic Random Access Memory Semiconductors (DRAMs) from Korea*	*US – Countervailing Duty Investigation on DRAMs*

WT/DS296/AB/R of 27 June 2005, *United States – Countervailing Duty Investigation on Dynamic Random Access Memory Semiconductors (DRAMs) from Korea*	*US – Countervailing Duty Investigation on DRAMs*
EC – Countervailing Measures on DRAM Chips	
WT/DS299/R of 17 June 2005, *European Communities – Countervailing Measures on Dynamic Random Access Memory Chips from Korea*	*EC – Countervailing Measures on DRAM Chips*
EC – Commercial Vessels	
WT/DS301/R of 22 April 2005, *EC – Measures Affecting Trade in Commercial Vessels*	*EC – Commercial Vessels*
EC and certain Member States – Large Civil Aircraft	
WT/DS316/R of 30 June 2010, *EC and certain Member States – Measures Affecting Trade in Large Civil Aircraft*	*EC and certain Member States – Large Civil Aircraft*
WT/DS316/AB/R of 18 May 2011, *EC and certain Member States – Measures Affecting Trade in Large Civil Aircraft*	*EC and certain Member States – Large Civil Aircraft*
WT/DS316/RW of 22 September 2016, *EC and certain Member States – Measures Affecting Trade in Large Civil Aircraft – Recourse to Article 21.5 of the DSU by the United States*	*EC and certain Member States – Large Civil Aircraft (Article 21.5)*
Japan – DRAMs (Korea)	
WT/DS336/R of 13 July 2007, *Japan – Countervailing Duties on Dynamic Random Access Memories from Korea*	*Japan – DRAMs (Korea)*
WT/DS336/AB/R of 28 November 2007, *Japan – Countervailing Duties on Dynamic Random Access Memories from Korea*	*Japan – DRAMs (Korea)*
Mexico – Olive Oil	
WT/DS341/R of 4 September 2008, *Mexico – Definitive Countervailing Measures on Olive Oil from the European Communities*	*Mexico – Olive Oil*
US – Customs Bond Directive	
WT/DS345/R of 29 February 2008, *United States – Customs Bond Directive for Merchandise Subject to Anti-Dumping/Countervailing Duties*	*US – Customs Bond Directive*

WT/DS343/AB/R and WT/DS345/AB/R of 16 July 2008, *United States – Measures Relating to Shrimp from Thailand* and *United States – Customs Bond Directive for Merchandise Subject to Anti-Dumping/ Countervailing Duties*	*US – Customs Bond Directive*
US – Large Civil Aircraft (2nd complaint)	
WT/DS353/R of 31 March 2011, *United States – Measures Affecting Trade in Large Civil Aircraft (Second Complaint)*	*US – Large Civil Aircraft (2nd complaint)*
WT/DS353/AB/R of 12 March 2012, *United States – Measures Affecting Trade in Large Civil Aircraft (Second Complaint)*	*US – Large Civil Aircraft (2nd complaint)*
US – Anti-Dumping and Countervailing Duties (China)	
WT/DS379/R of 22 October 2010, *United States – Definitive Anti-Dumping and Countervailing Duties on Certain Products from China*	*US – Anti-Dumping and Countervailing Duties (China)*
WT/DS379/AB/R of 11 March 2011, *United States – Definitive Anti-Dumping and Countervailing Duties on Certain Products from China*	*US – Anti-Dumping and Countervailing Duties (China)*
Canada – Renewable Energy & Feed-In Tariff Program	
WT/DS412/R and WT/DS426/R of 19 December 2012, *Canada – Certain Measures Affecting the Renewable Energy Generation Sector; Canada – Measures Relating to Feed-In Tariff Program*	*Canada – Renewable Energy & Feed-In Tariff Program*
WT/DS412/AB/R and WT/DS426/AB/R of 6 May 2013, *Canada – Certain Measures Affecting the Renewable Energy Generation Sector; Canada – Measures Relating to Feed-In Tariff Program*	*Canada – Renewable Energy & Feed-In Tariff Program*
China – GOES	
WT/DS414/R of 15 June 2012, *China – Countervailing and Anti-Dumping Duties on Grain-Oriented Flat-Rolled Electrical Steel from the United States*	*China – GOES*
WT/DS414/AB/R of 18 October 2012, *China – Countervailing and Anti-Dumping Duties on Grain Oriented Flat-Rolled Electrical Steel from the United States*	*China – GOES*

China – Broiler Products	
WT/DS427/R of 2 August 2013, *China – Anti-Dumping and Countervailing Duty Measures on Broiler Products from the United States*	*China – Broiler Products*
US – Carbon Steel (India)	
WT/DS436/R of 14 July 2014, *United States – Countervailing Measures on Certain Hot-Rolled Carbon Steel Flat Products from India*	*US – Carbon Steel (India)*
WT/DS436/AB/R of 8 December 2014, *United States – Countervailing Measures on Certain Hot-Rolled Carbon Steel Flat Products from India*	*US – Carbon Steel (India)*
US – Countervailing Measures (China)	
WT/DS437/R of 14 July 2014, *United States – Countervailing Duty Measures on Certain Products from China*	*US – Countervailing Measures (China)*
WT/DS437/AB/R of 18 December 2014, *United States – Countervailing Duty Measures on Certain Products from China*	*US – Countervailing Measures (China)*
China – Autos (US)	
WT/DS440/R of 23 May 2014, *China – Anti-Dumping and Countervailing Duties on Certain Automobiles from the United States*	*China – Autos (US)*
US – Washing Machines	
WT/DS464/R of 11 March 2016, *United States – Anti-Dumping and Countervailing Measures on Large Residential Washers from Korea*	*US – Washing Machines*
WT/DS464/AB/R of 7 September 2016, *United States – Anti-Dumping and Countervailing Measures on Large Residential Washers from Korea*	*US – Washing Machines*
US – Tax Incentives	
WT/DS487/R of 28 November 2016, *United States – Conditional Tax Incentives for Large Civil Aircraft*	*US – Tax Incentives*

Cases relating to other WTO provisions

Case	***Also quoted as***
WT/DS8/AB/R, WT/DS10/AB/R and WT/DS11/AB/R of 4 October 1996, *Japan – Taxes on Alcoholic Beverages*	*Alcoholic Beverages*
WT/DS27/AB/R of 9 September 1997, *European Communities – Regime for the Importation, Sale and Distribution of Bananas*	*EC – Bananas III*
WT/DS27/ARB of 9 April 1999, *European Communities – Regime for the Importation, Sale and Distribution of Bananas – Recourse to Arbitration by the European Communities under Article 22.6 of the DSU*	
WT/DS60/AB/R of 2 November 1998, *Guatemala – Anti-Dumping Investigation Regarding Portland Cement from Mexico*	*Guatemala – Cement I*
WT/DS121/AB/R of 14 December 1999, *Argentina – Safeguard Measures on Imports of Footwear*	*Argentina – Footwear*
WT/DS122/R of 28 September 2000, *Thailand – Anti-Dumping Duties on Angles, Shapes and Sections of Iron or Non-Alloy Steel and H-Beams from Poland*	*Thailand – H-Beams*
WT/DS122/AB/R of 12 March 2001, *Thailand – Anti-Dumping Duties on Angles, Shapes and Sections of Iron or Non-Alloy Steel and H-Beams from Poland*	*Thailand – H-Beams*
WT/DS132/R of 28 January 2000, *Mexico – Anti-Dumping Investigation into High Fructose Corn Syrup (HFCS) from the United States*	*Mexico – Corn Syrup*
WT/DS141/R of 30 October 2000, *European Communities – Anti-Dumping Duties on Imports of Cotton-Type Bed Linen from India*	*EC – Bed Linen*
WT/DS141/RW of 29 November 2002, *European Communities – Anti-Dumping Duties on Imports of Cotton-Type Bed Linen from India – Recourse to Article 21.5 of the DSU by India*	*EC – Bed Linen*
WT/DS156/R of 24 October 2000, *Guatemala – Definitive Anti-Dumping Measures on Grey Portland Cement from Mexico*	*Guatemala – Cement II*
WT/DS177/AB/R and WT/DS178/AB/R of 1 May 2001, *United States – Safeguard Measures on Imports of Fresh, Chilled or Frozen Lamb Meat from New Zealand and Australia*, para 124	*US – Lamb*

WT/DS184/R of 28 February 2001, *United States – Anti-Dumping Measures on Certain Hot-Rolled Steel Products from Japan*	*US – Hot-Rolled Steel*
WT/DS184/AB/R of 24 July 2001, *United States – Anti-Dumping Measures on Certain Hot-Rolled Steel Products from Japan*	*US – Hot-Rolled Steel*
WT/DS189/R of 28 September 2001, *Argentina – Definitive Anti-Dumping Measures on Imports of Ceramic Floor Tiles from Italy*	*Argentina – Ceramic Tiles*
WT/DS219/R of 7 March 2003, *European Communities – Anti-Dumping Duties on Malleable Cast Iron Tube or Pipe Fittings from Brazil*	*EC – Tube or Pipe Fittings*
WT/DS219/AB/R of 22 July 2003, *European Communities – Anti-Dumping Duties on Malleable Cast Iron Tube or Pipe Fittings from Brazil*	*EC – Tube or Pipe Fittings*
WT/DS241/R of 22 April 2003, *Argentina – Definitive Anti-Dumping Duties on Poultry from Brazil*	*Argentina – Poultry Anti-Dumping Duties*
WT/DS248/R, WT/DS249/R, WT/DS251/R, WT/DS252/R, WT/DS253/R, WT/DS254/R, WT/DS258/R and WT/DS259/R of 11 July 2003, *United States – Definitive Safeguard Measures on Imports of Certain Steel Products*	*US – Steel Products*
WT/DS264/R of 13 April 2004, *United States – Final Dumping Determination on Softwood Lumber from Canada*	*US – Softwood Lumber V*
WT/DS268/AB/R of 29 November 2004, *United States – Sunset Reviews of Anti-Dumping Measures on Oil Country Tubular Goods from Argentina*	*US – Oil Country Tubular Goods Sunset Reviews*
WT/DS294/AB/R of 9 May 2006, *United States – Laws, Regulations and Methodology for Calculating Dumping Margins (Zeroing)*	*US – Zeroing (EC)*
WT/DS295/AB/R of 29 November 2005, *Mexico – Definitive Anti-Dumping Measures on Beef and Rice / Complaint with Respect to Rice*	*Mexico – Anti-Dumping Measures on Rice*
WT/DS312/R of 28 October 2005, *Korea – Anti-Dumping Duties on Imports of Certain Paper from Indonesia*	*Korea – Certain Paper*
WT/DS331/R of 8 June 2007, *Mexico – Anti-Dumping Duties on Steel Pipes and Tubes from Guatemala*	*Mexico – Steel Pipes and Tubes*

WT/DS339/AB/R, WT/DS340/AB/R and WT/DS342/AB/R of 15 December 2008, *China – Measures Affecting Imports of Automobile Parts*	*China – Auto Parts*
WT/DS350/AB/R of 4 February 2009, *United States – Continued Existence and Application of Zeroing Methodology*	*US – Continued Zeroing*
WT/DS394/AB/R, WT/DS395/AB/R and WT/DS398/AB/R of 30 January 2012, *China – Measures Related to the Exportation of Various Raw Materials*	*China – Raw Materials*
WT/DS397/R of 3 December 2010, *European Communities – Definitive Anti-Dumping Measures on Certain Iron or Steel Fasteners from China*	*EC – Fasteners (China)*
WT/DS397/AB/R of 15 July 2011, *European Communities – Definitive Anti-Dumping Measures on Certain Iron or Steel Fasteners from China*	*EC – Fasteners (China)*
WT/DS405/R of 28 October 2011, *European Union – Anti-Dumping Measures on Certain Footwear from China*	*EU – Footwear (China)*
WT/DS425/R of 26 February 2013, *China – Definitive Anti-Dumping Duties on X-Ray Security Inspection Equipment from the European Union*	*China – X-Ray Equipment*

Pre WTO cases

Case	***Also quoted as***
Panel on Subsidies and State Trading, Report on Subsidies, L/1160 of 23 March 1960	
EC – Refunds on Exports of Sugar – Complaint by Australia, adopted on 6 November 1979, BISD 26S/290	
EC – Refunds on Exports of Sugar – Complaint by Brazil, adopted on 10 November 1980, BISD 27S/69	
European Economic Community – Payments and Subsidies Paid to Processors and Producers of Oilseeds and Related Animal-Feed Proteins, adopted on 25 January 1990, BISD 37S/86	*EEC – Oilseeds I*
United States – Countervailing Duties on Fresh, Chilled and Frozen Pork from Canada, adopted on 11 July 1991, BISD 38S/30	*US – Canadian Pork*
Korea – Anti-Dumping Duties on Imports of Polyacetal Resin from the United States, adopted on 27 April 1993, BISD 40S/205	*Korea – Resins*

I

INTRODUCTION

Principle Features of the ASCM and Intervention Logic

Principle Features of the ASCM

The subsidy disciplines set out in the ASCM apply to goods, but not to services.[1] Three constituent elements define a subsidy according to the ASCM, i.e.

(1) a financial contribution (or alternatively any form of income and price support in the sense of Article XVI of GATT 1994)
(2) given by the government or a public body that
(3) confers a benefit on the recipient of such contribution.[2]

Moreover, only subsidies that are specific to an enterprise or industry or groups of enterprises or industries (as opposed to being broadly available in the exporting country) fall under the remit of the ASCM.[3]

The ASCM distinguishes two types of subsidies. First, certain subsidies are prohibited *per se*. These are export subsidies and import substitution subsidies as defined by Article 3. Second, all other subsidies that meet the definition of Article 1 and that are specific can only be challenged if they cause certain negative effects. The ASCM, as it emerged from the Uruguay Round negotiations also contained a third type of subsidies, namely 'non-actionable' or 'green light' subsidies (certain R&D, environmental and regional subsidies). However, the provisions creating this carve-out expired by the end of 1999.[4]

As can be inferred from the aforementioned definition of a subsidy, the ASCM does not take into consideration whether or not the government pursues a legitimate purpose by granting the subsidy. Since the expiry of

[1] A detailed study on subsidies in the GATS context can be found in *Poretti* (2009).
[2] Article 1.
[3] Article 2.
[4] Articles 8, 9 and 31.

the provisions on green light subsidies, the objectives pursued by a government when providing subsidies are no longer relevant for the analysis under the ASCM.[5]

Under the WTO Dispute Settlement System, subsidies other than those that are prohibited pursuant to Article 3 can only be challenged if imports benefitting from such subsidies cause injury to the industry producing the like product in the importing country (cf. Article 15) or if the subsidies result in the adverse effects listed in Articles 5 and 6. Such phenomena include displacement or impedance of imports of the competing product into the market of the subsidizing WTO Member or a third country market, loss of market share, price undercutting etc. In short, and as *Hahn/Mehta* (2013) have put it, if a WTO Member grants a subsidy, the ASCM imposes only an obligation to do no harm to fellow Members, unless such subsidy is prohibited pursuant to Article 3.[6]

Self-help against subsidies is also permitted in the form of countervailing duties (a synonym for anti-subsidy duties). In other words, an importing country can impose an anti-subsidy duty on imports of a product found to be subsidized, if it has respected the provisions of Part V of the ASCM. This implies a number of steps. First, normally the industry of the importing country has filed an application containing sufficient *prima facie* evidence that the imports of a product are benefitting from a subsidy and that these imports have caused injury to the competing domestic industry of the importing country.[7] Second, if the investigating authority of the importing country considers the evidence submitted sufficient, it will open an investigation by giving public notice and requesting interested parties (including the government of the exporting country allegedly engaging in subsidization) to submit evidence (the information requirements are usually specified in a questionnaire issued by the investigating authority). Interested parties known to the investigating authority will also be informed directly. Parties have a minimum of 30 days to reply to the questionnaire.[8] Third, the investigating authority will then assure itself of the accuracy of the information submitted, typically by carrying out on-the-spot verifications on the premises of the government of the exporting country, exporters, the domestic industry and importers.[9] Fourth, based on the totality of the evidence on file, the investigating

[5] See also *Cosbey/Mavroidis* (2014) p. 16 *et passim*.

[6] *Hahn/Mehta* (2013) p. 141.

[7] Article 11.

[8] Article 12 (see also footnote 40 attached to Article 12.1.1).

[9] Articles 12.5 and 12.6.

authority will then draw up its conclusions as to the existence of injurious subsidization of the subject imports. Before imposing any definitive countervailing duties, all parties receive disclosure of these findings and have the possibility to comment.[10] The investigation can last up to a maximum of 18 months.[11] A countervailing duty can remain in force as long and to the extent necessary to counteract injurious subsidization. However, if the duty is to remain in force longer than five years, the investigating authority of the importing country will examine in a review whether there is a likelihood of continuation or recurrence of injurious subsidization. This type of review is commonly referred to as 'expiry review' or 'sunset review'.[12]

Four more features of countervailing action are noteworthy for the purposes of an introduction:

- In 'special circumstances' (which remain undefined in the ASCM), the investigating authority can also initiate an investigation on its own initiative, i.e. without an application submitted by the industry of the importing country. However, an investigating authority can only do so if it has sufficient *prima facie* evidence of injurious subsidization.[13]
- Exporting producers, the third country government and importers are not obliged to cooperate in a countervailing duty investigation. To the extent these parties do not cooperate, the investigating authority can use so-called 'facts available' in order to replace the information that was missing as a result of such non-cooperation. The possibility to use 'facts available' is therefore an important mechanism to induce cooperation by interested parties.[14]
- A provisional countervailing duty can be imposed not sooner than 60 days after initiation of the investigation. It can be applied for a maximum period of four months.[15]
- As an alternative to a countervailing duty, exporters and the government of the country of exports of the subsidized merchandise can also undertake to eliminate the subsidy or to raise export prices so that the effect of the subsidy is eliminated. The investigating authority enjoys considerable discretion when deciding whether or not to accept such an undertaking.[16]

[10] Article 12.8.
[11] Article 11.11.
[12] Articles 21.1 and 21.3.
[13] Article 11.6.
[14] Article 12.7.
[15] Articles 17.3 and 17.4.
[16] Article 18.

As can be inferred from the above, the ASCM generally structures any action against subsidies by linking them to a product and the effect of such subsidized merchandise on like products of other WTO Members. The term 'like product' is defined in Footnote 46 of the ASCM. A rough working hypothesis would suggest that the like product is typically the product competing with the subsidized export.

The WTO dispute settlement track is only open to governments of WTO Members while the countervailing duty track is normally triggered by an application of the industry in the importing country that competes with the subsidized merchandise. This differentiation is justified by the supposition that governments, when engaging in formal dispute settlement, will balance other considerations against the demand of its domestic industry to have relief from the effects of subsidized imports.[17]

Special rules apply with regard to subsidies provided by developing country Members (see Article 27) and to agricultural subsidies (see *infra* pp. 37–46).

Rationale of Anti-Subsidy Action

Subsidies as a Means to Influence Market Access

The object and purpose of the ASCM is described in more detail *infra* pp. 16–19. In a nutshell, and based on DSB rulings, its object and purpose can be summarized as to increase and improve disciplines relating to the use of both subsidies and countervailing measures.

The discussion of this topic amongst scholars is broader. Their position on subsidy control depends to a large extent on their perception of the aim and the effects of subsidies. At the outset, it should, however, be noted that economic theory has not provided yet a definition of the term 'subsidy' with sufficiently clear contours.[18]

Multilateral trade liberalization, and hence also the focus of the WTO project, is about creating opportunities for access to foreign markets. Prior to the Uruguay Round such improved market access was essentially achieved through various multilateral rounds of tariff reductions. These were conducted within the GATT framework. The Uruguay Round went beyond this by providing in addition market access in the fields of

[17] *Hufbauer/Erb* (1984) p. 24.
[18] *Rubini* (2009) p. 4.

services and public procurement.[19] It also resulted in a number of further agreements which had the purpose of further safeguarding agreed tariff reductions and services liberalization, e.g. the TRIPs Agreement and the ASCM.

Turning to the trade effects of a subsidy, the effect that first comes to mind is that a subsidy can have similar effects as an import tariff. A tariff increases the cost of the imported merchandise and thus makes it easier for the domestic industry to compete with imports. A government that subsidizes an industry simply reduces the costs of the subsidy recipient. This in turn allows the subsidized industry to lower its prices and to become more competitive *vis-à-vis* imports. Thus, a subsidy may represent a government-induced obstacle to international trade in the same way as an import tariff. Or, put differently, a government that has accepted to reduce or dismantle its import tariffs in a round of tariff liberalizations may undo its promise by providing subsidies.[20] This was the underlying logic for introducing some subsidy disciplines into the GATT 1947, notably its Articles VI and XVI.[21]

The effects of a subsidy may also be felt beyond the boundaries of the domestic market of the subsidizing country. Indeed, products benefitting from a subsidy can possibly compete more easily on overseas markets. This is true both with regard to overseas markets which do not have their own proper domestic production and which are therefore exclusively served by imports from various countries. But it is also true with regard to markets where domestic producers offer competing merchandise. Whether a subsidy for a given product has effects beyond the borders of the subsidizing country depends on the competitive position of the producers receiving such subsidies. The subsidy may indeed simply have the effect of fending off import competition if the domestic industry is not globally competitive. In short, in the context of influencing market access, the objectives pursued by the provision of a subsidy are structurally not much

19 The Agreement on Government Procurement is, however, only a plurilateral agreement.

20 According to *Janow/Staiger* (2003) p. 207, in order to replicate the economic effects of any particular (non-prohibitive) tariff on any particular import good, the removed tariff needs to be replaced not only by (i) a subsidy to domestic production of that particular good, but in addition also by (ii) a tax on domestic consumption of that particular good. Moreover, both the subsidy and the consumption tax must be applied at the same rate as the import tariff they replace.

21 See e.g. *Wouters/Coppens* (2010) p. 50 with further references and *Bagwell/Mavroidis* (2010) p. 170. Note, however, that the WTO system of remedies against actionable and prohibited subsidies is in no way linked to the level of tariff concessions made by the subsidizing country.

different as compared to those underlying tariffs, quotas and other more broader obstacles to market access.

But granting a subsidy does not necessarily only pursue 'defensive' purposes. It can also be a strategic tool to strengthen the competitive position of the domestic industry and to facilitate its expansion in overseas markets. A government may for instance attempt to create national champions which gradually develop into global champions, and this process is facilitated because the company operates from an incontestable home market base.[22] Producers benefitting from a protected home market have the possibility to earn enough money (combined with increased economies of scale because such a firm will produce and sell more than it would do without such protection) to challenge export markets. In addition to being able to charge lower prices (as described above) a company can also exploit the subsidy received to develop products which it could not have developed absent that subsidy, or market such products much earlier than without being subsidized.[23] In this context, subsidies used to bail out a company, i.e. to keep it artificially alive, can also play a role.[24]

In other words, subsidies can have a lasting impact on competition because they improve the competitive situation of exporters benefitting from them, at the expense of overseas competitors that do not enjoy such support.

Subsidies as a Means to Remedy Market Failures or to Pursue Other Policy Objectives

The purpose of providing a subsidy is not necessarily linked to the conquest of markets or to keep ailing industries on a lifeline. Subsidies can also be designed to remedy market failures (in particular, public goods and externalities). For instance, companies tend to spend on R&D only to the extent that they expect to internalize the benefits from such expenditure. Thus, the private sector underinvests in R&D and subsidies could compensate for this suboptimal level of R&D. By providing subsidies, a government can also pursue other policy objectives (e.g. those linked to equity and justice).

22 On the issue of strategic trade policy see also the next section.

23 See *infra* the commentary to Article 6, pp. 347–350.

24 See *infra* Article 1, pp. 115–122.

Therefore, subsidies may tackle a variety of objectives, e.g. reducing pollution, addressing climate change and environmental degradation, enhancing energy security, boosting R&D, encouraging the development of disadvantaged regions, facilitating the (re-)integration of unemployed in the labour market. Subsidies were indeed instrumental in promoting renewable energies. Note, however, that subsidies are not necessarily the only means to achieve these objectives.

The argument has been made that trade policy, in general, and subsidies, in particular, should be put at the service of infant industries in less developed countries and/or be used in developed countries to support high-technology industries and/or industries characterized by imperfect competition. These issues are sometimes discussed under the heading 'strategic trade policy', which, however, covers a broader range of issues. The special cases of market failures that are put forward in this context are imperfect capital markets and the problem of appropriability. The latter occurs if – in order to enter a market or develop a product – firms should generate knowledge that other firms can use without paying for it, e.g. by imitating the ideas of the first mover. A firm has normally no incentive to 'produce' such knowledge. Therefore, to make the development of the industry, the high-tech product etc. happen, there could be a case for subsidizing such industry. However, there are also a number of pitfalls associated with this approach. It will be difficult to identify good candidates, i.e. industries or companies that fit into this category because innovation and technological spillovers also happen in industries that are not all high-tech. Moreover, as described in the preceding section, this type of government intervention typically negatively affects overseas competitors that in turn will urge their governments to take appropriate counteractions. In short, this could provoke a 'subsidy war', i.e. the provision of subsidies by one government can trigger similar actions by other governments, or even risk trade wars. None of these are desirable.[25]

It is not the purpose of this book to review the discussion as to when subsidy action in the pursuit of policy objectives is economically efficient or politically justified let alone to develop a theory of such intervention.[26] Suffice it to mention that the current text of the ASCM does not distinguish between acceptable and non-acceptable subsidies on the basis of the policy

[25] *Krugman/Obstfeld/Melitz* (2015) p. 308 *et seq.*, p. 324 *et seq.*

[26] For a discussion of an intervention logic against subsidies (including appropriate remedies) based on economic criteria, see e.g. *Howse* (2010) p. 87 *et seq.* and *Coppens* (2014) pp. 588–600, *Cosby* (2013) pp. 8–10, all with further references.

objectives underlying the provision of the subsidy. Article 8 contained a number of provisions that classified certain subsidies as non-actionable. These non-actionable subsidies concerned assistance to R&D activities, assistance to disadvantaged regions and assistance to promote the adaptation of existing facilities to new environmental requirements. However, Article 8 expired by the end of 1999 by virtue of Article 31.[27] Therefore, today the scope of subsidy control under the ASCM is determined by its Article 1 that contains the definition of a subsidy and thus fixes the outer boundaries of the application of the ASCM. This definition does not distinguish between policy objectives. Rather, the ASCM employs a formal definition. The dividing line between government intervention that is permitted/not actionable and that is not permitted/actionable is essentially defined by criteria that are closely linked to the neutrality of such government action *vis-à-vis* the competitive process. Indeed, no subsidy exists if there is no financial contribution by the government to its industry (i.e. if the government action is purely regulatory),[28] if the government action is not specific (i.e. the subsidy is widely available in the economy),[29] or, if the recipient does not receive a benefit (i.e. if the financial contribution is given on market terms).[30] Moreover, with the exception of export subsidies and local content subsidies that are prohibited pursuant to Article 3, subsidies provided by a WTO Member can only be challenged if they create some sort of harm to the interests of another Member, i.e. injury to the domestic industry in the importing country as defined by Article 15 or if the subsidy causes one or more of the phenomena listed in Articles 5 and 6.

Why Anti-Subsidy Action?

The preceding two sections described the effects of subsidies on international trade as well as the function of subsidies to compensate for market failure. This section explores some of the rationales underlying the WTO system of remedies against subsidies (countervailing duties and the dispute settlement track). It would, however, go beyond the scope of this book to provide a comprehensive analysis as to why such action is taken or should (or should not) be taken.

Some scholars view action against subsidies (but also subsidies themselves – see the preceding section) in a much nuanced way. Certainly,

[27] See *infra* the commentary to Article 31.

[28] See *infra* pp. 73–105.

[29] See *infra* the commentary to Article 2.

[30] See *infra* pp. 125–160.

from the perspective of the welfare of an importing country that has no domestic industry competing with the subsidized imports, one could argue that such imports are beneficial (except in the rare case of predation). Consumers in such a third country simply get cheaper products while the negative effects of subsidies are felt elsewhere. Subsidies reduce the welfare of the subsidizing country and of exporters located in countries that do not receive subsidies and whose exports to that third country might therefore be displaced or be subject to increased price pressure.[31] Economic theory has also advanced the argument that subsidies have overall positive welfare effects for the importing country even if this country has a domestic industry competing with the imported subsidized product.[32] Or, as *Jackson* has so succinctly summarized this position, the importing country should just send a 'thank-you note' to the subsidizing nation.[33]

The system of remedies against subsidies provided for in the ASCM has also been viewed critically. Some recall the link between tariffs and subsidies and distinguish between 'new' and 'existing' subsidies in relation to the time when the tariff concession was made. As subsidies can frustrate tariff concessions made previously, they accept action against such new subsidies as a means to enhance the value of the tariff concession. However, challenges of subsidies that existed at the time when the tariff concession was made would not be compatible with that opinion.[34] Others that are critical against any anti-subsidy action point out that the ASCM does not necessarily distinguish adequately between 'good' subsidies (that address market failures) and 'bad' subsidies (that are trade distorting).[35] It is submitted that this criticism is ultimately not convincing. The text of Article 1 ASCM as interpreted by relevant DSB rulings has by and large ensured that anti-subsidy action does not hamper in any major way the pursuit of legitimate policy concerns.[36]

Using as a starting point the view that some subsidies are 'good', it has also been argued that action against subsidies as foreseen by the ASCM is overshooting. This view points out that the level of a countervailing duty is

[31] *Janow/Staiger* (2004) pp. 284–285.

[32] *Evaluation Study* (2012) p. 21; *Bagwell/Staiger* (2004) pp. 179–180.

[33] *Jackson* (2000) p. 281. See also *Janow/Staiger* (2003) p. 204 and p. 205.

[34] *Janow/Staiger* (2003) pp. 210–215. The appropriate action would, however, be something more in the form of a non-violation complaint pursuant to Article XXIII:1(b) GATT 1994 than the system of remedies provided in the ASCM.

[35] *Sykes* (2005) p. 105.

[36] See also *infra* pp. 12–16.

not mandatorily governed by the lesser-duty rule.[37] The lack of a mandatory lesser-duty rule means in practice that the level of a countervailing duty can be higher than what is necessary to remove from the industry of the importing country the injury resulting from the subsidized imports.[38] However, given that there is no universally accepted methodology to measure injury and that it is inherently difficult to quantify injury, and given that a countervailing duty typically only intervenes after a lengthy investigation, this criticism is not convincing either. The ASCM system is designed in such a way that some injury caused to the industry adversely affected by subsidies will necessarily remain unaddressed. Note also that under the WTO dispute settlement system, anti-subsidy action is prospective.[39]

However, the need for multilateral disciplines concerning the control of the provision of subsidies can be justified from a variety of angles that take a broader perspective than a purely economic one. First, as pointed out above, subsidies can have an effect very similar to import tariffs. Therefore, granting subsidies can frustrate market access expectations that originate in tariff concessions obtained in the WTO framework.[40] More generally, it would appear that the confidence in the WTO system of trade liberalization, its credibility and viability could be undermined in the absence of subsidy disciplines. Second, the danger of a subsidy 'race' or even a subsidy 'war' should be mentioned. Subsidies given by one country may generate requests by overseas competitors for similar or even higher levels of subsidies. In the political discourse, a plea for subsidies will often find support and even appear compelling if it is made by manufacturers (and their workers) that compete against subsidized overseas competitors. The resulting response to such unfair trade could prove more restrictive than the complicated subsidy disciplines under the ASCM.[41] In that

[37] See the second sentence of Article 19.2.

[38] *Hufbauer/Erb* (1984) p. 19.

[39] See *infra* Article 4, pp. 236–243.

[40] See *Sykes* (2010) pp. 496–497 who, however, also points out that this problem could be sufficiently addressed by non-violation complaints pursuant to Article XXIII of the GATT 1994, possibly combined with specific commitments limiting subsidies and modelled on the Agreement of Agriculture. Indeed, the ASCM subsidy disciplines apply across all products while market access expectations will typically be focused on the specific concessions obtained in a trade negotiation.

[41] *Hufbauer/Erb* (1984) p. 8, p. 17 and p. 21. According to *Sykes* (2010) p. 499, the aim to avoid competitive subsidization is not linked to the frustration of market access commitments. Rather, governments may have an interest in cooperating to reduce competitive subsidization to avoid unnecessary subsidy wars.

sense, if a government 'ties its hands' by accepting international subsidy disciplines, it can better fend off domestic demands for subsidies. Finally, research linked to public choice theory, a topic situated at a crossroads between economics and political science, has amply investigated incentives and mechanisms for private sector players to seek subsidies and for public administration and politicians to grant subsidies which cannot be justified on grounds of economic efficiency.[42] The very possibility of anti-subsidy action can contribute to limit the distribution of inefficient subsidies.[43] Perhaps even more importantly, subsidies distort market forces. This can result in enabling countries to gain first-mover advantages in new industries, in avoiding adjustment in old industries[44] and in frustrating efforts made by non-subsidizing countries to adjust such old industries. Moreover, if efficient industries in the importing country are forced out of the market because of the subsidized imports, the adjustment costs (restructuring of companies, social support of the workforce that had been made redundant, loss of tax revenue, negative impact on upstream suppliers etc.) are borne by the importing country including perhaps those consumers (in their capacity as taxpayers) that benefitted from the cheap and subsidized imports in the first place.[45] It follows from the above that there are a number of policy reasons justifying anti-subsidy action. But it is also worth recalling that any action against trade-distorting subsidies obviously should not be carried out in a way that is tantamount to protectionist abuse.[46]

In short, while, as mentioned above, economic theory has it that subsidies may create overall welfare effects in the importing country, political economy considerations may require action against subsidies because of their mix of negative social, political and economic effects.

Conclusion

There is a close and delicate link both between subsidies and their effects on trade etc. and between subsidy control and trade liberalization. The lack of disciplines on the provision of subsidies can potentially undo concessions given in the context of bilateral or multilateral trade liberalization. However, strong disciplines on the provision of subsidies also risk

[42] See the concise overview in *Rosenstock* (1995) pp. 44–54.
[43] Critical with regard to this argument *Sykes* (2005) p. 104.
[44] *Rubini* (2009) p. 43.
[45] See also *Rubini* (2009) p. 49.
[46] *Bhagwati* (1988) pp. 51–53.

increasing reluctance to further trade liberalization because they reduce the policy space of a country that is party to such trade agreement.

ASCM – Policy Constraints and Policy Space

A much debated topic is whether the ASCM leaves sufficient policy space to WTO Members. *Bagwell/Mavroidis* (2010) take the view that the ASCM regime goes too far towards disciplining subsidies, in particular through the absolute prohibition of export subsidies. They propose that an adequate response to subsidization should be limited to countervailing duties and non-violation complaints pursuant to Article XXIII:1(b) of GATT 1994.[47] Others propose more flexibility for developing countries because there is no single road to development and, moreover, it is claimed that today's developed countries have in their early stages of development also relied on subsidies that are disciplined today by the ASCM.[48]

A review of DSB rulings does not necessarily support such claims.

- **General infrastructure**: Nothing in the ASCM impedes public authorities to provide general infrastructure in their territory, such as streets, ports etc.[49]
- **Privatization of enterprises**: According to DSB rulings there is a rebuttable presumption that the privatization of an enterprise at a fair market price redeems the subsidies previously given to such an enterprise.[50] This jurisprudence has met with some criticism but it gives policy space to governments in that it facilitates a shift of economic activity from the public to the private sector.
- **R&D subsidies** are not exposed to challenge under the ASCM if they are not specific to 'certain enterprises' as defined by the chapeau of Article 2.1. Thus, the Panel in *EC and certain Member States – Large Civil Aircraft* did not consider subsidies as being specific that were available to a wide range of sectors and enterprises.[51] Moreover, like all other subsidies (unless they are prohibited export and local content subsidies), R&D subsidies can only be challenged in a resource

[47] *Bagwell/Mavroidis* (2010) p. 168 and p. 171.
[48] *Wouters/Coppens* (2010) p. 83.
[49] For details see *infra* Article 1 pp. 96–103.
[50] For details see *infra* Article 14 pp. 433–443.
[51] For details see *infra* Article 2 pp. 176–178 and pp. 188–193.

intensive adverse effects dispute settlement case pursuant or by a countervailing duty if they have trade distortive effects as defined in Articles 5, 6 and 15.

- **Renewable energy subsidies and subsidies for other environmental purposes**: The Appellate Body has adjusted its well-developed benefit analysis to reflect the particularities of the market of new energies (e.g. solar and wind power). The issue arose in the context of feed-in tariffs. The Appellate Body highlighted that the market for renewable energy was in fact created by the government. Therefore, the benefit analysis of feed-in tariffs could not simply focus on a comparison between prices paid to suppliers of renewable energy and prices paid to producers of conventional energy. Rather, the benefit analysis had to reflect the fact that the market for renewable energy was created by the government and that a non-distorted benchmark for purchases of renewable energy had to be found. Thus, while such feed-in tariffs can constitute a financial contribution, they are not necessarily a specific subsidy.[52]

As far as direct subsidies to manufacturers for R&D or the installation of environmentally friendly production equipment are concerned, Article 8.2 (a) and (c) contained (limited) carve-outs of such subsidies from the disciplines of the ASCM. However, Article 8 expired pursuant to Article 31 by the end of 1999. Such subsidies are in any event only challengeable if they have the trade distortive effects as defined in Articles 5, 6 and 15.

However, carbon leakage, or rather measures designed to avoid such leakage, is a somewhat more challenging problem. Governments that have subjected their domestic manufacturers to strict environmental standards may see these measures undermined by imports that have not been produced under such strict environmental conditions. Equally, a manufacturing industry subject to such conditions may find it very difficult to compete on those export markets where producers are not subject to similar strict conditions. One question that arises in the context of the ASCM is if and to what extent a government can make border adjustments to preserve the competiveness of its domestic producers. In other words, is it possible for a government to compensate its exporting manufacturers for their higher production costs resulting from such environmental standards by border adjustments (with a view to reduce

[52] See *infra* Article 1 pp. 132–136.

export prices) so as to ensure a level playing field for its manufacturers? And *vice versa* to increase the import price of products that have not been produced under such standards? DSB rulings have not addressed this issue yet. It would go beyond the scope of this book to discuss this topic in any detail. Note, however, that export subsidies are prohibited by virtue of Article 3, while footnote 1 of the ASCM allows for some border adjustments in relation to indirect taxes. More importantly, implementation of such a scheme issue would raise important challenges in terms of practicability.

Another issue is, if and to what extent the ASCM disciplines emission permits given by governments in the context of carbon trading schemes. The aforementioned ruling on whether or not feed-in tariffs confer a benefit appears also relevant for this issue.

As far as the import side is concerned, i.e. CVD action against imports that had not been manufactured in line with standards reducing greenhouse emissions, DSB rulings available so far would appear to suggest that the lack of government regulation setting such standards in the exporting country does not amount to a financial contribution or a system of income or price support. Hence, there is no subsidy.[53]

It is not possible to examine all conceivable forms of environmental support (e.g. tax incentives) in this chapter. For further references see *Rubini* (2012).

- **Regional subsidies**: It could be argued that the ASCM rules concerning the support of disadvantaged regions is less than optimal. Article 8.2(b), which expired by virtue of Article 31, classified regional aid as non-actionable if, *inter alia*, it was given to an area whose GDP per capita was not above 85 per cent of the average of the territory concerned or if the unemployment rate was at least 110 per cent of the average of the territory concerned. Based on the jurisprudence to Article 2.2, a financial contribution given by a public authority to certain enterprises located in a subset of its territory would automatically be specific.[54] And it would be actionable and countervailable if it also conferred a benefit. Thus, the current ASCM makes subsidies

[53] Numerous publications have addressed this subject but see in particular *Coppens* (2014) p. 492 *et seq.*; *Low/Marceau/Reinaud* (2012) p. 526 *et seq.*; *Hufbauer/Charnovitz/Kim* (2009) p. 65 *et seq.*; *Maruyama* (2011) pp. 717–726; *Henschke* (2012) p. 30 *et seq.*

[54] For details see *infra* Article 2 pp. 194–198.

open to challenge if they are given by public authorities to certain enterprises in designated parts of their territory in order to remedy a certain lack of economic development of such territory. However, much will depend on the particular circumstances of the case. First, a subsidy can only be challenged before the WTO pursuant to Articles 5 and 6 if it causes adverse effects as defined by these provisions or by a countervailing duty pursuant to Article 10 *et seq.* if the products benefitting from such subsidy cause injury to the industry of the importing country. Second, if subsidies are not given to certain enterprises in the disadvantaged region but instead are invested in general infrastructure (see *supra*), schools etc., they fall outside the remit of the ASCM.

- **Tax policies**: The ASCM leaves a WTO Member's autonomy largely intact when designing its tax system. Article 1.1(a)(1)(ii) classifies 'revenue foregone or not collected' as a financial contribution. Such financial contribution is a subsidy if it is also specific and confers a benefit to the recipient. When examining the application of this provision, the Appellate Body underlined that WTO Members are sovereign in determining the structure and rates of their domestic tax regimes. WTO rules do not oblige WTO Members to tax any categories of income, whether foreign-source or domestic-source income. However, as *US – FSC* and *US – Large Civil Aircraft (2nd complaint)* have shown, if a WTO Member sets a certain tax rate it cannot cut out certain sectors from the application of that general tax rate and treat these sectors differently.[55] Similarly, a case can be made for arguing that the ASCM is in principle neutral *vis-à-vis* tax systems (those that rely primarily on direct taxes as opposed to those that focus to an important extent also on indirect taxes; territorial versus worldwide tax systems). At least the facts underlying the DSB rulings rendered so far did not show that the ASCM manifestly discriminates in favour of the one or the other system.[56]

[55] For details see *infra* Article 1 pp. 88–96.

[56] WT/DS108/R of 8 October 1999, *United States – Tax Treatment for 'Foreign Sales Corporations'*, paras 7.121 and 7.122 *et passim* and *infra* Annex I pp. 604–609. However, many scholars hold the view that the distinction between indirect taxes and direct taxes underlying the ASCM is not adequate because both types of taxes could have similar effects while only some exemptions from indirect taxes are not subject to ASCM disciplines (see Article 1.1(a)(1)(ii) and footnote 1 to the ASCM as well as e.g. *Hufbauer* (2010) p. 767 *et seq*. Critical also *Sykes* (2010) pp. 506–508.

- **Regulatory failure**: There is some scholarly debate whether a regulatory failure by a government could constitute a subsidy. For instance, the failure to adopt adequate labour or environment protection laws which in turn benefit manufacturers in the country in question. There are no DSB rulings on this subject but the majority of contributions tends to argue that such failure does not constitute a subsidy because this type of government action (or rather lack thereof) does not fall within the list of financial contributions set out in Article 1.1(a)(1). The introduction of the requirement (and the definition) of a financial contribution into the ASCM as a result of the Uruguay Round negotiations has limited the types of government intervention that fall under the ambit of the ASCM. This has closed the possibility of a purely effect-based subsidy definition. Nor consider most scholars such social or environmental dumping as a form of income or price support.[57] The Panel ruling on *US – Export Restraints* seems to support this opinion.[58]
- **Exchange rates**: There is also some debate to what extent exchange-rate management (or manipulation as some prefer to argue) by a government falls under the scope of the ASCM. The majority of scholars tend to conclude it does not because it is not covered by the closed list of Article 1.1(a)(1). The application of Article XV of GATT 1994 that deals with exchange arrangements would also have to be examined in this context.[59]

Object and Purpose of the ASCM

The ASCM does not contain any express statement of its object and purpose. But the Appellate Body held in *US – Carbon Steel* that the object and purpose of the ASCM is 'to increase and improve GATT disciplines relating to the use of both subsidies and countervailing measures'.[60] The

[57] *Sykes* (2010) p. 473 and pp. 508–510.

[58] See *infra* Article 1 pp. 110–112.

[59] *Staiger/Sykes* (2010) pp. 609–611, 613–614. But see *Caryl* (2011) in particular on p. 195 and p. 218 and *Lima/Gaviria* (2012) p. 1022 *et seq.* *Thorstensen/Müller/Ramos* (2015) discuss some of the historical background (p. 118–124) and explore the scope of Article XV of GATT 1994 (p. 124–133).

[60] WT/DS213/AB/R of 28 November 2002 – *United States – Countervailing Duties on Certain Corrosion-Resistant Carbon Steel Flat Products from Germany*, paras 73 and 74. In this context, the Appellate Body recalled the 1986 Punta del Este Ministerial Declaration which initiated the Uruguay Round and which stated that the negotiations on subsidies

Appellate Body nuanced this statement somewhat in *Softwood Lumber IV* where it referred to the aforementioned statement but added 'while, recognizing at the same time the right of Members to impose such measures under certain conditions'.[61] *US – Countervailing Duty Investigation on DRAMs* added that the ASCM reflects a delicate balance between the Members that sought to impose more disciplines on the use of subsidies and those that sought to impose more disciplines on the application of countervailing measures.[62] *US – FSC (1st Article 21.5)* pointed out that it would be irreconcilable with the object and purpose of the ASCM to offer a Member carte blanche to evade any effective disciplines, thereby creating fundamental uncertainty and unpredictability.[63] *US – Anti-Dumping and Countervailing Duties (China)* attempts to summarize the various aforementioned rulings.[64]

Panel rulings on this issue have been slightly less nuanced. *Brazil – Aircraft* stated that the object and purpose of the ASCM is to impose multilateral disciplines on subsidies which distort international trade. Therefore, the Panel rejected an interpretation of the ASCM by Brazil according to which effectively a WTO Member could raise the provision of subsidies by a complaining Member as a defence justifying its own provision of subsidies ('matching').[65] *Canada – Aircraft* stated that the object and purpose of the ASCM could more appropriately be summarized as the establishment of multilateral disciplines on the premise that some forms

and countervailing measures shall be conducted 'with the objective of improving GATT disciplines relating to all subsidies and countervailing measures that affect international trade'. See also WT/DS296/AB/R of 27 June 2005, *United States – Countervailing Duty Investigation on Dynamic Random Access Memory Semiconductors (DRAMs) from Korea*, para 115.

[61] WT/DS257/AB/R of 19 January 2004, *United States – Final Countervailing Duty Determination with Respect to Certain Softwood Lumber from Canada*, paras 64 and 95.

[62] WT/DS296/AB/R of 27 June 2005, *United States – Countervailing Duty Investigation on Dynamic Random Access Memory Semiconductors (DRAMs) from Korea*, para 115. Very similar, but explicitly limited to Part V of the ASCM, WT/DS436/AB/R of 8 December 2014, *United States – Countervailing Measures on Certain Hot-Rolled Carbon Steel Flat Products from India*, paras 4.522 and 4.542.

[63] WT/DS108/RW of 20 August 2001, *United States – Tax Treatment for 'Foreign Sales Corporations' (Article 21.5, first recourse)*, para 8.39.

[64] WT/DS379/AB/R of 11 March 2011, *US – Definitive Anti-Dumping and Countervailing Duties on Certain Products from China*, para 573. Very critical *Cartland/Depayre/Woznowski* (2012) pp. 992/3 who consider this a self-invented preamble to the ASCM by the Appellate Body while the ASCM does not contain one, which in turn was a deliberate result of negotiations.

[65] WT/DS46/R of 14 April 1999, *Brazil – Export Financing Programme for Aircraft*, para 7.26.

of government intervention distort international trade, or have the potential to distort international trade.[66] *US – Export Restraints* agreed with these two statements. But it added that it does not follow from these two statements that every government intervention that might in economic theory be deemed a subsidy with a potential to distort trade is a subsidy within the meaning of the ASCM. Such an approach would mean that the 'financial contribution' requirement would effectively be replaced by a requirement that the government action in question be commonly understood to be a subsidy that distorts trade.[67] *US – Countervailing Measures Concerning Certain Products from the EC* is in line with the aforementioned rulings. It held that countervailing duties are not designed to counteract all market distortions or resource misallocations which might have been caused by subsidization.[68] *US – Carbon Steel* was of the view that paragraphs 3 and 6(a) of Article VI set out the purpose of countervailing duties and the general circumstances in which they may be levied. Moreover, these two provisions give some indication of the object and purpose of the ASCM.[69]

Note that in *US – Anti-Dumping and Countervailing Duties (China)*, the Appellate Body pointed out that considerations of object and purpose are of limited use to delimiting the scope of the term 'public body' in Article 1.1(a)(1). In the context of examining the meaning of the term 'public body' the Panel was concerned with the implications of too narrow an interpretation of this term. The Appellate Body thought that a too broad interpretation of the term 'public body' could equally risk upsetting the delicate balance embodied in the ASCM because it could empty the concepts of entrustment and direction by classifying entities with any connection to the government to be public bodies.[70] It also held that the object and purpose of the ASCM is not inconsistent with an approach that would accept that, in fixing the amount of countervailing duty to be imposed, it is appropriate to take account of anti-dumping

[66] WT/DS70/R of 14 April 1999, *Canada – Measures Affecting the Export of Civilian Aircraft*, para 9.119.

[67] WT/DS194/R of 29 June 2001, *United States – Measures Treating Export Restraints as Subsidies*, para 8.62.

[68] WT/DS212/R of 31 July 2002, *United States – Countervailing Measures Concerning Certain Products from the European Communities*, para 7.42.

[69] WT/DS213/R of 3 July 2002, *United States – Countervailing Duties on Certain Corrosion-Resistant Carbon Steel Flat Products from Germany*, para 8.31.

[70] WT/DS379/AB/R of 11 March 2011, *US – Definitive Anti-Dumping and Countervailing Duties on Certain Products from China*, paras 302 and 303.

duties that are being levied on the same products and that offset the same subsidization.[71]

In *Canada – Auto*, the Appellate Body had to decide whether there was a parallelism between Article 3.1(a) and (b) in the sense that the latter provision applied to import substitution contingency both in law and in fact. The Panel held that Article 3.1(b) only applied to import substitution contingency in law. In contrast, the Appellate Body considered that such a narrow interpretation would be contrary to object and purpose of the ASCM because it would make circumvention of the obligations by WTO Members too easy.[72]

See also *infra* p. 31–32.

Effectiveness of the ASCM

Action under the ASCM only offsets to a limited extent the distortive effects of subsidies. The neo-mercantilism currently pursued by some emerging economies was probably not even envisaged by the drafters of the ASCM. It is also difficult to address under the ASCM distortions prevailing in a comparatively recent type of organization of the economy, i.e. where the State retains a strong grip on the economy (*inter alia* via State-owned enterprises) which evolved from the Soviet style planned system and where private entrepreneurship coexists.

More fundamentally, unless a subsidy is prohibited, the negatively affected WTO Member can only take countervailing measures if there are some negative trade effects as defined in Article 15. However, at that stage, the effect of the subsidy might already be diluted in the sense that the subsidy margins found might not really reflect the trade-distortive effect of the subsidies. This is the result of the mechanics of a benefit calculation. The subsidization of an exporter is expressed as a percentage of the turnover of that company in the investigation period. Non-recurring subsidies such as grants (as opposed to, for instance, subsidized loans) are expensed over the normal lifetime of the assets of the company. As a result, if the subsidies have helped to establish a successful company with a large turnover that finally penetrated export markets, the rate of subsidization will often be fairly low. It will not necessarily reflect the fact that the subsidies

[71] WT/DS379/AB/R of 11 March 2011, *US – Definitive Anti-Dumping and Countervailing Duties on Certain Products from China*, paras 573 and 574.

[72] WT/DS139/AB/R and WT/DS142/AB/R of 31 May 2000, *Canada – Certain Measures Affecting the Automotive Industry*, para 142.

had an incubating effect on its recipient in that it enabled the exporter to develop products that it could not have developed (or only later) absent the subsidy. In extreme cases, the exporter would not even exist absent subsidization. Similar shortcomings can exist in relation to seeking relief under the dispute settlement track because the procedure can take a considerable period of time and, in case the challenge was successful, implementation can be elusive. Similar concerns apply in relation to adverse effects cases pursuant to Articles 5 and 6.

Temporal Application of the ASCM

There is no DSB ruling as to the temporal application of the ASCM. The issue arose in *Canada – Aircraft*. Canada requested a preliminary ruling that the ASCM does not apply to contributions and transactions that took place prior to 1 January 1995, the date of entry into force of the WTO Agreement. Canada's request was based on Article 28 of the Vienna Convention on the Law of Treaties. Brazil agreed with Canada that, with regard to prohibited subsidies, the ASCM did not apply to contributions made prior to 1 January 1995 and consequently withdrew its claim concerning a 1989 measure. As a result, there was no need for the Panel to decide on this issue.[73] But see the commentary to paragraphs 3 and 4 of Article 32 and the Appellate Body ruling in *Brazil – Desiccated Coconut*.

In relation to the temporal scope of Article 5 see *infra* p. 263.

Negotiating History of the ASCM

Anti-subsidy action as well as the first attempts to establish international subsidy disciplines date back to the end of the nineteenth century. The United States (US) were the first to adopt an explicit countervailing duty law in 1890. All this was in response to highly subsidized trade in sugar. And until 1979, the US was practically the only country applying countervailing duties.[74]

According to Article 32 of the Vienna Convention, the negotiating history of an agreement is a supplementary means of interpretation.[75] This is

[73] WT/DS70/R of 14 April 1999, *Canada – Measures Affecting the Export of Civilian Aircraft*, paras 9.42–9.44, 9.276.

[74] See e.g. Horlick (2013/2) p. 447.

[75] WT/DS436/AB/R of 8 December 2014, *United States – Countervailing Measures on Certain Hot-Rolled Carbon Steel Flat Products from India*, paras 4.395–4.396.

also a reason why this section describes the Tokyo Round Subsidies Code and the negotiation history leading to the ASCM.

Starting Point: Tokyo Round Subsidies Code

GATT subsidy disciplines could originally essentially be found in Articles VI and XVI of GATT 1947, in conjunction with Article XXIII. Article VI authorizes countervailing duties. Article XVI originally only contained a notification and consultation requirement in relation to subsidies. In the 1954/55 GATT review session some disciplines on export subsidies were added to Article XVI. Finally, the provision of new and unanticipated subsidies could be challenged pursuant to Article XXIII if it amounted to a nullification or impairment of tariff concessions that had been negotiated previously. In short, GATT 1947 was not very elaborate on subsidy disciplines.

In 1979, after five years of negotiation, the Tokyo Round Subsidies Code was added.[76] The GATT system was fundamentally different from the WTO system. The WTO system is an integrated system while the GATT system emerging from the Tokyo Round was not. The Tokyo Round Subsidies Code and the other eight Tokyo Round Agreements were treaties with different memberships, independent governing bodies and separate dispute settlement mechanisms. Thus, not all contracting parties to the GATT 1947 were signatories of the Tokyo Round Subsidies Code. In fact, by the end of the Uruguay Round, only 24 countries had ratified the Code. The GATT 1947 was administered by the contracting parties, whereas the Tokyo Round Subsidies Code was administered by the Committee on Subsidies and Countervailing Measures that was established pursuant to Article 16 of the Tokyo Round Subsidies Code. The Committee comprised the signatories of that Code. All disputes brought under Article XXIII of the GATT 1947 fell under GATT dispute settlement. In contrast, the Tokyo Round Committee on Subsidies and Countervailing Measures was responsible for administering and monitoring dispute settlement under Articles 12, 13, 17 and 18 of the Code. As a result of the separate legal identities of the GATT 1947 and the Tokyo Round Subsidies Code, a complaining party either had to bring a dispute under Articles VI and XVI of the GATT 1947 or under the provisions of the Code. Most disputes were brought under the Code.[77]

[76] Agreement on Interpretation and Application of Articles VI, XVI and XXIII of the General Agreement on Tariffs and Trade, BISD 26S/56. See also *Rivers/Greenwald* (1979).

[77] WT/DS22/AB/R of 21 February 1997, *Brazil – Measures Affecting Desiccated Coconut*, p. 11–12.

The basic deal underlying the Tokyo Round Subsidies Code was that the US agreed to impose countervailing duties only if there was a finding of injury to the domestic industry while the EC at the time accepted tighter rules on export subsidies as well as the principle that injurious subsidization could lead to countervailing duties.[78]

Neither the Tokyo Round Subsidies Code nor Articles VI and XVI of GATT 1947 contain a definition of the term 'subsidy'. Rather, they simply refer to this term. The Tokyo Round Subsidies Code also did not contain a definition of specificity.

Moreover, while the Tokyo Round Subsidies Code prohibited in its Article 9 export subsidies, it did not contain a definition of an export subsidy. It only set out in its Annex an illustrative list of practices that were deemed to constitute export subsidies. This Annex is essentially the same as Annex I of the ASCM. The Code did not stipulate a prohibition of import substitution subsidies.

Articles 2 through 6 of the Tokyo Round Subsidies Code contained the provisions governing the launch and the conduct of countervailing duty procedures as well as a definition of the notion of 'injury' to the industry of the importing country. These provisions were, however, much less detailed than those of the ASCM.

The substantive provisions of the dispute settlement track of the Tokyo Round Subsidies Code were also much less developed than those of the ASCM. In its Article 8, it already contained the various concepts, i.e. injury to the domestic industry of another signatory, nullification and impairment of benefits accruing and serious prejudice. However, with the exception of the concept of injury, the Code did not establish any clear and elaborate definitions of these concepts.

Note also that the Preamble and Article 11 of the Tokyo Round Subsidies Code not only recognized the harmful effects that subsidies may have, but they also acknowledged that subsidies are used by governments to promote important objectives of national policy.

Uruguay Round Negotiations

The Ministerial Declaration that launched in 1986 the Uruguay Round negotiations, the so-called Punta Del Este work programme, stipulated in its section D ('Subjects for Negotiations'):

[78] *Hufbauer/Erb* (1984) p. 15.

> Subsidies and countervailing measures
>
> Negotiations on subsidies and countervailing measures shall be based on a review of Articles VI and XVI and the MTN Agreement on subsidies and countervailing measures with the objective of improving GATT disciplines relating to all subsidies and countervailing measures that affect international trade. A negotiation group will be established to deal with these issues.

The reference to the 'MTN Agreement on subsidies and countervailing measures' is a reference to the Tokyo Round Subsidies Code. It was mainly the US that insisted on including subsidies and countervailing measures in the Punta Del Este work programme: the US *inter alia* considered that the Tokyo Round Subsidies Code did not impose any meaningful disciplines on subsidies and was therefore badly in need of an update. At the beginning of the negotiations and for a long time in the course of the negotiations, the US took the view that subsidies, whatever their form and purpose, are harmful because they are distorting competition and should consequently be banned. The US even went so far as to refuse to agree on a working agenda based on the Tokyo Round Subsidies Code on the grounds that this would prejudice its position, that the approach followed in the Code was totally wrong and that new rules had to be designed from scratch.[79]

The EC's position was more nuanced. It saw a need to strengthen the rules on countervailing measures. Note that the US initiated between the end of the Tokyo Round negotiations and the beginning of the Uruguay Round negotiations 281 CVD cases out of a total of 460 cases initiated by the totality of the GATT Membership.[80] Moreover, the EC accepted a ban on export subsidies. However, and based on its experience with its State Aid system, the EC also took the view that certain subsidies granted to promote social and economic objectives should be completely exempt from discipline. Moreover, the EC insisted that action against such subsidies could only be taken if the country defending itself could show some negative impact on its trade interests. According to the EC, and in sharp

[79] The US essentially pursued five negotiation objectives: (1) maintain and improve the prohibitions on the use of export subsidies, (2) increase and extend international discipline on the use of domestic subsidies, (3) improve the mechanisms to resolve disputes, including the creation of a credible and effective mechanism for multilateral dispute resolution in the subsidies area, (4) achieve, within the agreement, recognition of the subsidy-like nature of certain practices, such as targeting and dual energy-pricing, and (5) adopt appropriate disciplines in a new subsidies agreement to address such practices. See *Anderson/Husisian* (1996) p. 301 with further references.

[80] See *Anderson/Husisian* (1996) footnote 21 on p. 341.

contrast to the US position, the fact that a product was benefitting from aid at the expense of the government was not enough to justify countervailing measures. This position of the EC had the backing of the majority of the GATT Membership. At one stage in 1992, the EC also sought the exclusion of civil aircraft from the coverage of any new agreement.

Canada sought primarily to protect itself from the US countervailing duties and to limit regional specificity while the main concern of developing countries was to receive meaningful special and differential treatment.

Ambassador Michael Cartland (Hong Kong) was the chairman of the negotiation group on rules which included subsidies. The negotiations were characterized to a large extent by a certain antagonism between the US and the EC. In the first year, progress was sluggish not least because of the irreconcilable positions of the US, on the one hand, and the EC and other Members, on the other. During the negotiations he produced a number of draft agreements with the assistance of the GATT Secretariat. These proposals were subsequently discussed with the Membership who either bilaterally or within groups expressed their views on the texts. This in turn served as input to the chairman in order to further reduce the gaps between the different positions of Members. The last formal draft was incorporated in the so-called Dunkel draft, officially known as the 'Draft Final Act Embodying the Results of the Uruguay Round of Multilateral Trade Negotiations', released on 20 December 1991.[81]

It was Canada that came up with the principle to classify subsidies into three categories (i.e. banned subsidies, subsidies that are actionable if they affect negatively another Member's trade interests and subsidies that should be exempt from any action) that found its way into the new Agreement. This classification became known as the traffic light system. During the negotiations, considerable energy was spent on the 'green box' category, i.e. subsidies that were allowed (see Article 8 of the ASCM). A meaningful green box was considered crucial by the EC. A U-turn by the Clinton administration during the last weeks of the Round (the concluding meeting of the Uruguay Round negotiations took place in Geneva on 15 December 1993 at 3 pm) facilitated the final compromise. In its desire for a 'rejuvenation of the industrial base of the United States', the new administration, which only took office in January 1993, accepted a broadening of one group of non-actionable subsidies, i.e. R&D subsidies. Note

[81] GATT Doc. No. MTN.TNC/W/FA (Dec. 20, 1991). The draft alongside with the ASCM and the Tokyo Round Subsidies Code is also reproduced in *McDonough* (1999).

however that Article 8 expired by the end of 1999 pursuant to Article 31 ASCM.[82]

As pointed out above, the Tokyo Round Subsidies Code did not contain a definition of the term 'subsidy'. During the subsequent Uruguay Round, numerous participants in the Negotiating Group on Subsidies stressed the need to develop such a definition. The US took the view that a subsidy should be solely defined on the basis of the existence of a benefit conferred by any government action (effect-based definition). The view that finally prevailed was that in addition to a benefit (which also remained undefined in the Tokyo Round Subsidies Code), a government financial contribution was necessary as a means of limiting the universe of government actions that could be considered as a subsidy.[83]

Doha Development Agenda (DDA) Negotiations

The 4th Ministerial Conference in Doha launched the DDA. The renegotiation of the ASCM is conducted within the Rules Group, which also examines the WTO Anti-Dumping Agreement and rules on Regional Trade Agreements. The rules negotiations are part of the single undertaking under paragraph 47 of the Doha Declaration. Paragraph 28 of the Ministerial Decision reads:

> WTO Rules
>
> 28. In the light of the experience and the increasing application of these instruments by members, we agree to negotiations aimed at clarifying and improving disciplines under the Agreements on Implementation of Article VI of GATT 1994 and on Subsidies and Countervailing Measures, while preserving the basic concepts, principles and effectiveness of these Agreements and their instruments and objectives, and taking into account the needs of developing and least-developed participants. In the initial phase of the negotiations, participants will indicate the provisions, including disciplines on trade distorting practices, that they seek to clarify and improve in the subsequent phase. In the context of these negotiations, participants shall also aim to clarify and improve WTO disciplines on fisheries subsidies, taking into account the importance of this sector to developing countries. We note that fisheries subsidies are also referred to in paragraph 31.[84]

82 Detailed accounts of the Uruguay Round negotiations can be found in *Depayre* (1995) pp. 247–249, 252; *Paemen/Bensch* (1995) pp. 69, 158–160 and in particular *McDonough* (1999).

83 See e.g. WT/DS194/R of 29 June 2001, *United States – Measures Treating Export Restraints as Subsidies*, paras 8.65–8.69 with further references.

84 WT/MIN(01)/DEC/1 of 20 November 2001, adopted on 14 November 2001.

The WTO rules negotiations focused much more on the WTO Anti-Dumping Agreement than on the ASCM. In the course of the negotiations, the Chairman of the Rules Group produced two drafts. The first draft text was released in December 2007.[85] Its purpose was to give an overview over the state of play and to facilitate further work of the group. On 28 May 2008, the Chairman issued a second draft. The second draft again represented only an interim step but there was no consensus that it could constitute a possible balanced outcome of the negotiations.[86] In 2011, the Chairman issued a report on the status of the Group's work at that time. However, and contrary to his approach with regard to the WTO Anti-Dumping Agreement, he did not issue a revised draft legal text of the ASCM because he felt that there was insufficient basis to do so. The Chairman noted that – unlike in the negotiations of the Anti-Dumping Agreement where the issues before the Group have been narrowed down – there had been a significant number of new proposals, for instance, with regard to export financing benchmarks for developing members, countervail procedures, presumption of serious prejudice etc. Moreover, he referred also to the issues that remained bracketed in his previous proposals such as financing by loss-making institutions.[87]

The fate of the DDA negotiations was unclear when the manuscript of this book was finalized. While previous WTO Ministerial Conferences reaffirmed the DDA, ministers in Nairobi agreed to disagree on the further course of these negotiations. Paragraphs 30 and 31 of the Nairobi Ministerial Declaration read:

> 30. We recognize that many Members reaffirm the Doha Development Agenda, and the Declarations and Decisions adopted at Doha and at the Ministerial Conferences held since then, and reaffirm their full commitment to conclude the DDA on that basis. Other Members do not reaffirm the Doha mandates, as they believe new approaches are necessary to achieve meaningful outcomes in multilateral negotiations. Members have different views on how to address the negotiations. We acknowledge the strong legal structure of this Organization.
>
> 31. Nevertheless, there remains a strong commitment of all Members to advance negotiations on the remaining Doha issues. This includes advancing work in all three pillars of agriculture … , as well as non-agriculture market access, services, development, TRIPS and rules.[88]

[85] TN/RL/W/213 of 30 November 2007, Draft Consolidated Chair Texts of the AD and ASCM Agreements.

[86] TN/RL/W/232 of 28 May 2008, Working Document from the Chairman, Annex B.

[87] TN/RL/W/254 of 21 April 2011, pp. 37–45.

[88] WT/MIN(15)/DEC of 21 December 2015, Nairobi Ministerial Declaration, adopted on 19 December 2015.

Relationship of the ASCM with GATT 1994, Other Agreements and Relevance of Municipal Law

GATT 1994

The general interpretative note to Annex 1A of the WTO Agreement provides:

> In the event of conflict between the provision of the General Agreement on Tariffs and Trade 1994 and a provision of another agreement in Annex 1A to the Agreement Establishing the World Trade Organization (referred to in the agreements in Annex 1A as the 'WTO Agreement'), the provision of the other agreement shall prevail to the extent of a conflict.

Annex 1A includes also the ASCM. In other words, in the event of a conflict, the ASCM supersedes GATT 1994. To the extent that there is no conflict, the rights and obligations arising out of the ASCM and GATT 1994 exist in parallel.[89] In *Brazil – Desiccated Coconut*, the Appellate Body observed that the relationship between GATT 1994 and the other agreements in Annex 1A is complex and must be examined on a case-by-case basis. It referred also to Article 10 of the ASCM which stipulates that 'Members shall take all necessary steps to ensure that the imposition of a countervailing duty ... is in accordance with Article VI of GATT 1994'.[90]

Article III of GATT 1994

General Article III of GATT 1994 prohibits discrimination 'behind the border' of the imported product as compared to the domestic product. This lengthy provision establishes that the imported merchandise shall be accorded national treatment in relation to internal taxation and regulation.

The provision of subsidies can result in such discrimination. In *Indonesia – Autos*, Indonesia argued that there is a general conflict between the provisions of the ASCM and those of Article III of GATT 1994, and consequently that the ASCM is the only applicable law. The Panel did not accept this claim. It recalled that in international law there

[89] WT/DS267/R of 8 September 2004, *United States – Subsidies on Upland Cotton*, paras 7 255 and 7.256.

[90] WT/DS22/AB/R of 21 February 1997, *Brazil – Measures Affecting Desiccated Coconut*, p. 14 (the Appellate Body explained also that the provisions of GATT 1947 'are not the sum total of the rights and obligations of WTO Members concerning a particular matter'). See also WT/DS108/AB/R of 24 February 2000, *United States – Tax Treatment for 'Foreign Sales Corporations'*, para 116 and *infra* Article 10 pp. 371–372.

is a presumption against conflict. Moreover, Article III of GATT 1994 and the ASCM focus on different problems: the provision of a subsidy by a government does not imply that the subsidy itself will necessarily discriminate between imported and domestic products in contravention of Article III of GATT 1994. The Panel also referred to footnote 56 to Article 32.1. Nor would the application of Article III to the dispute in question have reduced the ASCM to inutility.[91]

Article III:8(b) provides a narrow carve-out for the disciplines contained in Article III (see *infra*).

Article III:2 of GATT 1994 *Indonesia – Autos* held that there is no conflict between the ASCM and Article III:2 of GATT 1994. Article 27.3 of the ASCM cannot reasonably be considered to authorize the imposition of discriminatory product taxes, contrary to Indonesia's claim. The ASCM does not deal with taxes on products (as Article III:2 of GATT 1994 does) but with subsidies to enterprises.[92]

Article III:8(b) of GATT 1994 Article III:8(b) reads:

> The provisions of this Article shall not prevent the payment of subsidies exclusively to domestic producers, including payments to domestic producers derived from the proceeds of internal taxes or charges applied consistently with the provisions of this Article and subsidies effected through governmental purchases of domestic products.

In other words, there is not necessarily a violation of the duty to accord national treatment to the imported merchandise if a government subsidizes only its domestic producers (including in the context of government procurement).[93] Note, however, that government procurement is subject to the subsidy disciplines because a government's purchase of goods for more than adequate remuneration constitutes a subsidy pursuant to Article 1.1(a)(1)(iii) of the ASCM.

DSB rulings have clarified this carve-out of the disciplines of Article III.

Indonesia – Autos, in line with previous GATT Panels and the Appellate Body, considered that the purpose of Article III:8(b) of GATT 1994 is to

[91] WT/DS54/R, WT/DS55/R, WT/DS59/R and WT/DS64/R of 2 July 1998, *Indonesia – Certain Measures Affecting the Automobile Industry*, paras 14.28–14.40.

[92] WT/DS54/R, WT/DS55/R, WT/DS59/R and WT/DS64/R of 2 July 1998, *Indonesia – Certain Measures Affecting the Automobile Industry*, paras 14.97–14.99.

[93] This is also the succinct description of the function of Article III:8(b) given by the Panel in WT/DS487/R of 28 November 2016, *United States – Conditional Tax Incentives for Large Civil Aircraft*, para 7.201.

confirm that subsidies to producers (as opposed, for instance, to a subsidy to consumers if they buy a domestically manufactured product) do not violate Article III of GATT 1994. Three points of the Panel's reasoning merit highlighting:

- In order to benefit from Article III:8(b) the subsidies may not have a component that introduces discrimination between imported and domestic products.
- The wording 'payment of subsidies exclusively to domestic producers' exists to ensure that only subsidies provided to producers, and not tax or other forms of discrimination on products, be considered subsidies for the purposes of Article III:8(b). In other words, Article III:8(b) does not cover a financial advantage that benefits producers indirectly (for example consumer subsidies, i.e. subsidies paid to consumers of products that are manufactured by domestic producers).
- If the subsidy to producers derives from indirect taxes, there must be a prior collection on a non-discriminatory basis of such taxes. The Panel noted approvingly the ruling of the Appellate Body in *Unites States – Malt Beverages*: Article III:8(b) limits the permissible producer subsidies to payments after taxes have been collected or payments otherwise consistent with Article III. This separation of tax rules, e.g. on tax exemptions or reductions, and subsidy rules makes sense economically and politically. Even if the proceeds from non-discriminatory product taxes may be used for subsequent subsidies, the domestic producer, like his foreign competitor, must pay the product taxes due. The separation of tax and subsidy rules contributes to greater transparency.

Note also that the Panel rejected Indonesia's view that the term 'the payment of subsidies' in Article III:8(b) must refer to all subsidies identified in Article 1 of the ASCM, not merely to the subset of direct subsidies to domestic producers, as opposed, for instance, to tax exemptions and tax reductions such as the ones granted by Indonesia in the case in question. If Indonesia's broad interpretation had been accepted, Article III of GATT 1994 would not have been applicable to the dispute at issue by virtue of its paragraph 8(b). Thus the discriminatory treatment of imported cars could not have been challenged under this provision.[94] In sum, it would appear that when a government only refrains from collecting taxes or fees

[94] WT/DS54/R, WT/DS55/R, WT/DS59/R and WT/DS64/R of 2 July 1998, *Indonesia – Certain Measures Affecting the Automobile Industry*, paras 14.41–14.46, 14.118 *et seq.*

that would otherwise be due, such non-collection cannot benefit from Article III:8(b) of GATT 1994.[95]

EC – Commercial Vessels understood Article III:8(b) to mean 'that a subsidy is not inconsistent with Article III:4 *merely* because it is granted only to domestic producers of a product and not to foreign producers of that product'.[96] Korea argued that the EU could not invoke Article III:8(b) in order to justify its 'Temporary Defensive Mechanism for Shipbuilding' (TDM) because it is a discriminatory regulatory framework. In other words, Korea's claim was not based on the subsidy as such. The Panel rejected this. It considered it sufficient that the TDM created the legal basis to authorize the adoption of aid schemes by the Member States providing for direct aid in support of contracts for the building of ships.[97] The Panel also rejected Korea's argument that Article III:8(b) only applies to subsidies that are general in nature.[98]

Article VI GATT 1994

Article VI[99] (together with Article XVI) is the central provision of GATT 1994 in relation to subsidies (and dumping) as well as countervailing (and anti-dumping) duties. However, it did not play any important role in disputes concerning the ASCM. Article 10 of the ASCM requires that any anti-subsidy investigations and countervailing measures are also in conformity with Article VI. Like Article XVI, Article VI does not contain a definition of a subsidy. Annex I to GATT 1994 contains an interpretative note to Article VI. It addresses, *inter alia*, the provision of a reasonable security for the payment of a countervailing duty pending final determination and rules. And it clarifies that multiple currency practices can constitute an export subsidy.

US – Carbon Steel was of the view that paragraphs 3 and 6(a) of Article VI set out the purpose of countervailing duties and the general circumstances in which they may be levied. Moreover, these two provisions give some indication of the object and purpose of the ASCM.[100]

95 See also *Wouters/Coppens* (2010) p. 21.

96 WT/DS301/R of 22 April 2005, *EC – Measures Affecting Trade in Commercial Vessels*, para 7.68 (emphasis added). See also WT/DS316/RW of 22 September 2016, *EC and certain Member States – Measures Affecting Trade in Large Civil Aircraft – Recourse to Article 21.5 of the DSU by the United States*, para 6.785 *et passim*.

97 WT/DS301/R of 22 April 2005, *EC – Measures Affecting Trade in Commercial Vessels*, paras 7.69–7.71.

98 WT/DS301/R of 22 April 2005, *EC – Measures Affecting Trade in Commercial Vessels*, para 7.72.

99 See Appendix 2.

100 WT/DS213/R of 3 July 2002, *United States – Countervailing Duties on Certain Corrosion-Resistant Carbon Steel Flat Products from Germany*, para 8.31.

Note that Article VI:3 contains, together with footnote 36 to Article 10 of the ASCM, a requirement to carry out in certain circumstances a pass-through analysis in relation to subsidized inputs of the product subject to investigation. The details are described *infra* Article 10 pp. 373–378.

According to the Appellate Body in *US – Anti-Dumping and Countervailing Duties (China)*, the obligation contained in Article VI:3 of GATT 1994 to establish the precise amount of the subsidy and the countervailing duty encompasses a requirement to conduct a sufficiently diligent investigation into, and solicitation of, relevant facts and to base any determination on positive evidence in the record.[101]

Article XVI GATT 1994

Introduction Article XVI contains two sections: Section A concerning subsidies in general and Section B setting out additional provisions on export subsidies. Section B was not contained in the original version of GATT 1947, but was only added in 1955.[102] Contrary to the ASCM, neither of the two sections contains a definition of the term 'subsidy'. However, Section A clarifies that any form of income or price support falls under the term 'subsidy' as used in Article XVI of GATT 1994. And Section B (Article XVI:4) contains a definition of some sort of the term 'export subsidy' that is, however, different from the one contained in Article 3.1(a) ASCM. Annex I to GATT 1994 also contains an interpretative note to Article XVI.

Section A, i.e. Article XVI:1, essentially stipulates that if a WTO Member grants or maintains a subsidy that has an effect on trade, it shall notify the other Members of such subsidy including the circumstances making such subsidization necessary and the estimated trade effect of the subsidy. In case such subsidy causes or threatens to cause serious prejudice to other Members, the WTO Member granting or maintaining such subsidy shall upon request discuss with the other WTO Members the possibility of limiting the subsidization. Given that each Member had to

[101] WT/DS379/AB/R of 11 March 2011, *US – Definitive Anti-Dumping and Countervailing Duties on Certain Products from China*, paras 601 and 602. See also WT/DS436/AB/R of 8 December 2014, *United States – Countervailing Measures on Certain Hot-Rolled Carbon Steel Flat Products from India*, para 4.152. See also WT/DS464/AB/R of 7 September 2016, *United States – Anti-Dumping and Countervailing Measures on Large Residential Washers from Korea*, para 5.204 *et seq.*, described *infra* the commentary to Article 19, pp. 526–528.

[102] For further details on Article XVI including references to disputes relating to this provision under the GATT see *Stoler* (2010) pp. 796–801.

select the subsidies to be notified based on its unilateral assessment of the trade effect, this was not a strong discipline. The notification disciplines under Article 25 of the ASCM are much more stringent. Note also that contrary to Article 6 of the ASCM, Article XVI of GATT 1994 does not contain a definition of 'serious prejudice'.

Section B covers paragraphs 2 to 5 of Article XVI. It deals with export subsidies but establishes different disciplines for primary and non-primary products. Article XVI:2 recognizes the harmful effects of export subsidies in general. Article XVI:3 stipulates that WTO Members should seek to avoid the use of subsidies on the export of primary products. At least, such subsidies should not be applied in a manner which gives the subsidizing WTO Member more than an equitable share of world export in the primary product in question. Thus, contrary to Article 3 of the ASCM, Article XVI:3 does not flatly prohibit export subsidies for primary products. Pre-Uruguay, there was some debate whether the 'equitable share' should be interpreted with reference to individual national markets or with reference to the overall world market.[103] Given that Article 6.3 of the ASCM has introduced a distinction between 'displacement' of imports in markets of individual Members (see subparagraphs a and b) and the 'world market share of the subsidizing Member' (see subparagraph d), this issue has lost importance.

Article XVI:4 requests that as from 1 January 1958 or from the earliest practicable date thereafter, parties should cease to grant any form of export subsidy on any non-primary product which results in an export price lower than the comparable domestic sales price in the exporting country (so-called 'bilevel pricing test').[104] Moreover, this paragraph also contains a standstill clause, i.e. the scope of export subsidization should not extend beyond that existing on 1 January 1955. Only in 1960, contracting parties could agree on a 'Declaration Giving Effect to the Provisions of Article XVI:4' that contained a non-exhaustive list of export subsidies on non-primary goods. Seventeen GATT Members accepted this Declaration which became effective as of 14 November 1962 and only applied to those 17 Members.[105]

[103] *Hufbauer/Erb* (1984) p. 38.

[104] A kind of subsidy-induced dumping, as *Stoler* (2010) p. 800 has put it. According to *Hufbauer/Erb* (1984) pp. 46–48, the bilevel pricing test proved unworkable both because subsidies do not necessarily have a price effect and because published data seldom permit a detailed comparison between domestic and export prices.

[105] *Wouters/Coppens* (2010) pp. 8 and 9. An updated version of this list found its way into the Tokyo Round Subsidies Code.

Primary products include agricultural products. The more lenient treatment of primary as compared to non-primary products is a result of US farm interests. At the time when Section B was added they were too powerful to be made subject to stricter disciplines.[106]

The interpretative note to Article XVI contains the following clarifications:

- A duty drawback system that does not result in excess remission shall not be considered as a subsidy. (Applies to both sections.)
- Section B does not preclude the use of multiple exchange rates in accordance with the Agreement of the IMF.
- Definition of a 'primary product'. This notion also covers agricultural products. (Applies to Section B only.)
- The fact that a WTO Member has not exported the primary product during a previous representative period does not exclude such Member from establishing its right to obtain a share in the trade of the product concerned. (Applies to Article XVI:3 of Section B only.)
- A system of stabilization of the domestic price of a primary product or of the return to domestic producers of such product shall be considered not to involve a subsidy if certain conditions are met. (Applies to Article XVI:3 of Section B only.)
- The intentions underlying Article XVI:4 are also clarified in the interpretative note, i.e. to reach agreement to abolish export subsidies as from 1 January 1958 or, failing this, to reach agreement on an extension of the standstill. (Applies to Article XVI:4 of Section B only.)

The table on the next page summarizes the scope of the various paragraphs of Article XVI of GATT 1994.

Relationship with the ASCM The ASCM refers six times to Article XVI:

- in footnote 1 to Article 1.1(a)(1)(ii) that deals with duty drawback,
- in Article 1.1(a)(2) that deals with income support,
- in footnote 13 to Article 5 that deals with the notion of serious prejudice,
- in Articles 25 and 26 concerning notifications of subsidies and review of such subsidies, and
- in Annex I item (l).

There is no provision of the ASCM that refers explicitly to Article XVI:4 of GATT 1994. *US – FSC* highlighted that the notion of an export subsidy in Article XVI of GATT 1994 is different to the one contained in Article 3.1(a) ASCM (see *infra*).

[106] *Hufbauer/Erb* (1984) p. 24.

Paragraph	Scope	Content
Section A, paragraph 1	All subsidies / all products	Every Member shall notify subsidies that have an effect on trade. It shall discuss the possibility of limiting subsidization with any other Member if the subsidy causes (or threatens to cause) serious prejudice to the interests of such Member
Section B, paragraph 2	Export subsidies / all products	This paragraph recognizes the negative effects of export subsidies
Section B, paragraph 3	Export subsidies / primary products	Members should seek to avoid the use of export subsidies; in any event, the subsidizing Member shall not, as a result of the subsidy, obtain more than an equitable share of world export trade in the subsidized product (as compared to previous representative periods)
Section B, paragraph 4	Export subsidies / non-primary products	As from 1 January 1958, Members shall cease to provide export subsidies that result in lower export prices than the price of a comparable product on the domestic market of the exporting country
Section B, paragraph 5	All subsidies / all products	Members shall review from time to time the operation of Article XVI

As can be seen from the DSB rulings listed in the next section, Article XVI of GATT 1994 provides little, if any, guidance for the interpretation of the ASCM.

Relevant Jurisprudence

- *US – Upland Cotton*

In this dispute, Brazil invoked *inter alia* Section B of Article XVI GATT 1994. It focused, amongst others, on the phrase in Article XVI:3

'any form of a subsidy which operates to increase the export of any primary product' and argued that the ordinary meaning of this phrase encompasses all subsidies with an export-enhancing effect, not just those that are contingent on export performance. The Appellate Body did not rule on this issue as it found it unnecessary for purposes of resolving the dispute, because the US would not have been under any additional obligation regarding implementation.[107] Note that the Panel believed that Article XVI:3 is limited to 'export subsidies'.[108] The Panel held that the provisions of Article XVI:1 and XVI:3 cannot be jointly applied but have to be examined separately.[109]

- *US – FSC*

The definition of the term 'export subsidy' in paragraph 4 differs substantially from the one in Article 3.1(a) of the ASCM. According to paragraph 4, the subsidy falling under paragraph 4 is 'any form of subsidy on the export of any product … which subsidy results in the sale of such product for export at a price lower than the comparable price charged for the like product to buyers in the domestic market'. Thus, whether a subsidy is an export subsidy under Article XVI:4 of GATT 1994 does not provide any guidance as to whether such measure is a prohibited export subsidy under Article 3.1(a) of the ASCM.[110] More generally, the preceding Panel in *US – FSC* has held that, in the light of *Brazil – Desiccated Coconut*, legal principles derived from Article XVI:4 of GATT 1994, read in isolation and without the benefit of the detailed provisions of the ASCM regarding the concepts of 'subsidy' and 'export subsidy', can be of little, if any, interpretative guidance in understanding the scope of a Member's obligations regarding export subsidies under the ASCM.[111]

According to the Appellate Body in *US – FSC*, the adoption of the GATT Panel reports by the GATT Council that solved four disputes known commonly and collectively as the Tax Legislation Cases that opposed Belgium, France, the Netherlands and the US, and that concerned export

[107] WT/DS267/AB/R of 3 March 2005, *United States – Subsidies on Upland Cotton*, paras 757–762.

[108] WT/DS267/R of 8 September 2004, *United States – Subsidies on Upland Cotton*, para 7.997 *et passim*.

[109] WT/DS267/R of 8 September 2004, *United States – Subsidies on Upland Cotton*, para 7.992.

[110] WT/DS108/AB/R of 24 February 2000, *United States – Tax Treatment for 'Foreign Sales Corporations'*, para 117.

[111] WT/DS108/R of 8 October 1999, *United States – Tax Treatment for 'Foreign Sales Corporations'*, para 7.82.

subsidies under Article XVI:4 of GATT 1947, was not an 'other decision' under paragraph 1(b)(iv) of the General Agreement on Tariffs and Trade 1994. On that ground, the Tax Legislation cases do not provide an authoritative interpretation of Article XVI:4 of GATT 1994, binding on all the contracting parties.[112] The previous Panel has also rejected the US claim that the 1981 Council Action represents 'subsequent practice' within the meaning of Article 31(3)(b) of the Vienna Convention on the Law of Treaties with respect to GATT Article XVI:4.[113] It found that it is a 'decision' within the meaning of Article XVI:4 of the Marrakesh Agreement Establishing the World Trade Organization.[114] However, that decision does not provide guidance in understanding detailed provisions of the ASCM which did not exist at the time when the understanding was adopted.[115]

- *Indonesia – Autos*

This Panel found that a WTO Member cannot claim that it has suffered serious prejudice with respect to products that have been produced abroad by its companies but do not originate in its country or customs territory.[116]

An overview of pre-WTO rulings concerning this provision can be found in *Adamantopoulos/Pereyra* (2007) pp. 8–10.

Article XX GATT 1994

Article XX contains general exceptions to the disciplines of GATT 1994, provided that a measure in question is not applied in a manner that would constitute a means of arbitrary or unjustifiable discrimination between countries where the same conditions prevail, or a disguised restriction on international trade, and if the measure falls under one of the subparagraphs of this provision, e.g. subparagraph '(g) relating to the conversation of exhaustible natural resources … '. The question is whether a

[112] WT/DS108/AB/R of 24 February 2000, *United States – Tax Treatment for 'Foreign Sales Corporations'*, paras 104–119. The precise reference of the decision in question is *Tax Legislation*, L/5271, 7–8 December 1981, BISD 28/S/114 and the four panel reports are listed in footnote 44 of the aforementioned Appellate Body ruling.

[113] WT/DS108/R of 8 October 1999, *United States – Tax Treatment for 'Foreign Sales Corporations'*, para 7.75.

[114] WT/DS108/R of 8 October 1999, *United States – Tax Treatment for 'Foreign Sales Corporations'*, paras 7.76–7.78.

[115] WT/DS108/R of 8 October 1999, *United States – Tax Treatment for 'Foreign Sales Corporations'*, paras 7.82–7.85.

[116] WT/DS54/R, WT/DS55/R, WT/DS59/R and WT/DS64/R of 2 July 1998, *Indonesia – Certain Measures Affecting the Automobile Industry*, paras 14.198–14.204.

subsidizing Member could invoke Article XX against an adverse effects claim (Articles 5 and 6 of the ASCM) or a claim against prohibited subsidies (Articles 3 and 4 of the ASCM). The Appellate Body in *China – Raw Materials* confirmed that Article XX could not be relied upon outside the GATT Framework unless textual support can be found within the specific legal regime. There is no jurisprudence with regard to the application of Article XX to the ASCM. Legal doctrine tends to exclude the applicability of Article XX.[117]

WTO Agreement on Agriculture

Introduction

The Agreement on Agriculture (AoA) is to a large extent about disciplining the use of subsidies for agricultural products. It binds the amounts of subsidies that WTO Members can provide to their farmers in a way which is not dissimilar to tariff bindings.[118] The product scope of the AoA is defined in Annex I of that Agreement.

Under the AoA, WTO Members are entitled to grant subsidies provided they are not in excess of the commitment levels specified in Part IV of each Member's schedule (see Article 3 AoA) or if they fall into the Green Box, the Blue Box, the S&D Box for developing country Members or the *de minimis* box (see *infra* pp. 40–41). The AoA distinguishes two types of commitments in relation to subsidies, i.e. domestic support and export subsidy commitments.

This contrasts with the ASCM, which prohibits export subsidies and import substitution subsidies and entitles WTO Members to act against other subsidies provided they produce negative effects as defined in Articles 5, 6 and 15. However, the ASCM also contains language that seems to subordinate, to a certain extent, anti-subsidy action to the conditions and provisions of the AoA. This chapter gives a short overview of the AoA rules on domestic and export support and explores the legal consequences of the web of cross-references between the two agreements.

117 For a good discussion with further references see *Coppens* (2014) p. 192 *et seq*. and *Farah/Cima* (2015) pp. 1113–1116 as well as WT/DS394/AB/R, WT/DS395/AB/R and WT/DS398/AB/R of 30 January 2012, *China – Measures Related to the Exportation of Various Raw Materials*, paras 303–306. More open to the application of Article XX of GATT 1994 *Rubini* (2012) pp. 559–570 in the context of renewable subsidies.

118 Sykes (2010) p. 486.

Note that the AoA does not contain a general subsidy definition such as the one contained in Article 1 ASCM. The Appellate Body has developed a definition for the purposes of the AoA but frequently refers – when examining whether or not there is a subsidy – to reports discussing the subsidy definition contained in the ASCM.[119]

Export Support

Contrary to the ASCM, the AoA does not *per se* prohibit export subsidies. They can be provided if they are in conformity with the schedule of the WTO Member in question and with the commitments as specified in the AoA.

The AoA defines export subsidies in Article 1(e) as 'subsidies contingent upon export performance, including the export subsidies listed in Article 9'. Article 9 lists six types of export subsidies and deals with the modalities of the export subsidy reduction commitments given by WTO Members. Article 10 AoA contains an obligation not to circumvent the export subsidy commitments. The Appellate Body in *US – FSC* held that the requirement of 'export-contingency' in the AoA and in the ASCM can

[119] WT/DS103/AB/R and WT/DS113/AB/R of 13 October 1999, *Canada – Measures Affecting the Importation of Milk and the Exportation of Dairy Products*, paras 84–102, in particular para 87 (a subsidy under the AoA 'involves a transfer of economic resources from the grantor to the recipient for less than full consideration'); WT/DS108/AB/R of 24 February 2000, *United States – Tax Treatment for 'Foreign Sales Corporations'*, paras 136 and 137. Note that the aforementioned definition does not include the type of governmental involvement normally associated with a subsidy. According to Article 9.1(c) AoA, payments ('transfer of economic resources', which can be in the form of monetary transfers or in kind) can also be funded or made by private parties, see WT/DS103/AB/RW2 and WT/DS113/AB/RW2 of 20 December 2002, *Canada – Measures Affecting the Importation of Milk and the Exportation of Dairy Products*, para 87. However, Article 9.1(c) requires that the payments are made 'by virtue of government action'. The Appellate Body has interpreted this condition in *Canada – Dairy (2nd Article 21.5)*, para 122 *et seq.* and held that there must be a demonstrable link or nexus between the government action and the payment. The scope of application of Article 9.1(c) is thus fairly far-reaching. In *EC – Export Subsidies on Sugar*, it covered sales of so-called C-sugar, i.e. sales of sugar that was not eligible for domestic price support nor export price support (A-sugar and B-sugar) and simply had to be exported by virtue of the market regulations. And in *Canada – Dairy (2nd Article 21.5)*, para 14, Canada had introduced a new category of milk for export processing (so-called 'commercial export milk' or 'CEM'). Export sales of CEM did not require a quota or any other form of permit from the Canadian government nor were they subject to any price regulation. Revenues obtained from sales of CEM were collected directly by the producers without any government involvement. However, if a dairy product derived from CEM was sold on the Canadian domestic market, the processor was liable for financial penalties. The supply of CEM by Canadian farmers to dairy processors qualified as an export subsidy under Article 9.1(c). In both *Canada – Dairy (2nd Article 21.5)* and *EC – Export Subsidies on Sugar* there was no payment by the public authorities.

be read in the same way.[120] However, the preceding Panel also concluded that a measure which is listed as an export subsidy in Article 9.1 AoA is an export subsidy for the purposes of the AoA independently of the subsidy definition of the ASCM.[121]

In relation to export subsidies, the central provision is Article 8 AoA, which stipulates:

> Each Member undertakes not to provide export subsidies otherwise than in conformity with this Agreement [on Agriculture] and with the commitments as specified in that Member's schedule.[122]

Article 3.3 AoA further clarifies:

> Subject to the provisions of paragraphs 2(b) and 4 of Article 9, a Member shall not provide export subsidies listed in paragraph 1 of Article 9 in respect of agricultural products or groups of products specified in Section II of Part IV of its Schedule in excess of the budgetary outlay and quantity commitments levels specified therein and shall not provide such subsidies in respect of any agricultural product not specified in that section of its Schedule.

Thus, under Article 3.3 AoA, WTO Members have undertaken two different types of export subsidy commitments. First, with regard to scheduled products they have committed that they will not provide export subsidies listed in Article 9.1 AoA in excess of the budgetary outlay and quantity commitments levels specified in their schedule. Second, with regard to unscheduled products, Members have committed not to provide any export subsidies listed in Article 9.1.[123] Article 9.1 AoA lists six types of

[120] See in detail *infra* Article 3 pp. 204–223 and WT/DS267/AB/R of 3 March 2005, *United States – Subsidies on Upland Cotton*, paras 513–584. See also WT/DS108/AB/R of 24 February 2000, *United States – Tax Treatment for 'Foreign Sales Corporations'*, para 141; WT/DS108/AB/RW of 14 January 2002, *United States – Tax Treatment for 'Foreign Sales Corporations' (Article 21.5, first recourse)*, para 190 *et seq*.

[121] WT/DS108/R of 8 October 1999, *United States – Tax Treatment for 'Foreign Sales Corporations'*, footnote 702 attached to para 7.150.

[122] WT/DS265/AB/R, WT/DS266/AB/R and WT/DS283/AB/R of 28 April 2005, *European Communities – Export Subsidies on Sugar*, para 216.

[123] WT/DS108/AB/R of 24 February 2000, *United States – Tax Treatment for 'Foreign Sales Corporations'*, paras 145 and 146. See also para 147 with regard to the interpretation of the terms 'export subsidy commitments' and 'reduction commitment levels'. WT/DS265/AB/R, WT/DS266/AB/R and WT/DS283/AB/R of 28 April 2005, *European Communities – Export Subsidies on Sugar*, para 189 *et seq*. clarified that a WTO Member can only benefit from Article 3.3 AoA if and to the extent it had actually specified budgetary outlay and quantity commitment levels in respect of subsidies listed in Article 9.1 AoA.

export subsidies that are subject to reduction commitments under the AoA.[124]

These obligations in relation to export subsidies are further reinforced by Article 10.1 AoA which provides:

> Export subsidies not listed in paragraph 1 of Article 9 shall not be applied in a manner which results in, or which threatens to lead to, circumvention of export subsidy commitments.

Note that Article 10.2 AoA does not exempt export credit guarantees from the export subsidy disciplines in Article 10.1 of the same Agreement.[125]

The Appellate Body in *US – FSC* had to interpret Article 10.1 AoA. It held that the term 'export subsidy commitments' in that provision covers commitments relating to both scheduled and unscheduled products. It also found that the FSC measures involved the application of export subsidies, not listed in Article 9.1 AoA, in a manner that, at the very least, threatened to lead to circumvention of the export subsidy commitment in Article 3.3 of that Agreement.[126]

Domestic Support

The system of domestic support established by the AoA is more complex. The AoA distinguishes five types of support:

- Green box subsidies (see Article 6.1 AoA and its Annex 2) are considered not or only minimally trade distorting. Therefore, they are not subject to the reduction requirements under the AoA. To fall within the green box, support must be (1) in conformity with the two horizontal requirements that are set out in paragraph 1 of Annex 2 (the support

[124] An example of subsidies falling under Article 9.1(a) can be found in WT/DS265/AB/R, WT/DS266/AB/R and WT/DS283/AB/R of 28 April 2005, *European Communities – Export Subsidies on Sugar*, para 206. The term 'financed by virtue of government action' contained in Article 9.1(c) was at issue in WT/DS265/AB/R, WT/DS266/AB/R and WT/DS283/AB/R of 28 April 2005, *European Communities – Export Subsidies on Sugar*, para 230 *et seq*. The same Appellate Body report examined the notion 'payment' in Article 9.1(c), see para 251 *et seq*. The notion of subsidies to reduce marketing costs (see Article 9.1(d)) was clarified in WT/DS108/AB/R of 24 February 2000, *United States – Tax Treatment for 'Foreign Sales Corporations'*, paras 128–132.

[125] See in detail *infra* Article 1 p. 15 and Annex I pp. 612–620 and WT/DS267/AB/R of 3 March 2005, *United States – Subsidies on Upland Cotton*, para 627. But see the dissenting opinion in para 631 *et seq*.

[126] WT/DS108/AB/R of 24 February 2000, *United States – Tax Treatment for 'Foreign Sales Corporations'*, paras 144–154. See also the Panel in WT/DS108/RW of 20 August 2001, *United States – Tax Treatment for 'Foreign Sales Corporations' (Article 21.5, first recourse)*, paras 8.111–8.122.

must be provided through a publicly-funded government programme and it shall not have the effect of providing price support to producers), and (2) it must be in conformity with one of the policy-specific criteria and conditions set out in paragraphs 2 to 13 of Annex 2. Paragraphs 2 to 13 cover a variety of programmes ranging from decoupled income support (paragraph 6) to domestic food aid (paragraph 4), government financial participation in income insurance and income safety-net programmes for farmers (paragraph 7) and payments under environmental and regional assistance programmes (paragraphs 12 and 13).[127]

- Blue box subsidies (see Article 6.5 AoA) cover payments based on fixed area and yields or a fixed number of livestock. They also cover payments that are made on 85 per cent or less of production in a defined base period. Thus, blue box subsidies are still coupled to production (contrary to green box subsidies) but the link between production and payments is somewhat loosened.
- *De minimis* support (see Article 6.4 AoA).
- Certain types of support provided by developing countries (see Article 6.3 AoA).
- Amber box subsidies: domestic subsidies other than the four aforementioned categories are put in the 'amber box' and are subject to the reduction commitments as set out in each WTO Member's schedule.

Relationship between the ASCM and the AoA

The basic question underlying this section is to what extent agricultural subsidies that are in conformity with the provisions of the AoA are shielded from the disciplines of the ASCM. In principle, the reply depends on the type of ASCM discipline in question. Three disciplines should be distinguished for this purpose, i.e. disciplines on prohibited subsidies (see Part II of the ASCM), disciplines concerning actionable subsidies (see Part III) and disciplines concerning countervailing measures (see Part V).

There can also be an interest to examine under the ASCM agricultural subsidies that are not in conformity with the AoA because the legal consequences of any violation established differ between the ASCM and the AoA. Most notably, the export subsidy disciplines under the ASCM as set out in its Articles 3 and 4 are more stringent than those under the AoA.

127 See also WT/MIN(13)/37 and WT/L/912 of 11 December 2013 concerning paragraph 2 of Annex 2 of the AoA and WT/MIN(13)/38 and WT/L/913 of 11 December 2013 on public stockholding for food security purposes and domestic food aid, both adopted at the Bali WTO Ministerial Conference.

The ASCM contains a number of references to the AoA, i.e. in Articles 3.1, 5, 6.9, 7.1 and 10. The AoA contains equally a number of references to the ASCM, i.e. Articles 21.1 and 13. The latter provision is the so-called 'peace clause' that expired in 2003 (see *infra* in this chapter).

The cross-references in the ASCM to the AoA can be classified in two groups, i.e. those that also include a reference to the peace clause of the AoA and those that do not contain such reference. Articles 5, 6.9 and 7.1 of the ASCM refer to the peace clause. Articles 5 and 6.9 of the ASCM both stipulate: 'This Article does not apply to subsidies maintained on agricultural products as provided in Article 13 of the Agreement on Agriculture.' Article 7.1 of the ASCM begins with the subordinate '[e]xcept as provided in Article 13 of the Agreement on Agriculture'.

By contrast, Articles 3.1 and 10 of the ASCM do not contain a cross-reference to the peace clause. The introductory phrase in Article 3.1 of the ASCM simply clarifies that export subsidies and import substitution subsidies are prohibited unless they are provided in the Agreement on Agriculture. Finally, Article 10 of the ASCM specifies: 'Countervailing duties may only be imposed pursuant to investigations initiated and conducted in accordance with the provisions of [the ASCM] and the Agreement on Agriculture.'

With regard to the references of the AoA to the ASCM, note first Article 21.1 AoA:

> The provisions of GATT 1994 and of the other Multilateral Trade Agreements in Annex 1A to the WTO Agreement shall apply subject to the provisions of this Agreement.[128]

Consequently, the provisions of the ASCM and GATT 1994 also apply to agricultural goods. However, in the event, and to the extent there is a conflict between the aforementioned provisions and those of the AoA, the latter prevail.

The Appellate Body in *US – Upland Cotton* examined whether such conflict existed in relation to import substitution subsidies falling under Article 3.1(b) of the ASCM. The preceding Panel did not find such a conflict. On appeal, the US argued that the Panel erred because it failed to give meaning to the introductory phrase '[e]xcept as provided in the Agreement on Agriculture' of Article 3.1 of the ASCM. The Appellate

[128] See also WT/DS265/AB/R, WT/DS266/AB/R and WT/DS283/AB/R of 28 April 2005, *European Communities – Export Subsidies on Sugar*, para 221.

Body upheld the Panel's findings. It agreed with the Panel's analysis as to what could constitute such an exception under the AoA:

> ... where, for example, the domestic support provisions of the *Agreement on Agriculture* would prevail in the event that an explicit carve-out or exemption from the disciplines in Article 3.1(b) of the *SCM Agreement* existed in the *text* of the *Agreement on Agriculture*. Another situation would be where it would be impossible for a Member to comply with its domestic support obligations under the *Agreement on Agriculture* and the Article 3.1(b) simultaneously. Another situation might be where there is an explicit authorization in the text of the *Agreement on Agriculture* that would authorize a measure that, in the absence of such an express authorization, would be prohibited by Article 3.1(b) of the *SCM Agreement*.

The Appellate Body also pointed out that there could be situations other than the three identified by the Panel where Article 21.1 of the AoA might apply. However, in the case at hand, neither the Panel nor the Appellate Body found in the AoA a provision (in particular not its paragraph 7 of Annex 3 and Article 6.3) that dealt specifically with the same matter (i.e. the prohibition of import substitution subsidies) or otherwise set aside for agricultural products the prohibition of such subsidies under Article 3.1(b) of the ASCM. Consequently, the contested US subsidies were prohibited pursuant to Article 3.1(b) although they were in conformity with the AoA.[129]

Article 13 of the AoA, i.e. the peace clause, contained a carve-out of certain subsidies for agricultural products from the disciplines of the ASCM.[130] Subparagraph (b)(i) was at issue in *Mexico – Olive Oil*[131] and subparagraph (c)(ii) in *Canada – Dairy (1st Article 21.5)*.[132] The peace clause was only applicable until 2003, i.e. during the so-called implementation

129 WT/DS267/AB/R of 3 March 2005, *United States – Subsidies on Upland Cotton*, paras 526–550 (in particular para 532). For details see *infra* Article 3 pp. 203–204.

130 WT/DS267/R of 8 September 2004, *United States – Subsidies on Upland Cotton*, paras 7 326–7.328 *et passim*, para 7.338 *et seq.* and 7.1030 *et seq.* as well as WT/DS267/AB/R of 3 March 2005, *United States – Subsidies on Upland Cotton*, para 310 *et seq.* The Panel concluded that Article 13(c) contained a carve-out for certain export subsidies but not for import substitution subsidies (see para 7.1050).

131 WT/DS341/R of 4 September 2008, *Mexico – Definitive Countervailing Measures on Olive Oil from the European Communities*, paras 7.51–7.81. See in particular the Panel's comments on 'due restraint', para 7.65 *et seq.*

132 WT/DS103/AB/RW and WT/DS113/AB/RW of 3 December 2001, *Canada – Measures Affecting the Importation of Milk and the Exportation of Dairy Products (1st Article 21.5)*, paras 122–125.

period of the AoA as defined in its Article 1(f) AoA.[133] In *Canada – Dairy (1st Article 21.5)*, the Appellate Body was unable to determine whether the contested measure was fully in conformity with Articles 9.1(c) and 10.1 of the AoA. The Appellate Body then recalled that the relationship between the AoA and the ASCM is defined, in part, by Article 3.1 of the ASCM which states that certain subsidies are prohibited except as provided in the AoA. In the view of the Appellate Body, Article 3.1 therefore indicates that the WTO consistency of an export subsidy for agricultural products has to be examined, in the first place, by the AoA. Given that the Appellate Body could not determine the consistency of the subsidy with the AoA, it declined to examine whether the measure constituted a prohibited subsidy under Article 3 of the ASCM. The Appellate Body's reference to the introductory phrase of Article 3.1 could be read to mean that the expiry of the peace clause did not render export subsidies prohibited under the ASCM.

The Appellate Body in *US – Upland Cotton* held with regard to the relationship between the ASCM and the AoA that to the extent that a WTO Member has not made an export subsidy reduction commitment, that Member is subject to a general prohibition of export subsidies.[134] Similarly, the Panel in *US – Upland Cotton (Article 21.5)* concluded that to the extent that such subsidies do not conform fully to the provisions of the AoA, i.e. they are provided for unscheduled products or in excess of export subsidy reduction commitments to exports of scheduled products, they are subject to the prohibition on export subsidies under Article 3.1(a).[135] Note, however, that the Implementation Panel did not need to address the question of whether after the expiry of the peace clause there may be a violation of Article 3.1(a) in respect of all agricultural export subsidies.[136]

[133] According to WT/DS341/R of 4 September 2008, *Mexico – Definitive Countervailing Measures on Olive Oil from the European Communities*, paras 7.52–7.54 the date of expiry of the implementation period might have been some point during 2004. The Panel did not see any need ultimately to determine the precise date of expiry.

[134] WT/DS267/RW of 18 December 2007, *United States – Subsidies on Upland Cotton (Article 21.5)*, paras 14.46 and 14.136 *et seq.*; WT/DS103/R and WT/DS113/R of 17 May 1999, *Canada – Measures Affecting the Importation of Milk and the Exportation of Dairy Products*, paras 7.20 and 7.21.

[135] WT/DS267/RW of 18 December 2007, *United States – Subsidies on Upland Cotton (Article 21.5)*, paras 14.154 and 14.155; confirmed in WT/DS267/AB/RW of 16 May 2008, *United States – Subsidies on Upland Cotton (Article 21.5)*, para 323.

[136] WT/DS267/RW of 18 December 2007, *United States – Subsidies on Upland Cotton (Article 21.5)*, footnote 785 attached to para 14.154.

The Panel in *US – Upland Cotton* is largely in line with the above. It concluded with regard to export subsidies for agricultural products that the web of cross-references discloses a scheme according to which an analysis of the same measures under the ASCM, the AoA and Article XVI of GATT 1994 should be first carried out under the AoA. According to the Panel, the same holds true with regard to allegedly actionable subsidies for agricultural products, at least during the implementation period for the purposes of Article 13.[137]

In *EC – Export Subsidies on Sugar* the Appellate Body held that a panel cannot exercise judicial economy in relation to a claim under Article 3 ASCM even if it had found that the export subsidies were prohibited under the AoA. The two situations are different, in particular because the AoA does not contain a rule similar to Article 4.7 ASCM. This provision stipulates that a Member providing a prohibited subsidy shall withdraw such subsidy without delay.[138] However, the Appellate Body could not complete the legal analysis. In this respect, the Appellate Body pointed out that in the light of Article 21 AoA and the chapeau of Article 3 ASCM, the question of the applicability of the ASCM to the export subsidies in

[137] WT/DS267/R of 8 September 2004, *United States – Subsidies on Upland Cotton*, paras 7.261–7.263 as well as para 7.673 *et passim*. WT/DS103/R and WT/DS113/R of 17 May 1999, *Canada – Measures Affecting the Importation of Milk and the Exportation of Dairy Products*, para 7.23; WT/DS103/AB/RW and WT/DS113/AB/RW of 3 December 2001, *Canada – Measures Affecting the Importation of Milk and the Exportation of Dairy Products (1st Article 21.5)*, paras 123–124. Note that not all prior DSB rulings followed this order of examination.

[138] WT/DS265/AB/R, WT/DS266/AB/R and WT/DS283/AB/R of 28 April 2005, *European Communities – Export Subsidies on Sugar*, paras 327–335. See also WT/DS103/R and WT/DS113/R of 17 May 1999, *Canada – Measures Affecting the Importation of Milk and the Exportation of Dairy Products*, paras 7.135–7.141 where the Panel declined to rule on a claim under Article 3 ASCM because (1) the US essentially argued that a violation of export subsidy commitments under the AoA automatically means a violation of Article 3 ASCM and (2) the US application was not in conformity with Article 4.2 of the ASCM because it did not contain a statement of available evidence. The implementation panel also declined to rule on a claim under Article 3 ASCM because according to that Panel, part of the export subsidy granted was within the budgetary outlay and quantity commitment levels under Article 9.1(c) AoA (see WT/DS103/RW and WT/DS113/RW of 11 July 2001, *Canada – Measures Affecting the Importation of Milk and the Exportation of Dairy Products (1st Article 21.5)*, paras 6.91–6.102). WT/DS103/RW2 and WT/DS113/RW2 of 26 July 2002, *Canada – Measures Affecting the Importation of Milk and the Exportation of Dairy Products (2nd Article 21.5)*, para 5.178 concluded that its findings concerning Articles 9.1(c) and 10.1 AoA were sufficient to resolve the matter of the dispute. The Panel declined to rule on the US claims relating to Article 3.1 ASCM. However, it deemed the factual record complete so that the Appellate Body could ultimately make a finding in relation to the ASCM if it disagreed with the Panel's finding made in relation to the AoA.

question raised a number of complex issues. These issues include whether the AoA contains 'specific provisions dealing specifically with the same matter', whether the ASCM applies to the agricultural export subsidy as a whole, or whether it applies only to the extent that the subsidy exceeds the responding Member's commitment levels etc.[139] The Appellate Body's statement could be taken as an indication that the relationship between the ASCM and the AoA is probably not fully clarified yet while some academics have painted the relationship between the two agreements with a broader brush. Their views vary but the debate is to a large extent about the effect of the expiry of the peace clause, i.e. Article 13 AoA.[140]

Article 10.3 AoA, that shifts in a dispute settlement procedure to the exporting Member the burden of proof of the absence of subsidization for any product exported in excess to the reduction commitments, does not apply to claims brought under the ASCM.[141]

The Panel in *US – Upland Cotton* also pointed out that Article 6.3 AoA does not provide that compliance with 'domestic support reduction commitments' shall necessarily be considered to be in compliance with other applicable WTO obligations. According to the Panel, Article 21.1 AoA does consequently not provide a carve-out in respect of domestic support reduction commitments.[142]

WTO Agreement on Trade-Related Investment Measures ('TRIMs Agreement')

Indonesia – Autos held that the ASCM and the TRIMs Agreement cannot be in conflict, as they cover different subject matters and do not impose mutually exclusive obligations. In the case of the ASCM, what was prohibited in the case at issue was the granting of an import substitution subsidy, not the requirement to use domestic goods as such. In the case of the TRIMs Agreement, what is prohibited are TRIMs in the form of local content requirements, not the grant of an advantage such as a subsidy. The

[139] See also WT/DS265/AB/R, WT/DS266/AB/R and WT/DS283/AB/R of 28 April 2005, *European Communities – Export Subsidies on Sugar*, paras 336–340.

[140] See e.g. *Wouters/Coppens* (2010) pp. 79–81 with further references.

[141] See in detail and WT/DS267/AB/R of 3 March 2005, *United States – Subsidies on Upland Cotton*, para 647. With regard to the relationship of the panel request and the burden of proof under Article 10.3 AoA see also WT/DS265/AB/R, WT/DS266/AB/R and WT/DS283/AB/R of 28 April 2005, *European Communities – Export Subsidies on Sugar*, para 154.

[142] WT/DS267/R of 8 September 2004, *United States – Subsidies on Upland Cotton*, paras 7.1058 and 7.1071 *et passim*.

Panel therefore rejected Indonesia's view that its car programmes were subsidies and consequently could not be TRIMs. According to the Panel, the obligations contained in the WTO Agreement are generally cumulative and can be complied with simultaneously. Different aspects and sometimes the same aspects of a legislative act can be subject to various provisions of the WTO Agreement.[143]

See also *Canada – Renewable Energy & Feed-In Tariff Program* (*infra* Article 1 pp. 132–136) where an input substitution subsidy was also a measure falling under the TRIMs Agreement.

WTO Anti-Dumping Agreement

Many provisions of the Agreement on Implementation of Article VI of GATT 1994 ('Anti-Dumping Agreement') and of Part V of the ASCM are identical or nearly identical. See for instance, the provisions on injury (Article 15 ASCM and Article 3 of the Anti-Dumping Agreement). Therefore, there is a need that such identical or nearly identical provisions are interpreted in a coherent manner. The 'Declaration on Dispute Settlement Pursuant to the Agreement on Implementation of Article VI of the General Agreement on Tariffs and Trade 1994 or Part V of the Agreement on Subsidies and Countervailing Measures' acknowledges this need. It reads:

> Ministers,
>
> *Recognize*, with respect to dispute settlement pursuant to the Agreement on Implementation of Article VI of the General Agreement on Tariffs and Trade 1994 or Part V of the Agreement on Subsidies and Countervailing Measures, the need for the consistent resolution of disputes arising from anti-dumping and countervailing duty measures.[144]

However, the need for a consistent resolution goes beyond countervailing duty measures. It is equally pertinent with regard to claims of adverse effects based on injury to the domestic industry of another WTO Member, according to Article 5(a) ASCM.[145] DSB rulings concerning

[143] WT/DS54/R, WT/DS55/R, WT/DS59/R and WT/DS64/R of 2 July 1998, *Indonesia – Certain Measures Affecting the Automobile Industry*, paras 14.47–14.56.

[144] This Declaration is part of the 'Final Act Embodying the Results of the Uruguay Round of Multilateral Trade Negotiations'.

[145] Footnote 11 to the ASCM specifies that the term 'injury to the domestic industry' in Article 5(a) is used in the same sense as it is used in Part V of the ASCM.

countervailing duty measures or adverse effects claims therefore routinely refer to Panel and Appellate Body reports that interpret the corresponding provisions of the Anti-Dumping Agreement.[146] However, Article 17.2 of the Anti-Dumping Agreement cannot be invoked under the ASCM.[147]

Prohibition of Double Remedies

The Notion of Double Remedy or Double Counting The issue of double remedies can arise when both countervailing duties and anti-dumping duties are imposed on the same imported product. More specifically, this refers to circumstances in which the simultaneous application of countervailing and anti-dumping duties on the same imported product results, at least to some extent, in the offsetting of the same subsidization twice.[148]

Double Remedies in Relation to Export Subsidies (Article VI:5 GATT 1994) The rationale underlying the prohibition to counter export subsidies concurrently via an anti-dumping duty and a countervailing duty is the following. An export subsidy will result in a pro rata reduction in the export price of the product, but will not affect the price of domestic sales of the product. In other words, the export subsidy will increase the price discrimination between the export price and the domestic price, i.e. it will result in a higher margin of dumping. Article VI:5 of GATT 1994 stipulates that '[n]o product of the territory of any contracting party imported into the territory of any other contracting party shall be subject to both anti-dumping and countervailing duties to compensate for the same situation of dumping and export subsidisation'. According to the Appellate Body in *US – Anti-Dumping and Countervailing Duties (China)*, in case of an export subsidy the situation of subsidization and the situation of dumping are the 'same situation', and the cumulative application of anti-dumping and countervailing duties would amount to the application of

[146] See e.g. WT/DS414/R of 15 June 2012, *China – Countervailing and Anti-Dumping Duties on Grain-Oriented Flat-Rolled Electrical Steel from the US*, para 7.289. WT/DS296/R/3 of 21 February 2005, *United States – Countervailing Duty Investigation on Dynamic Random Access Memory Semiconductors (DRAMs) from Korea*, para 7.350 *et seq*. This aspect was not appealed.

[147] WT/DS138/AB/R of 10 May 2000, *United States – Imposition of Countervailing Duties on Certain Hot-Rolled Lead and Bismuth Carbon Steel Products originating in the United Kingdom*, paras 42–51 and *infra* pp. 52–53 with further references.

[148] WT/DS379/AB/R of 11 March 2011, *US – Definitive Anti-Dumping and Countervailing Duties on Certain Products from China*, para 541.

'double remedies' to offset that export subsidy. By comparison, production subsidies (also referred to as 'domestic subsidies'), i.e. subsidies that are not conditional on the exportation of the product, will, in principle, affect in the same way the prices at which the producer sells its goods in both the export market and the domestic market. Thus, a production subsidy will lower in the same way the domestic price and the export price and thus will not lead to increased dumping. Therefore, the prohibition to cumulate countervailing duties and anti-dumping duties as contained in Article VI:5 of the GATT applies only in relation to export subsidies, but not to production subsidies. In relation to domestic subsidies, the countervailing duty and the anti-dumping duty would address different situations. The former would counter the domestic subsidy while the latter addresses the difference between export price and domestic price.[149]

Note, however, that the above rests on the assumption that an export subsidy and a domestic subsidy have distinct effects on prices. While this assumption may in some circumstances be correct there may be just as well cases where it is wrong. An exporter receiving an export subsidy is not obliged to decrease its prices commensurately. It could for instance invest the export subsidy in a project not related to its export activities (e.g. the acquisition of new machinery) or use the money in some other way, e.g. by buying a yacht and cruising in the Mediterranean. Having said this, there is no requirement under the ASCM for investigating authorities to establish the actual use to which individual subsidies are put. Only the conditions under which they are granted will be looked at. *Pauwelyn's* observation that Article VI:5 of GATT 1994 is a legal fiction which has the purpose of simplifying matters is perhaps an appropriate description of the function of this provision.[150]

Double Remedies in Relation to Subsidies in Non-Market Economy Countries The issue of double remedies may also arise in cases where a non-market economy methodology is used to calculate the margin of dumping. When investigating authorities calculate a dumping margin with regard to a product from a non-market economy country, they compare the export price to a normal value whose calculation is based on surrogate costs or prices from a third country with a market economy. The use of prices or costs established in such third country results

[149] WT/DS379/AB/R of 11 March 2011, *US – Definitive Anti-Dumping and Countervailing Duties on Certain Products from China*, para 568.

[150] *Pauwelyn* (2013) p. 237.

from the problem that prices and costs in a non-market economy country are usually considered unreliable. In other words, in dumping margin calculations, investigating authorities may compare a product's normal value (that is increased because it does not reflect the amount of subsidies received) with the product's actual export price (which, when subsidies have been received by the producer, is presumably lower than it would otherwise have been).

Therefore, the claim has been made that the dumping margin resulting from the surrogate country methodology is based on an asymmetric comparison and is generally higher than would otherwise be the case. This claim is based on the consideration that the surrogate country methodology reflects not only the price discrimination by the investigated producer between the export price and the normal value, i.e. dumping, but also economic distortions that affect the producer's cost of production. Such distortions may result from specific subsidies given to the investigated producer in respect of the product subject to an anti-dumping or CVD investigation. Therefore, an anti-dumping duty based on a surrogate country methodology might remedy or offset a domestic subsidy insofar as such subsidy has contributed to a lowering of the export price. When a countervailing duty is levied against the same imports, the same domestic subsidy is reflected in that duty. Thus, the additional countervailing duty might offset the subsidy twice.[151]

Double Remedies in Relation to Production Subsidies in Market Economy Countries The Appellate Body pointed out the issue of a double remedy may also arise in the context of domestic subsidies granted within market economies when anti-dumping and countervailing duties are concurrently imposed on the same product and an unsubsidized, constructed normal value is used.[152]

The Appellate Body on Double Remedies The Appellate Body took the view that the same subsidy cannot be remedied twice, i.e. by an anti-dumping duty and a countervailing duty. The Appellate Body saw the legal basis for this prohibition in Article 19.3 that specifies that a countervailing duty should be levied 'in the appropriate amounts in each case'. According

[151] WT/DS379/AB/R of 11 March 2011, *US – Definitive Anti-Dumping and Countervailing Duties on Certain Products from China*, paras 542 and 543.

[152] WT/DS379/AB/R of 11 March 2011, *US – Definitive Anti-Dumping and Countervailing Duties on Certain Products from China*, para 543 *in fine*. For more details see *Kelly* (2014/1) p. 120 *et seq.*

to the Appellate Body, the amount of a countervailing duty cannot be 'appropriate' in situations where that duty represents the full amount of the subsidy and where anti-dumping duties, calculated at least to some extent on the basis of the same subsidization, are imposed concurrently to remove the same injury to the domestic industry. The Appellate Body found relevant context *inter alia* in the following provisions:

- Article 10 (essentially for two reasons: (1) because footnote 35 specifies that with regard to the effects of a particular subsidy in the domestic market of the importing country only one form of relief shall be available, i.e. either a countervailing duty or a countermeasure under Articles 4 or 7; (2) because footnote 36 defines a countervailing duty as a special duty levied for the purpose of 'offsetting' a subsidy).
- Article 19.2 because this provision encourages investigating authorities to limit the amount of the countervailing duty to the injury to be removed.
- Article 19.3 because according to this provision a countervailing duty shall be levied on imports 'found to be subsidized and causing injury', i.e. this provision links the duty to the injury caused by the subsidized imports.
- Article 19.4 because this provision only provides for a quantitative ceiling of the countervailing duty, i.e. the duty cannot be higher than the subsidy found, but it does not require that the duty has to be equal to the subsidy found.
- Article 21.1 because this provision links the duty to the injury caused by the subsidized imports, like paragraphs 3 and 4 of Article 19.
- Article VI:5 of GATT 1994. This provision prohibits the parallel imposition of an anti-dumping and a countervailing duty 'to compensate for the same situation of dumping or export subsidization' (see also *supra* pp. 48–49). For the Appellate Body the term 'same situation' was of central importance to an understanding of the rationale underlying the prohibition of double remedies in case of export subsidization.
- The Anti-Dumping Agreement contains provisions that mirror the aforementioned provisions of the ASCM.[153]

In sum, the Appellate Body pleaded for an approach that the provisions of the Anti-Dumping Agreement and the ASCM 'should be interpreted

[153] WT/DS379/AB/R of 11 March 2011, *US – Definitive Anti-Dumping and Countervailing Duties on Certain Products from China*, paras 547–583, para 599.

together in a coherent and consistent manner, so as to avoid any possible circumvention of the rules governing, and ceilings on, anti-dumping and countervailing duties that are set forth in the respective provisions of the two agreements'.[154]

The Appellate Body was of the opinion that dumping margins established on a non-market economy methodology are likely to include some component that is attributable to subsidization. However, it also underlined that it was not convinced that double remedies necessarily result in every instance of a concurrent application of anti-dumping and countervailing duties. This depends rather on whether and to what extent domestic subsidies have lowered the export price of a product, and on whether the investigating authority has taken the necessary steps to adjust its methodology to take account of this factual situation. The burden of proof in this respect is on the investigating authority. According to the Appellate Body, an investigating authority is subject to an affirmative obligation to establish the appropriate duty under Article 19.3. However, in the case at issue, the Appellate Body could not finish its analysis because the record did not contain a sufficient basis in terms of factual findings of the panel and undisputed facts.[155]

Commentators were split on the question whether the Appellate Body's decision on double counting was appropriate.[156]

Differences in Dispute Settlement

The ASCM does not mirror Article 17.6 of the Anti-Dumping Agreement. The first subparagraph of this provision stipulates that in its assessment of the facts of the matter, the panel shall determine whether the authorities'

[154] WT/DS379/AB/R of 11 March 2011, *US – Definitive Anti-Dumping and Countervailing Duties on Certain Products from China*, para 589.

[155] WT/DS379/AB/R of 11 March 2011, *US – Definitive Anti-Dumping and Countervailing Duties on Certain Products from China*, para 592 *et seq.*

[156] *Cartland/Depayre/Woznowski* (2012) pp. 993–996 are very critical and refer, amongst others, to the context in which this provision was drafted and the negotiation history. Also critical *Pauwelyn* (2013) pp. 237–241 who noted *inter alia* that the text of Article 19.3 is not about determining the amount of the subsidy but levying a countervailing duty. In contrast, according to *Prusa/Vermulst* (2013) p. 225 *et passim*, the Appellate Body should have gone further, i.e. it should simply have concluded that the US' simultaneous use of AD and CVD remedies when applying the non-market economy methodology is illegal *tout court*. In their opinion, the Appellate Body probably did not adopt this radical solution because it seemed to have recognized that, in general, double remedies and pass-through are fundamentally empirical questions. *Ramanujan/Sampath* (2015) illustrate the problem of double counting by giving numerical examples and they also give an account on how the US administration finally resolved the issue.

establishment of the facts was proper and whether the evaluation of those facts was unbiased and objective. If all these conditions are met, a panel shall not overturn such a conclusion. The second subparagraph provides that the customary rules of interpretation of public international law shall apply. Moreover, it stipulates that where a panel finds that a relevant provision of the Anti-Dumping Agreement admits of more than one permissible interpretation, the panel shall find the anti-dumping measure in question in conformity with the Anti-Dumping Agreement if such measure rests upon one of those permissible interpretations. On this basis, *US – Softwood Lumber VI* held that there might well be cases in which the application of the Vienna Convention principles together with the additional provisions of Article 17.6 ADA could result in a different conclusion being reached in a dispute under the Anti-Dumping Agreement than under the ASCM. However, in the case in question it was not necessary to resolve this issue.[157]

1992 Agreement between the US and EU on Aircraft ('1992 Agreement')

In *EC and certain Member States – Large Civil Aircraft*, the EU invoked the above agreement on a number of issues. None of the claims was successful.

First, the EU argued that the US accepted in the 1992 Agreement in its bilateral relation with the EU an acceptable level of government support. Therefore, it cannot subsequently claim that this same support is actionable pursuant to Article 5 of the ASCM, causing adverse effects to its interests. The Appellate Body did not agree. While the 1992 Agreement stipulates that the parties shall seek to avoid any trade conflict on matters

[157] WT/DS277/R of 22 March 2004, *United States – Investigation of the International Trade Commission in Softwood Lumber from Canada*, paras 7.21 and 7.22. See also WT/DS277/AB/RW of 13 April 2006, *United States – Investigation of the International Trade Commission in Softwood Lumber from Canada – Recourse to Article 21.5 of the DSU by Canada*, paras 91 and 92 where the Appellate Body refers to *US – Hot-Rolled Steel*. The latter Appellate Body report did not really see any conflict between Article 17.6 Anti-Dumping Agreement and Article 11 DSU. *US – Lead and Bismuth II* also concluded that a party could not, by virtue of the Declaration on Dispute Settlement Pursuant to the Agreement on Implementation of Article VI of the General Agreement on Tariffs and Trade 1994 or Part V of the Agreement on Subsidies and Countervailing Measures, rely on Article 17.6 of the Anti-Dumping Agreement in an dispute concerning the ASCM, see WT/DS138/AB/R of 10 May 2000, *United States – Imposition of Countervailing Duties on Certain Hot-Rolled Lead and Bismuth Carbon Steel Products originating in the United Kingdom*, paras 44–51.

covered by it, it does not say that either party could not challenge subsidies provided to the aircraft industry if such support caused adverse effects. On the contrary, the agreement set out that it was the parties' intention to act without prejudice to their rights and obligations under the GATT and under other multilateral agreements negotiated under the auspices of the GATT.[158]

Second, the Appellate Body also rejected the EU's claims that the 1992 Agreement is relevant for the determination of whether or not the subsidies given to Airbus constituted a benefit under Article 1.1(b) of the ASCM. It held that the 1992 Agreement was not 'relevant' as it did not concern the subject matter that the Appellate Body had to examine, i.e. the question of benefit. The provision of the 1992 Agreement that the EU invoked referred to the maximum financial contribution that a party to the 1992 Agreement could give to its aircraft producers (which is not limited under the ASCM) but it did not deal with the question whether the amount to be paid by the recipient of the government loan was lower than the amount that would be paid for a comparable commercial loan.[159] The Panel has put this even more bluntly: '[The 1992 Agreement] contains no definition of a "subsidy" nor does it make any reference to the notion of "benefit".'[160] Its finding that the 1992 Agreement was not relevant for the question of benefit enabled the Appellate Body not to answer the question if the bilateral 1992 Agreement (as opposed to a multilateral agreement) could qualify under Article 31(3)(c) of the Vienna Convention. This provision provides that, when interpreting a treaty, there shall be taken into account, together with the context, any relevant rules of international law applicable in the relations between the parties. The US argued, based on the term 'parties', that this provision only refers to rules that are binding upon all parties to the treaty that should be interpreted, in the case at hand the ASCM and all WTO Members, and that consequently a bilateral agreement is not enough.

Third, the EU argued that any government support committed prior to 17 July 1992, the effective date of the 1992 Agreement, should be excluded from the scope of the DSB case because the 1992 Agreement grandfathered all the government support to large civil aircraft prior to its entry

[158] WT/DS316/AB/R of 18 May 2011, *EC and certain Member States – Measures Affecting Trade in Large Civil Aircraft*, paras 1301–1305.

[159] WT/DS316/AB/R of 18 May 2011, *EC and certain Member States – Measures Affecting Trade in Large Civil Aircraft*, para 839 *et seq.*

[160] WT/DS316/R of 30 June 2010, *EC and certain Member States – Measures Affecting Trade in Large Civil Aircraft*, para 7.389.

into force. The Panel did not accept this. It held that it had no jurisdiction pursuant to Articles 3.2 and 7.2 of the DSU to determine the rights and obligations arising out of the 1992 Agreement, that the EU's interpretation contradicted Article 30(3) of the Vienna Convention on the Law of Treaties and that in any event if the US had waived in the 1992 Agreement their rights under the ASCM any such waiver would need to be clear and unambiguous, which was not the case in the dispute at issue.[161]

Fourth, the Panel rejected an EU claim under Article 31(3) of the Vienna Convention on the Law of Treaties.[162]

Last but not least, the Panel also rejected the EU's argument that the 1992 Agreement gives rise to an estoppel preventing consideration of measures of support provided prior to the effective date of the 1992 Agreement. The Panel did not express a view whether this principle applied in the context of the WTO dispute settlement system but held that in any event there was no clear and unambiguous statement in the 1992 Agreement by which the US renounced having recourse to dispute settlement.[163]

WTO Dispute Settlement Understanding

Article 1.2 of the DSU states that the rules and procedures of the DSU shall apply subject to the special or additional rules and procedures on dispute settlement contained in the covered agreements as are identified in Appendix 2 of the DSU. Articles 4.2 through 4.12, 6.6, 7.2 through 7.10, 8.5, 24.4, 27.7, footnote 35 and Annex V the ASCM are such additional rules and procedures.

The rules and procedures of the DSU apply together with the special or additional provisions of the covered agreement except that in the case of a conflict between them, the special or additional provision prevails.[164]

–For details see *infra* the commentary to Article 30 of the ASCM. See also the 'Declaration on Dispute Settlement Pursuant to the Agreement

[161] WT/DS316/R of 30 June 2010, *EC and certain Member States – Measures Affecting Trade in Large Civil Aircraft*, paras 7.88–7.98. This point was not appealed.

[162] WT/DS316/R of 30 June 2010, *EC and certain Member States – Measures Affecting Trade in Large Civil Aircraft*, paras 7.99–7.100. This point was not appealed.

[163] WT/DS316/R of 30 June 2010, *EC and certain Member States – Measures Affecting Trade in Large Civil Aircraft*, paras 7.101–7.105. This point was not appealed.

[164] WT/DS108/AB/R of 24 February 2000, *United States – Tax Treatment for 'Foreign Sales Corporations'*, para 159 (in relation to Article 4.2 of the ASCM). With regard to the relationship between the special rules and the DSU see also WT/DS60/AB/R of 2 November 1998, *Guatemala – Anti-Dumping Investigation Regarding Portland Cement from Mexico*, para 65.

on Implementation of Article VI of the General Agreement on Tariffs and Trade 1994 or Part V of the Agreement on Subsidies and Countervailing Measures' reproduced *supra* pp. 47, 52–53.

Relevance of Municipal Law

Occasionally, the discussion of a concept under the ASCM may be influenced by the way municipal law of a WTO Member classifies or regulates matters or transactions. In *Softwood Lumber IV*, Canada argued that the provision of standing timber did not fall under the term 'good' in Article 1.1(a)(iii) because it did not constitute 'personal property'. The Appellate Body rejected this argument. It noted that municipal laws, in particular those relating to property, vary amongst WTO Members and that it would be inappropriate to characterize, for purposes of applying any provision of a WTO agreement, the same thing or transaction differently, depending on its legal categorization within the jurisdictions of different Members. Consequently, municipal law classifications are not determinative.[165]

In *Mexico – Beef and Rice*, the US claimed that certain provisions of the relevant Mexican law were inconsistent with the ASCM. Mexico argued that in Mexican law, international agreements such as the WTO agreements were self-executing and automatically applicable in Mexico, and that any domestic law had to be applied in a manner which was compatible with Mexico's international obligations. The Panel did not accept this argument. According to the Panel, the direct effect of the WTO Agreements in Mexican law may prove important in case the domestic law leaves the authority with discretion to apply the law in a WTO consistent manner. However, in case the domestic law is clear and manifestly conflicts with an agreement provision, as in the case at hand, then the direct effect of the WTO Agreements cannot shield the domestic law from scrutiny by WTO panels.[166]

[165] WT/DS257/AB/R of 19 January 2004, *United States – Final Countervailing Duty Determination with Respect to Certain Softwood Lumber from Canada*, paras 56 and 65.

[166] WT/DS295/R of 6 June 2005, *Mexico – Definitive Anti-Dumping Measures on Beef and Rice / Complaint with Respect to Rice*, para 7.224.

II

COMMENTARY

PART I

GENERAL PROVISIONS

Article 1

Definition of a Subsidy

Introduction

Overview

Article 1 defines the concept of subsidy. The concept of subsidy captures situations in which something of economic value is transferred by a government or a public body to the advantage of a recipient. Hence, a subsidy is deemed to exist pursuant to Article 1.1 where two distinct elements are present. First, there must be a financial contribution by a government or public body, or income or price support. Second, any financial contribution, or income or price support, must constitute a benefit.[1] The subsidy must also be specific (see Article 1.2 in conjunction with Article 2).

Situations involving exclusively private conduct – that is conduct that is not in some way attributable to a government or a public body – do not fall under the ASCM. Situations in subparagraphs (i) to (iii) refer to a financial contribution that is provided directly by the government or a public body. By virtue of subparagraph (iv), a financial contribution may also be provided indirectly by a government or a public body where it makes payments to a funding mechanism or where a government or a public body entrusts or directs a private body to carry out one or more of the functions illustrated in (i) to (iii).

Article 1.1 contains the definition of a subsidy and is thus central to the applicability of the remaining provisions of the ASCM. This definition applies wherever the word 'subsidy' occurs throughout the ASCM.[2] However, Article 1.1 itself does not impose any obligation on WTO Members with respect to the subsidies it defines. It is the provisions of the ASCM which follow, such as Articles 3 and 5, which impose obligations

1 WT/DS257/AB/R of 19 January 2004, *United States – Final Countervailing Duty Determination with Respect to Certain Softwood Lumber from Canada*, para 51.

2 WT/DS108/AB/R of 24 February 2000, *United States – Tax Treatment for 'Foreign Sales Corporations'*, para 93.

on WTO Members with respect to subsidies falling under the definition contained in Article 1.1.[3]

Article 1 limits the types of government action that fall under the disciplines of the ASCM by listing a number of acts by a government or public body that constitute a subsidy. Article 1.1 of the ASCM distinguishes three types of a financial contribution, i.e. (i) a direct transfer of funds or a potential direct transfer, (ii) government revenue that is otherwise due is foregone or not collected and (iii) a government provides goods or services other than general infrastructure, or purchases goods. By insisting on the condition of 'financial contributions' or alternatively on 'income or price support', Article 1 excludes a purely effect-based concept of subsidies. The requirement of a financial contribution was intended to ensure that not all government measures that confer a benefit could be deemed to be subsidies.[4]

The concepts of financial contribution, benefit and specificity are independent concepts. All must be present for a measure to be a subsidy in the sense of the ASCM.[5]

Can Several Acts of Subsidization Be Classified as a Single Programme?

This issue has consequences in terms of necessary evidence etc. If a number of financial contributions are part of a single programme, the investigating authority or a panel can, for instance, rely on evidence of alleged entrustment or direction of a creditor in respect of one financial contribution as evidence of alleged entrustment or direction of that creditor in respect of other financial contributions that form part of the same programme.[6] However, determining whether multiple subsidies are

[3] WT/DS108/AB/RW of 14 January 2002, *United States – Tax Treatment for 'Foreign Sales Corporations' (Article 21.5, first recourse)*, para 85.

[4] WT/DS257/AB/R of 19 January 2004, *United States – Final Countervailing Duty Determination with Respect to Certain Softwood Lumber from Canada*, footnote 35 attached to para 52. See also *infra* pp. 110–112.

[5] WT/DS379/R of 22 October 2010, *US – Definitive Anti-Dumping and Countervailing Duties on Certain Products from China*, para 9.29; WT/DS194/R of 29 June 2001, *United States – Measures Treating Export Restraints as Subsidies*, para 8.40; WT/DS46/AB/R of 2 August 1999, *Brazil – Export Financing Programme for Aircraft*, para 157.

[6] WT/DS296/R/3 of 21 February 2005, *United States – Countervailing Duty Investigation on Dynamic Random Access Memory Semiconductors (DRAMs) from Korea*, para 7.143. This point was not appealed. According to *Hahn/Mehta* (2013) p. 142, in case of a programme, new manifestations of that programme are covered by the relevant DSB decision. Thus,

part of the same subsidy programme is not always a clear-cut exercise. It requires careful examination of the relevant legislation – whether set out in one or several instruments – or the pronouncements of the granting authority(ies) to determine whether the subsidies are provided pursuant to the same subsidy scheme. Another factor that may be considered in this context is whether there is an overarching purpose behind the subsidies. But this overarching purpose must be something more concrete than a vague policy of providing assistance or promoting economic growth.[7]

In *US – Countervailing Duty Investigation on DRAMs*, the Panel had doubts as to the existence of a programme. The US considered the measures taken by the financial institutions that participated in Hynix's restructuring as part of a single programme that occurred over a short, ten-month period. This was based on the following points:

- The objective of the programme was the complete financial restructuring of Hynix in order to maintain the company as an ongoing concern.
- Each of the measures taken over the aforementioned period reflected a pattern of practices by the Government of Korea to ensure the continued viability of the company.
- Many of the events were overlapping and had the effect of reinforcing each other with respect to the goal of keeping Hynix operating.

The Panel did not take a final decision on this issue but warned that it was not necessarily true that any act of restructuring will form part of the same programme as other acts of restructuring simply because they all pursued the same objective.[8] Note that in the parallel investigation carried out by the European Union, various restructuring measures were examined as separate programmes.[9]

The US in *EC and certain Member States – Large Civil Aircraft* took the view that, in addition to the granting of launch aid for individual Airbus aircraft types, the EU operated a programme providing for subsidies for the launch of all Airbus models. According to the US, the four Airbus

a complainant can resort to procedures under Article 21.5 DSU instead of filing a new dispute.

[7] WT/DS353/AB/R of 12 March 2012, *United States – Measures Affecting Trade in Large Civil Aircraft (Second Complaint)*, para 752.

[8] WT/DS296/R/3 of 21 February 2005, *United States – Countervailing Duty Investigation on Dynamic Random Access Memory Semiconductors (DRAMs) from Korea*, paras 7.142 and 7.153 *et passim*. This aspect was not appealed.

[9] WT/DS299/R of 17 June 2005, *European Communities – Countervailing Measures on Dynamic Random Access Memory Chips from Korea*, para 7.63.

Member States operated a formal and institutionalized industrial policy towards Airbus. A central part of this policy has been the systematic and coordinated provision of launch aid subsidies to assist Airbus developing a family of large civil aircraft. The US acknowledged that there was no single written document that attested to such a coordinated system of financing but claimed that the existence of the programme could be evidenced by a series of facts or components that could in themselves be considered measures. The EU denied the existence of such a programme, arguing that each Member State took an individual decision on whether and under which terms and conditions to finance Airbus aircraft. The Panel accepted that the fact that the alleged existence of a programme is not evidenced in any single written document did not mean that it could not amount to a measure that may be challenged under the WTO Dispute Settlement System. In this respect it referred to the ruling of the Appellate Body in *US – Zeroing (EC)*.[10] However, and on the basis of the evidentiary standard established by the Appellate Body in the aforementioned ruling, it was not convinced that such a programme existed.[11] The Appellate Body set aside the Panel's ruling on this issue on the grounds that the alleged unwritten launch aid programme was not within the Panel's terms of reference. Note that the US, in its appeal, had raised the argument that the EU system constituted 'ongoing conduct' and was therefore a programme based on the Appellate Body's definition in *US – Continued Zeroing*.[12] Had the Panel found such a programme to exist as a separate measure, this would have brought the launch aid given for the development of the A350 under the scope of the Panel's ruling. Note that the US also attacked the aid for the A350 individually but the Panel did not find a clear and identifiable commitment by Airbus Member States to provide such aid at the time when the Panel was established.

The scope or breadth of the programme is also relevant for the specificity analysis. See *China – GOES* where China adopted a too narrow reading of the application of the subsidy programme and therefore concluded wrongly that the programme was specific.[13]

[10] WT/DS294/AB/R of 9 May 2006, *United States – Laws, Regulations and Methodology for Calculating Dumping Margins (Zeroing)*.

[11] WT/DS316/R of 30 June 2010, *EC and certain Member States – Measures Affecting Trade in Large Civil Aircraft*, para 7.513 *et seq.*

[12] WT/DS316/AB/R of 18 May 2011, *EC and certain Member States – Measures Affecting Trade in Large Civil Aircraft*, paras 781, 784–796.

[13] WT/DS414/R of 15 June 2012, *China – Countervailing and Anti-Dumping Duties on Grain-Oriented Flat-Rolled Electrical Steel from the US*, paras 7.105–7.112.

The ASCM uses the term 'programme' also in Articles 2.1, 28 and 29.[14]

When Does a Subsidy Come into Existence?

The chapeau of Article 1.1 specifies the circumstances pursuant to which 'a subsidy shall be deemed to exist'.

In *EC and certain Member States – Large Civil Aircraft*, the US claimed that prior to the establishment of the Panel, the EU Member States had already committed to finance the A350, and that this commitment constituted a financial contribution conferring a benefit on Airbus. In terms of financial contribution, the US claimed that the commitment could be classified as a 'potential direct transfer of funds or liabilities' (see Article 1.1(a)(1)(i)). However, while the Panel held that a commitment, if it existed, might well amount to a potential direct transfer of funds, it was not persuaded that such a commitment existed. There was evidence that the four Airbus Member States agreed in principle to contribute to the financing of the A350 but the precise terms and conditions were still subject to negotiation. The Panel also held that the US had not demonstrated that there would be a benefit because the US had not demonstrated that the terms and conditions of any commitment by Member States were more beneficial than what would have been available to Airbus on the market.[15]

The issue was also addressed by the Panel in *Brazil – Aircraft* where the circumstances were somewhat different. The Panel noted that according to Article 1.1(a)(1) a subsidy exists if a government practice involves a direct transfer of funds or a potential direct transfer of funds and not only when the government effectuates such a transfer or potential transfer. Otherwise the text of subparagraph (i) would read 'a government directly transfers funds ... ' instead of '*involves* a direct transfer of funds ... ' (emphasis added). The question as to when the subsidy is paid has to be distinguished from the question as to when the subsidy comes into existence.[16] See also the subsequent Appellate Body ruling that clarified that the issue of existence of a subsidy and the issue of the point at which the subsidy is granted pursuant to Article 27.4 are two legally distinct issues.[17]

[14] See, in particular, *infra* the jurisprudence relating to Article 2.1(c).

[15] WT/DS316/R of 30 June 2010, *EC and certain Member States – Measures Affecting Trade in Large Civil Aircraft*, para 7.296 *et seq*. This aspect was not appealed.

[16] WT/DS46/R of 14 April 1999, *Brazil – Export Financing Programme for Aircraft*, para 7.13.

[17] WT/DS46/AB/R of 2 August 1999, *Brazil – Export Financing Programme for Aircraft*, para 156 and *infra* Article 27 pp. 569–570.

Subsidy (Article 1.1)

Government or Public Body

Pursuant to Article 1.1(a)(1), the provision of a subsidy implies that the financial contribution is given by a government or a public body within the territory of a Member. The ASCM refers to both notions collectively as 'government'. A financial contribution given by a private body only qualifies as a subsidy if such private body is entrusted or directed by the government (see Article 1.1(a)(1)(iv)).[18] Public bodies can be located at national, regional and municipal level.

Contrary to the term 'public body', the term 'government' in the narrow sense does not normally raise any interpretative issues. The notion of 'public body' determines what acts carried out can be attributed to the government. This notion was extensively discussed in *US – Anti-Dumping and Countervailing Duties (China)*. In that case, the Appellate Body had to review a finding by the USDOC that Chinese State-owned enterprises and banks were public bodies that in turn provided to certain Chinese industries inputs for less than adequate remuneration and loans at preferential interest rates. The Appellate Body pointed out that 'being vested with governmental authority is the key feature of a public body' and that a public body 'must be an entity that possesses, exercises or is vested with government authority'.[19] Thus, the Appellate Body reversed the Panel's finding that a public body is an entity controlled by the government and that government ownership is highly relevant and indeed potentially dispositive. In short, the Appellate Body rejected the 'government control approach' and adopted the 'government authority approach' instead. It based its conclusion on the following considerations:

- There must be certain commonalities or overlaps between the terms 'government' *stricto sensu* and 'public body' because *inter alia* of the juxtaposition of the terms government and private body in Article 1 (para 288).
- Government is defined as the continuous exercise of authority over subjects, authoritative direction or regulation and control (definition found in the Shorter Oxford Dictionary, see also the Appellate Body in

[18] See *infra* Article 1 pp. 105–123.

[19] WT/DS379/AB/R of 11 March 2011, *US – Definitive Anti-Dumping and Countervailing Duties on Certain Products from China*, paras 310 and 317.

Canada – Dairy where it pointed out that the essence of government is that it enjoys the effective power to regulate, control or supervise individuals, or otherwise restrain their conduct through the exercise of lawful authority).[20]

- The definition of the word 'private' (paras 292 and 293).
- The notions of 'entrustment', 'direction' and 'which would normally be vested in the government' in Article 1.1(a)(1)(iv) (para 294).
- The International Law Commission's Articles on Responsibility of States for Internationally Wrongful Acts, via Article 31(3)(c) of the Vienna Convention (para 304 *et seq.*).

The Appellate Body made one important qualification. Based on the phrase 'which would normally be vested in the government' in subparagraph (iv), it held that the reference to 'normally' incorporates the notion of what would ordinarily be considered part of governmental practice in the legal order of the relevant Member. This suggests that whether the functions or conduct are of a kind that are ordinarily classified as government in the legal order of the relevant Member may be a relevant consideration for determining whether or not a specific entity is a public body (para 297). The Appellate Body also underlined that 'just as no two governments are exactly alike, the precise contours and characteristics of a public body are bound to differ from entity to entity, State to State, and case to case'. In order to decide whether an entity qualifies as a public body, it is necessary to conduct 'a proper evaluation of the core features of the entity concerned and its relationship with government in the narrow sense' (para 317).

> [P]anels and investigating authorities are called upon to engage in a careful evaluation of the entity in question to identify its common features and relationship with government in the narrow sense, having regard, in particular, to whether the entity exercises authority on behalf of the government. (para 319)

The Appellate Body also acknowledged that this may be a complex exercise (para 345). It gave further guidance as to the nature and outcome of such analysis:

> In some cases, such as when a statute or other legal instrument expressly vests authority in the entity concerned, determining that such an entity is a public body may be a straightforward exercise ... We do not, for example, consider that the absence of an express statutory delegation of

[20] WT/DS103/AB/R and WT/DS113/AB/R of 13 October 1999, *Canada – Measures Affecting the Importation of Milk and the Exportation of Dairy Products*, para 97.

> authority necessarily precludes a determination that a particular entity is a public body. What matters is *whether* an entity is vested with authority to exercise government functions, rather than *how* that is achieved … Evidence that an entity is, in fact, exercising governmental functions may serve as evidence that it possesses or has been vested with governmental authority, particularly where such evidence points to a sustained and systematic practice. It follows, in our view, that evidence that a government exercises meaningful control over an entity and its conduct may serve, in certain circumstances, as evidence that the relevant entity possesses governmental authority and exercises such authority in the performance of governmental functions. We stress, however, that, apart from an express delegation of authority in a legal instrument, the existence of mere formal links between an entity and government in the narrow sense is unlikely to suffice to establish the necessary possession of governmental authority. Thus, for example, the mere fact that a government is the majority shareholder of an entity does not demonstrate that the government exercises meaningful control over the conduct of the entity, much less that the government has bestowed it with governmental authority. In some instances, however, where the evidence shows that the formal indicia of government control are manifold, and there is also evidence that such control has been exercised in a meaningful way, then such evidence may permit an inference that the entity concerned is exercising governmental authority. (para 318)

See also para 310 where the Appellate Body stated that State ownership, while not being a decisive criterion, may serve as evidence indicating, in conjunction with other elements, the delegation of governmental authority.

The Appellate Body then applied the meaning of the term 'public body' as set out above to the facts of the case. It upheld the determination of the USDOC that the Chinese State-owned commercial banks were public bodies. The Department of Commerce based its determination on the following elements:

- Near complete State ownership of the banking sector.
- Article 34 of the Chinese Commercial Banking Law which provides that banks are required to carry out their loan business upon the needs of the national economy and the social development and under the guidance of State industrial policies.
- Record evidence indicating that State-owned commercial banks still lacked adequate risk management and analytical skills.
- During the investigation, the USDOC did not receive the evidence necessary to document in a comprehensive manner the process by which loans were requested, granted and evaluated to the paper industry.

- A 2005 OECD report according to which the chief executives of the head offices of the State-owned commercial banks are government appointed and the party retains significant influence in their choice.[21]

The USDOC did not make the aforementioned findings in the four investigations challenged (i.e. concerning circular welded carbon quality steel pipes, light-walled rectangular pipes and tubes, laminated woven sacks and certain new pneumatic off-road tires) before the WTO but in a previous investigation concerning coated paper. It incorporated these findings by reference into the investigations at issue. The Appellate Body clarified that merely incorporating findings by reference from one determination into another determination will normally not suffice as a reasoned and adequate explanation. However, in the case at hand, it saw a close temporal (only one year difference between the periods of investigation) and substantive (both investigations were concerned with the nature of State-owned commercial banks in China) overlap between the two investigations. Moreover, China had not challenged in the WTO dispute the reliance on findings made in a previous investigation.[22]

However, in relation to Chinese State-owned producers of steel, rubber and petrochemical inputs sold to the investigated companies or to trading companies (that in turn sold to the investigated companies), the Appellate Body did not accept the USDOC's determination. The USDOC found that the application of its five factors[23] test, which it traditionally applied, was not necessary absent information calling into question whether government ownership does not mean government control. Therefore, it considered that evidence of majority government ownership was sufficient to establish the existence of a public body. The Appellate Body referred to its interpretation of the term 'public body' set out above and noted that the investigating authorities have a duty to seek out relevant information and to evaluate it in an objective manner. The reasoning of an authority must be coherent and internally consistent and the conclusions reached and the inferences drawn

[21] WT/DS379/AB/R of 11 March 2011, *US – Definitive Anti-Dumping and Countervailing Duties on Certain Products from China*, para 348 *et seq.*

[22] WT/DS379/AB/R of 11 March 2011, *US – Definitive Anti-Dumping and Countervailing Duties on Certain Products from China*, para 354.

[23] See WT/DS379/R of 22 October 2010, *US – Definitive Anti-Dumping and Countervailing Duties on Certain Products from China*, para 8.18: (i) government ownership; (ii) the government's presence on the entity's board of directors; (iii) the government's control over the entity's activities; (iv) the entity's pursuit of governmental policies or interests; and (v) whether the entity is created by statute.

by the authority must be based on positive evidence.[24] *Ahn* correctly pointed out that the Appellate Body did not rule that State-owned enterprises might not be viewed as public bodies in countervailing duty investigations. Rather, it only ruled on the manner by which the USDOC examined whether or not these enterprises were public bodies. According to *Ahn*, given that governmental roles in the legal order of China are more intrusive, the task of the investigating authority simply becomes more challenging.[25]

The Appellate Body's ruling in *US – Anti-Dumping and Countervailing Duties (China)* has met strong criticism by some scholars and practitioners including three negotiators of the ASCM. For instance, *Pauwelyn* submits that by defining the term 'public body' as limited to entities that are exercising governmental authority the Appellate Body has essentially read out of the ASCM the words 'or any public body'.[26] *Ding* argues that this ruling has created a loophole by leaving some State-owned enterprises as being neither public nor private entities.[27] *Cartland, Depayre and Woznowski* point out, *inter alia*, that the ruling is not borne out by the negotiating history and that it is at odds with the internal logic of the ASCM.[28] To *Brink* it would appear that the Appellate Body's decision has expanded the scope of the information that is relevant to a determination of whether an entity is a public body and that investigating authorities will need to respond accordingly.[29]

In *US – Carbon Steel (India)*, the Appellate Body clarified its aforementioned interpretation of the term 'public body'. The US advanced that a public body may also include an entity controlled by the government such that the government may use the entity's resources as its own and that it is not necessary that the entity must be vested with authority from the government to perform governmental functions (see e.g. para 4.27 which describes also the reasoning underlying the US approach). The Appellate Body rejected this interpretation:

- The Appellate Body conceded that control over an entity and its conduct, including the government's possibility to use the entity's resources

[24] WT/DS379/AB/R of 11 March 2011, *US – Definitive Anti-Dumping and Countervailing Duties on Certain Products from China*, para 342 *et seq.*

[25] *Ahn* (2011) p. 4. See also the statements made by the Appellate Body in paragraphs 297 and 319 of its ruling.

[26] *Pauwelyn* (2013) pp. 235–237. In support of his opinion he also referred to paragraph 172 of China's Working Party Report.

[27] *Ding* (2014) p. 179.

[28] *Cartland/Depayre/Woznowski* (2012) pp. 1001–1013. See also *Ding* (2014) pp. 177–178.

[29] *Brink* (2011) p. 315.

as its own, may certainly be relevant evidence for the purposes of determining whether or not an entity is a public body. However, the Appellate Body also underlined that an investigating authority must avoid focusing exclusively or unduly on any single characteristic without affording due consideration to others that may be relevant (paras 4.19 and 4.20).

- It also conceded that an entity does not necessarily have to hold the power to regulate in order to be vested with governmental authority or exercising a governmental function, i.e. constitute a public body. Nor is it necessary that the relevant entity must have the power to entrust or direct private bodies to carry out the functions identified in Article 1.1(a) ASCM (paras 4.17 and 4.18).
- 'Whether the conduct of an entity is that of a public body must in each case be determined on its own merits, with due regard being had to the core characteristics and functions of the relevant entity, its relationship with the government, and the legal and economic environment prevailing in the country in which the entity operates. For example, evidence regarding the scope and content of governmental policies relating to the sector in which the investigated entity operates may inform the question of whether the conduct of the entity in question is that of a public body … [T]here are different ways in which a government could be understood to vest an entity with "governmental authority", and therefore different types of evidence may be relevant in this regard. [footnote omitted] In order properly to characterize an entity as a public body in a particular case, it may be relevant to consider "whether the functions or conduct [of the entity] are of a kind that are ordinarily classified as governmental in the legal order of the relevant Member", and the classification and functions of entities within WTO Members generally' (para 4.29).
- 'In sum, the USDOC did not evaluate the relationship between the NMDC [the National Mineral Development Corporation] and the GOI [Government of India] within the Indian legal order, and the extent to which the GOI in fact "exercised" meaningful control over the NMDC and over its *conduct* in order to conclude properly that the NMDC is a public body … Instead, the USDOC examined evidence which, in our view, would be seen more appropriately as evidence of "formal indicia of control" such as the GOI's ownership interest in the NMDC and the GOI's power to appoint or nominate directors. These factors are certainly relevant but do not provide a sufficient basis for a determination that an entity is a public body that possesses, exercises, or is vested with governmental authority. Moreover, the USDOC did

not refer in its determinations to evidence contained in the USDOC's administrative record that was referred to by the United States in the Panel proceedings as well as on appeal. Nor did the USDOC discuss in its determinations evidence on record regarding the NMDC's status as a *Miniratna* or *Navratna* company that could have been relevant to the question of whether the USDOC's determinations contain a sufficient and adequate evaluation of the relationship between the GOI and the NMDC, and, in particular, the degree of control exercised by the GOI over the *conduct* of the NMDC and the degree of autonomy enjoyed by the NMDC' (para 4.54).[30]

The issue of public body was also dealt with in *Korea – Commercial Vessels*. The Panel held that an entity is a public body if it is controlled by the government or other public bodies. The Panel considered that there was government control over the Export-Import Bank of Korea (KEXIM) *inter alia* because of government ownership, because the Korean President had the power to appoint and dismiss KEXIM's president and because KEXIM's annual operation programmes had to receive Ministerial approval.[31] The Panel dismissed attempts by Korea not to consider an entity as a 'public body' if such entity engages in market (non-official) activities on commercial terms. Korea's interpretation would have meant to mix separate legal elements, i.e. 'public body' and 'benefit', by making the private/public body determination entirely dependent on the existence of a benefit.[32] The Panel also held that IBK was controlled by the government.

> Here, we give particular weight to the fact that the IBK is almost fully (95 per cent) government owned [footnote omitted], a highly relevant and arguably determinative fact for the question of government control of IBK. In addition, we note that, pursuant to Article 35 of the IBK Act, both the IBK Business Plan and Operations Manual must be approved by a GOK

[30] WT/DS436/AB/R of 8 December 2014, *United States – Countervailing Measures on Certain Hot-Rolled Carbon Steel Flat Products from India*, paras 4.1–4.55 (the implications on the autonomy of a company classified as a miniratna or navratna are described in para 4.40). The Panel in WT/DS437/R of 14 July 2014, *United States – Countervailing Duty Measures on Certain Products from China*, paras 7.64–7.75 adopted a similar approach. It also found that a rebuttable presumption that majority government-owned enterprises are authorities (public bodies) is not compatible with Article 1.1(a)(1), see para 7.120 *et seq.*

[31] WT/DS273/R of 7 March 2005, *Korea – Measures Affecting Trade in Commercial Vessels*, para 7.50 *et seq.* See also para 7.172 in relation to the Korean Development Bank (KDB) and para 7.351.

[32] WT/DS273/R of 7 March 2005, *Korea – Measures Affecting Trade in Commercial Vessels*, paras 7.44 to 7.46.

> minister, and the Operations Manual itself must contain detailed provisions regarding the operations of the IBK, including 'the lending method, interest rates, loan terms, means of collection of loan principal and interest, and the maximum loan amount and payment guarantees to any one person'.[33]

The aforementioned approach taken by the Panel in *Korea – Commercial Vessels* is different to that of the Appellate Body in *US – Anti-Dumping and Countervailing Duties (China)* because it focuses on whether an entity is controlled by the government and not on whether it is vested with government authority and has therefore arguably been superseded by the Appellate Body rulings. Similar considerations apply for the more recent finding in *EC and certain Member States – Large Civil Aircraft* that the bank Credit Lyonnais was a public body because it was 'controlled' by the Government of France.[34]

A straightforward public body analysis can be found in *Canada – Renewable Energy & Feed-In Tariff Program*.[35]

'Within the Territory of a Member'

According to the chapeau of Article 1.1, the financial contribution has to be given by a government or a public body 'within the territory of a Member'. To date there are no rulings on the interpretation of this term. *Horlick* points out that this criterion was intended to exclude from the subsidy disciplines items such as World Bank loans, Japanese war reparations paid to Korea or US Marshall Plan aid paid to European countries. Hence, it was decided not to treat as countervailable subsidies those payments given by a government outside of its territory.[36]

'Financial Contribution'

Article 1.1(a)(1) defines and identifies in four subparagraphs the government conduct that constitutes a financial contribution for the

[33] WT/DS273/R of 7 March 2005, *Korea – Measures Affecting Trade in Commercial Vessels*, para 7.356.

[34] WT/DS316/R of 30 June 2010, *EC and certain Member States – Measures Affecting Trade in Large Civil Aircraft*, para 7.1359.

[35] WT/DS412/R and WT/DS426/R of 19 December 2012, *Canada – Certain Measures Affecting the Renewable Energy Generation Sector; Canada – Measures Relating to Feed-In Tariff Program*, paras 7.233–7.239.

[36] Horlick (2013/1) p. 298.

purposes of the ASCM. They cover a wide range of transactions. Some of the categories of conduct specified in subparagraphs (i) and (ii) are described in general terms with illustrative examples. These examples provide an indication of the common features that characterize the conduct more generally. Subparagraph (iii) does not contain such examples.[37]

Purpose of the Notion 'Financial Contribution'

According to the Appellate Body, an evaluation of the existence of a financial contribution involves consideration of the nature of the transaction through which something of economic value is transferred by a government. It pointed out that not all government measures capable of conferring a benefit, *per se*, would be subsidies. In this regard, the Appellate Body referred to the negotiation history of the ASCM as described in *US – Export Restraints*. The requirement of a financial contribution from the outset was intended to ensure that not all government measures that conferred benefits could be deemed subsidies.[38]

According to *US – Export Restraints*, the concept of financial contribution was included in the definition of subsidy in order to avoid an effects-based approach to the concept of subsidy.

> [B]y introducing the notion of financial contribution, the drafters foreclosed the possibility of the treatment of *any* government action that resulted in a benefit as a subsidy. Indeed, this is arguably the principal significance of the concept of financial contribution, which can be characterized as one of the 'gateways' to the SCM Agreement, along with the concepts of benefit and specificity. To hold that the concept of financial contribution is about the effects, rather than the nature, of a government action would be effectively to write it out of the Agreement, leaving the concepts of benefit and specificity as the sole determinants of the scope of the Agreement.[39]

It follows from the above that the list of government actions contained in Article 1 that constitute a financial contribution is exhaustive.

[37] WT/DS353/AB/R of 12 March 2012, *United States – Measures Affecting Trade in Large Civil Aircraft (Second Complaint)*, para 613.

[38] WT/DS257/AB/R of 19 January 2004, *United States – Final Countervailing Duty Determination with Respect to Certain Softwood Lumber from Canada*, para 52 including footnote 35. See also *supra* p. 25.

[39] WT/DS194/R of 29 June 2001, *United States – Measures Treating Export Restraints as Subsidies*, para 8.38 (footnote omitted).

Relationship between the Subparagraphs of Article 1.1(a)(1)

The ASCM does not explicitly spell out the relationship between the subparagraphs of Article 1.1(a)(1). Therefore, the structure of this provision does not explicitly preclude that a transaction could be covered by more than one subparagraph.[40] Most recently, the issue came to the fore in *Canada – Renewable Energy & Feed-In Tariff Program*. Japan argued that the support provided by Canada to its power generators when buying energy from renewable sources should be classified as a (potential) direct transfer of funds pursuant to Article 1.1(a)(1)(i). The Panel disagreed and considered that the purchase of electricity from renewable sources was a purchase of goods falling under Article 1.1(a)(1)(iii). The Appellate Body disagreed with an intermediate conclusion made by the Panel, i.e. that subparagraphs (i) and (iii) are mutually exclusive, but ultimately upheld the Panel's decision:

> When determining the proper legal characterization of a measure under Article 1.1(a)(1) of the SCM Agreement, a panel must assess whether the measure may fall within any of the types of financial contributions set out in that provision. In doing so, a panel should scrutinize the measure both as to its design and operation and identify its principal characteristics. [footnote omitted] Having done so, the transaction may naturally fit into one of the types of financial contributions listed in Article 1.1(a)(1). However, transactions may be complex and multifaceted. This may mean that different aspects of the same transaction may fall under different types of financial contribution. It may also be the case that the characterization exercise does not permit the identification of a single category of financial contribution and ... a transaction may fall under more than one type of financial contribution. We note, however, that the fact that a transaction may fall under more than one type of financial contribution does not mean that the types of financial contributions set out in Article 1.1(a)(1) are the same or that the distinct legal concepts set out in this provision would become redundant, as the Panel suggests. [footnote omitted] We further observe that, in *US – Large Civil Aircraft (2nd complaint)*, the Appellate Body did not address the question of whether, in the situation described above, a panel is under an obligation to make findings that a transaction falls under more than one subparagraph of Article 1.1(a)(1).[41]

[40] WT/DS353/AB/R of 12 March 2012, *United States – Measures Affecting Trade in Large Civil Aircraft (Second Complaint)*, para 613.

[41] WT/DS412/AB/R and WT/DS426/AB/R of 6 May 2013, *Canada – Certain Measures Affecting the Renewable Energy Generation Sector; Canada – Measures Relating to Feed-In Tariff Program*, para 5.120.

Consequently, the Appellate Body declared moot and of no legal effect the Panel ruling inasmuch it negated the possibility that a transaction may fall under more than one type of financial contribution under Article 1.1(a)(1).

Classification of the Government Support

The proper classification or characterization of the support is important both in relation to the concepts of 'financial contribution' and 'benefit'.[42] The Appellate Body held in *US – Large Civil Aircraft (2nd complaint)* that first the relevant characteristics of the measure should be determined. Only once the measures have been properly determined, the question can be addressed whether the measure, properly characterized, falls within the scope of Article 1.1(a)(1). The Appellate Body referred in this respect to its ruling on *China – Auto Parts*, where it pointed out that it was necessary first to identify all relevant characteristics of the measure, and to recognize which features are the most central to that measure itself, and which are to be accorded the most significance for purposes of characterizing the relevant measure and, thereby, properly determining the disciplines to which it is subject under the covered WTO agreements. In other words, a proper determination of which of the WTO agreements applies to a given measure must be grounded in a proper understanding of the measure's relevant characteristics. Based on the above, the Appellate Body took issue with the fact that the Panel found that certain measures were not a purchase of services or grants, but that the Panel did ultimately not specify how the measures at issue were properly characterized.[43] The Appellate Body in *Canada – Renewable Energy & Feed-In Tariff Program* also pointed out that the characterization of a transaction under Article 1.1(a)(1) may have implications for the manner in which the benefit analysis is to be conducted. Different characterizations may lead to different methods for determining whether a benefit has been conferred.[44]

[42] The issue in relation to benefit is dealt with *infra* pp. 136–137.

[43] WT/DS353/AB/R of 12 March 2012, *United States – Measures Affecting Trade in Large Civil Aircraft (Second Complaint)*, paras 585–589. The classification of these contracts by the Appellate Body is described *infra* pp. 82–84.

[44] WT/DS412/AB/R and WT/DS426/AB/R of 6 May 2013, *Canada – Certain Measures Affecting the Renewable Energy Generation Sector; Canada – Measures Relating to Feed-In Tariff Program*, para 5.130; WT/DS412/R and WT/DS426/R of 19 December 2012, *Canada – Certain Measures Affecting the Renewable Energy Generation Sector;*

Direct Transfer of Funds or Potential Direct Transfer of Funds or Liabilities (Article 1.1(a)(1)(i))

Introduction The first subparagraph of Article 1.1(a)(1) classifies as financial contribution any 'government practice [that] involves a direct transfer of funds' or 'potential direct transfers of funds or liabilities'. It also lists some examples of funds or liabilities, i.e. grants, loans and equity infusions. The Appellate Body has held that these examples do not exhaust the class of conduct captured by subparagraph (i). However, the inclusion of specific examples nevertheless provides an indication of the types of transactions intended to be covered by the more general reference to a 'direct transfer of funds'. The Appellate Body had found that debt forgiveness, the extension of loan maturity and debt-to-equity swaps are similar to the transactions expressly listed in subparagraph (i) and hence also covered by this provision.[45]

Subparagraph (i) also provides an example of a potential direct transfer of funds or liabilities, i.e. a loan guarantee. DSB rulings have examined whether a committed but not disbursed grant, a credit line, an equity guarantee as well as an export-credit insurance qualify as potential direct transfer of funds or liabilities.[46]

Government Practice In *Korea – Commercial Vessels*, Korea argued that there is only a financial contribution in the sense of Article 1.1(a)(1)(i) if the relevant government or public body is engaged in government practice such as regulation or taxation. Thus, in the opinion of Korea, even if a body is a public body, it does not make a financial contribution if it is not involved in 'government practice'. Korea considered that the term 'government practice' means the exercise of government authority such as regulatory powers and taxation authority. The Panel rejected this narrow interpretation. It held that the term 'government practice' only denoted the author of the action, rather than the nature of the action. It arrived at this conclusion *inter alia* in view of the term 'financial contribution' in the chapeau of Article 1.1(a)(1) that is written broadly.[47]

Canada – Measures Relating to Feed-In Tariff Program, para 7.194. See also *infra* pp. 136–137.

[45] WT/DS353/AB/R of 12 March 2012, *United States – Measures Affecting Trade in Large Civil Aircraft (Second Complaint)*, para 615, with references to previous Appellate Body rulings.

[46] See *infra* pp. 86–88.

[47] WT/DS273/R of 7 March 2005, *Korea – Measures Affecting Trade in Commercial Vessels*, paras 7.25, 7.28–7.31.

The phrase 'government practice involves' is also discussed extensively in *US – Carbon Steel (India)*, which is described in detail *infra* in the next section.

Direct Transfer of Funds This section first describes DSB rulings that discussed the term 'funds'. It then turns to *US – Carbon Steel (India)* that primarily focused on whether the transfer of funds was a direct one. The remainder of the section looks into various categories of a direct transfer of funds such as shares, equity infusions, grants and loans.

The notion of a 'fund' relates to *what* is to be transferred.[48] The Appellate Body in *Japan – DRAMs (Korea)* indicated that the term 'funds' in Article 1.1(a)(1)(i) encompasses not only money but also financial resources and other financial claims more generally. In that case, Japan and Korea disagreed as to whether the October 2001 and December 2002 restructurings of Hynix constituted 'direct transfers of funds' within the meaning of the aforementioned Article. Korea claimed that a direct transfer of funds arises only when there is an incremental flow of funds to the recipient that enhances the net worth of the recipient. According to Korea, when a creditor agrees to modify the terms of existing loans, or to write off loans entirely, existing claims are modified without providing any money to the borrower and there is no direct transfer of funds. For Korea, a transfer of funds occurs only when money changes hands from the government (or the entrusted/directed private body) to the subsidy recipient. For the same reason, Korea did not consider debt-to-equity swaps as a direct transfer of funds. The Panel and Appellate Body disagreed. The latter found that Korea's concept of funds was too narrow because it failed to encapsulate how financial transactions gave rise to an alteration of obligations from which an accrual of financial resources resulted. Debt forgiveness, which extinguishes the claims of a creditor, is a mechanism by which the borrower is taken to have repaid the loan to the lender. The extension of a loan maturity enables the borrower to enjoy the benefit of the loan for an extended period of time. An interest rate reduction lowers the debt servicing burden of the borrower. Similar considerations apply to debt-to-equity swaps. According to the Appellate Body, in all of these cases, the financial position of the borrower was improved and therefore there was a direct transfer of funds within the meaning of Article 1.1(a)(1)(i).[49]

[48] WT/DS436/AB/R of 8 December 2014, *United States – Countervailing Measures on Certain Hot-Rolled Carbon Steel Flat Products from India*, para 4.89.

[49] WT/DS336/AB/R of 28 November 2007, *Japan – Countervailing Duties on Dynamic Random Access Memories from Korea*, paras 250–252. See also WT/DS299/R of 17 June

Using *Japan – DRAMs (Korea)* as a starting point, the Appellate Body in *US – Large Civil Aircraft (2nd complaint)* generalized that a direct transfer of funds in subparagraph (i) captures conduct on the part of the government by which money, financial resources and/or financial claims are made available to a recipient. A direct transfer of funds will normally involve financing by the government to the recipient. The examples listed in subparagraph (i) provide an indication of the types of transactions intended to be covered by the more general reference to 'direct transfer of funds'.[50] The Appellate Body applied this approach to the case in question. Boeing entered into procurement contracts with NASA and agreed Assistance instruments with the US Department of Defense. These arrangements provided Boeing with

(a) funding and
(b) access to facilities, equipment and employees belonging to NASA and the Department of Defense.

The return expected from Boeing was not financial but rather took the form of scientific and technical information, discoveries and data expected as a result of Boeing's research performed under the arrangements. Like equity investors, NASA and the US Department of Defense had no certainty at the time they committed the funding etc. that the research would be successful. With regard to the funding provided to Boeing by NASA and the Department of Defense, the Appellate Body held this this would be most appropriately characterized as being akin to a species of joint venture. Furthermore, these joint venture arrangements had characteristics analogous to equity infusions, one of the examples of a direct transfer of funds listed in subparagraph (i). This commonality suggested to the Appellate Body that the measures fell within the concept of 'direct transfer of funds' under subparagraph (i). With regard to Boeing's access to NASA's facilities, equipment and employees and to the Department of Defense's facilities, these constituted the provision of goods and services under subparagraph (iii).[51]

US – Carbon Steel (India) also examined the notion of a 'direct transfer of funds'. This ruling looked at all the elements of this notion but

2005, *European Communities – Countervailing Measures on Dynamic Random Access Memory Chips from Korea*, paras 7.88 and 7.92.

[50] WT/DS353/AB/R of 12 March 2012, *United States – Measures Affecting Trade in Large Civil Aircraft (Second Complaint)*, paras 614, 615, 617 and 621.

[51] WT/DS353/AB/R of 12 March 2012, *United States – Measures Affecting Trade in Large Civil Aircraft (Second Complaint)*, paras 621–625 (see also *infra* pp. 83–84).

had a particular focus on whether the transfer was a 'direct' one. In the case in question, the USDOC had found in relation to the Indian Steel Development Fund (SDF) that a so-called Joint Plant Committee carried out the day-to-day management of the Fund. This included the collection of levies from the Indian steel industry and also the disbursement of loans to individual steel companies. However, the USDOC did not make a determination as to whether this Joint Plant Committee was a public body. Rather, the USDOC classified the so-called SDF Managing Committee as a public body. Only the latter entity had authority to making all decisions regarding the issuance of loans drawn from the fund, the terms of these loans and any waiver conditions. India argued, *inter alia*, that there was neither a transfer of funds nor, even if there had been one, that such transfer would be a 'direct' one because, *inter alia*, the actual transfer was made by the Joint Plant Committee and not by the SDF Management Committee. Neither the Panel nor the Appellate Body agreed with India.

The Appellate Body pointed out that a 'transfer' signifies a conveyance of something from one person or entity to another. It also noted that the term 'transfer' is further modified by the adjective 'direct', which indicates something occurring immediately, without intermediaries or interference. The phrase 'a direct transfer of funds' therefore 'suggests that what is at issue is the *manner* or *method* by which the funds are conveyed. While this phrase indicates a certain immediacy to the conveyance, it is not evident from the language of the provision under what circumstances a 'transfer' may be considered to be 'direct'. The immediacy of the conveyance of funds points to the existence of a close nexus concerning, for instance, the parties to, and/or actions relating to, the transfer of funds. The term 'direct' may refer to the immediacy of the link between the parties to the transfer, the immediacy of the mechanism by which the transfer is effectuated and/or possibly to some other basis. The Appellate Body examined in this context also the language preceding the phrase 'direct transfer of funds', i.e. '*government practice involves* a direct transfer of funds'. According to the Appellate Body, the term 'involves' suggests that the government practice need not consist, or be comprised, solely of the transfer of funds, but may be a broader set of conduct in which such a transfer is implicated or included. The term also appears to introduce an element suggesting a lack of immediacy to the extent that it does not prescribe that a government must necessarily make the direct transfer of funds, but only that there be a 'government practice' that 'involves' a direct transfer of funds. According to the Appellate Body, the juxtaposition of the term 'involves' with the term 'provides' in subparagraph (iii) also suggests that under the former term there is a potentially broadened framework for examining the government's role in respect of a direct transfer of funds. In sum, the combination of the terms 'government practice involves' and 'direct transfer of funds' suggests a more attenuated role of the government or public body for purposes of Article 1.1(a)(1)(i) as compared to the government's conduct that would qualify as a 'direct transfer of funds' in isolation. There is a tension between the elements of Article 1.1(a)(1)(i) that alternatively appears to narrow and broaden the scope of coverage as it relates to the parties to the transfer, and the nature of the transfer itself. Therefore, the Appellate Body considered that Article 1.1(a)(1)(i) does not rigidly prescribe the scope of its coverage. Rather, this provision reflects a balance of different considerations to be taken into account when assessing whether a particular transfer of funds constitutes a financial contribution.[52]

The Appellate Body understood India to argue that there is no direct transfer of funds if the governmental action consists of the decision-making on the issuance or terms of the transfer, and this action precedes the actual transfer of the funds by an intermediary. However, according to the Appellate Body, and based on the above interpretation of the notion 'government practices involves a direct transfer of funds', the conveyance of funds through an intermediary (such as the Joint Plant Committee) might still, depending on the circumstances relating to the nature and role of the intermediary, exhibit sufficient indicia of directness in order to establish that a government practice involves a direct transfer of funds. It also pointed out that its interpretation of the notion of a 'direct transfer of funds' did not render Article 1.1(a)(1)(iv) inutile, i.e. the provision dealing with entrustment and direction. According to the Appellate Body, although the SDF Managing Committee and the Joint Plant Committee are distinct entities serving different functions with respect to the SDF loans, the relationship between the SDF Managing Committee and the loan beneficiaries was not undermined by the nature of the involvement of the Joint Plant Committee as the former Committee made all critical decisions regarding the loans.[53]

[52] WT/DS436/AB/R of 8 December 2014, *United States – Countervailing Measures on Certain Hot-Rolled Carbon Steel Flat Products from India*, paras 4.89–4.92, 4.94. From the above it is only logical that the Appellate Body rejected India's definition that a transfer means that the rights or interest in the resources is terminated with the transferor and simultaneously created with the transferee.

[53] WT/DS436/AB/R of 8 December 2014, *United States – Countervailing Measures on Certain Hot-Rolled Carbon Steel Flat Products from India*, paras 4.94, 4.95.

Last but not least, the Appellate Body did not consider that Article 1.1(a)(1)(i) prescribes that the resources must necessarily be drawn from government resources or result in a charge to the public account. The Appellate Body held that, given its interpretation of the notion 'direct transfer of funds' as described in the preceding paragraphs, there may be limited situations in which a government is able to exercise control over resources pooled from non-government contributors in such a manner that the government's decision to transfer those resources could qualify as a financial contribution under Article 1.1(a)(1)(i). Therefore, it dismissed India's argument that the SDF loans could not constitute a financial contribution because the levies were collected from the participating steel companies. The Appellate Body also pointed out in this context that the primary focus of Article 1.1(a)(1)(i) is on the action taken by the government or public body.[54]

Canada – Renewable Energy & Feed-In Tariff Program dealt with the distinction between the purchase of a good for less than adequate remuneration and a potential direct transfer of funds. In the case in question the Appellate Body held that there was a financial contribution in the form of a purchase of a good for less than adequate remuneration and that Japan, one of the complainants, had not established that these measures should also have been classified as a potential direct transfer of funds.[55]

Shares, Equity Infusions and Joint Ventures

In *EC and certain Member States – Large Civil Aircraft*, the Panel recalled *Japan – DRAMs (Korea)* and held that shares in a company fall within the scope of the term 'funds' and a transfer of shares falls within the scope of the term 'direct transfer of funds'. The Panel based this conclusion on the consideration that shares in a company could be regarded as financial claims to a stream of income in the form of dividends and to a share in the capital of the company on its liquidation. The transaction in question consisted of a transfer of Airbus shares held by the Kreditanstalt für Wiederaufbau, i.e. a German public body, to MBB against an insufficient cash payment.[56]

[54] WT/DS436/AB/R of 8 December 2014, *United States – Countervailing Measures on Certain Hot-Rolled Carbon Steel Flat Products from India*, paras 4.96–4.98, 4.99–4.102.

[55] WT/DS412/AB/R and WT/DS426/AB/R of 6 May 2013, *Canada – Certain Measures Affecting the Renewable Energy Generation Sector; Canada – Measures Relating to Feed-In Tariff Program*, paras 5.130–5.132.

[56] WT/DS316/R of 30 June 2010, *EC and certain Member States – Measures Affecting Trade in Large Civil Aircraft*, para 7.1291. This aspect was not appealed.

In the same vein, the Panel held that the contribution of shares in a company (rather than a cash contribution) in exchange for newly-issued shares in the recipient company is a direct transfer of funds. In the case in question the French government transferred its 45.76 per cent interest in Dassault Aviation to Aérospatiale against new shares issued by Aérospatiale.[57]

The Appellate Body arrived at a similar conclusion in the parallel dispute *US – Large Civil Aircraft (2nd complaint)* where it underlined that equity infusions are characterized by reciprocity, like loans. The government's provision of capital to a recipient is made in return for the acquisition of shares. The provider of the capital thereby makes an investment in the recipient's enterprise and will be entitled to dividends or any capital gains that will be attributable to that investment. The returns on the investment will depend on the success of the recipient enterprise. At the time the government provides the capital, it does not know how the recipient enterprise will perform. The equity investor enjoys a return on its capital to the extent the enterprise succeeds, and suffers losses to the extent it fails.[58]

In the same dispute, the Appellate Body concluded that an agreement between NASA and Boeing was akin to a joint venture and was covered by Article 1.1(a)(1)(i). The main elements of the arrangement were:

- NASA paid Boeing for conducting R&D.
- Some of the transactions also involved that NASA provided Boeing with access to its equipment, facilities and employees to undertake the research project.
- Subjects to be researched were often determined in a collaborative arrangement.
- Both Boeing and NASA received access to the scientific information gathered as part of the research although Boeing enjoyed in some instances exclusive rights for a limited period of time.

In sum, the Appellate Body considered the transactions in question as a provision of funds from NASA, a pooling of non-monetary resources and some sharing of the fruits of the research conducted by Boeing. According to the Appellate Body, the transactions were collaborative arrangements that were composite in nature in that they involved

[57] WT/DS316/R of 30 June 2010, *EC and certain Member States – Measures Affecting Trade in Large Civil Aircraft*, para 7.1403. This aspect was not appealed.

[58] WT/DS353/AB/R of 12 March 2012, *United States – Measures Affecting Trade in Large Civil Aircraft (Second Complaint)*, para 616.

various elements that were interlinked. They were akin to a species of joint venture.[59]

Debt Settlement and Debt Forgiveness Are a Direct Transfer of Funds

See first *supra* the section on the direct transfer of funds (p. 79) with regard to *Japan – DRAMs (Korea)*.

In *EC and certain Member States – Large Civil Aircraft*, the Panel held that debt owed to a government is an asset held by the government consisting of certain financial claims (i.e. rights to payment of money or equivalents) that the government has against a debtor. A settlement of government-held debt essentially involves the transfer to the debtor of the government's financial claims against that debtor, resulting in the cancellation of the debt. The Panel also rejected the EU's claim that only a debt due (as opposed to one that is only payable after a certain period) could be forgiven and constitute a fund.[60] The debt in question concerned 9.4 billion Deutschmark owed by Deutsche Airbus to the German government. It consisted of (i) launch aid in respect of the A300/A310 and A330/A340 programmes, (ii) a loan to underwrite costs of producing the A320 and (iii) additional loans that the German government had provided to Deutsche Airbus in the 1980s and early 1990s, which had their origin in the 1989 restructuring of Airbus. Note, however, that a debt settlement does not automatically result in a benefit (see below p. 157).

In *Korea – Commercial Vessels*, Korea argued that debt-for-equity swaps, interest rate reductions, interest forgiveness and interest deferrals did not constitute a 'direct transfer of funds'. It claimed that these mechanisms did not constitute a transfer of pecuniary value but rather an increase in the value of recovery of the investment made by financial institutions. The Panel rejected this. It held that interest reductions and deferrals are similar to new loans, as they involve a renegotiation/extension of the terms of the original loan. Interest/debt forgiveness is also comparable to a cash grant, as funds that were previously provided as a loan, against interest, are now provided for free.[61]

[59] WT/DS353/AB/R of 12 March 2012, *United States – Measures Affecting Trade in Large Civil Aircraft (Second Complaint)*, paras 593–609. See also *infra* p. 85.

[60] WT/DS316/R of 30 June 2010, *EC and certain Member States – Measures Affecting Trade in Large Civil Aircraft*, paras 7.1316–7.1318 (these aspects were not appealed).

[61] WT/DS273/R of 7 March 2005, *Korea – Measures Affecting Trade in Commercial Vessels*, paras 7.408–7.413.

Korea – Commercial Vessels also rejected Korea's argument that various debt restructurings are a financial contribution to oneself and should consequently fall outside the scope of Article 1.1(a)(1). The Panel underlined that creditors and the debtor company are separate legal entities. It also pointed out that debt-for-equity swaps had the same effect as equity infusions which are listed in Article 1.1(a)(1)(i).[62]

Purchase of a Service as a 'Direct Transfer of Funds'?

The Panel in *US – Large Civil Aircraft (2nd complaint)* concluded that transactions properly characterized as a purchase of services by a public body did not qualify as financial contribution by means of a 'direct transfer of funds'. The Panel conceded that the ordinary meaning of the phrase 'a government practice involves a direct transfer of funds' in Article 1.1(a)(1)(i) might be broad enough to cover purchases of services. However, *inter alia* based on the immediate context provided by Articles 1.1(a)(1)(iii) and 14(d), it concluded that the drafters intended to exclude purchases of services from the definition of Article 1.1(a)(1)(i). Note that Articles 1.1(a)(1)(iii) and 14(d) refer to the provision of goods and services and the purchase of goods, i.e. the text of these provisions does not refer to the purchase of services.[63] The Appellate Body declared the Panel's interpretation to be moot and of no legal effect because the Appellate Body did not agree with the Panel's classification that the transactions aimed at the provision of a service. In the view of the Appellate Body, these transactions rather had characteristics akin to a joint venture contract which falls under Article 1.1(a)(1)(i).[64] In short, there is no definitive answer yet as to under what specific circumstances the purchase of a service could constitute a financial contribution.[65]

[62] WT/DS273/R of 7 March 2005, *Korea – Measures Affecting Trade in Commercial Vessels*, paras 7.419–7.422.

[63] WT/DS353/R of 31 March 2011, *United States – Measures Affecting Trade in Large Civil Aircraft (Second Complaint)*, paras 7.953–7.970.

[64] See *supra* the section on shares, equity infusion an joint ventures, pp. 83–84 [*Shares, Equity Infusions and Joint Ventures*]. A summary of the Panel's findings in this respect can also be found in WT/DS353/AB/R of 12 March 2012, *United States – Measures Affecting Trade in Large Civil Aircraft (Second Complaint)*, paras 555–563. The declaration that the Panel's findings are moot and without legal effect is set out in para 620. Note that the Appellate Body also took issue with the Panel's approach in determining whether a transaction is a purchase of services (see para 565 *et seq.*, in particular para 591). The characterization of the measures as joint venture contracts is set out in paras 592–611.

[65] See also *Coppens* (2014) pp. 44–45.

Grants

A grant will be provided by giving money or a money's worth to a recipient, normally without an obligation or expectation that anything will be provided to the grantor in return.[66] In *Australia – Automotive Leather II* there was agreement between the parties that payments made pursuant to a grant contract were subsidies within the meaning of Article 1. However, the parties disagreed whether the grant contract itself was a subsidy. The Panel held that each payment can be evaluated individually to determine whether it is a prohibited export subsidy, but only by reference to the criteria for disbursement set out in the grant contract. Thus, the Panel did not need to decide whether or not the grant contract was a subsidy in order to evaluate the individual payments.[67]

Loans

Loans are characterized by reciprocity. With a loan, a lender lends money or a money's worth on the basis that the principal, along with interest as may be agreed, is repaid. In addition, the lender will usually earn a return on the amount borrowed.[68]

In *EC and certain Member States – Large Civil Aircraft*, it was found that part of the launch aid committed by the Airbus Member States to the financing of the Airbus 380 had not been paid out yet. The Panel did not classify the funds that Member States had committed but not disbursed as a credit line but as a direct transfer of funds and treated them for all practical purposes as a loan.[69]

'Potential Direct Transfers of Funds or Liabilities'

Article 1.2(a)(1)(i) defines a financial contribution as including a 'potential direct transfer of funds or liabilities'. It identifies a loan guarantee as an example of a potential direct transfer of funds. The Panel in *EC and certain Member States – Large Civil Aircraft* held that this example is instructive

[66] WT/DS353/AB/R of 12 March 2012, *United States – Measures Affecting Trade in Large Civil Aircraft (Second Complaint)*, para 616.

[67] WT/DS126/R of 25 May 1999, *Australia – Subsidies Provided to Producers and Exporters of Automotive Leather*, paras 9.43–9.45.

[68] WT/DS353/AB/R of 12 March 2012, *United States – Measures Affecting Trade in Large Civil Aircraft (Second Complaint)*, para 616.

[69] WT/DS316/R of 30 June 2010, *EC and certain Member States – Measures Affecting Trade in Large Civil Aircraft*, paras 7.378 and 7.379. This aspect was not appealed.

for the purpose of understanding the types of measures that may constitute potential direct transfers of funds or liabilities. A loan guarantee may be described as a legally binding promise to repay the outstanding balance of a loan when the loan recipient defaults on its repayments. Thus, it is the promise to repay an outstanding loan in the event of a default that is the financial contribution, not the funds that may be transferred in the future in the event of default. Recalling that Article 14(c) provided useful context, the Panel concluded that

> when assessing whether a transaction involves a potential direct transfer of funds, the focus should be on the existence of a government practice that involves an obligation to make a direct transfer of funds which, *in and of itself*, is claimed and capable of conferring a benefit on the recipient that is separate and independent from the benefit that might be conferred from any future transfer of funds.[70]

The Panel made this statement in the context of the examination whether there was already a clear and identifiable commitment by Airbus Member States to provide launch aid for the A350 at the time of the establishment of the Panel.

The Panel also considered that funding, in the form of a grant under the German LuFo III R&D programme, that was committed but not yet disbursed to Airbus at the time of the establishment of the Panel, was a potential direct transfer of funds.[71]

Note also that the Panel in the aforementioned case classified a credit line from the European Investment Bank to EADS as a potential direct transfer of funds, within the meaning of Article 1.2(a)(1)(i), as the US alleged that Airbus had obtained a benefit from this credit line.[72]

Equity guarantees could also constitute a potential direct transfer of funds.[73]

The Panel in *EC – Countervailing Measures on DRAM Chips* classified a short-term export credit insurance as a 'potential direct transfer of funds'. The Korea Export Insurance Corporation, i.e. the official export credit

[70] WT/DS316/R of 30 June 2010, *EC and certain Member States – Measures Affecting Trade in Large Civil Aircraft*, para 7.304 (emphasis in original). This issue was not appealed.

[71] WT/DS316/R of 30 June 2010, *EC and certain Member States – Measures Affecting Trade in Large Civil Aircraft*, para 7.1495. This aspect was not appealed.

[72] WT/DS316/R of 30 June 2010, *EC and certain Member States – Measures Affecting Trade in Large Civil Aircraft*, paras 7.731–7.738. But see *infra* pp. 148–149.

[73] WT/DS222/R of 28 January 2002, *Canada – Export Credits and Loan Guarantees for Regional Aircraft*, para 7.320.

agency of Korea, provided this export credit insurance to 14 of Hynix's creditor banks that in turn provided an export credit facility to Hynix.[74]

In the case of a potential direct transfer of funds, a financial contribution exists regardless of whether the funds committed have to be paid in the end, i.e. whether the potential transfer materialized because the triggering event has happened. The actual amount of the subsidy resulting from such potential transfer is not, however, a question of whether a financial contribution exists, but relates to the question of benefit.

The Panel in *US – Large Civil Aircraft (2nd complaint)* also examined the term 'potential'. In the view of the Panel, a potential direct transfer of funds is a possibility due to uncertainty about whether the triggering event (e.g. default of the debtor in the case of a loan guarantee) will occur, rather than uncertainty about whether the transfer of funds will follow once the predefined or triggering event has taken place.[75]

Government Revenue Foregone or Not Collected (Article 1.1(a)(1)(ii))

Subparagraph (ii) deals essentially with tax exemptions. There is a financial contribution when government revenue that is otherwise due is foregone or not collected. Therefore, a government can grant a subsidy not only by positive action but also by some negative action, i.e. when it refrains from collecting revenue that is otherwise due. The ASCM lists one example that falls under this subparagraph, i.e. fiscal incentives such as tax credits.

This subparagraph is a recognition of the fact that a government that does not collect taxes etc. can achieve an effect that is similar if not identical to actively granting a subsidy by handing out a grant under Article 1.1(a)(1) etc.[76]

Whether or not there is a revenue foregone that is otherwise due requires a comparison between the tax treatment that applies in respect of the alleged subsidy and the tax treatment of comparable income of comparably situated taxpayers.

Footnote 1 that is attached to Article 1.1(a)(1)(ii) clarifies that the exemption of an exported product from duties or taxes borne by the like

[74] WT/DS299/R of 17 June 2005, *European Communities – Countervailing Measures on Dynamic Random Access Memory Chips from Korea*, para 7.87.

[75] WT/DS353/R of 31 March 2011, *United States – Measures Affecting Trade in Large Civil Aircraft (Second Complaint)*, para 7.164.

[76] WT/DS353/AB/R of 12 March 2012, *United States – Measures Affecting Trade in Large Civil Aircraft (Second Complaint)*, para 811.

product when destined for domestic consumption, or the remission of such duties or taxes in amounts not in excess of those which have accrued, shall not be deemed to be a subsidy. This footnote refers to the Note to Article XVI of GATT 1994 and to Annexes I–III of the ASCM, which contain identical text or at least reflect this text. Article VI:4 of GATT 1994 is also practically identical with footnote 1.[77] The rationale underlying this footnote is that producers in each nation should have access to internationally traded inputs at 'world' prices for use in export production and sales. By making the adjustments for duties and taxes on inputs as described above, an exporting producer should be able to charge approximately the world price for its exports.[78] Footnote 1 is one of the two examples contained in Article 1 that explicitly do not constitute a subsidy (the other being the provision of general infrastructure, see subparagraph (iii)). Thus, e.g. a proper duty drawback system or a refund of VAT upon exportation are not deemed to be a subsidy. This design falls in between the strict origin principle (prohibition to rebate any taxes or duties) and the strict destination principle (adjustment at the border for all taxes).[79] See also *infra* the FSC case described at pp. 95–96.

WTO Members are sovereign in determining the structure and rates of their domestic tax regimes[80] provided they respect their obligations in the ASCM. However, the Appellate Body has also made it clear that WTO Members are not obliged, by WTO rules, to tax any categories of income, whether foreign- or domestic-source income, and they may tax foreign-source income less than they tax domestic-source income.[81]

[77] Footnote 1 contains a reference to Annexes I–III of the ASCM as well as a reference to Article XVI of the GATT 1994. According to WT/DS108/AB/R of 24 February 2000, *United States – Tax Treatment for 'Foreign Sales Corporations'*, footnote 135 attached to para 117, the reference to Article XVI of the GATT 1994 is not a specific reference to Article XVI:4 of the GATT 1994 but to the Interpretative Note *Ad* Article XVI of the GATT 1994. WT/DS139/AB/R and WT/DS142/AB/R of 31 May 2000, *Canada – Certain Measures Affecting the Automotive Industry*, para 92 confirmed that footnote 1 deals with duty drawback issues.

[78] *Hufbauer/Erb* (1984) pp. 10–11.

[79] *Hufbauer/Erb* (1984) p. 51 *et seq.*

[80] WT/DS353/AB/R of 12 March 2012, *United States – Measures Affecting Trade in Large Civil Aircraft (Second Complaint)*, para 811.

[81] WT/DS108/AB/R of 24 February 2000, *United States – Tax Treatment for 'Foreign Sales Corporations'*, paras 90 and 98. See also the preceding Panel with regard to the neutrality of the ASCM concerning territorial and worldwide tax systems, WT/DS108/R of 8 October 1999, *United States – Tax Treatment for 'Foreign Sales Corporations'*, paras 7.121–7.123. Finally, see also WT/DS108/AB/RW of 14 January 2002, *United States – Tax Treatment for 'Foreign Sales Corporations' (Article 21.5, first recourse)*, para 86.

The leading cases with regard to Article 1.1(a)(1)(ii) are *US – FSC, US – FSC (Article 21.5)* and *US – Large Civil Aircraft (2nd complaint)*. One of the central issues under the second subparagraph is the test to be applied in order to determine whether government revenue was 'otherwise due'. A number of panels have tried to conceptualize this term by applying a 'but for' test. In other words, 'otherwise due' refers to a situation that would prevail but for the measure in question. The question was whether, absent the measure subject to dispute, would there be a higher tax liability?[82] The Appellate Body took a more nuanced view. For instance, in *US – FSC* the Appellate Body accepted that the 'but for' test worked in the case in question because there was a 'rule-exception' relationship. But it also pointed out that it may not work in other cases *inter alia* because it would not be difficult to circumvent such a test by designing a tax regime under which there would be no general rule.[83] The following should be borne in mind when applying subparagraph (ii):

- Foregoing of revenue otherwise due implies that less revenue has been raised by the government than would have been raised in a different situation.[84]
- The word 'foregone' suggests that the government has given up an entitlement to raise revenue that it could 'otherwise' have raised.[85]
- The purported entitlement cannot exist in the abstract. There must be some defined, normative benchmark against which a comparison can be made between the revenue actually raised and the revenue that would have been raised 'otherwise'.[86]
- The basis of comparison must be the prevailing domestic standard established by the tax rules applied by the WTO Member in question, because what is 'otherwise due' depends on the rules of taxation that each Member, by its own choice, establishes for itself.[87]

82 See e.g. WT/DS108/R of 8 October 1999, *United States – Tax Treatment for 'Foreign Sales Corporations'*, paras 7.45 and 7.46 *et passim*.

83 WT/DS108/AB/R of 24 February 2000, *United States – Tax Treatment for 'Foreign Sales Corporations'*, paras 90 and 91; WT/DS108/AB/RW of 14 January 2002, *United States – Tax Treatment for 'Foreign Sales Corporations' (Article 21.5, first recourse)*, para 91.

84 WT/DS108/AB/R of 24 February 2000, *United States – Tax Treatment for 'Foreign Sales Corporations'*, para 91.

85 WT/DS108/AB/R of 24 February 2000, *United States – Tax Treatment for 'Foreign Sales Corporations'*, para 90.

86 WT/DS108/AB/R of 24 February 2000, *United States – Tax Treatment for 'Foreign Sales Corporations'*, para 90.

87 WT/DS108/AB/R of 24 February 2000, *United States – Tax Treatment for 'Foreign Sales Corporations'*, para 90.

- A financial contribution does not arise under Article 1.1(a)(1)(ii) simply because a government does not raise revenue that it could have raised. Although a government might be said to 'forego' revenue when it chooses not to tax certain income, this alone is not determinative of whether the revenue foregone is 'otherwise due'. In other words, the mere fact that revenues are not due from a fiscal perspective does not determine that the revenues are otherwise due within the meaning of Article 1.1(a)(1)(ii).[88]
- Because WTO Members, in principle, have the sovereign authority to determine their own rules of taxation, the comparison under Article 1.1(a)(1)(ii) must necessarily be between the rules of taxation contained in the challenged measure of the Member concerned and other rules of taxation of the Member concerned.[89]
- It may be difficult to identify the appropriate benchmark for comparison under Article 1.1(a)(1)(ii) because domestic rules of taxation are varied and complex. Panels must ensure that they identify and examine fiscal situations which it is legitimate to compare. There must be a rational basis for comparing the fiscal treatment of the income subject to the contested measure and the fiscal treatment of certain other income.[90]
- In general terms, like will be compared with like and it is important to ensure that the examination involves a comparison of the fiscal treatment of the relevant income for taxpayers in comparable situations. For instance, if the measure at issue involves income earned in a sales transaction, it might not be appropriate to compare the treatment of this income with employment income. And if the measure at issue is concerned with the taxation of foreign-source income in the hands of a domestic corporation, it might not be appropriate to compare the measure with the fiscal treatment of such income in the hands of a foreign corporation. In other words, the normative benchmark for determining whether revenue foregone is otherwise due must allow a comparison of the fiscal treatment of comparable income, in the hands of taxpayers in similar situations. Panels should 'seek to compare the fiscal treatment of *legitimately comparable income* to determine whether the contested

[88] WT/DS108/AB/RW of 14 January 2002, *United States – Tax Treatment for 'Foreign Sales Corporations' (Article 21.5, first recourse)*, para 88.
[89] WT/DS108/AB/RW of 14 January 2002, *United States – Tax Treatment for 'Foreign Sales Corporations' (Article 21.5, first recourse)*, para 89.
[90] WT/DS108/AB/RW of 14 January 2002, *United States – Tax Treatment for 'Foreign Sales Corporations' (Article 21.5, first recourse)*, para 90.

measure involves the foregoing of revenue which is "otherwise due", in relation to the income in question' (see para 91, emphasis added).[91]

Based on the two FSC cases, *US – Large Civil Aircraft (2nd complaint)* has developed a three step test.

- First, a panel or investigating authority should identify the tax treatment that applies to the income of the alleged recipients of the subsidy. Identifying such tax treatment will entail consideration of the objective reasons behind that treatment and, where it involves a change in the tax rules, an assessment of the reasons underlying the change.
- Second, a benchmark for comparison should be identified. This benchmark is the tax treatment of 'comparable income of comparably situated taxpayers'. The task under this step is to develop an understanding of the structure of the domestic tax regime and its organizing principles that best explains the tax regime in question. This step also aims at providing a reasoned basis for identifying what constitutes comparable income of comparably situated taxpayers. Evidence relied upon in such an analysis must be located in the rules of taxation that each WTO Member establishes for itself. The Appellate Body recognized that this is not always a straightforward exercise, and may in some circumstances be exceedingly difficult. It may be that disparate tax measures, implemented over time, do not easily offer up coherent principles serving as a benchmark.
- Third, the reasons for the challenged tax treatment should be compared with the benchmark tax treatment that had been identified under step 2.[92]

Note that there was some dispute as to what extent the test under Article 1.1(a)(1)(ii) could be established on the basis of identifying the general rule of taxation and the exception(s). The Panel in *US – Large Civil Aircraft (2nd complaint)* interpreted previous Appellate Body rulings to say

- that where it is possible to identify a general rule of taxation, a 'but for' test could be applied;
- in other situations, the challenged taxation measure should be compared to the treatment applied to comparable income, for taxpayers in comparable circumstances, in the jurisdiction in issue.

[91] WT/DS108/AB/RW of 14 January 2002, *United States – Tax Treatment for 'Foreign Sales Corporations' (Article 21.5, first recourse)*, paras 90, 91, 92 and 98.

[92] WT/DS353/AB/R of 12 March 2012, *United States – Measures Affecting Trade in Large Civil Aircraft (Second Complaint)*, paras 812–815.

As already mentioned above, the Appellate Body was very critical about such a 'but for' test. It held that the Panel's approach suggested that, as long as a general rule of taxation is identified, it is sufficient to conduct an analysis limited to the determination that, but for the challenged measure, a higher tax liability would have applied by virtue of the general rule. Panels do not have a binary choice between a simplified and a more complex inquiry. The Appellate Body saw the following shortcomings of the general rule/exception approach. In identifying a general rule and exception relationship, a rule and an exception might be artificially created where no such distinction exists. The Appellate Body also warned about focusing too narrowly on the change that brought the challenged tax measure into existence. The departure of a benchmark identified solely by reference to historical rates might in reality only reflect evidence of shifting norms within that regime. Moreover, the domestic tax regime may be so replete with exceptions that the rate applicable to the general category of income in fact no longer represents the general rule but rather the exception. In sum, the Appellate Body recognized that there may be tax regimes pointing to such rule and exception relationship, but it also expected that an indication of such a relationship should not ordinarily end the analysis. Rather, a further examination of the structure of the domestic tax regime and its organizing principles would be appropriate, as described above in step 2.[93]

After reviewing the Panel's analysis on the basis of the above principles, the Appellate Body in *US – Large Civil Aircraft (2nd complaint)* confirmed the Panel's ruling. The Panel concluded that there was a general or normal Business and Occupation tax in Washington State with a rate of 0.484 per cent for manufacturing and wholesaling activities and 0.471 per cent for retailing activities, while Boeing, that carried out similar activities, only paid 0.2904 per cent. The Panel considered the latter to be an exceptional

[93] WT/DS353/AB/R of 12 March 2012, *United States – Measures Affecting Trade in Large Civil Aircraft (Second Complaint)*, paras 815, 823. Note that in *US – FSC (Article 21.5)*, the Appellate Body accepted (1) that in identifying a normative benchmark, there may be situations where the measure at issue might be described as an exception to the general rule of taxation and (2) to apply the 'but for' test. In that decision, it also pointed out that Article 1.1(a)(1)(ii) does not always require panels to identify with respect to any particular income the general rule of taxation prevailing. Given the variety and complexity of domestic tax systems, it will usually be very difficult to isolate a general rule of taxation, and exceptions to that general rule, and that an examination under Article 1.1(a)(1)(ii) must be sufficiently flexible to adjust to the complexities of a Member's domestic rules of taxation. See WT/DS108/AB/RW of 14 January 2002, *United States – Tax Treatment for 'Foreign Sales Corporations' (Article 21.5, first recourse)*, para 91 including footnote 66.

rate that differed from the general rates of 0.484 per cent and 0.471 per cent respectively. It noted that the law introducing this lower rate for aircraft manufacturers referred to this as a 'preferential tax rate'. The law also stipulated that if a company benefitting from such lower rate fails to comply with certain reporting requirements, there would be a reversion to the 'full taxes'. The Panel also considered that the scope of the general tax rates mentioned above to that of various lower tax rates did not alter its conclusion that the general rates reflected what would have been applied to aircraft manufacturers in the absence of the Business and Occupation tax reduction. The US submitted that the Business and Occupation tax system should have been examined as a whole, consisting of 36 activity classifications subject to this tax but at different rates. The appropriate benchmark should consist of the entire Business and Occupation tax regime. The Panel and Appellate Body were not impressed by this argument. They noted that there were four principal activity classifications (i.e. manufacturing, wholesaling and retailing with the tax rates mentioned above as well as services with a tax rate of 1.5 per cent), that accounted for 90 per cent of the Business and Occupation tax liability. This indicated that Washington State itself classified income from business activities into broad categories that, for purposes of the commercial aircraft sector, consist of manufacturing, wholesaling and retailing. To contend that the 36 tax rates together constitute the benchmark would amount to the contention that there is, in effect, no benchmark within the system. Rather, the inquiry should seek to identify a benchmark within the taxation system even in circumstances where there may be several, perhaps competing, principles operating within the taxation system, or where the existence of any coherent principle or principles is difficult to discern.[94] The US also submitted that account should be taken of 'pyramiding'. According to them, Boeing was subject to a particularly high effective rate because businesses are taxed at each stage of production and pay effectively higher rates in respect of later stages of production due to the accumulation of taxes paid on prior inputs in the production process. Again the Appellate Body was not impressed. There was no indication that adjusting tax rates to approximate the average tax rate reflected a principle under the Washington State Business and Occupation tax regime.[95] See

[94] WT/DS353/AB/R of 12 March 2012, *United States – Measures Affecting Trade in Large Civil Aircraft (Second Complaint)*, paras 816–828.

[95] WT/DS353/AB/R of 12 March 2012, *United States – Measures Affecting Trade in Large Civil Aircraft (Second Complaint)*, paras 829 and 830.

also the Panel in *US – Tax Incentives* that examined a number of tax reductions granted to Boeing including the Washington State Business and Occupation tax regime.[96]

Wouters/Coppens (2010) tried to summarize the two tests, i.e. the 'but for' test and the test referring to the normative benchmark. According to them, the former examines the matter from a legal viewpoint while the latter applies a policy viewpoint.[97] *Bohanes/Rueda Garcia* consider the third step of the test developed by the Appellate Body in *US – Large Civil Aircraft (2nd complaint)*, i.e. the reasons for the challenged tax treatment should be compared with the benchmark tax treatment that had been identified under the preceding step, as somewhat enigmatic and needlessly confusing. According to them, the third step could have just been a simple comparison while the type of examination envisaged by the Appellate Body would probably sit better in the specificity test.[98] Note finally that the aforementioned references by the Appellate Body to the 'structure of the domestic tax regime and its organizing principles' in *US – Large Civil Aircraft (2nd complaint)* and to the 'legitimately comparable income' in *US – FSC* will be of relevance, for instance, when it comes to the assessment of subsidies motivated by environmental considerations.[99]

In *US – FSC (1st Article 21.5)*, the Appellate Body had to establish the normative benchmark of US tax law with regard to the foreign-source income of US citizens or residents. It found that the US imposes tax on taxable income of each US citizen and resident and that taxable income means all income from whatever source derived. In other words, US law did not distinguish between income from US domestic sources or income from foreign sources. The Appellate Body then compared the taxation of foreign-source income as described in the preceding sentences with the taxation of so-called 'Qualifying foreign trade income', i.e. the contested measure. According to the Appellate Body, the US considered qualifying foreign trade income also as foreign-source income of US citizens and residents. However, US citizens and residents could elect, at their own discretion, to exclude such qualifying foreign trade income from taxation or to be taxed according to the otherwise applicable rules of taxation. The Appellate Body held that the possible

[96] WT/DS487/R of 28 November 2016, *United States – Conditional Tax Incentives for Large Civil Aircraft*, paras 7.44–7.165.

[97] See *Wouters/Coppens* (2010) p. 19.

[98] *Bohanes/Rueda Garcia* (2012/1) p. 369. Similar *Coppens* (2014) p. 47.

[99] *Rubini* (2012) pp. 533–540.

exclusion of qualifying foreign trade income from taxation met the conditions of Article 1.2(a)(1)(ii).[100]

Note that the Appellate Body in *US – FSC* did not accept the argument put forward by the US that footnote 59 (see item (e) of Annex I) qualifies the general interpretation of the term 'otherwise due'. Footnote 59 does not purport to establish an exception to the general definition of a subsidy as contained in Article 1.1.[101]

Canada – Autos again applied the principles established in *US – FSC*. The facts at issue in *Canada – Autos* were, however, less complex because the exemption from import duties of certain cars imported into Canada was clearly 'revenue foregone': in essence, established car manufacturers with production facilities in Canada benefited from the contested import duty exemption while manufacturers without such facility had to pay 6.1 per cent import duty.[102] Another straightforward example of 'government revenue that is otherwise due is foregone' is *Indonesia – Autos*, where import duty and luxury sales tax exemptions on certain cars and car parts granted by the Indonesian government represented revenue foregone.[103]

Government Provision of Goods or Services (Other Than General Infrastructure) and Purchase of Goods (Article 1.1(a)(1)(iii))

Introduction Subparagraph (iii) contemplates two distinct types of transaction: the first is where a government 'provides goods or services

[100] WT/DS108/AB/RW of 14 January 2002, *United States – Tax Treatment for 'Foreign Sales Corporations' (Article 21.5, first recourse)*, paras 93–102. See also the preceding Panel WT/DS108/RW of 20 August 2001, *United States – Tax Treatment for 'Foreign Sales Corporations' (Article 21.5, first recourse)*, paras 8.20–8.43. That Panel pointed out that by treating as non-taxable certain income on the basis of highly selective conditions and quantitative requirements, the contested measure effectively carves out such income from another situation and that the scope of the contested measure could not be rationally understood as a self-standing autonomous construct, but rather only by comparison with another situation to which the Act itself explicitly refers (para 8.26). The US invoked the Appellate Body ruling in *US – FSC* according to which Members are free not to tax any particular categories of revenues, and argued on this basis that the contested measure constituted a category of income that could be excluded. The Panel rejected this argument, *inter alia*, on the grounds that there would never be a foregoing of revenue otherwise due if that argument were to be accepted and that this would not be compatible with the object and purpose of the ASCM (paras 8.31–8.39).

[101] WT/DS108/AB/R of 24 February 2000, *United States – Tax Treatment for 'Foreign Sales Corporations'*, paras 92–94.

[102] WT/DS139/AB/R and WT/DS142/AB/R of 31 May 2000, *Canada – Certain Measures Affecting the Automotive Industry*, paras 87–94. The description of the programme can be found in para 7 *et seq.* of the report.

[103] WT/DS54/R, WT/DS55/R, WT/DS59/R and WT/DS64/R of 2 July 1998, *Indonesia – Certain Measures Affecting the Automobile Industry*, para 14.155.

other than general infrastructure'; and the second relates to situations in which the government 'purchases goods' from an enterprise. In the first type of transaction, the goods or services are provided *by* the government while in the second type of transaction the goods are provided *to* the government. The first type of transaction has the potential to lower artificially the cost of producing a product by providing, to an enterprise, inputs having a financial value. The second type of transaction has the potential to increase artificially the revenues gained from selling the product.[104]

With regard to the first type of transaction, i.e. the provision of goods and services, subparagraph (iii) does not specify whether the goods or services are provided free of charge or in exchange for consideration. By contrast, the term 'purchase' used for the second type of transaction is usually understood to mean that the person or entity providing the goods will receive some consideration in return.[105] A more recent example of a purchase of goods examined by the DSB is the feed-in tariff scheme operated by the Government of Ontario in order to purchase electricity produced from certain forms of renewable energy by which a guaranteed price was paid per kilowatt of electricity under 20-year or 40-year contracts.[106]

The provision of 'general infrastructure' does not constitute a financial contribution and hence not a subsidy.

Subparagraph (iii) does not list the purchase of services as a financial contribution. The question is whether the purchase of services can be classified as a 'direct transfer of funds falling under Article 1.1(a)(1)(i). There is no DSB ruling on this issue yet. See *supra* p. 85.

Goods The term 'goods' covers tangible items such as standing, unfelled trees which are made available under stumpage arrangements, i.e. a right of private parties to enter onto government lands, cut standing timber and enjoy exclusive rights over the timber that is harvested. In *US – Softwood Lumber IV* Canada argued that unfelled trees could not be classified as

[104] WT/DS257/AB/R of 19 January 2004, *United States – Final Countervailing Duty Determination with Respect to Certain Softwood Lumber from Canada*, para 53.

[105] WT/DS353/AB/R of 12 March 2012, *United States – Measures Affecting Trade in Large Civil Aircraft (Second Complaint)*, paras 618 and 619. See also *infra* pp. 103–104.

[106] WT/DS412/AB/R and WT/DS426/AB/R of 6 May 2013, *Canada – Certain Measures Affecting the Renewable Energy Generation Sector; Canada – Measures Relating to Feed-In Tariff Program*, para 5.109 *et seq*. For more details see *infra* pp. 103–104.

goods. The Appellate Body rejected this argument. It noted, *inter alia*, that the narrow interpretation put forward by Canada would permit the circumvention of subsidy disciplines in cases of financial contributions granted in the form other than money, such as through the provision of standing timber for the sole purposes of severing it from land and processing it. The Appellate Body also agreed with the previous Panel, that held that the ordinary meaning of the term 'good' as used in Article 1.1(a)(1)(iii) includes items that are tangible and capable of being possessed. According to the Appellate Body, in the context of Article 1.1(a)(1)(iii), all goods that might be used by an enterprise to its benefit – including even goods that might be considered as infrastructure – are to be considered 'goods' within the meaning of this provision, unless they are 'general infrastructure'.[107]

There are no rulings yet as to whether emission permits or intellectual property rights constitute a 'good'.[108]

To 'Provide' In *US – Softwood Lumber IV*, Canada argued that stumpage arrangements, i.e. rights to harvest timber, do not amount to the provision of a good, i.e. the supply of felled trees, logs or lumber. According to Canada, all that was provided by these stumpage arrangements was an intangible right to harvest. The term 'to provide' should be limited to the supplying or giving of goods or services. Making available a good is not enough. The Appellate Body disagreed with Canada that the granting of an intangible right to harvest standing timber cannot be equated with the act of providing timber. To 'provide' also includes granting a right to harvest standing timber under a stumpage arrangement because this puts the timber in question at the disposal of timber harvesters and allows those parties to make use of such resources. The Appellate Body held that the term 'provides' should be interpreted as meaning 'making available' or 'putting at the disposal of'. The Appellate Body also pointed out that 'making available' or 'putting at the disposal' requires the existence of a reasonably proximate relationship between the action of the government providing the good or service, on the one hand, and the use or enjoyment of the good or service by the recipient, on the other. A government must have some control over the availability of a specific thing

[107] WT/DS257/AB/R of 19 January 2004, *United States – Final Countervailing Duty Determination with Respect to Certain Softwood Lumber from Canada*, paras 57–67. See also *Horn/Mavroidis* (2005) pp. 226–229.

[108] But see *Henschke* (2012) pp. 32–35.

being made available. What matters for purposes of determining whether a government provides goods in the sense of Article 1.1(a)(1)(iii) is the consequence of the transaction (and in the case at issue making available timber was the *raison d'être* of the stumpage arrangements). On this basis, the Appellate Body confirmed the Panel ruling that the stumpage arrangements amounted to the provision of goods.[109]

US – Carbon Steel (India) had to address a similar issue. India contended that a grant of mining rights for iron ore and coal by the Government of India (GOI) could not be considered a provision of goods (iron ore and coal in the case in question) due to the intervening acts of non-government entities. According to India, the link between the grant of the mining rights and the actual iron ore or coal extracted was too remote to fulfil the 'reasonably proximate relationship' standard applied by the Appellate Body in *US – Softwood Lumber IV*. In India's view, specific action undertaken by the government or public body must be 'providing' the goods such that the governmental action itself, rather than the intervening acts of non-government bodies, directly results in the provision of goods. India submitted that there was no provision of goods because significant efforts, risks and investment had to be undertaken by the miner to actually make the mineral available for use or enjoyment. The Appellate Body therefore understood India to argue that the extraction process undertaken by the Indian steel producers, due to its complexity and uncertainty, was a significant intervening act so as to undermine such reasonably proximate relationship. The Appellate Body did not agree with India in the case at hand. According to the Appellate Body, in order to determine whether or not there is a reasonably proximate relationship between the grant of the mining rights and final extracted goods, an examination of the complexity and uncertainty of the mining rights arrangement is necessary. The Appellate Body referred in this context to the following elements:

- There is a difference between a general governmental act that simply facilitates the mining operation and, as in the case at hand, the grant of a right to mine that allows the beneficiary to extract government-owned minerals from the ground, and then use those minerals for its own purposes.

[109] WT/DS257/AB/R of 19 January 2004, *United States – Final Countervailing Duty Determination with Respect to Certain Softwood Lumber from Canada*, paras 68–75. See also *Horn/Mavroidis* (2005) pp. 226–229.

- A distinction could be drawn between the mining rights at issue which involve the right to extract minerals from known sites, as opposed to more tenuous arrangements such as exploration rights.
- The mining rights at issue involved the payment of royalties that were tied to the amount of extracted material.
- Rights over extracted iron ore and coal follow as a natural and inevitable consequence of the steel companies' exercise of their mining rights. This suggested that making available iron ore and coal was the *raison d'être* of the mining rights.
- India also tried to argue that the classification of mining rights as a provision of a good would permit other governmental acts, such as the granting of a business licence, to constitute a provision of goods, since, but for the governmental action, the mining company would not have been able to access the mineral in the first place. Given the aforementioned considerations, the Appellate Body was not impressed by this argument.[110]

In *EC and certain Member States – Large Civil Aircraft*, there was also disagreement as to what constitutes a provision of a good. Hamburg created the so-called Mühlenburger Loch industrial site (i) by conversion of wetlands into usable land, (ii) by the construction of certain flood protection measures and (iii) by building special purpose facilities. This site has subsequently been leased to Airbus who operated the adjacent Airbus facility, Finkenwerder. Thus, Airbus could expand its existing facilities. The EU argued that the creation of the Mühlenburger Loch industrial site was a creation of infrastructure that benefits the society as a whole and therefore reflects legitimate economic development policies with which, as long as the infrastructure is not provided to the recipient, the ASCM does not interfere. According to the EU, only the provision to an economic operator (as opposed to the creation) of infrastructure 'other than general infrastructure' is captured by the notion of financial contribution since only this government action is capable of distorting trade. The Appellate did not accept this argument. It argued that the creation of infrastructure is a precondition,

[110] WT/DS436/AB/R of 8 December 2014, *United States – Countervailing Measures on Certain Hot-Rolled Carbon Steel Flat Products from India*, paras 4.60–4.75. The Panel rejected India's argument that the granting of mining rights was too remote from the extracted minerals. In the Panel's view, India's approach *inter alia* lacked legal certainty for it would lead to different results depending on the complexity of the process required to extract the relevant minerals, or the uncertainty regarding the amount of minerals extracted (see paras 4.62 and 4.63). The Appellate Body disagreed with this part of the Panel's reasoning but ultimately upheld the Panel's finding.

and thus necessary, for the provision of infrastructure. According to the Appellate Body, the term 'provision' in Article 1.1(a)(1)(iii) does not exclude the possibility that circumstances of the creation of infrastructure may be relevant to a proper characterization of what it is that is provided. However, the Appellate Body did not go as far as the Panel that concluded that the financial contribution was the 'creation' of the Mühlenburger Loch. According to the Appellate Body, a proper characterization of the financial contribution provided to Airbus consisted of the lease of land and special purpose facilities at the Mühlenburger Loch industrial site.[111]

General Infrastructure In the context of the above Mühlenbuger Loch issue, the Panel in *EC and certain Member States – Large Civil Aircraft* had to clarify the term 'general infrastructure'. It held that this term refers to infrastructure that is not provided to or for the advantage of only a single entity or limited group of entities, but rather is available to all or nearly all entities. It also found that it is difficult if not impossible to define the concept of general infrastructure in the abstract. Rather, the determination must be made on a case-by-case basis based on all relevant facts. The Panel did not see any harm or problem in such lack of a precise definition because other disputes that had to interpret Article 1.1(a)(1) had similarly not resulted in precise or absolute definitions of terms in the abstract. The Panel recognized that the existence of limitations on access or use of infrastructure, whether *de jure* or *de facto*, is highly relevant in determining whether that infrastructure is 'general infrastructure'. It also found that this is not the only legally relevant consideration. Additional factors could include, *inter alia*, the circumstances under which the infrastructure in question was created and the nature and type of infrastructure in question, the recipients or beneficiaries of the infrastructure, and the legal regime applicable to such infrastructure. However, the Panel found that the following factors proposed by the EU did not provide useful guidance: (i) the substance of government action related to basic installations, facilities and services needed to support social as well as economic development; (ii) their public policy objective.

The Panel referred in this context approvingly to a submission made by the EU during the Uruguay Round negotiations that claimed that

[111] WT/DS316/AB/R of 18 May 2011, *EC and certain Member States – Measures Affecting Trade in Large Civil Aircraft*, paras 961–968. The Appellate Body also applied these principles when examining the Bremen Airport Runway extension and the Aéroconstellation Industrial Site in Toulouse.

contributions by the government could normally not be considered as subsidies if they merely contribute to the setting of terms and conditions of a country's economic and business environment and therefore do not alter the competitive position of firms. The Panel also pointed out that

- contrary to other subparagraphs of Article 1.1(a)(1) that provide examples as to what constitutes a financial contribution (see subparagraphs (i) and (ii)), it would not have been possible to give an example for 'general infrastructure' as there is no infrastructure that is inherently 'general' *per se*,
- as there is no infrastructure that is general *per se*, infrastructure may at some point in time be general, but not at another, depending on whether the government limits access or use,
- the fact that the authorities pursue a public interest in undertaking an infrastructure project does not render the project a general infrastructure.[112]

When the Panel applied the aforementioned principles to the facts of the case, it found that the Mühlenburger Loch and the Bremen runway extension could not be classified as 'general infrastructure'. The Mühlenburger Loch was tailor-made for Airbus and the runway extension was carried out to cater for Airbus's specific needs and, moreover, could *de jure* only be used by this manufacturer.[113] By contrast, the Panel held that in the case of publicly accessible and publicly used roads that form part of a general network of roads in a region, very strong evidence would be necessary to support the conclusion that improvements to such roads do not constitute general infrastructure. Merely that some users benefit more directly or more immediately than others does not in the view of the Panel suffice to turn the improved roads into a financial contribution. The roads in question were, *inter alia*, part of the general network of roads, allowing and/or improving access to all sites of the region.[114]

[112] WT/DS316/R of 30 June 2010, *EC and certain Member States – Measures Affecting Trade in Large Civil Aircraft*, paras 7.1035–7.1044, 7.1115, 7.117, 7.1176 *et seq.*

[113] WT/DS316/R of 30 June 2010, *EC and certain Member States – Measures Affecting Trade in Large Civil Aircraft*, paras 7.1084 and 7.1121.

[114] WT/DS316/R of 30 June 2010, *EC and certain Member States – Measures Affecting Trade in Large Civil Aircraft*, paras 7.1195. This aspect was not appealed. See also WT/DS353/R of 31 March 2011, *United States – Measures Affecting Trade in Large Civil Aircraft (Second Complaint)*, paras 7.444, 7.464–7.473.

Should a Multitude of Infrastructure Measures Be Considered Separately or Together?

The provision of infrastructure is often complex. Thus, the question may arise whether certain infrastructure measures should be considered together or separately. For example, in *EC and certain Member States – Large Civil Aircraft*, the parties disagreed whether the Bremen runway extension and noise reduction measures should be considered together (as advocated by the US) or separately (as the EU claimed). The Panel sided with the US because the EU did not provide any evidence to suggest that the noise reduction measures in question would have been undertaken even without the extension of the runway.[115]

To 'Purchase' A purchase of goods within the meaning of Article 1.1(a)(1)(iii) occurs when a government or public body obtains possession (including in the form of an entitlement) over a good by making a payment of some kind (monetary or otherwise). In *Canada – Renewable Energy & Feed-In Tariff Program*, Japan argued that the FIT did not constitute a 'purchase.' It alleged that the characterization of the measures at issue should be informed by the fact that one Ontario government entity made the payments for electricity while a different government entity received and transmitted electricity delivered by suppliers. In Japan's view, the first entity served as a financing entity, not a purchasing entity, because it never took possession of the electricity. According to Japan, the financial contribution amounted to a (potential) transfer of funds pursuant to subparagraph (i). Both Panel and Appellate Body did not agree. In the case in question, all entities involved were government public bodies and thus their activities were attributable to the Ontario government. It was not relevant whether the Government of Ontario acted through one or several of these entities. The Appellate Body also dismissed Japan's argument that the Government of Ontario's goals of achieving a stable supply of electricity and stimulating renewable energy are not addressed through purchases of electricity by the government, but rather through the allocation of distinct roles to the entities operating in Ontario's electricity system and the implementation of certain programmes. The Appellate Body noted, *inter alia*, that the Government of Ontario implemented these

[115] WT/DS316/R of 30 June 2010, *EC and certain Member States – Measures Affecting Trade in Large Civil Aircraft*, paras 7.1113 and 7.1114. A similar issue was discussed in paras 7.1173 to 7.1175 with regard to the zone d'aménagement concertée (ZAC) Aéroconstellation site and the équipement d'intérêt général (EIG) facilities.

policies amongst others through programmes involving purchases of electricity by the government. The Appellate Body was also not persuaded by Japan's argument that this mechanism should be examined in addition as a (potential) direct transfer of funds because there were no aspects of the measure that went beyond, or were different from, the payment of consideration in exchange for electricity.[116]

In the same dispute, at panel stage, the EU argued that the notion of a purchase of goods by the government implies that the government or the governmental entity is being supplied with something for its own use. Since the electricity that was purchased on the basis of FIT (Feed-In Tariff), was resold to electricity consumers in Ontario, there was – in the opinion of the EU – no government purchase of goods. The Panel did not accept this argument. It held that the act of purchasing a good might be described in terms of gaining possession of, acquiring, buying or obtaining a good. Moreover, the notion of a 'purchase' for the purpose of Article 1.1(a)(1)(iii) should involve some kind of payment (usually monetary) in exchange for a good.[117]

Is a Purchase of Services a Financial Contribution? Article 1.1(a)(1)(iii) classifies the provision of goods and services as a financial contribution. However, when it comes to purchases by the government, only the purchase of goods is mentioned, not that of services. The question whether the purchase of services by the government could constitute a financial contribution potentially falling under the disciplines of the ASCM is not settled yet. The issue was addressed by the Panel in *US – Large Civil Aircraft (2nd complaint)* but the subsequent Appellate Body ruling avoided this question by taking an entirely different route. The Panel essentially concluded that a transaction that is properly characterized as a government purchase of services does not fall within the scope of Article 1.1(a)(iii). The issue arose with regard to research activities that Boeing carried out for the US government. The US government

[116] WT/DS412/AB/R and WT/DS426/AB/R of 6 May 2013, *Canada – Certain Measures Affecting the Renewable Energy Generation Sector; Canada – Measures Relating to Feed-In Tariff Program*, paras 5.124, 5.125 and 5.131. See also WT/DS353/AB/R of 12 March 2012, *United States – Measures Affecting Trade in Large Civil Aircraft (Second Complaint)*, paras 618 and 619.

[117] WT/DS412/R and WT/DS426/R of 19 December 2012, *Canada – Certain Measures Affecting the Renewable Energy Generation Sector; Canada – Measures Relating to Feed-In Tariff Program*, paras 7.225–7.227 *et passim*.

contributed to this research not only by paying remuneration but also by allowing Boeing to use NASA and Department of Defense facilities etc. In order to classify the R&D work carried out by Boeing for the US government, the Panel construed the following test: was the research work principally for Boeing's own benefit and use, or was it principally for the benefit of the US government? Only in the latter case, the research would have been a purchase of a service by the government not constituting a financial contribution. In those cases where the research was for Boeing's own benefit, the Panel concluded that there was a direct transfer of funds.[118] The Appellate Body disagreed with the Panel's approach (on the grounds that it conflated the notions of financial contribution and benefit) and characterized the research carried out 'akin to a species of a joint venture'. See *supra* pp. 76 and 85.

While at first sight, it would appear that the ASCM contains an important loophole by not carving out the purchase of services by a government from the concept of a financial contribution, the issue is in reality less pressing. If a government attempts to provide a financial contribution in the disguise of a purchase of services, the issue will most likely be dealt with under the notion of a grant. *Neven/Sykes* (2014) construct in this respect the example of a government agency that pays a domestic industry USD 100 million a day for emptying an ash tray in its headquarters.[119]

Government Makes Payments to Funding Mechanism or Entrusts or Directs a Private Body to Carry Out Functions under Subparagraphs (i)–(iii) (Article 1.1(a)(1)(iv))

Entrustment or Direction

Introduction

Ordinarily, measures taken by private bodies may not be treated as subsidies. This is because Article 1.1(a)(1) defines a subsidy as a financial contribution that confers a benefit, and in general, only actions by a government, or a public body, may constitute financial contributions. Thus, if a government or a public body carries out an action falling under subparagraphs (i) to (iii) of Article 1.1(a)(1), such action constitutes a financial contribution. An action by a private body falling under the aforementioned

[118] WT/DS353/AB/R of 12 March 2012, *United States – Measures Affecting Trade in Large Civil Aircraft (Second Complaint)*, para 551.

[119] *Neven/Sykes* (2014) p. 286.

subparagraphs only constitutes a financial contribution if that private body has been entrusted or directed by the government. This is stipulated in subparagraph (iv). Thus, subparagraph (iv) covers situations where a private body is being used as a proxy by the government to carry out one of the types of functions listed in paragraphs (i) to (iii).[120] The scope of the actions covered by subparagraph (iv) is the same as those covered by subparagraphs (i) to (iii). Thus, the difference between subparagraphs (i) to (iii) on the one hand, and subparagraph (iv) on the other, has to do with the identity of the actor, and not with the nature of the action.[121] Subparagraph (iv) is intended to ensure that governments do not evade their obligations under the ASCM by using private bodies to take actions that would otherwise fall within Article 1.1(a)(1), were they to be taken by the government itself. Therefore, Article 1.1(a)(1)(iv) is in essence an anti-circumvention provision.[122]

If a government were to instruct a public body to entrust or direct a private body, such entrustment or direction would fall within the scope of Article 1.1(a)(1)(iv).[123]

The definition of a financial contribution in cases of entrustment or direction in subparagraph (iv) contains five requirements, i.e.

- a government 'entrusts or directs'
- a private body
- to carry out one or more of the type of functions illustrated in subparagraphs (i)–(iii) of Article 1.1(a)(1)
- which would normally be vested in the government and
- the practice, in no real sense, differs from practices normally followed by governments.

Korea – Commercial Vessels underlined like *US – Export restraints* that the second and third element (addressed to a particular private body and

[120] WT/DS296/AB/R of 27 June 2005, *United States – Countervailing Duty Investigation on Dynamic Random Access Memory Semiconductors (DRAMs) from Korea*, para 108; WT/DS336/R of 13 July 2007, *Japan – Countervailing Duties on Dynamic Random Access Memories from Korea*, para 7.49.

[121] WT/DS296/AB/R of 27 June 2005, *United States – Countervailing Duty Investigation on Dynamic Random Access Memory Semiconductors (DRAMs) from Korea*, para 112; WT/DS194/R of 29 June 2001, *United States – Measures Treating Export Restraints as Subsidies*, para 8.53.

[122] WT/DS296/AB/R of 27 June 2005, *United States – Countervailing Duty Investigation on Dynamic Random Access Memory Semiconductors (DRAMs) from Korea*, para 113.

[123] WT/DS296/R/3 of 21 February 2005, *United States – Countervailing Duty Investigation on Dynamic Random Access Memory Semiconductors (DRAMs) from Korea*, para 7.36. This aspect was not appealed.

of a particular task) are aspects of the first. For an interpretation of the term 'normally be vested in the government' see *supra* pp. 66–73. The remainder of this section focuses mainly on the notions of 'entrustment' and 'direction'.

A Government 'Entrusts or Directs'

Legal Standard

The Appellate Body in *US – Countervailing Duty Investigation on DRAMs* had to define the terms 'entrustment' and 'direction'. The interpretation adopted by the Panel whose findings were under appeal was in line with the one adopted by the Panel in *US – Export Restraints*. The latter Panel concluded that it follows from the ordinary meanings of the two words 'entrust' and 'direct' that the action of the government must contain a delegation (in the case of entrustment) or command (in the case of direction). According to the Panel, both the act of entrusting and that of directing therefore necessarily carry with them the following three elements: (i) an explicit and affirmative action, be it delegation or command, (ii) addressed to a particular party and (iii) the object of which action is a particular task or duty. The Panel in *US – Export Restraints* hastened to add that 'it is clearly the first element – an explicit and affirmative action of delegation or command – that is determinative. The second and third element – addressed to a particular party and of a particular task – are *aspects* of the first.'[124]

In the aforementioned DRAMs case the Appellate Body held that the definitions used by *US – Exports restraints* (i.e. entrustment = delegation; direction = command) were too narrow. According to the Appellate Body, 'entrusts' connotes the action of giving responsibility to someone for a task or an object. In the context of subparagraph (iv), the government gives responsibility to a private body 'to carry out' one of the types of functions listed in subparagraphs (i) to (iii). Delegation is only one of the possible means by which a government could give responsibility to a private body to carry out one of these functions. Similarly, the term 'to direct' is not identical with the notion of 'command'. Rather, the term 'to direct' has the sense of giving authoritative instructions or ordering a person to do something. This suggests that 'to direct' means exercising authority over a person or entity that is directed. In the context of subparagraph (iv)

124 WT/DS194/R of 29 June 2001, *United States – Measures Treating Export Restraints as Subsidies*, paras 8.29 and 8.30 (emphasis already in text).

the authority is exercised by a government or a public body over a private body. Again, a command is certainly one way in which a government can exercise authority over a private body, but governments are likely to have other means at their disposal to exercise authority over a private body.[125]

The Appellate Body also recognized that it may be difficult to identify precisely, in the abstract, the types of government action that constitute entrustment or direction and those that do not. The particular label used to describe the governmental action is not necessarily dispositive. In some circumstances, 'guidance' by a government can constitute direction. The Appellate Body also pointed out that in most cases, one would expect entrustment or direction of a private body to involve some form of threat or inducement, which could in turn serve as evidence of entrustment or direction. The determination of entrustment or direction will hinge on the particular facts of the case.[126]

Finally, the Appellate Body pointed out that the private body's refusal to carry out the function under subparagraphs (i) to (iii) may be evidence that the government did not give it responsibility for such function, or that the government did not exercise the requisite authority over it. This does not, however, on its own, mean that the private body was not entrusted or directed. Depending on the circumstances, a private body may decide not to carry out a function with which it was entrusted or directed, despite the possible negative consequences that may follow. However, the issue is somewhat theoretical because in such a case, nothing of economic value will have been transferred from the grantor to the recipient, i.e. there will not be any financial contribution.[127]

Finally, as subparagraph (iv) requires the participation of the government, albeit indirectly, there must be a demonstrable link between the government and the conduct of the private body.[128]

As far as the evidentiary standard is concerned, the Panel in *Japan – DRAMs (Korea)* pertinently noted that entrustment or direction will rarely

[125] WT/DS296/AB/R of 27 June 2005, *United States – Countervailing Duty Investigation on Dynamic Random Access Memory Semiconductors (DRAMs) from Korea*, paras 110 and 111. WT/DS299/R of 17 June 2005, *European Communities – Countervailing Measures on Dynamic Random Access Memory Chips from Korea*, para 7.52 adopted a similar approach.

[126] WT/DS296/AB/R of 27 June 2005, *United States – Countervailing Duty Investigation on Dynamic Random Access Memory Semiconductors (DRAMs) from Korea*, para 116.

[127] WT/DS296/AB/R of 27 June 2005, *United States – Countervailing Duty Investigation on Dynamic Random Access Memory Semiconductors (DRAMs) from Korea*, paras 124 and 125.

[128] WT/DS296/AB/R of 27 June 2005, *United States – Countervailing Duty Investigation on Dynamic Random Access Memory Semiconductors (DRAMs) from Korea*, para 112.

be formal or explicit (i.e. there is a 'smoking gun'). Therefore, allegations of entrustment or direction are likely to be based on pieces of circumstantial evidence.[129]

Affirmative Act

EC – Countervailing Measures on DRAM Chips took a different approach than *US – Export Restraints* as far the requirements relating to the act of entrustment or direction were concerned. The aforementioned *DRAM Chips* Panel held that any entrustment or direction should invariably take the form of an affirmative act. But contrary to *US – Export Restraints* such act did not necessarily need to be explicit. It could be explicit or implicit, informal or formal. The key was being able to identify such entrustment or direction in each factual circumstance.[130] *Korea – Commercial Vessels* came to similar conclusions.[131]

Government Exercise of Regulatory Powers Does Normally Not Amount to Entrustment or Direction

Both *US – Export Restraints* and *Korea – Commercial Vessels* underlined that government entrustment or direction is very different from a situation in which the government intervenes in the market in some way, which may or may not have a particular result simply based on the given factual circumstances and the exercise of free choice by the actors in that market. Both situations should not be confused.[132] In other words, entrustment or direction requires a higher standard than a simple government intervention in the market.[133] In the same vein, *US – Countervailing Duty Investigation on DRAMs* has underlined that mere policy announcements by a government would not, by themselves, constitute entrustment

[129] WT/DS336/R of 13 July 2007, *Japan – Countervailing Duties on Dynamic Random Access Memories from Korea*, paras 7.72–7.73.

[130] WT/DS299/R of 17 June 2005, *European Communities – Countervailing Measures on Dynamic Random Access Memory Chips from Korea*, para 7.57.

[131] WT/DS273/R of 7 March 2005, *Korea – Measures Affecting Trade in Commercial Vessels*, paras 7.370–7.373.

[132] WT/DS194/R of 29 June 2001, *United States – Measures Treating Export Restraints as Subsidies*, para 8.31; WT/DS273/R of 7 March 2005, *Korea – Measures Affecting Trade in Commercial Vessels*, paras 7.374 and 7.375. Confirmed by WT/DS296/AB/R of 27 June 2005, *United States – Countervailing Duty Investigation on Dynamic Random Access Memory Semiconductors (DRAMs) from Korea*, para 114.

[133] See also WT/DS273/R of 7 March 2005, *Korea – Measures Affecting Trade in Commercial Vessels*, para 7.407.

or direction for the purposes of subparagraph (iv). Furthermore, entrustment and direction imply a more active role than mere acts of encouragement by the government. They cannot be an inadvertent or mere by-product of government regulation.[134] This statement by the Appellate Body is probably in line with the statement of the preceding Panel that noted that an expression of a generalized wish does not amount to entrustment or direction because an expression of a wish does not amount to an affirmative act.[135] Moreover, the interpretation of subparagraph (iv) cannot be so broad as to allow WTO Members to apply countervailing measures to products whenever a government is merely exercising its general regulatory powers.[136]

Export Restraints

US – Export Restraints had to determine whether export restraints imposed by a government could be considered a financial contribution in the form of entrustment or direction. The US argued that where the effect of an export restraint (such as export taxes or export quotas) is to induce domestic producers of the upstream products to sell their product (in greater quantities or exclusively) to the domestic purchasers/users of the product subject to investigation, this was the same as if the government had explicitly and affirmatively ordered domestic producers of the upstream product to do so.[137] Thus, there is a financial contribution in the form of government-entrusted or government-directed provision of goods. The Panel did not agree. It argued, *inter alia*, as follows:

- The US standard focused primarily on the effects or the results of government action, rather than on the nature of the subsidies in order to determine whether that action constitutes a financial contribution. Thus, according to the US approach, the existence of a financial contribution in the case of an export restraint would depend entirely on the reaction thereto of the producers of the restrained good, and specifically on the extent to which they increase domestic sales of the restrained product because of the restraint (para 8.33).

[134] WT/DS296/AB/R of 27 June 2005, *United States – Countervailing Duty Investigation on Dynamic Random Access Memory Semiconductors (DRAMs) from Korea*, para 114.

[135] WT/DS296/R/3 of 21 February 2005, *United States – Countervailing Duty Investigation on Dynamic Random Access Memory Semiconductors (DRAMs) from Korea*, para 7.36.

[136] WT/DS296/AB/R of 27 June 2005, *United States – Countervailing Duty Investigation on Dynamic Random Access Memory Semiconductors (DRAMs) from Korea*, para 115.

[137] See also *Sykes* (2010) pp. 508–509.

- The US effect-based standard would mean in practice that a different standard would apply under subparagraph (iv) as compared to the standard under subparagraphs (i)–(iii) (para 8.34).
- The US standard would seem to imply that any government measure that creates market conditions favourable to or resulting in the increased supply of a product in the domestic market would constitute a government-entrusted or government-directed provision of goods, and hence a financial contribution. The Panel also compared the US approach to a hypothetical example where the government imposed a high customs tariff on a certain product that produced, in the Panel's opinion, similar effects as an export restraint, i.e. favouring certain domestic producers although it could clearly not be considered a financial contribution (paras 8.35–8.37).
- By introducing the notion of financial contribution in the ASCM, the drafters foreclosed the possibility to treat as a subsidy any government action that resulted in a benefit. A financial contribution and a benefit are two separate legal requirements in Article 1.1, which together determine whether a subsidy exists. The US approach would effectively eliminate the financial contribution as a separate legal element (paras 8.38 and 8.40).[138]

Note that the Panel preceded the above analysis by an interpretation of the notions 'entrustment' and 'direction'. However, this interpretation had subsequently been criticized by the Appellate Body in *US – Countervailing Duty Investigation on DRAMs* as being too narrow, as described *supra*.

In *China – GOES*, the question was whether US steel purchasers that paid higher prices as a result of a voluntary export restraint agreement were entrusted and directed. The agreement was signed by the US government and limited the market share of imports into the US to 18.5 per cent. The Panel did not accept that, when a government policy, such as a

[138] WT/DS194/R of 29 June 2001, *United States – Measures Treating Export Restraints as Subsidies*, para 8.33 *et seq.* The standard applied by *US – Export Restraints* in conjunction with the modifications expressed by *US – Countervailing Duty Investigations on DRAMs* was also used by WT/DS437/R of 14 July 2014, *United States – Countervailing Duty Measures on Certain Products from China*, para 7.392 *et seq.* However, the letter Panel made its findings in the context of examining whether the USDOC respected its obligations under Article 11.3 when it initiated various countervailing duty investigations based industry on applications alleging that export restraints constituted a subsidy. The Panel also highlighted that its conclusions were based on the particular facts of the case and it did not rule out that a different set of circumstances relating to export restraints could constitute a countervailable subsidy. This issue was not appealed.

border measure, has the indirect effect of increasing prices in a market, the government has entrusted or directed private consumers to provide direct transfers of funds to the industry selling the good in the affected market. In the view of the Panel, when an action of a private party (such as paying increased prices as a result of the export restraint agreement) is a mere side-effect resulting from a government measure, this does not come within the meaning of entrustment or direction under Article 1.1(a)(1)(iv).[139]

The treatment of export restraints under the ASCM is a difficult one and there is no obvious and straightforward solution. However, it could be argued that some of the Panel's reasoning that rejected the inclusion of export restraints in subsidy disciplines is not entirely convincing. The Panel's decision should perhaps be examined in the light of more 'extreme' cases in which the link between the government regulation and the favouring of exports is more direct than in *US – Export Restraints*. *Horlick* reports of an old US CVD case where the USDOC concluded that there was entrustment or direction because the Spanish government required Spanish banks to provide export financing at 2 percentage points less than domestic loans. The USDOC considered this tantamount to the Spanish government providing a 2 per cent interest rate subsidy, even though the government did not directly provide any money.[140] The discussion of export restraints in the economic literature points to some counterintuitive conclusions, i.e. such restraint is conceptually equivalent to a combination of an export subsidy and an import tariff, both of the same magnitude, on every product other than the one that is subject to an export restraint.[141]

Discretion Enjoyed by a Private Party Not Necessarily Incompatible with Entrustment or Direction

In *US – Countervailing Duty Investigation on DRAMs*, Korea argued that any time private bodies have a choice, it was hard to imagine how they could have been entrusted or directed to carry out an action. The Panel did not agree. Leaving discretion to a private body is not necessarily at odds with entrusting or directing that private body. In particular, it was possible that a government could entrust or direct a private body to make

139 WT/DS414/R of 15 June 2012, *China – Countervailing and Anti-Dumping Duties on Grain-Oriented Flat-Rolled Electrical Steel from the US*, paras 7.89–7.93.

140 *Horlick* (2013/1) p. 298.

141 *Janow/Staiger* (2003) pp. 229–234.

a loan, but leave the terms to the discretion of the private body. While there may be cases where the breadth of discretion left to the private body was such that it became impossible to properly conclude that it was entrusted or directed, this is a factual/evidentiary matter to be addressed on a case-by-case basis.[142]

Government Ownership in the Private Body

In *US – Countervailing Duty Investigation on DRAMs*, the Panel held, in line with the USDOC's finding, that government ownership or control in and of itself did not amount to entrustment or direction. Whereas government entrustment or direction refers to affirmative acts, government ownership might facilitate government entrustment or direction, but is not *per se* indicative of any affirmative act.[143]

In *EC – Countervailing Measures on DRAM Chips*, the Panel confirmed the EU's finding that five banks that participated in the October 2001 restructuring of Hynix and in which the Korean State had shareholdings, were directed. Two of the five cases are described here. With regard to Woori Bank the Panel pointed out that in the case of a 100 per cent government-owned bank (if it is not considered a public body), it needs to be demonstrated that the government actually exercised its shareholder power to direct the bank to provide the subsidy in question. Note that the Panel did not repeat this statement when reviewing the other banks. Moreover, the Panel accepted with regard to the Woori Bank circumstantial evidence, as it did with regard to the other four banks. The Panel upheld the EU's determination of direction as a reasonable and reasoned conclusion on the combination of the following grounds:

- the bank was 100 per cent government owned;
- Hynix (the creditor) was in a disastrous financial situation – in other words no reasonable market investor would have undertaken such investments;

[142] WT/DS296/R/3 of 21 February 2005, *United States – Countervailing Duty Investigation on Dynamic Random Access Memory Semiconductors (DRAMs) from Korea*, para 7.38. This aspect was not appealed.

[143] WT/DS296/R/3 of 21 February 2005, *United States – Countervailing Duty Investigation on Dynamic Random Access Memory Semiconductors (DRAMs) from Korea*, para 7.62 (this aspect was not appealed); WT/DS299/R of 17 June 2005, *European Communities – Countervailing Measures on Dynamic Random Access Memory Chips from Korea*, paras 7.119 and 7.128.

- recognized public interest considerations (reference to the impact on the national economy of Hynix going bankrupt) in deciding to participate in the programme; and
- the underlying legal framework for restructurings had changed – at the time when this restructuring took place, a government-driven policy considerably circumscribed the options for dissenting creditors.[144]

With regard to KEB, the Panel found relevant the EU's consideration that this bank used to be a specialized government bank, that the government of Korea remained the largest shareholder with 43.17 per cent of the shares, that Hynix was in a precarious financial state at the time of the restructuring programme but that the loans were nevertheless made available at rates for financially sound companies. The Panel did not accept Korea's argument that Commerzbank, the second largest KEB shareholder, controlled the lending practices of KEB, as only four out of the 20 directors were from Commerzbank, and that the government, as the largest shareholder, was able to influence the appointment of the other directors. In the view of the Panel, the combination of the important government control and the extremely negative financial state of Hynix justified, in the absence of strong evidence to the contrary, the EU's conclusion of government direction.[145]

In the parallel Japanese case, Japan based its finding on entrustment or direction, *inter alia*, on the lack of commercial reasonableness of the participation of four private creditors. The Panel was not convinced that the participation was commercially unreasonable and consequently did not find entrustment or direction. The Appellate Body reversed the Panel's finding. It criticized that the Panel did not adequately explain why a finding of commercial reasonableness, by itself, was indispensable for the ultimate finding of entrustment or direction as the Japanese investigating authority itself did not consider commercial reasonableness to be indispensable for its ultimate finding. However, the Appellate Body also recognized that the commercial unreasonableness of the financial transactions is a relevant factor in determining government entrustment or direction, in particular where an investigating authority seeks to establish government intervention based on circumstantial evidence. However, this did

[144] WT/DS299/R of 17 June 2005, *European Communities – Countervailing Measures on Dynamic Random Access Memory Chips from Korea*, paras 7.120–7.125. See also paras 7.126–7.132 and 7.205.

[145] WT/DS299/R of 17 June 2005, *European Communities – Countervailing Measures on Dynamic Random Access Memory Chips from Korea*, paras 7.133–7.135, 7.205.

not mean that a finding of entrustment or direction could never be made unless it was established that the financial transactions were on non-commercial terms. A government could entrust or direct a creditor to make a loan, which that creditor then does on commercial terms.[146]

If, on the one hand, the government or a public body and, on the other, private banks participate in restructurings, the nature of the operation has to be looked at in order to determine whether the involvement of the private banks is a relevant step for the subsidy determination. In *EC – Countervailing Measures on DRAM Chips*, the investigating authority, *inter alia*, had to assess to what extent the Debenture Programme by the Korean Development Bank (KDB) constituted a subsidy. Under this programme, that was set up by the Korean government in response to financial instability, the KDB purchased 80 per cent of maturing debt while the remaining 20 per cent had to be repaid by the company that had issued the bonds. Of the 80 per cent originally assumed by the KDB, 20 per cent of the bonds was then sold to the company's creditor banks in proportion to their debt exposure to the company. Seventy per cent was re-packaged for sale to investors as collateralized bond or loan obligations and guaranteed by the Korean Credit Guarantee Fund. The KDB retained the remaining 10 per cent. The participating company had to purchase at least 3 per cent of any collateralized bond and 5 per cent of any collateralized loan. The EU found that the purchase of the bonds by the KDB constituted a financial contribution (direct transfer of funds) by a public body. Hynix benefited from this programme. Korea argued before the Panel that the EU should have established entrustment or direction with regard to the numerous creditors that were also involved in the purchase of Hynix's corporate bonds in the framework of this programme. The Panel rejected Korea's view and sided with the EU, i.e. that this was a financial contribution by a public body. Whether or not the full cost of the financial contribution was borne by KDB was not relevant for the Panel in determining the existence of a financial contribution.[147]

Evidence in Relation to Entrustment and Direction/Examples

In *US – Countervailing Duty Investigation on DRAMs*, the US and Korea disagreed as to what constitutes the proper evidentiary standard in order

[146] WT/DS336/AB/R of 28 November 2007, *Japan – Countervailing Duties on Dynamic Random Access Memories from Korea*, paras 137–138.

[147] WT/DS299/R of 17 June 2005, *European Communities – Countervailing Measures on Dynamic Random Access Memory Chips from Korea*, paras 7.88–7.91.

to determine whether there was entrustment and direction. The question at issue was whether restructuring measures during the period 1998–2001 to save the Korean semiconductor manufacturer Hynix constituted a subsidy. The US held that the restructuring measures carried out by private creditors that were owned or controlled by the Government of Korea but not found to be public bodies (Group B creditors) and private entities in which the Korean government had a much smaller or even non-existent shareholdings (Group C creditors) were subsidies because these two types of creditors were entrusted or directed by the Korean government. The US based this conclusion on three factual inferences drawn from the evidence on the record:

(i) The Government of Korea maintained a policy of supporting Hynix's financial restructuring and thereby avoiding the firm's collapse.
(ii) The Government of Korea exercised the control or influence over Hynix's creditors necessary to implement this policy.
(iii) The Government of Korea at times used this control/influence to pressure or coerce Hynix's creditors to continue supporting the financial restructuring of the firm.[148]

The first issue at dispute was the evidentiary standard used by the Panel. The Panel held that evidence of entrustment or direction must be 'probative and compelling, in the sense that it demonstrates that each of the private creditors participating in the financial contributions was entrusted or directed to do so'. The US agreed that evidence, by its very nature, must be probative. But it argued that the standard of 'compelling' was contained neither in the ASCM nor in the DSU. The US interpreted the compelling standard as referring to evidence of such weight as to require the decision-maker to arrive at one given conclusion.

The Appellate Body agreed that neither the ASCM nor the DSU explicitly articulated a standard for the evidence required to substantiate a finding of entrustment or direction under Article 1.1(a)(1)(iv). The only requirement in relation to evidence that the ASCM establishes, can be found in Article 12, i.e. that a decision as to the existence of a subsidy can only be based on evidence on the record of the investigating authority. However, the Appellate Body ultimately did not agree with the US because the Panel did not use the term 'compelling' in the sense alleged by the US. Rather, in the opinion of the Appellate Body, the Panel examined

[148] WT/DS296/AB/R of 27 June 2005, *United States – Countervailing Duty Investigation on Dynamic Random Access Memory Semiconductors (DRAMs) from Korea*, para 131 *et seq.*

whether the evidence of the USDOC could support its conclusion that the evidence demonstrated entrustment or direction.[149]

The second issue at dispute was how the Panel reviewed the USDOC's decision that explicitly was based on the totality of evidence on the record. As stated above, the USDOC concluded that there was entrustment or direction based on three factual inferences which it drew from the totality of the evidence on the record. The Panel reviewed separately each individual piece of evidence on which the USDOC relied to support the particular premise. The Appellate Body did not see any fault as such in this approach even where the investigating authority drew its conclusion from the totality of the evidence. Indeed, in many cases a panel will be able to examine the sufficiency of the evidence supporting a particular conclusion only by looking at each individual piece of evidence. Errors in an investigating authority's examination of individual pieces of evidence undoubtedly could affect an examination of the totality of the evidence, as these pieces would constitute the evidence the panel would consider as a whole in assessing the evidentiary support of the investigating authority's decision on entrustment or direction. However, the Appellate Body found that the Panel erred in the manner in which it reviewed each individual piece of evidence. The Panel often appeared to examine whether each piece of evidence, viewed in isolation (!), demonstrated entrustment or direction. By following this approach, the Panel indeed appeared not to have considered seriously any evidence that did not amount to a 'smoking gun', as the US have put it. The Appellate Body pointed out that if an investigating authority relies on individual pieces of circumstantial evidence viewed together as support for a finding of entrustment or direction, a panel reviewing such a determination normally should consider that evidence in its totality, rather than individually, in order to assess the probative value of the investigating authority's determination. Like the investigating authority, the Panel should consider whether the individual piece of evidence being examined could support the conclusion that the agency was seeking to draw from it. In this context, the Appellate Body noted that a piece of evidence that may initially appear to be of little or no probative value, when viewed in isolation, could, when placed beside another piece of evidence of the same

[149] WT/DS296/AB/R of 27 June 2005, *United States – Countervailing Duty Investigation on Dynamic Random Access Memory Semiconductors (DRAMs) from Korea*, para 136 *et seq.* WT/DS299/R of 17 June 2005, *European Communities – Countervailing Measures on Dynamic Random Access Memory Chips from Korea*, para 7.59, also used the probative and compelling standard.

nature, form part of an overall picture that gives rise to a reasonable inference of entrustment or direction. When an investigating authority relies on the totality of circumstantial evidence, this imposes upon a panel the obligation to consider, in the context of the totality of the evidence, how the interaction of certain pieces of evidence may justify certain inferences that could not have been justified by a review of the individual pieces of evidence in isolation. Finally, in order to examine the evidence in the light of the investigating authority's methodology, a panel's analysis usually should seek to review the agency's decision on its own terms, in particular, by identifying the inference drawn by the agency from the evidence, and then by considering whether the evidence could sustain that inference.[150]

The third issue at dispute was whether the US could in the DSB proceeding rely on evidence that was on the USDOC's record but that was not explicitly quoted in the USDOC's determination, or whether such reliance amounted to an inadmissible *ex post* rationalization. The Panel refused to consider such evidence while the Appellate Body held that the US could invoke it. Article 22.5 ASCM does not require the investigating authority to cite or discuss every piece of supporting record evidence for each fact in the final determination as long as such reliance does not amount to a new reasoning or rationale.[151] This is in line with the ruling of the Appellate Body in the parallel DRAM case concerning Japan's determination. The Appellate Body held that it was on the basis of the rationale or explanation provided by the investigating authority that a panel must examine the consistency of the determination with the covered agreement, including whether the investigating authority has adequately explained how the facts support the determination it has made.[152]

Despite the fact that the Appellate Body reversed the Panel's findings on entrustment and direction to a considerable extent, the Panel's examination of the facts which the USDOC relied on for its entrustment/direction decision remains interesting reading. Indeed, the Panel report shows

[150] WT/DS296/AB/R of 27 June 2005, *United States – Countervailing Duty Investigation on Dynamic Random Access Memory Semiconductors (DRAMs) from Korea*, para 141 *et seq.* Confirmed in WT/DS336/AB/R of 28 November 2007, *Japan – Countervailing Duties on Dynamic Random Access Memories from Korea*, para 131.

[151] WT/DS296/AB/R of 27 June 2005, *United States – Countervailing Duty Investigation on Dynamic Random Access Memory Semiconductors (DRAMs) from Korea*, para 159 *et seq.*

[152] WT/DS336/AB/R of 28 November 2007, *Japan – Countervailing Duties on Dynamic Random Access Memories from Korea*, para 159.

the complexity of the considerations and determinations made by the USDOC.[153]

In the parallel case *Japan – DRAMs (Korea)*, the Japanese investigating authority took a somewhat different approach than the USDOC. It determined that four of Hynix's private creditors had been entrusted or directed by the Korean government. The Panel summarized Japan's reasoning in this respect as follows: the decisions of the four creditors to participate in the restructurings in October 2001 and December 2002 were not commercially reasonable and could therefore only be explained by some external, non-commercial factor, namely the Government of Korea's involvement in the restructurings. To support this explanation, Japan relied on the totality of the circumstantial evidence that consisted of a number of statements of government ministers and others as well as various circumstances relating to the restructurings. Korea criticized this finding by claiming that Japan relied on three premises that were all wrong:

- the Government of Korea's intent to keep Hynix alive;
- that no rational creditor would have entered into the restructuring transactions in view of Hynix's poor and deteriorating financial condition; and
- the lack of evidence establishing that the four creditors had conducted a sufficient analysis of the commercial reasonableness of the two restructurings before entering into them.

The Panel rejected Korea's argument with regard to the first premise, although not all record evidence pointed in that direction. With regard to the second premise, the Panel rejected Korea's argument in relation to the October 2001 restructurings, but not in relation to the December 2002 restructurings. It found that Japan's finding that the participation of the four creditors in the December 2002 restructurings was commercially unreasonable, was to a large extent based on Japan's rejection of the restructuring plan prepared by the Deutsche Bank (Deutsche Bank Report). The Panel disagreed with the rejection of the report. It recognized that Japan's determination of entrustment or direction was based on the totality of numerous items of evidence. However, the Panel concluded that it had no basis to assess whether Japan could have sustained its finding on entrustment or direction by using evidence other than

[153] WT/DS296/R/3 of 21 February 2005, *United States – Countervailing Duty Investigation on Dynamic Random Access Memory Semiconductors (DRAMs) from Korea*, para 7.47 *et seq.*

the evidence concerning commercial reasonableness. In the view of the Panel, had it done such an examination, this would have amounted to a *de novo* review. Japan claimed that this was not consistent with Article 11 DSU.

Japan claimed that the Panel erred by limiting the scope of its review to one piece of evidence in isolation (the Deutsche Bank Report) without considering whether the totality of the evidence supported Japan's finding on entrustment or direction. The Panel's approach would have as a consequence that a flaw in the investigating authority's assessment of one of many pieces of evidence would necessarily invalidate the entire determination.

Japan also took issue with the Panel's review of the intermediate finding on the commercial reasonableness (or rather lack thereof) of the four creditors' participation in the December 2002 restructurings.

The Appellate Body disagreed with the Panel. It pointed out that Japan's findings on entrustment or direction were based on the totality of evidence on the record, that it was not evident that Japan accorded such decisive weight to the issue of commercial reasonableness to render insignificant all other evidence and that it would not have been reasonable to expect the Japanese investigating authority to have carried out an enquiry into entrustment or direction on the basis that certain aspects of its reasoning would later be found to be faulty. Rather, the Panel should have considered whether the remaining evidence provided an objective basis for finding entrustment or direction. This was particularly so given the Panel's earlier finding that the Japanese investigating authority could properly have concluded that the balance of the record evidence indicated that the Korean government was prepared to intervene directly in the Hynix restructuring process and that it was prepared to maintain Hynix as a going concern at the time of the 2001/2 restructurings even if not all record evidence pointed in that direction. The Appellate Body also recognized that certain intermediate findings may be so central to the final finding that an error at such intermediate stage may invalidate the final decision but did not think that that was necessarily so in the case at issue.[154]

A number of intermediate conclusions made by the Panel in relation to entrustment or direction still appear to be relevant notwithstanding the

[154] WT/DS336/AB/R of 28 November 2007, *Japan – Countervailing Duties on Dynamic Random Access Memories from Korea*, para 117 *et seq*. See also *supra* pp. 113 the Appellate Body's view on the importance of the issue of commercial reasonableness for a determination on entrustment or direction.

fact that the Appellate Body reversed the Panel's findings on entrustment and direction.

The conduct of a private body which is contrary to its commercial interests might be indicative of government entrustment or direction. However, it could not be determinative in itself because it says nothing about the conduct of the government concerned. Evidence of non-commercial conduct would therefore need to be coupled with other evidence having sufficient probative value in order to arrive at a finding of entrustment or direction.[155]

In the assessment of circumstantial evidence, which could be taken to suggest entrustment or direction, an investigating authority must also take into account evidence, circumstantial or otherwise, which is contrary to that suggestion. This is the very nature of an investigating authority's obligation to evaluate the evidence before it in order properly to arrive at its conclusions.[156]

Korea – Commercial Vessels is also relevant with regard to the evidentiary standard but it should be borne in mind that the Panel's finding to equate the notions 'entrustment' and 'direction' with 'delegation' and 'command' was not in line with a later Appellate Body ruling (see above pp. 107–109). The Panel held that the delegation or command inferred by the terms entrustment and direction must take the form of an affirmative act. However, it saw nothing in Article 1.1(a)(1)(iv) that would require the act of delegation or command to be 'explicit'. The act in question could be explicit or implicit, formal or informal. The manner, or degree of detail, in which the addressee and object of the act of delegation or command is specified will depend on the form that the act of delegation or command may take. The fact that the addressee and object of the act of delegation or command is described in less detail does not preclude a finding of entrustment or direction, as a matter of law. Rather, it raises evidentiary issues. If an act of delegation or command is not specifically addressed to a particular private body it simply

155 WT/DS336/R of 13 July 2007, *Japan – Countervailing Duties on Dynamic Random Access Memories from Korea*, para 7.70. See also WT/DS299/R of 17 June 2005, *European Communities – Countervailing Measures on Dynamic Random Access Memory Chips from Korea*, paras 7.59 and 7.105.

156 WT/DS336/R of 13 July 2007, *Japan – Countervailing Duties on Dynamic Random Access Memories from Korea*, para 7.74. See also para 7.81 where the Panel rejected the idea that 'positive evidence' was needed as a basis for a finding of entrustment or direction, in so far as the application of such a standard would exclude the possibility to support such a finding with circumstantial evidence only.

means that it will be more difficult for a WTO Member or an investigating authority to properly demonstrate that such private party was entrusted or directed. The same applies with regard to the particular task or duty in question. But 'the evidence of entrustment and direction must in all cases be probative and compelling'.[157] Finally, the Panel saw no reason why a case of government entrustment or direction could not be premised on circumstantial evidence.[158] It is recalled that the Panel considered the second and third condition for a finding of entrustment or direction (addressed to a particular party and of a particular task) as aspects of the first (see *supra* p. 105). Note finally that in *Korea – Commercial Vessels* the evidence submitted by the EU was not considered sufficient to demonstrate entrustment or direction. It would appear that the standard applied by the Panel was a very high one.[159]

Private Body

Article 1.1(a)(1)(iv) further requires that a private body is entrusted or directed by the government. In *US – Export Restraints*, Canada initially argued that individual producers of a good subject to export restraints could not be considered a private body. For Canada, a private body was an organized group or collective entity that has a separate and independent existence. The fact that a given group of individuals can be described by a common characteristic (e.g. gold miners) would not transform the universe of such individuals into a private body. The Panel rejected this interpretation. It held that the term 'private body' is used in Article 1.1(a)(1)(iv) as a counterpoint to 'government' or 'public body' as the actor. Thus, any entity that is neither government nor a public body would be a private body. If Canada's initial narrow interpretation of the term 'private body' had been accepted, this would effectively have excluded from any subsidy disciplines actions by some entities, even if the government had ordered the entities in question to take those actions.[160]

[157] With regard to the notion of 'compelling' see above at the beginning of this section, p. 116.

[158] WT/DS273/R of 7 March 2005, *Korea – Measures Affecting Trade in Commercial Vessels*, paras 7.370–7.373.

[159] WT/DS273/R of 7 March 2005, *Korea – Measures Affecting Trade in Commercial Vessels*, paras 7.373 to 7.407.

[160] WT/DS194/R of 29 June 2001, *United States – Measures Treating Export Restraints as Subsidies*, paras 8.45–8.49. In the subsequent parts of the Panel proceeding, Canada seemed to have dropped this interpretation.

To Carry Out One or More of the Type of Functions Illustrated in (i) to (iii)

US – Export Restraints held that the scope of the actions covered by subparagraph (iv) must be the same as those covered by subparagraphs (i)–(iii). In the Panel's view, the difference between subparagraphs (i)–(iii) on the one hand, and subparagraph (iv) on the other, has to do with the identity of the actor, and not with the nature of the action.[161]

Which Would Normally Be Vested in the Government and the Practice, in No Real Sense, Differs from Practices Normally Followed by Governments

In *Korea – Commercial Vessels*, Korea argued that providing loans or loan guarantees was not covered by the condition 'which would normally be vested in the government and the practice, in no real sense, differs from practices normally followed by governments'. According to Korea, there is only a financial contribution in the sense of Article 1.1(a)(1)(i) if the relevant government or public body is engaged in government practice such as regulation or taxation. The Panel rejected this view. The Panel noted that the reference to functions normally vested in the government mirrors the reference to practices normally followed by governments. Accordingly, the reference to functions normally vested in the government should also be understood to mean functions of taxation and revenue expenditure. Since loans and loan guarantees involve revenue expenditure, they may be treated as functions normally vested in the government.[162] For a discussion of this term see also *US – Export Restraints*. Note that the Panel did not take a final view on this matter.[163] The term 'normally be vested in the government' was also discussed in *US – Anti-Dumping and Countervailing duties (China)*, see *supra* pp. 66–73.

Payments to a Funding Mechanism There is also a financial contribution pursuant to Article 1.1(a)(1)(iv) if a government makes payments to a funding mechanism. It would appear that there is no WTO jurisprudence concerning this issue.

[161] WT/DS194/R of 29 June 2001, *United States – Measures Treating Export Restraints as Subsidies*, paras 8.50–8.55. See however *supra* the chapter on export restraints (pp. 110–112) *in fine*.
[162] WT/DS273/R of 7 March 2005, *Korea – Measures Affecting Trade in Commercial Vessels*, paras 7.28–7.31.
[163] WT/DS194/R of 29 June 2001, *United States – Measures Treating Export Restraints as Subsidies*, paras 8.56–8.59.

Income or Price Support (Article 1.1(a)(2))

According to Article 1.1(a)(2), a subsidy shall be deemed to exist if there is any form of income or price support pursuant to Article XVI of GATT 1994. Article XVI:1 of GATT 1994 refers to 'any form of income or price support, which operates directly or indirectly to increase exports of any product from, or reduce imports of any products into' the territory of the subsidizing WTO Member. In practice, the concept of income or price support relates mainly to governmental action in the agricultural sector.[164]

The notion of 'income or price support' is not entirely clear but two WTO DSB rulings brought some clarifications. The Appellate Body has held that the concept of income or price support under Article 1.1(a)(2) broadens the range of measures capable of providing subsidies beyond those that constitute financial contributions.[165] The Panel in *China – GOES* had to determine whether a voluntary export restraint agreement by the US government constituted income or price support. This agreement capped steel imports at 18.5 per cent of market share and thus kept US domestic steel prices at a higher level. China argued that this constituted a subsidy for the benefit of the US steel industry. The Panel did not agree. First it pointed out that the term 'income or price support' in Article 1.1(a)(2) could be read to include also any government measure that has the effect of raising prices within a market. However, it finally did not retain this broad definition on the following grounds:

- The context of Article 1.1(a) suggests a more narrow interpretation. Each of the four types of financial contribution is determined by reference to an action by the government concerned, rather than by reference to the effects of the measure on a market. If the effect of the measures on prices were to be sufficient to constitute a financial contribution, the criterion of a financial contribution would no longer serve as a gateway to the ASCM but would be effectively written out of the ASCM.
- A GATT panel on Subsidies and State Trading (L/1160 of 23 March 1960) envisaged price support to involve a government setting and

[164] See *Adamantopoulos* in *Wolfrum/Stoll/Koebele* (2008), para 85 to Article 1.

[165] WT/DS257/AB/R of 19 January 2004, *United States – Final Countervailing Duty Determination with Respect to Certain Softwood Lumber from Canada*, para 52. *Luengo* (2007) p. 122 seems to be in general in favour of a more expansive definition of the notion 'income and price support' so as to cover a wide range of trade distortions caused by government.

maintaining a fixed price, rather than a random change in price merely being a side-effect of any government measure.

- A concept of 'market price support' is included in the Agreement on Agriculture. According to Annex 3 of that Agreement, the market price support is calculated as the difference between the external reference price and the applied administered price.
- The concept of price support also acts as a gateway to the ASCM and according to the Panel, its focus is on the nature of the government action, rather than upon the effects of such action.

Consequently, according to the Panel the concept of price support includes direct government intervention in the market with the design to fix the price of a good at a particular level, for example, through purchase of surplus production when price is set above equilibrium. But it does not include all government interventions that may have an effect on prices, such as tariffs or quantitative restrictions. A voluntary restriction agreement may have an incidental side-effect, of random magnitude, on prices, but the Panel did not consider this as being encompassed by the notion of 'price or income support'.[166] While the Panel's conclusion on the issue of voluntary restriction agreements may be a reasonable one, its narrow interpretation of the scope of income and price support could be called into question in future cases.

'Income or price support' was also at issue in *Canada – Renewable Energy / Feed-In Tariff Program*. However, both the Panel and the Appellate Body declined to rule on this issue.[167]

Benefit (Article 1.1(b))

The Notion of 'Benefit'

There is no subsidy if the recipient does not derive a benefit from the financial contribution or from the income or price support. The notion of benefit can perhaps most easily be understood by the following paradigmatic

[166] WT/DS414/R of 15 June 2012, *China – Countervailing and Anti-Dumping Duties on Grain-Oriented Flat-Rolled Electrical Steel from the US*, paras 7.83–7.88. *Coppens* (2014) pp. 58–59 agrees with the Panel's conclusions.

[167] WT/DS412/AB/R and WT/DS426/AB/R of 6 May 2013, *Canada – Certain Measures Affecting the Renewable Energy Generation Sector; Canada – Measures Relating to Feed-In Tariff Program*, paras 5.133–5.139; WT/DS412/R and WT/DS426/R of 19 December 2012, *Canada – Certain Measures Affecting the Renewable Energy Generation Sector; Canada – Measures Relating to Feed-In Tariff Program*, para 7.249.

example: if a government provides a loan, the benefit is determined by comparing the interest rate charged by the government with the interest rate the lender could obtain in the market. The ASCM itself does not define what constitutes a 'benefit' for the purposes of Article 1.1.(b).[168] However, the meaning of the term has been elucidated by Panel and Appellate Body rulings.

US – Lead and Bismuth II provides a good working hypothesis as to what constitutes a benefit. In that case, the Panel held that the term 'benefit' effectively represents the portion of a financial contribution that, by reference to a market benchmark, the recipient gets for free.[169] The purpose of the notion 'benefit' is to act as a screen to filter out commercial conduct from the scope of the ASCM.[170] Indeed, if the government acts like a normal commercial player on the market, then its action is not trade-distorting.

DSB rulings commonly refer to the definition of the term 'benefit' used by the Appellate Body in *Canada – Aircraft*. According to this definition, a financial contribution confers a benefit if the financial contribution makes the recipient better off than it would otherwise have been, absent that contribution. Furthermore, the marketplace provides an appropriate basis for comparison because the trade-distorting potential of a financial contribution can be identified by determining whether the recipient has received something on terms that would not be available to him on the market.[171] Like the specificity criterion, the requirement of a 'benefit' identifies government behaviour that has a potential to distort trade: if a recipient gets something for free from the government in a wider sense, it will tend to build its conduct on this fact, and not in response to market forces.

[168] See also WT/DS341/R of 4 September 2008, *Mexico – Definitive Countervailing Measures on Olive Oil from the European Communities*, para 7.151 *et seq.*

[169] WT/DS138/R of 23 December 1999, *United States – Imposition of Countervailing Duties on Certain Hot-Rolled Lead and Bismuth Carbon Steel Products originating in the United Kingdom*, footnote 80 to para 6.70.

[170] WT/DS273/R of 7 March 2005, *Korea – Measures Affecting Trade in Commercial Vessels*, para 7.28.

[171] WT/DS70/AB/R of 2 August 1999, *Canada – Measures Affecting the Export of Civilian Aircraft*, para 157. Confirmed in WT/DS316/AB/R of 18 May 2011, *EC and certain Member States – Measures Affecting Trade in Large Civil Aircraft*, paras 705, 832 and 849; WT/DS336/AB/R of 28 November 2007, *Japan – Countervailing Duties on Dynamic Random Access Memories from Korea*, paras 173 and 225; WT/DS412/AB/R and WT/DS426/AB/R of 6 May 2013, *Canada – Certain Measures Affecting the Renewable Energy Generation Sector; Canada – Measures Relating to Feed-In Tariff Program*, paras 5.163 and 5.165; WT/DS437/AB/R of 18 December 2014, *United States – Countervailing Duty Measures on Certain Products from China*, para 4.44.

Two issues are very topical in the context of a benefit analysis. First, the use of out-of-country benchmarks. This issue is essentially discussed *infra* in the commentary to Article 14. Second, it is not a straightforward exercise to determine the appropriate market benchmark for the purchase of products by a government, where the very market for this product has been created by the government. The Appellate Body had to address this issue when examining whether the government conferred a benefit when it purchased electricity obtained from solar or wind power on the basis of feed-in tariffs that were designed to boost the production of renewable energy (see *infra* Article 1 pp. 132–136).

The notion of 'benefit' cannot be equated with the notion of 'advantage', for instance, under the WTO TRIMs Agreement. It is true that the ordinary meaning of the term 'benefit' encompasses some sort of advantage. However, 'benefit' has a more specific meaning under the ASCM. 'Benefit' under the ASCM is linked to the concepts of 'financial contribution' and 'income or price support', and its existence requires a comparison in the marketplace. According to the Appellate Body, 'advantage' under the TRIMs Agreement may take other forms than a 'financial contribution' or a 'benefit' under the ASCM. Hence, there may be an 'advantage' under the TRIMs Agreement but not necessarily a benefit under the ASCM.[172]

According to *Mexico – Olive Oil*, as there is nothing in the language of Article 1.1 specifically relating to how the amount of the benefit is to be calculated in a countervail investigation, this provision does not establish a requirement to calculate in such investigation precisely the amount of benefit accruing to a particular recipient. Consequently, there is also no obligation flowing from this provision to conduct a pass-through analysis.[173] Article 14 which is directly applicable to countervailing duty investigations, contains provisions on calculating the amount of a benefit and is relevant context for any benefit analysis under Article 1 (see *infra* pp. 142–143).

[172] WT/DS412/AB/R and WT/DS426/AB/R of 6 May 2013, *Canada – Certain Measures Affecting the Renewable Energy Generation Sector; Canada – Measures Relating to Feed-In Tariff Program*, paras 5.205–5.210.

[173] WT/DS341/R of 4 September 2008, *Mexico – Definitive Countervailing Measures on Olive Oil from the European Communities*, para 7.151 *et seq.*; WT/DS353/R of 31 March 2011, *United States – Measures Affecting Trade in Large Civil Aircraft (Second Complaint)*, para 7.288. *De lege ferenda* see *Shadikhodjaev* (2012) p. 633 and p. 642 *et seq.* For details see *infra* the commentary to Article 10, pp. 373–379.

Note finally that the notion of benefit does not necessarily capture the trade effects of a subsidy. The trade effects comprise the additional sales that result from the provision of a subsidy.[174]

While the notion of benefit as interpreted by DSB rulings is, at least conceptually, a relatively straightforward exercise, some scholars have pointed out that the measurement of benefit should perhaps focus more closely on how the subsidy improved the situation of the recipient. For instance, did the subsidy lead to an expansion of the output of the recipient?[175] According to other scholars, a benefit exists when the subsidy confers a competitive advantage to a firm. In other words, for a benefit to exist, the financial contribution should not only make the recipient better off than it could be in the market place, but the position of the recipient should also be strengthened *vis-à-vis* its competitors. The benefit analysis should examine whether the competitive situation is improved but for the financial contribution.[176] The idea has also been advanced that a benefit should be determined by comparing the actual situation where a subsidy has been provided with a hypothetical situation absent such subsidy.[177] More generally, *François* criticizes that the current case law places too much emphasis on accounting definitions instead on economic analysis ('accountants captured the analytical high ground as countervailing (CVD) practice has evolved, seemingly at the expense of economic analysis').[178] None of the tests has been endorsed by DSB rulings.

[174] WT/DS267/ARB/1 of 31 August 2009, *United States – Subsidies on Upland Cotton (Arbitration under Article 22.6 DSU and 4.11 ASCM)*, paras 4.139–4.149. The issue was discussed in the context of determining the level of the countermeasures which Brazil requested following the lack of compliance by the US with prior DSB rulings.

[175] *Sykes* (2005) pp. 87–88. See also *Horn/Mavroidis* (2005) p. 230.

[176] *Grossman/Mavroidis* (2003) p. 187 *et passim*. On this basis, they reject the Appellate Body's ruling in *US – Lead and Bismuth II* that concluded that a benefit resulting from the provision of subsidies is extinguished if the company has been privatized at fair market value (see *infra* the commentary to Article 14, pp. 433–44). *Coppens* (2014) pp. 478/9 argues that the causation and the adverse effects analysis is better suited to examine the effect of a subsidy on competitors. Similar *Rubini* (2012) p. 546. See also *Sykes* (2005) pp. 86–87. Note that the Appellate Body in WT/DS336/AB/R of 28 November 2007, *Japan – Countervailing Duties on Dynamic Random Access Memories from Korea*, paras 257–278 rejected an argument to this effect (for details see *infra* the commentary to Article 15 p. 506.)

[177] *Horn/Mavroidis* (2005) pp. 231–234. They acknowledge, however, that such a benchmark can be impractical.

[178] *François* (2010) p. 103 *et passim*.

As the benefit test as applied by DSB rulings is a simple comparison between the terms of the financial contribution and what the recipient could obtain in the market, it is irrelevant whether or not the financial contribution is provided to compensate for disadvantages resulting from the regulatory framework of the exporting country, such as an uncompetitive environment resulting from high import tariffs etc.[179]

Benefit to a Recipient ...

In *Canada – Aircraft*, the Appellate Body held that a benefit does not exist in the abstract, but must be received and enjoyed by a beneficiary or a recipient. In other words, the term 'benefit' implies that there is a recipient, i.e. a person (natural or legal, group of persons), that has received something.[180]

Unless there is a pass-through scenario,[181] the recipient of the subsidy must be the producer of the product subject to a CVD investigation or of the product at issue in a dispute relating to Articles 3 and 5. In *Brazil – Aircraft (2nd Article 21.5)*, the government of Brazil made a non-refundable payment not to the buyers or producers of Brazilian Embraer aircraft but to financial institutions that provided export credit financing to the buyers of such aircraft. Therefore, the question was whether the payments conferred a benefit to the producers of the aircraft in question. The Panel held that whether the financial contribution has conferred a benefit to the producer of Embraer aircraft – as opposed merely to a benefit to suppliers of financial services – depended upon the impact of the payments on the terms and conditions of the export credit financing available to purchasers of Brazilian Embraer aircraft. Accordingly, the inquiry concentrated on whether, as a result of the payments, purchasers of Brazilian regional aircraft obtained export credits on terms more favourable than those available to them in the market. In the case in question, the Panel answered the question in the affirmative.[182]

179 See *Coppens* (2014) p. 468 and *Rubini* (2012) p. 546. See also *infra*. Indirect taxes and import tariffs borne by the like product when destined for domestic consumption can, however, be adjusted for exported products pursuant to footnote 1 to the ASCM.

180 WT/DS70/AB/R of 2 August 1999, *Canada – Measures Affecting the Export of Civilian Aircraft*, paras 154 and 155.

181 See *infra* the commentary to Article 10 pp. 373–379.

182 WT/DS46/RW/2 of 26 July 2001, *Brazil – Export Financing Programme for Aircraft (Article 21.5, second recourse)*, paras 5.27–5.29 and footnote 42. The application of the principles to the facts of the case can be found in the subsequent paragraphs of the Panel ruling. See also *infra* p. 150.

... and Not Cost to the Government

In *Canada – Aircraft*, Canada argued that a benefit cannot exist unless the granting of the financial contribution imposes a net cost to the government. In fact, Canada argued that a benefit is conferred when a financial contribution by a public body (i) imposes a net cost to the government and (ii) results in an advantage above and beyond what the market would provide.[183] The Appellate Body did not accept this and required instead that the inquiry should focus on the benefit to the recipient, and not on the net cost to the government.[184] Hence, the determining question is whether the terms of the financial contribution are more favourable to what is available to the recipient on the market. As the Appellate Body in *Japan – DRAMs (Korea)* has put it, there is but one standard, the market standard – according to which rational investors act.[185] A proper market benchmark is derived from an examination of the conditions pursuant to which the goods or services at issue would, under market conditions, be exchanged.[186]

However, in *EC and certain Member States – Large Civil Aircraft*, the Panel based its finding that there was a benefit on the fact that the costs of the Hamburg authorities providing each of the three infrastructure measures in question exceeded the amounts the city of Hamburg received in return for that investment. For instance, for the Mühlenburger Loch site (reclaimed land) the Panel calculated the benefit by comparing the difference between the actual rent paid by Airbus for the land and the facilities in question, and a reasonable return on the investment of the Hamburg authorities in creating that land and those facilities. It did so because the investment necessary in reclaiming the land was disproportionately large in comparison to any potential return – the cost of reclaiming the land amounted to around 700,000,000 EUR while the land had actually a value of between 71,600,000 and 85,000,000 EUR. The Appellate Body did not agree. It recalled *Canada – Aircraft* that endorsed the benefit-to-the-recipient standard while the Panel applied in reality a cost-to-government standard. It acknowledged that, in certain circumstances, a seller's costs

183 WT/DS70/R of 14 April 1999, *Canada – Measures Affecting the Export of Civilian Aircraft*, para 9.98 *et seq.* and para 9.311.

184 WT/DS70/AB/R of 2 August 1999, *Canada – Measures Affecting the Export of Civilian Aircraft*, paras 154–156.

185 WT/DS336/AB/R of 28 November 2007, *Japan – Countervailing Duties on Dynamic Random Access Memories from Korea*, para 172.

186 WT/DS316/AB/R of 18 May 2011, *EC and certain Member States – Measures Affecting Trade in Large Civil Aircraft*, para 975.

may be a relevant factor to consider in assessing whether goods or services were provided for less than adequate remuneration. However, the Panel's analysis had the shortcoming that it did not refer to these costs as a factor in its analysis, but rather as the sole basis for its findings. Thus, the Panel wrongly applied a net cost to government standard. The Appellate Body also underlined that the marketplace reflects a sphere in which goods and services are exchanged between willing buyers and sellers. It continued to state that a calculation of benefit in relation to prevailing market conditions thus demands an examination of behaviour on both sides of a transaction, and in particular in relation to the conditions of supply and demand as they apply in that market. Even where a market is limited for a particular good or service, that market price is not dictated solely by the price a seller wishes to charge or a buyer wishes to pay. The fact that a market actor would seek a return on its investment does not mean that it could necessarily obtain that return on the market. The price of a good or service must reflect the interaction between the supply-side and the demand-side considerations under prevailing market conditions. In sum, the investment costs borne by the relevant authorities are an insufficient basis upon which to establish the market value of the sale or lease of the infrastructure at issue.[187] With regard to the extended runway at Bremen airport, the Appellate Body concluded that Airbus had obtained a benefit because it did not pay additional fees for the extended runway, which it could use exclusively. Airbus paid only the level of fees other users of Bremen airport had to pay although the latter were not allowed to use the extended runway.[188] Note that the introduction of supply-side considerations by the Appellate Body in *EC and certain Member States – Large Civil Aircraft* has met with a certain criticism (see *infra* Article 1, pp. 132–136).

The manner in which an investigating authority or panel evaluates market evidence will be a function of the particular context of each case, and of the information that is adduced by the parties to the dispute.[189]

[187] WT/DS316/AB/R of 18 May 2011, *EC and certain Member States – Measures Affecting Trade in Large Civil Aircraft*, paras 977–983. The completion of the benefit analysis can be found in paras 984–993. According to the Panel (see WT/DS316/R of 30 June 2010, para 7.1091), the appropriate question to be addressed in resolving the question of benefit is whether a market actor would have provided the good or service to the recipient at the time, on the same terms and conditions as the government provision at issue. The Panel's statement is probably not entirely compatible with the standard set by the Appellate Body.

[188] WT/DS316/AB/R of 18 May 2011, *EC and certain Member States – Measures Affecting Trade in Large Civil Aircraft*, para 991.

[189] WT/DS316/AB/R of 18 May 2011, *EC and certain Member States – Measures Affecting Trade in Large Civil Aircraft*, para 974.

Need to First Define the Relevant Market

The Appellate Body highlighted that a panel should not start its benefit analysis by reviewing the various market benchmarks proposed by the various parties. Rather, it should start the benefit analysis with the definition of the relevant market. The definition of the relevant market is central to, and a prerequisite for, a benefit analysis under Article 1.1(b). The existence of a benefit can properly be established only by comparing the prices of goods and services in the relevant market where they compete.[190] The Appellate Body also pointed out that an analysis not only of demand-side but also supply-side factors can be relevant. Indeed, in the case in question such analysis covering also supply-side factors would have shown the significance of the government intervention.[191]

The Appellate Body made the aforementioned statements in *Canada – Renewable Energy & Feed-In Tariff Program*. The Panel and Appellate Body had to determine whether there was a benefit that resulted from Feed-In Tariffs (FIT) paid by the Ontario Power Authority to producers of electricity generated from wind power and solar energy. These tariffs were only available if the electricity was produced with equipment that met certain local content rules. The applicants (Japan and the EU) argued that the proper benchmark in order to define whether or not there is a benefit should have been the Ontario electricity wholesale market.

The majority of the Panellists and the Appellate Body did not agree. According to the Appellate Body, the definition of the market in which these two types of electricity generators operated was of primordial importance. The particular challenge was that the markets for electricity obtained from wind and solar power only existed and received their shape at the time because of the Government of Ontario's intervention in the market. Without that intervention, the production of electricity from solar or wind power would not have been economically viable. In fact, the markets for these two particular sources of electricity existed because the Ontario government imposed on the electricity distribution company an energy supply mix that included electricity from solar and

190 WT/DS412/AB/R and WT/DS426/AB/R of 6 May 2013, *Canada – Certain Measures Affecting the Renewable Energy Generation Sector; Canada – Measures Relating to Feed-In Tariff Program*, paras 5.169, 5.197.

191 WT/DS412/AB/R and WT/DS426/AB/R of 6 May 2013, *Canada – Certain Measures Affecting the Renewable Energy Generation Sector; Canada – Measures Relating to Feed-In Tariff Program*, para 5.172 *et passim*. The Appellate Body referred in this context also to the market analysis that is carried out for the purposes of examining serious prejudice claims under Article 6.

wind energy. In other words, the electricity distribution company had to purchase electricity not only from fossil energy but also from these two renewable sources of energy. Therefore, from the purchasing perspective of the electricity distribution company (i.e. at the wholesale level), electricity obtained from sources other than solar and wind power was not substitutable while there was substitutability from the perspective from the final consumers of electricity.

The Appellate Body considered that Article 14(d) provided relevant context and pointed out that the text of that provision referred to 'prevailing market conditions'. It held that the relevant market was not the wholesale market for electricity from all sources of energy (including fossil energy), but rather the markets for wind- and solar-generated electricity which are defined by the Government of Ontario's choice of energy supply mix. According to the Appellate Body, the relevant question is whether wind power and solar electricity suppliers would have entered the electricity markets absent the Feed-In programmes, not whether they would have entered the blended wholesale electricity market. The Appellate Body also noted that a 'but for' approach in the context of establishing a benefit, i.e. what would be the remuneration of solar and wind power electricity providers absent the FIT, would not be appropriate if solar and wind power electricity production would not occur absent the government's definition of the energy supply mix. Indeed, such an approach would not measure what the producers of solar and wind power electricity would get in the two types of markets. The 'but for' approach would only measure what remuneration they would receive in the market of electricity generated from all sources, including fossil ones.[192]

According to the Appellate Body, a distinction should be drawn between, on the one hand, government interventions that create markets that would otherwise not exist and, on the other hand, other types of government interventions in support of certain players in markets that already exist or to correct market distortions therein. Where a government creates a market, it cannot be said that the government intervention distorts the market, as there would not be a market if the government would not have created it. Creating a market by defining the energy supply mix as including wind power and solar electricity cannot in and of

[192] WT/DS412/AB/R and WT/DS426/AB/R of 6 May 2013, *Canada – Certain Measures Affecting the Renewable Energy Generation Sector; Canada – Measures Relating to Feed-In Tariff Program*, paras 5.195, 5.199. The facts surrounding the case are described in detail by *Rubini* (2014) pp. 897–901.

itself be considered as conferring a benefit (as would have been the case if the wholesale electricity price would have been used as a benchmark). Moreover, the fact that a government sets prices does not in itself establish the existence of a benefit. The Appellate Body went on to say that if it becomes necessary to identify a market benchmark or to construct a proxy, such benchmark or proxy may be administered prices for the same product (in the country of purchase or other countries, subject to adjustments) provided that it is based on a price-setting mechanism that ensures a market outcome. The Appellate Body highlighted that an analysis of the methodology that was used to establish the administered prices may provide evidence as to whether the price does or does not provide more than adequate remuneration. It referred in this context to a market-based price-discovery mechanism.[193] The Appellate Body also pointed out that the comparison with an undistorted benchmark would have to refer to prices referring to the same period, the same type of generation technology, the same overall supply mix, projects of the same or similar scale and supply contracts of a similar duration. If any of these conditions were not met, adjustments in the light of the factors in Article 14(d) and of the supply mix defined by the government might be necessary.[194] The Appellate Body also hinted at (but without taking a position) what could be considered a benchmark in case of a government's choice of a particular supply mix, i.e. administered prices based on principles of cost recovery and a reasonable margin of profit.[195] However, the Appellate Body was not able to complete the analysis.[196]

[193] WT/DS412/AB/R and WT/DS426/AB/R of 6 May 2013, *Canada – Certain Measures Affecting the Renewable Energy Generation Sector; Canada – Measures Relating to Feed-In Tariff Program*, paras 5.185, 5.188, 5.225, 5.227 and 5.228.

[194] WT/DS412/AB/R and WT/DS426/AB/R of 6 May 2013, *Canada – Certain Measures Affecting the Renewable Energy Generation Sector; Canada – Measures Relating to Feed-In Tariff Program*, para 5.235. By stating that the benchmark has to reflect the broader supply mix in which the contested FIT is embedded, it appears that the Appellate Body has accepted that the supply mix is an autonomous government decision.

[195] WT/DS412/AB/R and WT/DS426/AB/R of 6 May 2013, *Canada – Certain Measures Affecting the Renewable Energy Generation Sector; Canada – Measures Relating to Feed-In Tariff Program*, para 5.175.

[196] WT/DS412/AB/R and WT/DS426/AB/R of 6 May 2013, *Canada – Certain Measures Affecting the Renewable Energy Generation Sector; Canada – Measures Relating to Feed-In Tariff Program*, para 5.223 *et seq.*, in particular para 5.240. See also paras 5.217 (where the Appellate Body expressed explicitly no view about the merits of comparing the rates of return obtained by FIT with the average cost of capital in Canada for projects having a similar risk profile in the same period) and 5.228 (where it pointed out that an analysis of the methodology that was used to establish the administered prices may provide evidence as to whether the price does or does not provide more than adequate remuneration).

Note that the FIT was not in conformity with Article III of GATT 1994 as well as the TRIMs Agreement. The interest to invoke the ASCM in this case was probably linked to the fact that had the financial contribution of the Government of Ontario conferred a benefit, it would have been classified as a prohibited local content subsidy pursuant to Article 3.1(a) for which – by virtue of Article 4 – the remedy is more expeditious than for the concurrent violations under Article III:4 of GATT 1994 and Article 2.1 of the TRIMs Agreement.

Two points merit mentioning. First, at Panel stage, one of the Panellists made a dissenting opinion arguing that, as essentially also the complainants did, the proper benchmark for determining the existence of a benefit should be the competitive wholesale market for electricity that could exist in Ontario. According to the dissenting opinion, facilitating the entry of certain technologies into the market such as solar and wind power energy by way of a financial contribution can itself be considered to confer a benefit.[197] In other words, according to this opinion, government support to make a product competitive would automatically have amounted to a subsidy. Second, the Appellate Body's benefit analysis has been considered by some as abandoning the longstanding series of rulings according to which benefit is determined in relation to the market, and that this change had been motivated by policy considerations, i.e. the promotion of renewable energy.[198] It is submitted that

[197] WT/DS412/R and WT/DS426/R of 19 December 2012, *Canada – Certain Measures Affecting the Renewable Energy Generation Sector; Canada – Measures Relating to Feed-In Tariff Program*, paras 9.1–9.23.

[198] Very critical is *Coppens* (2014) pp. 463–468 *et passim* who, *inter alia*, considers that it would have been more appropriate to establish the benefit by comparing the FIT with a 'normal' wholesale electricity purchasing price and then to deal with the difference between electricity from renewable sources and electricity from fossil sources in the context of an adverse effects claim when defining the market. According to him, the Appellate Body's approach is not necessarily limited to the implementation of legitimate policy considerations by the government and is thus too broad. The Appellate Body's reliance on supply-side considerations was also criticized – with varying decrees – by *Rubini* (2014) pp. 910–919; *Rubini* (2015); *Pal* (2014) p. 128 *et seq.* and *Weber/Koch* (2015) p. 758, p. 774, p. 779 *et passim*. According to them, the Appellate Body's new approach enables governments to pick and promote the production methodology they like without the risk of falling under the subsidy disciplines because the market could be defined fairly narrowly as a result of supply-side considerations. In other words, this approach allegedly weakens the subsidy disciplines. *Rubini* (2015) p. 224 *et seq.* also argues that by focusing on the price-discovery mechanism to determine the adequacy of remuneration, the ruling brings the notion of benefit closer to EU State Aid law as interpreted by the *Altmark* decision. According to him, the application of procurement rules focuses more on administrative efficiency and does not necessarily result in a market benchmark. The introduction

this criticism does not seem to be borne out by the Appellate Body's report. Indeed, the Appellate Body has pointed out that it could not accept a statement that policy objectives underlying electricity production and supply entirely prevent a market-based approach to the determination of a benefit. To do so would read an exception into Article 1.1(b).[199] Indeed, the Appellate Body insists on a market-based benchmark for the purposes of the benefit analysis, but as described above, a much targeted one. It would appear that by taking the above-mentioned approach, the Appellate Body has given policy space to governments to correct market distortions (the lack of production of renewable energy absent government intervention) by creating new markets (the renewable energy market).[200] However, the pursuit of such legitimate policy objectives is not a pre-condition for the application of the Appellate Body's new approach.[201]

Proper Classification of the Support

A meaningful benefit analysis can only be built on a proper classification of the financial contribution (e.g. is it a loan, or an equity infusion etc., see *supra* p. 76). The reason for this is that the benchmark for determining whether the recipient of the subsidy received a benefit will depend on the nature of the contribution. The market benchmark used for a loan will differ from the one used for an equity infusion. The issue arose in *EC and certain Member States – Large Civil Aircraft* where there was some

of supply-side considerations inadequately imports a methodology appropriate for antitrust cases into the realm of subsidy law. *Piérola* (2013) p. 295 focuses on alternatives if no market benchmark is available. *Cosbey/Mavroidis* (2014) point out that the distinction between new markets created by government intervention and existing markets is a tenuous one. They also examine, *inter alia*, the relationship between subsidy disciplines and the relevant rules under the TRIMs Agreement and in their opinion there is a need to update the ASCM by redrafting Article 8 which provided for a limited safe haven for environmental subsidies. Finally, *Charnovitz/Fischer* (2015) p. 204 *et passim*, while not absolutely rejecting the Appellate Body's approach, highlight that markets can be created in more or less efficient ways, and that distortions associated with government intervention are equally possible in markets created by the government. They argue that by avoiding a finding of whether a programme based on environmental motivations confers a benefit, the Appellate Body might have opened the door for a number of well or poorly intentioned interventions.

[199] WT/DS412/AB/R and WT/DS426/AB/R of 6 May 2013, *Canada – Certain Measures Affecting the Renewable Energy Generation Sector; Canada – Measures Relating to Feed-In Tariff Program*, para 5.223 *et seq.*, para 5.182.

[200] *Coppens* (2014) p. 461.

[201] *Coppens* (2014) p. 82.

discussion as to how the launch aid given to Airbus should be qualified. In almost all cases, Airbus was required to reimburse all funding contributions, plus any interest at the agreed rate, exclusively from revenues generated by sales of the aircraft model that was financed. Repayment took place through per-aircraft levies and followed a pre-established repayment schedule. It started usually with the delivery of the first aircraft but in some instances repayment began only after Airbus had made a specified number of deliveries. The Panel and Appellate Body concurred that the launch aid had particular features that distinguished it from a conventional loan. These features that related to the transfer of certain risks from Airbus to the Member States can be found in some equity instruments. However, since the characterization of the launch aid was not under appeal, the Appellate Body treated it as an unsecured loan.[202]

Determination of Benefit is an *ex ante* Analysis

Article 14 suggests that the assessment of benefit should focus on the relevant market benchmark at the time the financial contribution was granted to the recipient. Thus, the benchmark will be based on what a market participant would have been able to secure at that time. In other words, the assessment of benefit must examine the terms and conditions of the challenged transaction and compare them to the terms and conditions that would have been offered in the market at the time when the challenged transaction was made.

Therefore, the determination of benefit under Article 1.1(b) is an *ex ante* analysis that does not depend on how the particular financial contribution actually performed after it was granted. For instance, in relation to a loan, the assessment must rather look as to how the loan is structured and how risk is factored in. A benefit analysis is a forward-looking exercise and focuses on future projections.[203]

202 WT/DS316/AB/R of 18 May 2011, *EC and certain Member States – Measures Affecting Trade in Large Civil Aircraft*, paras 826 and 830 (a short description of the launch aid / Member State financing is given in paras 822–825, 834 of the report). See also WT/DS412/AB/R and WT/DS426/AB/R of 6 May 2013, *Canada – Certain Measures Affecting the Renewable Energy Generation Sector; Canada – Measures Relating to Feed-In Tariff Program*, para 5.130.

203 WT/DS316/AB/R of 18 May 2011, *EC and certain Member States – Measures Affecting Trade in Large Civil Aircraft*, paras 706, 707 and 835 *et seq.*, 999, 1019. Confirmed in WT/DS353/AB/R of 12 March 2012, *United States – Measures Affecting Trade in Large Civil Aircraft (Second Complaint)*, para 636.

Benefit Analysis Must Be Evidence Based

In *US – Large Civil Aircraft (2nd complaint)*, the Appellate Body criticized the Panel's benefit test in the case of NASA and Department of Defense (DOD) research, on the grounds that it was not based on evidence. The ruling shows the complexities and difficulties that can be encountered even in cases that at first sight appear to be straightforward. According to the Appellate Body, the Panel's test for the financial contribution and for benefit revolved around the same question, i.e. which party derived the principal benefit and use from the research. The Panel found that the contract in question provided that NASA paid Boeing for conducting R&D that was principally for Boeing's benefit and use. On that basis, the Panel examined whether, in a commercial transaction, one entity would pay another entity to conduct R&D on these same terms. The Panel reasoned that no commercial entity would provide payments to another commercial entity on the condition that the other entity performs R&D activities principally for the benefit and use of that other entity. The Appellate Body took issue with the Panel's ruling in several respects.

- First, the approach adopted by the Panel, i.e. that the transaction in question was not a purchase of services because the R&D was principally for the benefit of the commissioned party rather than the commissioning government, makes the determination of benefit almost a foregone conclusion.
- Second, the Panel's approach was not consistent with a market benchmark. Under the contract in question, Boeing also provided funding and made other contributions. Therefore, the Panel should not only have looked at the distribution of the results of the R&D but also at the relationship between what the parties have contributed and how the results of the research have been shared. The distribution of the returns under the NASA procurement contracts did not indicate by itself what the distribution of the returns would be in the market.
- Third, the Panel did not indicate what evidence there was on the record to sustain its view that a private entity acting pursuant to commercial considerations would not provide payments to another commercial entity (here Boeing) where (i) the other entity performs R&D activities principally for its own benefit and use and that, at a minimum, (ii) it would be expected that the private party is required to make some form of royalties or repayment. Panels cannot base determinations as to what would occur in the marketplace only on their own intuition of what rational economic actors would do.

- Finally, the Panel did not explain how it reached the conclusion that the EU had established a *prima facie* case that the transaction would not take place in the market (e.g. by referring to evidence on record of what was the prevailing commercial practice or otherwise reflects market behaviour).

The Appellate Body was able to complete its review. It found that the NASA contracts indeed conferred a benefit on Boeing for the following reasons:

- US law constrained NASA's ability to negotiate ownership over any intellectual property developed under the relevant contract. The allocation of intellectual property rights is pre-determined under the US legal framework and could thus not be negotiated – the contractor (here Boeing) will obtain ownership over any such rights.
- By contrast, in a transaction between two market actors, the party undertaking the research would have to bargain to obtain ownership of any intellectual property.
- The allocation of intellectual property rights in the examples of market transactions on record has been more favourable to the commissioning party and less favourable to the commissioned party than under the NASA procurement contracts. In other words, Boeing obtained more and NASA obtained less than they would have obtained in the market.[204]

What Type of Evidence Is Relevant? In *Japan – DRAMs (Korea)*, four private creditors were found to be entrusted or directed by the Korean government with regard to the October 2001 restructuring of Hynix. The question was whether Hynix received a benefit resulting from the restructuring of its debts. For the purpose of determining whether or not there was a benefit, the Japanese investigating authority relied on evidence relating to the question whether the financial contribution was given on the basis of commercial considerations. The same evidence was used for the purposes of determining entrustment and direction.

The Panel agreed with Japan's approach. It pointed out that in certain circumstances, an investigating authority might determine the existence

[204] WT/DS353/AB/R of 12 March 2012, *United States – Measures Affecting Trade in Large Civil Aircraft (Second Complaint)*, para 639 *et seq*. *Neven/Sykes* (2014) pp. 288–289 criticize the Appellate Body's focus on the distribution of the intellectual property rights and suggest alternative approaches. See also *Bohanes/Rueda Garcia* (2012/1) pp. 371–372.

of a benefit by gathering available evidence on the terms the market would have offered, and by comparing those terms with those of the financial contribution at issue (this was the approach advocated by Korea). In other circumstances, an investigating authority might for the benefit issue rely on evidence of whether or not the financial contribution was provided on non-commercial considerations (this was the approach followed by Japan). The second type of evidence, i.e. reliance on non-commercial considerations, indicates terms more favourable than those available from the market as the market is presumed to operate on the basis of commercial considerations. Depending on the particular circumstances of a case, an investigating authority might also rely on other types of evidence that could be equally relevant. The Panel also concluded that Japan properly determined, on the basis of available evidence, that the mere participation of other creditors in the October 2001 restructuring should not outweigh the evidence directly relating to the four entrusted/directed creditors that indicated that these four participated in the restructuring on the basis of non-commercial considerations.

Korea took issue with the Panel's determinations. First, it argued that the Panel conflated the concepts of a financial contribution and benefit. A finding of entrustment or direction is not by itself sufficient to conclude that there is a benefit. Second, Korea claimed that the benchmark used by the Panel was wrong as the creditors' failure to undertake an analysis might be probative for entrustment or direction but not for the question whether the recipient received a benefit. And finally Korea referred to a report by an accounting firm. It claimed that this report demonstrated that the Korean government did not confer a benefit to Hynix because the terms from the four entrusted/directed creditors were comparable with what Hynix would have been able to obtain from other creditors that were not entrusted/directed. Korea also submitted that the report was already available to the Japanese investigating authority at the time when it conducted its benefit analysis.

The Appellate Body rejected Korea's appeal. It held that relying on the same or similar evidence for assessing distinct legal requirements did not amount to a conflation of the benefit requirement with the financial contribution requirement. In particular with regard to Korea's third point, the Appellate Body acknowledged that an investigating authority might be confronted with different types of evidence, and that one type of evidence might not support the conclusion suggested by the other. However, in the case at hand, the Japanese investigating authority had undertaken to investigate whether creditors acting in accordance with the usual practice in the relevant market would have restructured Hynix on the same terms as the four entrusted/directed creditors did. To this end, the Japanese investigating authority addressed questionnaires to non-entrusted/non-directed creditors that also participated in the October 2001 restructuring, i.e. other creditors than the four that were found to be entrusted/directed. With one exception, none replied to these questionnaires. Therefore, the investigating authority had to use facts available pursuant to Article 12.7. In other words, there was no direct evidence on the record regarding the reasons why other creditors had participated in the October 2001 restructuring. In these circumstances, the mere participation of other creditors in the October 2001 restructuring (absent evidence establishing that their participation was based on commercial considerations) did not preclude a finding by Japan that the participation of the four creditors in that restructuring conferred a benefit on Hynix.[205]

The question is also whether a market benchmark can be appropriate if it is only based on a limited number of transactions. The Panel in *Korea – Commercial Vessels* concluded in relation to so-called Advance Payment Refund Guarantees (APRGs), that the exceptional nature of any particular market APRG should not preclude its use as an appropriate benchmark for the purposes of determining the existence of a benefit. Any APRG should be admissible as a market benchmark provided that it is negotiated on a commercial basis by a market operator, and is comparable in terms of duration etc.[206]

Benchmark Must Not Be Distorted

The benchmark that is chosen in order to determine whether the recipient is better off must not itself be distorted by the financial contribution. Rather, the benchmark must reflect conditions in the market absent the financial contribution. Otherwise, it would not be possible to determine whether the financial contribution placed the recipient in an advantageous position, because the benchmark used in the comparison itself reflects the financial contribution.[207]

205 WT/DS336/AB/R of 28 November 2007, *Japan – Countervailing Duties on Dynamic Random Access Memories from Korea*, para 216 *et seq.*
206 WT/DS273/R of 7 March 2005, *Korea – Measures Affecting Trade in Commercial Vessels*, para 7.155.
207 WT/DS316/AB/R of 18 May 2011, *EC and certain Member States – Measures Affecting Trade in Large Civil Aircraft*, para 900. The facts underlying this statement are described *infra* pp. 157–160.

Adjustments May Be Necessary to Make a Benefit Analysis

When examining whether transactions are subsidies because they are given below a market benchmark, the conditions of the transaction and the proposed benchmark have to be comparable. Factors that are relevant in this respect include the comparability of the collaterals and guarantees given, the credit ratings, the maturity, the currency and other terms. If they are not comparable, it has to be examined whether adjustments can be made to account for the differences.[208] See also *infra* pp. 144–148.

Precise Quantification of a Benefit

There is no obligation under the ASCM to quantify the precise amount of the subsidy for purposes of an adverse effects claim. While a Panel should have regard to the magnitude of the challenged subsidy and for instance its relationship to prices of the product, as this may be relevant to the assessment of a claim of serious prejudice, a precise, definitive quantification of the subsidy is not required for purposes of a serious prejudice analysis.[209] Thus, a review of a Panel ruling by the Appellate Body will not necessarily result in a reversal if the ruling is based on a mistake as to the amount of the estimated benefit.[210]

Article 14 Is Relevant Context for Any Benefit Analysis

The chapeau of Article 14 states that the guidelines of this provision apply for the purposes of part V of the ASCM, i.e. countervailing measures. However, the Appellate Body took the view that Article 14 also provides relevant context for the interpretation of the term 'benefit' in Article 1.1(b), e.g. for the purposes of an Article 5 claim. The explicit textual

[208] WT/DS273/R of 7 March 2005, *Korea – Measures Affecting Trade in Commercial Vessels*, para 7.224 *et seq.* WT/DS412/AB/R and WT/DS426/AB/R of 6 May 2013, *Canada – Certain Measures Affecting the Renewable Energy Generation Sector; Canada – Measures Relating to Feed-In Tariff Program*, paras 5.216, 5.218, 5.228 and 5.235.

[209] WT/DS353/AB/R of 12 March 2012, *United States – Measures Affecting Trade in Large Civil Aircraft (Second Complaint)*, para 697; WT/DS267/AB/R of 3 March 2005, *United States – Subsidies on Upland Cotton*, para 467; WT/DS412/AB/R and WT/DS426/AB/R of 6 May 2013, *Canada – Certain Measures Affecting the Renewable Energy Generation Sector; Canada – Measures Relating to Feed-In Tariff Program*, paras 5.162–5.166; WT/DS341/R of 4 September 2008, *Mexico – Definitive Countervailing Measures on Olive Oil from the European Communities*, para 7.151 *et seq.*

[210] WT/DS353/AB/R of 12 March 2012, *United States – Measures Affecting Trade in Large Civil Aircraft (Second Complaint)*, paras 697–700.

reference to Article 1.1 in Article 14 indicates that 'benefit' is used in the same sense in the two provisions. Panels followed and adopted the same approach.[211] Nevertheless, Article 1.1(b) is concerned with the existence of a benefit while Article 14 is concerned with the calculation of the amount of the benefit.[212]

Note that Article 14(d) has been interpreted as allowing for the use of out-of-country benchmarks.[213]

Recipient of Financial Contribution Not Necessarily Identical with Recipient of Benefit

In order for a subsidy to exist, the recipient of the financial contribution is not necessarily identical with the recipient of benefit.[214] However, in such a set of circumstances there is a need to conduct a pass-through analysis. Two configurations exist. First, a subsidy could be given to a producer of an input that is subsequently used in the manufacturing of downstream products. The question is whether the subsidy passed through from the input producer to the producer of the downstream product that incorporates that input (for details see *infra* the commentary to Article 10, pp. 373–378). Second, the pass-through issue arises in the so-called privatization cases, i.e. a subsidy is given to company or its shareholders and subsequently, the ownership of the company is transferred. Here, the question is whether the privatized company benefits from a subsidy bestowed prior to privatization (see *infra* the commentary to Article 14, pp. 433–443).

[211] WT/DS70/AB/R of 2 August 1999, *Canada – Measures Affecting the Export of Civilian Aircraft*, para 155. Confirmed in WT/DS316/AB/R of 18 May 2011, *EC and certain Member States – Measures Affecting Trade in Large Civil Aircraft*, paras 833, 972, 998 and 1019. See also WT/DS299/R of 17 June 2005, *European Communities – Countervailing Measures on Dynamic Random Access Memory Chips from Korea*, para 7.173; WT/DS412/AB/R and WT/DS426/AB/R of 6 May 2013, *Canada – Certain Measures Affecting the Renewable Energy Generation Sector; Canada – Measures Relating to Feed-In Tariff Program*, para 5.165.

[212] WT/DS299/R of 17 June 2005, *European Communities – Countervailing Measures on Dynamic Random Access Memory Chips from Korea*, paras 7.178 and 7.179.

[213] See e.g. WT/DS412/AB/R and WT/DS426/AB/R of 6 May 2013, *Canada – Certain Measures Affecting the Renewable Energy Generation Sector; Canada – Measures Relating to Feed-In Tariff Program*, paras 5.227 and 5.239 *et passim*. For a comprehensive discussion see *infra* the commentary to Article 14, pp. 454–468.

[214] WT/DS379/R of 22 October 2010, *US – Definitive Anti-Dumping and Countervailing Duties on Certain Products from China*, para 12.36.

Specific Issues

Tax Exemptions and Other Tax Issues The Appellate Body held that tax exemptions provided by the FSC measure confer upon the recipient the obvious benefit of reduced tax liability and, therefore, reduced tax payments.[215]

In *EC and certain Member States – Large Civil Aircraft*, the EU argued that effects of taxation should be taken into account when determining the benefit. The EU's argument was that the taxation of income generated through economic activity facilitated by launch aid must be taken into account when calculating the benefit. The Panel dismissed this argument. It did not see any basis in the ASCM to reduce the amount of a financial contribution for any tax payments made to the government on income generated from economic activity that is facilitated by that financial contribution.[216]

Loans In relation to loans,[217] the Appellate Body held that the comparison between the (interest) amount the recipient pays on the government loan and the amount the recipient would pay on a comparable commercial loan is to be performed as though the loans were obtained at the same time. Because the assessment focuses on the moment in time when the lender and the borrower commit to the transaction, it must look at how the loan is structured and how risk is factored in, rather than looking at how the loan actually performed over time.[218]

The determination of the appropriate market benchmark used to assess whether or not the loan confers a benefit can be quite a complex exercise. The benchmark should be established on the basis of a similar type of commercial financing. Considerations to be taken into account when establishing the benchmark of an undistorted loan are:

- selection of a comparable market interest benchmark, e.g. Eurodollar market, Swap market (these benchmarks distinguish between the location of the borrower);
- date of the loan, i.e. there should be a temporal correlation;[219]

[215] WT/DS108/AB/R of 24 February 2000, *United States – Tax Treatment for 'Foreign Sales Corporations'*, para 140.

[216] WT/DS316/R of 30 June 2010, *EC and certain Member States – Measures Affecting Trade in Large Civil Aircraft*, para 7.429.

[217] See also *infra* the commentary to Article 14, pp. 446–450.

[218] WT/DS316/AB/R of 18 May 2011, *EC and certain Member States – Measures Affecting Trade in Large Civil Aircraft*, paras 835–838.

[219] WT/DS273/R of 7 March 2005, *Korea – Measures Affecting Trade in Commercial Vessels*, para 7.179.

- nature of the credit: loan or bond;
- interest regime, i.e. fixed, variable, floating etc.;
- amortization schedule;
- maturity;
- securities and collaterals;[220]
- currency;
- rating of borrower according to rating agencies;
- risk premium;
- changes in the loan conditions over time.

See also *Korea – Commercial Vessels* concerning the inclusion of a country-risk spread in the market benchmark.[221]

EC and Certain Member States – Large Civil Aircraft is a perfect demonstration of the complexities associated with the determination of the benchmark and the comparison between the interest rate actually charged and the benchmark rate. In general, a two-step-approach was used. First, a comparable market interest benchmark was selected. Second, as this benchmark did not exactly reflect the nature of the loans at issue under the benefit analysis, the necessary adjustments were made to the benchmark so selected. The following points of the Panel report are worth mentioning:

EADS Loan Obtained in 2002 from the European Investment Bank (EIB): In line with the arguments made by the US, the Panel first examined the specific features of the EIB's lending operations. The Panel noted the non-profit-making nature of the EIB's operations and its mandate to provide financing to the extent funds are not available on reasonable terms. It considered these two elements as features that suggest that the bank grants loans for projects that would be more difficult to successfully realize, or simply unfeasible, on the basis of commercial financing. This indirectly supported the view that the rate of return the EIB obtained on the loans it grants to borrowers was below the rate of return that would be demanded by a commercial lender (para 7.753). The Panel then examined the appropriateness of the specific benchmark advanced by the US. The US alleged that the market benchmark would be 5.68 per cent based on a Eurodollar bond with a ten-year maturity to a borrower rated A-. According to the EU, the benchmark was inappropriate for a number of

[220] WT/DS273/R of 7 March 2005, *Korea – Measures Affecting Trade in Commercial Vessels*, para 7.164 *et seq.* See also paras 7.175, 7.176. 7.178, 7.184.

[221] WT/DS273/R of 7 March 2005, *Korea – Measures Affecting Trade in Commercial Vessels*, para 7.142 *et seq.*

reasons, *inter alia*, because EADS had an A rating and not A-, that cheaper credit rates would have been available to EADS (on the so-called Yankee market and the SWAP market) as opposed to the Eurodollar market, and that the costs associated with a bond were higher than those associated with a loan. While accepting some of the points made by the EU, the Panel concluded that overall, on the basis of the arguments and evidence submitted by the parties, the market interest rate proxy provided by the US came closest to the 2002 EIB loan to EADS in terms of key characteristics and features, at least closer than the alternatives proposed by the EU.[222]

Commitment Fees and Non-utilization Fees: The US claimed that the EADS obtained an additional benefit in relation to the aforementioned loan because it did not have to pay any commitment fees and non-utilization fees for the loans obtained. With regard to the non-utilization fees, the US did not substantiate its claim and the Panel consequently dismissed this claim. With regard to the commitment fees, the following should be noted: if a company receives a credit line that is not used (as was in part here the case), it must normally pay a commitment fee for the unused credit amount. In exchange for this fee, the company has guaranteed access to the bank's money even if its own creditworthiness deteriorates or the cost of credit rises after the credit line was agreed. To the extent the loan agreed between EADS and the EIB was not disbursed but fully committed, the bank did not charge a fee to cover the risk of a deterioration of EADS' creditworthiness. Hence, the Panel considered the absence of such fee as a benefit conferred on EADS. Note that the agreed interest rate adequately reflected all other risks associated with contracting a credit line, such as the risk that interest rates rise after the credit line was agreed.[223]

Market Interest Rate Benchmark Should Be a Spread of Rates and Not a Single Interest Rate: The EU contended that because a borrower will typically consider the terms and conditions offered by different finance providers before taking out a loan, the market interest rate benchmark should be a spread of rates and not a single interest rate. According to the EC, a difference of 20 to 50 basis points above or below the single benchmark rate should not be taken as a sign of benefit. The Panel agreed in principle. According to the Panel, it would not be unreasonable to expect that two or more different commercial lenders may charge slightly

[222] WT/DS316/R of 30 June 2010, *EC and certain Member States – Measures Affecting Trade in Large Civil Aircraft*, paras 7.747–7.787. This aspect was not appealed.

[223] WT/DS316/R of 30 June 2010, *EC and certain Member States – Measures Affecting Trade in Large Civil Aircraft*, paras 7.788–7.800. This aspect was not appealed.

different rates of interest for loans having the same terms and conditions. There are many factors that might affect the level at which a commercial lender will set its interest rates to customers, e.g. any reserve requirements, differences in the risk assessment, access to liquidity, the lender's desired risk exposure and business model, as well as the commercial relationship it has or wants to build with the potential customer. However, the Panel held that the EU failed to present evidence that validated its proposed parameters and consequently rejected the request.[224]

Loans vs Bonds: Loans seem to be slightly cheaper than bonds and this might require an adjustment to the benchmark selected.[225]

Risk Premium: The Panel has accepted that the EIB failed to charge a risk premium on any loans prior to 1999 and found that the EU had not presented sufficient evidence to show that other instruments compensated for this. To the extent that such a risk premium had not been charged, the loans in question were considered to confer a benefit.[226] Note that this issue was ultimately not relevant for the case because the EIB loans were not found to be specific.

Loan Guarantees Given by Spanish Government's Industrial Holding: The benchmark for loans by the EIB to CASA (an Airbus member company at the time) were based on the cost of borrowing to the Spanish government because of loan guarantees provided by INI, the Spanish government's industrial holding. According to the Panel, the loan guarantees given by INI transformed the loans to CASA into loans that were akin to loans to the Spanish government.[227]

Loan as grant in disguise: In *EC – Countervailing Measures on DRAM Chips*, the EU found that Hynix had received a benefit to the extent that three banks participated in a syndicated loan. The EU considered the loans grants because the record showed that the financial situation of Hynix was such that no reasonable private investor would have been willing to provide funds to this company, as it was clear that the chances of ever recovering the money invested were minimal. The Panel did not agree. It pointed out that at

[224] WT/DS316/R of 30 June 2010, *EC and certain Member States – Measures Affecting Trade in Large Civil Aircraft*, paras 7.786–7.787, 7.856. But see also para 7.851. This aspect was not appealed.

[225] WT/DS316/R of 30 June 2010, *EC and certain Member States – Measures Affecting Trade in Large Civil Aircraft*, paras 7.780–7.783. This aspect was not appealed.

[226] WT/DS316/R of 30 June 2010, *EC and certain Member States – Measures Affecting Trade in Large Civil Aircraft*, paras 7.815, 7.816 and 7.878–7.880. This aspect was not appealed.

[227] WT/DS316/R of 30 June 2010, *EC and certain Member States – Measures Affecting Trade in Large Civil Aircraft*, paras 7.785–7.786. This aspect was not appealed.

the provisional stage of the countervailing duty investigation the EU did not find that the Syndicated Loan conferred a benefit. The only changes between the provisional stage and the definitive stage were that there was an allegation of pressure exercised by the Korean government to participate in the loan, the fact that three banks received a waiver from Korean Supervisory Financial Institutions to increase the lending limit with regard to Hynix and that without lifting the lending limit, the three banks could not have given the loans. The Panel held that the lifting of the lending limit was uninformative for the question whether a benefit existed. However, it found it very relevant that another seven banks participated in the Syndicated Loan and extended loans on similar terms to Hynix. Some of these banks were not considered public bodies. The EU ignored the loans provided by the seven other banks without examining whether these loans were commercial or whether their provision was so influenced by the alleged government intervention that these loans could actually not be obtained in the market.[228]

Net interest margin: Note that in *Canada – Aircraft*, the Panel held in the context of debt financing that the net interest margin is the more appropriate measure of performance than the financial institution's return on equity. According to the Panel, return on equity is the more appropriate measure of performance in the investment sector, where equity shares are held by the investor.[229]

If loans are provided by a public body in order to finance sales of a private company and if that private company has also organized itself such type of financing, the complaining party in an Article 4 or Article 5 case can normally not argue that the conditions stipulated in those latter transactions should be used as a benchmark in order to determine whether or not the financing provided by the public body of the defending party confers a benefit. The public body in question is not a party to such transaction, and has no right to obtain details of those transactions. It is likely that the terms of those transactions are viewed as confidential by the parties.[230]

Credit Lines The Panel in *EC and certain Member States – Large Civil Aircraft* held that a 700 million EUR credit line was a financial contribution

[228] WT/DS299/R of 17 June 2005, *European Communities – Countervailing Measures on Dynamic Random Access Memory Chips from Korea*, paras 7.181–7.186.

[229] WT/DS70/R of 14 April 1999, *Canada – Measures Affecting the Export of Civilian Aircraft*, para 9.165 *et passim*.

[230] WT/DS222/R of 28 January 2002, *Canada – Export Credits and Loan Guarantees for Regional Aircraft*, para 7.224.

because it amounted to a potential direct transfer of funds,[231] but that the US did not substantiate the claim that the credit line constituted a benefit.

> [The US] has adduced no evidence nor advanced any particular argument to identify and explain the alleged benefit of the *promise* to obtain liquidity on favourable terms for EADS. We are not convinced that simply showing that a credit line has been granted on beneficial terms is enough to establish that it has placed its recipient in a better position than it otherwise would have been in absent availability of the particular credit line. In our view, something more is required to demonstrate that a promise to provide 'cheap' financing, *in and of itself*, confers a benefit. (emphasis in original)[232]

The Panel took the same view in relation to funds under the LuFo III programme that were committed but not disbursed yet to Airbus as of 1 July 2005, i.e. the cut-off date used by the US in its first written submission.[233] See also *supra* pp. 144–148.

Credit Ratings With regard to the use of credit ratings for the purposes of establishing a benefit, see also *Canada – Aircraft Credits and Guarantees*.[234]

Export Credits The so-called OECD Arrangement[235] prescribes minimum credit rates for export credits. The central element of the OECD Arrangement is the 'Commercial Interest Rate Reference' or 'CIRR'. An official export credit that respects the CIRR can constitute a benefit because the CIRR is a constructed interest rate for a particular currency, at a particular time, that does not always reflect the actual state of credit markets. It is constructed on the basis of government bond yields plus a fixed margin. Because of the method of the fixation of the CIRR, it may also lag behind the market. Moreover, the CIRR is designed to correspond to commercial interest rates for first-class borrowers while according to the OECD Arrangement, the premium charged should, in addition, reflect a number of risks such as the applicable country risk classification and the buyer risk (see its Article 24 'Minimum Premium Rates for Credit Risk'). Thus, the

[231] See *supra* p. 146.

[232] WT/DS316/R of 30 June 2010, *EC and certain Member States – Measures Affecting Trade in Large Civil Aircraft*, para 7.884. This aspect was not appealed.

[233] WT/DS316/R of 30 June 2010, *EC and certain Member States – Measures Affecting Trade in Large Civil Aircraft*, para 7.1502. This aspect was not appealed.

[234] WT/DS222/R of 28 January 2002, *Canada – Export Credits and Loan Guarantees for Regional Aircraft*, paras 7.205–7. 211, 7.249 *et seq*.

[235] A more detailed description of the OECD Arrangement can be found *infra* the commentary to Annex I, pp. 628–633.

prescription of a CIRR floor for financing operations does not establish *per se* the absence of a benefit for the buyers of the product in question. Indeed, what is relevant for the question of benefit is whether, as a result of the export credit programme, purchasers of the good in question obtain export credits on terms more favourable than those available to them in the market.[236] However, the financing operation in accordance with the CIRR (plus all the interest rate provisions of the OECD Arrangement) is protected by the safe haven as set out in the second paragraph of item (k) of Annex I. The second paragraph operates as an affirmative defence and precludes a finding of a prohibited export subsidy, even if the transaction in question is not strictly in line with 'market' benchmarks. Hence, exporting countries may have an interest to demonstrate that they fall within this safe haven as was the case in *Brazil – Aircraft (2nd Article 21.5)*.[237]

Repayment terms that extend beyond the maximum repayment terms provided for in the relevant Sector Understanding on Export Credits for Civil Aircraft are not in itself evidence of a benefit within the meaning of Article 1.1(b) ASCM.[238]

In *Brazil – Aircraft (2nd Article 21.5)*, the Brazilian government provided non-refundable payments to the financing institution that loaned money to the purchaser for the purpose of buying the Brazilian aircraft. The Panel noted that, while there was no doubt that the payments conferred a benefit, the question was whether they conferred a benefit to the Brazilian producers of the aircraft. In the opinion of the Panel, if Canada (the applicant in that dispute) could establish that the payments to the lenders passed through to the purchasers of the aircraft in the form of improved terms of credit, this would constitute a *prima facie* case that the payments benefited the Brazilian producers of the aircraft.[239]

[236] WT/DS46/RW/2 of 26 July 2001, *Brazil – Export Financing Programme for Aircraft (Article 21.5, second recourse)*, paras 5.29, 5.34–5.37. WT/DS222/R of 28 January 2002, *Canada – Export Credits and Loan Guarantees for Regional Aircraft*, paras 7.237–7.241 has also held that CIRR compliance does not necessarily mean the absence of a benefit. Note finally that WT/DS70/R of 14 April 1999, *Canada – Measures Affecting the Export of Civilian Aircraft*, para 9.117 rejected the argument made by Canada that item (k) constitutes contextual guidance for determining the existence of a benefit in the specific context of government credit under Article 1.

[237] WT/DS46/RW/2 of 26 July 2001, *Brazil – Export Financing Programme for Aircraft (Article 21.5, second recourse)*, para 5.56.

[238] WT/DS222/R of 28 January 2002, *Canada – Export Credits and Loan Guarantees for Regional Aircraft*, paras 7.232–7.236.

[239] WT/DS46/RW/2 of 26 July 2001, *Brazil – Export Financing Programme for Aircraft (Article 21.5, second recourse)*, paras 5.29, 5.34–5.37 including footnote 42. See also WT/

Guarantees in Particular in the Context of an Export Credit Guarantee Programme In *EC – Countervailing Measures on DRAM Chips*, KEIC, a Korean public body, provided an export guarantee to Hynix. The EU concluded that the benefit conferred on Hynix equalled the full amount of the guarantee. Without the guarantee, no further financing would have been available for Hynix. Moreover, no party raised the possibility of alternative financing, absent the guarantee. Thus, there was no benchmark for the cost comparison. It also appeared that even KEIC was hesitant to provide the guarantee and needed a governmental assurance, which it received. The Panel agreed with these findings. Korea also argued in front of the Panel that item (j) of Annex I to the ASCM required that in a government export guarantee situation, the benefit had to be assessed by examining whether the fees paid by the recipient of the guarantee were adequate to cover long-term operating costs and losses. The Panel also dismissed this claim. It held that item (j) of Annex I did not operate as an affirmative defence. Item (j) was relevant in determining whether a prohibited export subsidy existed, but not whether a benefit existed. The question of benefit had to be determined in relation to the market place, e.g. by comparing the guarantee provided by the government with a comparable guarantee provided by the market place. Alternatively, the principles set out in Article 14(c) could be used in order to determine whether or not a benefit existed.[240]

In *Korea – Commercial Vessels*, the EU claimed that Advance Payment Refund Guarantees (APRGs) given by banks should be considered a subsidy. These guarantees provided that buyers of ships will be refunded of any advance payment made to a Korean shipyard in case the shipyard defaults under the relevant export contract. The Panel held that guarantees that were given by banks that the buyer of the ship had designated could not serve as a market benchmark in order to determine subsidization because there was a risk that such guarantee was not negotiated at arm's length. Indeed, the shipyard was a captive buyer of such guarantee as it had to accept the bank designated by the purchaser of the ship.[241]

DS353/R of 31 March 2011, *United States – Measures Affecting Trade in Large Civil Aircraft (Second Complaint)*, paras 7.278–7.280.

240 WT/DS299/R of 17 June 2005, *European Communities – Countervailing Measures on Dynamic Random Access Memory Chips from Korea*, paras 7.187–7.193. The export credit guarantee arrangement is described in para 7.85. WT/DS299/R of 17 June 2005, *European Communities – Countervailing Measures on Dynamic Random Access Memory Chips from Korea*, para 7.191 arrived at a similar conclusion.

241 WT/DS273/R of 7 March 2005, *Korea – Measures Affecting Trade in Commercial Vessels*, para 7.135.

According to *Korea – Commercial Vessels*, the absence of a credit risk spread in the fee for a guarantee can constitute a benefit.[242]

Restructurings outside versus inside investor benchmark In *Japan – DRAMs (Korea)*, one of the specific benefit calculation issues was whether the investigating authority should use an outside investor benchmark or an inside investor benchmark in the context of Hynix's restructuring. The restructuring was achieved because existing creditors of Hynix gave new loans, extended the maturity of existing loans, accepted debt-to-equity swaps etc. Japan concluded that four creditors that participated in the restructurings were entrusted or directed by the Korean government. Before the Panel, Korea essentially argued that the Japanese investigating authority wrongly calculated the amount of benefit, which accrued to Hynix and which resulted from the four creditors, from the perspective of outside investors. The Panel accepted Korea's claim. It recalled that the Japanese investigating authority explicitly accepted the premise that existing creditors would possibly provide additional funding in order to maximize the recovery of credit. The Panel held that an objective and impartial investigating authority, which itself had accepted that existing creditors might engage in restructuring measures that new, outside investors would not, could not properly calculate the amount of benefit conferred by restructurings undertaken by inside creditors on the basis of an exclusively outside investor benchmark.[243]

Equity Infusions A government confers a benefit by making a financial investment if the terms of such investment are more favourable than those available on the market. Article 14(a) gives guidance in order to determine whether or not an equity infusion confers a benefit.

> [G]overnment provision of equity capital shall not be considered as conferring a benefit, unless the investment decision can be regarded as inconsistent with the usual investment practice (including the provision of risk capital) of private investors in the territory of that Member.

The Appellate Body in *EC and certain Member States – Large Civil Aircraft*, when examining equity infusions in Aérospatiale, understood the term 'usual practice' to describe common or customary conduct of private investors in respect of equity investment. Moreover, as Article 14(a)

[242] WT/DS273/R of 7 March 2005, *Korea – Measures Affecting Trade in Commercial Vessels*, para 7.157.

[243] WT/DS336/R of 13 July 2007, *Japan – Countervailing Duties on Dynamic Random Access Memories from Korea*, para 7.304 *et seq.*

focuses on the investment decision, the Appellate Body was of the view that an *ex ante* approach is necessary when assessing the equity investment by comparing the decision, based on the costs and the expected returns of the transaction, to the usual practice of private investors at the moment the decision to invest is undertaken. The notion 'investment decision' is key because it identifies what is to be compared to a market benchmark, and when the comparison is to be situated.[244] The Appellate Body also confirmed the Panel's approach, i.e.:

- When evaluating an equity investment in an enterprise, a private investor will be seeking to achieve a reasonable rate of return on its investment.
- Information relevant to such an evaluation would include current and past indicators of an enterprise's financial performance (including return on equity, debt-to-equity and debt coverage ratios) calculated from the enterprise's financial statements and accounts, information as to the future financial prospects of the enterprise, including market studies, economic forecasts and project appraisals, equity investment in the enterprise by other private investors, and marketplace prospects for the products produced by the enterprise. These points are customarily taken into account by private investors. In order to demonstrate that a private investor would not have invested in Aérospatiale, the US not only submitted information on the bad financial performance of Aérospatiale but also corresponding information for certain alleged peer companies for the same period that had in many instances significantly superior ratios. Owing to the cyclical nature of the markets in which Aérospatiale operated, the Panel regarded indicators of Aérospatiale's performance in comparison to a peer group of companies operating in the same industries, presumably subject to the same business risks and cycles as Aérospatiale, as particularly probative of the question whether a private investor would have made a similar investment.
- In sum, the question is whether a private investor would not have made the capital investment in question based on the information available at the time when the decision was taken, or, to the contrary, could the private investor have expected to achieve a reasonable return on its investment?

[244] WT/DS316/AB/R of 18 May 2011, *EC and certain Member States – Measures Affecting Trade in Large Civil Aircraft*, paras 998, 1019 *et passim*.

On this basis, the Appellate Body upheld the Panel's decision that equity infusions in the form of four capital investments totalling 5.9 billion French francs by the French government and by Credit Lyonnais (that at the time was controlled by the French government) in Aérospatiale constituted a benefit to Airbus.[245] With regard to these equity infusions, there was some disagreement between the parties as to what weight the Panel should have given to evidence relating to Boeing's prospects as a proxy for Airbus's prospects. The Appellate Body accepted that the Panel attributed to the Boeing evidence less weight than to other evidence more indicative of Aérospatiale's future prospects because the Boeing evidence did not reflect the same range of business activities as those of Aérospatiale.[246] Note finally that the Panel did not regard the fact that Aérospatiale was undercapitalized by the French government, its sole shareholder, to necessarily mean that a private investor would not have provided capital to the company.[247]

But the Appellate Body did not agree with the Panel's assessment that there was a benefit in relation to an equity infusion by the French government into Aérospatiale that was achieved by transferring the government's shares in Dassault Aviation to Aérospatiale against the issuance of new shares by Aérospatiale. However, the Appellate Body was unable to complete the analysis. The share transfer was a preliminary step in the planned consolidation of the French aeronautic, defence and space industries through the combination of Aérospatiale and Matra Hautes Technologies, and the subsequent partial public offering of shares in the combined Aérospatiale-Matra entity. The Panel based its conclusion that there was a benefit *inter alia* on the following considerations:

- While there was an improvement of Aérospatiale's financial conditions and prospects, Aérospatiale's capitalization brought about by the aforementioned share transfer was necessary in order to increase the chances that the planned privatization could occur as soon as possible.
- The transfer was regarded as necessary to improve the French government's position in its negotiations with other Airbus governments over the terms of the consolidation of the European aerospace industry.

[245] WT/DS316/AB/R of 18 May 2011, *EC and certain Member States – Measures Affecting Trade in Large Civil Aircraft*, paras 1000–1003.

[246] WT/DS316/AB/R of 18 May 2011, *EC and certain Member States – Measures Affecting Trade in Large Civil Aircraft*, paras 1004–1012.

[247] WT/DS316/R of 30 June 2010, *EC and certain Member States – Measures Affecting Trade in Large Civil Aircraft*, para 7.1364. This aspect was not appealed.

- A party may successfully rebut a claim that an equity infusion conferred a benefit by showing that the transaction in question was a preliminary step in, or otherwise part of, a restructuring or consolidation project and that the equity investment was consistent with the usual investment practice of a private investor.
- While there were valuations of the various transfers, these valuations had all been made after the French government had decided to make the transfers.

In the opinion of the Appellate Body, the Panel failed to identify the correct investment decision and to assess it in relation to the usual investment practice because the attractiveness of an investment will be determined in relation to the particular costs and expected returns associated with that decision. The Appellate Body first referred to the standard already established previously with regard to the equity infusions by the French government and Credit Lyonnais. There was basic agreement between the parties that the investment decision at issue was the transfer of the government's shares in Dassault Aviation to Aérospatiale in anticipation of returns from the consolidation and subsequent public offerings of shares. As a consequence of this transfer, the French government lost control over Dassault Aviation. The parties disagreed over the value to be associated to the loss of control, and the value to be associated to the returns generated as a result of the consolidation and eventual privatization. The US argued that not only Aérospatiale continued to be in poor financial condition, but also that the costs associated with the investment were not outweighed by the expected return from the eventual public offering of Aérospatiale-Matra shares. However, the Panel had incorrectly limited its conclusion to an assessment of the financial health of Aérospatiale immediately prior to the share transfer and found that it was not in a position to attract private investors. But the Panel did not examine the costs and expected returns associated with the French government's investment decision and whether the expected returns outweighed the costs.[248] The Panel seemed to have asked the right question (a private investor contemplating such an investment would be seeking to achieve a reasonable rate of return on its investment; the French government's investment in Aérospatiale by the transfer of shares in Dassault Aviation against newly issued Aérospatiale shares only made sense if the rate of return on the

[248] WT/DS316/AB/R of 18 May 2011, *EC and certain Member States – Measures Affecting Trade in Large Civil Aircraft*, para 1018 *et seq.*

newly issued Aérospatiale shares exceeded the expected return on the Dassault shares).[249] But the Panel failed to reply to these questions.

Only the Panel, but not the Appellate Body, examined various share transfers in Airbus in Germany. According to the Panel, they constituted a benefit.[250]

In *Korea – Commercial Vessels*, the Panel had to decide whether Daewoo's shipbuilding activities obtained a benefit as a result of the debt restructurings carried out by a number of Korean public bodies. The Panel examined whether the EU had demonstrated that each of the restructurings in question were commercially unreasonable. The Korean public bodies relied on a report by Anjin that claimed that Daewoo's going concern value exceeded its liquidation value. The EU claimed that this report contained a number of shortcomings and that creditors had insufficient time to review the report. According to the EU, the report was therefore not suitable as a justification for accepting the restructurings. Therefore, the Panel examined whether a reasonable commercial actor could have used the report as the basis to decide that restructuring made better economic sense than liquidation. The Panel concluded that the EU had not established a case, thereby applying a very demanding standard in order to determine whether the report could serve such a basis. The Panel also conceded that while another analyst performing the same task might have used assumptions closer to those preferred by the EU, this did not mean that the assumptions used by Anjin were demonstrably incorrect.[251] The Panel also held, in the absence of detailed arguments, that a simple reference to the non-participation of foreign investors in the restructuring of another Korean shipyard was insufficient to establish that the terms of the restructuring were commercially unreasonable, especially given that the evidence was mixed as to the reasons for and significance of this non-participation.[252]

Equity Guarantees See *Canada – Aircraft Credits and Guarantees*.[253]

[249] WT/DS316/R of 30 June 2010, *EC and certain Member States – Measures Affecting Trade in Large Civil Aircraft*, paras 7.1407 and 7.1412).

[250] WT/DS316/R of 30 June 2010, *EC and certain Member States – Measures Affecting Trade in Large Civil Aircraft*, para 7.1264 *et seq.*

[251] WT/DS273/R of 7 March 2005, *Korea – Measures Affecting Trade in Commercial Vessels*, paras 7.427–7.493. See, for instance, the Panel's examination as to the amount of time that creditors had for review of the report, para 7.445 *et seq.*

[252] WT/DS273/R of 7 March 2005, *Korea – Measures Affecting Trade in Commercial Vessels*, para 7.498.

[253] WT/DS222/R of 28 January 2002, *Canada – Export Credits and Loan Guarantees for Regional Aircraft*, para 7.331 *et seq.*

Purchase of Equity from Government There is no benefit when a purchaser is required to pay for an equity share valued in the negative.[254]

Privatizations See *infra* the commentary to Article pp. 433–443. Both the report of the Panel and the Appellate Body in *EC and certain Member States – Measures Affecting Trade in Large Civil Aircraft* also contain an overview of the benefit issue in privatization cases.[255]

Debt Forgiveness Does Not Necessarily Confer a Benefit In *EC and certain Member States – Large Civil Aircraft*, the US argued that Airbus has obtained a benefit because the German government cancelled a debt of DM 9.4 billion that was to be repaid in 2001 against a cash payment of DM 1.7 billion in 1998. This amount was based on an independent evaluation of probable future revenues from the aircraft concerned. In the particular circumstances of the case, the Panel found that Airbus did not obtain a benefit out of this debt settlement because the debt settlement was based on the present value of the claims and consistent with the terms that Airbus could have obtained in the market for the settlement of the claims.[256]

Grants As a usual matter, a non-refundable payment will confer a benefit.[257]

R&D Funding See *supra* pp. 138–141 concerning *US – Large Civil Aircraft (2nd complaint).*

Appropriate Benchmark for Launch Aid Given to Airbus In *EC and certain Member States – Large Civil Aircraft*, the parties agreed that the benchmark for the launch aid given to Airbus should reflect the

[254] WT/DS70/R of 14 April 1999, *Canada – Measures Affecting the Export of Civilian Aircraft*, paras 9.232–9.246.

[255] WT/DS316/R of 30 June 2010, *EC and certain Member States – Measures Affecting Trade in Large Civil Aircraft*, para 7.224 *et seq.*; WT/DS316/AB/R of 18 May 2011, *EC and certain Member States – Measures Affecting Trade in Large Civil Aircraft*, para 722 *et seq.* The leading cases are *US – Lead and Bismuth II* and *US – Countervailing Measures Concerning Certain Products from the EC.*

[256] WT/DS316/R of 30 June 2010, *EC and certain Member States – Measures Affecting Trade in Large Civil Aircraft*, paras 7.1318–7.1321. This aspect was not appealed.

[257] WT/DS46/RW/2 of 26 July 2001, *Brazil – Export Financing Programme for Aircraft (Article 21.5, second recourse)*, para 5.27.

government borrowing rate, the general corporate risk premium for the Airbus companies in question (i.e. the difference between the rate of return on a corporate bond and the government borrowing rate) and a project-specific risk premium. However, they disagreed as to how this third element should be calculated. The Panel found a number of deficiencies in the methods proposed by both the US and the EU in relation to the project-specific risk premia. It opined that the US methodology generally overstated the benefit while the EU methodology generally understated it. Moreover, the Panel criticized that the EU and the US applied a single risk premium to all Airbus models. It would have preferred a variable risk premium that took into account the particularities of each Airbus model. Ultimately, the Panel determined different risk premia for each of the three segments or groups of Airbus models. The Appellate Body reviewed under Article 11 DSU the EU's claims in respect of the quantification of the risk premium. It held that the Panel's reasoning in this respect was internally inconsistent because:

- The Panel dismissed venture capital financing as a source from which to derive the project-specific risks of the various Airbus models because it considered venture capital financing to be inherently more risky than launch aid given to Airbus by France, Germany, Spain and the UK. At the same time, the Panel used the data provided by the US that were based on returns from venture capital financing as an upper limit for the risk premia associated with the launch aid.
- Moreover, in relation to some Airbus models the Panel left the upper limit of the range of project-specific risk premia unbounded, thus going even potentially beyond the level of the risk premium associated with venture capital financing, although it held the venture capital financing standard inappropriate.
- Finally, with regard to one group of Airbus models (A320, A330 and A340 including their derivatives), the Panel determined the same upper limit for a risk premium for all models although the projects were very diverse: some concerned the development of completely new aircraft while others concerned the development of derivatives. In relation to the latter, the Panel found that launching them was less risky than launching completely new models. In this respect, the Appellate Body also pointed out that the span of time during which these models were launched covered 13 years, i.e. the level of experience of Airbus and thus the risk associated with each model changed over time (when Airbus launched the A320 at the beginning of that period, it had previously

developed two Airbus models; when it launched 13 years later the A340-500/600, it had previously developed five models). The Panel did not give an explanation as to how it accounted for the experience acquired by Airbus for each successive launch although it recognized that the project risk is reduced as the firm gains experience.[258]

The Appellate Body also rejected the benchmark proposed by the EU in relation to the project-related risk, i.e. deriving the project risk on the basis of the returns that risk-sharing suppliers to Airbus expected to achieve on the financing they provided for the development of the A380. The Appellate Body concurred with the Panel that that rate of return would underestimate the amount that would be demanded by a market lender in the absence of launch aid given by the Airbus Member States. Rather, that rate is distorted by the launch aid and could therefore not serve as a reliable benchmark that reflects the terms of a comparable commercial loan that Airbus could have actually obtained in the market. The terms that these suppliers negotiate with Airbus depend on how risky they perceive the specific project. Launch aid given by Airbus Member States reduces the risk that the project will fail (e.g. by reducing the risk that it will run into financial difficulties) and that it will not generate the revenues necessary to pay suppliers. The Appellate Body nevertheless found some flaws in the reasoning of the Panel underlying the aforementioned conclusion.[259]

The Appellate Body held that all launch aid programmes conferred a benefit. In all but two programmes the rates of return of the governments of the Airbus Member State were lower than a market benchmark based only on the first two elements of the risk premium, i.e. the government borrowing rate and the general corporate risk premium for the Airbus companies, but leaving aside the project-specific risk premium. The remaining two programmes were also below the benchmark if the project specific risk premium were to be calculated as suggested by the EU.[260]

The Panel and Appellate Body finally examined the question as to whether a royalty-based financing granted on the basis of a reasonable repayment forecast *per se* confers a benefit. The Panel's view was

[258] WT/DS316/AB/R of 18 May 2011, *EC and certain Member States – Measures Affecting Trade in Large Civil Aircraft*, paras 860–895.

[259] WT/DS316/AB/R of 18 May 2011, *EC and certain Member States – Measures Affecting Trade in Large Civil Aircraft*, paras 896–922.

[260] WT/DS316/AB/R of 18 May 2011, *EC and certain Member States – Measures Affecting Trade in Large Civil Aircraft*, paras 923–929.

somewhat ambiguous. It held that a reasonable repayment forecast (in the case in question a reasonable number of sales over which a market lender could expect full repayment of the principal of the loan plus interest) cannot alone be determinative of whether a royalty-based financing confers a benefit. It went on to state that while it could accept that an unreasonable repayment forecast may signal that a loan confers a benefit, it did not believe that the opposite will necessarily be true. This was because the number of sales over which full repayment is expected says little, if anything, about the appropriateness of the rate of return that will be achieved by the lender. The Appellate Body took issue with the last statement because it could also be understood to suggest that the number of sales is irrelevant to the calculation of the rate of return of the government of the Airbus Member State. Consequently, it reversed the Panel's statement.[261]

Feed-In Tariffs in Case Electricity from Renewable Energy Sources Is Produced with Equipment That Must Meet Minimum Domestic Content Levels See the Appellate Body in *Canada – Renewable Energy & Feed-In Tariff Program*[262] and *Charnovitz/Fischer* (2015) pp. 197–198. See also *supra* pp. 132–136.

A Public Body Receiving Subsidies Does Not Automatically Provide Loans Conferring a Benefit The legal standard for 'benefit' is benefit to the recipient, and not the cost to the government. Therefore, the fact that a public body providing financing to private parties may receive subsidized funding does not mean that such public body will inevitably provide subsidized financing to its customers.[263]

[261] WT/DS316/AB/R of 18 May 2011, *EC and certain Member States – Measures Affecting Trade in Large Civil Aircraft*, paras 930–936. The Panel examined also footnote 16 of the ASCM that has lapsed since and that deals with royalty-based financing. It concluded that this footnote did not inform the meaning of benefit under Article 1.1(b), see WT/DS316/R of 30 June 2010, *EC and certain Member States – Measures Affecting Trade in Large Civil Aircraft*, para 7.396.

[262] WT/DS412/AB/R and WT/DS426/AB/R of 6 May 2013, *Canada – Certain Measures Affecting the Renewable Energy Generation Sector; Canada – Measures Relating to Feed-In Tariff Program*, paras 5.223–5.245.

[263] WT/DS273/R of 7 March 2005, *Korea – Measures Affecting Trade in Commercial Vessels*, para 7.84.

Article 2

Specificity

Introduction

Subsidies only fall under the disciplines of the ASCM if they are specific. This follows from Article 1.2 which stipulates that a subsidy shall only be subject to the provisions of Parts II, III or V if it is specific. Article 2 elaborates the concept of specificity.

Article 2.1 deals with specificity in general, and Article 2.2 deals with regional specificity. Article 2.3 clarifies that any subsidy that is prohibited pursuant to Article 3 (i.e. which is export contingent or contingent on import substitution) is deemed to be specific. Article 2.4 finally contains a procedural provision by underlining that any determination of specificity 'shall be clearly substantiated on the basis of positive evidence'. Specificity under Article 2.1 can be *de jure* (see subparagraphs (a) and (b)) or *de facto* (see subparagraph (c)).

In order for a subsidy to be specific, it must not be generally available to economic operators within the jurisdiction of the granting authority, but it has to be limited to 'certain enterprises'. The chapeau of Article 2.1 defines for the entire ASCM 'certain enterprises' as 'an enterprise or industry or group of enterprises or industries'.

As the Panel in *US – Anti-Dumping and Countervailing Duties (China)* has so pertinently put it, the specificity requirement is not about the existence of a subsidy, which is dealt with in Article 1.1, but rather about access thereto.[1] According to *US – Upland Cotton*, non-specific subsidies are broadly available throughout an economy, in contrast to specific subsidies to which access is limited to a 'sufficiently discrete segment' of an economy as to constitute 'certain enterprises'.[2] The Panel in *EC and certain*

[1] WT/DS379/R of 22 October 2010, *US – Definitive Anti-Dumping and Countervailing Duties on Certain Products from China*, para 9.22. See also WT/DS437/AB/R of 18 December 2014, *United States – Countervailing Duty Measures on Certain Products from China*, para 4.144.

[2] WT/DS267/R of 8 September 2004, *United States – Subsidies on Upland Cotton*, paras 7.1142, 7.1143 and 7.1151.

Member States – Large Civil Aircraft pointed out that this understanding of what specificity means serves as the beacon which guides the entirety of Article 2, including the question of *de facto* specificity pursuant to Article 2.1(c).[3] In the context of *de jure* specificity (see Article 2.1(a)(b)), this Panel has nuanced *US – Upland Cotton* by highlighting that a finding of specificity requires the establishment of the existence of a limitation that expressly and unambiguously restricts the availability of the subsidy to certain enterprises, and thereby does not make the subsidy sufficiently broadly available throughout an economy.[4] In other words, the subsidy is specific if, as a result of the limitation, the subsidy is no longer broadly available throughout an economy.

The question of the 'programme' underlying the subsidy is also highly relevant for the specificity analysis. If several individual legal acts constitute a programme, they should be analysed together. See *infra* pp. 178–182 and *supra* the commentary to Article 1, pp. 62–65. The notion of a 'programme' is also relevant in the context of the first *de facto* specificity factor under Article 2.1(c).

The examination of specificity follows logically after the determination of a financial contribution under Article 1.1. In *US – Large Civil Aircraft (2nd Complaint)*, the Panel, having found that there was no specificity, did not examine the financial contribution issue further. The Appellate Body gave to understand that the determination of a financial contribution under Article 1.1 was a preliminary issue on which the subsequent specificity analysis depended. According to the Appellate Body, the assessment of specificity under Article 2.1 depends on how the subsidy was defined. The Panel's *arguendo* approach (i.e. assuming that there is a financial contribution) led to an uncertainty as to what precisely the Panel assumed to be a self-standing subsidy for the purposes of the assessment of specificity.[5]

It is not necessary that the granting authority specifies all the elements of a subsidy in order to explicitly limit access to it.

There are a number of policy arguments underlying the specificity requirement. First, specific subsidies are more trade distortive than subsidies that are generally available throughout the economy. Indeed, a

[3] WT/DS316/R of 30 June 2010, *EC and certain Member States – Measures Affecting Trade in Large Civil Aircraft*, para 7.970. This aspect was not appealed.

[4] WT/DS316/R of 30 June 2010, *EC and certain Member States – Measures Affecting Trade in Large Civil Aircraft*, para 7.919. This aspect was not appealed.

[5] WT/DS353/AB/R of 12 March 2012, *United States – Measures Affecting Trade in Large Civil Aircraft (Second Complaint)*, paras 738–740 *et passim*, e.g. para 753.

subsidy provided to a limited number of beneficiaries or sectors of the economy or even to only one recipient will have a more intensive impact on the competitive situation than subsidies that are generally available.[6] However, subsidies that are generally provided across the board in a country, i.e. to all of the society and/or sectors of the economy (and thus are not specific), can also change the competitive situation of that country. Pertinent examples are e.g. subsidies for general infrastructure and education. They clearly have an effect on costs and prices in that country and can thus impact international trade. Therefore, the aspect of trade distortion is not in itself sufficient to fully justify the specificity requirement. Second, it would appear, as *Jackson* has put it, that the specificity test 'is useful as a tool of administration (albeit sometimes blunt) to get rid of a number of cases which really ought not to be brought into a countervailing duty or other international rule process'. Under this perspective, the specificity test has the function to keep general activities that all governments undertake (such as societal infrastructure like police, fire protection and road construction) outside the scope of the ASCM. In short, this perspective focuses on the correction of market failures, such as the provision of public goods.[7] The case law described in this chapter does not necessarily reflect the aforementioned two rationales.

The specificity test as designed by the ASCM is, according to some scholars, not without flaws. They claim, amongst others, that it is a poor device for identifying subsidies that are inefficient from an economic standpoint, that the treatment of regional subsidies is not coherent[8] and in more general that 'it turns in a murky way on the degree of industrial targeting'.[9]

Limitation of the Subsidy to a Certain Subgroup of Enterprises within an Industry Is Not the Relevant Benchmark

The issue discussed in this chapter has been raised under two different angles, i.e. with regard to the concept of specificity in general and when interpreting the first *de facto* specificity factor listed in Article 2.1(c) ('use of a subsidy

[6] *Jackson* (2000) pp. 296–297.
[7] *Jackson* (2000) p. 297.
[8] See, for instance, *Neven/Sykes* (2014) p. 292.
[9] *Sykes* (2010) p. 482 and p. 512 *et seq.*

programme by a limited number of certain enterprises'). The remainder of this chapter summarizes the relevant rulings concerning specificity in general while DSB findings concerning the first *de facto* specificity factor are set out *infra* in this chapter pp. 185–187. The rulings concerning these two aspects are coherent.

In *US – Softwood Lumber IV*, Canada argued that any subsidies provided for stumpage harvesters would not be specific. Canada claimed that a subsidy which consists of the provision of a good that can only be used as an input by a particular industry should not be considered to be specific unless the granting authority has deliberately limited its use to a certain subgroup of enterprises in that industry. The Panel rejected this argument because it did not see any basis for this position in the text of Article 2 in general, and Article 2.1(c) in particular. Article 2 speaks of the use of a subsidy by a limited number of certain enterprises or the predominant use by certain enterprises, not of the use by a limited number of certain eligible enterprises. In the case of a good that is provided by the government and that has utility only for certain enterprises (because of the inherent characteristics of the good), it is all the more likely that a subsidy conferred via the provision of that good is specifically provided to certain enterprises only. The Panel hastened to add that it did not consider that this would imply that any provision of a good in the form of a natural resource automatically would be specific, precisely because in some cases, the goods provided (for example oil, gas, water etc.) may be used by an indefinite number of enterprises.[10]

In the case at hand, the USDOC found that only a group of wood product industries consisting of the pulp and paper mills and the lumber industry used the stumpage programme. The Panel agreed with the US that the wood product industries constituted at most only a limited group of industries. It did not consider determinative that these industries may be producing many different end-products. Specificity is to be determined at the enterprise or industry level, not at the product level. The Panel also noted that it is not necessary that the subsidy is specific to only the producers of the product subject to the CVD investigation. In other words, the subsidy may be available also to other producers provided that all eligible producers constitute 'certain enterprises'. Nor is it required under Article 2 that the subsidy be specifically targeted at subsidizing only the subject merchandise of producers who produce both subject merchandise and non-subject

[10] WT/DS257/R of 29 August 2003, *United States – Final Countervailing Duty Determination with Respect to Certain Softwood Lumber from Canada*, para 7.116.

merchandise.[11] For instance, a subsidy paid to producers of both laptop computers and smartphones would still be specific in a CVD investigation involving only laptop computers. But see also *infra* that the concept of an industry relates to producers of certain products.[12]

The Appellate Body in *US – Carbon Steel (India)* confirmed the Panel in *US – Softwood Lumber IV*. In the former case, subsidies in the form of a provision of iron ore were considered as being *de facto* specific. India argued that such a specificity finding would have required that the subsidy is only given to a sub-set of iron ore users. Both the Panel and Appellate Body rejected India's claim. They did not see any basis for India's claim. The Appellate Body recognized that it may be that, in respect of a provision of goods, there is a greater likelihood of a finding of specificity in instances where the input good is used by only a circumscribed group of entities and/or industries. However, the Appellate Body was not persuaded by India's argument that there will necessarily be a finding of specificity with regard to every provision of a good with inherent limitations on its use due to the product characteristics.[13]

General Specificity (Article 2.1)

Chapeau of Article 2.1

Introduction

The general rules on specificity are set out in Article 2.1, which consists of a chapeau and three subparagraphs. The subparagraphs specify how

[11] WT/DS257/R of 29 August 2003, *United States – Final Countervailing Duty Determination with Respect to Certain Softwood Lumber from Canada*, para 7.117 *et seq.*

[12] WT/DS267/R of 8 September 2004, *United States – Subsidies on Upland Cotton*, para 7.1142. The Panel also pointed out: 'To us, the concept of an "industry" relates to producers of certain products. The breadth of this concept of "industry" may depend on several factors in a given case. At some point that is not made precise in the text of the agreement, and which may modulate according to particular circumstances of a given case, a subsidy would cease to be specific because it is sufficiently broadly available throughout an economy as not to benefit a particular limited group of producers of certain products. The plain words of Article 2.1 indicate that specificity is a general concept, and the breadth or narrowness of specificity is not susceptible to rigid quantitative definition.' In para 7.1151, the Panel examined whether the production in question (growers and producers of certain agricultural crops as well as – in certain regions and under certain conditions – growers and producers of livestock) was 'a sufficiently discrete segment of the United States economy in order to qualify as "specific" within the meaning of Article 2'.

[13] WT/DS436/AB/R of 8 December 2014, *United States – Countervailing Measures on Certain Hot-Rolled Carbon Steel Flat Products from India*, paras 4.391–4.398.

access to the subsidy could be limited, i.e. explicit (*de jure* specificity) or *de facto*. The chapeau clarifies first that for a subsidy to be specific, access must be limited to an enterprise or an industry, or group of enterprises or industries – both jointly referred to throughout the ASCM as 'certain enterprises'. Second, the chapeau points out that the three subparagraphs contain 'principles' (as opposed for instance to 'rules'). Third, it makes it clear that the limitation of the subsidy to certain enterprises is within the jurisdiction of the granting authority.

'Certain Enterprises'

The chapeau of Article 2.1 defines for the entire ASCM the term 'certain enterprises' as 'an enterprise or industry or group of enterprises or industries'. The Appellate Body in *US – Anti-Dumping and Countervailing Duties (China)* defined 'certain' as 'known and particularized but not explicitly identified … '. The Appellate Body referred approvingly to the definition of the term 'industry' used by the Panel in *US – Upland Cotton*. Therefore an industry or group of industries may be generally referred to by the type of products they produce. The concept of an industry relates to producers of certain products.[14] On that basis, the Appellate Body concluded that the term 'certain enterprises' referred to a single enterprise or industry or a class of enterprises or industries that are known and particularized.[15] It also recognized that the aforementioned concept involved a certain amount of indeterminacy at the edges and that a determination in this respect can only be made on a case-by-case basis.[16] The ordinary meanings of the terms 'group' and 'certain' do not indicate any numerical thresholds pointing to a minimum or maximum number in order to qualify as a 'certain group'.[17]

While Article 2.1(a) requires an explicit limitation, it does not address the related but separate question of the breadth or narrowness of the term 'certain enterprises'.[18] In *US – Upland Cotton*, the subsidy was available to approximately 100 different agricultural commodities

[14] WT/DS267/R of 8 September 2004, *United States – Subsidies on Upland Cotton*, paras 7.1142 and 7.1151. See also *supra* footnote 12.

[15] WT/DS379/AB/R of 11 March 2011, *US – Definitive Anti-Dumping and Countervailing Duties on Certain Products from China*, para 373.

[16] WT/DS379/AB/R of 11 March 2011, *US – Definitive Anti-Dumping and Countervailing Duties on Certain Products from China*, para 373.

[17] WT/DS436/AB/R of 8 December 2014, *United States – Countervailing Measures on Certain Hot-Rolled Carbon Steel Flat Products from India*, para 4.365.

[18] WT/DS379/R of 22 October 2010, *US – Definitive Anti-Dumping and Countervailing Duties on Certain Products from China*, para 9.33.

(which included crops as well as livestock). According to the Panel, this was a sufficiently discrete segment of the US economy to qualify as specific. Indeed, the subsidies were only available for a subset of agricultural products. *US – Upland Cotton* also emphasized the case-by-case nature of the analysis of the breadth of availability of the subsidy in the context of a specificity finding. The Panel cautioned against interpreting the concept of specificity too narrowly.[19] However, the Panel did not make a finding on whether a subsidy available to the agricultural sector as a whole is specific.

US – Anti-Dumping and Countervailing Duties (China) is very similar to *US – Upland Cotton*. China argued that its subsidies were available to a diversity of recipients, i.e. 539 'encouraged' industries in China spanning 26 broad sectors of economic activity (the industries in question only covered a part of each sector). According to China, any such subsidy could not be specific given the diversity of recipients and the breadth of availability of the subsidy. The Panel rejected this reasoning. The sheer diversity of economic activities supported by a given subsidy was not sufficient by itself to preclude that subsidy from being specific. Also this Panel underlined, following *US – Upland Cotton*, that the dividing line between a subsidy to which access is limited enough to be specific, as opposed to broadly enough available throughout an economy to be non-specific, is not precisely defined in the ASCM and can only be determined on a case-by-case basis.[20]

Subparagraphs (a) to (c) Contain Principles

The chapeau of Article 2.1 and the first sentence of Article 2.1(c) refer to 'principles' that apply in order to determine whether a subsidy is specific to certain enterprises. The Appellate Body in *US – Anti-Dumping and Countervailing Duties (China)* held that the use of the term 'principles' instead of, for instance, 'rules' suggests that subparagraphs (a) to (c) are to be considered within an analytical framework that recognizes and accords appropriate weight to each principle. A proper understanding of specificity must allow for a concurrent application of the three subparagraphs. The specificity analysis will ordinarily proceed in a sequential order by

[19] WT/DS267/R of 8 September 2004, *United States – Subsidies on Upland Cotton*, paras 7.1142–7.1152. See also *supra* footnote 12.

[20] WT/DS379/R of 22 October 2010, *US – Definitive Anti-Dumping and Countervailing Duties on Certain Products from China*, para 9.38 *et passim* (see in particular the example given in para 9.39). The facts of the case are described *infra* on pp. 175–176.

which subparagraph (c) is examined following the assessment under subparagraphs (a) and (b). Consequently, according to the Appellate Body, the application of one of the subparagraphs of Article 2.1 may not by itself be determinative in arriving at a conclusion that a particular subsidy is specific or is not specific. With regard to any individual subsidy there may indeed be indications pointing both to subparagraph (a) and to subparagraph (b) and the specificity analysis must accord appropriate consideration to both principles. However, the Appellate Body also recognized that there may be instances in which the evidence under consideration unequivocally indicates specificity or non-specificity under one of the subparagraphs, and in such circumstances further consideration under the other subparagraphs may be unnecessary. The Appellate Body pointed out that the examination of subparagraph (b) is not necessary if the subsidy is not specific under subparagraph (a). Note finally that this limitation of the specificity examination to an individual subparagraph of Article 2.1 does obviously not apply if, in the light of the nature and content of the measures challenged in a particular case, there is also potential to apply another subparagraph of Article 2.1.[21]

'[W]ithin the Jurisdiction of the Granting Authority'

This issue was discussed in *US – Countervailing Measures (China)*.[22]

Discriminatory Access to the Subsidy

The key question in relation to specificity is whether or not the law or the granting authority discriminates access to the subsidy among operators or sectors of the economy.[23] The central focus of the analysis under

[21] WT/DS379/AB/R of 11 March 2011, *US – Definitive Anti-Dumping and Countervailing Duties on Certain Products from China*, paras 366, 369 and 371. Confirmed in WT/DS316/AB/R of 18 May 2011, *EC and certain Member States – Measures Affecting Trade in Large Civil Aircraft*, para 950 and in WT/DS353/AB/R of 12 March 2012, *United States – Measures Affecting Trade in Large Civil Aircraft (Second Complaint)*, para 796 *et seq*., paras 873 and 876; WT/DS436/AB/R of 8 December 2014, *United States – Countervailing Measures on Certain Hot-Rolled Carbon Steel Flat Products from India*, paras 4.366–4.367; WT/DS437/AB/R of 18 December 2014, *United States – Countervailing Duty Measures on Certain Products from China*, paras 4.117–4.126, 4.130. See also WT/DS436/R of 14 July 2014, *United States – Countervailing Measures on Certain Hot-Rolled Carbon Steel Flat Products from India*, para 7.119.

[22] WT/DS437/AB/R of 18 December 2014, *United States – Countervailing Duty Measures on Certain Products from China*, paras 4.164–4.173.

[23] See WT/DS379/AB/R of 11 March 2011, *US – Definitive Anti-Dumping and Countervailing Duties on Certain Products from China*, para 367. But see WT/DS436/AB/R of 8 December

subparagraphs (a) and (b) of Article 2.1 are the eligibility requirements for the subsidy in the particular legal instrument or the government conduct. In other words, it does not matter for the specificity analysis under these two subparagraphs whether a subsidy has been *granted* to certain enterprises. What matters is whether *access* has been explicitly limited. The examination must seek to discern from the legislation and/or the express acts of the granting authority(ies) which enterprises are eligible to receive the subsidy and which are not.[24]

US – Countervailing Measures (China) has highlighted that a specificity analysis focuses not only on whether a subsidy has been provided to particular recipients, but also on all enterprises or industries eligible to receive that same subsidy. As such, an inquiry into whether a particular subsidy is specific to certain enterprises may require determining what other enterprises or industries also have access to that same subsidy under that subsidy scheme. Therefore, it is relevant to consider not only the actual, but also the past and potential recipients of a particular subsidy.[25]

In *Japan – DRAMs (Korea)*, Korea argued that the restructurings of Hynix were made using the same procedures and on the same terms that were generally available to other companies in a similar condition. Hence, the restructurings should not be classified as being specific because they were limited to one company. These terms, conditions and procedures were, *inter alia*, provided for in the Korean Corporate Restructurings Promotion Act. Korea claimed by focusing on Hynix only, the Japanese investigating authority missed the broader picture. Rather, Japan should have assessed the restructurings at the level of the Korean Corporate Restructuring Promotion Act. The Panel rejected Korea's arguments. In the view of the Panel, the aforementioned Act merely provided the procedural framework within which the October 2001 and the December 2002 Hynix restructurings took place, rather than actually determining the terms of those restructurings. The evidence on the record indicated that the substantive terms of restructurings were the prerogative of the Councils for Creditor Financial

2014, *United States – Countervailing Measures on Certain Hot-Rolled Carbon Steel Flat Products from India*, paras 4.381–4.390 and *infra* in this chapter, pp. 183–185.

[24] WT/DS379/AB/R of 11 March 2011, *US – Definitive Anti-Dumping and Countervailing Duties on Certain Products from China*, para 368; WT/DS353/AB/R of 12 March 2012, *United States – Measures Affecting Trade in Large Civil Aircraft (Second Complaint)*, paras 750 and 753.

[25] For details see WT/DS437/AB/R of 18 December 2014, *United States – Countervailing Duty Measures on Certain Products from China*, para 4.140.

Institutions, which were set up for each restructured company separately. The Panel also added that in general, subsidies which were provided pursuant to government entrustment or direction motivated by an intention to save a single company, as was the case here, might reasonably be found to be specific to that company.[26]

De jure *Specificity (Article 2.1(a) and (b))*

Introduction

The focus of the inquiry under subparagraph (a) is whether the legislation or the granting authority explicitly limits access to a subsidy to certain enterprises. An explicit limitation points to *de jure* specificity. Subparagraph (b) narrows the scope of *de jure* specificity as defined in subparagraph (a) by stipulating that specificity shall not exist if the legislation or the granting authority establish objective criteria or conditions governing the eligibility for, and the amount of, the subsidy. The exemption set out in subparagraph (b) (i.e. objective criteria concerning eligibility and the amount of subsidies) is, however, only applicable if three conditions are met:

- Eligibility for the subsidy must be automatic.
- Criteria and conditions concerning eligibility must be strictly adhered to.
- The criteria or conditions must be clearly spelled out in the law, regulation or other official document, so as to be capable of verification.

Despite the finding in *US – Anti-Dumping and Countervailing Duties (China)* that the subparagraphs (a) to (c) contain principles and should be applied concurrently (see *supra* pp. 167–168) the relationship between subparagraphs (a) and (b) is probably not fully elucidated yet.[27]

The subsequent sections explain in more detail the following:

- when the limitation in the access to the subsidy is 'explicit';
- the notions of 'granting authority' and 'legislation';

[26] WT/DS336/R of 13 July 2007, *Japan – Countervailing Duties on Dynamic Random Access Memories from Korea*, para 7.362 *et seq.*

[27] See *Coppens* (2014) pp. 106–107 with references to WT/DS316/AB/R of 18 May 2011, *EC and certain Member States – Measures Affecting Trade in Large Civil Aircraft*, para 951 (this case is also described *infra* this chapter, pp. 176–178), and WT/DS353/AB/R of 12 March 2012, *United States – Measures Affecting Trade in Large Civil Aircraft (Second Complaint)*, para 857.

- the type of 'discretion' that is compatible with the requirement that the eligibility for the subsidy must be 'automatic'.

'Explicitly'

The text of Article 2.1(a) requires that the limitation in the access to the subsidy must be explicit. A subsidy is specific according to Article 2.1(a) if either the legislation or the granting authority explicitly limits access to the subsidy to certain enterprises.

A typical example of a subsidy that is explicitly limited to certain enterprises can be found in *EC and certain Member States – Large Civil Aircraft*: the *ad hoc* equity infusions in question were limited to Aérospatiale, i.e. an Airbus parent company.[28]

In *US – Anti-Dumping and Countervailing Duties (China)*, the question was what the word 'explicitly' meant. The Appellate Body held that there is an 'explicit' limitation on access to the subsidy to certain enterprises if this limitation is 'express, unambiguous or clear from the content of the relevant instrument, and not merely 'implied' or 'suggested'.[29]

An explicit limitation on access to the subsidy is only required in relation to 'certain enterprises'. There are many ways in which access to a subsidy can be explicitly limited. The necessary limitation on access to the subsidy can be effected through an explicit limitation on access to the financial contribution, on access to the benefit or on access to both. However, it is not a precondition for a subsidy that the granting authority or the legislation explicitly limits access *both* to the financial contribution *and* to its corresponding benefit. In sum, what must be made explicit under Article 2.1(a) is the limitation on access to the subsidy to certain enterprises, regardless of how the explicit limitation is established. According to the Appellate Body, the purpose of Article 2 is not to identify the elements of a subsidy as set out in Article 1.1, but to establish whether the availability of the subsidy is limited *inter alia* by reason of the eligible recipients (Article 2.1(a)) or by reason of geographical location of beneficiaries (Article 2.2).[30] The Panel gave a number of

[28] WT/DS316/R of 30 June 2010, *EC and certain Member States – Measures Affecting Trade in Large Civil Aircraft*, para 1379. This aspect was not appealed.

[29] WT/DS379/AB/R of 11 March 2011, *US – Definitive Anti-Dumping and Countervailing Duties on Certain Products from China*, para 372 *et seq.* WT/DS316/R of 30 June 2010, *EC and certain Member States – Measures Affecting Trade in Large Civil Aircraft*, para 7.919 has adopted a very similar definition. This aspect of the Panel's ruling was not appealed.

[30] WT/DS379/AB/R of 11 March 2011, *US – Definitive Anti-Dumping and Countervailing Duties on Certain Products from China*, para 374 *et seq.*, para 408 *et seq.*

examples to illustrate this point although they ultimately appear not to be convincing.[31]

'[G]ranting Authority, or the Legislation Pursuant to Which the Granting Authority Operates' Limits Access

According to the Appellate Body, the reference in subparagraphs (a) and (b) to 'granting authority, or the legislation pursuant to which the granting authority operates' is critical because it situates the analysis for assessing any limitations on eligibility in the particular legal instrument or government conduct effecting such limitation. In other words, the source of any limitation is the legislation pursuant to which the granting authority operates, or the granting authority itself.

The relationship between 'granting authority' and 'legislation' was at issue in *US – Large Civil Aircraft (2nd Complaint)*. The EU argued that specificity under Article 2.1 may be assessed either from the perspective of the 'granting authority' or from the perspective of 'the legislation pursuant to which the granting authority operates'. According to the Appellate Body, Article 2.1 did not establish such a mutually exclusive choice. In the majority of cases involving an allegation of an express limitation, the alleged limitation will be reflected in the legislation pursuant to which the granting authority operates. It is difficult to conceive of many situations in which an express limitation can be identified from the decisions or actions of the granting authority where such limitation is not explicit in the corresponding legislation. Furthermore, even where the focus is on the pronouncements or actions of the granting authority, these pronouncements or actions would have to be examined in the light of the corresponding legislation. For this reason, the Appellate Body held the view that the assessment of specificity under Article 2.1 should not proceed on the basis of a binary choice between looking at the granting authority or looking at the legislation. Rather, the assessment should normally look at both.[32]

What legal instruments and/or what actions by the granting authority have to be analysed depends on the particular circumstances of the case. This analysis is, however, framed by the particular subsidy that has been

[31] WT/DS379/R of 22 October 2010, *US – Definitive Anti-Dumping and Countervailing Duties on Certain Products from China*, para 9.27.

[32] WT/DS353/AB/R of 12 March 2012, *United States – Measures Affecting Trade in Large Civil Aircraft (Second Complaint)*, paras 755–760.

found pursuant to Article 1.1. For a pertinent example in this respect, see the analysis of the allocation of patent rights to Boeing in *US – Large Civil Aircraft (2nd Complaint)* (see *infra* in this chapter, pp. 178–181.

Automatic Eligibility Versus Discretion

In *EC and certain Member States – Large Civil Aircraft*, the US claimed that loans given by the European Investment Bank (EIB) are *de jure* specific because the Bank explicitly limits access to its loans by negotiating them individually, and by granting them on a discretionary basis on terms and conditions that are not pre-determined, but tailored to each individual project. The US considered that the panel findings in *Japan – DRAMS* supported their claim. The Panel did not agree for the following reasons:

- It rejected *Japan – DRAMS (Korea)* to the extent that it held that the application of discretion would automatically lead to *de jure* specificity (see *supra* pp. 168–170). The Panel recalled that *Japan – DRAMS (Korea)* did not specify as to which precise paragraph or sub-paragraph of Article 2 it referred – the statements related to the notion of specificity under Article 2.1 as a whole. It then noted that *Japan – DRAMS (Korea)* viewed as determinative for a specificity finding the existence of discretion (i.e. a conscious decision) when a subsidy is granted to an individual company under a generally available subsidy programme. The Panel went on to say that if this were the correct standard for finding a subsidy *de jure* specific, the implication would be that all subsidies would be explicitly specific under Article 2.1(a) if they are granted to certain enterprises on the basis of the exercise of discretion, irrespective of how that discretion was actually exercised. This would not sit well with Article 2.1(c) where the exercise of discretion does not automatically lead to *de facto* specificity. Rather, according to the latter provision, what matters is the manner in which a granting authority exercises its discretion.
- The contractual terms and conditions of the EIB loans are to a large degree prescribed *ex ante* in its standard templates. Where dates and values are left blank in the contract templates, methodologies are in some cases described for arriving at the relevant figure(s), or other general guidance is given to finalize the relevant clauses.
- A number of factual differences exist between *Japan – DRAMS (Korea)* and *EC and certain Member States – Large Civil Aircraft*.

- The EIB's lending objectives,[33] although very broad, do establish an explicit limitation on its lending activities, but these limitations do not result in a limitation on the availability of the loans to 'certain enterprises'. In the Panel's view, the wide array of economic sectors covered by the EIB's explicit lending objectives means that its operations are expressly intended to benefit recipients well beyond a particular enterprise or industry or group of enterprises or industries. Moreover, the fact that the loans given by the EIB to Airbus (and other borrowing entities) may contain one or more terms and conditions that are not exactly the same, does not render access to those loans explicitly limited to particular recipients.[34]

How to Carry Out a *de jure* Specificity Analysis?

The Panel in *US – Anti-Dumping and Countervailing Duties (China)* described how a *de jure* specificity analysis has to be carried out. First, the investigating authority has to establish, on the basis of evidence, whether the various documents identified 'certain enterprises'. Obviously, the industry whose exports are examined in the CVD investigation (in this case off-road tyres from China) has to be part of the 'certain enterprises' that benefit from the subsidy in question. Thus, in the circumstances of the case, the first step could consist in establishing for instance that documents in relation to government plans identify the tyre industry as beneficiary of subsidized loan financing in order to foster its development. Second, in the case of the aforementioned loan scenario, it has to be examined whether the banks (which were considered as public bodies in the case in question) were acting pursuant to the prescriptions of the planning documents when they provided the loan financing to the industry under investigation. Any panel reviewing the findings of an investigating authority will review whether the findings under both steps are supported by sufficient evidence.[35] The review by a panel must not be a *de novo* review of the evidence but should be a 'critical and searching' examination.[36] Clearly, the nature of the relevant evidence will depend on the particular measures and the government structure in the exporting

[33] See WT/DS316/R of 30 June 2010, *EC and certain Member States – Measures Affecting Trade in Large Civil Aircraft*, paras 7.904–7.905.

[34] WT/DS316/R of 30 June 2010, *EC and certain Member States – Measures Affecting Trade in Large Civil Aircraft*, paras 7.918–7.935. This aspect was not appealed.

[35] WT/DS379/R of 22 October 2010, *US – Definitive Anti-Dumping and Countervailing Duties on Certain Products from China*, para 9.47.

[36] WT/DS379/R of 22 October 2010, *US – Definitive Anti-Dumping and Countervailing Duties on Certain Products from China*, para 9.50 *et seq.*

country. In some cases, e.g. where eligibility of the subsidy is limited by a law, e.g. to the textile sector, the analysis will be more straightforward.

See also *infra* in this chapter, pp. 178–181.

Examples in Which an Explicit Limitation on Access to the Subsidy Was Examined

US – Anti-Dumping and Countervailing Duties (China): **Preferential Lending** The USDOC found that China's preferential lending to its off-road tyre industry was *de jure* specific because a number of central, provincial and municipal laws, plans and policies explicitly limited access to these subsidies to this industry. Both the Panel and the Appellate Body upheld this conclusion. However, it is not easy to reconstruct precisely the reasoning of both the Panel and the Appellate Body in this respect. Two issues can perhaps be distinguished.

First, does it play a role that Chinese State-owned commercial banks (SOCB) gave preferential loans not only to so-called encouraged industries (to which the Chinese off-road tyre industry belonged, i.e. the industry whose exports to the US were subject to the contested CVD measures), but also to other industries? The Chinese planning system in question distinguished four categories of industries, i.e. encouraged, restricted, eliminated and permitted projects/industries. SOCB were instructed to provide financing to encouraged industries. China argued that the fact that SOCB were instructed to provide financing to encouraged projects did not, by its own terms, identify an explicit *limitation of access* to the relevant financial contribution. China underlined that SOCB also provided loans to the industries under the permitted category, i.e. industries that are neither encouraged, restricted nor eliminated. Therefore, according to China, the financial contribution was not specific because it was not explicitly limited to encouraged industries but also open to permitted industries. The Appellate Body did not accept this because the laws and policy documents under consideration were silent as to how financial institutions were to conduct themselves with regard to industries falling under the permitted category. In other words, it was not found that the projects and industries under the 'permitted' category were eligible to receive the same loans as the encouraged projects and industries.[37]

[37] WT/DS379/AB/R of 11 March 2011, *US – Definitive Anti-Dumping and Countervailing Duties on Certain Products from China*, paras 379–385.

Second, the Panel's confirmation of the USDOC's approach seems to contain two different strands of reasoning both of which seem relevant to address China's provision of loans. The USDOC based its finding of specificity on the totality of evidence on the record. This evidence consisted of a number of documents related to central, provincial and municipal levels. The USDOC concluded that the off-road tyre industry was explicitly identified in the planning documents at all government levels as a target for the development and that all financial institutions were instructed to provide financing to that industry. The Panel and the Appellate Body accepted that all the documents, taken together, demonstrated a clear lending policy directed to favour the tyre industry.[38] Moreover, the Panel embarked also upon an examination of the so-called Government of China catalogue that established the specific projects falling under the encouraged, restricted and eliminated categories. The Panel considered this catalogue as mandatory and that a principal function of this catalogue was the allocation of loan financing by financial institutions. As the three aforementioned categories did not describe all economic activity – there was also a permitted category covering all remaining activities not falling under the three categories contained in the catalogue – the Panel held that a reasonable and objective investigating authority could conclude that the encouraged projects constitute a sufficiently discrete segment of the economy as to be limited to 'certain enterprises'. The Appellate Body, while upholding the Panel's finding of specificity, took issue with the latter approach by the Panel as this did not mirror the USDOC's determination (which was based on the totality of the evidence on file and not only on the investment catalogue).[39] It seems that this part of the Panel's analysis was perhaps not really necessary as the first line of the Panel's reasoning provided already a sufficient basis to dispose of China's claim.

Subsidies Granted to Airbus under the EC's Second to Sixth Framework Programmes The legal regime of these programmes consisted of several layers. First, the decision establishing the Framework Programme sets out overall guidelines but does not indicate how funds authorized

[38] WT/DS379/AB/R of 11 March 2011, *US – Definitive Anti-Dumping and Countervailing Duties on Certain Products from China*, paras 399–401 and paras 391–394.

[39] WT/DS379/AB/R of 11 March 2011, *US – Definitive Anti-Dumping and Countervailing Duties on Certain Products from China*, paras 389–398. See also the description of the Investment catalogue by the preceding Panel *supra* in this chapter, pp. 160–167.

under the programme can be accessed by individual applicants. Second, there are decisions concerning specific programmes in order to implement the Framework Programmes. These specific programmes contained detailed rules and methodologies for the distribution of funds. There were also specific programmes for 'aeronautics' or 'aeronautics and space', i.e. an amount of funding dedicated to research to these sectors was provided for under each of the relevant Framework Programmes. Third, there were work programmes and calls for proposals in order to implement the specific programmes. The Panel noted that the effect of allocations to 'aeronautics' or 'aeronautics and space' was equivalent to setting aside a portion of the total budget of the Framework Programme that was ostensibly intended to fund research activities in all sectors of the economy, for the sole purpose of the research efforts of enterprises in the aeronautics sector. Thus, the legal regimes explicitly limited access to the dedicated portion of budgeted funds only to these enterprises or industries undertaking research in the field of aeronautics and were therefore specific pursuant to Article 2.1(a). In other words, there was a closed system of subsidization that focused on 'aeronautics' and 'aeronautics and space'.

On appeal, the EU argued that the Panel was required to rely on the Framework Programmes as a whole as a benchmark for determining the existence of specificity. Therefore, the specificity does not result from the allocation of funding to aeronautics-related research as the Framework Programme as a whole establishes a broad-based allocation that ensures equal access to a wide range of sectors and enterprises. The funding amounts allocated to the aeronautics sector could not be accessed by entities seeking support for projects other than those concerning aeronautics while entities involved in aeronautics could not access funds under the remainder (and great majority) of the Framework Programme budgets.

The Appellate Body rejected the appeal. It did not accept that explicit limitations on access to a subsidy to entities active in one sector of the economy could be compensated by virtue of the fact that separate groupings of entities have access to other pools of funding under that programme. In short, where access to certain funding under a subsidy programme is explicitly limited to a grouping of enterprises or industries that qualify as 'certain enterprises' this leads to a provisional indication of specificity under Article 2.1(a), irrespective of how other funding under that programme is distributed. The Appellate Body then tested this provisional indication of specificity found under Article 2.1(a) by analysing the claim under Article 2.1(b). However, it did not find any objective criteria that could have led to a reversal of the provisional conclusion found under Article 2.1(a).[40]

However, in the same dispute the Panel found that subsidies under the Spanish PROFIT I and II given to the aeronautics industry were not *de jure* specific. Like the EU's Framework Programmes, PROFIT was an umbrella programme that supported a wide range of different research areas. One of the numerous sub-programmes concerned research in the aeronautics sector. Unlike the EU's Framework Programme, PROFIT did not provide for ring-fencing of funds for particular sub-programmes. Therefore, the entirety of the funding available under the umbrella programme was, in principle, accessible for eligible projects under any particular sub-programme and thus not *de jure* specific. The Panel also pointed out that funds that are, on the face of it, available to all projects equally under an umbrella subsidy programme might in substance be ring-fenced for a particular purpose or industry sector, if, for instance, different decision-making procedures or eligibility criteria apply without justification to limit the availability of funds to 'certain enterprises'.[41] The UK Technology Programme was also not found to be *de jure* specific on the basis that funding was not reserved for the aeronautics industry.[42]

Launch Aid Granted to Airbus This aid was found to be specific pursuant to Article 2.1(a). Each of the launch aid contracts concluded between Airbus and the Airbus government in question involved a unique transfer of funds to one particular company, i.e. Airbus, and was consequently limited to 'certain enterprises'.[43]

Allocation of Patent Rights to Boeing under NASA and US Department of Defense Contracts In *US – Large Civil Aircraft (2nd Complaint)*,

[40] WT/DS316/AB/R of 18 May 2011, *EC and certain Member States – Measures Affecting Trade in Large Civil Aircraft*, paras 937–952. This finding contrasts with the Panel ruling in the EU's European Investment Bank loans, see *supra* in this chapter, pp. 173–174.

[41] WT/DS316/R of 30 June 2010, *EC and certain Member States – Measures Affecting Trade in Large Civil Aircraft*, para 7.1571 *et seq.* The PROFIT programme was, however, found to be specific pursuant to Article 2.1(c) because the EU did not furnish sufficient information neither in the Annex V process nor in response to a question posed by the Panel. This aspect was not appealed.

[42] WT/DS316/R of 30 June 2010, *EC and certain Member States – Measures Affecting Trade in Large Civil Aircraft*, para 7.1584 *et seq.* This aspect was not appealed.

[43] WT/DS316/R of 30 June 2010, *EC and certain Member States – Measures Affecting Trade in Large Civil Aircraft*, para 7.497.

Boeing obtained patent rights as a result of the research conducted under the aforementioned contracts. However, the technical transfer of the patent rights to Boeing was not provided for in the contracts it concluded with NASA and the USDOC. Rather, the transfer was the result of 'patent waivers' that were administered centrally (one for NASA and one for the remaining US Federal Government) and that applied in relation to research conducted for federal agencies. The Panel assumed for the sake of argument that the allocation of patent rights under the waivers was in some respects a self-standing subsidy that is separate from the payments under the contracts. But it concluded that such subsidy would not be *de jure* specific.

The Appellate Body proceeded somewhat reluctantly on the basis of the Panel's assumption about the self-standing nature of the subsidy although it fully agreed with the Panel's conclusion that such subsidy would not be *de jure* specific. This finding was based on an analysis of the legislative and regulatory framework that applied to R&D activities performed by all enterprises for US government departments and agencies. In other words, the analysis was not limited to the work carried out by Boeing for NASA and the US Department of Defense. It accepted that it does not amount to *de jure* specificity if the legislative framework is administered by a number of granting authorities and if authority-specific regulations are merely measures implementing the broader legislation pursuant to which these authorities operate. The Appellate Body noted that all enterprises performing R&D for the US government in all industry sectors have been and are granted patent rights over their inventions discovered as a result of the research. The allocation of patent rights under the NASA and US Department of Defense contracts operates within a legislative and regulatory framework that applies to R&D activities performed by all enterprises in all sectors in respect of all US government departments and agencies. The Appellate Body also underlined that the patent rights allocation did not present the same 'compartmentalization' of funding to aeronautics R&D as under the EC Framework Programmes in *EC and certain Member States – Large Civil Aircraft*. The following parts of the Appellate Body's reasoning merit particular attention:

> 749. Article 2.1(a) refers to limitations on access to 'a subsidy'. Although the use of this term in the singular might suggest a limited conception, we note that, if construed too narrowly, any individual subsidy transaction would be, by definition, specific to the recipient. Other context in Article 2.1 suggests a potentially broader framework within which to examine specificity. As we have noted, subparagraphs (a) and (b) of Article 2.1 refer

to 'the granting authority, or the legislation pursuant to which the granting authority operates'. The second sentence of subparagraph (c) refers both to 'a subsidy' and to 'a subsidy programme'. Similarly, examining economic diversification or the duration of a subsidy programme under the last sentence of Article 2.1(c) also entails consideration of the broader framework pursuant to which a particular challenged subsidy has been issued. We do not consider that the use of the term 'granting authority' in the singular limits the inquiry. The use of the term 'granting authority', in our view, does not preclude there being multiple granting authorities. Rather, this is likely where a subsidy is part of a broader scheme.

750. The foregoing indicates that the scope of the inquiry called for under Article 2.1(a) is not necessarily limited to the subsidy as defined in Article 1.1. Although the subsidy as defined in Article 1.1 is the starting point of the analysis under Article 2.1(a), the scope of the inquiry is broader in the sense that it must examine the legislation pursuant to which the granting authority operates, or the express acts of the granting authority. We note that a granting authority will normally administer subsidies pursuant to legislation. Thus, we would expect that most claims of specificity under Article 2.1(a) would focus on limitations set out in the legislation pursuant to which the granting authority operates. Members may design the legal framework for the distribution of subsidies in many ways. However, the choice of the legal framework by the respondent cannot predetermine the outcome of the specificity analysis. For instance, a Member may choose to authorize the distribution of subsidies to eligible enterprises or industries in the same legal instrument. In such cases, the inquiry may focus solely on that legal instrument. In other circumstances, a Member may set up a more complex regime by which the same subsidy is provided to different recipients through different legal instruments. It may also be that a Member may administer the distribution of subsidies through multiple granting authorities. In these cases, the inquiry may have to take into account this legal framework. This framework may be set out in laws, regulations, or other official documents, all of which may be part of the 'legislation' pursuant to which the granting authority operates. We find support for this reading of 'legislation' in Article 2.1(b), which provides that, '{w}here the granting authority, or the legislation pursuant to which the granting authority operates, establishes objective criteria or conditions governing the eligibility for, and the amount of, a subsidy' [note omitted], these criteria or conditions 'must be clearly spelled out in law, regulation, or other official document, so as to be capable of verification'.

751. Having said that, the chapeau of Article 2.1 makes it clear that the assessment of specificity is framed by the particular subsidy found to exist under Article 1.1. This means that the assessment of specificity under Article 2.1 should not examine subsidies that are different from those challenged by the complaining Member. A subsidy, access to which is limited to 'certain enterprises', does not become non-specific merely because there

are other subsidies that are provided to other enterprises pursuant to the same legislation. [note omitted]

752. Determining whether multiple subsidies are part of the same subsidy is not always a clear-cut exercise. As we have explained, it requires careful scrutiny of the relevant legislation – whether set out in one or several instruments – or the pronouncements of the granting authority(ies) to determine whether the subsidies are provided pursuant to the same subsidy scheme. Another factor that may be considered is whether there is an overarching purpose behind the subsidies. Of course, this overarching purpose must be something more concrete than a vague policy of providing assistance or promoting economic growth.[44]

Individual Legal Acts Versus Programmes – Washington Special Business and Occupation Tax Rates for the Aircraft Industry *US – Large Civil Aircraft (2nd Complaint)* also had to examine the question of *de jure* specificity. The state of Washington had special preferential Business and Occupation tax rates for the aircraft industry which had been found to be subsidies. The US argued that these subsidies were not specific because the Panel should have examined the special rates for the aircraft industry together with the other differential Business and Occupation tax rates as part of the same subsidy programme and it should have given consideration to the fact that such differential rates were all contained in the Washington State Tax Code. The Appellate Body did not agree with the US. Where multiple subsidies are part of the same subsidy scheme, one would expect to find links or commonalities between those subsidies. It was true that the Washington State Business and Occupation Tax stipulated that a number of manufacturing activities (such as manufacturing wheat into flour, manufacturing semi-conductors and nuclear fuel assemblies, manufacturing of timber etc.) were subject to differential rates. However, the Appellate Body noted that the Washington State Tax Code reflected a gradual accumulation of tax rate adjustments over time, each implemented through separate pieces of legislation. The fact that a series of differential taxes are located in the same section of the tax code cannot be dispositive as to whether they constitute part of the same subsidy scheme for purposes of the specificity analysis under Article 2.1(a). The amendment that introduced the differential rate for aircraft manufacturing was

[44] WT/DS353/AB/R of 12 March 2012, *United States – Measures Affecting Trade in Large Civil Aircraft (Second Complaint)*, paras 749–752, 761–789. See also *infra* in this chapter, p. 193 and *Bohanes/Rueda Garcia* (2012/1) p. 376.

not enacted as part of a broader subsidy scheme. It stated that the differential rate was aimed at retaining and attracting the aerospace industry to Washington State. While some of the other differential tax rates were designed to retain certain business activities in Washington State, others appeared to have been adopted for entirely different purposes, e.g. to address low profit margins experienced by firms in those industries.[45] In other words, while the Appellate Body examined the broader framework both with regard to the Business and Occupation Tax and the grant of patent rights under NASA and US Department of Defense contracts in order to determine whether access to the financial contribution was limited to certain enterprises, it did find *de jure* specificity in the former case but not in the latter.

More generally, the question may arise whether several individual subsidies within a single piece of legislation or measure should be analysed together or separately. The Panel in *China – GOES* concluded that a subsidy programme should be considered as a whole. The programme should define the breadth of the specificity analysis, rather than the legislation through which it was enacted. Otherwise, a broadly available subsidy programme could be found to be specific if extended to each industry through separate pieces of legislation.[46]

US – Offset Act (Byrd Amendment) Neither the Byrd Amendment nor any disbursements under the Byrd Amendment were considered as being specific. Payments were available in principle to any US producer of any product on which anti-dumping or anti-subsidy duties would be collected. The Panel also pointed out that the source of funding for disbursements under the Byrd Amendment (i.e. duties paid by US importers) was not relevant.[47]

[45] WT/DS353/AB/R of 12 March 2012, *United States – Measures Affecting Trade in Large Civil Aircraft (Second Complaint)*, paras 838–858. The criteria developed by the preceding Panel were perhaps somewhat more precise than the test applied by the Appellate Body. The Panel opined that if the differential Business and Occupational tax rates were truly implemented as part of a common subsidy programme, it would be reasonable to expect some links between the individual tax reductions, for example, in the timing of their introduction, in their purpose or in their levels (see WT/DS353/R of 31 March 2011, *United States – Measures Affecting Trade in Large Civil Aircraft (Second Complaint)*, para 7.205).

[46] WT/DS414/R of 15 June 2012, *China – Countervailing and Anti-Dumping Duties on Grain-Oriented Flat-Rolled Electrical Steel from the US*, para 7.108 *et seq.*

[47] WT/DS217/R and WT/DS234/R of 16 September 2002 – *United States – Continued Dumping and Subsidy Offset Act of 2000*, paras 7.108–7.116. For a description of the functioning of the Byrd Amendment see *infra* the commentary to Article 32, pp. 596–598.

De facto Specificity (Article 2.1 (c))

Introduction

The inquiry under Article 2.1(c) focuses on whether a subsidy, although not apparently limited to certain enterprises, is nevertheless allocated in a manner that belies the apparent neutrality of the measure. This inquiry requires an examination of the reasons as to why the actual allocation of amounts of subsidies differs from an allocation that would be expected if the subsidy were administered in accordance with the conditions for eligibility for that subsidy.[48] Put differently, while a *de jure* analysis examines concrete evidence relating to explicit limitations on access to the subsidy in the legal instruments or by the granting authority, a *de facto* analysis focuses on indicia of such limitations.[49] As *US – Carbon Steel (India)* put it most pertinently, the focus of Article 2.1(c) is on *de facto* circumstances surrounding the use of the subsidy.[50]

Article 2.1(c) does not require a finding of discrimination between 'certain enterprises' and other, similarly situated enterprises. In *US – Carbon Steel (India)*, India essentially argued that in order for a subsidy to be specific, the recipients and some category of non-recipients of the subsidy must be 'like' or 'similarly situated'. Both the Panel and the Appellate Body did not accept India's argument as it was not in line with the text of Article 2 nor with the aim of determining whether the subsidy is specific to 'certain enterprises' under Article 2.1.[51]

Subparagraph (c) has a curious structure. It stipulates that if, notwithstanding the appearance of non-specificity pursuant to subparagraphs (a) and (b), there are reasons to believe that the subsidy may in fact be specific, other factors may be considered. It then lists four such factors:

- use of a subsidy programme by a limited number of certain enterprises;
- predominant use by certain enterprises;
- granting of disproportionately large subsidy amounts to certain enterprises;

[48] WT/DS353/AB/R of 12 March 2012, *United States – Measures Affecting Trade in Large Civil Aircraft (Second Complaint)*, para 877.

[49] WT/DS436/AB/R of 8 December 2014, *United States – Countervailing Measures on Certain Hot-Rolled Carbon Steel Flat Products from India*, para 4.373.

[50] WT/DS436/AB/R of 8 December 2014, *United States – Countervailing Measures on Certain Hot-Rolled Carbon Steel Flat Products from India*, paras 4.391–4.398.

[51] WT/DS436/AB/R of 8 December 2014, *United States – Countervailing Measures on Certain Hot-Rolled Carbon Steel Flat Products from India*, paras 4.381–4.390.

- manner in which discretion has been exercised by the granting authority in the decision to grant a subsidy.

However, this list of four factors is not exhaustive. The last sentence then adds that in applying subparagraph (c), account shall be taken of the extent of diversification of economic activities within the jurisdiction of the granting authority, as well as the length of time during which the subsidy programme has been in operation.

Which of the four factors are relevant to the analysis of specificity under subparagraph (c) will be a function of what reasons there are to believe that the subsidy may in fact be specific. The conclusion may, depending on the circumstances of the case, rely on the assessment of one, several or all of the factors listed in subparagraph (c) and an investigating authority must remain open to the applicability of each of the elements in this subparagraph.[52]

One will normally examine subparagraph (c) after it has been determined that there are no explicit limitations pursuant to subparagraph (a) as to which enterprises or industries have access to the subsidy. However, there may be more special configurations where the analysis stops with the examination of subparagraph (a) or where it might be appropriate to limit the analysis to an examination of subparagraph (c). The first of these special configurations was at issue in a DSB proceeding about actionable subsidies, i.e. where the panel was the first trier of facts. According to the Appellate Body, a panel must consider whether, in the light of the arguments made by the parties, there are 'reasons' for it to believe that an assessment under Article 2.1(c) is warranted. These reasons would have to relate to the factors mentioned in subparagraph (c). However, where the panel finds that the arguments and evidence submitted by the parties do not sufficiently demonstrate reasons to indicate specificity under Article 2.1(c), a more exhaustive analysis of the specificity factors set out in that provision may not be warranted.[53] The second configuration was at issue in a US countervailing duty investigation. China argued that the US investigating authority should have first examined subparagraphs (a) and (b)

[52] WT/DS353/AB/R of 12 March 2012, *United States – Measures Affecting Trade in Large Civil Aircraft (Second Complaint)*, para 878; WT/DS436/AB/R of 8 December 2014, *United States – Countervailing Measures on Certain Hot-Rolled Carbon Steel Flat Products from India*, para 4.369.

[53] WT/DS353/AB/R of 12 March 2012, *United States – Measures Affecting Trade in Large Civil Aircraft (Second Complaint)*, paras 796–797.

before looking into *de facto* specificity. The Appellate Body disagreed. It held that there may be circumstances where the analysis can go straight to subparagraph (c) without first examining subparagraphs (a) and (b); for instance, when the subsidy is given pursuant to an unwritten measure. In other words, to analyse specificity exclusively under Article 2.1(c) is not necessarily inconsistent with the ASCM, despite the language at the beginning of this subparagraph which states 'notwithstanding any appearance of non-specificity resulting from the application of the principles laid down in subparagraphs (a) and (b) ... '.[54]

A straightforward example of *de facto* specificity can be found in *EC – Countervailing Measures on DRAM Chips*. Korea applied the so-called KDB Debenture Programme. The EU considered all four factors mentioned in Article 2.1(c) and concluded that under all four factors the programme was *de facto* specific to Hynix, the subsidized exporter in question. It determined:

- The subsidy programme was used by a very limited number of companies, as only six out of an eligible 200 companies used the programme.
- It was predominantly used by the Hyundai group to which Hynix belonged.
- A disproportionate 41 per cent of the total subsidy amount was granted to Hynix.
- There was considerable criticism within Korea from companies in similarly difficult situations complaining about the lack of transparency and the eligibility criteria.

The Panel agreed with the EU's assessment.[55]

The Four *de facto* Specificity Factors Listed in Subparagraph (c)

'[U]se of a Subsidy Programme by a Limited Number of Certain Enterprises' This factor was first discussed in *US – Carbon Steel (India)*. India argued that it is not sufficient for a subsidy to be *de facto* specific if it is only available to 'certain enterprises'. Rather, the use of the words 'limited number' in conjunction with 'of certain enterprises' suggests a 'sub-set – super-set' relationship. In other words, a limited number of users of

[54] WT/DS437/AB/R of 18 December 2014, *United States – Countervailing Duty Measures on Certain Products from China*, paras 4.117–4.126, 4.130. See also *supra* pp. 167–168.

[55] WT/DS299/R of 17 June 2005, *European Communities – Countervailing Measures on Dynamic Random Access Memory Chips from Korea*, paras 7.223–7.232.

the subsidies must be understood as forming a subset of certain enterprises. India pointed out that in the case in question 'certain enterprises' were users of iron ore. Consequently, Article 2.7(c) required that the US investigating authority should have demonstrated that the alleged subsidy programme was used by a limited number of entities within the set of users of iron ore. Both Panel and Appellate Body rejected India's interpretation. The Appellate Body considered, *inter alia*, that a better reading of the term 'limited number of certain enterprises' simply refers to the quantity of certain enterprises that must be found to have used the subsidy programme in order to indicate the existence of *de facto* specificity.[56]

The notion 'use of a subsidy programme' was at issue in *US – Countervailing Measures (China)*. The Appellate Body held that the reference to 'use of a subsidy programme' suggests that it is relevant to consider whether subsidies have been provided to recipients pursuant to a plan or a scheme of some kind. However, the mere fact that financial contributions had been provided to certain enterprises is not sufficient to demonstrate a plan or a scheme because the question of a financial contribution is about the existence of a subsidy, and not about its specificity. The relevant evidence regarding the nature and scope of a subsidy programme may be found in a wide variety of forms, for instance, in the form of law, regulations, or other official document or act setting out criteria or conditions governing the eligibility for a subsidy. A subsidy scheme or plan may also be evidenced by a systematic series of actions pursuant to which financial contributions that confer a benefit are provided to certain enterprises. Last but not least, the examination of the existence of a plan or scheme may also require assessing the operation of such plan or scheme over a period of time. However, the Appellate Body rejected China's argument that in order to demonstrate the existence of a programme the investigating authority is required to identify an explicit subsidy programme implemented through law or regulation, or through other explicit means.[57] Note that the factual question at issue was whether the provision of specific inputs by Chinese

[56] WT/DS436/AB/R of 8 December 2014, *United States – Countervailing Measures on Certain Hot-Rolled Carbon Steel Flat Products from India*, paras 4.371–4.380. See also WT/DS257/R of 29 August 2003, *United States – Final Countervailing Duty Determination with Respect to Certain Softwood Lumber from Canada*, para 7.116.

[57] For details see WT/DS437/AB/R of 18 December 2014, *United States – Countervailing Duty Measures on Certain Products from China*, paras 4.141–4.151. The preceding Panel followed a largely similar concept as the Appellate Body by stating that the term 'subsidy programme' should be interpreted broadly given that subsidies can take many forms and can be provided through many different kinds of mechanisms, some more and some less

State-owned enterprises for less than adequate remuneration to Chinese exporters of subject products constituted a programme.

'[P]redominant Use by Certain Enterprises' According to *EC and certain Member States – Large Civil Aircraft*, 'predominant use' refers to the use of a subsidy programme. Moreover, the ordinary meaning of 'predominant' includes 'constituting the main or strongest element, prevailing'. Thus, predominant use of a subsidy programme may be simply understood to be a situation where a subsidy programme is mainly, or for the most part, used by certain enterprises.[58]

The last sentence of Article 2.1(c) is relevant for the determination as to whether there is a predominant use. In relation to the diversification of the economy the Panel gave the following example. Where a subsidy programme operates in an economy made up of only a few industries, the fact that those industries may have been the main beneficiaries of a subsidy programme may not necessarily demonstrate predominant use. Rather the use of a subsidy by those industries may simply reflect the limited diversification of economic activities within the jurisdiction of the granting authority. On the other hand, the same subsidy programme operating in the context of a highly diversified economy that is used mainly, or for the most part, by only a few industries, would tend to indicate predominant use.[59]

In relation to the length of time during which the subsidy programme has been in operation, the Panel gave the same guidance as with regard to the third *de facto* specificity factor, i.e. granting of disproportionately large amounts of subsidy to certain enterprises.[60]

The Panel did not find that the loan given in 2002 to EADS constituted a predominant use of the subsidy programme in question. Note that the programme identified by the Panel in its predominant use analysis was the same as the one used when at issue in the analysis of the third *de facto* specificity factor ('granting of disproportionately large amounts').[61]

explicit. According to the Panel, evidence of systematic activity (or a series of systematic activities) provided an objective basis to identify a subsidy programme.

58 WT/DS316/R of 30 June 2010, *EC and certain Member States – Measures Affecting Trade in Large Civil Aircraft*, para 7.974.

59 WT/DS316/R of 30 June 2010, *EC and certain Member States – Measures Affecting Trade in Large Civil Aircraft*, para 7.975.

60 See *infra* pp. 188–193 of this chapter.

61 WT/DS316/R of 30 June 2010, *EC and certain Member States – Measures Affecting Trade in Large Civil Aircraft*, paras 7.992–7.996.

'[T]he Granting of Disproportionately Large Subsidy Amounts to Certain Enterprises' The Appellate Body examined this criterion in *US – Large Civil Aircraft (2nd Complaint)*. It summarized its interpretation and the tests to be applied as follows:

> 879. In this dispute, the Panel conducted an analysis of the IRBs under each of the factors set out in Article 2.1(c). However, the factor on which the Panel based its specificity finding, and which is directly at issue on appeal, concerns 'the granting of disproportionately large amounts of subsidy to certain enterprises'. Article 2.1(c) does not offer clear guidance as to how to measure whether certain enterprises are 'grant{ed} disproportionately large amounts of subsidy'. The language of Article 2.1(c) indicates that the first task is to identify the 'amounts of subsidy' granted. Second, an assessment must be made as to whether the amounts of subsidy are 'disproportionately large'. This term suggests that disproportionality is a relational concept that requires an assessment as to whether the amounts of subsidy are out of proportion, or relatively too large.[note omitted] When viewed against the analytical framework set out above regarding Article 2.1(c), this factor requires a panel to determine whether the actual allocation of the 'amounts of subsidy' to certain enterprises is too large relative to what the allocation would have been if the subsidy were administered in accordance with the conditions for eligibility for that subsidy as assessed under Article 2.1(a) and (b). In our view, where the granting of the subsidy indicates a disparity between the expected distribution of that subsidy, as determined by the conditions of eligibility, and its actual distribution, a panel will be required to examine the reasons for that disparity so as ultimately to determine whether there has been a granting of disproportionately large amounts of subsidy to certain enterprises.[62]

In short, in order to apply the criterion of the disproportionate use, the Appellate Body requests a comparison between the actual and the expected distribution of the subsidy. While the actual distribution is a fairly straightforward concept, the notion of the expected distribution is less so. The application of the test set out by the Appellate Body is heavily evidence-based.[63]

The application of the principles established by the Appellate Body in *US – Large Civil Aircraft (2nd Complaint)* resulted in the following findings. It is recalled that the Appellate Body had to determine whether the City of Wichita Industrial Revenue Bonds were specific under the

[62] WT/DS353/AB/R of 12 March 2012, *United States – Measures Affecting Trade in Large Civil Aircraft (Second Complaint)*, para 879. The application of these principles to the facts of the case can be found at the end of this chapter.

[63] See also *Bohanes/Rueda/Garcia* (2012/1) pp. 377 and 378.

disproportionality criterion. The Bonds were potentially available to enterprises that sought to purchase, construct or improve various types of commercial or industrial property. The relevant law provided that the subsidy was broadly available throughout the economy. However, 69 per cent of all funds paid under this scheme between 1979 and 2005, i.e. during a 25-year period, went to Boeing and its successor company Spirit. The parties to the dispute focused on determining what share of employment Boeing and Spirit had within the Wichita economy. Boeing/Spirit only represented 3.5 per cent of total employment and 32 per cent of total manufacturing employment in Wichita. On this basis, the Panel concluded that the subsidy was *de facto* specific. The Appellate Body did not consider this as particularly relevant in order to determine whether these subsidies were disproportionately large. The Appellate Body criticized that the Panel should rather have focused on the reasons that explained any disparity between the actual and the expected distributions of a subsidy. In any event, on appeal the US argued that it would have made more sense to take a look at investments that qualified for the Wichita Industrial Revenue Bonds, i.e. to compare the investments made by Boeing/Spirit with the total investments subsidized under the scheme. The Appellate Body agreed in principle with this suggestion but rejected the appeal on the grounds that the US did not place on the Panel record evidence that supported a conclusion that Boeing/Spirit could have been expected to receive over two-thirds of the subsidy. The submissions made by the US were only of a relatively high level of generality.[64] Thus, it would seem that – given the evidence on file – the Appellate Body has accepted the Panel's conclusion as a sort of *prima facie* case that shifted the burden of proof to the US.[65]

The Panel in *EC and certain Member States – Large Civil Aircraft* also dealt extensively with this criterion. It pointed out that assessing whether the amount of the subsidy is disproportionately large will involve (i) identifying the relationship between the amount of the subsidy at issue and something else that is a whole and (ii) determining whether that relationship demonstrates that the amount of the subsidy is greater than the amount it would need to be in order to be proportionate. There was some dispute between the US and the EU as to what this 'something else' or baseline could be. The EU was of the opinion that this should be the total

[64] WT/DS353/AB/R of 12 March 2012, *United States – Measures Affecting Trade in Large Civil Aircraft (Second Complaint)*, paras 871–889.

[65] See *Bohanes/Rueda Garcia* (2012/1) p. 378.

amount paid out under the subsidy programme pursuant to which the challenged subsidy is granted while the US held the view that also the use of a reference other than the subsidy programme may be permitted. The Panel held that where the subsidy at issue has been granted pursuant to a subsidy programme, that programme should normally be used as that 'something else'. However, the Panel acknowledged that, as the US had pointed out, the absence of any explicit reference to a 'subsidy programme' in this third *de facto* specificity factor (as opposed to the first one) suggests that it does not require that a subsidy programme be used for this purpose in each and every factual circumstance.

Moreover, the Panel clarified, based on the last sentence of Article 2.1(c), that even where a subsidy programme is used to determine the 'something else', the total amount paid out under the subsidy programme is not necessarily decisive. The relevant part of the last sentence of Article 2.1(c) provides: 'in applying this subparagraph, account shall be taken of ... the length of time during which the subsidy programme has been in operation'. According to the Panel, in the context of the third *de facto* specificity factor, this last sentence requires that the length of time during which the subsidy programme has been in operation must form part of the consideration or reckoning of whether the amount of a subsidy granted to certain enterprises pursuant to that same subsidy programme is disproportionately large. The Panel also provided two examples for which it would not be appropriate to use the total amount of the subsidy programme as the 'something else'. First, if the subsidy programme has not operated long enough to understand the impact on the economy. Second, to use the total amount under a long-standing subsidy programme might not be appropriate if there has been a material change in the importance of the subsidized activities in the wider economy and/or the granting authority's economic priorities over the life of the subsidy programme. In this regard, subsidies targeted towards certain enterprises in an emerging sector might not appear to be disproportionately large when compared with an extremely broad universe that includes subsidies to enterprises in sectors that do not play as significant a role in the economy today as they did over previous decades.

Once the correct baseline is identified the examination of disproportionality can be established by comparing the share of the total amount of subsidies granted under the generally available subsidy programme to one or more recipients with the proportion of economic activity attributable to the same recipient(s) within the jurisdiction of the granting authority. Where the portion of the subsidy granted to the recipient(s) out of the total subsidy programme (or the relevant part thereof) exceeds significantly the economic activity attributable to the recipient(s) in the broader economy, the amount of the subsidy at issue would be disproportionately large.[66]

The Panel's analysis of whether a loan given by the European Investment Bank (EIB) in 2002 to EADS falls under this *de facto* specificity criterion is most interesting as far as the determination of the baseline is concerned. The US argued that the subsidy programme in question was the Bank's loans in 2002 under the 'Innovation 2000 Initiative', or alternatively, the loans in 2000, 2001 and 2002 under this initiative. The Panel disagreed.

First, the Panel had to select a 'unit of measurement', an indicator, in order to check whether disproportionately large amounts were given. The Panel considered the amount of the principal transferred under the loan a useful indicator of the amount of subsidy in particular because the interest rate terms of loans followed a standard methodology and the parties did not argue that there was any material difference in the subsidy intensity of the loans. Thus, the Panel did not focus on the benefit derived from the loans.

Second, the Panel held that the Innovation 2000 Initiative could not be considered as a programme and thus the total amount given under this initiative could not be used as a baseline to determine disproportionately granting. As a consequence, the entire programme of EIB lending as mandated under the EC Treaty and the EIB statute constituted the baseline. The facts underlying this conclusion do not need to be presented here. The Panel found it *inter alia* relevant that loans given under the Innovation 2000 Initiative were not approved under a different application, review or decision-making procedure compared with other loans given by the EIB. The same was true with regard to the terms and conditions of the loan contracts. According to the Panel, an understanding of the legal regime pursuant to which an alleged subsidy is granted is relevant and an important consideration when making a specificity determination under Article 2.1(c) as it helps to define the relevant programme.

Third, as part of the determination of the baseline, the Panel had to decide on the time period for which it would establish the EIB's lending activities and compare it with the loan to EADS in question. The Panel opted for the year when the loan was disbursed to EADS but added that

[66] WT/DS316/R of 30 June 2010, *EC and certain Member States – Measures Affecting Trade in Large Civil Aircraft*, paras 7.961–7.973.

one calendar year was perhaps too short a period within which to assess whether the amount of the loan was disproportionately large.[67]

The Panel had also to decide whether loans granted to Airbus between 1988 and 1993 fall under the third *de facto* specificity criterion. The Panel first examined to what extent it would be appropriate to aggregate entirely or in part the loan amounts given in this period and what should be the appropriate baseline. There was again a dispute between the parties as to what constituted the appropriate baseline. The Panel first compared the total value of the loans given to EADS during 1988 and 1993 with the total value of individual loans granted by the EIB during this period and found that the EADS loans constituted 2 per cent of the total value of all loans given by the Bank. It added that given that the subsidy amount at issue related to 11 loans granted between 1988 and 1993, and because the EIB operates a lending programme that is long-standing, it would be reasonable and appropriate to consider the relative importance of the loans to Airbus over a longer period than the period of 1988–1993. Finally, the Panel was not impressed by the argument raised by the US that Airbus was the largest recipient of individual loans given by the EIB. It held that it could see no apparent reason why the simple fact that Airbus might have been the largest private recipient of funds in the period in question demonstrated, in the light of the EU's highly diversified economy and the long duration of the EIB's lending programme, that the Bank's subsidies were in fact not sufficiently broadly available throughout the economy to warrant a finding of specificity.[68]

The disproportionality criterion was also at issue in *US – Washing Machines*. The Panel ruled that the USDOC had not conducted the necessary relational analysis. It acknowledged that the USDOC considered how the amount of tax credits received by Samsung related to the amounts received by other Korean recipients as it was found that Samsung received many times more than the average Korean recipient. However, the USDOC failed to consider how the amount of subsidies received by Samsung related to a benchmark that was indicative of the amount that Samsung would have been expected to receive, taking account of all factors having a bearing on that amount were the subsidy distributed proportionately.[69]

[67] WT/DS316/R of 30 June 2010, *EC and certain Member States – Measures Affecting Trade in Large Civil Aircraft*, paras 7.980–7.991.

[68] WT/DS316/R of 30 June 2010, *EC and certain Member States – Measures Affecting Trade in Large Civil Aircraft*, paras 7.997–7.1007.

[69] WT/DS464/R of 11 March 2016, *United States – Anti-Dumping and Countervailing Measures on Large Residential Washers from Korea*, paras 7.231–7.250.

Discretion The fourth *de facto* specificity factor is the manner in which discretion has been exercised by the granting authority in the decision to grant a subsidy. In *US – Large Civil Aircraft (2nd Complaint)*, the question was whether the allocation of patent rights was *de facto* specific as NASA and the US Department of Defense enjoyed a certain discretionary authority with respect to the allocation of patent rights. For example, a contractor of NASA did not receive automatically any patents obtained under the work carried out for NASA. Rather, it had to request that NASA waives its rights to such patents and NASA had in principle the authority to reject such a waiver. However, in practice and in line with its regulations, NASA regularly waived such rights and the EU did not point to any evidence to the contrary. Therefore, the Appellate Body did not see any reason why the fourth *de facto* specificity factor 'discretion' was met.[70]

Extent of Diversification of Economic Activities and Duration of Subsidy

The last sentence of Article 2.1(c) requires that when examining *de facto* specificity, account shall be taken of the extent of diversification of economic activities within the jurisdiction of the granting authority, as well as of the length of time during which the subsidy programme has been in operation. In other words, diversification of economic activities and duration of the subsidy shall be looked at when e.g. examining the four *de facto* specificity factors. See the Panel in *EC and certain Member States – Large Civil Aircraft* as described *supra* pp. 188–192.

In *US – Countervailing Measures (China)* the question was whether the investigating authority must take into account in every Article 2.1(c) analysis the two factors listed in the final sentence of this provision. The Panel answered the question in the affirmative. However, it agreed with previous panel rulings in *US – Softwood Lumber IV* and *EC – Countervailing Measures on DRAM Chips* that taking into account the two factors need not be done explicitly but could also be done implicitly. Note also that the Panel rejected the US's claim that the requirement in the final sentence of

[70] WT/DS353/AB/R of 12 March 2012, *United States – Measures Affecting Trade in Large Civil Aircraft (Second Complaint)*, paras 798–799. See also *supra* in this chapter pp. 178–181 and *Neven/Sykes* (2014) pp. 291–292 more generally with regard to the EU's claim that the allocation of intellectual property rights constituted a subsidy.

Article 2.1(c) is dependent upon whether an interested party raised the relevance of the two factors.[71]

Regional Specificity (Article 2.2)

Article 2.2 deals with regional specificity. Its first sentence stipulates that a subsidy is specific if it is limited to 'certain enterprises' located within a designated geographical region within the jurisdiction of the granting authority. Its second sentence points out that it is understood that the setting or change of generally applicable tax rates by all levels of government entitled to do so shall not be deemed to be a specific subsidy for the purposes of the ASCM. WTO rulings have considerably clarified the various concepts of Article 2.2.

The Panel in *US – Anti-Dumping and Countervailing Duties (China)* had to define the meaning of the reference to 'certain enterprises' in the first sentence of Article 2.2. Did that reference mean that for a subsidy to be regionally specific, there must be a limitation of a subsidy to a *subset* of enterprises located within a designated geographical region (so the opinion of China)? Or is a subsidy regionally specific if it is limited, on a purely geographic basis, to part of the territory within the jurisdiction of the granting authority (so the opinion of the US)? The Panel sided with the US. Had it accepted China's interpretation it would have meant that subsidies limited to a designated geographical region within the jurisdiction of the granting authority would have to be further limited to a subset of the enterprises located within that region in order to be specific. This would have deprived Article 2.2 of its meaning and purpose, as any such subsidy already would have been specific pursuant to Article 2.1. The Panel based its conclusion also on the first and the second paragraph of Article 8 which, however, has expired pursuant to Article 31. Indeed, the two paragraphs taken together suggest that subsidies limited to a designated geographical region within the jurisdiction of the granting authority are specific.[72] These findings of the Panel are in line with those made

[71] WT/DS437/R 14 July 2014, *United States – Countervailing Duty Measures on Certain Products from China*, paras 7.250–7.256. This aspect was not appealed. WT/DS436/R of 14 July 2014, *United States – Countervailing Measures on Certain Hot-Rolled Carbon Steel Flat Products from India*, para 7.136 and WT/DS464/R of 11 March 2016, *United States – Anti-Dumping and Countervailing Measures on Large Residential Washers from Korea*, para 7.252, followed the same approach.

[72] WT/DS379/R of 22 October 2010, *US – Definitive Anti-Dumping and Countervailing Duties on Certain Products from China*, paras 9.125–9.135.

by the Panel in *EC and certain Member States – Large Civil Aircraft* in relation to what constitutes 'certain enterprises'.[73] The latter Panel held that grants provided by the European Regional Development Fund (ERDF) were regionally specific because they were only available to enterprises in designated geographical regions within the territory of the granting authority. In contrast, certain subsidies granted by Andalucia and Wales to their entire respective territory were classified as not being specific because they were available in the entire territory of the granting authority.[74] The Appellate Body endorsed this approach.[75] In short, the decisive question in relation to regional specificity is whether the subsidy given by the granting authority is available in its entire jurisdiction (then there is no regional specificity) or only in a sub-region of its jurisdiction (then the subsidy would be regionally specific).

The notion of 'certain enterprises' in the first sentence of Article 2.2 was also at issue in *US – Washing Machines*. Korean companies could receive a corporate income tax credit equal to 7 per cent of the value of all qualifying business assets investments. Only investments outside the Seoul Metropolitan Area (which accounts for approximately 2 per cent of the Korean territory) qualified. The tax credit could be obtained irrespective of whether or not the company had a legal personality in the qualifying area, i.e. outside the Seoul Metropolitan Area. Korea took the view that regional specificity has to be established based on the geographical location of the recipient of the subsidy. Such recipient must be a natural or legal person, i.e. an entity with legal personality. Conversely, an enterprise's facility does not qualify as a subsidy recipient because it does not have legal personality. On that basis, the subsidy provided by Korea would not be regionally specific because the recipient in question (Samsung) was located in Seoul while the qualifying investments related to a branch of the recipient located outside the Seoul Metropolitan Area. Both the Appellate Body and the Panel disagreed with Korea. The Appellate Body held that the term 'certain enterprises' is not limited to entities with legal personality. Rather, in particular the definition of the term 'enterprise' suggests a broader reading, as this term means a business firm or a company. The term 'business' in turn also includes a reference to a company's premises.

[73] WT/DS316/R of 30 June 2010, *EC and certain Member States – Measures Affecting Trade in Large Civil Aircraft*, para 7.1220 *et seq*. This aspect was not appealed.

[74] WT/DS316/R of 30 June 2010, *EC and certain Member States – Measures Affecting Trade in Large Civil Aircraft*, para 7.1237 *et seq*. This aspect was not appealed.

[75] WT/DS437/AB/R of 18 December 2014, *United States – Countervailing Duty Measures on Certain Products from China*, para 4.165.

The Appellate Body also agreed with the Panel that the term 'industry' in the chapeau of Article 2.1 encompasses a 'group of enterprises' and a 'group of industries', i.e. entities that do not have legal personality by their very nature. Finally, the Appellate Body found support for its interpretation in the term 'located' in Article 2.2. The core function of Article 2.2 is to address limitations on access to a subsidy by virtue of the geographical location of the enterprise eligible for that subsidy.[76]

Both the Panel in *US – Anti-Dumping and Countervailing Duties (China)* and the Appellate Body in *US – Washing Machines* had to decide as to what constitutes a 'designated geographical region'. In the former case, for China, this language referred to a formal administrative entity, whereas for the US it referred to any specified, identified large piece of land (whether or not it has a separate administrative identity or apparatus). The Panel sided with the US. In sum, specificity in the sense of Article 2.2 refers to limitation of access to a subsidy on the basis of geographic location alone.[77] As a next step, and building on the finding that a designated geographical region could be 'any piece of land', the Panel in *US – Anti-Dumping and Countervailing Duties (China)* also analysed the regional specificity determination made by the US Department of Commerce in respect to land-use rights located in an 'Industrial Park'. The Panel concluded that there was no regional specificity because the US did not identify that the provision of land-use rights within the designated area followed or constituted a distinct regime compared with the provision of land-use rights outside the area. Differences in land-use prices within and outside the Industrial Park could have been indication for such a different regime.[78] Had the Panel followed the US view, this would have led to the problem that land-use rights would have been necessarily specific because the PRC government was the ultimate owner of all land in China. The Appellate Body confirmed this by making it clear that the Panel ruling did not imply that the mere existence of a distinct regime makes a subsidy specific to a designated geographical region, even

[76] WT/DS464/AB/R of 7 September 2016, *United States – Anti-Dumping and Countervailing Measures on Large Residential Washers from Korea*, paras 5.218–5.225.

[77] WT/DS379/R of 22 October 2010, *US – Definitive Anti-Dumping and Countervailing Duties on Certain Products from China*, paras 9.140–9.144, 9.157.

[78] WT/DS379/R of 22 October 2010, *US – Definitive Anti-Dumping and Countervailing Duties on Certain Products from China*, para 9.152 *et seq*. Confirmed in WT/DS437/R 14 July 2014, *United States – Countervailing Duty Measures on Certain Products from China*, paras 7.349–7.354. This part was not appealed.

if the identical subsidy were also available to enterprises outside that designated geographical region.[79]

The Appellate Body in *US – Washing Machines* held in relation to the term 'designated' geographical area that the identification of a region for purposes of Article 2.2 may be explicit or implicit, provided that the relevant region is clearly discernible from the text, design, structure and operation of the subsidy measure at issue.[80] *US – Washing Machines* also examined whether the concept of 'geographical region' for the purposes of Article 2.2 depended on the territorial size of the area covered by the subsidy. Korea argued that the region in question covered 98 per cent of Korea, i.e. the entire territory of Korea with the exception of the Seoul Metropolitan Area. In the opinion of Korea, this was too large, too unbound and insufficiently demarcated or cohesive to be considered a designated geographical region. A subsidy that is available in 98 per cent of the national territory is in fact broadly available. Again both the Panel and the Appellate Body did not agree. The term 'geographical region' in Article 2.2 is not qualified. It can be, as the Panel in *US – Anti-Dumping and Countervailing Duties (China)* pointed out, any identified tract of land within the jurisdiction of the granting authority. According to the Appellate Body, the territorial size is not a relevant criterion for the applicability of Article 2.2. The Appellate Body also pointed out that this interpretation is in line with the function of Article 2.2, which is to address subsidy schemes by which Members direct resources to certain geographical regions within their jurisdiction, thereby interfering with the market's allocation of resources. The Appellate Body also addressed a more fundamental question in this context. Korea argued that the subsidy was broadly available and therefore not trade distortive. This argument was not accepted. Articles 2.1 and 2.2 set forth two distinct and independent ways in which a subsidy may be specific. Therefore, the fact that a subsidy may be distributed according to neutral and objective criteria (see Article 2.1(b)) with respect to a certain region does not, in and of itself, exclude regionally specificity.[81]

Note that the meaning of the second sentence has not been clarified yet by DSB rulings.[82]

[79] WT/DS379/AB/R of 11 March 2011, *US – Definitive Anti-Dumping and Countervailing Duties on Certain Products from China*, para 415 *et seq.*

[80] WT/DS464/AB/R of 7 September 2016, *United States – Anti-Dumping and Countervailing Measures on Large Residential Washers from Korea*, paras 5.226–5.232.

[81] WT/DS464/AB/R of 7 September 2016, *United States – Anti-Dumping and Countervailing Measures on Large Residential Washers from Korea*, paras 5.233–5.238.

[82] *Coppens* (2014) p. 114 considers that the second sentence of Article 2.2 has probably no specific meaning.

It could be argued that the text of Article 2.2 as interpreted by DSB rulings is perhaps overshooting. The following example illustrates the problem: suppose that in a country entrepreneurs would gladly invest in a port city while the government seeks to promote a landlocked province. To the extent that the government only compensates entrepreneurs accepting to invest in the landlocked province for the additional cost of transport between the port city and the land-locked company site, no distorted trade effects arise.[83] However, such subsidy would be specific on the basis of the aforementioned DSB rulings. Admittedly, it may be difficult in practice to design the subsidy in a way that it only compensates for the additional cost of transport. The concept of regional specificity as embodied in the ASCM has also been criticized from a more fundamental angle. Some have expressed the view that regionally specific subsidies should only be actionable if there is a distortion of trade across the border and not only within the country providing the subsidy.[84]

Deemed Specificity of Export and Local Content Subsidies (Article 2.3)

Article 2.3 clarifies that any subsidy that is prohibited pursuant to Article 3 (i.e. which is export contingent or contingent on import substitution) is deemed to be specific.

China's Accession Protocol to the WTO

China's Protocol of Accession contains in Section 10.2 a special provision concerning specificity. It reads:

> 2. For purposes of applying Articles 1.2 and 2 of the SCM Agreement, subsidies provided to State-owned enterprises will be viewed as specific if, inter alia, state-owned enterprises are the predominant recipients of such subsidies or state-owned enterprises receive disproportionately large amounts of such subsidies.[85]

There is no explicit stipulation that Section 10.2 is to expire at some date. To date no jurisprudence exists with regard to this text.

[83] *Jackson* (2000) p. 299.

[84] *Jackson* (2000) p. 299; *Neven/Sykes* (2014) p. 292.

[85] WT/L/432 of 23 November 2001, Protocol on the Accession of the People's Republic of China. See also *Yamaoka* (2013) p. 128.

PART II

PROHIBITED SUBSIDIES

Article 3

Prohibition

Introduction

Article 3 defines what subsidies are prohibited, i.e. export subsidies and import substitution subsidies.

Article 3.1(a), in conjunction with Article 3.2, contains a general prohibition of granting or maintaining export subsidies. The ASCM defines export subsidies as subsidies contingent upon export performance. Under Part II of the ASCM, the prohibition does not depend on the amount of the subsidy[1] or on its impact on competitors in third countries. Annex I to the ASCM contains an illustrative list of export subsidies and any subsidy that falls under this list is deemed to be prohibited. In other words, it is not necessary to demonstrate export contingency of a subsidy listed in Annex I.[2] The prohibition of export subsidies in Article 3.1(a) is not without exceptions. First, exceptions can be found in the Agreement on Agriculture.[3] Second, Part VIII of the ASCM (which consists of Article 27) in conjunction with Annex VII contains the special and differential treatment provisions for developing countries. The prohibition of granting or maintaining export subsidies pursuant to Article 3 only applies under certain circumstances to developing countries.[4]

Article 3.1(b), in conjunction with Article 3.2, contains a general prohibition of import substitution subsidies, i.e. subsidies that are contingent upon the use of domestic over imported goods. The Panel in *US – Upland Cotton* considered this provision a fundamental prohibition and a cornerstone of the subsidy disciplines imposed by the ASCM. According to the Panel, this prohibition relates to the basic national treatment provision in

[1] WT/DS213/AB/R of 28 November 2002, *United States – Countervailing Duties on Certain Corrosion-Resistant Carbon Steel Flat Products from Germany*, para 80.

[2] For details, see *infra* the commentary to Annex I.

[3] See *supra* pp. 37–46.

[4] See *infra* the commentary to Article 27, pp. 567–573.

Article III:4 of GATT 1994, which in its turn is a cornerstone of the WTO multilateral trading system.[5] However, it is clear that a subsidy measure which is in breach of Article III:4 of GATT 1994 is not necessarily prohibited under Article 3.1(b). Article 27.3 contained a special and differential treatment for developing country Members that has, however, expired in the meantime.

In short, the expression 'contingent … upon' is used in both Articles 3.1(a) and 3.1(b).

Subsidies that are prohibited pursuant to Article 3 are deemed to be specific pursuant to Article 2.3. Article 4 provides for a specific remedy track (special dispute settlement rules) in relation to prohibited subsidies. The characteristic features of this remedy track are essentially expedited dispute settlement and implementation. In actual fact, dispute settlement is not necessarily expedited because a panel might be obliged to look at both claims under Article 3 and claims under other provisions of the ASCM.

In order for a subsidy to be prohibited, it not only has to fall within the description of either Article 3.1(a) or 3.1(b) but it also has to meet the definition provided by Article 1 of the ASCM.[6] Prohibited subsidies are also actionable under Parts III and V of the ASCM.[7] In *Korea – Commercial Vessels*, Korea argued that it was legally and factually impossible for a given measure to be at the same time both a prohibited and an actionable subsidy. The Panel did not accept this view.[8]

The WTO-consistency of an export subsidy for agricultural products normally has to be examined, in the first place, under the Agreement on Agriculture. Examination under the ASCM would follow if necessary.[9]

Note finally that Section B of Article XVI of GATT 1994 also deals with export subsidies. However, it defines differently an export subsidy and

[5] WT/DS267/R of 8 September 2004, *United States – Subsidies on Upland Cotton*, para 7.1073.

[6] WT/DS487/R of 28 November 2016, *United States – Conditional Tax Incentives for Large Civil Aircraft*, para 7.196.

[7] See e.g. WT/DS126/RW of 21 January 2000, *Australia – Subsidies Provided to Producers and Exporters of Automotive Leather (Article 21.5)*, para 6.33.

[8] WT/DS273/R of 7 March 2005, *Korea – Measures Affecting Trade in Commercial Vessels*, para 7.334.

[9] WT/DS267/AB/R of 3 March 2005, *United States – Subsidies on Upland Cotton*, paras 570 and 571. But see WT/DS108/R of 8 October 1999, *United States – Tax Treatment for 'Foreign Sales Corporations'*, where the claims under the AoA seemed to be of a more accessory nature and where the Panel first examined the measures under Article 3 of the ASCM and afterwards under the AoA.

also does not contain a flat prohibition of such subsidies with regard to primary products.[10]

'Except as Provided in the Agreement on Agriculture' (Chapeau of Article 3.1)

The chapeau of Article 3.1 stipulates that except as provided in the Agreement on Agriculture (AoA), export subsidies and import substitution subsidies, within the meaning of Article 1, shall be prohibited.

In *US – Upland Cotton*, the question arose whether the prohibition of import substitution subsidies provided in Article 3.1(b) applies to agricultural products if the subsidies in question are counted in the 'Aggregate Measurement of Support' (also referred to as AMS) pursuant to Articles 1(a) and 6.3 of the AoA and paragraph 7 of its Annex 3. The US argued indeed that Article 3.1(b) does not apply to such subsidies. Both the Panel and the Appellate Body rejected this claim. The Appellate Body pointed out that the introductory language of the chapeau of Article 3.1 makes it clear that the AoA prevails over Article 3 of the ASCM, but only to the extent that the former contains an exception. The Appellate Body next examined whether the AoA indeed contains such an exception. It started its analysis with Article 21.1 AoA, which deals more broadly with the relationship of that Agreement and the other covered agreements relating to the trade in goods. Article 21.1 AoA provides: 'The provisions of GATT 1994 and of the other Multilateral Trade Agreements in Annex 1A to the WTO Agreement shall apply subject to the provisions of this Agreement.' According to both Panel and Appellate Body, there could at least be three situations where the domestic support provisions prevail pursuant to Article 21.1 AoA over Article 3.1(b) ASCM:

- where the text of the AoA contains an explicit carve-out or exemption from the disciplines in Article 3.1(b) of the ASCM;
- where it would be impossible for a Member to comply with its domestic support obligations under the AoA and the Article 3.1(b) ASCM prohibition simultaneously;
- where there is an explicit authorization in the text of the AoA of a measure that, in the absence of such an express authorization, would be prohibited by Article 3.1(b) of the ASCM.

[10] See *supra* pp. 31–37.

The Appellate Body also referred to a previous ruling on Article 21.1 AoA where it had interpreted this provision to mean that the provisions of GATT 1994 and of other multilateral trade agreements in Annex 1A apply, 'except to the extent that the Agreement on Agriculture contains specific provisions dealing specifically with the same matter'.[11] The Appellate Body therefore concluded that the key issue before it was whether the AoA contains specific provisions dealing specifically with the same matter as Article 3.1(b) of the ASCM, i.e. subsidies contingent upon the use of domestic over imported goods. It then examined Article 6.3 AoA and paragraph 7 of its Annex 3, but found that these provisions did not deal with the same matter as Article 3.1(b). Hence, it rejected the US claim.

It is interesting to note that the US claimed that if domestic support payments are not exempted from the prohibition of Article 3.1(b), paragraph 7 of Annex 3 AoA would be rendered inutile. According to the US, if US cotton users could claim the subsidy regardless of the origin of the cotton, the benefit to producers would 'evaporate' and the subsidy to cotton producers would become a simple input subsidy for textile mills. The Panel and the Appellate Body rejected this argument because, *inter alia*, there could be other measures that do not necessarily have an import substitution component.[12]

Further details with regard to the carve-out contained in the chapeau of Article 3.1 are described *supra* pp. 41–46.

Export Subsidies (Article 3.1(a))

Introduction

A prohibited export subsidy exists where (i) there is a subsidy within the meaning of Article 1.1, i.e. there is a financial contribution by a government, and a benefit is thereby conferred, and (ii) the subsidy is contingent upon export performance ('export contingency').[13] The subsidy elements

[11] WT/DS27/AB/R of 9 September 1997, *European Communities – Regime for the Importation, Sale and Distribution of Bananas*, para 155.

[12] WT/DS267/AB/R of 3 March 2005, *United States – Subsidies on Upland Cotton*, paras 513–584. Note that the import substitution subsidies were given to textile mills and not to cotton producers.

[13] WT/DS46/RW/2 of 26 July 2001, *Brazil – Export Financing Programme for Aircraft (Article 21.5, second recourse)*, para 5.19; WT/DS108/R of 8 October 1999, *United States – Tax*

set out in Article 1.1 are discussed in the commentary to that provision. Note also that export subsidies are deemed to be specific pursuant to Article 2.3.

Contrary to a production subsidy, an export subsidy tends to create a difference in prices at which a good is traded: the price on the world market will be lower than the price on the domestic market of the exporting country. Indeed, export subsidies provide an incentive to export because as a result of such subsidy, exporters will be more competitive on their export markets.[14] This is also the reason why in cases of parallel anti-dumping and anti-subsidy measures on imports of the same product from the same source, the combined duty level cannot be based on the simple addition of the dumping and the subsidy margin as this would amount to remedying the same situation twice.[15]

A subsidy can be *de jure* or *de facto* export contingent. The two types of export subsidies can be distinguished by the type of evidence necessary.[16] According to Article 3.1(a), export contingency can be the sole condition for granting the subsidy, or it can be one of several conditions. Annex I to the ASCM contains an illustrative list of export subsidies. Article 3.1(a) also contains two footnotes, i.e. Footnotes 4 and 5 to the ASCM. Footnote 4 further clarifies the standard of *de facto* export contingency. Footnote 5 recalls that Annex I also contains a number of examples that do not constitute export subsidies and provides that subsidies conforming to these examples shall not be prohibited, neither under Article 3 nor under any other provision of the ASCM. Footnote 5 does not specify exactly which measures constitute such an 'affirmative' defence (see in detail *infra* p. 210 in the commentary to Annex I, pp. 601–604).

Maintaining prohibited export subsidies leads to a violation of Article 3.2.[17]

Treatment for 'Foreign Sales Corporations', para 7.39; WT/DS139/R and WT/DS142/R of 11 February 2000, *Canada – Certain Measures Affecting the Automotive Industry*, para 10.155.

[14] *Krugman/Obstfeld/Melitz* (2015) p. 249 *et seq*.

[15] For details, see *supra* pp. 48–49.

[16] WT/DS139/AB/R and WT/DS142/AB/R of 31 May 2000, *Canada – Certain Measures Affecting the Automotive Industry*, para 100. For details see *infra* in this chapter, pp. 210–211.

[17] WT/DS108/RW of 20 August 2001, *United States – Tax Treatment for 'Foreign Sales Corporations' (Article 21.5, first recourse)*, para 8.110.

Section B of Article XVI GATT 1994 also contains provisions on export subsidies. However, the definition of the term 'export subsidy' under Article XVI GATT 1994 differs from the one under Article 3.[18]

Rationale of the Prohibition

Article XVI:2 of GATT 1994 states:

> [t]he contracting parties recognize that the granting … of a subsidy on the export for any product may have harmful effects for other contracting parties, both importing and exporting, may cause undue disturbance to their normal commercial interests, and may hinder the achievement of the objectives of this Agreement.

Export subsidies are prohibited because of their direct trade-distortive effects. Indeed, the most obvious reason for giving an export subsidy is the desire to promote the domestic industry at the expense of foreign competing industries. *Brazil – Aircraft (Arbitration)* has described these direct trade-distorting effects in that export subsidies usually operate with a multiplying effect. In other words, a given amount of subsidies allows a company to make a number of sales, thus gaining a foothold in a given market with the possibility to expand and gain market shares.[19]

Hahn/Mehta take a more nuanced view by arguing that many export subsidies are perhaps better dealt with outside the rules of Part II of the ASCM. According to them, in many instances of State support, measures would be far too complex to be adequately addressed by the complete prohibition of Article 3.[20] *Janow/Staiger* point out that according to standard economic reasoning, an export subsidy can always be shown to confer a net benefit to the rest of the world, i.e. the non-subsidizing countries. For them, there is no justification for a prohibition of export subsidies – the general rules set out in Parts III and V of the ASCM should be sufficient. Export subsidies harm an importing country only if there is injury to the competing domestic industry and if this injury cannot be addressed via the use of tariffs (including their renegotiation

[18] See *supra* pp. 31–37.

[19] WT/DS46/ARB of 28 August 2000, *Brazil – Export Financing Programme for Aircraft (Arbitration under Articles 22.6 DSU and 4.11 ACSM)*, para 3.54. See also WT/DS353/AB/R of 12 March 2012, *United States – Measures Affecting Trade in Large Civil Aircraft (Second Complaint)*, paras 1183–1186.

[20] *Hahn/Mehta* (2013) p. 154 *et passim*.

in the WTO), countervailing duties or other policy instruments. They acknowledge, however, that this does not take account of concepts that are less analysed in economics such as transaction costs, stage of economic development or the perception that export subsidies are particularly aimed at transferring the costs of adjustment abroad.[21] *Green/Trebilcock* review the economic analysis of export subsidies and conclude that they are normally globally inefficient although there may be cases in which they are efficient. With respect to the latter, they notably refer to cases of an oligopoly, situations in which the export subsidy overcomes an existing distortion in the importing country by reducing the net tariff for a particular good, and some examples relating to export subsidies provided by developing countries.[22] *Sykes* is also critical with regard to an across-the-board prohibition of export subsidies[23] while his opinion towards export subsidies as such was more negative in a previous publication.[24] According to *Flett*, the logic underlying the prohibition of export subsidies was that trade negotiators cared first and foremost for their own markets and, therefore, the subsidization of exports by others could be very problematic. But he questions whether this motivation is still relevant today given the globalization of markets: if a company operates in a global market, injury sustained in any part of that global market as a result of competitors' (production) subsidies, i.e. subsidies that are not prohibited but actionable under the ASCM, becomes equally problematic as export subsidies. However, export subsidies can also contribute to market partitioning along territorial lines while removing such partitioning and preventing its return is a systemic objective. On this basis, the prohibition of export subsidies is defendable although not necessarily coherent because other types of subsidies may have similar effects without being prohibited.[25]

Export Contingency

The Appellate Body in *Canada – Aircraft* has clarified a number of basic concepts concerning export contingency:

[21] *Janow/Staiger* (2004) pp. 280–285 and footnote 70. See also *Janow/Staiger* (2003) p. 204 *et passim* and *Bagwell/Staiger* (2004) pp. 179–180.

[22] *Green/Trebilcock* (2010).

[23] *Sykes* (2010) pp. 516–518.

[24] *Sykes* (2005) pp. 90–92 and p. 99.

[25] *Flett* (2012) pp. 50–51 and p. 58. See also *Sun/Wang* (2013).

- The term 'contingent' in Article 3.1(a) means 'conditional' or 'dependent for its existence on something else'. This understanding of the word 'contingent' is borne out by the text of Article 3.1(a) which makes an explicit link between 'contingency' and 'conditionality' by stating that export contingency can be the sole or one of several other conditions for granting the subsidy. This understanding also follows from the wording of footnote 4 that stipulates that the anticipation of exports is not enough. Thus, there is export contingency if export is a necessary condition for the receipt of a subsidy.
- The legal standard for export contingency in Article 3.1(a) is the same for both *de jure* and *de facto* contingency.[26] Footnote 4 does not introduce other types of relationship between subsidy and export.[27] As pointed out above, the two types of export subsidies can be distinguished by the type of evidence necessary.[28]

This term 'export contingency' has been further elaborated in *Canada – Aircraft (Article 21.5 – Brazil)*, that held that subsidies 'conditional upon export performance' means that they are 'dependent for their existence on export performance'.[29]

No Single Class of Recipients

WTO Members allegedly granting export subsidies occasionally argued that their financial contributions did not qualify as export subsidies because the subsidies were also available if the product was used domestically.

The relevant legal standard is whether there is a single class of recipients of the payments, i.e. whether the definition of an eligible person is the same on the domestic and the export side and whether the condition for receiving the subsidies are the same for eligible exporters and eligible domestic users. If there is such single class of recipients on both the domestic and the export side, there is no export subsidy. Conversely,

[26] WT/DS70/AB/R of 2 August 1999, *Canada – Measures Affecting the Export of Civilian Aircraft*, para 166. Confirmed in WT/DS316/AB/R of 18 May 2011, *EC and certain Member States – Measures Affecting Trade in Large Civil Aircraft*, para 1037.

[27] See *Flett* (2012) p. 51.

[28] WT/DS139/AB/R and WT/DS142/AB/R of 31 May 2000, *Canada – Certain Measures Affecting the Automotive Industry*, para 100.

[29] WT/DS70/AB/RW of 21 July 2000, *Canada – Measures Affecting the Export of Civilian Aircraft (Article 21.5 – Brazil)*, para 47. Confirmed in WT/DS267/AB/R of 3 March 2005, *United States – Subsidies on Upland Cotton*, paras 572 and 574.

if there are two distinct sets of recipients (exporters and domestic users) in two distinct factual situations (export and domestic use), there would be an export subsidy.

The most recent decision on this issue can be found in *US – Upland Cotton*. An exporter of upland cotton was eligible for the subsidy, if they were regularly engaged in selling eligible upland cotton for *exportation* from the US. By contrast, an eligible domestic user was a person regularly engaged in the business of opening bales of eligible upland cotton for the purpose of *manufacturing* such cotton into cotton products in the US. In other words, the statute and the regulations pursuant to which the subsidy was granted involve two distinct sets of recipients (exporters or domestic users) in two distinct factual situations (export or domestic use). The subsidy granted to exporters was therefore classified as an export subsidy.[30]

A similar situation was encountered in *US – FSC (1st Article 21.5)*. The measure in question granted a tax exemption in two different sets of circumstances, i.e. (a) where property was produced within the US and held for use outside the US and (b) where property was produced outside the US and held for use outside the US. The EU pointed out that firms which only manufacture in the US could only obtain the subsidy by exporting. The US argued that export contingency was not a necessary condition for receiving the subsidy. The Appellate Body rejected the US's argument. The fact that a measure grants export contingent subsidies in the first set of circumstances is not affected by the fact that the subsidy can also be obtained in the second set of circumstances. The fact that the subsidy granted in the second set of circumstances might not be export contingent does not dissolve the export contingency arising in the first set of circumstances. The distinctiveness of the two situations was confirmed by the presence of two provisions in the US Internal Revenue Code, each addressing one of the factual situations.[31]

[30] WT/DS267/AB/R of 3 March 2005, *United States – Subsidies on Upland Cotton*, para 572 *et seq*.

[31] WT/DS108/AB/RW of 14 January 2002, *United States – Tax Treatment for 'Foreign Sales Corporations' (Article 21.5, first recourse)*, paras 107–120. See also the reasoning of the preceding Panel WT/DS108/RW of 20 August 2001, *United States – Tax Treatment for 'Foreign Sales Corporations' (Article 21.5, first recourse)*, paras 8.49–8.75. The US tried to use an analogy between export contingency and specificity, arguing that just as the conventional way of making a specific subsidy non-specific is to expand the universe of beneficiaries, the way to cure an export subsidy is to ensure that the benefit is provided to a larger group than just exporters. This argument was not accepted by the Panel.

Footnote 5

Footnote 5 stipulates that measures referred to in Annex I as not constituting export subsidies shall not be prohibited under Article 3.1(a) or any other provision of the ASCM. The only measures in Annex I that are explicitly referred to as not constituting export subsidies are export credit practices in conformity with the interest rate provisions of the OECD Arrangement under the second paragraph of item (k). DSB rulings have rejected any claims to extend this exception and to apply a general *a contrario* argument for instance to the first paragraph of item (k). The *a contrario* argument means that subsidies would not be prohibited if they do not fall exactly under an item of Annex I.[32]

Export Contingency in Law

Introduction

The Appellate Body in *Canada – Autos* concluded that the evidence that may demonstrate *de jure* export contingency is different from evidence that may show *de facto* export contingency. The former can be demonstrated from the very words of the relevant legislation, regulation or other legal instrument constituting the measure. However, it is not necessary that *de jure* contingency be set out expressly – it can also be derived by necessary implication from the wording of a legal instrument.[33]

Whether the words of the relevant legislation, regulation or other legal instrument actually demonstrate, either explicitly or implicitly, export contingency in law is not always easy to determine.

In *Canada – Autos* the Appellate Body found export contingency by law in relation to certain import duty exemptions to the extent that a car manufacturer could only benefit from such exemption if it exported merchandise for a value equivalent to the imports. In other words, the more motor vehicles a manufacturer exported, the more vehicles that manufacturer was entitled to import duty-free. The Appellate Body considered

[32] WT/DS46/R of 14 April 1999, *Brazil – Export Financing Programme for Aircraft*, footnote 197 to para 7.18. See also WT/DS46/RW of 9 May 2000, *Brazil – Export Financing Programme for Aircraft (Article 21.4, first recourse)*, paras 6.33–6.41; WT/DS139/R and WT/DS142/R of 11 February 2000, *Canada – Certain Measures Affecting the Automotive Industry*, paras 10.196 and 10.197. See in more detail *infra* the Commentary to Annex I pp. 601–604.

[33] WT/DS139/AB/R and WT/DS142/AB/R of 31 May 2000, *Canada – Certain Measures Affecting the Automotive Industry*, para 100. Confirmed in WT/DS267/AB/R of 3 March 2005, *United States – Subsidies on Upland Cotton*, para 572.

this a clear relationship of dependency or conditionality.[34] With regard to subsidies under Article 3.1(b) see *infra*.

The issue also arose at Panel stage in *EC and certain Member States – Large Civil Aircraft* with regard to launch aid given to Airbus by France, Germany, Spain and the United Kingdom. The US claimed that the launch aid was contingent in law upon export performance because the sales levels of Airbus aircraft that had to be reached in order to trigger a full repayment of the launch aid could only be achieved if aircraft were also exported. In order to establish the necessary share of export sales of Airbus aircraft, the US relied on Airbus's Global Market Forecasts and project appraisals prepared by the Airbus governments, i.e. documents other than the legal instruments pursuant to which the subsidies were granted. The US invoked the Appellate Body report in *Canada – Autos* but the Panel did not accept this:

> We note that the arguments the United States has advanced in support of its claims are based on more than simply the text of the LA/MSF contracts, or the implications that can be necessarily drawn from *that text*. The United States clearly relies upon facts that are extraneous to the LA/MSF contracts themselves, most notably, information contained in the Global Market Forecasts and the government project appraisals. In our view, by relying upon such facts, the United States' claim strays from a complaint about what can be understood from the legal obligations written into the LA/MSF contracts, to a complaint about how those legal obligations can be understood *in the light of the relevant facts and circumstances*. Whereas the former represents what we consider the essence of an in law export contingency claim, the latter, in our view, defines the contours of a claim that a subsidy measure is contingent in fact upon export performance. (Emphasis in original.)[35]

What Is the Relevance of Footnote 4 for the Concept of 'Export Contingency in Law'?

Footnote 4 is placed after the word 'fact' in Article 3.1(a) and defines the standard of *de facto* export contingency. According to the Panel in *EC and certain Member States – Large Civil Aircraft*, footnote 4 is not directly

[34] WT/DS139/AB/R and WT/DS142/AB/R of 31 May 2000, *Canada – Certain Measures Affecting the Automotive Industry*, paras 104–108. A detailed description of the programme can be found in WT/DS139/R and WT/DS142/R of 11 February 2000, *Canada – Certain Measures Affecting the Automotive Industry*, para 10.184 *et seq.*

[35] WT/DS316/R of 30 June 2010, *EC and certain Member States – Measures Affecting Trade in Large Civil Aircraft*, para 7.313 *et passim*. This aspect was not appealed.

applicable to *de jure* contingent subsidy claims.[36] However, it has been held that footnote 4 informs the notion of export contingency in law.

First, the Appellate Body has found in *Canada – Autos* that the words 'tied to' in footnote 4 are a synonym for 'contingent' or 'conditional'. As the legal standard is the same for *de facto* and *de jure* export contingency, a tie amounting to a relationship of contingency, between the granting of the subsidy and actual or anticipated exportation meets the legal standard of 'contingent' in Article 3.1(a).[37]

Second, the Panel in *EC and certain Member States – Large Civil Aircraft* was of the view that footnote 4 also informs the notion of 'export performance' in Article 3.1(a). It held that the concept of export performance in Article 3.1(a) can be understood to refer to actual or anticipated exportation or export earnings as set out in footnote 4.[38]

Examples of Export Contingency in Law

- A guarantee given for the specific purpose of guaranteeing down payments made by oversees customers for Korean goods intended for export.[39]
- Pre shipment loans (PSL) that are provided for the specific purpose of assisting companies with the production of goods intended for exports.[40]
- The exporter will only receive the subsidy if it shows proof of exportation.[41]

Examples of an Absence of Export Contingency in Law

The Appellate Body has held in *US – FSC* that WTO Members are not obliged, by WTO rules, to tax any categories of income, whether foreign- or domestic-source income, and that they may tax foreign-source income

[36] WT/DS316/R of 30 June 2010, *EC and certain Member States – Measures Affecting Trade in Large Civil Aircraft*, para 7.707.

[37] WT/DS139/AB/R and WT/DS142/AB/R of 31 May 2000, *Canada – Certain Measures Affecting the Automotive Industry*, para 107.

[38] WT/DS316/R of 30 June 2010, *EC and certain Member States – Measures Affecting Trade in Large Civil Aircraft*, paras 7.696–7.701 This aspect was not appealed.

[39] WT/DS273/R of 7 March 2005, *Korea – Measures Affecting Trade in Commercial Vessels*, paras 7.189–7.191.

[40] WT/DS273/R of 7 March 2005, *Korea – Measures Affecting Trade in Commercial Vessels*, paras 7.305–7.307.

[41] WT/DS267/AB/R of 3 March 2005, *United States – Subsidies on Upland Cotton*, para 582.

less than they tax domestic-source income.[42] However, they are not allowed to carve out an export-contingent exemption from the category of foreign-source income that is taxed under its other rules of taxation.[43]

See also the examples given by *Flett*.[44]

Export Contingency in Fact

Introduction

A subsidy that is contingent *in fact* upon export performance is also prohibited. The Uruguay Round negotiators have, through the prohibition of export subsidies that are contingent *in fact* upon export performance, sought to prevent circumvention of the prohibition of subsidies contingent in law upon export performance. According to footnote 4, the standard 'contingent in fact upon export performance' is met 'when the facts demonstrate that the granting of a subsidy … is in fact tied to actual or anticipated exportation or export earnings'. Footnote 4 also clarifies that '[t]he mere fact that a subsidy is granted to enterprises which export shall not for that reason alone be considered to be an export subsidy'.

According to the Appellate Body in *Canada – Aircraft*, it follows from footnote 4 that the standard of determining *de facto* export contingency requires proof of three elements, i.e. that (1) the 'granting of a subsidy', is (2) 'tied … to' (3) 'actual or anticipated exportation or export earnings'.[45] It is submitted that there is some overlap in the margins of the contours of these three elements. The three elements are discussed *infra* in the next two sections.[46]

The Appellate Body in *Canada – Aircraft* held:

- To satisfy the standard for *de facto* export contingency, a relationship of conditionality or dependence must be demonstrated between the subsidization and the actual or anticipated exportation or export earnings.[47]

[42] WT/DS108/AB/R of 24 February 2000, *United States – Tax Treatment for 'Foreign Sales Corporations'*, para 98.

[43] WT/DS108/AB/R of 24 February 2000, *United States – Tax Treatment for 'Foreign Sales Corporations'*, para 99.

[44] *Flett* (2012) p. 52.

[45] WT/DS70/AB/R of 2 August 1999, *Canada – Measures Affecting the Export of Civilian Aircraft*, para 169.

[46] With regard to *de facto* export contingency see also the excellent overview by *Hahn/Mehta* (2013) p. 147 *et seq.*

[47] WT/DS70/AB/R of 2 August 1999, *Canada – Measures Affecting the Export of Civilian Aircraft*, para 171.

- The legal standard for export contingency in Article 3.1(a) is the same for both *de jure* and *de facto* contingency. Footnote 4 that is directly applicable to *de facto* export contingency claims only, does not alter the contingency standard.
- The difference between the *de jure* and *de facto* export contingency can be found in the type of the relevant evidence. *De jure* export contingency is derived explicitly or implicitly from the legal instrument. The relevant evidence for *de facto* export contingency goes beyond a legal instrument and includes a variety of factual elements concerning the granting of the subsidy in a given case. Proving *de facto* export contingency is a much more difficult task. The existence of the relationship of contingency between the subsidy and the export performance must be inferred from the total configuration of the facts constituting and surrounding the granting of the subsidy, none of which on its own is likely to be decisive in any given case.
- Footnote 4 makes it clear that *de facto* export contingency must be demonstrated by the facts. What facts should be taken into account in a particular case will depend on the circumstances of that case. There can be no general rule as to what facts or what kind of facts must be taken into account.[48]

Australia – Automotive Leather II also pointed out that the terms 'contingent ... in fact' and 'in fact tied to' suggest an interpretation that requires a close connection between the grant or maintenance of a subsidy and export performance.[49]

Note that there is no jurisprudence as to whether footnote 4 defines exhaustively the standard of export contingency in fact, i.e. whether this standard is only met if there is a subsidy that is 'tied to actual or anticipated exportation or export earnings' or whether other configurations not explicitly covered by footnote 4 might also meet the standard.

As will be explained in the next two sections, the standard developed by the Appellate Body in *Canada – Aircraft* and *EC and certain Member States – Large Civil Aircraft* seems to be a rather narrow one: only

[48] WT/DS70/AB/R of 2 August 1999, *Canada – Measures Affecting the Export of Civilian Aircraft*, paras 167 and 169, confirmed in WT/DS316/AB/R of 18 May 2011, *EC and certain Member States – Measures Affecting Trade in Large Civil Aircraft*, para 1046. As to what constitute relevant facts see *infra* pp. 216–223 of this chapter.

[49] WT/DS126/R of 25 May 1999, *Australia – Subsidies Provided to Producers and Exporters of Automotive Leather*, para 9.55.

supporting an export-oriented firm to increase its sales levels (including its export sales) does not meet the *de facto* export contingency test. Hence, while such support can be actionable under Parts III and V of the ASCM, it is not prohibited pursuant to Article 3.1(a).

'Actual or Anticipated Exportation or Export Earnings'

The Appellate Body in *Canada – Aircraft* held that the meaning of the term 'anticipated' in footnote 4 is 'expected' and whether exports are expected or anticipated is to be gleaned from an examination of objective evidence.[50]

When interpreting the notions of 'actual' and 'anticipated' exportation contained in Footnote 4, the Appellate Body in *EC and certain Member States – Large Civil Aircraft* ruled that 'actual exportation' means exportation that has occurred at the time the subsidy is granted. By contrast, 'anticipated exportation' means exportation that a granting authority considers, expects or foresees will occur in the future, after it has granted the subsidy.[51]

Anticipated exportation within the meaning of footnote 4 is to be demonstrated by way of objective evidence, such as the fact that a government is in possession of a company's sales forecasts showing significant export sales. It does not entail a determination of what the government's motivation is, but simply whether the prospect of future exports exists and whether the government is aware of that prospect.[52] The EU challenged the evidence on which the Panel relied in this respect, but was not successful. The reason for this was that the governments, at the time when they concluded with Airbus the contracts for the financing of the A380, the A340-500/600 and the A330-200, were fully aware that Airbus was a global company operating in a global market, and that the Airbus projects in question would involve Airbus selling much if not most of its production in export markets.[53]

[50] WT/DS70/AB/R of 2 August 1999, *Canada – Measures Affecting the Export of Civilian Aircraft*, para 172. WT/DS70/AB/RW of 21 July 2000, *Canada – Measures Affecting the Export of Civilian Aircraft (Article 21.5 – Brazil)*, para 48.

[51] WT/DS316/AB/R of 18 May 2011, *EC and certain Member States – Measures Affecting Trade in Large Civil Aircraft*, paras 1058 and 1059.

[52] WT/DS316/AB/R of 18 May 2011, *EC and certain Member States – Measures Affecting Trade in Large Civil Aircraft*, para 1061.

[53] WT/DS316/AB/R of 18 May 2011, *EC and certain Member States – Measures Affecting Trade in Large Civil Aircraft*, para 1070 *et seq*. The type of evidence examined is, for instance, described in para 1073.

The relationship between the notions of export contingency and anticipated export performance was also examined in *Canada – Aircraft*. The Appellate Body held that use of the word 'anticipated' does not transform the standard for 'contingent … in fact' into a standard that is satisfied by merely ascertaining expectations of exports on the part of the granting authority. A subsidy may well be granted in the knowledge, or with the anticipation, that exports will result. Yet, that alone is not sufficient for a finding of export contingency in fact because that alone is not proof that the granting of the subsidy is *tied to* the anticipation of exportation.[54] This book examines the 'tied to' criterion in the next section.

'Granting of the Subsidy … Tied To'

The question as to when the granting of a subsidy is 'tied to' exportation or export earnings is perhaps the most difficult issue in relation to export subsidies. Two Appellate Body rulings are of particular relevance, i.e. *Canada – Aircraft* and *EC and certain Member States – Large Civil Aircraft*. It is in particular the latter that sets out best the applicable standard while the former is perhaps more illustrative of the complexity of the facts that underpin the 'tied to' language. According to *EC and certain Member States – Large Civil Aircraft*, a subsidy is 'tied to' exportation or export earnings if the subsidy provides an incentive to the recipient to export in a way that is not simply reflective of the conditions of supply and demand in the domestic and export markets undistorted by the granting of the subsidy. In other words, the subsidy is tied to exportation or export earnings if it is geared to induce the promotion of export performance.

The interpretation of the 'tied to' criterion across the various relevant rulings as well as the facts underlying these cases are described in the remainder of this section.

The Appellate Body in *Canada – Aircraft* held:

- The notion 'tied to' is at the very heart of the legal standard in footnote 4 (para 171).
- The notion 'granting of the subsidy' shows that the inquiry whether a subsidy is *de facto* tied to a future exportation must focus on the expectation of the granting authority and not, as Canada claimed, on the reasonable knowledge of the recipient (para 170).

[54] WT/DS70/AB/R of 2 August 1999, *Canada – Measures Affecting the Export of Civilian Aircraft*, para 172. WT/DS70/AB/RW of 21 July 2000, *Canada – Measures Affecting the Export of Civilian Aircraft (Article 21.5 – Brazil)*, para 48.

- It follows from the second sentence of footnote 4 that although a subsidy may well be granted in the knowledge, or with the anticipation, that exports will result, that alone is not sufficient. Such knowledge or anticipation alone is not proof that the granting of the subsidy is 'tied' to the anticipation of exportation (para 172). '[M]erely knowing that a recipient's sales are export oriented does not demonstrate, without more, that the granting of a subsidy is tied to actual or anticipated exports' (para 173).
- Rather, the export orientation of a recipient may be taken into account as a relevant fact, provided that it is one of several facts which are considered and is not the only fact supporting a finding (para 173).[55]

The Appellate Body not only agreed with the legal standard established by the Panel, but also with the Panel's application of that standard. The Panel concluded, by taking into account 16 different factual elements that covered a variety of matters, that the subsidy programme in question, Technology Partnerships Canada (TPC), was tied to anticipated exportation because:

- Terms and Conditions of the programme required that funding decisions be based on, *inter alia*, whether the funded projects would generate export sales and increase the international competitiveness of the funded companies.
- Applicants were required to indicate whether the project to be funded would increase exports, and to distinguish between export sales and domestic sales when reporting actual and future sales.[56]
- The Appellate Body nuanced, however, the Panel's statements that (a) the closer a subsidy brings a product to sale on the export market,[57]

[55] WT/DS70/AB/R of 2 August 1999, *Canada – Measures Affecting the Export of Civilian Aircraft*. In order to examine whether the granting of the subsidy was 'tied to' to exports the Panel also used the formula whether the subsidy was given '*but for* anticipated exportation or export earnings', see WT/DS70/R of 14 April 1999, *Canada – Measures Affecting the Export of Civilian Aircraft*, paras 9.332, 9.339 and 9.340. The Appellate Body was critical about such a 'but for' test, see WT/DS70/AB/R of 2 August 1999, *Canada – Measures Affecting the Export of Civilian Aircraft*, para 171 footnote 102. In relation to export orientation see also WT/DS70/AB/RW of 21 July 2000, *Canada – Measures Affecting the Export of Civilian Aircraft (Article 21.5 – Brazil)*, para 49.

[56] The facts that the Panel considered relevant are listed in detail in WT/DS70/R of 14 April 1999, *Canada – Measures Affecting the Export of Civilian Aircraft*, para 9.340.

[57] The Panel distinguished in this regard between subsidies for pure research, or for general purposes such as improving efficiency or adopting new technologies, on the one hand, and subsidies that directly assist companies in bringing specific products to the (export) market, on the other. See WT/DS70/R of 14 April 1999, *Canada – Measures Affecting the Export of Civilian Aircraft*, para 9.339.

the greater the possibility that the facts may demonstrate that the subsidy is contingent in fact upon export performance and that (b) the further removed a subsidy is from sales on the export market, the less the possibility that the facts may demonstrate that the subsidy is contingent in fact upon export performance. According to the Appellate Body, by these statements the Panel appeared to apply what could be read to be a legal presumption. The Appellate Body agreed that the nearness-to-the-export-market factor may, in certain circumstances, be a relevant fact, but it did not believe that this should be regarded as a legal presumption. If a panel takes this factor into account, it should treat it with considerable caution.[58]

Note that the revised TPC programme at issue in the Article 21.5 proceeding was found not to constitute an export subsidy. Canada removed the selection and objective criteria related to exportation. The revised TPC listed three eligible sectors, i.e. the aerospace and defence industry (which was export oriented), environmental technologies and enabling technologies. In the opinion of the Appellate Body, this was not enough to find an export contingency of fact. This result is in line with the jurisprudence developed previously and follows clearly from the second sentence of footnote 4 of the ASCM.[59]

In *EC and certain Member States – Large Civil Aircraft*,[60] the parties disagreed as to whether financing given to Airbus by France, Germany, Spain and the United Kingdom could be considered *de facto* export subsidies. The Panel sided with the US, as far as the A380 financing by Germany, Spain, and the United Kingdom was concerned, by taking into account the following:

- At the time the relevant governments concluded the financing contracts they were fully aware that Airbus was a global company operating

[58] WT/DS70/AB/R of 2 August 1999, *Canada – Measures Affecting the Export of Civilian Aircraft*, para 174. See also WT/DS70/RW of 9 May 2000, *Canada – Measures Affecting the Export of Civilian Aircraft (Article 21.5 – Brazil)*, paras 5.19–5.26 and WT/DS222/R of 28 January 2002, *Canada – Export Credits and Loan Guarantees for Regional Aircraft*, paras 7.368–7.378.

[59] WT/DS70/AB/RW of 21 July 2000, *Canada – Measures Affecting the Export of Civilian Aircraft (Article 21.5 – Brazil)*, paras 48–50. See also para 5.33 of the preceding Panel ruling where it was pointed out that the selection panel did not even have specific information about the volume of exports that might result from the project for which funding was sought.

[60] WT/DS316/AB/R of 18 May 2011, *EC and certain Member States – Measures Affecting Trade in Large Civil Aircraft*, para 1029 *et seq.*

on a global market, and that the various Airbus projects would involve Airbus selling most, if not all, of its production on export markets.

- It was clear from the repayment provisions of the financing contracts, the market forecasts at the time of concluding the contracts and highly sensitive business information that achieving the level of sales needed to repay fully each loan would require Airbus making a substantial amount of exports.
- The EU Member States expected that the loans granted under the financing contracts would be fully repaid.
- In sum, Member States, in granting the loans, must have counted on Airbus selling a sufficient number of aircraft so as to repay the loans and that such sales necessarily included a substantial number of exports. Therefore, the evidence supported the view that the provision of large aircraft on sales-dependent repayment terms was, at least in part, 'conditional' or 'dependent for its existence' upon the EU Member States' anticipated exportation or export earnings.
- The Panel did not consider the aforementioned evidence as being decisive, but it ultimately based its finding of a *de facto* export contingency of the Airbus financing on additional evidence relating to certain provisions in the financing contracts, statements by government officials etc.

The EU challenged the Panel findings. In front of the Appellate Body, the parties agreed with the legal standard set by *Canada – Aircraft*, i.e. that *de facto* export contingency requires a relationship of conditionality between the subsidies and exportation. However, they disagreed as to *what* must be demonstrated in order to demonstrate that the subsidy is tied to anticipated exportation within the meaning of footnote 4 of the ASCM. The Appellate Body sided with the EU. The Appellate Body applied the following test in order to determine *de facto* export contingency under Article 3.1(a) and footnote 4: 'Is the granting of the subsidy geared to induce the promotion of future export performance by the recipient?' (para 1044 *et passim*, e.g. para 1067).

- It underlined that the aforementioned test is not met 'merely because the granting of the subsidy is designed to increase a recipient's production, even if the recipient's production is exported in whole'. Rather, *de facto* export contingency 'would be met if the subsidy is granted so as to provide an incentive to the recipient to export in a way that is not simply reflective of the conditions of supply and demand in the domestic and export markets undistorted by the granting of the subsidy' (para 1045).

- Based on *Canada – Aircraft*, *de facto* export contingency must be inferred from the total configuration of facts constituting and surrounding the granting of the subsidy. The following factors may be relevant: (i) design and structure of the measure granting the subsidy; (ii) the modalities of operation set out in such measure; (iii) the relevant factual circumstances surrounding the granting of the subsidy that provide the context for understanding the measure's design, structure and modalities of operation (para 1046).[61]
- The Appellate Body held that the necessary assessment could be based on a comparison between, on the one hand, the ratio of anticipated export and domestic sales of the subsidized product that would come about in consequence of granting the subsidy and, on the other hand, the situation in the absence of the subsidy. The latter situation may be understood on the basis of historical sales of the same product by the same recipient in both markets or, in the absence of such data, on the performance a profit-maximizing company would hypothetically be expected to achieve in both markets in the absence of such subsidy. The Appellate Body tried to illustrate the test whether the subsidy is geared to induce exports by the recipient by providing numerical examples. It explained that if a subsidy is designed to allow an increase of the recipient's production by five units and if the ratio of the recipient's export to domestic sales at the time of the granting of the subsidy is 2:3, it would be indicative that the subsidy is 'not tied' to anticipated exportation if the recipient would not be expected to export more than two units out of the additional production of five units. By contrast, the granting of the subsidy would be tied to anticipated exportation if, all other things being equal, the recipient is expected to export at least three of the additional five units. In short, the question is whether the increase of the recipient's higher output as a result of the subsidy would lead to a disproportionate increase of export sales? In the words of the Appellate Body the subsidy is tied to exports if 'the subsidy is designed in such a way that it is expected to skew the recipient's future sales in favour of export sales, even though the recipient may also be expected to increase its domestic sales' (para 1048).

[61] Note that WT/DS126/R of 25 May 1999, *Australia – Subsidies Provided to Producers and Exporters of Automotive Leather*, paras 9.56 and 9.57 already used these criteria. That Panel in para 9.70 also pointed out that the focus should be on the facts at the time the subsidy was granted, and not on possible subsequent developments. See also WT/DS70/R of 14 April 1999, *Canada – Measures Affecting the Export of Civilian Aircraft*, paras 9.337 and 9.338.

- The Appellate Body also underlined that the above test sets an 'objective standard'. Therefore, this standard is not satisfied by the subjective motivation of the granting authority to promote the future export performance of the recipient or any other reason the granting authority may have had, but by assessing the subsidy itself in the light of the relevant factual circumstances. Note, however, that evidence regarding the policy reasons of a subsidy is not necessarily excluded from the inquiry into *de facto* export contingency (paras 1050 and 1051).
- The Appellate Body found relevant context in the list of export subsidies set out in Annex I of the ASCM in that a common feature of all the examples is that the subsidy gives certain advantages to exported products and favours exported products over products destined for domestic consumption (para 1053).
- See also the summary in para 1056.[62]

On the basis of the above analytical framework, the Appellate Body rejected the Panel's interpretation that 'contingency may be demonstrated where the subsidy was granted *because* the granting authority anticipated export performance' (original in italics). According to the Appellate Body, the Panel has equated its standard of export contingency with the reason(s) for granting a subsidy – in the Panel's view, export contingency requires anticipation of exportation as a reason for granting the subsidy. This is not the same as the Appellate Body's standard of export contingency, i.e. 'geared to induce the promotion of future export performance by the recipient'.[63]

The US argued in favour of a standard that was altogether different. According to the US there is export contingency if the subsidy encourages more exports even if it also encourages domestic sales as well e.g. because contracts tie the repayment of the subsidy to reaching certain sales levels that can only be attained by export sales.[64] In other words, if the subsidy results, by its very nature, in more exports, it would have been *de facto* export contingent if the US approach had been adopted. Obviously, this standard is much broader than the one adopted by the Panel and the Appellate Body.

[62] See also *Flett* (2012) p. 57 who, while agreeing with the standard set by the Appellate Body, points out that the evidentiary standard to demonstrate such 'hidden contingency' may be difficult to meet.

[63] WT/DS316/AB/R of 18 May 2011, *EC and certain Member States – Measures Affecting Trade in Large Civil Aircraft*, para 1066.

[64] WT/DS316/AB/R of 18 May 2011, *EC and certain Member States – Measures Affecting Trade in Large Civil Aircraft*, paras 487 and 488.

Hahn/Mehta agree with the Appellate Body's standard because, according to them, only such a restrictive interpretation avoids the absurdity that, say, most Singaporean subsidies would *a priori* fall into the category of prohibited subsidies, as subsidies in a small country with an export-oriented economy will more often than not be granted in expectation of export performance and in order to increase such performance.[65]

The Appellate Body's findings are highly significant because they seem to have moved the *Canada – Aircraft* standard to one which requires inducement of exports in preference to domestic sales. To put it another way, *de facto* export contingency seems to require a measure effectively to discriminate in favour of exports over domestic sales.

The Appellate Body also examined if it could complete the analysis as to whether the financing granted to Airbus was *de facto* export contingent. It found that it was not in a position to do so because there were not enough facts on the record to examine whether the standard it set ('is the granting of the subsidy geared to induce the promotion of future export performance by the recipient?') was met. There was sufficient evidence to demonstrate that at the time when the subsidy was granted Airbus was anticipated to make a sufficient number of export sales. It was clear that Airbus was an export-oriented company. However, the Panel's findings did not shed any light on the question whether these anticipated exports were not simply reflective of conditions of supply and demand undistorted by the granting of subsidies.[66] The issue continues to be litigated in the compliance proceedings.[67]

Australia – Leather II took a somewhat different approach than *EC and certain Member States – Large Civil Aircraft*. In the former case, the Panel found that a grant contract was export contingent. This contract was awarded by the Australian government to the Australian manufacturer Howe Leather. The Panel was of the view that the export contingent in fact language in Article 3.1(a) including its footnote 4 required the Panel to examine all the facts that actually surround the granting or maintenance of the subsidy in question, including the terms, structure, the nature and

[65] *Hahn/Mehta* (2013) p. 153.

[66] WT/DS316/AB/R of 18 May 2011, *EC and certain Member States – Measures Affecting Trade in Large Civil Aircraft*, para 1081 *et seq.* (in particular paras 1091, 1092, 1097).

[67] The implementation Panel found that the US has failed to demonstrate a *prima facie* case that launch aid for the A380 and the A350XWB were prohibited export subsidies, see WT/DS316/RW of 22 September 2016, *EC and certain Member States – Measures Affecting Trade in Large Civil Aircraft – Recourse to Article 21.5 of the DSU by the United States*, paras 6.671–6.774.

the operation of the subsidy, and the circumstances under which it was granted or maintained. Taken together, the facts considered must demonstrate that the grant or maintenance of the subsidy was export contingent. By contrast, an examination of the terms of the legal instruments or administrative arrangements would not be sufficient.[68]

With regard to the grant contract itself, the Panel noted:

- The overwhelming majority of Howe's sales were for export.
- The Australian government was concerned that Howe remains in business, and determined to give it financial assistance in order to ensure that it did so.
- The Australian market was too small to absorb Howe's production, much less any expanded production that might result from the financial benefits that might result from the grant payments, and the required investments.
- Howe Leather would have to continue and probably increase exports in order to meet (best endeavour) sales performance targets set out in the grant contract.

In short, the Panel seems to have based its conclusion of a *de facto* export contingency on a factual necessity to export instead of asking the question of whether the grant contract would provide an incentive to export rather than sell domestically, as required by *EC and certain Member States – Large Civil Aircraft*.[69]

Import Substitution Subsidies (Article 3.1(b))

Import substitution subsidies (also referred to as local content subsidies) are the second category of subsidies that the ASCM prohibits. Article 3.1(b) defines them as subsidies contingent upon the use of domestic over imported goods. Note that import substitution subsidies are production subsidies. The trade distortion of this type of subsidy results from the explicit design to replace imports (as opposed to a normal production subsidy that may or may not have such an effect). Moreover, this type of subsidy rather favours the upstream industry and not the industry using

[68] WT/DS126/R of 25 May 1999, *Australia – Subsidies Provided to Producers and Exporters of Automotive Leather*, paras 9.56–9.57.

[69] WT/DS126/R of 25 May 1999, *Australia – Subsidies Provided to Producers and Exporters of Automotive Leather*, paras 9.62–9.72. The way the Panel addresses the subsidy schemes that have been replaced by the grant contract is also interesting. The facts surrounding the case are described in *Moulis/O'Donnell* (2000) pp. 1–2.

the substituted input in question. In other words, this type of subsidy distorts trade in the input market.[70] It would appear that the prohibition of import substitution subsidies is not really contentious among economists, contrary to the prohibition of export subsidies.[71] According to *US – Tax Incentives*, the purpose of Article 3.1(b) is to prohibit certain subsidies that have been considered particularly trade-distorting by Members. That Panel also pointed out that Article 3.1(b) protects competitive opportunities of imported products, rather than existing trade flows of such products.[72]

Note that the disciplines of Article 3.1(b) in conjunction with Article 1.1(a)(1)(iii) apply to government procurement, unlike many of the obligations set out in GATT 1994 and the TRIMs Agreement.[73]

According to *Canada – Autos*, Article 3.1(b) in some sense has its roots in Article III:4 of GATT 1994, i.e. the national treatment provision. However, Article 3.1(b) has obviously not the same scope as Article III:4. The Panel was therefore unwilling to import into Article 3.1(b) legal principles derived from the interpretation of Article III:4, a text that differs markedly from that of Article 3.1(b).[74] Article 3.1(b) requires that the actual use of domestic over imported goods must be a condition for receipt of the subsidy. In contrast, the standard set out in Article III:4 of GATT 1994 is easier to meet, as it encompasses subsidies contingent upon domestic value-added requirements. Such domestic value-added requirements may be designed merely to promote or encourage the use of domestic goods while Article 3.1(b) would require that the conditions make the use of domestic goods unavoidable (see *Canada – Autos* below).

The legal standard for 'contingent' in Article 3.1(b) is the same as in subparagraph (a).[75] The Panel in *Canada – Autos* held that the ASCM only

[70] Local content subsidies are not only prohibited pursuant to Article 3.1(b), but they may also be incompatible with several other provisions of the WTO legal order, notably the TRIMs Agreement and Article III of GATT 1994, see *Hestermeyer/Nielsen* (2014) for a comprehensive overview. They also describe what forms such local content measures may take.

[71] *Janow/Staiger* (2003) pp. 205–207.

[72] WT/DS487/R of 28 November 2016, *United States – Conditional Tax Incentives for Large Civil Aircraft*, paras 7.222 and 7.225. See also the reference to *Brazil – Aircraft* in para 7.198. The Panel's view on the purpose of Article 3.1(b) had consequences for the interpretation of the term 'goods', see *infra*.

[73] See *Hestermeyer/Nielsen* (2014) p. 584.

[74] WT/DS139/R and WT/DS142/R of 11 February 2000, *Canada – Certain Measures Affecting the Automotive Industry*, para 10.215.

[75] WT/DS139/AB/R and WT/DS142/AB/R of 31 May 2000, *Canada – Certain Measures Affecting the Automotive Industry*, para 123; WT/DS267/R of 8 September 2004, *United*

extends to import substitution contingency in law because subparagraph (b) did not reproduce the words 'in law or in fact' that can be found in subparagraph (a). In the view of the Panel, this omission was deliberate and must have some meaning. The Appellate Body did not agree, not least because it would run counter to the object and purpose of the ASCM if Article 3.1(b) only extended to import substitution contingency in law. A limitation to import substitution contingency in law would make circumvention of obligations by WTO Members too easy.[76]

The specific facts in *Canada – Autos* also merit to be mentioned here. Canadian car manufacturers could obtain an import duty exemption if, *inter alia*, the value added in Canada to their manufactured cars was above a certain threshold. The law specified in detail a large list of costs which constituted Canadian value added such as the costs of parts produced in Canada, transportation costs, wages, rent for factory premises in Canada, depreciation etc. The Appellate Body was not able to complete the analysis as to whether this configuration constituted an import substitution subsidy in law or in fact. This was due to the fact that the file did not contain any findings as to whether the Canadian value added requirement was so high that the use of domestic over imported goods may well have been a necessity.[77] This is an important point: production subsidies that are conditional upon meeting general domestic value added levels do not necessarily fall under the scope of Article 3.1(b) if that added value can easily be met by using domestic services etc. In other words, the requirement to use domestic goods is different to a requirement to add domestic value.

US – Tax Incentives had to address whether certain tax incentives given to Boeing by the state of Washington constituted import substitution

States – Subsidies on Upland Cotton, para 7.1081; WT/DS487/R of 28 November 2016, *United States – Conditional Tax Incentives for Large Civil Aircraft*, paras 7.208 7.211, 7.320. This applies for the term 'contingency' as well as for both *de jure* and *de facto* contingency, see *supra* pp. 204–223 of this chapter.

[76] WT/DS139/AB/R and WT/DS142/AB/R of 31 May 2000, *Canada – Certain Measures Affecting the Automotive Industry*, paras 135–143.

[77] WT/DS139/AB/R and WT/DS142/AB/R of 31 May 2000, *Canada – Certain Measures Affecting the Automotive Industry*, para 124 *et seq*. See also the preceding Panel ruling WT/DS139/R and WT/DS142/R of 11 February 2000, *Canada – Certain Measures Affecting the Automotive Industry*, paras 10.217–10.219. A similar issue arose in WT/DS412/R and WT/DS426/R of 19 December 2012, *Canada – Certain Measures Affecting the Renewable Energy Generation Sector; Canada – Measures Relating to Feed-In Tariff Program*, paras 7.161 and 7.162, in relation to Annex 1(a) of the TRIMs Agreement. In that case, it was, however, clear that the domestic value added requirement could not be met by procuring solely Canadian services. It was also necessary to purchase domestically produced merchandise.

subsidies. It first had to solve some interpretational issues that were never discussed before. Article 3.1(b) refers to the '*use* of domestic *over* imported *goods*' (emphasis added). The Panel held that the word 'over' can be read in the sense of 'in preference to' (or 'instead of' or 'rather than'), so that Article 3.1(b) prohibits any subsidy that is conditional on the use of domestic goods in preference to (or 'instead of' or 'rather than') imported goods.[78] As for the term 'use', the Panel noted that neither the text of this provision nor any relevant context indicates that this verb is confined to a particular manner of using or employing a given good, or that the good 'used' in this context must possess certain characteristics in order to be capable of being 'used' within the meaning of Article 3.1(b). Accordingly, a subsidy to be covered by Article 3.1(b) could be conditional upon 'consuming' the good, or it could be conditional in any other way on the use or employment of domestic goods, in preference to imported goods.[79] Finally, as far as the term 'goods' is concerned, the Panel considered it to be synonymous with 'products', and the goods in question must be at least potentially tradable. However, there is no requirement under Article 3.1(b) that the goods in question must be actually traded. Hence there is no need to demonstrate present trade in a specific product as it exists at a given moment in time to establish a prohibited contingency under Article 3.1(b).[80]

The Panel did not find *de jure* contingency. The legal instruments underlying the tax reductions provided by the state of Washington were silent as to the use of imported or domestic products. Nor could conditionality be implied, in the sense that it resulted inevitably from the terms of these instruments. The legal instruments did not speak of component sourcing decisions (in this case wings and fuselage), but of the location of certain manufacturing activities of Boeing.[81]

[78] WT/DS487/R of 28 November 2016, *United States – Conditional Tax Incentives for Large Civil Aircraft*, para 7.218.

[79] WT/DS487/R of 28 November 2016, *United States – Conditional Tax Incentives for Large Civil Aircraft*, para 7.222.

[80] WT/DS487/R of 28 November 2016, *United States – Conditional Tax Incentives for Large Civil Aircraft*, para 7.225. In para 7.368 the Panel pointed out that Article 3.1(b) does not require the identification of a specific good in order that it can be applied to a particular situation. The Panel made this statement because it was confronted with a counterfactual situation as to what action by Boeing would trigger the removal of certain tax concessions given by the state of Washington. The evidence suggested that the import of wings would trigger such a removal but that there could be a broad variety of configurations of how such imports could take place, see paras 7.322–7.369.

[81] WT/DS487/R of 28 November 2016, *United States – Conditional Tax Incentives for Large Civil Aircraft*, paras 7.272–7.315.

The Panel then proceeded to examine *de facto* contingency. It first set out the legal standard based on previous rulings in relation to Article 3.1(a):

> 7.320. In summary, the legal standard expressed by the word 'contingent' is the same for both *de jure* or *de facto* contingency.[598] However, there is a difference in the type of evidence that may be employed to establish *de jure* or *de facto* contingency. *De jure* contingency is demonstrated on the basis of the words of the relevant legislation, regulation or other legal instrument. The evidence needed to establish *de facto* contingency goes beyond the relevant legal instruments and includes a variety of factual elements concerning the granting of the subsidy in a specific case.[599] *De facto* contingency must be established from the total configuration of the facts constituting and surrounding the granting of the subsidy, including the design, structure, and modalities of operation of the measure granting the subsidy, none of which on its own is likely to be decisive in any given case.[600] That configuration of the facts may include the following factors: (i) the design and structure of the measure granting the subsidy; (ii) the modalities of operation set out in such a measure; and (iii) the relevant factual circumstances surrounding the granting of the subsidy that provide the context for understanding the measure's design, structure, and modalities of operation.[601] Moreover, the determination of contingency must be based on an assessment of *the subsidy itself*, in the light of the relevant factual circumstances, rather than by reference to the granting authority's subjective motivation for the measure. Reviewable expressions of a government's policy objectives for granting a subsidy may, however, constitute relevant evidence in the inquiry.[602]
>
> 7.321. For the Panel to find a violation of Article 3.1(b) of the SCM Agreement, the European Union will need to make a *prima facie* case that the aerospace tax measures are granted subject to the condition that domestic products must be used instead of, or in preference to, imported products. It would not be sufficient to demonstrate, for example, that a subsidy is being granted to a firm that uses domestic instead of imported goods or even that the subsidy would negatively affect the competitive opportunities of foreign producers. Such facts would not in themselves support a determination that the challenged measures are subject to a prohibited contingency (although they might be relevant in the context of actions pursuant to Parts III and V of the SCM Agreement). Rather, the European Union will need to demonstrate that there is something about the design and structure of the challenged measures and their operation, in the circumstances in which the measures have been introduced and exist, that establishes the contingency, and does so with the requisite standard of certainty. The Panel recalls, in this regard, the Appellate Body's warning against blurring 'the line drawn by the [SCM] Agreement between *prohibited* … subsidies and *actionable* … subsidies', in a manner 'contrary to the overall design and structure of the Agreement'.[604]

(Emphasis in original.)[82]

[598] Appellate Body Report, *Canada – Aircraft*, para. 167.
[599] Ibid. and Appellate Body Report, *EC and certain Member States – Large Civil Aircraft*, para. 1038.
[600] Appellate Body Reports, *Canada – Aircraft*, para. 167; *EC and certain Member States – Large Civil Aircraft*, para. 1051.
[601] Appellate Body Report, *EC and certain Member States – Large Civil Aircraft*, para. 1046.
[602] Ibid. paras. 1051–1052.
[604] Appellate Body Report, EC and certain Member States – Large Civil Aircraft, para. 1054.

When applying this standard to the facts of the case, the Panel found the measure to be *de facto* contingent because according to the evidence on record some of the tax reductions were only maintained if Boeing continued the assembly of wings for the 777X aircraft in the state of Washington. However, they would be revoked if Boeing imported wings.[83]

See also *EC and certain Member States – Large Civil Aircraft (Article 21.5)*.[84]

Article 3.2

According to paragraph 2, a WTO Member shall neither grant nor maintain export subsidies or import substitution subsidies. According to the Panel in *Brazil – Aircraft (1st Article 21.5)*, the term 'grant' is to be interpreted in the same way as in Article 27.4.[85] The notion of 'granting' is legally distinct from the notion of when the subsidy is 'deemed to exist' pursuant to Article 1.1.[86]

[82] WT/DS487/R of 28 November 2016, *United States – Conditional Tax Incentives for Large Civil Aircraft*, paras 7.320 and 7.321. See also paras 7.327 and 7.347.
[83] WT/DS487/R of 28 November 2016, *United States – Conditional Tax Incentives for Large Civil Aircraft*, paras7.322–7.369.
[84] WT/DS316/RW of 22 September 2016, *EC and certain Member States – Measures Affecting Trade in Large Civil Aircraft – Recourse to Article 21.5 of the DSU by the United States*, paras 6.752–6.791.
[85] WT/DS46/RW of 9 May 2000, *Brazil – Export Financing Programme for Aircraft (Article 21.4, first recourse)*, para 6.11. See also *infra* the commentary to Article 27, p. 572.
[86] WT/DS46/RW of 9 May 2000, *Brazil – Export Financing Programme for Aircraft (Article 21.4, first recourse)*, paras 6.12–6.14.

Article 4

Remedies

Introduction

Article 4 is applicable to prohibited subsidies as defined in Article 3, i.e. export subsidies and local content subsidies. It deals with remedies against such subsidies by setting out a number of procedural provisions that are specific to dispute settlement of claims relating to such subsidies. The procedural provisions cover the various stages of dispute settlement: consultations (paragraphs 1 to 4), panel process (paragraphs 4 to 7), adoption of the panel report and appeal (paragraphs 8 to 9) as well as compensation and suspension of concessions (paragraphs 10 and 11).

One of the main features of Article 4 is that it aims at accelerating dispute settlement as compared to a normal dispute under the DSU. This is achieved in two ways. First, many of the provisions of Article 4 provide for shorter time periods than those foreseen under the DSU. For instance, under Article 4.4 ASCM, a panel can be requested after 30 days of the request for consultations; while according to Article 4.7 DSU, such period is 60 days. Second, Article 4.12 ASCM stipulates that time periods other than those specifically addressed in the preceding paragraphs shall be half the time prescribed in the DSU.

However, Article 4 ASCM provides for other special rules, most notably those in Article 4.7 concerning the withdrawal of the subsidy (as opposed to a recommendation pursuant to Article 19.1 to bring the measure into conformity with the WTO provision in question) and in Articles 4.10 and 4.11 concerning compensation and suspension of concessions.

Articles 4.2 through 4.12 are special and additional rules or procedures identified in Appendix 2 to the DSU.[1]

[1] See *supra* pp. 55–56.

Pursuant to Article 27.7, Article 4 does not apply to a developing country Member in the case of export subsidies that are in conformity with Article 27.2 through Article 27.5. Instead Article 7 applies.

Some of the controversies surrounding Article 4, in particular the duty to withdraw a prohibited subsidy pursuant to Article 4.7 and the rules concerning compensation and suspension set out in Articles 4.10 and 4.11, should also be viewed in the light of the objective of dispute settlement. Article 4 does not state an objective. Article 3.7 of the DSU stipulates that – in the absence of a mutually agreed solution – the first objective of the dispute settlement mechanism is usually to secure the withdrawal of the measures concerned if these are found to be inconsistent with the provisions of the covered agreements. This requires compliance *ex nunc* as of the expiry of the specified reasonable period of time and countermeasures should induce such compliance.[2] Even the Panel report *Australia – Automotive Leather II (Article 21.5)*, that was heavily criticized because it ordered Australia to claim back from the recipient the subsidies paid, acknowledged that the remedy under Article 4.7 was not intended to fully restore the *status quo ante* by depriving the recipient of the benefits it may have enjoyed in the past. Nor was it intended to provide reparation or compensation in any sense.[3] Similarly, when it comes to defining the 'appropriate countermeasures' under Article 4.11, *US – FSC (Arbitration)* held that

- such measures should at least entitle the complaining Member to counter the injurious effect of the illegal measure;
- such measures should contribute to the ultimate objective of withdrawal of the subsidy without delay;
- the object and purpose of countermeasures is a temporary response to a lack of compliance.[4]

In sum, it would seem that the objective of dispute settlement under Article 4 is to induce compliance, but not to achieve reparation of the harm suffered resulting from the provision of prohibited subsidies.[5]

2 WT/DS27/ARB of 9 April 1999; *European Communities – Regime for the Importation, Sale and Distribution of Bananas – Recourse to Arbitration by the European Communities under Article 22.6 of the DSU*, para 6.3.

3 WT/DS126/RW of 21 January 2000, *Australia – Subsidies Provided to Producers and Exporters of Automotive Leather (Article 21.5)*, para 6.49.

4 WT/DS108/ARB of 30 August 2002, *United States – Tax Treatment for 'Foreign Sales Corporations' (Arbitration under Articles 22.6 DSU and 4.11 ASCM)*, paras 5.41, 5.57 and 5.60.

5 *Guan* (2014) p. 822 *et passim* is of the view that this applies to all subsidy-related retaliation issues, i.e. also those under Article 7. See also *Grané* (2001) pp. 759–763.

Consultations (Paragraphs 1 to 4 of Article 4)

Introduction

The special rules on consultations contained in Article 4 include the following:

- *Statement of available evidence*: Pursuant to Article 4.2 of the ASCM, the request for consultation must include a 'statement of available evidence' while Article 4.4 of the DSU stipulates that the request for consultations give reasons for the request including identification of the measure at issue and an indication of the legal basis of the complaint.
- *Expedited consultations and request for the establishing a panel*: According to Article 4.3 of the ASCM, the parties shall enter into the consultations 'as quickly as possible'. Moreover, according to Article 4.4 of the ASCM, if no mutually agreed solution has been reached within 30 days of the request for consultations, any Member to such consultations may request a panel. By contrast, according to Article 4.3 of the DSU, the Member to which the request for consultation is addressed shall reply to the request within ten days after the date of the receipt and consultations shall start within a period of no more than 30 days. A panel can be requested pursuant to Article 4.7 of the DSU if consultations fail to settle the dispute within 60 days after the date of receipt of the request for consultations.

Statement of Available Evidence (Article 4.2)

Article 4.2 requires that the request for consultations 'include a statement of available evidence with regard to the existence and nature of the subsidy in question'. According to the Appellate Body in *US – FSC*, this requirement is distinct from – and not satisfied by compliance with – the requirements of Article 4.4 of the DSU. Article 4.4 of the DSU requires that all requests for consultations give reasons for the request, including identification of the measure at issue and an indication of the legal basis for the complaint. Article 4.4 of the DSU and Article 4.2 of the ASCM should be read together and applied together, so that a request for consultations relating to a prohibited subsidy claim under the ASCM must satisfy both provisions. This requirement of a 'statement of available evidence' is important given the accelerated timeframes for disputes involving claims of prohibited subsidies and given that the question whether a subsidy is a prohibited one often requires a detailed examination of facts. The Appellate Body held that it is available evidence of the character of the measure as a subsidy that must be indicated, and not – contrary to the view of the preceding Panel – merely evidence of the existence of the measure (e.g. by simply referring to the legal instrument under dispute).[6]

The Appellate Body furthermore noted that Article 4.2 requires the provision of a statement of the evidence but not the evidence itself.[7] The adequacy of the statement of available evidence must be determined on a case-by-case basis.[8] On the sufficiency of the statement see also the Panel report in *US – FSC*.[9]

Article 4.2 was also at issue in *Australia – Automotive Leather II*. Australia argued that this provision imposes an obligation on the complainant to disclose, in its request for consultation, not only facts, but also the argumentation why such facts lead the complainant to believe that there is a violation of Article 3.1. According to Australia, because of the accelerated dispute settlement procedure under Article 4, the complainant must 'show its hand' at the outset of the proceedings in order to guarantee that information necessary for the respondent to defend itself is provided. Therefore, the complaining Member should disclose in its consultation request all facts and evidence on which it will rely in the course of the dispute. The Panel did not agree. It held that Article 4.2 requires considerably less than what Australia opined. According to the Panel, the ordinary meaning of the terms of Article 4.2 requires a complaining Member to include in its request for consultations an expression in words of the facts at its disposal at the time it requests consultations. The facts relate to the conclusion made by the complaining Member that it has reason to believe that a prohibited subsidy is being granted or maintained.[10]

[6] WT/DS108/AB/R of 24 February 2000, *United States – Tax Treatment for 'Foreign Sales Corporations'*, paras 155–161. As to the purpose of the statement of available evidence see also WT/DS267/R of 8 September 2004, *United States – Subsidies on Upland Cotton*, para 7.98 ('serves to provide a responding Member with a better understanding of the matter in dispute'; 'serves as a basis for consultations' etc.).

[7] WT/DS267/AB/R of 3 March 2005, *United States – Subsidies on Upland Cotton*, para 308.

[8] WT/DS267/AB/R of 3 March 2005, *United States – Subsidies on Upland Cotton*, para 308.

[9] WT/DS108/R of 8 October 1999, *United States – Tax Treatment for 'Foreign Sales Corporations'*, paras 7.5 and 7.6. The Panel held e.g. that there is no need to annex the available evidence. An identification of the evidence is sufficient. Moreover, it is not necessary according to the Panel to explicitly use the term 'statement of available evidence'.

[10] WT/DS126/R of 25 May 1999, *Australia – Subsidies Provided to Producers and Exporters of Automotive Leather*, paras 9.16–9.22.

Note also that neither Article 4.2 nor the remainder of Article 4 contains a rule that a complaining Member can only rely, in presenting its case to the panel, on the facts and arguments explicitly set out in its request for consultation. *Australia – Automotive Leather II, inter alia*, referred to Article 13.2 of the DSU which provides that a panel has the right to seek information from any relevant source. According to the Panel, this right is not somehow limited by the expedited nature of the relief sought under Article 4.[11]

The Appellate Body held that a defending party cannot invoke for the first time Article 4.2 one year after the submission of the request for consultations and after consultations had been held on three occasions and the case was on the agenda of two DSB meetings. This would not be in line with the principle of good faith. Therefore, the Appellate Body rejected a claim by the US that the EU's claim under Article 3 should be dismissed because the request for consultations did not include an explicit statement of available evidence.[12]

Relationship between the Requests for Consultations and for Establishing a Panel

According to the Appellate Body in *Brazil – Aircraft*, the first four paragraphs of Article 4 (as well as Articles 4 and 6 of the DSU) set forth a process, by which a complaining party must request consultations, and consultations must be held, before a matter may be referred to the DSB for the establishment of a panel. However, these provisions do not require a precise and exact identity between the specific measures that were the subject of consultations and the specific measures identified in the request for establishment of a panel. The Appellate Body quoted approvingly the preceding Panel that found that one purpose of consultations, as set forth in Article 4.3 of the ASCM, is to clarify the facts of the situation. Therefore, it can be expected that information obtained during the course of consultations may enable the complainant to focus the scope of the matter with respect to which it seeks establishment of a panel.

[11] WT/DS126/R of 25 May 1999, *Australia – Subsidies Provided to Producers and Exporters of Automotive Leather*, paras 9.23–9.30. Ditto WT/DS267/R of 8 September 2004, *United States – Subsidies on Upland Cotton*, para 7.99. Confirmed by WT/DS267/AB/R of 3 March 2005, *United States – Subsidies on Upland Cotton*, para 308.

[12] WT/DS108/AB/R of 24 February 2000, *United States – Tax Treatment for 'Foreign Sales Corporations'*, paras 162–166.

In the case in question, Brazil argued that certain regulatory instruments relating to Brazil's PROEX export financing programme of Embraer aircraft were not properly before the Panel because these instruments came into effect after consultations had been held. The Appellate Body dismissed Brazil's claim. The request for consultations covered 'certain export subsidies granted under the Brazilian Programa de Financiamento às Exportações (PROEX) to foreign purchasers of Brazil's Embraer aircraft'. The request for the establishment of a panel related to 'the payment of export subsidies through interest rate equalization and export financing programmes under PROEX'. According to the Appellate Body, the specific measures at issue were the Brazilian export subsidies for regional aircraft under PROEX. Both, the request for consultations and the request for establishment of a panel referred to these subsidies. Note that Brazil confirmed that the regulatory instruments that came into effect after consultations did not change the essence of the PROEX regime.[13]

Panel Process (Paragraphs 4 to 7 of Article 4)

Introduction

The special rules on the panel process contained in Article 4 include:

- *Establishment of a panel by the DSB*: Under Article 4.4 of the ASCM, any Member may refer the matter to the DSB for the immediate establishment of the panel, as opposed to Article 6 DSU according to which a panel shall be established at the latest at the DSB meeting following that at which the request first appears on the agenda.
- *Assistance by the Permanent Group of Experts*: According to Article 4.5 of the ASCM, a panel can request the assistance of the so-called Permanent Group of Experts as established in Article 24.3 of the ASCM. The recommendations of the Permanent Group of Experts have to be accepted by the panel without modification. There is no such equivalent in the DSU. However, it would appear that up to now, no panel made use of this possibility. The reference to the 'nature of the subsidy' in Article 4.5 appears to refer to whether or not a subsidy is prohibited.[14]

[13] WT/DS46/AB/R of 2 August 1999, *Brazil – Export Financing Programme for Aircraft*, paras 131–133. *Ditto* WT/DS70/R of 14 April 1999, *Canada – Measures Affecting the Export of Civilian Aircraft*, para 9.12.

[14] WT/DS414/R of 15 June 2012, *China – Countervailing and Anti-Dumping Duties on Grain-Oriented Flat-Rolled Electrical Steel from the US*, para 7.61.

- *Circulation of the final panel report*: Pursuant to Article 4.6 of the ASCM, the panel shall circulate its final report within 90 days of the date of its composition and establishment of its terms of reference.[15] The corresponding time-period under the DSU is six months (or three months in cases of extreme urgency) but it should not exceed nine months, see Article 12.9 of the DSU.
- *Withdrawal without delay*: According to Article 4.7 of the ASCM, where it is found that a prohibited subsidy has been provided, the panel shall recommend that the subsidizing Member withdraw the subsidy without delay. The panel shall also specify a time period for the withdrawal. In contrast, Article 19.1 of the DSU specifies that the panel shall recommend that the Member concerned shall bring the measure into conformity with the violated agreement in question and Article 21.3 of the DSU clarifies how the time period for implementation of the ruling should be determined. Article 4.7 of the ASCM also differs from Article 7.8 of the ASCM. The latter provision stipulates that the Member granting or maintaining a subsidy that results in adverse effects shall either withdraw the subsidy (this is also provided for in Article 4.7) or it shall take appropriate steps to remove the adverse effects of such subsidy.
- *Adoption of the panel report*: Article 4.8 of the ASCM provides for an accelerated adoption of the panel report that has found a prohibited subsidy. Adoption shall be within 30 days of the issuance of the report to all Members. In contrast, Article 16 DSU prescribes that the panel report shall not be considered for adoption by the DSB until 20 days after the date it has been circulated to the Members and it shall be adopted within 60 days of that date.
- *Appeal*: Article 4.8 of the ASCM specifies the duration of the appeal phase (the Appellate Body report should be issued within 30 days but no later than 60 days) and the adoption of the Appellate Body's report by the DSB (within 20 days of the issuance of the report to the Members). This contrasts with Articles 17.6 (the Appellate Body report should be issued within 60 days but no later than 90 days) and 17.14 of the DSU (adoption by the DSB within 30 days) that are applicable to 'standard' dispute settlement procedures.

[15] This requirement is not always respected, see WT/DS487/R of 28 November 2016, *United States – Conditional Tax Incentives for Large Civil Aircraft*, para 1.7 *et seq.*

Withdrawal of the Subsidy (Article 4.7)

Notion of Withdrawal

If the measure is found to be a prohibited subsidy, the Panel shall recommend that the subsidizing Member withdraw the subsidy without delay. The Panel shall also specify in its recommendation the time period within which the measure must be withdrawn. Therefore, Article 4.7 of the ASCM goes beyond Article 19.1 of the DSU. The latter provision only stipulates that where a panel concludes that a measure is inconsistent with a covered agreement, it shall recommend that the Member concerned bring the measure into conformity with that agreement. In other words, according to Article 19.1 of the DSU, a panel is not required to make a recommendation as to how the Member should implement its obligations or as to the time frame for implementation.[16]

Because the remedies are different under Article 4.7 of the ASCM as compared to Article 19.1 of the DSU, a Panel cannot necessarily apply judicial economy in case claims have been made pursuant to Articles 3 and 8 of the Agreement of Agriculture as well as Article 3 of the ASCM and if the panel has already found that there was a violation of the two provisions of the Agreement of Agriculture.[17]

Most DSB rulings rejected to read into Article 4.7 an obligation to withdraw the subsidy retroactively. The Appellate Body held that the withdrawal of a subsidy, under Article 4.7, refers to the 'removal' or 'taking away' of that subsidy.[18] Thus, according to *US – Upland Cotton (Article 21.5)*, the decisive question is whether the country in question continues, or continued, after the end of the implementation period, to provide export subsidies, or whether they have ceased to provide such subsidies.[19] As the parties in *Canada – Aircraft (Article 21.5)* agreed, withdrawal of the subsidy normally implies some sort of prospective action.[20] This case

[16] WT/DS265/AB/R, WT/DS266/AB/R and WT/DS283/AB/R of 28 April 2005, *European Communities – Export Subsidies on Sugar*, para 332.

[17] WT/DS265/AB/R, WT/DS266/AB/R and WT/DS283/AB/R of 28 April 2005, *European Communities – Export Subsidies on Sugar*, para 335.

[18] WT/DS46/AB/RW of 21 July 2000, *Brazil – Export Financing Programme for Aircraft (Article 21.4, first recourse)*, para 45; confirmed in WT/DS316/AB/R of 18 May 2011, *EC and certain Member States – Measures Affecting Trade in Large Civil Aircraft*, para 754.

[19] WT/DS267/RW of 18 December 2007, *United States – Subsidies on Upland Cotton (Article 21.5)*, para 14.32; WT/DS70/RW of 9 May 2000, *Canada – Measures Affecting the Export of Civilian Aircraft (Article 21.5 – Brazil)*, paras 5.10, 5.64.

[20] WT/DS70/RW of 9 May 2000, *Canada – Measures Affecting the Export of Civilian Aircraft (Article 21.5 – Brazil)*, para 5.9.

made it clear that removal of the export contingency is sufficient, even if the subsidy continues to be granted.[21] In contrast, *Australia – Automotive Leather II (Article 21.5)* which is described *in fine* of this section, argued that granted export subsidies should be repaid.

If the disputed subsidy is given on the basis of a policy guideline or a similar instrument, withdrawal of the subsidy is more than the simple absence of financing transactions. It also includes an examination of such guidelines in order to ensure that such export subsidies can no longer be granted under the programme in question.[22]

In the implementation proceeding in *US – Upland Cotton*, the US provided after the implementation deadline (i.e. the date by which the US had to comply with the DSB recommendations) payments under outstanding export guarantee commitments. Brazil argued that Article 4.7 included an obligation to abstain from performing on financial commitments outstanding under a programme as of the implementation deadline, or, to put it simply, to refrain from making such payments after that date. The Panel did not agree with Brazil. First, it held that making payments is inconsistent with a Member's obligation to 'withdraw the subsidy' when the payments themselves amount to the granting of the subsidy. However, the subsidies at issue in the dispute were not the payments made by the US government but the issuance of export credit guarantees. Note also that Article 4.7 does not refer to the withdrawal of payments but to the withdrawal of subsidies.[23] Second, Brazil argued that the reference to 'withdraw' in Article 4.7 also referred to a prohibition to maintain an export subsidy. According to Brazil, the obligation to fully withdraw a prohibited subsidy is not achieved if the WTO Member leaves the entirety or part of the prohibited subsidy in place. Brazil submitted that by continuing to perform on its commitments under the prohibited subsidies, the US maintained them unchanged. The Panel held that there was no precedent according to which a Member was required to withdraw an individual subsidy that had already been granted in the past. Ultimately, the Panel saw no need to decide this question as Brazil was not seeking a retroactive remedy but claimed that its request was entirely prospective.[24]

[21] WT/DS70/RW of 9 May 2000, *Canada – Measures Affecting the Export of Civilian Aircraft (Article 21.5 – Brazil)*, para 5.12.

[22] WT/DS70/RW of 9 May 2000, *Canada – Measures Affecting the Export of Civilian Aircraft (Article 21.5 – Brazil)*, paras 5.132 and 5.133.

[23] WT/DS267/RW of 18 December 2007, *United States – Subsidies on Upland Cotton (Article 21.5)*, para 14.22 *et seq.*

[24] WT/DS267/RW of 18 December 2007, *United States – Subsidies on Upland Cotton (Article 21.5)*, para 14.35 *et seq.*

Whether the withdrawal of an export subsidy would amount to retroactivity was also examined in *Brazil – Aircraft (1st Article 21.5)*. However, the situation in that case was different to *US – Upland Cotton*. In the former case, the Brazilian authorities issued first a 'letter of commitment'. At that point, the export subsidy was not granted. But Brazil had entered into a contractual obligation at that point to provide the subsidy once all conditions were met. According to the Appellate Body, export subsidies are granted when all legal conditions have been fulfilled to entitle the beneficiary to receive the subsidies. Two of these conditions were the conclusion of the sales contract and the execution of the export shipments. Only at that stage would the Brazilian authorities issue the relevant bonds. According to the Appellate Body, the export subsidies at issue were therefore only granted at the time of the issuance of the bonds. Note that the subsidies at issue were the issuance of bonds under the so-called PROEX-programme. Under that programme, the Brazilian government granted interest equalization payments, notably on the export of regional aircraft.[25] In short, there was no question of retroactivity of the recommendation to withdraw the subsidy.

A similar situation as in *Brazil – Aircraft (1st Article 21.5)* arose in *US – FSC (1st Article 21.5)*. The US had to withdraw its export subsidy, i.e. the favourable treatment of a company as a Foreign Sales Corporation, by 1 October 2000. However, the US measure implementing the ruling provided that for Foreign Sales Corporations in existence as of that date, the repeal of the original Foreign Sales Corporation measure was not to be applied to any transaction that occurred before 1 January 2002. Moreover, even after that date, existing Foreign Sales Corporations could continue

[25] WT/DS46/AB/R of 2 August 1999, *Brazil – Export Financing Programme for Aircraft*, para 158 *et seq*. In the Article 21.5 proceeding, the Appellate Body pointed out that Brazil's arguments about when a subsidy is deemed to exist under Article 1.1 and when it is granted under Article 3.2 of the ASCM were not relevant for the inquiry of a withdrawal of the subsidy under Article 4.7. Rather, for the purposes of Article 4.7, the Appellate Body examined whether Brazil continued to make payments under the prohibited subsidy programme. In practice, however, the Appellate Body focused on the continued issuance of bonds under the PROEX programme by Brazil, pursuant to letters of commitments made before the implementation date of the original DSB ruling. See WT/DS46/AB/RW of 21 July 2000, *Brazil – Export Financing Programme for Aircraft (Article 21.4, first recourse)*, para 46, that also clearly spelled out that private contractual obligations that a WTO Member may have under its domestic law, are not relevant to the issue of whether the DSB's recommendation to 'withdraw' the prohibited export subsidies permits the continued granting of subsidies. The ruling of the preceding Panel was in line with the Appellate Body ruling, see WT/DS46/RW of 9 May 2000, *Brazil – Export Financing Programme for Aircraft (Article 21.5, first recourse)*, paras 6.15 and 6.16.

to use the original measure for transactions pursuant to a binding contract between the Foreign Sales Corporation and any unrelated person provided that contract was in effect on and after 30 September 2000. The Appellate Body held that this arrangement did not amount to a full withdrawal of the subsidy pursuant to Article 4.7. The US argument was essentially that it should be able to continue to grant prohibited subsidies to protect the contractual interests of private parties and to ensure an orderly transition to the regime of the new measure. The Appellate Body did not agree. A Member's obligation to withdraw a subsidy pursuant to Article 4.7 cannot be affected by contractual obligations which private parties may have assumed between themselves in reliance on laws conferring prohibited export subsidies.[26]

To summarize, the three rulings are coherent. The Appellate Body treated *US – FSC (1st Article 21.5)* in a similar way as *Brazil Aircraft (Article 21.5)*. The US and Brazil had violated their obligation to withdraw the subsidy to the extent they continued after the implementation period to pay out the subsidies in question. The common denominator in both cases is that not all conditions for receiving the subsidy had been met prior to the end of the implementation period. Hence the subsidies could not be disbursed after the end of that period. Note, however, that Brazil had already taken on a sort of contractual obligation prior to the expiry of the implementation period. Note also that the FSC dispute concerned transitional provisions which allowed legislative measures that had been found, in the original dispute to confer prohibited export subsidies, to continue to apply with respect to certain transactions. It did not make any difference that the Brazilian case was about contractual obligations between private parties and the FSC case about an obligation of a WTO Member itself under municipal law. In contrast, *US – Upland Cotton* was different to the Brazilian Aircraft and the US FSC case. In *US – Upland Cotton*, the US did not grant any export subsidies after the implementation period but rather executed outstanding export guarantee commitments (the subsidy in question) that had already been made prior to the end of the implementation period.

Australia – Automotive Leather II (Article 21.5) examined the issue of withdrawal of a prohibited subsidy under two angles. First, Australia argued that it had withdrawn its *de facto* export subsidy by releasing the recipient from the remaining export obligations under the grant contract.

[26] WT/DS108/AB/RW of 14 January 2002, *United States – Tax Treatment for 'Foreign Sales Corporations' (Article 21.5, first recourse)*, paras 224–231.

The Panel was not persuaded by Australia's argument. It opined that where the prohibited subsidy is a non-recurring one and where the export performance has already been achieved, as in the case under review, it would be a logical impossibility to change the facts and circumstances surrounding the decision to provide the subsidy and which led to the conclusion that the subsidy was *de facto* export contingent and thus prohibited. Second, the US, i.e. the complaining party, requested that a withdrawal of the non-recurring subsidy should be understood to mean only the prospective portion of the prohibited subsidy. In other words, the amount of the subsidy should be allocated over the useful life of the production assets and the amount to be withdrawn would cover only that portion which covers the period following adoption of the DSB report plus interest. Australia agreed with this approach in principle. Thus, both parties to the dispute argued that the repayment of the financial contribution in full was not at issue. The Panel went beyond the US request arguing, *inter alia*, that the allocation approach would give rise to 'complicated questions' for which there were no guidelines in the ASCM. It concluded that the withdrawal of the subsidy may encompass repayment of the entire amount of the financial contribution and is not limited to prospective action only. The Panel based itself on the ordinary meaning of the term 'withdraw the subsidy', read in context, and in light of its object and purpose, and in order to give it effective meaning.[27] The Panel also held that repayment of the subsidy does not include any interest component, since the remedy does not involve restoring the *status quo ante* and thus depriving the subsidy recipient of any benefits it may have enjoyed in the past.[28] The parties ultimately came to a settlement, one element of which involved the partial repayment of the subsidy.[29] Many WTO Members have been very reluctant to accept the Panel's retrospective approach.[30]

[27] WT/DS126/RW of 21 January 2000, *Australia – Subsidies Provided to Producers and Exporters of Automotive Leather (Article 21.5)*, para 6.39 *et passim*. See also the concise summary of the Panel ruling in *Goh/Ziegler* (2003) p. 547.

[28] WT/DS126/RW of 21 January 2000, *Australia – Subsidies Provided to Producers and Exporters of Automotive Leather (Article 21.5)*, para 6.49.

[29] WT/DS126/11 of 31 July 2000, *Australia – Subsidies Provided to Producers and Exporters of Automotive Leather*, Notification of Mutually Agreed Solution. *Moulis/O'Donnell* (2000) give a detailed account of the dispute surrounding implementation of the Panel's ruling including the NAFTA dimension.

[30] See e.g. Brazil in WT/DS70/RW of 9 May 2000, *Canada – Measures Affecting the Export of Civilian Aircraft (Article 21.5 – Brazil)*, paras 5.46–5.48. See also the negative reactions by the US, Australia, Canada ('one-time aberration of no precedential value'), Brazil and Japan in the DSB meeting adopting the Panel report, WT/DSB/M/75 of 7 March 2000, pp. 5–9.

Canada – Aircraft Credits and Guarantees observed that it is not entirely clear that the WTO Dispute Settlement System only provides for prospective remedies in cases involving export subsidies,[31] but given the numerous rulings quoted above, *Australia – Automotive Leather II (Article 21.5)* is probably outdated.[32]

Time Period within Which the Measure Must Be Withdrawn

Article 4.7 stipulates that the panel shall recommend that the subsidizing Member withdraw the subsidy without delay and that the panel shall specify the time period within which the measures must be withdrawn. In *Brazil – Aircraft*, the Appellate Body confirmed the Panel ruling that the requirement 'without delay' meant 90 days in the circumstances of the case. Thus, the Appellate Body also rejected Brazil's claim that Article 4.7 does not entitle a Panel to determine a specific time period. Moreover, the Appellate Body held that Article 21.3 of the DSU was not relevant for determining the specific period.[33]

Canada – Autos also specified a 90-day period. In doing so, the Panel took into account the nature of the steps necessary to withdraw the prohibited subsidy. It highlighted that the acts to be revocated were acts of the executive, and not the legislative branch of the government. The amendment or revocation of an act by the executive branch can normally be effectuated more quickly than would be the case if legislative action were required. In line with normal DSU rules, the Panel did not specify a time period during which Canada should bring its measures into conformity with its obligations under GATT 1994 and the GATS that Canada did not respect.[34]

Australia – Automotive Leather II considered as well that a 90-day period would be appropriate for the withdrawal of the measures and

[31] WT/DS222/R of 28 January 2002, *Canada – Export Credits and Loan Guarantees for Regional Aircraft*, para 7.170. See also *Goh/Ziegler* (2003) p. 564 *et passim*.

[32] See also *Grané* (2001) p. 766 *et seq.* on the question of retroactivity (or rather the opposite) in WTO law.

[33] WT/DS46/AB/R of 2 August 1999, *Brazil – Export Financing Programme for Aircraft*, paras 188–194.

[34] WT/DS139/R and WT/DS142/R of 11 February 2000, *Canada – Certain Measures Affecting the Automotive Industry*, paras 11.3–11.7. The 90-day period for the withdrawal of the prohibited export subsidy was not at issue in the arbitration award, see WT/DS139/12 and WT/DS142/12 of 4 October 2000, *Canada – Certain Measures Affecting the Automotive Industry (Arbitration under Article 21(c) of the Understanding on Rules and Procedures Governing the Settlement of Disputes*, paras 34 and 35.

thus rejected a request for an implementation period of seven and a half months.[35]

More generally, a number of rulings highlighted that the duration of the period was influenced, on the one hand, by the stipulation in Article 4.7 that the contested subsidy had to be withdrawn 'without delay' and, on the other, by the nature of the measures necessary to implement (such as whether the action required is one of the executive or one of the legislative branch – see *supra*).[36] Rulings did not accept that the duration of the period should be influenced by the respect of contractual obligations into which the respondent Member or private parties of that Member had entered.[37]

No Recommendation Pursuant to Article 4.7 if the Subsidy Is Already Extinguished

According to the Appellate Body in *EC and certain Member States – Large Civil Aircraft*, Panels or the Appellate Body are not required to make recommendations pursuant to Articles 4.7 and 4.8 with respect to a subsidy that was found to be extinguished or extracted from the recipient.[38]

No Need for a Recommendation Pursuant to Article 4.7 in an Implementation Panel

Article 4.7 obliges a Member to achieve full withdrawal of the prohibited subsidy. Consequently, a Member remains under the obligations of Article 4.7 if it either leaves the entirety or part of the original prohibited subsidy in place, or if it replaces the prohibited subsidy with another subsidy prohibited under the ASCM. The Appellate Body opined, in an *obiter dictum* concerning the question whether an implementation panel could

[35] WT/DS126/R of 25 May 1999, *Australia – Subsidies Provided to Producers and Exporters of Automotive Leather*, paras 10.4–10.7.

[36] WT/DS222/R of 28 January 2002, *Canada – Export Credits and Loan Guarantees for Regional Aircraft*, para 8.4; WT/DS139/R and WT/DS142/R of 11 February 2000, *Canada – Certain Measures Affecting the Automotive Industry*, paras 11.6 and 11.7; WT/DS46/R of 14 April 1999, *Brazil – Export Financing Programme for Aircraft*, para 8.5; WT/DS46/AB/R of 2 August 1999, *Brazil – Export Financing Programme for Aircraft*, paras 192–194; WT/DS126/R of 25 May 1999, *Australia – Subsidies Provided to Producers and Exporters of Automotive Leather*, paras 10.4 and 10.6. The Appellate Body also referred to this standard (but other considerations could also play a role), see WT/DS265/AB/R, WT/DS266/AB/R and WT/DS283/AB/R of 28 April 2005, *European Communities – Export Subsidies on Sugar*, para 340.

[37] WT/DS108/AB/RW of 14 January 2002, *United States – Tax Treatment for 'Foreign Sales Corporations' (Article 21.5, first recourse)*, paras 228–230.

[38] WT/DS316/AB/R of 18 May 2011, *EC and certain Member States – Measures Affecting Trade in Large Civil Aircraft*, paras 756 and 757.

make a new recommendation pursuant to Article 4.7, that this could have the effect of extending implementation periods through new Article 4.7 recommendations and successive Article 21.5 implementation proceedings. And this could lead to a potentially never-ending cycle of dispute settlement proceedings and inordinate delays in the implementation of recommendations and rulings of the DSB.[39] The preceding Panel rejected the proposition that an implementation panel was required to make a new recommendation.[40]

Compensation and Suspension of Concessions (Paragraphs 10 and 11 of Article 4)

Introduction

Article 4.10 stipulates that if a recommendation by the DSB to withdraw the prohibited subsidy is not followed within the time period specified, the DSB shall grant authorization to the prevailing WTO Member to take appropriate countermeasures. Footnote 9, which is attached to the term 'appropriate' in Article 4.10, clarifies that the term 'appropriate' is 'not meant to allow countermeasures that are disproportionate in the light of the fact that the subsidies dealt with under these provisions are prohibited'. Article 22.4 and 22.7 of the DSU would apply in the absence of Article 4.10 of the ASCM. The two aforementioned DSU provisions require that the level of the suspension of concessions shall be equivalent to the level of the nullification or impairment.

Article 4.11 stipulates that in the event a party to the dispute requests arbitration under Article 22.6 of the DSU, the arbitrator shall determine whether the countermeasures are appropriate. Footnote 10 is attached to the term 'appropriate' and it is identical to footnote 9.

According to *US – FSC (Arbitration)*, Articles 4.10 and 4.11 complement each other, and the arbitrator's mandate in relation to countermeasures concerning prohibited subsidies under Article 4 is defined with reference to the notion embodied in the underlying provision in Article 4.10.[41]

[39] WT/DS108/AB/RW2 of 13 February 2006, *United States – Tax Treatment for 'Foreign Sales Corporations' (Article 21.5, second recourse)*, para 81 *et seq.*, in particular paras 83, 84, 86 and 88.

[40] WT/DS108/RW2 of 30 September 2005, *United States – Tax Treatment for 'Foreign Sales Corporations' (Article 21.5, second recourse)*, paras 7.40–7.46, 7.51–7.56.

[41] WT/DS108/ARB of 30 August 2002, *United States – Tax Treatment for 'Foreign Sales Corporations' (Arbitration under Articles 22.6 DSU and 4.11 ASCM)*, para 4.3; WT/DS267/

Articles 7.9 and 7.10 are the provisions equivalent to Articles 4.10 and 4.11 for actionable subsidies.[42]

Up to now, there has been no disagreement as to the types of countermeasures.[43] The typical countermeasure is a suspension of tariff concessions.[44] Rather, the discussions focused on what would constitute an appropriate level of countermeasures. The relevant rulings described below can be distinguished on the basis of whether they determine the level of such countermeasures more from the perspective of the trade effects of the subsidy in question on the complaining Member (so *US – Upland Cotton (Arbitration)*) or from the perspective of the amount of the prohibited subsidy (so the other arbitral awards[45]). In contrast, the corresponding provision in the DSU, i.e. Article 22.4, stipulates that the level of the suspension of concessions authorized by the DSB shall be 'equivalent' to the level of the nullification or impairment and Article 7.9 provides that the countermeasures should be 'commensurate' with the degree and nature of the adverse effects found. Note also that all arbitral awards relating to Article 22.4 found that the purpose of countermeasures under this provision is to induce compliance with the ASCM obligation not to provide prohibited subsidies. Moreover, while it depends on the particular circumstances of the case whether the amount of the subsidy is higher than its trade effects or *vice versa* none of the arbitrators' decisions attempted to justify its decision by systematically choosing the higher of the two amounts.

The well-established WTO practice on the burden of proof in arbitration proceedings also applies in relation to disputes under Article 4.10. If

ARB/1 of 31 August 2009, *United States – Subsidies on Upland Cotton (Arbitration under Article 22.6 DSU and 4.11 ASCM)*, para 4.16.

42 WT/DS46/ARB of 28 August 2000, *Brazil – Export Financing Programme for Aircraft (Arbitration under Articles 22.6 DSU and 4.11 ACSM)*, para 3.49. Note that in *United States – Subsidies on Upland Cotton* Brazil introduced two separate recourses to arbitration, i.e. one under Articles 22.6 DSU and 4.11 ASCM for prohibited subsidies and another one under Articles 22.6 DSU and 7.9 ASCM for actionable subsidies.

43 For a definition of the term 'countermeasure' see WT/DS222/ARB of 17 February 2003, *Canada – Export Credits and Loan Guarantees for Regional Aircraft (Arbitration under Articles 22.6 DSU and 4.11 ASCM)*, para 3.7; WT/DS108/ARB of 30 August 2002, *United States – Tax Treatment for 'Foreign Sales Corporations' (Arbitration under Articles 22.6 DSU and 4.11 ASCM)*, paras 5.4–5.7.

44 But see WT/DS222/ARB of 17 February 2003, *Canada – Export Credits and Loan Guarantees for Regional Aircraft (Arbitration under Articles 22.6 DSU and 4.11 ASCM)*, para 1.3.

45 Note, however, that these other arbitral awards did not entirely rule out a calculation based on trade effects, see the detailed description of these awards *infra* pp. 246–253.

a WTO Member proposes to suspend certain concessions or other obligations as 'appropriate countermeasures', it is for the other WTO Member to submit evidence sufficient to establish a *prima facie* case that the proposed countermeasures are not appropriate.[46] According to *US – Upland Cotton (Arbitration under Articles 22.6 DSU and 4.11 ASCM)*, in the event that an arbitrator finds that the proposed countermeasures are not appropriate within the meaning of Article 4.10 of the ASCM, the arbitrator would be required also to determine what could constitute appropriate countermeasures.[47]

Article 4.10 and 4.11 are special or additional rules identified in Appendix 2 of the DSU. The aforementioned provisions may embody different rules that prevail in the case of conflict with the DSU. Nonetheless, Article 22.6 of the DSU remains relevant, as the general legal basis under which the proceedings are conducted. Indeed, Article 4.11 of the ASCM refers expressly to Article 22.6 of the DSU as the legal basis for arbitral proceedings concerning countermeasures in relation to prohibited subsidies.[48]

US – Upland Cotton (Arbitration under Articles 22.6 DSU and 4.11 ASCM) would suggest that once the prohibited subsidy is withdrawn, countermeasures can no longer be authorized by an arbitrator. In the case in question, the US had maintained prohibited subsidies until 31 July 2006 although these subsidies should have been withdrawn by 1 July 2005. Already on 4 July 2005, Brazil had recourse to arbitration under Article 4.10 of the ASCM and Article 22.2 of the DSU. On 18 August 2006, Brazil also requested a compliance panel whose report was circulated on 18 December 2007. Concerning the withdrawn subsidies, the compliance panel declined to make findings as to any US non-compliance because it saw no useful purpose in addressing non-compliance during a past period. Such finding would have had no additional operational value in terms of the nature of the obligations of the Member in question. The arbitrator relied on similar considerations. It classified countermeasures as a temporary remedy available only where compliance has not

[46] WT/DS46/ARB of 28 August 2000, *Brazil – Export Financing Programme for Aircraft (Arbitration under Articles 22.6 DSU and 4.11 ACSM)*, para 2.8; WT/DS267/ARB/1 of 31 August 2009, *United States – Subsidies on Upland Cotton (Arbitration under Article 22.6 DSU and 4.11 ASCM)*, paras 4.19–4.23.

[47] WT/DS267/ARB/1 of 31 August 2009, *United States – Subsidies on Upland Cotton (Arbitration under Article 22.6 DSU and 4.11 ASCM)*, paras 4.25, 4.128, 4.129.

[48] WT/DS267/ARB/1 of 31 August 2009, *United States – Subsidies on Upland Cotton (Arbitration under Article 22.6 DSU and 4.11 ASCM)*, para 4.31 *et passim*.

been achieved. Countermeasures should induce compliance and according to Article 22.1 of the DSU, neither compensation nor the suspension of concessions or other obligations is preferred to full implementation. Therefore, the arbitrator, whose report is dated 31 August 2009, i.e. a date after the withdrawal of the prohibited subsidy, saw no legitimate basis for such countermeasures in relation to past payments. According to the arbitrator, the entitlement to countermeasures arises as of the end of the implementation period, if there has been no compliance by that moment, and it continues to exist for so long as compliance has not been achieved in relation to the measure at issue.[49]

Relevant Rulings

This section does not describe separately each sub-concept contained in Articles 4.10 and 4.11, i.e. the notions of 'appropriate' and 'countermeasures' as well as 'disproportionate in the light of the fact that the subsidies dealt with under these provisions are prohibited', on the basis of the relevant arbitration awards. Rather, each ruling is described in its entirety because it would have been difficult and artificial to split it up based on the aforementioned sub-concepts. This is to a large extent due to the fact that every case was argued in a very specific way by the parties to the arbitration. A common denominator of all the rulings described below is that the arbitrator enjoys considerable discretion given the broad concepts on which the decisions are based.

Brazil – Aircraft (Arbitration)

Canada requested to be authorized to take countermeasures in the amount of 700 million Canadian dollars per year.

- Canada claimed that the level of countermeasures was directly proportionate to the size of the prohibited subsidies Brazil paid out in support of its regional aircraft exports. As an alternative, Canada also provided a calculation based on the value of the harm caused by the subsidy to the Canadian industry. Although this harm was higher than the amount based on the subsidies paid out by Brazil, Canada preferred

[49] WT/DS267/ARB/1 of 31 August 2009, *United States – Subsidies on Upland Cotton (Arbitration under Articles 22.6 DSU and 4.11 ACSM)*, paras 3.16–3.50. The conclusion of the arbitration proceeding took such a long time because the proceeding was suspended for nearly three years. Critical *vis-à-vis* the award, *Guan* (2014) p. 833 wonders whether in view of the arbitrator's decision the 'reasonable period of time' would still have meaning.

the option based on the amount of the subsidy paid out (paras 3.19, 3.21 and 3.22).

- Brazil agreed in principle with Canada's approach that the countermeasures could be based on the subsidies paid. Brazil also agreed that Canada could have requested the authorization to grant a counter-subsidy. However, it requested that the countermeasures only be based on the subsidies paid for aircraft sales that the competing Canadian industry actually could have obtained itself. Brazil argued that subsidies paid for Brazilian aircraft and for which, for instance, no competing Canadian model existed, should not give rise to countermeasures. Moreover, as Brazil's export subsidies consisted in interest equalization payments, Brazil claimed that only the amount of the interest equalization paid that was above the benchmark of acceptable export financing pursuant to Annex I item k (i.e. CIRR or US Treasury ten-year bond plus 20 basic points rate) could be a basis for calculating the amount of countermeasures. In the opinion of Brazil, only the part of the payments used to 'secure a material advantage in the field of export credit terms' within the meaning of item k constituted a prohibited export subsidy (paras 3.23 *et seq.*, 3.30, 3.32, 3.41).
- First, the arbitrator noted that it did not need to identify a generally applicable definition of the term 'countermeasures' because both parties agreed that this term as used in Article 4 may include suspension of concessions or other obligations and that there was no reason to disagree with the parties (para 3.29).
- The core legal argument centred around the question as to what be considered an 'appropriate' level of countermeasures.
- The arbitrator held that, when dealing with a prohibited export subsidy, an amount of countermeasures which corresponds to the total amount of the subsidy (as opposed to the level of nullification or impairment suffered by Canada) is 'appropriate'. The following considerations appear to be the most important ones in this context:

  (i) Based on the work of the International Law Commission on State responsibility, the arbitrator concluded that a countermeasure is 'appropriate' *inter alia* if it induces compliance. In the case of a prohibited subsidy, inducing compliance means withdrawal of the subsidy without delay pursuant to Article 4.7. In contrast, other illegal subsidies do not have to be withdrawn without delay (paras 3.44 and 3.45).
  (ii) Meaning must be given to the fact that there is no explicit reference to the concept of nullification or impairment in Articles 3

and 4, whilst this concept is expressly mentioned in Article 5. The requirement to withdraw a prohibited subsidy is of a different nature than removal of the specific nullification or impairment caused to a Member by a measure which in turn would be based on the trade effect.[50] Moreover, Articles 7.9 and 7.10, which are with regard to actionable subsidies the provisions equivalent to Articles 4.9 and 4.10 use the term 'commensurate with the degree and nature of the adverse effects'. Finally, the reference in footnotes 9 and 10 that the subsidies dealt with are prohibited can most probably be considered more as an aggravating factor than as a mitigating factor (paras 3.41–3.51).

- The arbitrator also dismissed Brazil's argument that the countermeasures should not cover the full interest rate equalization payments but only the portion above the benchmark rate. The previous Panel and Appellate Body rulings considered the entire amount a prohibited subsidy. And it is the prohibited subsidy that should be withdrawn (paras 3.32–3.40, 3.54).
- The arbitrator also did not accept Brazil's request to take only subsidies into account that financed the sale of Brazilian aircraft that competed with Canadian aircraft. Such a limitation would only have been appropriate if the benchmark had been nullification and impairment (para 3.62).
- Based on the above, the arbitrator calculated a present value of the subsidy provided by Brazil of 344.2 million Canadian dollars per year.[51]

US – FSC (Arbitration)

In *US – FSC (Arbitration)*, the US were found not to have withdrawn export subsidies. The EC requested authorization to take appropriate countermeasures and to suspend concessions in the amount of USD 4.043 billion per year. This corresponded to the amount of the subsidies (i.e. the financial contribution) given by the US. The US argued that the countermeasure should be limited to the trade effects of the prohibited

[50] The Appellate Body also noted in para 3.54 that given that export subsidies usually operate with a multiplying effect (a given amount enables a company to make a number of sales, thus gaining a foothold in a given market with the possibility to expand and gain market shares), the calculation of the countermeasures based on the trade effect could produce higher figures than a calculation based on the amount of the subsidy.

[51] WT/DS46/ARB of 28 August 2000, *Brazil – Export Financing Programme for Aircraft (Arbitration under Articles 22.6 DSU and 4.11 ACSM).*

subsidy. The arbitrator did not agree with the US but instead authorized the amount requested by the EC. It held:

- In the context of Article 4, the term 'countermeasures' is used to define temporary measures which a prevailing Member may be authorized to take in response to a persisting violation of Article 3, pending full compliance with the DSB's recommendations (para 5.5).
- A 'countermeasure' in Article 4.10 can be directed at either countering the measure at issue (in the case in question effectively neutralizing the export subsidy) or countering the effects of the prohibited subsidy in the affected party, or both (para 5.6).
- The adjective 'appropriate' in Article 4.10 does not predefine which of the aforementioned two possible interpretations should be selected. The relevant provisions do not lay down a precise formula or otherwise quantified benchmark or amount of countermeasures which might be legitimately authorized in each and every instance. Based on the plain meaning of the word 'appropriate' ('especially suitable or fitting'), countermeasures should be adapted to the particular case at hand; they should be suitable or fitting by way of response to the case. There is an intent not to prejudge what the circumstances might be in the specific context of dispute settlement in a given case (paras 5.8–5.13).
- However, footnote 9 effectively clarifies that countermeasures that would be 'disproportionate in the light of the fact that the subsidies dealt with under these provisions are prohibited' could not be considered appropriate (para 5.16). There should be no manifest imbalance or incongruity between the wrongful act and the countermeasure. But this does not require exact equivalence (para 5.18).
- The final part of footnote 9 provides that, when assessing countermeasures under Article 4.10, account must be taken of the fact that the export subsidy at issue is prohibited pursuant to Part II of the ASCM and has to be withdrawn (para 5.22).
- An export subsidy has, in itself, the effect of upsetting the balance of rights and obligations between the parties, irrespective of what might be the actual trade effects of the prohibited subsidies. This consideration can only be reasonably construed to be an aggravating rather than a mitigating factor (para 5.23).
- Footnote 9 makes it clear that the text cannot be construed to confine the appropriateness test to the element of countering the injurious effects on a party. The entitlement to countermeasures is also to be assessed taking into account the legal status of the wrongful act and

that it has upset the balance of rights and obligations between WTO Members (para 5.24).

- Footnote 9 does not allow countermeasures that would be disproportionate but it does not require strict proportionality (para 5.26).
- In terms of relevant context, the arbitrator noted that there is no reference whatsoever in the remedies foreseen under Article 4 to concepts such as 'trade effects', 'adverse effects' or 'trade impact' while Articles 5, 7.9 and 9.4 refer to such concepts. The latter provisions refer to subsidies that are actionable but not prohibited. While these other subsidies are acceptable in themselves, other Members are nevertheless entitled to protection from their possible adverse effects (para 5.32 *et seq.*).
- Article 22.4 and 22.7 of the DSU which are the provisions that would apply in the absence of Article 4.10 of the ASCM, stipulate that the level of the suspension of concessions shall be equivalent to the level of nullification or impairment (para 5.44 *et seq.*).
- Pursuant to Article 4.7, the DSB may only recommend that the subsidizing WTO Member withdraw the subsidy without delay. Therefore, the object and purpose of the ASCM in relation to Article 4.10 is to secure compliance with the DSB's recommendation to withdraw the subsidy without delay (para 5.52).

On the basis of the above, the arbitrator rejected the view of the US and concluded that a Member is entitled to act with countermeasures that properly take into account the gravity of the breach and the nature of the upset in the balance of rights and obligations in question. This cannot be reduced to a requirement that constrains countermeasures to trade effects. At the same time, Article 4.10 does not amount to a blank cheque – there is nothing in the text or the context which suggests an entitlement to manifestly punitive measures. The interpretation proposed by the US would effectively have read the specific language of Article 4.10 out of the text (paras 5.61 and 5.62).[52]

When analysing the countermeasures proposed by the EU, the arbitrator first analysed the elements of the wrongful US act:

- The arbitrator considered fundamental the financial contribution, as this is a core element of the subsidy definition. The amount of the financial contribution given by the US and the amount of the proposed

[52] WT/DS108/ARB of 30 August 2002, *United States – Tax Treatment for 'Foreign Sales Corporations' (Arbitration under Articles 22.6 DSU and 4.11 ASCM).*

countermeasures were virtually identical and there was thus a manifest relationship of proportionality (paras 6.14–6.17).

- The arbitrator noted that the financial contribution given is, *stricto sensu*, the measure at issue, i.e. the wrongful act that breached the US's obligation owed to the EU. Thus, there was not only a more arithmetic proportionality but also an underlying more structural element of proportionality between measure and proposed countermeasure (paras 6.18–6.19).
- On that basis, it appeared to the arbitrator that 'this is a proper manner from which to judge the congruence of the countermeasure to the measure at issue, i.e. to view it under its legal category: on the one hand an expense to the government of a certain value constituting an upsetting of the balance of rights and obligations; and therefore, on the other hand, a congruent duty imposed by a responding government as a mirror withdrawal of an obligation' (para 6.19).
- The arbitrator also noted that there was a certain correlation between the benefits initially conferred to US firms and the EU's proposed response. He added that it would in many situations be impracticable to devise a countermeasure that would exactly counter the benefits conferred. Moreover, there was no requirement to do so because Article 4.10 takes the perspective of countering the legal breach as a wrongful act, and not its effects (paras 6.21–6.25).
- The FSC subsidy did not only affect the EU but also other trading partners of the US. However, there was no need for the arbitrator to examine this issue of an allocation of the countermeasures because, *inter alia*, the EU was the only complainant (paras 6.26–6.32 and 6.37–6.42).

The arbitrator also examined the trade effects of the FSC subsidy on the EU because Article 4.10 does not preclude a WTO Member from taking countermeasures that are tailored to counter the adverse effects that it has suffered as a result of the illegal measure. Thus, trade effects are not *a priori* ruled out as relevant when examining the appropriateness of the countermeasure. But the arbitrator found that it had no reliable basis to conclude that the amount of countermeasures would be out of proportion with the trade effects.[53]

[53] WT/DS108/ARB of 30 August 2002, *United States – Tax Treatment for 'Foreign Sales Corporations' (Arbitration under Articles 22.6 DSU and 4.11 ASCM)*, paras 6.33–6.60.

Canada – Aircraft Credits and Guarantees (Arbitration)

In *Canada – Aircraft Credits and Guarantees (Arbitration)*, Brazil sought an authorization to impose countermeasures in an amount of USD 3.36 billion. This amount was an estimate of the value of the contracts for Canadian Bombardier aircraft not delivered as of the date that the subsidies at issue should have been withdrawn (and implicitly of lost sales for Brazil's aircraft manufacturer Embraer). The arbitrator awarded a significantly lower amount, i.e. around USD 248 million. The following considerations are of broader importance:

- The arbitrator noted that countermeasures based on trade effects or competitive harm, as requested by Brazil, may be consistent with Article 4.10 (para 3.20).
- The arbitrator pointed out that in past cases where a lost sales or a trade effect methodology was proposed, a counterfactual approach was used, comparing the existing situation with that which could have occurred had implementation taken place as of the expiration of a reasonable period of time. The arbitrator was persuaded that withdrawal of the subsidy would not have resulted in Embraer obtaining the remainder of the contract relating to Bombardier aircraft that had not been delivered yet at the end of a reasonable period of time. Therefore, countermeasures based on a trade effects/competitive harm methodology as proposed by Canada were not appropriate (paras 3.21–3.26).
- The arbitrator also recalled *US – FSC (Arbitration)*, which pointed out that countermeasures should be adapted to the particular case at hand. On that basis the arbitrator considered the appropriateness of the level of the proposed countermeasures in the light of the following five factors: (i) the level of the proposed countermeasures authorized in the parallel case *Brazil – Aircraft*; (ii) the total value of goods imported from Canada into Brazil; (iii) the gravity of Canada's breach of its WTO obligations; (iv) the need to induce Canada to comply with its WTO obligations; and (v) whether the countermeasures were manifestly excessive. Note in this context that Brazil's proposed countermeasures were a multiple of the amount that was awarded to Canada in the parallel case and at least three times higher than the total Canadian exports to Brazil. Moreover, the gravity of the breach of WTO obligations does not only refer to the nature of the subsidy (i.e. a prohibited export subsidy), but could also cover characteristics of the subsidy such as whether the subsidy programme was limited in time etc. (paras 3.27–3.51).

- For the above reasons, the arbitrator used as a starting point for calculating the appropriate amount of a countermeasure a methodology based on the amount of the subsidy. Brazil requested to base the countermeasures on the value of the loan. Instead, the arbitrator calculated the amount of the subsidy as the discounted present value of the difference in payment streams under the subsidized financing compared to an estimated market financing. It considered Article 14 of the ASCM relevant for this exercise (paras 3.52–3.90). The net present value so calculated amounted to USD 206 million.
- The arbitrator finally examined whether adjustments to the amount of subsidy were necessary in order to arrive at the appropriate level of countermeasures. It held that mere non-compliance with the recommendations and rulings of the DSB were not aggravating factors justifying a higher level of countermeasures. However, Canada stated that, for the moment, it did not intend to withdraw the subsidy at issue. Therefore, and in order to induce compliance in the case at hand, a higher level of countermeasures than that based on the amount of the subsidy was necessary and appropriate. Brazil also tried to justify an upward adjustment on the grounds that the lower the anticipated level of countermeasures, the higher the chances of hit and run actions. The arbitrator rejected this based on the particular circumstances of the case (paras 3.91–3.122).[54]

US – Upland Cotton (Arbitration under Articles 22.6 DSU and 4.11 ASCM)

Brazil sought an authorization to take countermeasures in an amount that corresponded to the total of (i) the export subsidies received by US exporters (in the form of interest rate discounts) in the most recent fiscal year and that the US had not withdrawn yet and (ii) the estimated additional export sales obtained by US exporters as a result of these discounts (so-called 'additionality') (para 4.6). In other words, Brazil's claims were not limited to the amount of the prohibited subsidy but – contrary to previous arbitration awards – they also took into account the trade effects of the subsidy. The US had proposed an altogether different approach, i.e. that the countermeasures should be calculated on the basis of the cost to the government of the subsidies at issue, and not on the benefits as requested by Brazil (paras 4.9–4.11, 4.18).

[54] WT/DS222/ARB of 17 February 2003, *Canada – Export Credits and Loan Guarantees for Regional Aircraft (Arbitration under Articles 22.6 DSU and 4.11 ASCM).*

The arbitrator followed in principle the line taken by Brazil, i.e. not only the amount of the prohibited subsidy (in the sense of the benefit to the recipient) is relevant for determining what constituted 'appropriate' countermeasures, but also the trade effects of the prohibited subsidy. Thus, *US – Upland Cotton (Arbitration under Articles 22.6 DSU and 4.11 ASCM)* has departed from previous decisions, notably from *US – FSC (Arbitration)*, by clearly limiting the amount of authorized countermeasures to the trade effect (as opposed to the full amount of the prohibited subsidies) suffered by Brazil both on its domestic market and on its export markets. At the same time, the arbitrator's decision suggests that the standard to determine the level of countermeasures is more flexible that the one contemplated by Article 7.8 ASCM or Article 22.4 of the DSU. The following considerations of the arbitrator merit being highlighted:

- The term 'countermeasures' essentially characterizes the nature of the measures to be authorized, i.e. temporary measures that would otherwise be contrary to the obligations under the WTO Agreement and that are taken in response to a breach of an obligation under the ASCM (para 4.42).
- The term 'countermeasures' does not necessarily connote an intention to refer to retaliatory action that goes beyond the mere rebalancing of trade interests, contrary to what was suggested by Brazil (para 4.38).
- The permissible level of countermeasures is primarily defined through the term 'appropriate' and the wording of footnote 9 (para 4.43).
- The term 'appropriate' suggests that all the circumstances of a particular case should be taken into account in assessing the appropriateness of proposed countermeasures, and it also suggests a degree of flexibility in what might be considered appropriate in a given case (para 4.47; see also paras 4.104 and 4.107).
- The question is what countermeasures will be 'appropriate' for that complainant in the specific dispute at hand. This implies that it is appropriate to take into account not only the existence of the violation in itself, but also the specific circumstances that arise from the breach for the complaining party seeking to apply countermeasures (para 4.54).
- The actual economic consequences of the breach may vary significantly from case to case. In particular, the trade-distorting impact of a prohibited subsidy on a WTO Member may vary depending on the nature and design of the subsidy as well as various economic factors (para 4.57).
- The trade-distorting impact of the prohibited subsidy at issue on the complaining Member effectively reflects the manner in which the

economic position of the complaining party to the dispute has been disrupted and harmed by the illegal measure. This provides a measure of the extent to which the balance of rights and obligations between the parties has been upset (para 4.58).

- An interpretation that would not take due account of the extent to which the complaining Member has been affected by the illegal measure would lead to the result that countermeasures could in principle be identical, irrespective of whether the Member at issue has been significantly affected or not at all by the measure (para 4.60).
- The initiation of dispute settlement proceedings in relation to a prohibited subsidy is not conditional on the demonstration of adverse trade effects. This does not imply, however, that the manner in which the complaining Member is affected by the breach is not relevant to dispute settlement proceedings, or that it should not be an important consideration in determining the level of countermeasures if the dispute reaches the stage of such countermeasures (para 4.63).
- The proportionality requirement in footnote 9 is a protection against excessive countermeasures. While the expression 'appropriate countermeasures' allows a degree of flexibility in assessing what may be appropriate in the circumstances of a given case (as opposed to an exact equivalence with the level of the adverse trade effects on the complaining Member, see paras 4.87, 4.88, 4.97, 4.107, 4.178), this flexibility is not unbounded.
- Countermeasures under Article 4.10 serve to induce compliance. However, this purpose does not, in and of itself, distinguish Article 4.10 from the other comparable provisions in the WTO Agreement, and does not in and of itself provide specific indications as to the level of countermeasures that may be permissible under this provision (para 4.112).
- Countermeasures that are suited to the circumstances could mean countermeasures authorized at a level that is within the range of the trade-distorting impact that can fairly be said to arise for the complaining Member from the failure to withdraw the illegal measure (paras 4.114, 4.132–4.135).
- The arbitrator accepted basing the level of countermeasures on the amount of the subsidies *and* the trade effects. The trade effects had been defined as the additional sales as a result of the subsidies and had been referred to in the Award as so-called 'additionality'. These trade effects had been further broken down to sales to creditworthy obligors (marginal additionality) and sales to uncreditworthy obligators

(full additionality), both in Brazil and in third country markets (paras 4.173–4.198, 4.245–4.279).
- The arbitrator rejected the idea that its interpretation could 'dull' the effectiveness of countermeasures under Article 4.10 thereby making them less powerful for the inducement of compliance (para 4.116).

Note that US exports benefitting from the prohibited subsidies had displaced not only Brazilian exports, but also exports from other sources (see also paras 4.192, 4.199 and 4.244). As a result, the arbitrator apportioned the full amount and awarded to Brazil only USD 147.4 million for the financial year 2006 instead of USD 3 billion as requested by Brazil.[55] Some commentators have welcomed this decision.[56]

DSB Rulings Have Been Wary to Deduce from Article 4 Additional Procedural Obligations

On a number of occasions, the defending party to a dispute tried to argue that the accelerated nature of dispute settlement under Article 4 has consequences on the panel procedure that go beyond the explicit obligations listed in Article 4. So far, DSB rulings have dismissed these attempts.

- Article 4 does not prevent a party from adducing new evidence or invoking new allegations (including affirmative defences) after the first substantive meeting of the panel with the parties (provided the allegations fall within the panel's terms of reference and respect due process rights).[57]
- There is nothing in either the DSU or the ASCM that a request for a fast-track panel under Article 4 ASCM should be more precise than a request for establishing a panel under the 'standard' WTO dispute settlement. Such a requirement also cannot be inferred from the duty to provide a 'statement of available evidence' pursuant to Article 4.2.[58]

[55] WT/DS267/ARB/1 of 31 August 2009, *United States – Subsidies on Upland Cotton (Arbitration under Article 22.6 DSU and 4.11 ASCM)*. The formula for subsequent years is set out in Annex 4 of the decision. See also the very good discussion of this arbitration award (as well as the parallel award concerning Brazil's claims under Article 7.9) by *Grossman/Sykes* (2011); the formula is discussed in their article on p. 162.

[56] *Grossman/Sykes* (2011) p. 141.

[57] WT/DS70/R of 14 April 1999, *Canada – Measures Affecting the Export of Civilian Aircraft*, paras 9.70–9.74, 9.77.

[58] WT/DS70/R of 14 April 1999, *Canada – Measures Affecting the Export of Civilian Aircraft*, para 9.29.

Adverse Inferences from a Member's Refusal to Provide Information

Article 4, which deals with remedies against prohibited subsidies, does not specifically address the matter of drawing adverse inferences from a Member's refusal to provide information. However, paragraphs 6 to 9 of Annex V of the ASCM, which deal with procedures for developing information about serious prejudice in cases involving actionable subsidies, do address the drawing of adverse inferences under certain circumstances. The Appellate Body in *Canada – Aircraft* saw no 'logical reason' why Panels should not have the power to draw adverse inferences in prohibited subsidy cases while such power existed in dispute settlement proceedings in relation to actionable subsidies.[59]

[59] WT/DS70/AB/R of 2 August 1999, *Canada – Measures Affecting the Export of Civilian Aircraft*, para 201 *et seq*. The various instances where the issue of adverse inferences arose are described in WT/DS70/R of 14 April 1999, *Canada – Measures Affecting the Export of Civilian Aircraft*, para 9.181 and para 9.189 *et seq*.

PART III

ACTIONABLE SUBSIDIES

Article 5

Adverse Effects

Introduction

Article 5 obliges WTO Members not to cause, through the use of any subsidy, adverse effects to the interests of other Members. This provision distinguishes three types of adverse effects:

- injury to the domestic industry of another Member (see *infra* pp. 269–275 of this chapter);
- nullification or impairment of benefits accruing directly or indirectly to other Members under GATT 1994 (see *infra* pp. 275 of this chapter);
- serious prejudice to the interests of another Member (see *infra* the commentary to Article 6, pp. 278–355).

The definition of a subsidy is set out in Article 1, which applies for the purposes of the entire ASCM. For the purposes of interpreting the term 'use of any subsidy', Article 7.1 provides useful context. This provision equates the use of a subsidy with granting or maintaining a subsidy.[1]

The three types of adverse effects identified in Article 5 are quite distinct. First, they can be distinguished in terms of how the effects of a subsidy are to be assessed. If the adverse effects consist of 'injury to the domestic industry of another Member', it has to be demonstrated that the subsidized exports (and not the subsidy as such) have caused injury of the domestic industry in the importing country. By contrast, in a claim concerning serious prejudice, the subsidy(ies) as such have to cause the effects that are considered a serious prejudice, e.g. the *effect of the subsidy* is to displace or impede exports of a like product of another Member into the third country market of the subsidizing

[1] WT/DS217/R and WT/DS234/R of 16 September 2002, *United States – Continued Dumping and Subsidy Offset Act of 2000*, para 7.122.

Member. Second, the geographical area where the adverse effects occur differs depending on which subparagraph is examined. In case of injury to the domestic industry of another Member, it is obviously the domestic market of that other Member for which injury should be found. By contrast, in a serious prejudice claim the adverse effects can occur on the market of the subsidizing Member, on the market of the competing Member or on a third country market, depending on which subparagraph of Article 6.3 the claim is based. Finally, if the adverse effects claim is based on nullification and impairment, the adverse effects should typically be felt in the market of the subsidizing WTO Member.

Article 7 specifies the remedies that are at the disposal of any Member in case it suffers such adverse effects. These remedies consist essentially of consultations, and if these do not result in a mutually agreed solution, dispute settlement proceedings.

The last sentence of Article 5 stipulates that this provision does not apply to subsidies maintained on agricultural products as provided in Article 13 of the Agreement on Agriculture.[2]

Finally, Articles 5 and 6 apply subject to the special and differential treatment provisions for developing country Members as contained in Articles 27.8, 27.9 and 27.13.[3]

Prohibited Subsidies Can Also Be Actionable under Part III of the ASCM

In *Korea – Commercial Vessels*, Korea argued that it was legally and factually impossible for a given measure to be at the same time both a prohibited and an actionable subsidy. The Panel did not accept this view.[4] This Panel also held that a subsidy that is specific under Article 2.3 (here as a result of export contingency) is specific for the purpose of both Part II (prohibited export subsidy) and Part III (actionable subsidy) claims.[5]

[2] See *supra* pp. 37–46.

[3] See *infra* the commentary to Article 27, pp. 573–574.

[4] WT/DS273/R of 7 March 2005, *Korea – Measures Affecting Trade in Commercial Vessels*, para 7.334.

[5] WT/DS273/R of 7 March 2005, *Korea – Measures Affecting Trade in Commercial Vessels*, para 7.514.

Temporal Scope of Article 5

In *EC and certain Member States – Large Civil Aircraft*, the EU took the view that Article 5 did not apply to subsidies granted prior to 1 January 1995 as they fall outside the scope of Article 5. To cover them would be inconsistent with the principle of non-retroactivity embodied in Article 28 of the Vienna Convention. Both the Panel and the Appellate Body disagreed. The Appellate Body essentially argued that Article 5 requests that '[n]o Member should cause, through the use of any subsidy … adverse effects to the interests of other Members'. According to the Appellate Body, this means that pre-1995 measures are not precluded from challenge because from 1995 on WTO Members have been under an obligation not to cause, 'through the use of any subsidy', adverse effects to the interests of other Members. The Appellate Body arrived at this conclusion *inter alia* by considering Article 7.8 and paragraph 7 of Annex IV of the ASCM.[6]

Adverse Effects Must Be 'Present'

General

Adverse effects must be 'present', as opposed to such effects occurring in the past. But Articles 5 and 6.3 do not specify any particular time period for a panel to consider when determining adverse effects. However, a determination pursuant to Article 6.3 in conjunction with Article 6.4 requires the establishment of an appropriately representative period. Such period shall be sufficient to demonstrate clear trends in the development of the market for the product concerned and normally shall be at least one year. None of these provisions defines a starting date or an end date of such period. Moreover, it also has to be borne in mind that there is typically a time lag until data become available.[7] As shown *infra*, this is

[6] WT/DS316/AB/R of 18 May 2011, *EC and certain Member States – Measures Affecting Trade in Large Civil Aircraft*, para 650 *et seq*. Before the Panel the EU also argued that the launch aid given to Airbus should be judged against the provisions of the Tokyo Round Subsidies Code. The Panel dismissed this claim – see WT/DS316/R of 30 June 2010, *EC and certain Member States – Measures Affecting Trade in Large Civil Aircraft*, para 7.320 *et seq*. This aspect was not appealed.

[7] See e.g. WT/DS267/AB/RW of 16 May 2008, *United States – Subsidies on Upland Cotton (Article 21.5)*, paras 237, 244; WT/DS316/R of 30 June 2010, *EC and certain Member States – Measures Affecting Trade in Large Civil Aircraft*, paras 7.1693–7.1694. See also *infra* the commentary to this chapter p. 270.

a recurring theme in DSB rulings concerning all three types of adverse effects. Note, however, that there is no need to demonstrate current benefit in an adverse effects claim (see *infra* pp. 267–268). By contrast, countervailing duties can only offset the benefit still found to exist (see *infra* the commentary to Article 19, pp. 526–531).

Adverse Effects Depend on How the Subsidy Accrues or Diminishes over Time

In *EC and certain Member States - Large Civil Aircraft*, the parties agreed that a subsidy has a life which may come to an end, through either the removal of the financial contribution and/or the expiration of the benefit. Based on this, the Appellate Body pointed out that the adverse effect analysis, which is distinct from the benefit analysis, has to take into account the fact that a subsidy provided accrues and diminishes (e.g. by depreciation of the assets purchased with the subsidy) over time, and will have a finite life. Intervening events that occurred after the grant of the subsidy and that may affect the projected value of the subsidy as determined under the *ex ante* analysis, must be taken into account.[8]

In this dispute the EU argued that a number of intervening events reduced or brought to an end the subsidies provided to the Airbus companies. First, the EU claimed that shares in Aérospatiale-Matra, EADS and Airbus SAS, firms that have previously received subsidies, were subsequently bought by new private owners in sales transactions conducted at arm's length and for fair market value, resulting in the extinction of subsidies. Note that this dispute was not about full privatizations but about partial privatizations, contrary to previous 'privatization' cases (*US - Countervailing Measures Concerning Certain Products from the EC* and *US - Lead and Bismuth II*) that concerned a complete transfer of ownership and control. Moreover, the Airbus case was about sales of shares between private entities. Finally, the previous cases concerned CVD measures and not, as here, an Article 5 determination.[9]

[8] WT/DS316/AB/R of 18 May 2011, *EC and certain Member States - Measures Affecting Trade in Large Civil Aircraft*, paras 709–715.

[9] For a discussion of *US - Countervailing Measures Concerning Certain Products from the EC* and *US - Lead and Bismuth II*, see *infra* the commentary to Article 14, pp. 433–443.

The members of the Appellate Body division hearing the case could not agree on a common view and consequently set out separate opinions. One Member took the view that the rules developed in previous full privatization cases do not apply to partial privatization or to private-to-private sales while another thought they did. A third Member finally considered that the subsidy continued to benefit the recipient, even if the ownership of the recipient's shares changes. In other words, the third Member seemed to have doubts that any privatization could extinguish the subsidy. There was no need for the Appellate Body to finally decide on this point because the Panel had not sufficiently examined the circumstances surrounding the partial privatizations and private-to-private sales transactions at issue. The Panel should have assessed whether each of the sales was on arm's-length terms and for fair market value, and to what extent these sales involved a transfer of ownership and control to new owners. For doing this, a fact-intensive inquiry into the circumstances surrounding the changes in ownership would have been necessary. Moreover, a Panel would have had to examine whether the transactions are of a nature, kind and amount so as to affect an adverse effects analysis and attenuate the link under Articles 5 and 6 of the ASCM between the alleged subsidies and their alleged effects. Note that the EU only invoked extinction of the subsidy in relation to significant sales of shares in Airbus companies, i.e. transactions in the assets of an enterprise by strategic shareholders rather than day-to-day sales of shares held as investments.[10]

Second, the EU claimed that the removal of cash or cash equivalents from a wholly owned subsidiary that has previously received subsidies, results in an extraction of subsidies that should be taken into account in an adverse effects analysis under Article 5. Unlike the Panel, the Appellate Body did not *a priori* exclude the possibility that all or part of a subsidy may be removed from a firm by the removal of cash or cash equivalents. The Appellate Body also hastened to add that it is not the case that every time cash leaves a company the benefit of prior financial contributions would be correspondingly diminished. Rather, a consideration of whether the cash removed from a company eliminates past subsidies is a fact-specific inquiry that must be assessed in the light of the circumstances of the case. Such inquiry could consider matters such as whether the cash extracted was in the form of dividends representing the profits of a company. The Panel developed a two-pronged test in this respect

[10] WT/DS316/AB/R of 18 May 2011, *EC and certain Member States – Measures Affecting Trade in Large Civil Aircraft*, paras 716–736.

that the Appellate Body found 'a useful point of departure'. According to the Panel, in order for a cash disbursement to be capable of removing or reducing the benefit of prior financial contributions,

- there must be causal relationship of some sort between the cash extraction and the subsidy and
- the extraction must effectively move the money beyond the reach of the company-shareholder unit.

In relation to the first point the EU argued that any benefit from prior subsidies would have enhanced the balance sheet of the Airbus companies and consequently, the removal of cash had the effect of reducing these companies' value and extracting any incremental value created by prior subsidies. The Appellate Body held that the EU's standard was not sufficient. At a minimum, the EU was required to explain how the specific subsidies received were reflected in the balance sheets of the companies in question, and how the cash removed or extracted represented the remaining or unused value of these subsidies.[11]

Repayment of a Subsidized Loan

In *EC and certain Member States – Large Civil Aircraft*, the EC requested the Panel to dismiss US claims in relation to all but three loans provided by the European Investment Bank because the loans had already been fully repaid, often before the establishment of the Panel. The Panel did not agree. It referred to the rulings by the Appellate Body in *US – Upland Cotton* and by a Panel in *Indonesia – Autos* (both of which did not involve the granting of loans) and argued that while the European Communities may be correct in characterizing a fully repaid loan as a measure that no longer exists, the nature of an adverse effects claim does not preclude the possibility of finding that the loan may have a consequential impact on the relevant market after its full repayment and, as such, cause adverse effects within the meaning of Article 5.[12]

Loan Granted to a Predecessor Company

In *EC and certain Member States – Large Civil Aircraft*, the EC requested the Panel to dismiss US claims in relation to a loan given to British

[11] WT/DS316/AB/R of 18 May 2011, *EC and certain Member States – Measures Affecting Trade in Large Civil Aircraft*, paras 737–749.

[12] WT/DS316/R of 30 June 2010, *EC and certain Member States – Measures Affecting Trade in Large Civil Aircraft*, paras 7.720–7.723. This issue was not appealed.

Aerospace because the company's Airbus activities had been transferred to Airbus SAS. According to the EU it followed that any benefit conferred by this loan could not have been transferred to Airbus SAS and be causing present adverse effects to the US. The Panel did not agree. It pointed out that any benefit conferred by the loan would have been enjoyed for the most part between 1991 and October 2006, and therefore was directly connected with the production and sale of Airbus large civil aircraft. This was enough for the Panel to dispose of the EU's argument.[13]

Article 5 Does Not Require the Demonstration of a 'Continuing Benefit'

In *EC and certain Member States – Large Civil Aircraft*, the EU was of the view that the application of Article 5 (as well as Articles 1 and 6) requires, in addition to the finding of a subsidy, that such subsidy confers a present or continuing benefit. To put it differently: according to the EU, when a benefit to a recipient arising from prior subsidies diminishes over time (e.g. by using amortization rules to allocate the amount of benefit over time) or is removed or taken away, there is a significant change that must be taken into account in the application of the ASCM and, in particular, in the examination of a causal link between the granting of the subsidy and the alleged adverse effects. The EU referred in this respect to a number of transactions involving Airbus companies that it alleged had the effect of removing all or part of the subsidies provided to the companies. The EU based its position on the use of the present tense in Articles 5 ('cause') and 6.3 ('is').

Therefore, the dispute was about whether and, if so, how an assessment of the benefit established pursuant to Article 1.1(b) relates to the adverse facts analysis. Both the Panel and the Appellate Body disagreed with the EU, although the Appellate Body slightly modified the Panel's interpretation. The Appellate Body held that the EU confused present adverse effects (which must be demonstrated under Articles 5 and 6.3) with present subsidization (which is not necessary to demonstrate). The use or provision of a subsidy and the adverse effects are not necessarily contemporaneous but

[13] WT/DS316/R of 30 June 2010, *EC and certain Member States – Measures Affecting Trade in Large Civil Aircraft*, paras 7.725–7.728. This issue was not appealed. In 2006, Airbus and EADS placed their Airbus-related design, engineering, manufacturing and production activities and their membership rights under the common control of the newly created holding company Airbus SAS (the Panel report contains a description of all corporate changes in Airbus after para 7.289).

there may be a time lag, as *US – Upland Cotton* has already pointed out. The Appellate Body explicitly did not exclude that, under certain circumstances, a past subsidy that no longer exists may be found to cause or have caused adverse effects that continue to be present during the reference period. At the same time, the Appellate Body also recognized that the effects of a subsidy will ordinarily dissipate over time and will end at some point after the subsidy has expired and that this aspect should be considered by any panel carrying out an adverse effects analysis (see *infra* the commentary to Article 6 pp. 326–328).[14]

Is a Pass-through Test Necessary for an Article 5 Claim?

In *EC and certain Member States – Measures Affecting Trade in Large Civil Aircraft*, the EU argued that the US should have demonstrated that any subsidies paid to the Airbus Consortium, i.e. the predecessor company of Airbus SAS, passed through to the latter. The Appellate Body held for a number of reasons that this was not necessary.

- Subsidies provided in the past can continue to have adverse effects at a later point in time.
- There was no suggestion that subsidies were provided to a different input product that was separate or distinct from the downstream subsidized product (as opposed to the configuration dealt with by *US – Softwood Lumber IV*).
- Despite the different legal organization, the economic realities of production of Airbus planes demonstrated that the Airbus Consortium and Airbus SAS were the 'same producer'.
- The Appellate Body underlined that it was not faced with a situation where the predecessor and successor companies were unrelated and operating at arm's length and where a pass-through analysis might therefore have been required.[15]

Note that while *US – Upland Cotton* was ambiguous in that it could have been interpreted as saying that a pass-through analysis is never necessary in serious prejudice claims under Articles 5 and 6.3,[16] the Appellate Body

[14] WT/DS316/AB/R of 18 May 2011, *EC and certain Member States – Measures Affecting Trade in Large Civil Aircraft*, para 698 *et seq.*

[15] WT/DS316/AB/R of 18 May 2011, *EC and certain Member States – Measures Affecting Trade in Large Civil Aircraft*, para 769 *et seq.*

[16] WT/DS267/AB/R of 3 March 2005, *United States – Subsidies on Upland Cotton*, para 472 *et passim.*

in *EC and certain Member States – Large Civil Aircraft* did not categorically rule out the need for such an analysis with regard to such claims.

Increase in Consumer Welfare Does Not Constitute a Defence to a Claim of Adverse Effects Caused by Subsidies

Subsidies often contribute positively to consumer welfare because they reduce the price paid by consumers. However, this does not constitute a defence to an adverse effects claim.[17]

Injury to the Domestic Industry of Another Member (Subparagraph (a) of Article 5)

Footnote 11 to the ASCM clarifies that the term 'injury to the domestic industry' as used in Article 5(a) is the same as it is used in Part V of the Agreement, i.e. for the purposes of countervailing duty investigations.[18] For presentational purposes DSB rulings relating to injury in CVD investigations are set out in the commentary to Article 15 while rulings in relation to injury under adverse effects claims are set out in the commentary to Article 5. The commentary to Article 5 does not repeat the descriptions of the general analytical framework of an injury analysis that is set out under Article 15.

Note also that rulings relating to injury and threat of injury concerning anti-dumping measures are also relevant here as the relevant provisions on injury of the ADA and the ASCM are almost identical.[19]

EC and certain Member States – Large Civil Aircraft is the first case where a panel has been requested to consider adverse effects under Article 5(a). The Panel noted that when examining a claim under Article 5(a) it essentially fulfils the role of an investigating authority in countervailing duty investigations. Consequently, the Panel must base itself on positive

[17] WT/DS316/R of 30 June 2010, *EC and certain Member States – Measures Affecting Trade in Large Civil Aircraft*, para 7.1991. This issue was not appealed.

[18] WT/DS316/R of 30 June 2010, *EC and certain Member States – Measures Affecting Trade in Large Civil Aircraft*, paras 7.2068, 7.2080. This aspect was not appealed.

[19] WT/DS316/R of 30 June 2010, *EC and certain Member States – Measures Affecting Trade in Large Civil Aircraft*, paras 7.2057 and 7.2159. This aspect was not appealed. See also the 'Declaration on Dispute Settlement Pursuant to the Agreement on Implementation of Article VI of the General Agreement on Tariffs and Trade 1994 or Part V of the Agreement on Subsidies and Countervailing Measures', adopted by Ministers at Marrakesh. The Declaration can be downloaded from the WTO website.

evidence and carry out an objective examination when examining and determining injury.[20]

Reference Period

A Panel must establish whether there are 'present' adverse effects, in the case in question present material injury or threat thereof. In *EC and certain Member States – Large Civil Aircraft*, there was some dispute as to what should be the reference period for establishing present material injury. The EU argued that the US must demonstrate present material injury in 2008, on the basis of the most recent complete and reliable data. The year 2008 was well after the start of the panel proceeding and one year before the Panel released the interim report. The Panel did not agree. Note that the Panel did not select a reference period for the purposes of the injury analysis under Article 5(a) but rather examined the evidence and arguments put forward by the US and the rebuttal evidence and arguments presented by the EU. The Panel did not request any evidence beyond the calendar year 2006 (the US filed its first written submission in that dispute in November 2006) and considered the end of that year as a reasonable cut-off date. The Panel recognized that at the time of its decision there was a degree of historicity in relation to the data used. However, it considered that the interests of due process, in allowing the parties an opportunity to comment on the information used for the decision, justified putting an end date to the information sought. It is impossible to establish the 'present' situation as immediately current data is not, and can never be, available as of the date of a panel's decision. Therefore, a review of the past is necessary to draw conclusions for the present.[21]

When Is the Injury 'Material'?

Footnote 45 establishes that any form of 'injury' under the ASCM shall, unless otherwise specified, be taken to mean material injury. The ASCM does not contain any elaboration of the word 'material' and consequently, there is no standard for determining whether a particular degree of injury is material. The Panel in *EC and certain Member States – Large Civil*

[20] WT/DS316/R of 30 June 2010, *EC and certain Member States – Measures Affecting Trade in Large Civil Aircraft*, para 7.2080. This aspect was not appealed.

[21] WT/DS316/R of 30 June 2010, *EC and certain Member States – Measures Affecting Trade in Large Civil Aircraft*, para 7.2045 *et seq*. This aspect was not appealed. See also *supra* p. 263.

Aircraft held the determination whether a particular degree of injury, as evidenced by the Article 15.4 factors, is 'material' is fact-specific in each case, depending on the nature of the product and the industry in question. Developments in various of the relevant factors, for instance a particular decline in production, sales or profit levels, that in one industry may support a finding of material injury, may not in another industry. Therefore, the determination must be based on an overall evaluation of the condition of the industry at issue, taking into account the particularities brought to the attention of the panel concerning the operations and the relative importance of the relevant factors with respect to the industry's performance. Furthermore, an explanation is necessary of how the facts support the determination.[22]

Evaluation of the Article 15.4 Factors

The Panel in *EC and certain Member States – Large Civil Aircraft* held that it was not necessary that all relevant factors, or even most or a majority of them, must show declines in order to make a finding of injury. The Panel derived this conclusion from the last sentence of Article 15.4 that stipulates, *inter alia*, that no one or several factors can necessarily give decisive guidance. The Panel did not rule out that injury may also be found in the case of an industry whose performance is improved or improving, based on an overall evaluation of the information, in context, as well as an explanation of how the facts support the determination.[23]

Before concluding on injury, the Panel had first to solve a number of methodological questions. First, it found that deliveries of aircraft are a more appropriate basis for consideration of market share than orders, *inter alia*, because Boeing's financial performance was to a large extent linked to deliveries, when the bulk of revenues were recorded (see para 7.2094). Second, the Panel concluded that information relating to a period subsequent to the cut-off date of December 2006 (see *supra* p. 270), to the extent that it was relevant, pertained to the question of threat of material injury (paras 7.2095 and 7.2097). Third, in relation to production capacity, the parties did not disagree on the basic fact that in the large aircraft industry, production capacity is planned

[22] WT/DS316/R of 30 June 2010, *EC and certain Member States – Measures Affecting Trade in Large Civil Aircraft*, para 7.2083. This aspect was not appealed.

[23] WT/DS316/R of 30 June 2010, *EC and certain Member States – Measures Affecting Trade in Large Civil Aircraft*, para 7.2084. This aspect was not appealed.

and established years in advance based on actual orders and anticipated demand. However, there was disagreement as to how the capacity should be calculated. The Panel agreed with the US that claimed that Boeing's production capacity remained unchanged during the period considered (paras 7.2100 and 7.2101).

The Panel held, on the basis of an evaluation of the Article 15.4 factors, that Boeing, i.e. the US domestic industry, was not materially injured. Boeing's condition deteriorated significantly from 2001 to 2003. Thereafter, it improved, with significantly better performance in 2006, although not all factors reached again the 2001 levels. Production, sales, capacity utilization and cash flow remained in 2006 well below the 2001 levels. By contrast, operating income, return on assets and productivity not only improved after early declines, but were in 2006 well above the levels reported in 2001. In sum, Boeing's performance began to recover in 2004, and by 2006, it was operating at levels which in the Panel's view did not warrant a finding that the US industry was materially injured. As the Panel pointed out elsewhere (see para 7.2157) it is possible for a domestic industry to compete with subsidized imports and not be materially injured. Note that Boeing's order books in 2006 reached record levels.

The US disputed this finding by pointing out that wages and employment declined steadily throughout the period, ending at levels just slightly above half of those reported in 2001, i.e. the beginning of the injury examination period. The Panel dismissed this argument. It was of the view that this decline clearly reflected significant and successful cost-cutting and efficiency programmes instituted by Boeing, as well as increased outsourcing. The US also invoked that the significant improvement of Boeing's financial health must be viewed in the context of unusual high demand in 2005 and 2006, and asserted that Boeing remained competitive despite lost market share in the US by cutting costs and improving productivity. The Panel considered that these arguments were of little weight for the injury determination. Note in this context that the Panel held that decreasing demand and the injury resulting therefrom would be an argument relating to other factors which may be causing injury and did not address the question whether the industry was injured.[24]

[24] WT/DS316/R of 30 June 2010, *EC and certain Member States – Measures Affecting Trade in Large Civil Aircraft*, para 7.2083 *et seq*. This aspect was not appealed.

Causal Link Analysis – One Step Versus Two Steps

The question is whether a one-step analysis or whether a two-step analysis is appropriate for a finding under Article 5(a). If the latter approach is adopted a panel would first establish whether or not the domestic industry has suffered material injury. In a second step it would examine whether the injury was caused by the subsidized imports. The Panel in *EC and certain Member States – Large Civil Aircraft* followed a two-step approach as neither party requested a different method of analysis and as this method is commonly employed by investigating authorities, although the Panel held that such two-step analysis was not mandatory. The Panel considered it not necessary to opine on the question of the nature of the two-step analysis.[25]

Causal Link Analysis – Injury Must Be Caused by the Subsidized Imports and Not by the Effect of Subsidies

In *EC and certain Member States – Large Civil Aircraft*, the EU argued that the injury must be caused by the use of the subsidies. The US contested this by arguing that the EU tried to read the 'effect of the subsidy' standard under Article 6.3 into a material injury inquiry under Article 5(a) and that Article 15.3 requires that the material injury be the effect of the subsidized imports. The Panel sided with the US. The Panel essentially arrived at this conclusion by referring to the numerous references in Article 15 that all made it clear that the injury must be caused by the subsidized imports and not by the subsidy itself. Hence, it also rejected the EU's claims that a panel must consider the nature and effect of the subsidies and their magnitude when evaluating the question of injury under Article 5(a).[26]

Threat of Injury

The Panel in *EC and certain Member States – Large Civil Aircraft* examined also whether there was threat of injury to the US large aircraft industry,

[25] WT/DS316/R of 30 June 2010, *EC and certain Member States – Measures Affecting Trade in Large Civil Aircraft*, para 7.2058. This aspect was not appealed. See also *infra* the commentary to Article 6, pp. 311–315.

[26] WT/DS316/R of 30 June 2010, *EC and certain Member States – Measures Affecting Trade in Large Civil Aircraft*, para 7.2059 *et seq.* and para 7.2143. This aspect was not appealed.

i.e. Boeing. The Panel first referred to the two dispute settlement cases concerning threat of injury.[27] One of these two cases dealt with the corresponding provision of the WTO Anti-Dumping Agreement, but given that that provision is quasi identical with the ASCM this ruling also constituted guidance for the Panel. The Panel concluded that there was no such threat. Based on the two aforementioned DSB rulings, the Panel held that an industry that is not materially injured, and whose performance is robust and improving, is less vulnerable to a deterioration of its performance which might be considered material injury in the near future. Conversely, an industry whose performance, while not reflecting present material injury, is generally weak and declining, would be more vulnerable to such deterioration, and the likelihood of its being materially injured in the near future would be greater. Whether any such future material injury would be caused by subsidized imports must also be considered, as well as the Article 15.7 factors pertinent to this aspect of the analysis (para 7.2167). With regard to the case at hand, the Panel noted that Boeing improved its performance towards the end of the injury examination period and that the significant number of orders booked suggested that Boeing's performance would continue to be strong.

The Panel then examined the four factors listed in Article 15.7. With regard to the first factor (nature of the subsidy and trade effects likely to arise therefrom), the Panel noted that Airbus aircraft in the near future would continue to be subsidized. However, there was nothing to suggest that there was likely to be an increase in subsidization in the near future or that there was likely to be an increase in subsidized imports in the near future as a consequence of the subsidies themselves. With regard to the second criterion (significant rate of increase of subsidized imports indicating the likelihood of substantially increased importation) the Panel examined orders of aircraft. At the outset it stated that orders of Airbus aircraft by US companies were not necessarily resulting in imports in the US as many of these orders had been made by leasing companies that intended to lease the aircraft to non-US airlines. Furthermore, orders are sometimes cancelled. Moreover, in view of the long lead time between the order of an aircraft and the delivery, the Panel considered future events as 'imminent' if they could occur in a time frame of two to three years. With all these considerations in mind, the Panel

[27] WT/DS132/R of 28 January 2000, *Mexico – Anti-Dumping Investigation of High Fructose Corn Syrup (HFCS) from the United States*, para 7.124 *et seq.*; WT/DS277/R of 22 March 2004, *United States – Investigation of the International Trade Commission in Softwood Lumber from Canada*, para 7.67 *et seq.*

did not think it likely that there would be a substantial increase in imports of Airbus aircraft into the US. With regard to the third criterion, i.e. capacity, the Panel accepted the US argument that Airbus's capacity was increasing because it was adding two production lines and it had announced further capacity increases and that at least some of this capacity could be expected to supply additional aircraft to the US. However, the Panel concluded that these capacity increases would not have a significant imminent effect on imports. Finally, with regard to the fourth criterion (continued price depression and suppression), the Panel found it difficult to draw any conclusions about likely future pricing, particularly given the evidence of improvement in the market and Boeing's order backlog. It consequently ruled that the information did not demonstrate that subsidized imports did likely have a price depressing or supressing effect in the near future.[28]

Nullification or Impairment of Benefits (Subparagraph (b) of Article 5)

Article 5(b) stipulates that no WTO Member should cause, through the use of any subsidy referred to in the first two paragraphs of Article 1, nullification or impairment of benefits accruing directly or indirectly to other Members under GATT 1994 and in particular the benefits of concessions bound under Article II of GATT 1994. Footnote 12 to Article 5(b) clarifies that the term 'nullification or impairment' is used in the ASCM in the same sense as it is used in the relevant provisions of GATT 1994, and the existence of such nullification or impairment shall be established in accordance with the practice of application of these provisions. Article XXIII of GATT 1994 and Article 26 of the Understanding on Rules and Procedures Governing the Settlement of Disputes are the central provisions concerning nullification and impairment. Note that nullification and impairment does not depend on a finding of a breach of a legal obligation. Rather it is about reasonable expectations of a WTO Member, e.g. an action of a WTO Member that harmed the trade of another and that could not have been reasonably anticipated by the other at the time it negotiated the concession. The use of subsidies to inhibit imports in certain cases was considered a *prima facie* case for nullification and impairment.[29]

[28] WT/DS316/R of 30 June 2010, *EC and certain Member States – Measures Affecting Trade in Large Civil Aircraft*, para 7.2158 *et seq*. This aspect was not appealed.

[29] See *Jackson* (2000) pp. 114–115 with further references.

It would appear that since 1994 this provision has only been at issue in one DSB ruling, i.e. in *US – Offset Act (Byrd Amendment)*. The Panel reviewed Mexico's claims under two different angles. First, it examined whether the nullification or impairment resulted from a violation of GATT 1994. Mexico invoked a violation of Articles VI:2 and X:3(a) in conjunction with Article 3.8 DSU. The Panel was not convinced. It first pointed out that it had already found a violation of Articles 11.4 and 32.1 of the ASCM (and the corresponding provisions of the ADA) as well as of GATT 1994. This was not sufficient to demonstrate nullification or impairment for the purpose of Article 5(b). The presumption arising under Article 3.8 DSU relates to nullification or impairment caused by the violation of the provision at issue. By contrast, pursuant to Article 5(b), a complaining party must show that the use of the subsidy (and not the violation of a provision) caused nullification or impairment. The US also pointed out, and the Panel agreed, that reliance on the presumption of nullification or impairment resulting from Article 3.8 DSU in the context of an Article 5 ASCM claim would eliminate the primary distinction between prohibited subsidies under Article 3, where effects are presumed, and actionable subsidies under Article 5, where the complaining party must demonstrate adverse effects.

Second, with regard to the claim concerning a 'non-violation' nullification or impairment, both Mexico and the Panel relied on the GATT Panel *EEC – Oilseeds* dating from 1990, i.e. a pre-WTO Panel. In the view of the Panel, *EEC – Oilseeds* suggested that non-violation nullification or impairment would arise when the effect of a tariff concession is systematically offset or counteracted by a subsidy programme. The Panel considered this as a reasonable approach because the standard of 'systematically offsetting/counteracting' would preserve the exceptional nature of the 'non-violation/impairment remedy'. However, the Byrd Amendment did not provide for product-specific subsidies (unlike the subsidy programme in *EEC – Oilseeds*) and the amount of such subsidies was not directly linked to the level of tariff concessions made for the specific product at issue (but to the amount of AD or countervailing duties collected). In short, there was no certainty that the grant of offset payments under the Byrd Amendment would systematically offset or counteract benefits accruing to Mexico, i.e. the WTO Member that made this claim, under Articles II and VI of GATT 1994. The Panel also highlighted the tension between the right of a WTO Member to subsidize (except prohibited subsidies), on the one hand, and the legitimate expectations of improved market access resulting from negotiated tariff concessions. It pointed out that any subsidy to domestic producers is likely to have some adverse effect on the competitive relationship between domestic and imported products. However, this is not enough for an Article 5(b) claim. Otherwise, any specific domestic subsidy programme which is related to a product on which there is a tariff concession could constitute the non-violation nullification or impairment of benefits.[30] Note also that under GATT 1947 (when neither the ASCM nor its predecessors existed) non-violation complaints were considered useful because they could be used when a Member undermined its tariff concessions by systematically using subsidies.[31]

Serious Prejudice to the Interests of Another Member (Subparagraph (c) of Article 5)

The commentary with regard to adverse effects in the form of 'serious prejudice' is set out *infra* Article 6.

[30] WT/DS217/R and WT/DS234/R of 16 September 2002, *United States – Continued Dumping and Subsidy Offset Act of 2000*, paras 7.118–7.131.

[31] *Coppens* (2014) p. 146.

Article 6

Serious Prejudice

Introduction

General

Serious prejudice is listed in Article 5 as one of the three types of adverse effects to the interests of other WTO Members that could be caused through the use of subsidies. Footnote 13 attached to Article 5(c) stipulates that the term 'serious prejudice to the interests of another Member' is used in the ASCM in the same sense as it is used in Article XVI:1 of GATT 1994, and includes threat of serious prejudice.[1] Article 6 elaborates further the concept of serious prejudice.

Article 6 is the central provision in case a WTO Member challenges under the WTO dispute settlement system a subsidy as defined in Article 1 and provided by another Member, instead of imposing countervailing measures. In case a Panel or the Appellate Body finds serious prejudice, the remedies available are those set out in Article 7, i.e. the Member granting the actionable subsidy shall take appropriate steps to remove the adverse effects or shall withdraw the subsidy.

For the historical background of Article 6, see *Piérola* in *Wolfrum/Stoll/Koebele* (2008), paras 8–12 to Article 6.

Article 6, in particular its structure, is not a provision that is easily accessible. Paragraph 1 which contained a rebuttable presumption of serious prejudice in well-defined circumstances (for certain types of subsidy, notably those exceeding 5 per cent *ad valorem*), expired at the end of 1999 by virtue of Article 31 (see *infra* this chapter pp. 281–282). Because of this expiry, paragraph 2 seems to be devoid of any

[1] See also WT/DS267/R of 8 September 2004, *United States – Subsidies on Upland Cotton*, paras 7.1486–7.1503 with regard to the relationship between serious prejudice and threat thereof. The Panel report examines also whether there is a need to address a claim of threat if there is already a finding of actual serious prejudice. See also *infra* pp. 346–347 of this chapter.

purpose.[2] Therefore, today the most essential part of Article 6 is its paragraph 3. This paragraph identifies four types of serious prejudice, depending on the effect of the subsidy, which a subsidizing Member can cause to other Members. Paragraphs 4, 5 and 7 elaborate further on these four types of serious prejudice. The four types of serious prejudice can be summarized as follows:

Type of serious prejudice	Displacement or impedance of imports	Displacement or impedance of imports	Significant price under-cutting, significant price suppression, significant price depression; lost sales	Increase of world market share of the subsidizing Member in a particular subsidized primary product or commodity
Relevant subparagraph	(a)	(b)	(c)	(d)
Where is the effect of the subsidy felt?	Market of the subsidizing Member	Third country market	'Same' market	World market
Related provisions	Article 6.7	Articles 6.4, 6.7	Article 6.5	

These four situations are described in detail *infra* in this chapter. The focus of a serious prejudice claim under Article 6.3 is different to that of a countervailing duty investigation. Countervailing duties can only remedy the effects of subsidization by a third country on the domestic market of the importing country. Article 6.3 deals essentially with a substantial damage to the export opportunities of a WTO Member on third country markets but the 'same market' in subparagraph (c) can also cover the market of the importing Member.

[2] See *infra* pp. 281–282.

Subparagraphs (a) and (b) as well as the concept of price undercutting in subparagraph (c) generally distinguish between the product benefitting from subsidies granted by a Member and the like product. The term 'like product' is defined in footnote 46 (see *infra* the commentary to Article 15, pp. 471–473). The like product is in competition with the subsidized product and the issue is whether this like product suffers the market phenomena set out in one or several of the subparagraphs of Article 6.3. The definition of the relevant market is of primary importance (see *infra* this chapter, pp. 333–339)

The examination of an Article 6 claim by a panel is different to many other challenges under the WTO dispute settlement system. For instance, in the case of a challenge of an anti-dumping or a countervailing duty, the panel reviews a decision by a domestic investigating authority. However, a panel conducting an analysis under Article 6 is the 'first trier of facts', rather than a reviewer of factual determinations made by such authority. Thus, the panel has a particular responsibility in gathering and analysing the necessary evidence.[3]

Article 6.6 obliges a WTO Member in the market in which serious prejudice is alleged to have arisen, to make available relevant information.[4] Article 6.8 deals with the establishment of the facts by a panel. Both provisions specify that the discovery process under Annex V is available.

According to Article 6.9, Article 6 does not apply to subsidies maintained on agricultural products as provided in Article 13 of the Agreement on Agriculture, i.e. the so-called peace clause. Article 13, however, expired.

Serious prejudice only exists if the situation described in one of the four subparagraphs is the effect of the subsidy. There must be a 'genuine and substantial relationship of cause and effect' between the subsidy and the situation in question. See *infra* this chapter pp. 307–332. This begs the question how the causal link is analysed. The issue is commonly referred to as the choice between the unitary approach versus a two-step analysis. In the latter case, the panel will first establish the phenomena under the relevant subparagraph of Article 6.3 and subsequently it will examine whether these phenomena have been caused by the subsidy. The unitary

[3] See e.g. WT/DS267/AB/R of 3 March 2005, *United States – Subsidies on Upland Cotton*, para 458.

[4] See *Piérola* in *Wolfrum/Stoll/Koebele* (2008), paras 78–80 to Article 6.

approach merges the two steps and relies typically on a counterfactual analysis. See *infra* this chapter pp. 284–285. In the case of multiple subsidies one single causal link analysis is sufficient if the conditions for a cumulation or aggregation of these subsidies are met. Otherwise, a causal link has to be established for each subsidy separately. See *infra* this chapter pp. 315–323.

A panel must establish whether the serious prejudice is 'present', as opposed to such effects occurring in the past.[5] This also applies to proceedings pursuant to Article 21.5 of the DSU.[6] However, for all practical purposes, the determination of 'present' serious prejudice will be based on data established for a reference period (see *infra* this chapter pp. 339–343). But temporal considerations are not limited to the duration of the reference period. The age of a subsidy (see *infra* this chapter pp. 326–328) and events intervening between the grant of the subsidy and the present adverse effects (see supra the commentary to Article 5, pp. 264–266) may equally play a role for any serious prejudice finding. Finally, it is not necessary to show a continuation of the benefit in the reference period used to demonstrate adverse effects (see *supra* the commentary to Article 5, pp. 267–268).

Article 6.6 is a special and additional rule or procedure identified in Appendix 2 to the DSU.

Deemed Serious Prejudice Provision Expired in 1999 (Article 6.1)

Article 6.1 expired in 1999 by virtue of Article 31 because WTO Members could not agree to its continuation. It listed a number of circumstances in which serious prejudice in the sense of Article 6.3 was deemed to exist, e.g. total *ad valorem* subsidization of a product exceeding 5 per cent or subsidies covering operating losses by an industry.

[5] See e.g. WT/DS316/R of 30 June 2010, *EC and certain Member States – Measures Affecting Trade in Large Civil Aircraft*, para 7.1714; WT/DS267/AB/RW of 16 May 2008, *United States – Subsidies on Upland Cotton (Article 21.5)*, paras 237, 244. See also *supra* the commentary to Article 5 pp. 263–268.

[6] WT/DS267/AB/RW of 16 May 2008, *United States – Subsidies on Upland Cotton (Article 21.5)*, para 447. However, if relevant circumstances in the Article 21.5 proceeding have not changed since the original proceedings, it is proper for a panel not to deviate from the approach followed in the original proceedings, see para 422. See also WT/DS267/RW of 18 December 2007, *United States – Subsidies on Upland Cotton (Article 21.5)*, para 10.18 with further references.

Although a provision has lapsed, it may still be relevant in indicating the original architecture of the ASCM.[7]

Article 6.2 is linked to Article 6.1. It specified that any deemed serious prejudice pursuant to Article 6.1 could in fact be rebutted. Note, however, that the limited period of application of Article 6.1 by virtue of Article 31 does not extend to Article 6.2. Given the expiry of Article 6.1, it would therefore appear that Article 6.2 is now devoid of any purpose. The Panel in *US – Upland Cotton* pointed out in respect of the latter provision that a massive inefficient subsidy of a certain design may have relatively miniscule effects, whereas a smaller subsidy of a different nature may have relatively greater effects.[8] Articles 6.1 and 6.2 were also referred to in *Korea – Commercial Vessels*.[9]

Relationship between Articles 5(c) and 6

The chapeau of Article 6.3 stipulates that serious prejudice in the sense of Article 5(c) *may* arise in any case where the conditions of one or several subparagraphs of Article 6.3 are met. In *US – Upland Cotton* there was disagreement between the parties whether an examination under Article 6.3(c) was determinative of serious prejudice for the purposes of Article 5(c). The US took the view that the use of 'may' in the introductory sentence of Article 6.3 indicated that serious prejudice need not arise even if one or more of the circumstances listed in Article 6.3 is met. The Panel did not agree. It did not believe that once it had concluded that the conditions in Article 6.3(c) are fulfilled, and thus that serious prejudice 'in the sense of paragraph (c) of Article 5 may arise' (see chapeau of Article 6.3), a separate examination of the existence of serious prejudice under the chapeau of Article 6.3 or Article 5(c) was necessary. Note, however, that the Panel dealt only with one of the items in Article 6.3. Thus, the Panel saw no need to decide on whether or not there might exist situations – other than those enumerated in Article 6.3 – in which serious prejudice could be established. According to the Panel, the significant price suppression

[7] WT/DS267/R of 8 September 2004, *United States – Subsidies on Upland Cotton*, footnote 1309 to para 7.1192.

[8] WT/DS267/R of 8 September 2004, *United States – Subsidies on Upland Cotton*, para 7.1190.

[9] WT/DS273/R of 7 March 2005, *Korea – Measures Affecting Trade in Commercial Vessels*, para 7.616.

under Article 6.3 amounted to serious prejudice within the meaning of Article 5(c).[10] See also *infra* this chapter pp. 344–346 regarding *Korea – Commercial Vessels.*

Relationship between the Subparagraphs of Article 6.3

The Appellate Body in *EC and certain Member States – Large Civil Aircraft* acknowledged that, when looked at from a broader, market-wide perspective, there could be some overlap between the concept of lost sales (see subparagraph (c)) and the concepts of displacement and impedance (see subparagraphs (a) and (b)). But it also saw two distinctions between these three concepts. First, the assessment of displacement or impedance has a well-defined geographic focus while the reference to the 'same market' in subparagraph (c) allows more flexibility in defining the relevant market. Therefore, the 'same market' can include the world market. The Appellate Body referred in this context to its ruling in *US – Upland Cotton*. Second, the requirement in subparagraph (c) that the lost sales be 'significant' implies that the assessment can have quantitative and qualitative dimensions while the assessment of displacement and impedance under subparagraphs (a) and (b) is primarily quantitative in nature.[11] Note that the Appellate Body in *US – Large Civil Aircraft (2nd Complaint)* rejected the Panel's conclusion that the phenomena of displacement and impedance necessarily follow from a finding of significant lost sales.[12]

Serious Prejudice Claims Can Only Be Entertained for Products Originating in the Territory of the Complaining Member

Indonesia – Autos found that the US could not claim that it has suffered serious prejudice with respect to products that have been produced abroad by subsidiaries of US companies but do not originate in the US.[13] Similarly,

[10] WT/DS267/R of 8 September 2004, *United States – Subsidies on Upland Cotton*, paras 7.1364–7.1395. See also WT/DS54/R, WT/DS55/R, WT/DS59/R and WT/DS64/R of 2 July 1998, *Indonesia – Certain Measures Affecting the Automobile Industry*, para 14.255.

[11] WT/DS316/AB/R of 18 May 2011, *EC and certain Member States – Measures Affecting Trade in Large Civil Aircraft*, para 1218. Confirmed in WT/DS353/AB/R of 12 March 2012, *United States – Measures Affecting Trade in Large Civil Aircraft (Second Complaint)*, para 1241.

[12] WT/DS353/AB/R of 12 March 2012, *United States – Measures Affecting Trade in Large Civil Aircraft (Second Complaint)*, para 1241.

[13] WT/DS54/R, WT/DS55/R, WT/DS59/R and WT/DS64/R of 2 July 1998, *Indonesia – Certain Measures Affecting the Automobile Industry*, paras 14.198–14.204.

in *US – Upland Cotton*, the question arose whether the complainant Brazil could claim serious prejudice to the interests of countries other than Brazil. The Panel rejected this claim. It based its conclusion *inter alia* on Article 7.2 that limits serious prejudice claims to the interests of the Member requesting consultations. However, the Panel took into account serious prejudice allegations of Members other than Brazil to the extent these constituted evidentiary support of the effect of the subsidy suffered by Brazil as a WTO Member whose producers are involved in the production and trade in upland cotton in the world market. Note that these Members other than Brazil had been third parties in the DSB proceeding.[14]

Structure of the Serious Prejudice Analysis – Unitary Versus Two-Step Approach

The Appellate Body in *US – Upland Cotton* has found that panels, when analysing serious prejudice pursuant to Article 6, may apply either a unitary or a two-step approach.[15]

Under a unitary approach, the analysis of the particular market phenomena of Article 6.3 is not conducted separately from the analysis of whether there is a causal relationship between those market phenomena and the challenged subsidies. Following the Appellate Body in *EC and certain Member States – Large Civil Aircraft*, the unitary approach uses a counterfactual.[16]

Under a two-step approach, the analysis first seeks to identify the phenomena of Article 6.3 and then, as a second step, examines whether there is a causal relationship.

The Appellate Body has indicated a preference for the unitary approach claiming that it has a sound conceptual foundation and explaining that it

[14] WT/DS267/R of 8 September 2004, *United States – Subsidies on Upland Cotton*, paras 7.1396–7.1416.

[15] WT/DS267/AB/R of 3 March 2005, *United States – Subsidies on Upland Cotton*, paras 431–434; WT/DS267/AB/RW of 16 May 2008, *United States – Subsidies on Upland Cotton (Article 21.5)*, para 354. *US – Upland Cotton* and WT/DS273/R of 7 March 2005 *Korea – Measures Affecting Trade in Commercial Vessels*, paras 7.617 and 7.618 are examples of a two-step approach. In *Korea – Commercial Vessels*, the Panel examined whether factors other than the subsidy would 'attenuate' any affirmative causal link that it may find, or render insignificant any price suppression or price depression effect of the subsidy that it may find.

[16] WT/DS316/AB/R of 18 May 2011, *EC and certain Member States – Measures Affecting Trade in Large Civil Aircraft*, paras 1109, 1234 and footnote 2655 attached thereto. See also *infra* this chapter pp. 311–315.

may be difficult to ascertain the existence of some of the market phenomena in Article 6.3 without considering the effect of the subsidy at issue. It went on to say that any attempt to identify one of the market phenomena in Article 6.3 without considering the subsidies at issue could only be preliminary in nature since Article 6.3 requires that the market phenomenon be the effect of the challenged subsidy. It claimed that a two-step approach simply deferred the core of the analysis to the second step. By artificially leaving aside the question of whether the market phenomenon is the effect of the subsidy, one could overlook market phenomena that are in fact occurring.[17]

The difference between the two approaches is perhaps not significant. For instance, in *EC and certain Member States – Large Civil Aircraft*, the Panel used the two-step approach. However, the causal link analysis was based on a counterfactual, i.e. the core of the methodology ascribed to the unitary approach. Ultimately, the difference between the two approaches seems to be more of a presentational nature. Whatever method is chosen, it is key that the alleged market phenomena are properly identified.

It is also true that it might be difficult under a two-step-analysis to separate the phenomena in Article 6.3 and the causal link. A two-step examination under Article 6.3(c) examining the question whether the effect of the challenged subsidy is significant price suppression illustrates the problem. The definition of price suppression (prices do not increase when they otherwise would have) refers to a hypothetical situation, i.e. absence of the subsidies. In a first step, the price suppression analysis would address prices without reference to the subsidies and their effects. In a second step, the effects analysis would address causal factors related to the nature of the subsidies, their relationship to prices, their magnitude and their impact on production and exports. The analysis in this second step would also address factors other than the challenged subsidies that may have an impact on prices. Therefore, the definition of price suppression may lead a panel to address some of the same or similar factors in its reasoning both under the first step (price suppression) and under the second step (effects analysis).[18]

[17] WT/DS316/AB/R of 18 May 2011, *EC and certain Member States – Measures Affecting Trade in Large Civil Aircraft*, para 1109 and para 1163 *et seq.* In WT/DS267/AB/RW of 16 May 2008, *United States – Subsidies on Upland Cotton (Article 21.5)*, para 354, the opinion of the Appellate Body was still somewhat more nuanced. It pointed out that because of the counterfactual nature of price suppression, it is difficult to separate price suppression from its causes. Hence, a unitary analysis has a sound conceptual foundation, at least in respect of identifying price suppression and its causes.

[18] WT/DS267/AB/R of 3 March 2005, *United States – Subsidies on Upland Cotton*, paras 432–434.

Displacement and Impedance (Articles 6.3(a), 6.3(b), 6.4 and 6.7)

General

Subparagraph (a) of Article 6.3 refers to a situation where the 'effect of the subsidy is to displace or impede the imports of a like product of another Member into the market of the subsidizing Member'. Subparagraph (b) of Article 6.3 refers to a situation where the 'effect of the subsidy is to displace or impede the exports of a like product of another Member from a third country market'. In other words, the difference between the two subparagraphs is whether the effect of the subsidy concerns the territory of the subsidizing Member or a third country market.

The Appellate Body recognized that it might be difficult to draw a clear demarcation between the concepts of displacement and impedance. It suggested that evidence that actual sales declined would be relevant for a determination of displacement whereas evidence that sales would have increased more than they did, or would have declined less than they did, would be relevant for a claim of impedance.[19]

Neither subparagraph (a) nor subparagraph (b) expressly qualifies the level of degree of displacement or impedance required for a finding under these provisions (as opposed to subparagraph (c) that requires that the phenomena described therein are 'significant'). However, displacement must be discernible.[20]

There is both a geographic and product market component to the assessment of displacement and impedance.[21]

Sales and market share data are highly relevant for claims of displacement and impedance.[22] But it is not necessary to demonstrate displacement or impedance on a sale-by-sale basis.[23] In *EC and certain Member*

[19] WT/DS316/AB/R of 18 May 2011, *EC and certain Member States – Measures Affecting Trade in Large Civil Aircraft*, para 1162. See also WT/DS353/AB/R of 12 March 2012, *United States – Measures Affecting Trade in Large Civil Aircraft (Second Complaint)*, para 1071 *in fine*.

[20] WT/DS316/AB/R of 18 May 2011, *EC and certain Member States – Measures Affecting Trade in Large Civil Aircraft*, para 1169.

[21] WT/DS353/AB/R of 12 March 2012, *United States – Measures Affecting Trade in Large Civil Aircraft (Second Complaint)*, para 1076. For details see *infra* this chapter pp. 333–339.

[22] WT/DS316/R of 30 June 2010, *EC and certain Member States – Measures Affecting Trade in Large Civil Aircraft*, para 7.1739 (this issue was not appealed); WT/DS54/R, WT/DS55/R, WT/DS59/R and WT/DS64/R of 2 July 1998, *Indonesia – Certain Measures Affecting the Automobile Industry*, para 14.211.

[23] WT/DS316/R of 30 June 2010, *EC and certain Member States – Measures Affecting Trade in Large Civil Aircraft*, para 7.1751. This issue was not appealed.

States – Large Civil Aircraft, the parties disagreed as to whether order data or delivery data would be more relevant for the displacement and impedance analysis. The Panel held that the focus on deliveries was appropriate, *inter alia*, because subparagraphs (a) and (b) refer to imports and exports.[24]

Displacement and impedance in third country markets, i.e. the configuration defined in subparagraph (b), are also dealt with in Article 6.4. The relationship between Articles 6.3(b) and 6.4 has been clarified in *EC and certain Member States – Large Civil Aircraft*. The EU argued that a finding of displacement or impedance under Article 6.3(b) required that in addition to the conditions set out in Article 6.3(b), also those in Article 6.4 be met. This would have meant that displacement or impedance of exports to a third country market could have been demonstrated only if the complaining WTO Member did not provide a subsidy within the meaning of Article 1 in respect of the like product whose exports were displaced or impeded. Indeed, Article 6.4 refers to the 'non-subsidized like product'. In other words, the EU argued that a Member could have introduced a claim under Article 6.3(b) only if it had 'clean hands'. The US and the Panel disagreed. The Panel held that displacement or impedance under Article 6.3(b) can be demonstrated without reference to Article 6.4. The reason for this is that the scope of Article 6.3(b) is broader and the 'non-subsidized like product' provision only applies in the specific circumstances of Article 6.4. Therefore, the provisions of Article 6.4 are only one way of demonstrating serious prejudice in cases of displacement or impedance. This follows from the text of Article 6.4 that stipulates that '[f]or the purpose of paragraph 3(b), the displacement or impeding of exports *shall include* … ' (emphasis added). However, if the circumstances set out in Article 6.4 are satisfied, a further assessment of whether the changes in market share are 'the effect of the subsidy', as required by Article 6.3(b), is not necessary.[25] *Indonesia – Autos* held that Article 6.4 does not apply to the configuration dealt with in Article 6.3(a), i.e. displacement or impedance in the market of the WTO Member whose subsidies are subject to a serious prejudice

[24] WT/DS316/R of 30 June 2010, *EC and certain Member States – Measures Affecting Trade in Large Civil Aircraft*, para 7.1745 *et seq*. This issue was not appealed. See also WT/DS353/AB/R of 12 March 2012, *United States – Measures Affecting Trade in Large Civil Aircraft (Second Complaint)*, para 1243, where the Appellate Body concluded that order data may be more relevant for a threat of displacement or impedance.

[25] WT/DS316/R of 30 June 2010, *EC and certain Member States – Measures Affecting Trade in Large Civil Aircraft*, paras 7.1760–7.1771. This aspect was not appealed). Doubtful *Coppens* (2014) p. 159 *et seq*.

claim. That does not, however, mean that market share data are irrelevant to the analysis of displacement or impedance into a subsidizing Member's market. Note that Article 6.4 is a powerful provision in the sense that a complainant can make a *prima facie* case of displacement or impedance simply by demonstrating that the market share of the subsidized product has increased over an appropriately representative period.[26]

Finally, pursuant to Article 6.7 displacement and impedance shall not arise in any of the circumstances listed in that provision. The six sets of circumstances have as a common denominator that they all describe reasons other than the subsidy which impact on exports of a complaining WTO Member, e.g. natural disasters or other *force majeure* events that impact negatively on exports to the market of the subsidizing Member or to a third country market.[27] Footnote 18 is attached to the chapeau of Article 6.7 and clarifies this provision further by stipulating, *inter alia*, that the circumstances preventing exports etc. must not be isolated, sporadic or otherwise insignificant.[28] *US – Upland Cotton* has classified Article 6.7 as a defence to a displacement/impedance claim.[29] It would appear that the application of Article 6.7 to the facts of a particular case was only considered once in a dispute settlement proceeding, i.e. in *EC and certain Member States – Large Civil Aircraft*.[30]

Displacement

Displacement is a situation where imports or exports of a like product are replaced by the sales of the subsidized product. Thus, the concept of displacement relates to, and arises out of competitive engagement between products in a market. Aggressive pricing of certain products may, for example, lead to displacement of imports or exports, but only if the products in question compete in the same market.[31] Therefore, displacement

[26] WT/DS54/R, WT/DS55/R, WT/DS59/R and WT/DS64/R of 2 July 1998, *Indonesia – Certain Measures Affecting the Automobile Industry*, paras 14.209–14.211.

[27] See also WT/DS273/R of 7 March 2005, *Korea – Measures Affecting Trade in Commercial Vessels*, para 7.586.

[28] For details see *Piérola* in Wolfrum/Stoll/Koebele (2008) paras 85–125 to Article 6.

[29] WT/DS267/R of 8 September 2004, *United States – Subsidies on Upland Cotton*, footnote 1503 attached to para 7.1405.

[30] WT/DS316/R of 30 June 2010, *EC and certain Member States – Measures Affecting Trade in Large Civil Aircraft*, paras 7.1693–7.1713. The case is described *infra* this chapter pp. 339–343.

[31] WT/DS316/AB/R of 18 May 2011, *EC and certain Member States – Measures Affecting Trade in Large Civil Aircraft*, para 1119. Confirmed in WT/DS353/AB/R of 12 March 2012,

under Article 6.3(a) arises where the effect of the subsidy is that imports of a like product of the complaining WTO Member are substituted by the subsidized product in the market of the subsidizing Member. Similarly, displacement under Article 6.3(b) arises where exports of the like product of the complaining WTO Member are substituted in a third country market by exports of the subsidized product.[32]

The Appellate Body in *EC and certain Member States – Large Civil Aircraft* held that the examination of trade volumes and market share data over a reference period was appropriate in the light of the manner in which the US presented its claim and under the two-step approach (see *supra* this chapter pp. 284–285). Indeed, it is not sufficient to examine trade volumes to determine whether the imports or exports of the like product are being substituted by the subsidized product, in particular when total consumption increases or decreases. By contrast, loss of market share can be an indication of displacement. The analysis of market shares is rather straightforward in a duopoly situation, but more difficult when there are more than two competitors. The identification of displacement should focus on trends in the markets. The trend has to be clearly identifiable. Moreover, an assessment based on a static comparison of the situation of the subsidized product and the like product at the beginning and at the end of the reference period would be inadequate.[33]

Where a two-step approach is used and displacement has been shown on a preliminary basis, the complaining WTO Member will have to establish, in addition, that such displacement is the effect of the challenged subsidies.[34]

When applying the above principles to *EC and certain Member States – Large Civil Aircraft*, the Appellate Body carried out its displacement analysis by classifying all large aircraft in three groups (single-aisle, twin-aisle and large aircraft) and in relation to a period of six years (from 2001

United States – Measures Affecting Trade in Large Civil Aircraft (Second Complaint), para 1071; WT/DS54/R, WT/DS55/R, WT/DS59/R and WT/DS64/R of 2 July 1998, *Indonesia – Certain Measures Affecting the Automobile Industry*, para 14.218.

32 WT/DS316/AB/R of 18 May 2011, *EC and certain Member States – Measures Affecting Trade in Large Civil Aircraft*, para 1160; WT/DS353/AB/R of 12 March 2012, *United States – Measures Affecting Trade in Large Civil Aircraft (Second Complaint)*, para 1071.

33 WT/DS316/AB/R of 18 May 2011, *EC and certain Member States – Measures Affecting Trade in Large Civil Aircraft*, paras 1165, 1170 and 1293.

34 WT/DS316/AB/R of 18 May 2011, *EC and certain Member States – Measures Affecting Trade in Large Civil Aircraft*, para 1170.

to 2006). Given the particular situation in the large civil aircraft market (existence of a duopoly between Boeing and Airbus), and because the Panel (which considered all large aircraft to be one group of products) entertained the US claim of displacement on the basis of an assessment of whether there was an observable decline in the sales of Boeing, the Appellate Body followed the following rules:

- no displacement where Boeing's sales increased during the reference period in a particular market;
- no displacement where Boeing made no sales in a product group throughout the period;
- no displacement where Boeing was the sole supplier during the reference period;
- no displacement where sales were sporadic (for instance, where sales were only in two years out of six so that no trend could be established).

On this basis, the Appellate Body reversed the Panel's findings that there was displacement of Boeing's sales in relation to the markets of Brazil, Korea, Mexico, Singapore and Chinese Taipei. The Panel arrived at its findings by reasoning that Airbus was the only competitor of Boeing in these markets during the relevant period, and consequently any market share achieved by Airbus in those markets was at the expense of Boeing. Note that the Panel recognized that the evidence at its disposal in relation to these markets was less compelling because sporadic sales and relatively small sales volumes in these markets made the identification of trends more difficult.[35]

The Appellate Body in *US – Large Civil Aircraft (2nd Complaint)* summarized its position taken in *EC and certain Member States – Large Civil Aircraft* with regard to displacement by saying that a finding of displacement will normally require, first, that at least a portion of the market share of the exports of the like product of the complaining Member must have been taken over or substituted by the subsidized product; and, second, it must be possible to discern trends in volume and market share. On this basis, it accepted that Boeing displaced Airbus's sales in Australia because Airbus lost market share to Boeing over the period in question.

[35] WT/DS316/AB/R of 18 May 2011, *EC and certain Member States – Measures Affecting Trade in Large Civil Aircraft*, para 1173 *et seq.* (para 1189 contains, for instance, an interesting example). Note that one Member of the Appellate Body was of the opinion that Article 17.6 DSU did not allow the Appellate Body to complete the analysis of displacement but he agreed with the interpretation of the concept of displacement, see paras 1149 and 1205.

However, with regard to the three other third country markets at issue, i.e. Ethiopia, Kenya and Iceland, there was no evidence that Airbus made or was projected to make deliveries prior to, during or after the reference period. Boeing had a 100 per cent market share in these three countries and only the number of its deliveries fluctuated. On this basis alone, the Appellate Body found that it could not sustain the Panel's finding of a threat of displacement. Consequently, the Appellate Body reversed the Panel's finding.[36]

See also *US – Large Civil Aircraft (2nd Complaint)*, in which the Appellate Body, *inter alia*, pointed out that the Panel erred in not identifying or discussing the third country markets in which displacement occurred.[37]

Indonesia – Autos is a case that demonstrates clearly that an examination of simple trends of market shares might occasionally be misleading. Indonesia's subsidized passenger vehicle, the Timor, captured within a very short period a significant market share, i.e. in the year of its launch it already achieved a market share of 16.9 per cent and in the second quarter of the subsequent year its market share climbed to 47.7 per cent. By contrast, the market share of the competing European cars increased from 2.4 to 5.7 per cent and subsequently dropped to 3.7 per cent. The Panel concluded that the conditions of Article 6.3(a) were not met because the quantity of exports of European cars to Indonesia remained relatively stable. The loss of market share by European cars was not the effect of the subsidy but of the introduction of the Timor which created a new market segment.

Impedance

The concept of competitive engagement would seem to apply also to the concept of impedance.[38] The Appellate Body held that the term 'impede' in Article 6.3 connotes a broader array of situations than the term 'displace'. It refers to situations where the exports or imports of the like product of the complaining WTO Member would have expanded had they not been obstructed or hindered by the subsidized product. Impede could

[36] WT/DS353/AB/R of 12 March 2012, *United States – Measures Affecting Trade in Large Civil Aircraft (Second Complaint)*, para 1082 *et seq.*

[37] WT/DS353/AB/R of 12 March 2012, *United States – Measures Affecting Trade in Large Civil Aircraft (Second Complaint)*, paras 1237–1244 and para 1217 *et seq.*

[38] WT/DS316/AB/R of 18 May 2011, *EC and certain Member States – Measures Affecting Trade in Large Civil Aircraft*, para 1119 and footnotes 2465 and 2466.

also refer to a situation where the exports or imports of the like product of the complaining WTO Member did not materialize at all because production was held back by the subsidized product.[39] While there may be some overlap between them, displacement and impedance are therefore not interchangeable concepts.[40]

The Panel in *EC and certain Member States – Large Civil Aircraft* also clarified that the same market share data that could show displacement could not, on its own, demonstrate impedance. The notion of impedance involves understanding whether sales which would otherwise have taken place were impeded, i.e. hindered or obstructed. Thus, in order to conclude that imports were impeded over the relevant reference period, a panel would, *inter alia*, have to be satisfied that those sales would have actually taken place absent the subsidization.[41]

According to the Appellate Body in *US – Large Civil Aircraft (2nd Complaint)*, Article 6.4 requires that a finding of impedance should be supported by evidence of changes in the relative market share in favour of the subsidized product, over a sufficiently representative period, to demonstrate clear trends in the development of the market concerned. However, unlike displacement, impedance is not necessarily a visible phenomenon. Therefore, evidence of trends may not be dispositive, or may be of less probative value, for a finding of impedance than for a finding of displacement. In any event, the Appellate Body did not find any evidence for clear trends with regard to Ethiopia, Kenya and Iceland, i.e. the very same countries for which it did not find displacement either (see *supra* this chapter pp. 288–291). The Panel's finding of a threat of impedance seemed to have been based exclusively on Boeing's actual and projected sales to these countries. However, Boeing's market share remained at 100 per cent during the reference period and there were no discernible trends, *inter alia*, because sales were too sporadic.[42]

[39] WT/DS316/AB/R of 18 May 2011, *EC and certain Member States – Measures Affecting Trade in Large Civil Aircraft*, para 1161. Confirmed in WT/DS353/AB/R of 12 March 2012, *United States – Measures Affecting Trade in Large Civil Aircraft (Second Complaint)*, para 1071; WT/DS54/R, WT/DS55/R, WT/DS59/R and WT/DS64/R of 2 July 1998, *Indonesia – Certain Measures Affecting the Automobile Industry*, para 14.218.

[40] WT/DS353/AB/R of 12 March 2012, *United States – Measures Affecting Trade in Large Civil Aircraft (Second Complaint)*, para 1071.

[41] WT/DS316/R of 30 June 2010, *EC and certain Member States – Measures Affecting Trade in Large Civil Aircraft*, para 7.1739. This issue was not appealed. WT/DS54/R, WT/DS55/R, WT/DS59/R and WT/DS64/R of 2 July 1998, *Indonesia – Certain Measures Affecting the Automobile Industry*, paras 14.223–14.235.

[42] WT/DS353/AB/R of 12 March 2012, *United States – Measures Affecting Trade in Large Civil Aircraft (Second Complaint)*, paras 1086–1089.

See also *US – Large Civil Aircraft (2nd Complaint)*, in which The Appellate Body, *inter alia*, pointed out that a Panel erred in not identifying or discussing the third country markets in which impedance occurred.[43]

Price Effects and Lost Sales (Article 6.3(c) and 6.5)

Introduction

Article 6.3(c) sets out the third form of serious prejudice, i.e. the effect of the subsidy is (1) significant price undercutting by the subsidized product as compared with the price of a like product of another Member in the same market or (2) significant price suppression, (3) price depression or (4) lost sales in the same market.

The Notions 'in the Same Market' and 'Significant' Apply to All Four Situations of Subparagraph (c)

The Appellate Body in *US – Upland Cotton* concluded that the phrase 'in the same market' in subparagraph (c) applies to all four situations covered by this provision, i.e. significant price undercutting, significant price suppression and price depression as well as lost sales.[44]

Article 6.3(c) lists the adjective 'significant' only twice explicitly, i.e. in conjunction with price undercutting and price suppression, but WTO jurisprudence held that the term 'significant' applies to all four situations in this provision, i.e. also to price depression and lost sales.[45]

Relationship between Paragraphs 3(c) and 5 of Article 6

The Panel in *EC and certain Member States – Large Civil Aircraft* held that the relationship between Articles 6.3(c) and 6.5 is the same as the one between Articles 6.3(b) and 6.4. In other words, Article 6.5 does not set further conditions that have to be met in order to present a successful claim under Article 6.3(c). Therefore, it is not necessary for a claim under

[43] WT/DS353/AB/R of 12 March 2012, *United States – Measures Affecting Trade in Large Civil Aircraft (Second Complaint)*, paras 1237–1244 and para 1217 *et seq.*

[44] WT/DS267/AB/R of 3 March 2005, *United States – Subsidies on Upland Cotton*, paras 400–414. WT/DS316/R of 30 June 2010, *EC and certain Member States – Measures Affecting Trade in Large Civil Aircraft*, para 7.1794 agreed. This issue was not appealed.

[45] WT/DS316/R of 30 June 2010, *EC and certain Member States – Measures Affecting Trade in Large Civil Aircraft*, para 7.1795. This aspect was not appealed.

Article 6.3(c) to demonstrate that the products of the complaining WTO Member are not subsidized, as requires the first sentence of Article 6.5. Rather, Article 6.5 sets out a particular set of circumstances in which price undercutting can be found without further consideration of whether the price difference is the effect of the subsidy.[46] This follows in fact directly from the wording of Article 6.5 that stipulates that '[f]or the purposes of paragraph 3(c), price undercutting *shall include* any case in which such price undercutting has been demonstrated through a comparison of prices of the subsidized product with prices of the non-subsidized like product' (emphasis added). As set out below, and irrespective of whether the claim is based on Article 6.5, this provision contains useful guidance for the price undercutting analysis.[47]

Price Undercutting

Article 6.5 provides useful guidance for the nature of the analysis of price undercutting in general, when it describes in its second and third sentence the type of price comparison that should be undertaken, i.e. the comparisons should relate to transactions made at the same level of trade, at comparable times and concerning comparable products, due account being taken of any other factor affecting price comparability.[48]

The difficulties of carrying out a price undercutting analysis are well described in *EC and certain Member States – Large Civil Aircraft*. The US presented considerable evidence on sales campaigns to airlines that have been lost by Boeing and won by Airbus. The Panel recognized that price, in the sense of the overall value of the offer, remained one of the determinative factors, if not the only one, in the customer's purchasing decision. The Panel also had at its disposal evidence as to the price offers made by both Airbus and Boeing. For instance, Czech Airlines's strategic director explained that both the offers from Airbus and from Boeing met all of their technical requirements without exception, but that Airbus offered the better price. However, airlines also took account of a number of other considerations when purchasing aircraft such as

[46] WT/DS316/R of 30 June 2010, *EC and certain Member States – Measures Affecting Trade in Large Civil Aircraft*, para 7.1799. This issue was not appealed.

[47] WT/DS316/R of 30 June 2010, *EC and certain Member States – Measures Affecting Trade in Large Civil Aircraft*, para 7.1834. This issue was not appealed.

[48] WT/DS316/R of 30 June 2010, *EC and certain Member States – Measures Affecting Trade in Large Civil Aircraft*, para 7.1834. This issue was not appealed.

existing fleets, their route structure and forecasts for changes in routes and traffic patterns, operating costs, maintenance costs, training costs etc. The Panel also found that personal or political factors appeared to have occasionally played a role. Many of these non-price considerations were reflected in public statements made by the airlines at or around the time of the purchases. On the basis of all this the Panel found that the information at its disposal was not sufficient to make a price undercutting analysis between Airbus's and Boeing's offers.[49] However, the information was enough to conclude that Boeing had lost significant sales to Airbus.

Indonesia – Autos is another example of a complex price undercutting analysis that also required a number of adjustments to the prices of Indonesian and imported cars to make them comparable.[50]

Price Suppression and Price Depression

Price Depression. The following definitions have been used in WTO dispute settlement rulings with regard to the term 'price depression': price depression refers to a situation where prices are pressed down, or reduced;[51] price reductions, i.e. prices decline when they should have remained stable or even increased;[52] a situation where prices are observed to fall.[53]

EC and certain Member States – Large Civil Aircraft is an example for a price depression analysis in practice. The Panel concluded that the prices of three of Boeing's aircraft, i.e. the vast majority of Boeing's sales, were significantly depressed. However, in relation to one model (B777), the prices declined only in one of five years. In all other years, prices increased roughly in line with the changes of the United States Aircraft Manufacturers Producer Price Index (PPI), with the exception of 2006 when prices rose by significantly more, leaving them at approximately the same level as the PPI.

[49] WT/DS316/R of 30 June 2010, *EC and certain Member States – Measures Affecting Trade in Large Civil Aircraft*, paras 7.1833–7.1840. This issue was not appealed.

[50] WT/DS54/R, WT/DS55/R, WT/DS59/R and WT/DS64/R of 2 July 1998, *Indonesia – Certain Measures Affecting the Automobile Industry*, para 14.237 *et seq.*

[51] WT/DS267/R of 8 September 2004, *United States – Subsidies on Upland Cotton*, para 7.1277.

[52] WT/DS273/R of 7 March 2005, *Korea – Measures Affecting Trade in Commercial Vessels*, para 7.534.

[53] WT/DS316/R of 30 June 2010, *EC and certain Member States – Measures Affecting Trade in Large Civil Aircraft*, para 7.1854. This issue was not appealed.

Thus, the Panel was not convinced that there was price depression in relation to the B777.[54]

Price Suppression. The Appellate Body in *US – Upland Cotton* has recognized that Article 6.3(c) does not set forth any specific methodology for determining whether the effect of the subsidy is significant price suppression. There may well be different ways to make this determination.[55] Price suppression exists if price increases are lower than expected, i.e. prices have not increased, or less, when they otherwise would have.[56] The Panel in *US – Upland Cotton* adopted a similar line: 'Thus, "price suppression" refers to the situation where "prices" ... either are prevented or inhibited from rising (i.e. they do not increase when they otherwise would have) or they do actually increase, but the increase is less than it otherwise would have been.'[57] The Appellate Body approved of this definition[58] and in *US – Upland Cotton (Article 21.5)* elaborated further:

> While price depression is a directly observable phenomenon, price suppression is not. Falling prices can be observed; by contrast, price suppression concerns whether prices are less than they would otherwise have been in consequence of various factors, in this case, the subsidies. The identification of price suppression, therefore, presupposes a comparison of an observable factual situation (prices) with a counterfactual situation (what prices would have been) where one has to determine whether, in the absence of the subsidies (or some other controlling phenomenon), prices would have increased or would have increased more than they actually did ... Thus, counterfactual analysis is an inescapable part of analyzing the effect of a subsidy under Article 6.3(c) of the *SCM Agreement*.[59]

[54] WT/DS316/R of 30 June 2010, *EC and certain Member States – Measures Affecting Trade in Large Civil Aircraft*, paras 7.1854 and 7.1855. This issue was not appealed.

[55] WT/DS267/AB/R of 3 March 2005, *United States – Subsidies on Upland Cotton*, para 427; WT/DS267/AB/RW of 16 May 2008, *United States – Subsidies on Upland Cotton (Article 21.5)*, para 441. In the implementation proceeding, the US claimed that the Panel should have examined the effects of the bundle of price-contingent subsidies at issue in the original proceeding and then subtracted the impact of the repeal of the subsidy as a result of US implementation. By contrast, the Panel analysed the effect of the remaining subsidies that were not withdrawn by the US. The Appellate Body agreed with the Panel's approach.

[56] WT/DS273/R of 7 March 2005, *Korea – Measures Affecting Trade in Commercial Vessels*, para 7.534.

[57] WT/DS267/R of 8 September 2004, *United States – Subsidies on Upland Cotton*, para 7.1277.

[58] WT/DS267/AB/R of 3 March 2005, *United States – Subsidies on Upland Cotton*, paras 423 and 424.

[59] WT/DS267/AB/RW of 16 May 2008, *United States – Subsidies on Upland Cotton (Article 21.5)*, para 351. This definition of price depression was confirmed by WT/DS316/R of 30

In *US – Large Civil Aircraft (2nd Complaint)*, the Appellate Body further highlighted the value of a counterfactual analysis: '[A] counterfactual analysis is likely to be of particular utility for panels faced with claims that subsidies have caused price suppression.'[60] In order to demonstrate that there was price suppression, the US in *EC and certain Member States – Large Civil Aircraft* compared the development of their aircraft prices (on an indexed basis) with the PPI. The PPI reflects the development of production costs in terms of material and labour. The EU challenged this, claiming that the PPI was a theoretical construct and thus provided little information about Boeing's actual manufacturing costs, that Boeing had introduced a number of cost-cutting and restructuring measures over the past decade and that Boeing could take advantage of learning curve effects. Instead, Boeing's operating margin, i.e. a function of actual cost and revenue, should have been used. The Panel sided with the US. It said that one would expect that in any manufacturing industry, all else being equal, prices would tend to increase when production costs increase. The Panel found that the aircraft industry shared this expectation. In particular, both Airbus and Boeing typically tried to ensure that the final price paid by a customer for an aircraft delivered some years after the date it was ordered kept pace with any increase in the costs of production over the intervening period by including a price escalation clause in their sales contracts. The factors that went into the PPI were to a large extent also used for the purposes of the price escalation clause. Therefore, the PPI represented a reasonable benchmark for the price trends and levels that would have been expected over the reference period.[61]

US – Large Civil Aircraft (2nd Complaint) had to examine whether the US subsidies for the Boeing Aircraft 787 suppressed prices of the Airbus A330 (which was the market leader at the time the B787 was launched in 2004) and the more recent model A350. The Panel answered this in the affirmative. It considered trends in prices and market shares in the light of

June 2010, *EC and certain Member States – Measures Affecting Trade in Large Civil Aircraft*, para 7.1854 (this issue was not appealed) and WT/DS353/AB/R of 12 March 2012, *United States – Measures Affecting Trade in Large Civil Aircraft (Second Complaint)*, paras 1091 and 1092; WT/DS273/R of 7 March 2005, *Korea – Measures Affecting Trade in Commercial Vessels*, paras 7.536–7.537.

60 WT/DS353/AB/R of 12 March 2012, *United States – Measures Affecting Trade in Large Civil Aircraft (Second Complaint)*, para 1092; WT/DS267/AB/RW of 16 May 2008, *United States – Subsidies on Upland Cotton (Article 21.5)*, para 354.

61 WT/DS316/R of 30 June 2010, *EC and certain Member States – Measures Affecting Trade in Large Civil Aircraft*, para 7.1856 *et seq*. This issue was not appealed.

its economic logic, i.e. that the introduction of a superior product at comparable prices (the B787) would normally be accompanied by decreases in prices of the incumbent competing product (the Airbus products).

The US contested the Panel's finding by claiming that the Panel was required to establish a direct and continuous correlation between the B787's market share in the reference period and the A330 prices during these years. The Appellate Body did not agree with the US. It pointed out that the fact that the A330 prices were not affected immediately by the launch of the B787, or did not drop to the same degree as Airbus's market share declined, might well reflect the fact that Airbus did not change its pricing strategy immediately upon the introduction of the B787, but did so with a time-lag, and only after appreciating the extent of the market share lost to Boeing.[62]

The US also challenged the Panel's conclusion that prices of the A350 were suppressed because of the subsidized B787. It claimed that the Panel's conclusion was based on insufficient evidence as there were no pricing data of any kind and only anecdotal evidence that covered barely 30 per cent of sales of the original A350. Thus, according to the US, the EU had not established a *prima facie* case of price suppression. The US relied on the Appellate Body ruling in *US – Upland Cotton* according to which an '[a]ssessment of general price trends is clearly relevant to significant price suppression although ... price trends are not conclusive'.[63] The Appellate Body understood the US to argue that a finding of price suppression had to be based on price trend data for the original A350. The Appellate Body did not agree with the US. It pointed out that its ruling in *US – Upland Cotton* could not be interpreted to require such data. The Appellate Body's statement in *US – Upland Cotton*, that general price trends are 'clearly relevant', was a function of the particular counter-cyclical and price-contingent nature of the subsidies at issue in that dispute. Moreover, pricing trends of the original A350 would not have been particularly probative given that prices of the original A350 were never unaffected by the existence of the B787. The original A350 was launched in 2005 in the market where the effects of the subsidies – through the presence of the B787 – were already

[62] WT/DS353/AB/R of 12 March 2012, *United States – Measures Affecting Trade in Large Civil Aircraft (Second Complaint)*, paras 1104–1113.

[63] See also WT/DS273/R of 7 March 2005, *Korea – Measures Affecting Trade in Commercial Vessels*, para 7.534.

being felt. Therefore, any subsequent price trends would not have been particularly probative as to the effects on Airbus prices of the R&D subsidies given to Boeing.[64]

Finally, with regard to the necessary level of evidence, i.e. on what percentage of sales should a finding of significant price suppression be based, see *US – Large Civil Aircraft (2nd Complaint)*.[65]

A pass-through analysis 'is not critical for the assessment of significant price suppression' under Article 6 if the subsidy is given to an upstream producer. However, the subsidized product must be properly identified for the purposes of the price suppression analysis.[66]

Can world market prices be the relevant price for the suppression analysis? According to the Appellate Body in *US – Upland Cotton*, the analysis of world market prices (as opposed to prices in the same market of another WTO Member) such as internationally accepted price indices can be sufficient if prices for the product concerned throughout the world are largely determined by such index.[67]

The *relationship between the subsidies and the price effects* as defined in Article 6.3(c) can be of a more *indirect nature*, which in turn adds to the complexity of the analysis. *US – Upland Cotton (Article 21.5)* is such an example. The question was whether certain subsidies given by the US, i.e. a marketing loan and countercyclical payments, had an impact on the prices of upland cotton on the world market that could be considered significant price suppression. The Panel opted for a unitary analysis, contrary to the two-step analysis followed in the original case, and a counterfactual approach (i.e. whether 'but for the subsidies' the world market prices of upland cotton would not have been suppressed). Brazil did not claim that these subsidies had a direct impact on world market upland cotton prices. Rather, Brazil alleged that the subsidies had an impact on farmers' planting decisions and, consequently, on US upland cotton production levels which in turn led to suppressed prices. The Panel therefore tried to answer the question whether there was marginal production attributable to the subsidies, and whether the corresponding increase in supply of cotton

[64] WT/DS353/AB/R of 12 March 2012, *United States – Measures Affecting Trade in Large Civil Aircraft (Second Complaint)*, paras 1114–1119.

[65] WT/DS353/AB/R of 12 March 2012, *United States – Measures Affecting Trade in Large Civil Aircraft (Second Complaint)*, paras 1120–1125.

[66] WT/DS267/AB/R of 3 March 2005, *United States – Subsidies on Upland Cotton*, paras 471–472. See also *infra* this chapter pp. 344–346.

[67] WT/DS267/AB/R of 3 March 2005, *United States – Subsidies on Upland Cotton*, paras 415–418. See in detail *infra* this chapter pp. 336–338.

had effects on prices in the world market. All else being equal, the marginal production attributable to the subsidy would be expected to have an effect on world prices, particularly if the subsidy is provided by a country with a meaningful share of world output. The Appellate Body approved of this approach and also noted that there is some inherent difficulty in quantifying the effects of subsidies, because in a price suppression analysis, the increase in prices cannot be directly observed. Therefore, one way to undertake the analysis is to use economic modelling or other quantitative techniques.

The Panel based its conclusion that US subsidies caused significant price suppression on the following main elements:

- US share of world upland cotton production (around 20 per cent) and share of world upland cotton exports (40 per cent of exports). On this basis, the Panel found that the US exerted a substantial proportionate influence on the world market for upland cotton.
- Structure, design and operation of the subsidies. The Panel found that subsidies affected US production as a result of their price-contingent nature and revenue stabilizing effect.
- Large magnitude of the subsidies (more than USD 2 billion per year).
- Discernible temporal coincidence of suppressed world market prices and the US subsidies.
- Significant price gap between the total cost of production of US upland cotton producers and their market revenue. The subsidies accounted in marketing year 2004 for 35 per cent and in marketing year 2005 for 27 per cent of total revenue of US upland cotton farmers, and the costs exceeded market revenues by 3.7 per cent and 71.9 per cent, respectively. According to the Panel, this suggested that the subsidies were an important factor affecting the economic viability of US upland cotton farming.
- The Appellate Body recognized that the US had, in order to implement the original DSB decision, removed one subsidy but the amounts paid under this subsidy were much smaller than the ones that were paid under the schemes that continued to exist.
- Economic simulations estimated that the subsidies that were not repealed following the original DSB ruling had an effect on world market prices (9.3–10.7 per cent according to Brazil and 1.41–2.26 per cent according to the US). The significance of even relatively small changes in price for commodity products such as upland cotton was also noted.

- The subsidies resulted in additional production of 12–18 per cent, even when using the US parameters of the economic model.

Because of the 'but for' approach, the Panel did not consider it necessary to undertake a comprehensive analysis of other factors affecting the world market price of upland cotton although it examined the effect of China's destocking of upland cotton. The Appellate Body upheld the Panel's ruling.[68] See also *infra* this chapter pp. 354–355 the discussion of price suppression by the Panel in *US – Upland Cotton*. Note, however, that the existence of a correlation between a subsidy and a particular level of prices is not in and of itself sufficient to establish that the subsidy causes significant price suppression.[69]

The analysis under Article 6.3(c) may require the *calculation of the cost of production*. DSB rulings held that the total cost of production is relevant (as opposed to only the variable costs).[70] The Appellate Body accepted also that non-cash opportunity costs such as unpaid labour and owned land can be included in the calculation of the cost of production.[71] DSB rulings have not accepted to reduce the cost of production by income from activities not related to the product concerned.[72]

Is the concept of 'like product' a required element in the analysis of price suppression/price depression? Korea – Commercial Vessels answered this to the negative, not least because Article 6.3(c) refers to this concept only for the purposes of the price undercutting analysis, but not in relation to a price suppression/depression analysis. According to the Panel, the principal analytical purpose of the concept of like product would seem to ensure that such a price-to-price comparison would be made in all cases. Notwithstanding the Panel's conclusion that the concept of like product does not apply, this does not mean in the Panel's view that product

[68] WT/DS267/AB/RW of 16 May 2008, *United States – Subsidies on Upland Cotton (Article 21.5)*, para 353 *et seq*. See also *infra* this chapter pp. 311–314.

[69] WT/DS267/RW of 18 December 2007, *United States – Subsidies on Upland Cotton (Article 21.5)*, para 10.133.

[70] WT/DS267/AB/RW of 16 May 2008, *United States – Subsidies on Upland Cotton (Article 21.5)*, para 423 *et seq*.; WT/DS103/AB/RW2 and WT/DS113/AB/RW2 of 20 December 2002, *Canada – Measures Affecting the Importation of Milk and the Exportation of Dairy Products (2nd Article 21.5)*, para 88.

[71] WT/DS267/AB/RW of 16 May 2008, *United States – Subsidies on Upland Cotton (Article 21.5)*, para 428; WT/DS103/AB/RW2 and WT/DS113/AB/RW2 of 20 December 2002, *Canada – Measures Affecting the Importation of Milk and the Exportation of Dairy Products (2nd Article 21.5)*, paras 99–110.

[72] WT/DS267/AB/RW of 16 May 2008, *United States – Subsidies on Upland Cotton (Article 21.5)*, paras 429–432.

considerations are irrelevant. On the contrary, product is an inherent element of price. Therefore, according to the Panel, it is always for the complaining party to a WTO dispute to determine the basis and the nature of its complaint in terms of the breadth or narrowness of the description of the product whose prices allegedly are suppressed or depressed, and the relationship of the price levels and trends with the subsidy in question. Note that the Panel viewed the product issue ultimately as pertaining to the demonstration of causation under Article 6.3(c).[73] The Panel in *EC and certain Member States – Large Civil Aircraft* adopted a similar position by concluding that it is not, strictly speaking, necessary to identify a 'like product' within the meaning of footnote 46 of the Agreement for purposes of assessing price suppression, price depression or lost sales under Article 6.3(c).[74] The Appellate Body in *US – Upland Cotton* could leave the question open whether the like product requirement applied to a price suppression analysis.[75]

Miscellaneous. In *Korea – Commercial Vessels*, the question arose as for whose prices the Panel should establish price suppression or depression, i.e. Korean prices, world prices or EU prices. In the case at hand, the parties seemed to have agreed that the subsidizer's (i.e. Korean) prices *inter alia* were also relevant.[76]

Korea – Commercial Vessels also held that a finding of price suppression/depression under Article 6.3(c) requires an examination of the cause of the observed price trend. Accordingly, price depression is not simply a decline in prices. Rather, prices must have been pushed down by subsidies. Similarly, a finding of price suppression requires a finding that prices have been restrained by subsidies. In other words, what would have been the price movements for the product in the absence ('but for') of subsidies?[77] This in fact refers ultimately to the question of causation (see *infra*)

[73] WT/DS273/R of 7 March 2005, *Korea – Measures Affecting Trade in Commercial Vessels*, paras 7.543–7.560.

[74] WT/DS316/R of 30 June 2010, *EC and certain Member States – Measures Affecting Trade in Large Civil Aircraft*, para 7.1671. This aspect was not appealed.

[75] WT/DS267/AB/R of 3 March 2005, *United States – Subsidies on Upland Cotton*, para 407 and footnote 453.

[76] WT/DS273/R of 7 March 2005, *Korea – Measures Affecting Trade in Commercial Vessels*, paras 7.535.

[77] WT/DS273/R of 7 March 2005, *Korea – Measures Affecting Trade in Commercial Vessels*, para 7.537 and para 7.612 *et seq.* See also WT/DS54/R, WT/DS55/R, WT/DS59/R and WT/DS64/R of 2 July 1998, *Indonesia – Certain Measures Affecting the Automobile Industry*, para 14.255.

and the question of a unitary versus a two-step analysis (see *supra* this chapter pp. 284–285).

See also *US – Large Civil Aircraft (2nd Complaint)*.[78]

Lost Sales

Serious prejudice pursuant to Article 6.3(c) can also arise if the effect of the subsidy is lost sales in the same market. The Appellate Body examined the concept of 'lost sales' for the first time in *EC and certain Member States – Large Civil Aircraft*. It considered a lost sale as one that a supplier failed to obtain. It further understood lost sales to be a relational concept that includes consideration of the behaviour of both the subsidized firm(s), which must have won the sales, and the competing firm(s), which allegedly lost the sales. As pointed out above, the notions 'same market' and 'significant' also apply in relation to lost sales.

In *EC and certain Member States – Large Civil Aircraft*, the EU argued that the concept of lost sales implied significant price undercutting. According to the EU, lost sales can only be demonstrated on the basis of price undercutting. When applying this principle to the facts of the case, this means that Boeing lost a sale if Airbus has won that sale on the basis of a price that was significantly lower than the one offered by Boeing and if that significantly lower price is caused by subsidies. The Panel disagreed by finding that there is no legal basis for the EU's claim.[79]

The Appellate Body held that it may be appropriate to assess lost sales by focusing on an examination of specific sales campaigns (like in the sale of large commercial aircraft) given the particular characteristics of a market. Sometimes, it will be necessary to also look beyond individual sales campaigns to fully understand the competitive dynamics that are at play in a particular market. Thus, an approach in which sales are aggregated by supplier, or examined on a country-wide or even global basis, rather than individually, is also permissible.[80]

There is no DSB decision yet determining whether 'lost sales' can also refer to a lost sale of a single unit. A lost sales campaign comprising several units does not raise the single unit issue.

[78] WT/DS353/AB/R of 12 March 2012, *United States – Measures Affecting Trade in Large Civil Aircraft (Second Complaint)*, paras 1223–1227 and para 1217 *et seq*.

[79] WT/DS316/R of 30 June 2010, *EC and certain Member States – Measures Affecting Trade in Large Civil Aircraft*, para 7.1841 *et seq*. This aspect was not appealed.

[80] WT/DS316/AB/R of 18 May 2011, *EC and certain Member States – Measures Affecting Trade in Large Civil Aircraft*, para 1217 and footnote 2627.

The Appellate Body acknowledged that the causal link analysis can be carried out in a one-step approach (which is its preferred option) or in two steps. Under the two-step approach, a Panel would first examine whether there had been significant lost sales. Moreover, as it must be assessed whether the lost sales are the effect of a subsidy, a counterfactual analysis would be appropriate. This would involve a comparison of the sales actually made by the competing firms of the complaining Member with a counterfactual scenario in which the firms of the subsidizing WTO Member would not have received the subsidy. Obviously, there would be lost sales where the counterfactual analysis shows that sales won by the subsidized firm would not have been made in the absence of the subsidy.[81]

See also *US – Large Civil Aircraft (2nd Complaint)*.[82]

'Significant'

The term 'significant' means 'important, notable, or consequential', and has both quantitative and qualitative dimensions.[83] According to *Korea – Commercial Vessels*, only price suppression or price depression of a sufficient magnitude or degree, seen in the context of a particular product at issue, is meaningfully able to affect suppliers.[84] This is in line with previous rulings in *Indonesia – Autos*[85] and *US – Upland Cotton*.[86]

[81] WT/DS316/AB/R of 18 May 2011, *EC and certain Member States – Measures Affecting Trade in Large Civil Aircraft*, para 1216. See *supra* this chapter pp. 284–285. The Appellate Body's review of the Panel's findings made in relation to the first step can be found in para 1221 *et seq.*

[82] WT/DS353/AB/R of 12 March 2012, *United States – Measures Affecting Trade in Large Civil Aircraft (Second Complaint)*, paras 1228–1236, and para 1217 *et seq.*

[83] WT/DS316/AB/R of 18 May 2011, *EC and certain Member States – Measures Affecting Trade in Large Civil Aircraft*, paras 1213–1220. Confirmed in WT/DS353/AB/R of 12 March 2012, *United States – Measures Affecting Trade in Large Civil Aircraft (Second Complaint)*, para 1052. See also WT/DS273/R of 7 March 2005, *Korea – Measures Affecting Trade in Commercial Vessels*, para 7.571.

[84] WT/DS273/R of 7 March 2005, *Korea – Measures Affecting Trade in Commercial Vessels*, para 7.571.

[85] WT/DS54/R, WT/DS55/R, WT/DS59/R and WT/DS64/R of 2 July 1998, *Indonesia – Certain Measures Affecting the Automobile Industry*, para 14.254. The Panel held that the insertion of 'significant' in this context presumably was intended to ensure that undercutting margins should not give rise to serious prejudice if they are so small that they could not meaningfully affect domestic competitors of the imported subsidized product.

[86] WT/DS267/R of 8 September 2004, *United States – Subsidies on Upland Cotton*, paras 7.1326–7.1330. The Appellate Body approved of the Panel's definition in WT/DS267/AB/R of 3 March 2005, *United States – Subsidies on Upland Cotton*, para 427.

In relation to 'lost sales', the assessment of 'significant' can have quantitative and qualitative dimensions. For instance, the winning of a particular sale can have strategic importance. Significance can also result from consequences beyond the revenue effect of lost sales, e.g. in the aircraft business, because:

- lost sales can delay a manufacturer's ability to benefit from the important learning effects and economies of scale in the industry in question; or
- not becoming the incumbent supplier can also have negative effects on future rounds of procurement.[87]

The Panel in *US – Upland Cotton* also clarified considerably as to how the concept of 'significant' can be applied in practice. First, it specified that it is the degree of price suppression or depression itself that must be significant and that such significance may vary from case to case, depending upon the factual circumstances, and may not solely depend upon a given level of numerical significance. Other considerations, including the nature of the 'same market' and the product under consideration may also enter into such an assessment. Second, when applying this standard to the facts of the case the Panel held:

> We cannot believe that what may be significant in a market for upland cotton could necessarily also be applicable or relevant to a market for a very different product. We consider that, for a basic and widely traded commodity, such as upland cotton, a relatively small decrease or suppression of prices could be significant because, for example, profit margins may ordinarily be narrow, product homogeneity means that sales are price sensitive or because of the sheer size of the market in terms of the amount of revenue involved in large volumes traded on the markets experiencing the price suppression.[88]

In case of a finding of price suppression that is based on several factors, only the price suppression needs to be significant. There is no requirement that each factor is significant.[89]

[87] WT/DS316/AB/R of 18 May 2011, *EC and certain Member States – Measures Affecting Trade in Large Civil Aircraft*, paras 1218 and 1219.

[88] WT/DS267/R of 8 September 2004, *United States – Subsidies on Upland Cotton*, para 7.1330. See also the preceding three paras of the Panel report as well as para 7.1332. The Appellate Body approved of the Panel's definition in WT/DS267/AB/R of 3 March 2005, *United States – Subsidies on Upland Cotton*, para 427.

[89] WT/DS267/AB/RW of 16 May 2008, *United States – Subsidies on Upland Cotton (Article 21.5)*, para 416.

Increase in World Market Share (Article 6.3(d))

A serious prejudice claim can be based on an increase in the world market share of the subsidizing Member in a particular subsidized primary product or commodity if this increase is the effect of the subsidy. The increase is to be measured against the average world market share that the subsidizing Member had during the previous period of three years, and the increase must follow a consistent trend over the period when subsidies have been granted. Footnote 17 is attached to paragraph 3(d) and is essentially self-explanatory.

Paragraph 3(d) covers only primary products and commodities while the other subparagraphs of paragraph 3 may cover any type of product. Therefore, paragraph 3(d) is reminiscent of Article XVI:3 of GATT 1994 which refers to a 'contracting party having more than an equitable share of world export trade in that product'. Note that the latter provision is also limited to primary products (a definition of the term 'primary product' is contained in the notes and supplementary provisions to Article XVI). However, Article XVI:3 only covers export subsidies while – given the prohibition of export subsidies under the ASCM – paragraph 3(d) covers actionable subsidies.

In *US – Upland Cotton*, there was some disagreement over how the term 'world market share' had to be defined. Brazil submitted that this meant a Member's market share of the world market for exports only. The US contended that its share of the world market for upland cotton encompassed all consumption of upland cotton, including consumption by a country of its own production. The Panel rejected both proposed definitions and held that the phrase 'world market share of a subsidizing Member' in Article 6.3(d) refers to the share of the world market supplied by the subsidizing Member of the product concerned, thus excluding the subsidizing Member's own consumption.[90] The Appellate Body exercised judicial economy in this respect.[91]

Article 6.3(d) was again at issue in the Article 21.5 proceeding. Brazil argued that the US world market share had increased in the marketing year 2005, as compared to the US average in marketing years 2002–2004, by 1.53 percentage points. The Panel considered this a small increase

[90] WT/DS267/R of 8 September 2004, *United States – Subsidies on Upland Cotton*, paras 7.1436 and 7.1454. See also footnote 1527 of the Panel's report.

[91] WT/DS267/AB/R of 3 March 2005, *United States – Subsidies on Upland Cotton*, paras 497–512.

that was part of the ordinary fluctuations in the US market share and not the effect of the subsidy. It also pointed out that there was even a decrease if data for the marketing year 2006 were to be used. On this basis, it rejected Brazil's claim without examining whether the second condition of Article 6.3(d) was met, i.e. whether the increase followed a consistent trend.[92]

Causation

General

The issue here is whether the subsidies caused serious prejudice within the meaning of Article 6.3, i.e. whether the 'effect of the subsidy' is

- to displace or impede imports of a like product of another WTO Member into the market of the subsidizing Member (subparagraph (a));
- to displace or impede exports of a like product of another WTO Member from a third country market (subparagraph (b));
- a significant price undercutting by the subsidized product as compared with the price of a like product of another WTO Member in the same market or significant price suppression, price depression or lost sales in the same market (subparagraph (c));
- or an increase in the world market share of the subsidizing Member in a particular subsidized primary product or commodity (subparagraph (d)).

In *US – Upland Cotton*, the Appellate Body held that although Article 6.3(c) does not use the word 'cause', an analysis as to whether the 'effect of the subsidy is … significant price suppression' requires the establishment of a causal link.[93] This causal link analysis must establish a 'genuine and substantial relationship of cause and effect' between the subsidies and the alleged market phenomenon in subparagraph (c). Moreover, such analysis must contain a non-attribution analysis, i.e. that the effects of factors other than the subsidy are not improperly attributed to the challenged subsidies. The particular market phenomena alleged under Article 6.3(c) must result from a chain of causation that is linked to the impugned

[92] WT/DS267/RW of 18 December 2007, *United States – Subsidies on Upland Cotton (Article 21.5)*, paras 10.260–10.268.

[93] WT/DS267/AB/R of 3 March 2005, *United States – Subsidies on Upland Cotton*, paras 435–438. WT/DS267/AB/RW of 16 May 2008, *United States – Subsidies on Upland Cotton (Article 21.5)*, para 372.

subsidy.[94] Finally, the Appellate Body also pointed out that Article 6.3(c) leaves some discretion to panels in choosing the methodology used for the causal link assessment. In the Article 21.5 case, the Appellate Body observed that in the light of this flexibility it would not have been improper for the Panel to have assessed the effect of other factors as part of its counterfactual analysis, rather than conducting a separate analysis of non-attribution.[95] In *EC and certain Member States – Large Civil Aircraft*, the Appellate Body concluded that the standards for causation and non-attribution were also applicable to subparagraphs (a) and (b).[96] Note also that, contrary to the causal link standard under Article 15.5, it is the effect of the subsidy, rather than the subsidized product, that must cause the market phenomena in Article 6.3.[97]

In *US – Large Civil Aircraft (2nd Complaint)*, the Appellate Body set out extensively the causal link standard for serious prejudice claims:

> 913. … The Appellate Body has consistently articulated the causal link required as 'a genuine and substantial relationship of cause and effect'. [footnote omitted] In other words, the subsidies must contribute, in a 'genuine'[1865] and 'substantial'[1866] way, to producing or bringing about one or more of the effects, or market phenomena, enumerated in Article 6.3.
>
> 914. When tasked with determining whether the causal link in question meets this requisite standard of a 'genuine and substantial' causal relationship, a panel will often be confronted with multiple factors that may have contributed, to varying degrees, to that effect. Indeed, in some circumstances, it may transpire that factors other than the subsidy at issue have caused a particular market effect. Yet the mere presence of other causes that contribute to a particular market effect does not, in itself, preclude the subsidy from being found to be a 'genuine and substantial' cause of that effect. Thus, as part of its assessment of the causal nexus between the subsidy at issue and the effect(s) that it is alleged to have had, a panel must seek to understand the interactions between the subsidy at issue and the various other causal factors, and make an assessment of their connections to, as well as the relative importance of the subsidy and of the other factors in bringing about, the relevant effects. In order to find that the subsidy is a genuine and substantial cause, a panel need not determine it to be the *sole* cause of that effect, or even that it is the *only* substantial cause of that effect. A panel must, however, take care to ensure

[94] WT/DS267/AB/R of 3 March 2005, *United States – Subsidies on Upland Cotton*, paras 435–438. WT/DS267/AB/RW of 16 May 2008, *United States – Subsidies on Upland Cotton (Article 21.5)*, para 375.

[95] WT/DS267/AB/RW of 16 May 2008, *United States – Subsidies on Upland Cotton (Article 21.5)*, paras 370, 375 *et passim*.

[96] WT/DS316/AB/R of 18 May 2011, *EC and certain Member States – Measures Affecting Trade in Large Civil Aircraft*, para 1232 *et passim*, e.g. para 1376.

[97] WT/DS267/R of 8 September 2004, *United States – Subsidies on Upland Cotton*, para 7.1227.

that it does not attribute the effects of those causal factors to the subsidies at issue [footnote omitted], and that the other causal factors do not dilute the causal link between those subsidies and the alleged adverse effects such that it is not possible to characterize that link as a genuine and substantial relationship of cause and effect. [footnote omitted] The subsidy at issue may be found to exhibit the requisite causal link notwithstanding the existence of other causes that contribute to producing the relevant market phenomena if, having given proper consideration to all other relevant contributing factors and their effects, the panel is satisfied that the contribution of the subsidy has been demonstrated to rise to that of a genuine and substantial cause.

915. Finally, we note that a demonstration that subsidies are a genuine and substantial cause of the alleged serious prejudice is a fact-intensive exercise, and one that inevitably involves extensive, case-specific evidence. The manner in which a complainant may seek to demonstrate the existence of the effects and links between the subsidies at issue and those effects, and the type of supporting evidence that may be adduced, are likely to vary considerably. Even though each panel's assessment will turn very much on the particular facts and considerations of the case, it must not deviate from the requirements outlined above.[98]

[1865] The 'genuine' nature of the causal link requires a complainant to show that the nexus between cause and effect is 'real' or 'true'. Dictionary definitions of 'genuine' include '{h}aving the character claimed for it: real, true, not counterfeit', and '{n}atural or proper to a person or thing' (Shorter Oxford English Dictionary, 6th edn, A. Stevenson (ed.) (Oxford University Press, 2007), Vol. 1, p. 1094).

[1866] As for the 'substantial' component of the causal relationship, this concerns the relative importance of the causal agent (the subsidies at issue) in bringing about the adverse effect(s) in question. Dictionary definitions of 'substantial' include '{h}aving solid worth or value, of real significance; solid; weighty; important, worthwhile' and '{o}f ample or considerable amount or size; sizeable, fairly large' (Shorter Oxford English Dictionary, 6th edn, A. Stevenson (ed.) (Oxford University Press, 2007), Vol. 2, p. 3088).

In the case in question, the EU's theory of causation was that the tied tax subsidies received by Boeing led this firm to lower its aircraft prices, and that such price effects led to lost aircraft sales and suppressed aircraft prices for Airbus. The Panel accepted this proposition. According to the Appellate Body, the Panel should in these circumstances have examined *whether* Boeing indeed lowered its prices by using the tied tax subsidies.

[98] WT/DS353/AB/R of 12 March 2012, *United States – Measures Affecting Trade in Large Civil Aircraft (Second Complaint)*, paras 913–915. See also paras 984 and 1206. See also WT/DS316/AB/R of 18 May 2011, *EC and certain Member States – Measures Affecting Trade in Large Civil Aircraft*, para 1232; WT/DS267/AB/R of 3 March 2005, *United States – Subsidies on Upland Cotton*, para 437 (in relation to non-attribution).

However, the Appellate Body did not consider as relevant the question *why* Boeing lowered its prices in the context of particular sales campaigns.[99]

According to the Panel in *Korea – Commercial Vessels*, there is no single approach to determining causation for all claims of serious prejudice. Each case presents a unique combination of kinds of subsidies, of products, of markets and of forms of serious prejudice, which operate together in an unique way. Consequently, the causation analysis thus necessarily must be case-by-case, tailored to the particular situation presented in each individual dispute. The Panel also conducted a non-attribution analysis but insisted that such other factors must be identified by the parties.[100] Whatever the factual situation in a given case, the burden will be on the complainant to furnish specific factual evidence affirmatively demonstrating the alleged causal link. The difficulty and the ways to meet this standard may be very different from one case to another.[101]

For the purposes of a causal link analysis, DSB rulings accept both a *quantitative* analysis (economic modelling) and a *qualitative* analysis. There is no precise guidance as to whether both types of analysis must be employed or the precise mix thereof. Thus, the Appellate Body underlined in *US – Large Civil Aircraft (2nd Complaint)* that the precise way in which a counterfactual reasoning is deployed will vary depending on how the causal problem presents itself in the dispute. The counterfactual analysis may be highly quantitative, or predominantly qualitative in nature, or it may involve quantitative and qualitative elements.[102] And previously in *US – Upland Cotton*, in the context of a price suppression analysis, the Appellate Body noted that there is some inherent difficulty in quantifying the effects of a subsidy because the increase in prices, absent the subsidies, cannot be directly observed. One way to undertake the analysis is economic modelling or other quantitative techniques.[103]

[99] WT/DS353/AB/R of 12 March 2012, *United States – Measures Affecting Trade in Large Civil Aircraft (Second Complaint)*, para 1212.

[100] WT/DS273/R of 7 March 2005, *Korea – Measures Affecting Trade in Commercial Vessels*, para 7.617 *et seq*. The case-by-case nature of the causation analysis was also underlined by WT/DS353/AB/R of 12 March 2012, *United States – Measures Affecting Trade in Large Civil Aircraft (Second Complaint)*, para 915.

[101] WT/DS273/R of 7 March 2005, *Korea – Measures Affecting Trade in Commercial Vessels*, para 7.560.

[102] WT/DS353/AB/R of 12 March 2012, *United States – Measures Affecting Trade in Large Civil Aircraft (Second Complaint)*, para 1019.

[103] WT/DS267/AB/RW of 16 May 2008, *United States – Subsidies on Upland Cotton (Article 21.5)*, para 356.

Elements that can be relevant for the purpose of the causation analysis are:

- nature of the subsidy;[104]
- the way in which the subsidy operates;
- magnitude of the subsidy;
- the extent to which the subsidy is provided in respect of a particular product;
- conditions on the market;
- conceptual distance between the activities of the subsidy recipient and the products in respect of which price suppression/depression is alleged;
- supply and demand factors;
- production costs;
- relative efficiency.[105]

This is explained in detail *infra* this chapter pp. 323–326.

Note, however, that in the pre WTO cases concerning *EC – Sugar Exports* no such analysis was conducted. The Panels in these cases concluded that the EC export refunds had contributed to depressing world sugar prices, and also constituted a source of uncertainty on world markets.[106]

'But for' Analysis

The Appellate Body in *US – Upland Cotton (Article 21.5)* and in *EC and certain Member States – Large Civil Aircraft* stated that one possible approach to the assessment of causation is an inquiry that

[104] WT/DS267/AB/R of 3 March 2005, *United States – Subsidies on Upland Cotton*, para 450 (for instance, whether subsidies are price-contingent and thus insulate the recipients from the development of world market prices).

[105] See also WT/DS273/R of 7 March 2005, *Korea – Measures Affecting Trade in Commercial Vessels*, paras 7.560 and 7.615; WT/DS267/AB/R of 3 March 2005, *United States – Subsidies on Upland Cotton*, para 434 (the Panel examined the relative magnitude of the US production and exports in the world upland cotton market, general price trends and the nature of the subsidies at issue – all this is described *infra* this chapter pp. 354–355.

[106] GATT Panel Report, *EC – Refunds on Exports of Sugar – Complaint by Australia*, adopted 6 November 1979, BISD 26S/290, points (g) and (h) of the conclusions; GATT Panel Report, *EC – Refunds on Exports of Sugar – Complaint by Brazil*, adopted 10 November 1980, BISD 27S/69, points (f) and (g) of the conclusions.

seeks to identify what would have occurred 'but for' the subsidies. In other words, the effects of other factors would be assessed as part of a properly designed counterfactual that adjusts for the subsidies while maintaining everything else equal. The counterfactual analysis entails comparing the actual market situation with the market situation that would have existed in the absence of the challenged subsidies. This requires undertaking a modelling exercise as to what the market would have looked like in the absence of the subsidies. For instance, in relation to displacement and impedance, this involves estimating what the sales of the complaining WTO Member would have been in the absence of the challenged subsidy. The counterfactual sales would then be compared to the actual sales. Displacement or impedance would arise where the counterfactual analysis shows that the sales of the complaining WTO Member would have declined less or would have been higher in the absence of the challenged subsidy. The Appellate Body also recognized that, as with other factual assessments, panels clearly have a margin of discretion in conducting the counterfactual analysis.[107]

Economic modelling or other quantitative techniques estimate whether there are higher levels of production resulting from the subsidies and, in turn, the price effects of that production. They provide a framework to analyse the relationship between the subsidies, other factors and price movements.[108]

According to the Appellate Body, in some contexts, including in assessing claims of price suppression and impedance, a counterfactual analysis is an inescapable part of a causation analysis.[109] However, the

[107] WT/DS316/AB/R of 18 May 2011, *EC and certain Member States – Measures Affecting Trade in Large Civil Aircraft*, paras 1110 and 1163. WT/DS353/AB/R of 12 March 2012, *United States – Measures Affecting Trade in Large Civil Aircraft (Second Complaint)*, paras 1019 and 1020. See also WT/DS267/AB/RW of 16 May 2008, *United States – Subsidies on Upland Cotton (Article 21.5)*, paras 357 and 370 and *et passim;* WT/DS273/R of 7 March 2005, *Korea – Measures Affecting Trade in Commercial Vessels*, para 7.615.

[108] WT/DS267/AB/RW of 16 May 2008, *United States – Subsidies on Upland Cotton (Article 21.5)*, para 356.

[109] WT/DS267/AB/RW of 16 May 2008, *United States – Subsidies on Upland Cotton (Article 21.5)*, paras 351 and 371. See also WT/DS273/R of 7 March 2005, *Korea – Measures Affecting Trade in Commercial Vessels*, para 7.537; WT/DS353/AB/R of 12 March 2012, *United States – Measures Affecting Trade in Large Civil Aircraft (Second Complaint)*, para 1020.

Appellate Body has also underlined the limits of this approach. In *US – Upland Cotton (Article 21.5)*, it explained that a 'but for' test may be too undemanding if the subsidy is necessary but not sufficient to bring about a market phenomenon listed in subparagraph (c) of Article 6.3. It also pointed out that the test would be too rigorous if it required the subsidy to be the only cause. Therefore, the 'but for' test should determine that there is a genuine and substantial relationship of cause and effect.[110]

EC and certain Member States – Large Civil Aircraft endorsed the aforementioned test and gave further guidance as to its application. In some circumstances, a determination that the market phenomena in Article 6.3 would not have occurred 'but for' the challenged subsidies will suffice to establish causation. This is because, in some circumstances, the 'but for' analysis will show that the subsidy is both a necessary cause of the market phenomenon in question and a substantial cause. The Appellate Body hastened to add that, however, there are circumstances in which the 'but for' approach does not suffice – for example, where the necessary cause is too remote and other intervening causes substantially account for the market phenomenon. A proper non-attribution analysis is essential in such circumstances.[111]

In *US – Upland Cotton (Article 21.5)*, the Appellate Body also recognized that a separate non-attribution analysis is not necessarily required under a 'but for' analysis. Rather, the Panel could have assessed the effect of factors other than the subsidies as part of its counterfactual analysis.[112] And in *EC and certain Member States – Large Civil Aircraft*, the Appellate Body opined that a 'but for' test generally reflects the unitary approach to causation.[113] See also *supra* this chapter pp. 284–285.

The precise way in which counterfactual reasoning is deployed will vary depending on how the causal problem presents itself in a particular dispute, that is, according to *inter alia* the scenarios, arguments raised and evidence on the record. A counterfactual analysis may be highly

[110] WT/DS267/AB/RW of 16 May 2008, *United States – Subsidies on Upland Cotton (Article 21.5)*, paras 374 and 375.

[111] WT/DS316/AB/R of 18 May 2011, *EC and certain Member States – Measures Affecting Trade in Large Civil Aircraft*, para 1233.

[112] WT/DS267/AB/RW of 16 May 2008, *United States – Subsidies on Upland Cotton (Article 21.5)*, paras 369, 371 and 375 *et seq.*

[113] WT/DS316/AB/R of 18 May 2011, *EC and certain Member States – Measures Affecting Trade in Large Civil Aircraft*, note 2655 attached to para 1234.

quantitative, or predominantly qualitative in nature or it may involve both quantitative and qualitative elements.[114]

A panel evaluating the claims and defences of the parties will have to give due consideration to the use of a counterfactual analysis, especially when such an analysis forms part of the arguments submitted by the parties. However, a panel is not required to identify and explore every possible hypothetical market scenario, especially where the parties themselves have not elaborated upon, or substantiated the likelihood of such possible scenarios.[115]

When it comes to the amount of R&D subsidies given in relation to the total development costs of a product and/or the financial strength of the recipient, care has to be taken not to be misled by a simplistic comparison of amounts. In *US – Large Civil Aircraft (2nd Complaint)*, the US argued that the subsidies given to Boeing could not have caused adverse effects to Airbus because Boeing was in a position to finance the development of the B787 model entirely itself. In this context, the US pointed out that the magnitude of subsidies received (around USD 2 billion) was inconsequential when compared to the USD 16 billion spent by Boeing in repurchasing shares between 1986 and 2006. Thus, according to the US, one could not argue that absent the R&D subsidies, Boeing would not have been able to launch an aircraft incorporating all the technologies that were incorporated on the B787 in 2004, with promised deliveries commencing in 2008. The Panel and Appellate Body disagreed. They held that the value of the subsidies was not directly comparable to the cash amounts paid to shareholders, and the effects of the subsidies were not reducible to their cash value. Rather, the R&D subsidies were intended to have multiplier effects. They also allowed Boeing to overcome the significant disincentives that it otherwise faced to start the development of a new airplane. Thus, a simple comparison of dollar amounts of the R&D subsidies with Boeing's available financial resources over the same period would not have been an appropriate measurement by which to predict Boeing's likely commercial behaviour in the absence of the subsidies.[116]

[114] WT/DS353/AB/R of 12 March 2012, *United States – Measures Affecting Trade in Large Civil Aircraft (Second Complaint)*, paras 1019, 1039. WT/DS267/AB/RW of 16 May 2008, *United States – Subsidies on Upland Cotton (Article 21.5)*, para 330 *et seq.*

[115] WT/DS353/AB/R of 12 March 2012, *United States – Measures Affecting Trade in Large Civil Aircraft (Second Complaint)*, para 1020.

[116] WT/DS353/AB/R of 12 March 2012, *United States – Measures Affecting Trade in Large Civil Aircraft (Second Complaint)*, para 1033 *et seq.*

Relevant Factors and Configurations

Aggregation and Cumulation – Causal Link Analysis in the Case of Multiple Subsidies

In past serious prejudice cases, often a multitude of countervailable subsidies has been found. The issue in this section is whether the effects of these subsidies can be analysed collectively, and if so, under what circumstances. The Appellate Body in *US – Large Civil Aircraft (2nd Complaint)* has summarized the law. Before describing the different possible methodologies and their conditions it pointed out:

- The way in which a panel structures its evaluation of a claim that multiple subsidies have caused serious prejudice will necessarily vary from case to case.
- Relevant circumstances that will guide a panel's choice include the design, structure and operation of the subsidies at issue, the alleged market phenomena and the extent to which the subsidies are provided with regard to a particular product or products.
- A panel must also take account of the manner in which the claimant presents its case, and the extent to which it claims that multiple subsidies have similar effects on the same product.
- A panel enjoys a degree of methodological latitude in selecting its approach to analysing the collective effects of multiple subsidies.
- A panel must be careful not to combine multiple subsidies in such a way as to absolve a complainant of its burden to demonstrate that the subsidies have caused the market phenomena of Article 6.3.

According to the Appellate Body, a panel may at least select between two ways of conducting a collective causation analysis, i.e. aggregation or cumulation of subsidies. However, irrespective of the methodology chosen, the standard of a 'genuine and substantial relationship' of cause and effect between the subsidies and the alleged market phenomena of Article 6.3 must always be met.[117]

The aggregation approach has been selected in *US – Upland Cotton* while the cumulation approach had been used for the first time in *EC and certain Member States – Large Civil Aircraft*. The following table summarizes the main differences between the two methodologies.[118] The remainder of this section describes the details.

[117] WT/DS353/AB/R of 12 March 2012, *United States – Measures Affecting Trade in Large Civil Aircraft (Second Complaint)*, para 1284.

[118] WT/DS353/AB/R of 12 March 2012, *United States – Measures Affecting Trade in Large Civil Aircraft (Second Complaint)*, paras 1285–1287, para 1290.

	Aggregation	Cumulation
Specific condition for analysing together the effects of multiple subsidies	Subsidies must be sufficiently similar in their design, structure, and operation.	None
Structure of the causal link analysis	Genuine and substantial causal relationship between the multiple subsidies, taken together, and the relevant market phenomena in Article 6.3.	1st step: Panel analyses whether there is a genuine and substantial causal relationship between the effects of a single subsidy, or an aggregated group of subsidies, and the market phenomena in Article 6.3. 2nd step: Are there other subsidies (either individually or in aggregated groups) that have a *genuine* causal connection to the market phenomena in Article 6.3, and *complement and supplement* the effects of the subsidy – or group of subsidies – at issue in step 1?
Not required	Finding that each subsidy is, individually, a genuine and substantial cause of the market phenomena in Article 6.3. Assessment of the relative contribution of each subsidy within the group of subsidies to the market phenomena of Article 6.3.	The other subsidy (or subsidies) examined under the 2nd step need not, in itself, amount to a substantial cause in order to cumulate it with the subsidy (or subsidies) at issue in the 1st step. However, the other subsidy has to be a genuine cause.

The Appellate Body pointed out that a decision to aggregate subsidies that share a similar design, structure and operation is a useful tool that a panel can use to avoid having to repeat the same analysis for each and every subsidy at issue. Moreover, it is a substantive recognition that the subsidies in question are of a kind that they are likely to lead to the same result. An aggregate analysis of such a group of subsidies may establish a genuine and substantial causal link in circumstances where no such link could have been established for each subsidy analysed in isolation. Thus, aggregation is appropriate if, given the degree of similarity among the subsidies, there is a reasonable likelihood that the examination of the causal relationship between each such subsidy and the alleged Article 6.3 effects will be largely similar, and that the Article 6.3 effects of each subsidy will be largely the same. In adopting the aggregation approach, a panel must explain why it considers that the aforementioned similarities exist. Such explanation should be grounded in the characteristics of the subsidies at issue (in particular the nature and design of the subsidies, the implications of that nature and design for the operation of the subsidies), their relationship to the subsidized product, and the structure of the market in which that product competes.[119]

In contrast, cumulation of the effects of different subsidies is only possible after it has been determined that, for at least one subsidy or group of aggregated subsidies, it has a genuine and substantial link to the alleged market phenomena under Article 6.3. Once such a causal link has been established, a panel will have to address in its cumulation analysis whether the other subsidies have a genuine connection to the Article 6.3 phenomena. Considerations that are relevant in the context of this causal link analysis include the design, structure, magnitude and operation of the subsidy, as well as the nexus between the subsidy and the subsidized product. According to the Appellate Body, a genuine causal connection can be established in different ways. One way is to demonstrate that the subsidy or subsidies cause effects that follow the same causal pathway (e.g. technology effects or price effects of the subsidy/ies) as the subsidy that has already been found to be a substantial and genuine cause of the alleged Article 6.3 market phenomena. Alternatively, a genuine causal connection may also be found if it can be demonstrated that, even though other subsidies do not operate along the same causal pathway, those other subsidies nevertheless, either in isolation or in combination, made a real or

[119] WT/DS353/AB/R of 12 March 2012, *United States – Measures Affecting Trade in Large Civil Aircraft (Second Complaint)*, para 1291.

meaningful contribution to, and thereby complement and supplement, the adverse effects within the meaning of Article 6.3. In other words, the effect of such other subsidy or group of subsidies must be shown to be non-trivial in order to reach the 'supplement or complement standard'.[120] The Appellate Body also pointed out that the characteristics of the market may be relevant for the analysis whether the effects of different subsidies complement and supplement each other. For example, when a subsidy recipient exercises market power, it may be more likely to be able to take advantage of potential interaction between different subsidies, and to exploit these effects to the disadvantage of its competitors, than would be the case in a perfectly competitive market.[121]

Moreover, the Appellate Body noted that it did not see any *a priori* reason – such as, that different subsidies operate through distinct causal mechanisms – why cumulation would be precluded outright.[122] The Appellate Body also pointed out that in a duopoly market (in which Airbus and Boeing operate) it may be that the product and technology effects of subsidies[123] can be examined separately from their price effects. The Appellate Body nevertheless questioned whether such a segmented analysis is capable of fully reflecting market dynamics and taking account of the scope for subsidies and their effects to interact in these types of markets. Moreover, in many other markets the structure of competition will be such that it will simply be impossible meaningfully to conduct a separate analysis of, or distinguish between, product effects and price effects.[124] The introduction of cumulation strengthens the subsidy disciplines. Indeed, cumulation reduces Members' possibility to unduly segment the serious prejudice analysis by distributing their subsidies via different programmes or different levels of government.[125]

[120] WT/DS353/AB/R of 12 March 2012, *United States – Measures Affecting Trade in Large Civil Aircraft (Second Complaint)*, paras 1292 and 1319.

[121] WT/DS353/AB/R of 12 March 2012, *United States – Measures Affecting Trade in Large Civil Aircraft (Second Complaint)*, para 1293.

[122] WT/DS353/AB/R of 12 March 2012, *United States – Measures Affecting Trade in Large Civil Aircraft (Second Complaint)*, para 1319.

[123] In summary, 'product' effects of subsidies are where the subsidy enables a product to be launched in a certain form and at a certain time. 'Technology' effects are where the subsidy enables a product to be launched with certain technological features at a certain time. In the absence of the subsidy, such launches would not have been possible. See *infra* this chapter pp. 333–339.

[124] WT/DS353/AB/R of 12 March 2012, *United States – Measures Affecting Trade in Large Civil Aircraft (Second Complaint)*, para 1319.

[125] *Bohanes/Rueda Garcia* (2012/3) p. 401.

EC and certain Member States – Large Civil Aircraft thus confirms the Panel in *US – Upland Cotton*. That Panel held in the latter case that the reference to the effect of the subsidy in the singular in Article 6.3(c) did not mean that a serious prejudice analysis of price suppression must clinically isolate each individual subsidy and its effects. It concluded:

> textual references to 'any subsidy' and 'the effect of the subsidy' permit an integrated examination of effects of any subsidies with a sufficient nexus with the subsidized product and the particular effects-related variable under examination. Thus, in our price suppression analysis under Article 6.3(c), we examine one effects-related variable – prices – and one subsidized product – upland cotton. To the extent a sufficient nexus with these exists among the subsidies at issue so that their effects manifest themselves collectively, we believe that we may legitimately treat them as a 'subsidy' and group them and their effects together.[126]

Korea – Commercial Vessels also examined the issue of aggregation of subsidies. It justified aggregation by invoking Article 6.1(a) and Annex IV. According to the Panel, in determining the *ad valorem* subsidization of a product, subsidies under different programmes are to be aggregated.[127]

Cumulation: Case Study *EC and certain Member States – Large Civil Aircraft*. In this case it was found that specific financing provided by certain EU Member States to Airbus to launch a number of aircrafts had caused the effects listed in subparagraphs (a) to (c) of Article 6.3. In addition, Airbus benefitted from subsidies in the form of equity infusions, infrastructure measures and R&D subsidies. The question was as to how these latter three types of subsidies should be examined in the causal link analysis under Article 6.3. The EU took the view that the effects of these subsidies could not be considered aggregately with the effect of the launch aid because not all of the former subsidies had a nexus to a particular subsidized Airbus model, they were not contemporaneous, and some were recurring while others were not. According to the EU, there was no evidence to suggest that the launch of a particular Airbus model was contingent on the aforementioned three types of subsidy, i.e. that the subsidy was necessary to enable the launch of a particular Airbus model.

126 WT/DS267/R of 8 September 2004, *United States – Subsidies on Upland Cotton*, para 7.1192. See also WT/DS267/RW of 18 December 2007, *United States – Subsidies on Upland Cotton (Article 21.5)*, para 10.51.

127 WT/DS273/R of 7 March 2005, *Korea – Measures Affecting Trade in Commercial Vessels*, para 7.616.

The Panel and Appellate Body disagreed. The Panel considered that the ability to consider the effects of subsidies together extends to all aspects of a claim of adverse effects under Articles 5(a) and (b) and Articles 6.3(a), (b) and (c). The Panel examined whether the three types of subsidies in question complemented and supplemented the product effect[128] of the specific launch aid for Airbus's aircraft. The Appellate Body first confirmed the Panel's approach that cumulation is in principle possible. It held that once the Panel had established that the launch aid was a genuine and substantial cause of the observed displacement and lost sales, it was not necessary to establish that the three other types of subsidy were themselves also substantial causes to the same phenomena or necessary to enable a launch decision at a particular point in time. Moreover, the fact that launch aid was a substantial cause of adverse effects does not exclude that the other types of subsidies had similar effects. Rather, it was conceivable that the three other types complemented or *supplemented* the effects of launch aid. The Panel had to establish that subsidies other than launch aid 'had a genuine causal connection' (!) with Airbus's ability to launch and bring to the market its aircraft models, thus contributing to the adverse effects of launch aid.[129] The terms 'connection' and 'contribution' used by the Appellate Body can be considered paraphrases of the terms 'complement and supplement'.

When applying the 'complement and supplement standard' to the three subsidies in question, the Appellate Body confirmed the Panel's conclusions in relation to equity infusions. The Panel found that equity infusions in two companies that were part of the Airbus consortium, i.e. Aérospatiale and Deutsche Airbus, provided support to Airbus's efforts in developing and bringing to the market various Airbus models, with corresponding effects on Boeing's sales. While the equity infusions were not tied to a particular Airbus model, they were undertaken with the specific purpose of addressing the undercapitalization of both Aérospatiale and Deutsche Airbus, which, during the 1990s, threatened the investment capacity and even the very existence of both companies. Given the nature and structure of the Airbus consortium, it would have been unlikely that Airbus could have continued to develop and bring to the market its successive aircraft models without the participation of each

[128] See *supra* this chapter, p. 319.

[129] WT/DS316/AB/R of 18 May 2011, *EC and certain Member States – Measures Affecting Trade in Large Civil Aircraft*, para 1357 *et seq.* (in particular paras 1378 and 1379).

of the national companies engaged in Airbus.[130] The Appellate Body also upheld the Panel's findings that some of the infrastructure measures of various Airbus governments had the effect of displacing Boeing's aircraft from the EU and relevant third country markets, and of significant sales lost by Boeing. It reasoned that these infrastructure measures had a genuine causal link with the creation and expansion of Airbus's production facilities and that these infrastructure measures complemented or supplemented launch aid given by Member States, thus contributing to Airbus's ability to introduce its large civil aircraft into the market.[131]

In relation to certain R&D subsidies, the Panel claimed that these subsidies enabled Airbus to develop features and aspects of its aircraft on a schedule that otherwise it would have been unable to accomplish. The Appellate Body reversed the Panel's findings and ruled that R&D subsidies would not have any impact on Airbus's (and consequently on Boeing's) sales unless they provide Airbus aircraft with a competitive advantage in relation to Boeing's aircraft. Such competitive advantage must be reflected either in technologies incorporated in Airbus aircraft, or in technologies that make the production process of those aircraft more efficient. Only in these circumstances would R&D subsidies have complemented and supplemented the 'product effect' of the launch aid given to Airbus enabling it to launch particular aircraft models. The Appellate Body ultimately concluded that there was insufficient evidence on the record to reach this conclusion.[132]

Cumulation: Case Study *US – Large Civil Aircraft (2nd Complaint)*. The Panel refused to make an aggregated analysis of three groups of subsidies, i.e. so-called tied tax subsidies, R&D subsidies received by Boeing and the remaining subsidies.[133] The tied subsidies in relation to the B787 consisted of the so-called Business and Occupation tax reduction subsidies granted in Washington State. The Panel declined to aggregate these subsidies with Boeing's R&D subsidies on the grounds that the two groups of subsidies operated in very different ways. When looking at the effects of the Business and Occupation tax reduction subsidies in isolation, the Panel concluded that there was insufficient evidence that this subsidy

[130] WT/DS316/AB/R of 18 May 2011, *EC and certain Member States – Measures Affecting Trade in Large Civil Aircraft*, paras 1381–1391.

[131] WT/DS316/AB/R of 18 May 2011, *EC and certain Member States – Measures Affecting Trade in Large Civil Aircraft*, para 1392 *et seq.*

[132] WT/DS316/AB/R of 18 May 2011, *EC and certain Member States – Measures Affecting Trade in Large Civil Aircraft*, paras 1401–1409.

[133] Note, however, that the Panel aggregated several subsidies within each group.

had, on its own, such an impact on Boeing's prices that would lead to the Article 6.3 effects. By contrast, the Appellate Body held that the Panel should not have limited its analysis as to whether the different subsidies could be aggregated. Rather, it should also have examined whether the subsidies could be cumulated.[134]

The analysis of the relationship between tied tax subsidies (FSC/ETI subsidies and Business and Occupation Tax subsidies) and the remaining subsidies[135] was similar. The Appellate Body found it appropriate not to aggregate these two types of subsidies in particular because they were different in nature. However, according to the Appellate Body, the Panel should have examined whether these two types of subsidies could have been cumulated for the purpose of the serious prejudice analysis.[136]

US – Large Civil Aircraft (2nd Complaint) also contains an example of cumulation. The City of Wichita gave so-called Industrial Revenue Bonds (IRBs). IRBs were designed to assist Boeing in raising revenue to fund the purchase, construction or improvement of industrial property used for manufacturing purposes. The subsidies from IRBs were aimed at, and used, for the purpose of enhancing Boeing's manufacturing facilities in Wichita. The Wichita manufacturing facilities produced important parts of the Boeing B737NG. The Appellate Body found that the IRB complemented and supplemented the price effects of the FSC/ETI subsidies and the state of Washington Business and Occupation tax reductions and should therefore be cumulated with the latter subsidies. The Appellate Body's analysis was based on the following considerations:

- Subsidies that are not directly contingent upon production or sale can nevertheless affect pricing decisions in some circumstances.
- The subsidies in question affected Boeing's pricing decisions in relation to sales campaigns to JAL and a Singaporean leasing firm concerning the B737NG. This was based on the conclusion that Boeing would have used all available means to reduce its prices to the extent necessary to secure those sales.

[134] WT/DS353/AB/R of 12 March 2012, *United States – Measures Affecting Trade in Large Civil Aircraft (Second Complaint)*, para 1294 *et seq.*

[135] The remaining subsidies are described in WT/DS353/R of 31 March 2011, *United States – Measures Affecting Trade in Large Civil Aircraft (Second Complaint)*, paras 7.1825–7.1827.

[136] WT/DS353/AB/R of 12 March 2012, *United States – Measures Affecting Trade in Large Civil Aircraft (Second Complaint)*, paras 1326, 1327–1329.

- The IRBs could not be considered trivial in terms of their overall magnitude or duration, and they had a genuine link to Boeing's production of the B737NG as described above.
- In sum, Boeing's benefits resulting from the IRBs increased its pricing flexibility that it already enjoyed by virtue of the effects of FSC/ETI subsidies and the state of Washington Business and Occupation tax reductions.[137]

Aggregation: Case Study *US – Upland Cotton*. The details can be found in the Panel's report. The analysis distinguished between price-contingent and non-price-contingent subsidies and found that only the former caused significant price suppression.[138] In this regard, the Panel departed from the 'money is fungible' theory, under which all subsidies, whatever their nature, ultimately make the recipient better off and thus enable it to reduce prices. According to the 'money is fungible' theory, a subsidy, for instance, granted to fund a firm's Christmas party will save the firm money that it would otherwise have spent on this function, thus lowering its costs and enabling it to reduce prices.

Nature of the Subsidies in Terms of Their Structure, Design and Operation, Subsidy Amounts and Magnitudes, Conditions of Competition, Evidence Concerning Individual Sales Campaigns

Nature of the Subsidies – Prohibited Subsidies Subsidies falling under Article 3 are prohibited and must be withdrawn without there being any need to show adverse effects resulting from such subsidies. However, prohibited subsidies can also play a central role in the causation analysis in serious prejudice cases, notably when other subsidies are cumulated with prohibited subsidies for the purposes of establishing a causal link.

The US claimed in *US – Large Civil Aircraft (2nd Complaint)* on appeal that the Panel applied a presumption that subsidies found to be prohibited

[137] WT/DS353/AB/R of 12 March 2012, *United States – Measures Affecting Trade in Large Civil Aircraft (Second Complaint)*, paras 1347 and 1348. However, the Appellate Body criticized the Panel for not having considered cumulation of the technology effects of the R&D subsidies and the price effects of the Business and Occupational Tax rate reductions in causing significant lost sales, price suppression and threat of displacement and impedance in the 200–300 seat aircraft market because the EU had consistently taken the position that both groups of subsidies had similar effects on Boeing's pricing and contributed to the same market phenomena, see paras 1309–1330, 1349.

[138] WT/DS267/R of 8 September 2004, *United States – Subsidies on Upland Cotton*, para 7.1280 *et seq*. (including para 7.1355).

under Part II of the ASCM cause adverse effects within the meaning of Part III of the ASCM. The Appellate Body held that the Panel did not apply such a presumption. It considered the Panel's findings rather as an examination of the nature of the subsidies and agreed with the Panel's evaluation that export subsidies are by virtue of their very nature more likely to cause adverse effects. According to the Appellate Body, the Panel had been elaborating upon its view that the nature of subsidies in question (export subsidies) increases the likelihood that they will produce adverse effects. Furthermore, the Panel indicated that it would for the aforementioned reason accord to this factor considerable weight in the serious prejudice analysis. The Appellate Body added that an analysis of the export-contingent nature of a subsidy may reveal elements that are highly pertinent to an assessment of its trade effects. At the same time, a finding of export contingency would not, by itself, establish the existence of adverse effects phenomena such as those at issue in the appeal.[139]

See also *US – Upland Cotton* concerning the nature of subsidies, for instance whether subsidies are price-contingent and thus insulate the recipients from the development of world market prices.[140]

Amount of the Subsidies ('Magnitude') In *US – Large Civil Aircraft (2nd Complaint)*, there was also some dispute whether the Panel appropriately addressed the amount of the subsidies. The Appellate Body held:

> In our view, both the absolute and the relative magnitudes of the subsidies are likely to be relevant to a panel's analysis of the effects of subsidies on prices. Both considerations may shed light on the impact that those subsidies have on price, although the extent to which either or both considerations shed light on this relationship will depend on the particular subsidies, products and markets at issue. Through scrutinizing magnitude in the light of and as part of an analysis of the particular subsidies, the particular products, and the particular characteristics of the market within which those products compete, a panel can gain an understanding of the effects that the subsidies have on prices, and of the relevance of the subsidies' magnitude to such effects. In other words, what it means to take account of the considerations of 'magnitude' will also depend upon the circumstances of each case and the market phenomena at issue.[2442] Depending on the circumstances an assessment of whether the subsidy amounts are significant should not necessarily be limited to a mere inquiry into *what* those amounts are, either in absolute or per-unit terms. Rather, such an analysis may be situated within a

[139] WT/DS353/AB/R of 12 March 2012, *United States – Measures Affecting Trade in Large Civil Aircraft (Second Complaint)*, paras 1183–1186.

[140] WT/DS267/AB/R of 3 March 2005, *United States – Subsidies on Upland Cotton*, para 450.

> larger inquiry that could, for instance, entail viewing these amounts against considerations such as the size of the market as a whole, the size of the subsidy recipient, the per-unit price of the subsidized product, the price elasticity of demand, and, depending on the market structure, the extent to which a subsidy recipient is able to set its own prices in the market, and the extent to which rivals are able or prompted to react to each other's pricing within that market structure. Considerations of some of these elements formed part of the Appellate Body's analysis of the magnitude of price-contingent subsidies in *US – Upland Cotton (Article 21.5 – Brazil)*.[141]
>
> 2442 Like the Panel, we use the term 'magnitude' here in its broad sense ('{t}he "magnitude" of something is generally understood as a reference to its size, extent, degree, or numerical quantity or value') and not in the specialized sense that it was at times used by the European Communities before the Panel, meaning a per-LCA [large commercial aircraft] amount calculated by allocating the total amounts of subsidies over time and across aircraft models.

The Appellate Body found the Panel's reasoning concerning the magnitude of the subsidies 'somewhat opaque'. The parties presented arguments and evidence regarding the relative significance of the subsidies. In particular, their arguments focused on whether these subsidies were of a size that, when considered in relation to product values or prices, could produce market effects amounting to serious prejudice. The Appellate Body did not exclude that subsidies of a relatively small magnitude in relation to product values or prices could have such effects, or that such effects could be found in the case at issue. But the Panel should have explained why it rejected certain evidence concerning the relative magnitude of subsidies in relation to aircraft values.[142]

Moreover, the Panel should have examined pertinent factors other than the subsidies that could have explained the effects of lost sales and price suppression suffered by Airbus. The Appellate Body had in mind factors that suggested the existence of competitive dynamics that advantaged Boeing or disadvantaged Airbus in aircraft sales campaigns. For example, the fact that Boeing's 777 plane benefits from a fuel burn efficiency would have been an important factor that should have been taken into account when assessing whether Boeing used the subsidies to lower its prices and thereby causing serious prejudice. This operating cost advantage could suggest that Boeing was not subject to the same sort of pricing pressure as Airbus in this product market as opposed to other product markets where

[141] WT/DS353/AB/R of 12 March 2012, *United States – Measures Affecting Trade in Large Civil Aircraft (Second Complaint)*, para 1193.

[142] WT/DS353/AB/R of 12 March 2012, *United States – Measures Affecting Trade in Large Civil Aircraft (Second Complaint)*, paras 1194 and 1246.

the competing aircraft of both producers were more similar. Similarly, the fact that Boeing was the 'incumbent supplier' to an airline might constitute an advantage for Boeing indicating that it would not have been under the same pressure to lower prices as it would have been in a more competitive sales campaign.[143]

The Appellate Body had already previously in *US – Upland Cotton* found that the magnitude of the subsidies is one relevant factor (but not the only one) that may be relevant for the determination of the effects of the challenged subsidy. Under Article 6, it is not necessary to quantify exactly the amount of the subsidy. However, given that Article 6.3(c) for instance requires that the effect of a subsidy is significant price suppression, a panel will need to consider the effects of a subsidy on prices. The magnitude of the subsidy is an important factor in this analysis. A large subsidy that is closely linked to prices of the relevant product is likely to have a greater impact on prices than a small subsidy that is less closely linked to prices. All other things being equal, the smaller the subsidy for a given product, the smaller the degree to which it will affect the costs or revenue of the recipient, and the smaller its likely impact on the prices charged by the recipient for the product.[144]

Age of Subsidies

In a countervailing duty investigation under Part V of the ASCM, it is well established that a subsidy which has been fully allocated over time (i.e. for which the allocation period expired) can no longer be subject to measures. This follows notably from *Japan – DRAMs (Korea)*. In this situation, there is no subsidy to 'offset' within the meaning of Article VI:3 of the GATT 1994.[145]

However, in an adverse effects case under Part III of the ASCM, there is no similar 'cut-off' provision. While the situation is somewhat more complex in adverse effects cases than in countervailing duty investigations, it is, however, clear that the age of the subsidy plays a role in the causation analysis conducted by any panel or the Appellate Body. A panel must take into account in its analysis under Articles 5 and 6 how a subsidy is expected to materialize over time. A panel is also required to consider

[143] WT/DS353/AB/R of 12 March 2012, *United States – Measures Affecting Trade in Large Civil Aircraft (Second Complaint)*, para 1214.

[144] WT/DS267/AB/R of 3 March 2005, *United States – Subsidies on Upland Cotton*, paras 459–473.

[145] See *infra* the commentary to Article 19 pp. 526–531.

whether the life of a subsidy has ended, for example, by reason of amortization of the subsidy over the relevant period or because the subsidy was removed from the recipient. Moreover, the Appellate Body has emphasized that the effects of a subsidy will generally diminish and come to an end with the passage of time.[146]

In *EC and certain Member States – Large Civil Aircraft*, there was some disagreement as to the effects over time of the subsidies given to finance each of the Airbus models. The Panel conceded that the effect of a single subsidy may well dissipate over time. However, it argued that the fact that the subsidies at issue in the dispute were granted over the entire history of Airbus to the same product (but successively for various models) has had rather the opposite effect. Through the learning and spillover effects and production synergies that are inherent in this industry the effect of subsidies for the development of one model allegedly spread to subsequent models. The Appellate Body disagreed. The effects of any subsidy can be expected to diminish and eventually come to an end with the passage of time. This applies both to single as well as multiple acts of subsidization. The Appellate Body accepted, however, as well that there may be residual effects of old subsidies, but that this is a fact-specific matter. Turning to the facts of the case, it concluded that the subsidies given for the A300 and A310 were likely to have caused minimal, if any, adverse effects during the reference period 2001–2006 as the models were first delivered in 1974 and 1985 respectively, the subsidies were fully disbursed between 1988 and 1992 (depending on the Airbus Member State) and the marketing life of an aircraft was 17 years.[147]

Linked to the question of the age of subsidies is the question as to how to treat recurring subsidies under Article 6.3. In *US – Upland Cotton*, the US took the view that recurring price-contingent subsidies do not confer a benefit after the year for which they were paid, and hence are no longer a subsidy under Article 1. A subsidy that is paid annually must be allocated or expensed to the year for which payments were made and the effect of such subsidy cannot be significant price depression in any other year. The Appellate Body did not agree. It pointed out that whether the effect of a subsidy begins and expires in the year in which it was paid, or whether the subsidy has effects beyond that year, is a fact-specific question. It also

[146] WT/DS316/AB/R of 18 May 2011, *EC and certain Member States – Measures Affecting Trade in Large Civil Aircraft*, para 1236.

[147] WT/DS316/AB/R of 18 May 2011, *EC and certain Member States – Measures Affecting Trade in Large Civil Aircraft*, para 1237 *et seq.*

referred to Article 6.2 that points to a time lag between the provision of the subsidy and its effect,[148] as well as Article 6.4 that suggests that the effect of the subsidy must be examined over a sufficiently long period of time and is not limited to the year in which it was paid. In sum, the Appellate Body did not agree with the proposition that, if subsidies are paid annually, their effects are also extinguished annually.[149] The preceding Panel also noted that subsidies granted under expired measures or subsidy programmes may still have lasting adverse effects.[150]

Subsidies Given throughout the Reference Period

In *US – Large Civil Aircraft (2nd Complaint)*, Boeing received subsidies under the FSC/ETI programme before and throughout the reference period. The US claimed that even if the FSC/ETI subsidies were provided over a long time, there was no correlation between the subsidies and the price levels for aircraft and that there was consequently no causal link. The Panel reasoned that it was impossible for it to determine the effects of the FSC/ETI subsidies through direct observation of market share and price trend data because of the long period over which these subsidies were provided. The underlying concern was that any observations that could be made about aircraft prices before and during the reference period would not have assisted the Panel in establishing the price effects of the subsidies since any such effects would have always been present throughout the period. For this reason, the Panel considered that the US's evidence of causal factors other than the subsidies could not 'reverse or attenuate the pervasive and consistent pricing advantage that Boeing had'.

As the subsidies were given throughout the reference period, the Panel believed that it saw itself confronted with the following choice: it could decline to make a serious prejudice finding because of the difficulty of calculating with mathematical certitude the precise degree to which Boeing's pricing of the 737 and 777 families were affected by the tax subsidies.

[148] According to the Appellate Body, the word 'resulted' in Article 6.2 ('the subsidy in question has not resulted in any of the effects enumerated in paragraph 3') highlights the temporal relationship between the subsidy and its effect, in that one might expect a time lag between the provision of the subsidy and the resulting effect.

[149] WT/DS267/AB/R of 3 March 2005, *United States – Subsidies on Upland Cotton*, paras 474–484.

[150] WT/DS267/R of 8 September 2004, *United States – Subsidies on Upland Cotton*, para 7.1201. See also WT/DS54/R, WT/DS55/R, WT/DS59/R and WT/DS64/R of 2 July 1998, *Indonesia – Certain Measures Affecting the Automobile Industry*, para 14.206 (the Panel pointed out that the issue under Article 6.3 is not the effect of the subsidy programme but the 'effect of the subsidy').

Alternatively (in one such exceptional case), it could deduce the effects of those subsidies on Airbus's sales and prices 'based on common sense reasoning and the drawing of inferences' from its conclusions regarding the nature and duration of the subsidies, and the nature of competition between Boeing and Airbus. It chose to take the latter course of action.

The Appellate Body did not agree. It rejected the Panel's view that considerations of market share and price trends during the period of sustained subsidization, and of 'other factors' potentially contributing to such shares or trends, were of no assistance in analysing the effects of the subsidies. The Appellate Body referred to its ruling in *US – Upland Cotton*, in which it concluded that one would normally expect a discernible correlation between significantly suppressed prices and the challenged subsidies. The question of correlation was a relevant one even if the subsidies had been provided over a long time and the Panel should have explained why, in the absence of such correlation, it arrived at the finding of a genuine and substantial causal relationship.

Moreover, the Appellate Body was somewhat puzzled by the Panel's alleged choice between declining to make a finding and using common sense reasoning. The Panel should have assessed whether it had arguments and evidence before it that could have allowed it to estimate the effects of the subsidies on Boeing's prices with something less than mathematical certitude. The Appellate Body did not see that the use of common sense and inferences in the course of adjudicating a claim could be characterized as somewhat exceptional. It is not uncommon for a panel to draw inferences and conclusions from the evidence before it but it is for the Members to provide reasoning engaging with the evidence to support those inferences and conclusions.[151]

How Direct Should Be the Link between the Subsidies and the Product in Question – Pre-competitive Subsidies etc.?

In *US – Large Civil Aircraft (2nd Complaint)*, the US argued that certain NASA subsidies could not have benefitted the B787 e.g. because they were directed at supersonic civil air transport. The B787 is not a supersonic aircraft and Boeing had indeed abandoned the development of a supersonic aircraft for civil use, i.e. the technology subsidized was not one of the key technologies used in that airplane. The Panel did not agree and the

[151] WT/DS353/AB/R of 12 March 2012, *United States – Measures Affecting Trade in Large Civil Aircraft (Second Complaint)*, para 1205 *et seq.*, in particular paras 1209 and 1217 *et seq.* The Appellate Body was able to complete the analysis, see e.g. para 1253.

Appellate Body upheld the Panel's findings. The Panel perceived a causal link as encompassing not only research conducted pursuant to subsidy programmes that could be traced directly to the B787 technologies, but also research that was less directly related, and even resulted in failure. The Appellate Body pointed out that it could identify one way in which the programme focusing on supersonic technologies contributed to advancing the research into the B787 technologies: prior to 2000, Boeing was working on a high-speed aircraft – the Sonic Cruiser. That project gained little support from airlines because customers were more interested in aircraft with lower operating costs than aircraft flying at supersonic speed. In line with this feedback, Boeing decided to build a more efficient airplane that was capable of flying at the same speed as existing aircraft but at lower cost. Therefore, the research into the high-speed Sonic Cruiser, even if it ultimately resulted in failure, helped Boeing to eliminate those technologies that were not commercially attractive, and to concentrate efforts instead on research into technologies that were of more interest to customers and were actually used on the B787.[152]

The US also argued that the NASA R&D subsidies were too far removed from the commercial technologies used on the B787. Both Panel and Appellate Body rejected this argument. The subsidies in question referred indeed to projects with a low technological readiness level. That is, it can take a considerable time (often several years) until such technologies are sufficiently mature to be used in commercial applications. Early and potentially unsuccessful research is financially more risky for private investors than research relating to more advanced technologies. Nevertheless, the subsidies accelerated the technology development process by some amount of time, and, therefore, gave Boeing an advantage in bringing the technologies to market. The exact amount of time was not critical. The subsidies reduced the large disincentives for the private sector to invest in early stage aeronautics R&D. Without the subsidies, Boeing would not have been willing to invest as much, and as soon, in early stage R&D, and it would have taken Boeing longer to bring the B787 technologies to commercial readiness without such subsidies.[153]

[152] WT/DS353/AB/R of 12 March 2012, *United States – Measures Affecting Trade in Large Civil Aircraft (Second Complaint)*, paras 960–971.

[153] WT/DS353/AB/R of 12 March 2012, *United States – Measures Affecting Trade in Large Civil Aircraft (Second Complaint)*, paras 972–981.

In the same vein, both Panel and Appellate Body rejected the US's argument that Boeing conducted a substantial amount of research on its own to develop and launch the B787, including at the early stages of the research effort, and that the NASA-funded research was small in comparison to Boeing's own contributions. What *inter alia* was crucial was that Boeing gained a significant advantage from performing the R&D work itself, in collaboration with NASA, as well as from conducting research under the R&D subsidies in tandem with its own related R&D efforts. Moreover, the NASA subsidies provided a boost to the development of technologies at the earliest, most fundamental stages of research. To focus too narrowly on Boeing's own efforts would sever artificially the contribution of earlier significant research efforts with NASA and/or financed with subsidies. NASA's role in the early stages lay precisely in the fact that it shouldered the initial burden for the private sector when technology was at its lowest stage of maturity and where risk was highest. Note, however, that the Appellate Body could conceive of different ways in which an advantage provided by subsidies might dissipate over time or might be severed. This might happen for instance through the intervention of other, more important, causal factors. However, in the view of the Appellate Body, the US did not put forward any arguments to this effect.[154]

See also *Korea – Commercial Vessels* where the Panel noted that product definition issues could 'create a significant, if not insurmountable hurdle in respect of causation' where the alleged subsidy was given for an input product while significant price suppression/depression was alleged in relation to a downstream product, or where the subsidy in respect of one product was alleged to cause significant price suppression/depression in respect of a completely unrelated product.[155]

Irrelevant Considerations

Price War. In *US – Large Civil Aircraft (2nd Complaint)*, the question was whether certain tied subsidies received by Boeing caused serious prejudice in the sense that Airbus lost sales, was impeded to sell and/or suffered from price suppression. The US claimed that any serious prejudice was not caused by its subsidies but by an 'other factor', i.e. that Airbus

[154] WT/DS353/AB/R of 12 March 2012, *United States – Measures Affecting Trade in Large Civil Aircraft (Second Complaint)*, paras 982–989. See also paras 1003–1011 of the Appellate Body report.

[155] WT/DS273/R of 7 March 2005, *Korea – Measures Affecting Trade in Commercial Vessels*, para 7.560.

initiated a downward pricing trend, and that Boeing simply responded by becoming more competitive on price. The Appellate Body did not consider this as a relevant argument. The aforementioned behaviour merely reflects the competitive conditions in a duopolistic market whereby price changes by one firm affect the pricing behaviour of its competitor. In sales campaigns that are waged and won principally on the basis of price, Boeing and Airbus typically set prices through a series of successively lower offers until a final price is accepted by a customer. What mattered was whether the subsidies were used by Boeing to further reduce prices, resulting in lost sales and price suppression for Airbus.[156]

Does a Panel Have to Define the Subsidized Product?

In *EC and certain Member States – Large Civil Aircraft*, the Panel had to resolve the question whether it should examine the adverse effects claims on the basis of the subsidized product as defined in the application of the US or whether it was required to make an independent assessment as to the appropriate subsidized product, as the EU requested. The US position meant that there should be only one adverse effects analysis based on all Airbus large commercial aircraft while the EU argued that there should be an individual adverse effects analysis for each different model family of Airbus large commercial aircraft. In fact, the EU proposed five separate markets for large civil aircraft. The Panel espoused the US position because

- there is no specific guidance in Articles 5 or 6, or in any other provision of the ASCM, regarding the identification of the subsidized product or a panel's role in that process and it was unlikely that the drafters of this Agreement intended panels to make independent, fact-based determinations of the appropriate subsidized product in disputes under the aforementioned provisions;
- the acceptance of the EU's position would have meant that the Panel had to apply relevant criteria and apply them to the facts of the case;
- there is no linkage in Article 6.3 between the terms like product, subsidized product and market;
- it is not the role of a panel to direct a WTO Member with respect to how it presents its complaint in a dispute (i.e. it is for the complainant to define the product);

[156] WT/DS353/AB/R of 12 March 2012, *United States – Measures Affecting Trade in Large Civil Aircraft (Second Complaint)*, para 1213.

- in trade remedy cases it was not necessary for a panel to review the scope of the product under consideration, as *EC – Salmon (Norway)* has found: even if it had been necessary in trade remedy cases, it would still be unnecessary and inappropriate to address this in an adverse effects dispute;
- the US had presented evidence concerning the linkages and spillover effects of the subsidies in question between the different Airbus models. In other words, a subsidy given for a particular Airbus model benefits also other models, and an examination based on models would preclude the examination whether the linkages and spillovers exist;
- there was no obvious basis for dividing large civil aircraft into segments and, if a segmentation would be carried out, there is in any event competition between adjacent product groups.[157]

The above question is ultimately irrelevant as an analysis under Article 6.3 requires an examination of adverse effects in the same market. Indeed, the Appellate Body concluded that the conclusion that there is a single subsidized product and a single like product cannot stand in the absence of an objective determination of the market by the applicant. The determination of the product component of the relevant market will also have to address the question whether the subsidized product can be assessed in its totality or whether the analysis has to be carried out on the basis of segments of the subsidized product.[158]

See also *US – Upland Cotton.*[159]

Relevant Market

The notion of the market is key for the analysis under Article 6.3. The phenomena listed in all four subparagraphs of this provision, i.e. displacement, impedance, price undercutting, price suppression, price depression and lost sales, can only be observed for products that compete in the same market.[160]

[157] WT/DS316/R of 30 June 2010, *EC and certain Member States – Measures Affecting Trade in Large Civil Aircraft*, paras 7.1651–7.1670.

[158] WT/DS316/AB/R of 18 May 2011, *EC and certain Member States – Measures Affecting Trade in Large Civil Aircraft*, point (k) of the Findings and Conclusions See also *infra* this chapter, pp. 338–339.

[159] WT/DS267/AB/R of 3 March 2005, *United States – Subsidies on Upland Cotton*, para 472.

[160] WT/DS316/AB/R of 18 May 2011, *EC and certain Member States – Measures Affecting Trade in Large Civil Aircraft*, para 1214; WT/DS267/AB/R of 3 March 2005, *United States – Subsidies on Upland Cotton*, para 407.

Therefore, the relevant market both in terms of the product scope and the geographical scope has to be defined carefully.

Product Component

The principal question is what products form part of the same market. According to *EC and certain Member States – Large Civil Aircraft*, the word 'market' in Article 6.3 must be read together with the term 'like product'. Subparagraphs (a) to (c) of Article 6.3 refer to imports or exports of the like product. This means that first the subsidized product has to be identified and then the like imported or exported product. The definition for the term 'like product' is set out in footnote 46 and applies throughout the ASCM.[161]

Footnote 46, that is attached to Article 15 ('Determination of Injury') stipulates that the term 'like product' shall be interpreted to mean a product which is identical, i.e. alike in all respects to the product under consideration, or in the absence of such a product, another product which, although not alike in all respects, has characteristics closely resembling those of the product under consideration. Therefore, footnote 46 suggests that identity or close resemblance of characteristics is one factor to consider in assessing whether products are in the same market. However, the focus on physical, chemical characteristics etc. is not in itself sufficient. In addition, the various products identified by reference to footnote 46 must be analysed under the discipline of the product market as set out below in order to be able to determine whether displacement is occurring.[162]

The notion 'displacement' plays also a role in this context. As stated above, displacement is a situation where imports or exports of a like product are replaced by the sales of the subsidized product. Thus, the concept of displacement relates to, and arises out of competitive engagement between products in a market. Aggressive pricing of certain products may, for example, lead to displacement of imports or exports, but only if the products in question compete in the same market.[163]

On this basis, the Appellate Body defined a market within the meaning of subparagraphs (a) and (b) of Article 6.3 as a set of products in a

[161] WT/DS316/AB/R of 18 May 2011, *EC and certain Member States – Measures Affecting Trade in Large Civil Aircraft*, para 1118.

[162] WT/DS316/AB/R of 18 May 2011, *EC and certain Member States – Measures Affecting Trade in Large Civil Aircraft*, paras 1118 and 1119.

[163] WT/DS316/AB/R of 18 May 2011, *EC and certain Member States – Measures Affecting Trade in Large Civil Aircraft*, para 1119.

particular geographical area that are in actual or potential competition with each other. This requires an examination of a competitive relationship between products in order to determine whether and to what extent one product may displace another. In the absence of actual or potential competition between two products in a market place it is not conceivable that the effect of the subsidy provided to one of the products could be found to be the displacement of the other product.[164] The Appellate Body also added that the scope of a market is likely to vary from case to case depending on the particular factual circumstances, including the nature of the product at issue.[165] The notion of substitutability is not necessarily delineated by reference to physical characteristics, end-uses and consumer preferences. Other factors may also be relevant, e.g. whether customers demand a range of products (as is often the case in the aircraft sector) or whether they are interested in only a particular product type. In the former case, this may give an indication that all such products could be competing in the same market. It may also be necessary to examine substitutability on the supply side. For instance, evidence on whether a supplier can switch production at limited or prohibitive cost from one product to another in a short period of time may also inform the question of whether two products are in a single market.[166]

The Appellate Body found that its definition was consistent with the fundamental economic proposition that a market comprises only those products that exercise competitive constraint on each other.[167]

The market definition used by the Appellate Body in *EC and certain Member States – Large Civil Aircraft* is in line with the one used in *US – Upland Cotton*. The latter case concerned only Article 6.3(c), i.e. price undercutting etc. in the same market and the Appellate Body defined a market as follows:

- Market is the area of economic activity in which buyers and sellers come together and the forces of supply and demand affect prices.

[164] WT/DS316/AB/R of 18 May 2011, *EC and certain Member States – Measures Affecting Trade in Large Civil Aircraft*, paras 1119, 1122 and 1123. Confirmed in WT/DS353/AB/R of 12 March 2012, *United States – Measures Affecting Trade in Large Civil Aircraft (Second Complaint)*, para 1076.

[165] WT/DS316/AB/R of 18 May 2011, *EC and certain Member States – Measures Affecting Trade in Large Civil Aircraft*, para 1123.

[166] WT/DS316/AB/R of 18 May 2011, *EC and certain Member States – Measures Affecting Trade in Large Civil Aircraft*, paras 1120 and 1121.

[167] WT/DS316/AB/R of 18 May 2011, *EC and certain Member States – Measures Affecting Trade in Large Civil Aircraft*, paras 1120 and 1123.

- Two products would be in the same market if they were engaged in actual or potential competition in that market. Thus, two products may be in the same market even if they are not necessarily sold at the same time or in the same place or country;
- The scope of the market, for determining the area of competition between two products, may depend on several factors such as the nature of the product, the homogeneity of the conditions of competition and transport costs.

In the Airbus case, the Appellate Body held that similar considerations would also be relevant in claims of serious prejudice under the remainder of Article 6.3 (e.g. displacement, impedance, lost sales) because all subparagraphs of this provision are concerned with the effect of the subsidy in a market.[168]

Geographic Component

Subparagraph (a) refers to the market of the subsidizing Member, subparagraph (b) to a third country market (i.e. neither the subsidizing Member nor that of the complaining party), subparagraph (c) refers to the same market (i.e. it does not contain any explicit geographical limitation) and finally subparagraph (d) refers to the world market.

The Appellate Body pointed out that the manner in which the geographic dimension of a market is determined will depend on a number of factors. In some cases, the geographic market may extend to cover the entire country concerned. In others, an analysis of the conditions of competition for sales of the product in question may lead to the conclusion that a geographic market exists within that country, for example, a region. There may also be cases where the geographic dimension of a particular market exceeds national boundaries or could be even the world market. However, according to subparagraphs (a) and (b) the focus of the analysis of displacement and impedance is the territory of the subsidizing Member or third countries involved. Accordingly, findings of displacement and impedance are to be made only with regard to the territory of the relevant country, even though, from an economic perspective, the geographic market may not be national in scope.[169] The Appellate Body enumerated

[168] WT/DS316/AB/R of 18 May 2011, *EC and certain Member States – Measures Affecting Trade in Large Civil Aircraft*, para 1122 and WT/DS267/AB/R of 3 March 2005, *United States – Subsidies on Upland Cotton*, para 408.

[169] WT/DS316/AB/R of 18 May 2011, *EC and certain Member States – Measures Affecting Trade in Large Civil Aircraft*, para 1117. Confirmed in WT/DS353/AB/R of 12 March

as potentially relevant factors for determining the area of competition, and thus the scope of the market, for instance the nature of the product, the homogeneity of the conditions of competition and transport costs. It also underlined that two products may be in the same market even if they are not necessarily sold at the same time in the same place or country.[170]

The geographic dimension of a market under subparagraph (c) seems to allow more flexibility than the one under subparagraphs (a) and (b). Subparagraph (c) contains only one express qualification on the type of market, i.e. that it must be the 'same' market. This contrasts with the reference to the geographic dimension in subparagraphs (a) and (b). According to *US – Upland Cotton*, this difference may indicate that the drafters did not intend to confine, *a priori*, the market under subparagraph (c) to any particular area. Thus, the ordinary meaning of the word 'market' in subparagraph (c), when read in the context of the other paragraphs of Article 6.3, neither requires nor excludes the possibility of a national market or a world market. Therefore, the Appellate Body rejected an argument made by the US that the relevant market cannot be the world market.[171] Finally, the Panel in *US – Upland Cotton* noted that it is not the task of a panel to select the appropriate market. It is for the complaining Member to identify the market for the purposes of its claim. The Panel then determines whether it is a market within the meaning of Article 6.3(c) and whether the effect of the subsidy is proven on that market.[172]

Korea – Commercial Vessels is in line with the aforementioned Appellate Body ruling. The parties disagreed as to what would constitute the same market in relation to a claim based in subparagraph (c). The EU was of the view that the 'same market' would be the world market. Korea objected. The Panel pointed out that the ACSM does not contain a geographical

2012, *United States – Measures Affecting Trade in Large Civil Aircraft (Second Complaint)*, para 1076.

[170] WT/DS267/AB/R of 3 March 2005, *United States – Subsidies on Upland Cotton*, para 408. These are the same criteria that are also relevant for defining the product component, see *supra* this chapter pp. 334–336.

[171] WT/DS267/AB/R of 3 March 2005, *United States – Subsidies on Upland Cotton*, paras 406 and 411. The US also argued that no world market for upland cotton can exist if there is no world price for actual cotton. The Appellate Body dismissed this argument as a factual question beyond its remit. The Panel's analysis whether or not there is a world market price for upland cotton can be found in WT/DS267/R of 8 September 2004, *United States – Subsidies on Upland Cotton*, para 7.1260 *et seq*. Confirmed in WT/DS316/AB/R of 18 May 2011, *EC and certain Member States – Measures Affecting Trade in Large Civil Aircraft*, para 1118.

[172] WT/DS267/R of 8 September 2004, *United States – Subsidies on Upland Cotton*, para 7.1246. See also *infra* this chapter, pp. 338–339.

qualifier in relation to the term 'same market'. It held that the market in question must be the one where the WTO members compete for sales of the product in question. According to the Panel, the lack of modifiers to the term 'the same market' in Article 6.3(c) has the consequence that this provision encompasses (at least) all of the possibilities referred to in the other subparagraphs of Article 6.3 (national market of the subsidizer, of the complaining Member, or of a third country, and the world market).[173]

Time Component

As to the relationship between individual sales campaigns and the relevant market, see *US –Large Civil Aircraft (2nd Complaint).*[174]

Market Definition Submitted by the Complainant of an Article 6.3 Claim Is Not Necessarily Controlling

As described above, the Panel in *EC and certain Member States – Large Civil Aircraft* stated that making an independent and objective assessment of the complaining Member's definition of the subsidized product was not required. Therefore, it deferred to the US's subsidized product definition and then determined a like product simply by reference to the previously identified subsidized product. The Panel consequently grouped all large civil aircraft together for the purposes of the examination of a claim under Article 6.3.

The Appellate Body disagreed with the Panel's interpretation because the Panel defined in a second step the relevant market on the basis of the complainant's product definition. According to the Appellate Body, the Panel should have made its own independent assessment of whether all Airbus large civil aircraft compete in the same market or not. Or put more generally, the identification of a subsidized product and the like product cannot determine whether such products compete in the same market. Therefore, as the EU has put it, the specific question was whether the identified universe of allegedly subsidized products should be treated as a single subsidized product, or multiple subsidized products. The Appellate Body was not impressed by the fact that the US challenged

[173] WT/DS273/R of 7 March 2005, *Korea – Measures Affecting Trade in Commercial Vessels*, paras 7.564 and 7.565.

[174] WT/DS353/AB/R of 12 March 2012, *United States – Measures Affecting Trade in Large Civil Aircraft (Second Complaint)*, para 1079.

subsidies provided to all Airbus large aircraft claiming that they were causing adverse effects to their interests. In other words, the US did not contend that subsidies provided to a single Airbus model were causing adverse effects only to the corresponding or most closely resembling Boeing model. Nor was the Appellate Body impressed by the fact that two Panels that previously had to review an EU anti-dumping measure and a US CVD measure respectively, rejected a claim that the product subject to investigation must be a single homogeneous product, i.e. that there must be likeness within both the product under consideration and within the like product. The Appellate Body recalled that in a case relating to Part III of the ASCM, the panel is required to establish the facts and to make a 'full and objective assessment'. Therefore, in a serious prejudice case there is no need to apply the 'same degree of deference' to the complainant's product definition as would be appropriate when reviewing a countervailing duty measure under Part V of the ASCM. Note that the Appellate Body could not complete the analysis whether all large aircraft models constituted a single product market or several such markets. However, it completed the displacement analysis for three product groups proposed by the EU for which there was adequate information on the record, while one Member of the Appellate Body dissented with this approach.[175]

In short, it is possible that a complainant chooses to define the subsidized and the like product so broadly that it is necessary to analyse these products in different markets.[176]

Reference Period

Adverse effects need to be present (see *supra* this chapter p. 281 but immediate data concerning the effect of the subsidy will normally not be available. Therefore, a recent reference period will typically be used in order to establish adverse effects.

Article 6 mentions the need for a reference period only in its paragraph 4. This provision establishes for the purposes of Article 6.3(b), i.e. when examining displacement and impedance of exports in a third country market, that a change in relative shares in the market to the disadvantage

[175] WT/DS316/AB/R of 18 May 2011, *EC and certain Member States – Measures Affecting Trade in Large Civil Aircraft*, paras 1119–1150. See also *supra* this chapter, pp. 333–339.

[176] WT/DS316/AB/R of 18 May 2011, *EC and certain Member States – Measures Affecting Trade in Large Civil Aircraft*, para 1124 *et seq.*

of the non-subsidized like product has to be demonstrated over an appropriately representative period, which in normal circumstances shall be at least one year. In contrast, Articles 5(a) and (c) and 6.3(a) and (c) do not mention a particular time period that panels should use in examining adverse effects claims.

In relation to Article 6.4 the Appellate Body observed that this provision requires that displacement or impedance is demonstrated over an appropriately representative period so that clear trends in changes in market share can be demonstrated. It then held that the foregoing suggested that the effect of the subsidy must be examined over a sufficiently long period of time and is not limited to the year in which it was paid because consideration of developments over a longer period provides a more robust basis for a serious prejudice evaluation.[177] *EC and certain Member States – Large Civil Aircraft* also approvingly quoted the safeguard case *Argentina – Footwear* in which the Appellate Body clarified that investigating authorities are required to consider trends in imports over a period of investigation (rather than just comparing end points), as this may mask trends developing in the intervening period. A panel assessing a claim of displacement would have to look at clearly discernible trends during the reference period.[178]

In *EC and certain Member States – Large Civil Aircraft*, the effect of the challenged subsidies (some of them dating back to 1969/1970) was examined in relation to a reference period lasting from 2001 to 2006.[179] The Appellate Body held that the identification of a trend will be more accurate the larger the data set used in the analysis. At the same time it recognized that too strict a requirement concerning the size of the data set could preclude a Member from timely challenging subsidies that cause adverse effects to its interests. But most recent available data should not be excluded from consideration.[180] Note, however, that the duration of the reference period as such was not subject to appeal.

[177] WT/DS267/AB/R of 3 March 2005, *United States – Subsidies on Upland Cotton*, para 478. Confirmed, *inter alia*, in WT/DS353/AB/R of 12 March 2012, *United States – Measures Affecting Trade in Large Civil Aircraft (Second Complaint)*, para 1081.

[178] WT/DS316/AB/R of 18 May 2011, *EC and certain Member States – Measures Affecting Trade in Large Civil Aircraft*, paras 1166 and 1167 *in fine*.

[179] WT/DS316/AB/R of 18 May 2011, *EC and certain Member States – Measures Affecting Trade in Large Civil Aircraft*, para 1234.

[180] WT/DS316/AB/R of 18 May 2011, *EC and certain Member States – Measures Affecting Trade in Large Civil Aircraft*, para 1167.

At Panel stage, the EU took issue with the US approach to base its adverse effects claims on data covering a period from 2001 to 2006. It requested that data be excluded for the initial three years of that period (2001 to 2003) because of the events of 9/11. The Panel disagreed:

- The EU claimed that the events of 9/11 constituted *force majeure* in the sense of Article 6.7(c). The Panel first pointed out that this provision does not concern the determination of the relevant period but only precluded a finding of serious prejudice if the circumstances identified therein were present. Next it noted that subparagraph (c) did not define *force majeure*. On the basis of the examples listed in subparagraph (c), this term contemplates events that have a substantial effect on supply (and not on demand), thereby limiting the ability of the complaining WTO Member to export its product for reasons that have nothing to do with subsidies. Thus, when a *force majeure* event unrelated to subsidization substantially affects production, qualities, quantities or prices of the product available for export from the complaining WTO Member, a decrease in that Member's market share in an export market shall not constitute serious prejudice. As 9/11 did not substantially impact on Boeing's ability to supply aircraft, the Panel concluded that subparagraph (c) did not apply. The Panel also noted that even assuming that the types of *force majeure* under subparagraph (c) included shocks affecting demand for particular products, the events of 9/11 would not constitute *force majeure* for the purposes of subparagraph (c), as such events would have to concern limitations on exports that do not also affect the product of the defending WTO Member in the same or similar way.
- The second argument by the EU was that any claim under Articles 5(a) and (c) and 6.3(a) to (c) would have to be based on present adverse effects in the form of both injury and serious prejudice. As a consequence, the Panel should reject the data from 2001 to 2003 as irrelevant or give that data very little probative value for the purpose of demonstrating present adverse effects. The Panel disagreed because of the idiosyncrasies of the aircraft industry (long lead times for development of new aircraft, each model has a long life once put into service, orders are often placed well in advance of deliveries, long period during which subsidies supported Airbus's development and production of aircraft). Therefore, the Panel found that a longer period better informed its understanding of the industry and market, and helped in evaluating adverse effects and causation although it did not dispute that it must assess whether subsidies presently caused adverse effects.

- The Panel also rejected the EU's argument that WTO jurisprudence preferred shorter reference periods in assessing trade remedies cases.
- The Panel also referred to the Appellate Body in *US – Upland Cotton* that recognized that there may well be a time lag between the payment of a subsidy and the consequential adverse effects (see *supra* this chapter pp. 326–328). This is particularly true in a dispute where subsidies have been granted over a long period and where the industry operates on long time-frames.
- The Panel noted that an improvement in the situation in the most recent period does not preclude a finding of present adverse effects. To the contrary, such a finding can also be made if the present situation is worse than it would have been in the absence of the subsidies, and by a sufficient degree.
- In sum, the Panel believed that it was more appropriate to consider all the information that has been put before it, and assess it in the light of the arguments of the parties, than to make *a priori* judgments as to a defined and limited reference period, beyond which it would not look. But the Panel also highlighted that its approach to consider the evidence relating to a longer period was not to suggest that adverse effects manifested at some time in the past were sufficient to support a finding of violation of Article 5.[181]

The Panel also rejected a US claim that a determination concerning adverse effects should be made 'as of' the date of the establishment of the panel in July 2005. While the collection, submission and analysis of information will necessarily be based on a past period, the panel's determination had to relate to present adverse effects. The Panel also referred to *US – Upland Cotton* where the Panel took into account information from a period beyond the date of its establishment.[182] On this basis, it would seem that the most recent period for which complete data exist could and should be used.

Particular difficulties arise if the subsidization already started before the reference period and continued throughout this period. In such

[181] WT/DS316/R of 30 June 2010, *EC and certain Member States – Measures Affecting Trade in Large Civil Aircraft*, paras 7.1693–7.1713.

[182] WT/DS316/R of 30 June 2010, *EC and certain Member States – Measures Affecting Trade in Large Civil Aircraft*, para 7.1714. See also WT/DS267/R of 8 September 2004, *United States – Subsidies on Upland Cotton*, para 7.1198 and WT/DS267/RW of 18 December 2007, *United States – Subsidies on Upland Cotton (Article 21.5)*, paras 10.18, 10.57 and 10.265. In the latter case the Panel even took a period for which in part only production forecasts were available as the margin of error of these forecasts was very low.

circumstances, it is not possible to determine the effects of subsidies through direct observation of market share and price trend data. However, this does not mean that such data could not contribute to the analysis. For details see *supra* this chapter, pp. 328–329.

The Panel in *US – Upland Cotton* also used a reference period for a claim under Article 6.3(c), i.e. where the alleged effect of the subsidy is price undercutting, price suppression and price depression. The reference period used was the marketing year 2002 which represented the most recent period for which essentially complete data existed. According to the Panel, significant price suppression cannot be identified in the abstract. Rather, discerning adverse effects of subsidies requires reference to a recent historical period. The Panel also pointed out that subsidies granted prior to the marketing year 2002 were relevant for its evaluation. Consideration of developments over a period longer than one year, while not necessarily required (at least not in Articles 5(c) and 6.3(c)) provides a more robust basis for a serious prejudice evaluation than merely paying attention to developments in a single recent year. It may, for example, be that the market may well have been already distorted in a given year due to subsidies.[183]

Serious Prejudice Finding Does Not Require a Deterioration of the Situation of the Industry beyond the Factors Listed in Paragraph 3

In *EC and certain Member States – Large Civil Aircraft*, the EU argued that the US or Boeing could not suffer serious prejudice caused by the EU's subsidies because of the alleged improvements in and the excellent condition of Boeing over the period 2006 to 2007. The Panel disagreed. It concluded that there is nothing in the text of Article 6 or any other provision of the ASCM that would even suggest, much less require, consideration of the state of the industry of the complaining Member in the context of a serious prejudice analysis. The relevant harm is defined in Article 6.3. Article 15, i.e. the provision on the determination of injury for the purposes of countervailing measures, does not apply. Accordingly, any improvements in Boeing's profitability are not relevant.[184]

[183] WT/DS267/R of 8 September 2004, *United States – Subsidies on Upland Cotton*, para 7.1195 *et seq*. WT/DS267/RW of 18 December 2007, *United States – Subsidies on Upland Cotton (Article 21.5)*, paras 10.18, 10.19 and 10.83.

[184] WT/DS316/R of 30 June 2010, *EC and certain Member States – Measures Affecting Trade in Large Civil Aircraft*, paras 7.1733–7.1737 (this issue was not appealed). The Panel in

In *Korea – Commercial Vessels*, a similar argument was made. Korea claimed that the existence of one or several of the situations listed in Article 6.3 is a necessary but not a sufficient condition for a finding of serious prejudice. It argued that a finding of serious prejudice requires a two-step analysis, i.e. first whether the conditions of one of the four subparagraphs of Article 6.3 are met and second that the elements set forth in Articles 11 to 15 must be demonstrated. Korea thus claimed that 'serious prejudice' is a similar but more severe standard than 'material injury'. Korea relied *inter alia* on the text of the chapeau of Article 6.3 that states that serious prejudice 'may' arise in any case falling under subparagraphs (a) to (d). Korea also claimed that the WTO Member relying on serious prejudice had to demonstrate that its domestic industry that suffers as a result of the subsidies given by a third country is vital to its overall interests.

The Panel dismissed all these claims. It held that serious prejudice is an entirely different concept from injury as set out for instance in the Safeguards Agreement or in Articles 11 to 15 of the ASCM. It saw support for this conclusion *inter alia* in Articles 6.2, 6.6, 6.7, 27.8 and Annex V of the ASCM. It also relied on prior dispute settlement in relation to Article XVI:1 of GATT 1947 and the negotiating history. In sum, the Panel concluded that serious prejudice does not concern the condition of a particular domestic industry. Rather, it concerns the effects of subsidies on a complaining country's trade in a given product as such, i.e. the volumes and prices of such trade, in markets variously defined. But the Panel also underlined that its conclusion did not mean to suggest that particular effects on a given industry (e.g. employment, profitability etc.) could not be examined in the context of serious prejudice.[185] Specifically with regard to the term 'may' see para 7.582 of *Korea – Commercial Vessels*.

Serious Prejudice Finding Does Not Require a Precise Calculation or Allocation of the Benefit of the Subsidies at Dispute

A serious prejudice finding does not require a precise calculation of the benefit flowing from the subsidies, or a pass-through analysis. This is

WT/DS267/R of 8 September 2004, *United States – Subsidies on Upland Cotton*, paras 7.1389 and 7.1390 *et passim* took the same position in relation to a claim under Article 6.3(c). See also *Piérola* in *Wolfrum/Stoll/Koebele* (2008), paras 3 and 40 to Article 6.

185 WT/DS273/R of 7 March 2005, *Korea – Measures Affecting Trade in Commercial Vessels*, paras 7.531, 7.572–7.603. The Panel in WT/DS316/R of 30 June 2010, *EC and certain Member States – Measures Affecting Trade in Large Civil Aircraft*, paras 7.1733–7.1737 was even more categorical on this issue by pointing out that it would not take into account

based on the consideration that, contrary to a countervailing duty which pursuant to Article 19.4 cannot be levied in excess of the subsidy amount, a successful Article 6 claim obliges the Member giving such subsidy either to remove the adverse effects or to withdraw the subsidy (see Article 7.8). The Appellate Body in *US – Upland Cotton* did not find it relevant that Annexes IV (paragraph 1) and V (paragraph 2) contained references to the amounts of subsidies given. However, the magnitude of the subsidy can be relevant for the causal link analysis under Article 6.[186] As the preceding Panel has so aptly put it: 'Allocating absolutely precise proportions of the subsidy to the product concerned, or trying to trace with precision where each subsidy dollar may be spent by a recipient, is not a necessary exercise on the part of the panel. Broader considerations are at play in a serious prejudice analysis than those involved in a countervailing duty sense.'[187] These two rulings had been handed down in relation to Article 6.3(c).

In *EC and certain Member States – Large Civil Aircraft*, the Panel held that the principle established in *US – Upland Cotton* should apply not only to Article 6.3(c) but also to other claims of serious prejudice under the remainder of Article 6, and indeed, to the entire universe of claims of adverse effects. The Panel hastened to add that the finding that a precise quantification is not necessary does not mean that the magnitude of the subsidy is irrelevant. Whether a particular subsidy or subsidies cause particular alleged adverse effects is clearly not a function simply of their magnitude, but must also take into account the nature and effects of the particular subsidies in question, and the nature of the subsidized product and market, in order to assess whether a causal link exists. While logic may indicate that a larger subsidy is likely to have more significant effects, in some circumstances, even a relatively small subsidy may have significant effects, for instance, where it enables market participation that would otherwise not occur. In relation to the case at issue, the Panel concluded that the magnitude of the specific subsidies was certainly sufficient to

in the serious prejudice analysis any improvements in the condition of Boeing (this issue was not appealed).

186 WT/DS267/AB/R of 3 March 2005, *United States – Subsidies on Upland Cotton*, paras 459–473.The preceding Panel report lists in detail the differences between a claim under Part III and a claim under Part V of the ASCM, see WT/DS267/R of 8 September 2004, *United States – Subsidies on Upland Cotton*, paras 7.1166–7.1190. See also *supra* this chapter pp. 323–326.

187 WT/DS267/R of 8 September 2004, *United States – Subsidies on Upland Cotton*, para 7.1173 (subsequently confirmed by the Appellate Body).

have had the effect of enabling Airbus to launch successive models of aircraft at a pace it could otherwise not have achieved.[188]

Note finally that pass-through of a benefit may also be relevant under an Article 6 claim because it relates to one of the definitional elements of a subsidy, but it is not directly applicable to the examination of serious prejudice under Articles 5(c) and 6.3(c).[189]

Threat of the Phenomena in Article 6.3

The question is whether a claim under Article 6.3 can only be based on the existence of the phenomena listed in this provision or whether a threat is sufficient. Article 6.3 does not refer to threat of displacement etc. However, it refers back to Article 5(c) ('[s]erious prejudice in the sense of paragraph (c) of Article 5 may arise … '). Footnote 13 of Article 5 in turn stipulates that the term serious prejudice to the interests of another Member is used in the ASCM in the same sense as it is used in paragraph 1 of Article XVI of GATT 1994, and includes threat of serious prejudice. Therefore, the Appellate Body in *EC and certain Member States – Large Civil Aircraft* held that a threat of displacement may be sufficient under subparagraphs (a) and (b) of Article 6.3. It also considered Article 15.7 as context and that it was therefore reasonable to require that a determination of threat of serious prejudice 'be based on facts and not merely on allegation, conjecture or remote possibility' and that the change in circumstances that would create a situation in which the subsidy would cause displacement 'must be clearly foreseen and imminent'.[190] Note that there is no explicit ruling yet as to whether threat is also sufficient under subparagraphs (c) and (d).

See also *US – Large Civil Aircraft (2nd Complaint)*, where threat was discussed in the light of the specific situation relating to the commercial aircraft market. This market *inter alia* is characterized by the fact that the time between the order of the aircraft and its delivery is quite substantial.

[188] WT/DS316/R of 30 June 2010, *EC and certain Member States – Measures Affecting Trade in Large Civil Aircraft*, paras 7.1966–7.1968. This issue was not appealed. Confirmed by the Appellate Body in WT/DS353/AB/R of 12 March 2012, *United States – Measures Affecting Trade in Large Civil Aircraft (Second Complaint)*, para 1006.

[189] WT/DS267/R of 8 September 2004, *United States – Subsidies on Upland Cotton*, para 7.1181. Confirmed by WT/DS267/AB/R of 3 March 2005, *United States – Subsidies on Upland Cotton*, para 472. See also WT/DS353/R of 31 March 2011, *United States – Measures Affecting Trade in Large Civil Aircraft (Second Complaint)*, paras 7.289–7.300.

[190] WT/DS316/AB/R of 18 May 2011, *EC and certain Member States – Measures Affecting Trade in Large Civil Aircraft*, para 1171 (the application of the principles can be found in para 1200).

Orders that had been made during the reference period would normally only be delivered after the reference period, although there is a possibility that orders are also cancelled subsequently. The Appellate Body considered that information relating to orders may be pertinent for a finding of threat of displacement and impedance.[191]

See also *US – Upland Cotton*[192] and *US – Upland Cotton (Article 21.5)*. The latter ruling clarifies that threat of serious prejudice relates to prejudice that does not yet exist but is imminent such that it will materialize in the near future.[193]

Evidence

Paragraphs 6 and 8 of Article 6 address the question of evidence. Both provisions refer to the discovery procedure set out in Annex V. Moreover, a WTO Member in whose market serious prejudice is alleged to have arisen shall supply all relevant information that can be obtained as to the changes of market shares of the parties to the dispute as well as concerning prices of the products involved.

Examples of specific types of evidence that have been discussed in dispute settlement rulings:

- Role of econometric modelling, see *inter alia US – Upland Cotton*.[194]
- Role of studies, see *inter alia US – Upland Cotton*.[195]

Examples of a Serious Prejudice Analysis

EC and certain Member States – Large Civil Aircraft

In this case, the Panel concluded (and the Appellate Body upheld) that the launch aid given by various EU Member States has caused serious prejudice in the sense of subparagraphs (a) to (c) of Article 6.3.

[191] WT/DS353/AB/R of 12 March 2012, *United States – Measures Affecting Trade in Large Civil Aircraft (Second Complaint)*, para 1243.

[192] WT/DS267/R of 8 September 2004, *United States – Subsidies on Upland Cotton*, paras 7.1486–7.1503.

[193] WT/DS267/AB/RW of 16 May 2008, *United States – Subsidies on Upland Cotton (Article 21.5)*, para 244.

[194] WT/DS267/R of 8 September 2004, *United States – Subsidies on Upland Cotton*, paras 7.1202–7.1209.

[195] WT/DS267/R of 8 September 2004, *United States – Subsidies on Upland Cotton*, paras 7.1210–7.1215.

The US put forward two theories on causation, one referred to as the 'product theory' and the other as the 'pricing theory'. The Panel found no causal link under the pricing theory but found that the product theory was substantiated. The EU appealed and so the appeal only concerned the product theory. Under this theory, the US claimed that the subsidies had an impact on Airbus's ability to launch and bring to the market, in that particular form, models of large civil aircraft that would not have been possible at the time and in that way had there not been any subsidies. For the US, market distortion and adverse effects flow directly from Airbus's entry at a particular time with a particular aircraft, which would not have been possible but for the subsidies. The US relied on a series of public statements and one state aid decision of the European Commission. These documents allegedly revealed the views held by various officials from Airbus and other public bodies on the impact of the subsidies on the ability of Airbus to launch the various aircraft. Moreover, the US submitted a report (the 'Dorman Report') which purportedly demonstrated the impact of the subsidies on the decision to launch an aircraft. The EU essentially accepted that three of the Airbus models could not have been launched without subsidies but three other models could have been offered with a delay of three or four years. The Panel concluded:

- The subsidies were necessary for Airbus to have launched the A300, the A310 and the A330/340 as originally designed and at the time that it did.
- In respect of the A320, it would have been extremely difficult, if not impossible, for Airbus to launch this aircraft as originally designed and at the time it did.
- The particular grant specific to the A330-200 may not have been necessary to its launch, but without subsidies to the models preceding it, Airbus could not have launched the A330-200 when it did so without significantly higher costs.
- Subsidies were essential to the development of the A340-500/600 because it was derived from the A340, whose launch depended on the provision of subsidies.
- Subsidies were either directly or indirectly a necessary precondition for Airbus's launch in 2000 of the A380 because Airbus's technical capabilities derived in part from its experience in the development of its earlier models funded in turn by subsidies. Airbus would not have been in a position to obtain market financing for the A380 because it would have accumulated a significant amount of debts had it not financed the

> development of its earlier models in significant part through the various subsidies at issue. Thus, it was considered irrelevant that there was a positive net present value for this LCA even in a worst case scenario in the Airbus business case.

The Panel then proceeded to examine competition in the aircraft industry in the absence of subsidies. It based its conclusions on four different scenarios. In scenarios 1 and 2, Airbus would not have entered the market without subsidies. Boeing would have been a monopolist (scenario 1) or would have competed with another US manufacturer (scenario 2). In scenario 2, Boeing would not necessarily have had a higher market share than in reality but the US still would have had 100 per cent of the market. In scenario 3, Boeing would have competed with Airbus. Finally, in scenario 4, Boeing and another US manufacturer would have competed with Airbus. The Panel ascribed different probabilities to these scenarios. It described the first two scenarios as plausible and the last two scenarios as unlikely. The Panel further explained that, in the unlikely event that Airbus would have entered the market without subsidies, it would have been a significantly different aircraft manufacturer: Airbus could not conceivably have been present in the market with the same aircraft and at the same time as it actually was given the Panel's earlier conclusions concerning the cumulative effects of the various subsidies on Airbus's ability to launch successive models as and when it did. In sum, the Panel concluded that a non-subsidized Airbus would not have achieved the market presence it had over the period 2001–2006. This conclusion followed from the Panel's views that a non-subsidized Airbus would have been a much weaker aircraft manufacturer with at best a more limited range of models. On this basis, the Panel also rejected the claims by the EU that factors other than the competition from subsidized Airbus contributed to Boeing's loss of market share, such as the events of 9/11. Similarly, the Panel also rejected the EU's view that the US should have shown that Boeing's loss of sales must be by reason of Airbus's lower price in order to constitute adverse effects.

The Appellate Body held that this conclusion of the Panel provided enough of a basis to establish a genuine and substantial relationship of cause and effect. In other words, Airbus's sales would have been significantly lower in this counterfactual scenario. According to the Appellate Body, it was not necessary for the Panel to have made a precise quantification of the extent of the displacement or loss of sales caused by the subsidies. Based on a number of complex factual arguments that are worth reading the Appellate Body was also not convinced that a non-subsidized Airbus company could have launched the various models as claimed by the EU. Note that the Panel relied in its assessment also on an *ex post* fact (actual problems encountered by Airbus when executing the A380 programme, i.e. after the financing decisions had been made) and a wrong assumption about the A380 business case. However, according to the Appellate Body these mistakes were not of such a nature as to invalidate the Panel's overall analysis.[196]

In relation to the pricing theory, the US argued that the challenged subsidies, in particular the launch aid, provided Airbus with funds that in turn allowed it to be flexible with its pricing of aircraft when competing with Boeing so that Airbus could win sales, capture market share and significantly depress and suppress prices during the reference period. The Panel found that, given the circumstances of the case, it would be too simplistic to conclude that because of the subsidies that improved Airbus's financial condition, credit rating and perhaps reduced its marginal cost of production, Airbus was able to offer its aircraft at lower prices and that this reduction in prices caused Boeing to lose sales.[197]

US – Large Civil Aircraft (2nd Complaint)

In this case, the EU alleged the existence of 31 US subsidy measures amounting to a total of USD 19.1 billion that caused serious prejudice within the meaning of Articles 5(c) and 6.3(a), (b) and (c). The Panel found that 15 of these 31 measures constituted specific subsidies totalling at least USD 5.3 billion. The Panel separated the subsidies into three groups, identified three relevant product markets and considered two mechanisms through which the subsidies caused serious prejudice. The two mechanisms in question were that the subsidies affected Boeing's prices and that the subsidies affected the development of technologies for use on a new Boeing aircraft, the B787 family.

[196] WT/DS316/AB/R of 18 May 2011, *EC and certain Member States – Measures Affecting Trade in Large Civil Aircraft*, para 1242 *et seq.* Critical *Hahn/Mehta* (2013) pp. 158/159. They take the view that it would have been necessary to develop a global demand growth evolution corresponding to delayed development of product families by Airbus. The reason for this is that the core dynamics in the large civil aircraft industry would have been different without Airbus's competitive pressure.

[197] WT/DS316/R of 30 June 2010, *EC and certain Member States – Measures Affecting Trade in Large Civil Aircraft*, para 7.1997 *et seq.*

The EU claimed technology effects of NASA/DOD subsidies only in relation to one group of subsidies, i.e. aeronautics R&D subsidies. The Panel examined the technology effects of these subsidies in two stages. First, it analysed the effect of the subsidies on Boeing's offering of the B787 (i.e. Boeing's prices, the performance characteristics of Boeing's aircraft and the launching date of the aircraft). Second, it carried out an analysis of the effect of the R&D subsidies, through their effect on Boeing's commercial behaviour, on Airbus's prices and sales. This second step comprised the various types of serious prejudice as defined in Article 6.3. The Panel examined at each step possible relevant non-attribution factors, and it clarified that the overall approach was counterfactual in nature. It concluded that Boeing could not have launched the B787 when it did (in 2004) and in that form in the absence of subsidies. The Appellate Body confirmed the Panel's analysis.[198]

The approach in establishing causation with regard to the price effects of the so-called tied subsidies (FSC/ETI subsidies, i.e. export subsidies, and the Business and Occupation tax rate reductions) received by Boeing was somewhat different. The Appellate Body found that the Panel erred on a number of issues. Therefore, it completed the analysis where possible, i.e. where the Panel's factual findings or the uncontested facts on the record provided a sufficient basis. The Appellate Body based its analysis on facts relating to the nature and magnitude of the subsidies, and the conditions of competition in the relevant markets. It followed a two-step approach as described in detail below. First, it established the relevant facts and dynamics on a generalized basis. In a second step, it examined whether the pricing dynamic described in the general part occurred in particular aircraft sales campaigns. The Appellate Body found that the tied subsidies received by Boeing had caused serious prejudice pursuant to Article 6.3(b) and (c) only in respect of those specific sales campaigns, where the pricing dynamic described in the general part occurred.

Nature of the Subsidies

Each aircraft sale of Boeing lowered directly the taxes Boeing had to pay and commensurately increased its after-tax profit. Therefore, the tied subsidies had a more direct and immediate relationship to aircraft prices and sales

[198] See summary in WT/DS353/AB/R of 12 March 2012, *United States – Measures Affecting Trade in Large Civil Aircraft (Second Complaint)*, para 890 *et seq.*, para 1054. Critical about the Appellate Body's approach with regard to R&D subsidies *Neven/Sykes* (2014) pp. 293–294. In order to determine that the subsidies had a material effect on Boeing's R&D strategy, a cash flow analysis of the R&D projects should have been undertaken, with and without the subsidies.

than other subsidies at dispute, e.g. the R&D subsidies received by Boeing. Moreover, as those tied subsidies were export subsidies, they were likely to produce more adverse effects in the market. Generally speaking, subsidies contingent on export modify the incentives faced by a domestic producer, reward discrimination in favour of export markets over the domestic market, and thereby reduce export prices. Last but not least, the Appellate Body also noted the long duration of the tied subsidies – they dated back to 1989.

Magnitude of the Subsidies

The tied subsidies amounted to 2.2 billion over the period from 1989 to 2002. The subsidy amounts appear substantial in absolute amounts. The Appellate Body found also relevant the relative magnitude and relative significance. However, there was little on the Panel record in this respect. The Appellate Body noted, at a high level of generalization, that the annual value of Boeing's sales was many times higher than the annual value of the subsidies. However, it found that this alone did not tell much about the significance of the subsidy amounts. This is because even relatively small subsidies may have significant effects, depending on the nature of the subsidies, and the circumstances in which these subsidies are received, including the relevant market structure and conditions of competition in that market. The Appellate Body referred in this context to the nature of the subsidies, the dynamics of price competition between Boeing and Airbus in a duopolistic market, and whether the benefits received by Boeing from these subsidies were applied across the board to all sales, or whether they were disproportionately applied to lower prices in respect of certain sales. Such evidence was not on the record. However, there was anecdotal evidence showing that Boeing itself considered the FSC subsidies an important aspect of its ability to compete. On this basis, the Appellate Body considered that the record supported the view that the absolute amount of the tied tax subsidies was significant. And there was also some support for the proposition that these amounts had a relative significance: when deployed strategically, the benefits were of a significant magnitude to contribute to Boeing's ability to win sales in particular campaigns or to suppress Airbus's prices in such campaigns.

Conditions of Competition in the Aircraft Industry

Here the Appellate Body pointed out that each relevant aircraft product market operated as a duopoly, and that Airbus and Boeing each possessed market power. In a duopolistic market, the effects of one firm's commercial behaviour – including the price effects from subsidies – will necessarily impact the rival firm. Differences in price, capacity and direct operating cost of competing aircraft are the most significant factors that determine the outcome of a sales campaign. The relative importance of these factors can, however, vary considerably from one campaign to another. They might be smaller for instance, because an aircraft producer is the incumbent supplier to an airline and the airline would incur so-called switching costs if it wants to source from the rival supplier. The principal variable that can be modified during a campaign are the price and price-related concessions – price concessions can offset disadvantages associated with non-price factors.[199]

The Appellate Body did not consider that the above was sufficient to establish the causal connection between the tied tax subsidies and the effects on Airbus's sales and prices because it was not persuaded that the above dynamic occurred in each and every sales campaign. It considered that Boeing had both the ability and the incentive to use the tied tax subsidies to lower prices, and that there was a substantial likelihood that this occurred in sales campaigns that were particularly competitive and sensitive in terms of prices. However, in the view of the Appellate Body, a causal link could only be found if Boeing was under particular pressure to reduce its prices in order to secure particular aircraft selling campaigns, and if there were no other non-price factors that explained Boeing's success in obtaining the sale or suppressing Airbus's prices. In other words, the Appellate Body held that it could only reach a finding of serious prejudice if it could also identify uncontested facts on the Panel record that showed that the general pricing dynamic described above also occurred in particular aircraft sales campaigns. Therefore, it examined each individual aircraft sales campaign in the light of the above. For each campaign where there was enough uncontested evidence showing that factors other than the subsidies (e.g. switching cost or importance of certain technical features of the aircraft at offer) were not present, the Appellate Body concluded that the subsidies caused serious prejudice.[200]

Korea – Commercial Vessels

This case is also a good example as to the applicable standard. The EU claimed that certain financing and restructuring arrangements that Korea provided for its shipyards had caused serious prejudice to it pursuant to Article 6.3(c) in the form of price suppression and price depression. The

[199] But see *Neven/Sykes* (2014) pp. 295–296.

[200] WT/DS353/AB/R of 12 March 2012, *United States – Measures Affecting Trade in Large Civil Aircraft (Second Complaint)*, paras 1250–1274.

claim was limited to Liquified Natural Gas tankers (LNGs), product/chemical tankers and container ships. The Panel first determined as to what support schemes operated by Korea constituted subsidies in the sense of Articles 1 and 3. It then proceeded for each of the three categories of ships to examine whether these subsidies had caused significant price depression/suppression to the EC in the same market. In this context, the Panel established to what extent Korean ships benefited from these subsidies. The analysis was limited to a certain period of time relevant for the subsidies given. The Panel concluded that for none of these types of ships the prevailing market prices would have been significantly higher in the absence of the subsidies found. For instance, with regard to LNGs the Panel found that three ships produced by Korean shipyards benefitted from subsidies. The subsidies in the form of guarantees were given in 2000 and 2001 and expired between 2002 and 2004. The benefit from these subsidies was relatively small although the precise amount was not given for reasons of confidentiality. As of January 2004, 62 LNGs were on order around the world, 37 of them with Korean yards. The Panel looked for evidence of a relationship between the subsidized transaction for a given ship type, on the one hand, and the prevailing market price for that ship type, on the other. It did not find evidence of such a relationship. However, had it found one, it would have gone on to consider in more detail questions of product definition, geographic markets, timing of subsidization, movements in prices, evidence pertaining to costs etc. for each product category subject of a serious prejudice claim. Note however that the EU did not make any claim as to the aggregate effect of subsidies on all product categories.[201]

US – Upland Cotton

The original case of *US – Upland Cotton* is an example of a two-step analysis in relation to price suppression. First, the Panel found that price suppression existed in the world market, i.e. the relevant market in this case. The Panel's examination covered the following considerations: (a) the relative magnitude of the US's production and exports in the world upland cotton market; (b) general price trends; and (c) the nature of the subsidies at issue, in particular, whether or not the nature of these subsidies is such as to have discernible price suppressive effects. Several of the US subsidies were directly linked to world market prices, thereby delinking to a

[201] WT/DS273/R of 7 March 2005, *Korea – Measures Affecting Trade in Commercial Vessels*, para 7.676 *et seq.*

certain extent the US farmers' production decisions from world market prices when the latter were low. Moreover, the price-contingent subsidies were large. In the Panel's view, the collective operation of these subsidies was akin to a large, counter-cyclical, deficiency payment laced with additional payments. In the Panel's words, the structure, design and operation particularly of the price-contingent subsidies constituted strong evidence supporting a finding of price suppression. There was also evidence on the record that increased production and supply which reaches world markets will have an effect on prices. Moreover, price movements and trends originating from the US market were closely tracked by prices on the world market, as *inter alia* confirmed by two globally used price indices.[202]

Second, the Panel also found that price suppression and price depression were the effect of price-contingent subsidies.

On appeal, the US essentially criticized that Panel for ignoring or failing to take proper account of certain evidence and arguments in analysing the effect of the price-contingent subsidies, e.g.:

- that farmers' planting decisions depended upon the expected market price and not the subsidies;
- that the US share in world cotton production remained stable;
- that the Panel did not consider how the cotton production of other countries would have developed in the absence of the US payments;
- that the Panel should not have looked at the relative size of US cotton production in relation to that of other countries but at the competition between the various cotton producing countries;
- that the temporal coincidence between suppressed world market prices and the price-contingent subsidies was not convincing;
- that, for the purposes of the examination whether the US farmers would have been economically capable of remaining in the cotton production had it not been for the subsidies, a comparison should have been done between the US farmers' variable cost of production and their sales revenue from cotton and not with their total cost of production.

Given the facts of the case, the Appellate Body did not find any of these arguments convincing.[203]

[202] WT/DS267/R of 8 September 2004, *United States – Subsidies on Upland Cotton*, paras 7.1280–7.1314. Upheld by the Appellate Body.

[203] WT/DS267/AB/R of 3 March 2005, *United States – Subsidies on Upland Cotton*, para 419 *et seq.*, in particular paras 439–457. The Panel's analysis can be found in WT/DS267/R of 8 September 2004, *United States – Subsidies on Upland Cotton*, paras 7.1347–7.1363.

Article 7

Remedies

Introduction

Article 7 sets out special and additional rules with regard to actionable subsidies that cause adverse effects pursuant to Article 5 and that are challenged under the dispute settlement track (as an alternative to countervailing measures pursuant to Part V of the ASCM). The function of Article 7 in relation to actionable subsidies is similar to the one of Article 4 in relation to prohibited subsidies.

The entirety of Articles 7.2 through 7.10 are special and additional rules or procedures identified in Appendix 2 to the DSU. They provide in some cases for an accelerated procedure compared to the normal DSU rules, e.g. circulation of the panel report within 120 days. Annex V procedures on the development of evidence are available for claims under Article 7.

The provisions of Article 7 deal with requests for consultations (paragraph 2), the ensuing consultations (paragraph 3), requests for the establishment of a panel (paragraph 4), the panel phase including its duration (paragraph 5), the adoption of the panel report (paragraph 6), the duration of the appeal phase (paragraph 7), the remedies that a WTO Member has to take in case it has caused adverse effects (paragraph 8), the conditions for granting countermeasures in case the losing Member has not taken appropriate steps to remove the adverse effects or to withdraw the subsidy (paragraph 9). Last but not least Article 7 contains rules concerning arbitration to determine whether countermeasures are commensurate with the degree and nature of the adverse effects found to exist (paragraph 10).

Footnote 19 refers to Article 6.1, i.e. the provision listing the circumstances in which serious prejudice is deemed to exist. As Article 6.1 has expired by virtue of Article 31, footnote 19 would seem to be devoid of any purpose.

Article 6 applies subject to the special and differential treatment provisions for developing country Members as contained in Articles 27.9 and 27.13.

Article 7 is essentially self-explanatory. Therefore, the remainder of the commentary to Article 7 only sets out relevant DSB rulings.

Request for Consultations (Article 7.2)

According to Article 7.2, a request for consultation shall include a statement of available evidence. In line with the conditions of a successful claim under Article 7, the statement shall cover not only the evidence with regard to the existence and nature of the subsidy (as in Article 4.2), but also the evidence concerning adverse effects as defined in Article 5. Article 4.2 contains a similar obligation to provide a statement of available evidence (see *supra* the commentary to Article 4, pp. 231–233).

Article 7.2 does not explicitly refer to the magnitude or amount or value of the subsidy, let alone to any precise quantitative methodologies pertaining to its allocation. However, according to the Panel in *US – Upland Cotton*, Article 7.2 calls for qualitative, and, to some extent, quantitative analysis of the existence and nature of the subsidy and the serious prejudice caused.[1]

Consultations (Article 7.3)

The last sentence of Article 7.3 stipulates: 'The purpose of the consultations shall be to clarify the facts of the situation and to arrive at a mutually agreed solution.' According to the Panel in *US – Upland Cotton*, these facts would necessarily pertain to the subject of the request for consultations, including the statement of available evidence. They would thus logically pertain to the existence and nature of the subsidy but not necessarily to the precise quantification of the amount of the subsidy.[2]

Removal of Adverse Effects or Withdrawal of Subsidy (Article 7.8)

Article 7.8 informs the meaning and the scope of the DSB's recommendations and rulings arising from the original proceedings (as opposed to proceedings under Article 21.5 of the DSU). It specifies what a Member has to do if it had been found that a subsidy granted or maintained by that

[1] WT/DS267/R of 8 September 2004, *United States – Subsidies on Upland Cotton*, para 7.1173 (subsequently confirmed by the Appellate Body).

[2] WT/DS267/R of 8 September 2004, *United States – Subsidies on Upland Cotton*, para 7.1175.

Member has resulted in adverse effects to the interests of another Member pursuant to Article 5. According to Article 7.8, the Member granting or maintaining such subsidy

- shall take appropriate steps to remove the adverse effects of such subsidy or
- shall withdraw the subsidy.

The function of Article 7.8 is to some extent similar to the one of Article 4.7. The latter provision specifies that a Member found to have given a prohibited subsidy shall withdraw the subsidy without delay and that the Panel shall specify in its recommendation the time period within which the measure must be withdrawn. However, Article 7.8 gives Members, in contrast to Article 4.7, the option of removing the adverse effects as an alternative to withdrawing the subsidy because actionable subsidies are not prohibited *per se*.[3] For instance, in *US – Upland Cotton*, the arbitrator recalled that the US subsidies in the form of marketing loans and countercyclical payments had adverse effects in the form of significant price suppression for upland cotton in the world market. This price suppression had in turn two effects. First, the sales value obtained by farmers of upland cotton was lower because of the lower and suppressed prices. Second, lower prices resulted in shift on the supply curve of upland cotton, i.e. the production quantity at the suppressed price levels was lower than it would have been at non-suppressed prices.[4]

For an interpretation of the notion to 'withdraw the subsidy' see the commentary to Article 4.7.

The Panel in *EC and certain Member States – Large Civil Aircraft (Article 21.5)* also discussed the notions of a withdrawal of a subsidy and the removal of its adverse effects.[5] This ruling is currently subject to appeal.

Challenge of a Subsidy Paid after the Implementing Period under Article 21.5 of the DSU. Article 7.8 was at issue in *US – Upland Cotton (Article 21.5)*. The question was whether a subsidy that was given after the end of the reasonable period of time within which the Member had

[3] WT/DS267/AB/RW of 16 May 2008, *United States – Subsidies on Upland Cotton (Article 21.5)*, para 238.

[4] WT/DS267/ARB/2 of 31 August 2009, *United States – Subsidies on Upland Cotton (Arbitration under Article 22.6 DSU and 7.10 ASCM)*, paras 4.90 and 4.128 *et seq.*

[5] WT/DS316/RW of 22 September 2016, *EC and certain Member States – Measures Affecting Trade in Large Civil Aircraft – Recourse to Article 21.5 of the DSU by the United States*, paras 6.752–6.791.

to comply with the DSB recommendations, could be challenged in a dispute pursuant to Article 21.5 of the DSU. The reasonable period of time elapsed on 21 September 2005 while the US had implemented recommendations with regard to certain recurring subsidies only as of 1 August 2006 and others not at all. The Appellate Body held:

- In order to determine whether there is compliance with the DSB's recommendations and rulings in a case involving actionable subsidies, a panel would have to assess whether the Member concerned has taken one of the actions foreseen under Article 7.8.
- The use of the terms 'shall take' and 'shall withdraw' in Article 7.8 indicate that compliance with this provision will usually involve some action by the respondent Member.
- Such action is certainly expected with respect to subsidies granted in the past and which may have formed the basis for the panel's determination of present serious prejudice and adverse effects.
- The obligation in Article 7.8 also covers recurring annual payments made by a Member as a result of subsidies that it 'maintains' beyond the time period examined by the panel for purposes of determining the existence of serious prejudice, as long as those payments continue to have adverse effects. Otherwise, a complaining Member that has demonstrated that subsidies provided by another Member have resulted in adverse effects would obtain relief only with respect to any lingering effects of the subsidies provided during the period examined by the panel. And it would have to initiate another dispute to obtain relief with respect to payments made after the period examined by the panel, even if those subsidies are recurring payments or otherwise of the same nature as those found to have resulted in adverse effects.
- A Member would not comply with its obligation in Article 7.8 to withdraw the subsidy if it leaves an actionable subsidy in place, either entirely or partially, or replaces that subsidy with another actionable subsidy.[6]

Subsidy Programmes Versus Payments under Such Programmes. In *US – Upland Cotton (Article 21.5)*, there was also some dispute as to what extent the findings of the original Panel extended to the subsidy *programmes* or whether they were limited to the *payments* made under these

[6] WT/DS267/AB/RW of 16 May 2008, *United States – Subsidies on Upland Cotton (Article 21.5)*, para 237 *et passim*.

programmes. The Appellate Body was critical with regard to this distinction. It had some difficulty accepting the notion that a subsidy programme and the payments under that programme could be assessed separately. This is because the terms and conditions, beneficiaries, amounts and other aspects of a payment will be set in the programme or authorizing legislation, especially in the case of recurring payments. Therefore, the Appellate Body found it difficult to conceive how an analysis of whether a programme 'as such' resulted in adverse effects would differ from an analysis of whether payments under a programme had resulted in such effects.[7]

Countermeasures in Case the Adverse Effects Are Not Removed or the Subsidy Is Not Withdrawn (Articles 7.9 and 7.10)

Paragraphs 9 and 10 of Article 7 entitle the complaining Member to request authorization to take 'countermeasures, commensurate with the degree and nature of the adverse effects determined to exist'. These two provisions dealing with actionable subsidies serve a similar function as paragraphs 10 and 11 of Article 4 that apply if the subsidizing Member does not withdraw a prohibited subsidy. Articles 4.10 and 4.11 refer to 'appropriate countermeasures' while footnote 9 further clarifies the term 'appropriate'. In contrast, Article 7.9 does not qualify further the term 'countermeasures'.

The arbitrator in *US – Upland Cotton (Arbitration under Article 22.6 DSU and 7.10 ASCM)* has extensively dealt with Article 7.9.

With regard to the various theoretical foundations of countermeasures (essentially inducing compliance versus 'efficient breach') see *Grossman/Sykes* (2011) pp. 149–162.

Countermeasures

The arbitrator interpreted the term 'countermeasures' in the same way under Article 7 and under Article 4.[8] The reader is therefore referred to the relevant section in the commentary of Article 4.

[7] WT/DS267/AB/RW of 16 May 2008, *United States – Subsidies on Upland Cotton (Article 21.5)*, paras 233, 234, 241, 242, 243.

[8] See WT/DS267/ARB/1 of 31 August 2009, *United States – Subsidies on Upland Cotton (Arbitration under Article 22.6 DSU and 4.11 ASCM)*, paras 4.34–4.43 and WT/DS267/ARB/2 of 31 August 2009, *United States – Subsidies on Upland Cotton (Arbitration under Article 22.6 DSU and 7.10 ASCM)*, paras 4.24–4.33.

'[C]ommensurate with the Degree and Nature of the Adverse Effects Determined to Exist'

According to the arbitrator, 'commensurate' essentially connotes a correspondence between two elements. In Article 7.9, these two elements are (1) the countermeasures and (2) the 'degree and nature of the adverse effects determined to exist'.[9]

Moreover, the term 'commensurate' does not suggest that exact or precise equality is required between the countermeasures and the degree and nature of the adverse effects determined to exist. The term 'commensurate' has a less precise degree of equivalence than exact numerical correspondence. Nonetheless, the term 'commensurate' does indicate a relationship of correspondence and proportionality between the two elements, and not merely a relationship of adequacy or harmony as suggested by Brazil, i.e. the party seeking countermeasures. The relationship may be qualitative as well as quantitative. However, the exact nature of the correspondence at issue is identified by the next element, i.e. 'the degree and nature of the adverse effects determined to exist'.[10]

In relation to '*degree and nature*', the arbitrator noted that 'degree' of the adverse effects could be understood as a quantitative element whereas the reference to the 'nature' of the adverse effects seemed to point to something more qualitative. More specifically, the reference to the nature of the adverse effects may refer to the different types of adverse effects that are foreseen in Articles 5 and 6. With regard to the degree of the adverse effects, the US (the defendant) argued that 'degree' means that the proposed countermeasures may not exceed the scope of the findings while Brazil (the applicant) submitted that the full extent of the degree and nature of the adverse effects must be taken into account. The arbitrator agreed in principle with both of these propositions.[11]

The '*adverse effects determined to exist*' refer back to the precise findings on adverse effects made by a panel and/or the Appellate Body, be they in the form of injury to the domestic industry, nullification or impairment of benefits or serious prejudice (see Article 7.1).[12]

9 WT/DS267/ARB/2 of 31 August 2009, *United States – Subsidies on Upland Cotton (Arbitration under Article 22.6 DSU and 7.10 ASCM)*, para 4.37.

10 WT/DS267/ARB/2 of 31 August 2009, *United States – Subsidies on Upland Cotton (Arbitration under Article 22.6 DSU and 7.10 ASCM)*, para 4.39.

11 WT/DS267/ARB/2 of 31 August 2009, *United States – Subsidies on Upland Cotton (Arbitration under Article 22.6 DSU and 7.10 ASCM)*, paras 4.41, 4.43, 4.46.

12 WT/DS267/ARB/2 of 31 August 2009, *United States – Subsidies on Upland Cotton (Arbitration under Article 22.6 DSU and 7.10 ASCM)*, paras 4.49–4.53.

The arbitrator considered Articles 4.10, 5 and 6 of the ASCM as well as Article 22 of the DSU as relevant context that confirmed the above understanding. They also highlighted that there is no suggestion in Article 7.9 that would allow taking into account any consideration other than the 'degree and nature of the adverse effects determined to exist'.[13]

Finally, the arbitrator concluded that the object and purpose of Article 7.9 is to induce compliance, i.e. the same object and purpose as that of Article 22.1 of the DSU and that of Article 4.10 of the ASCM. They hastened to add that this purpose did not give, in and of itself, any indication as to the level of countermeasures because this purpose is common to all three legal bases for countermeasures or suspension of obligations and each of these three provisions defines itself the level of countermeasures. In other words, the term 'degree and nature of the adverse effects determined to exist' does not empower the arbitrator to increase the level of the countermeasures to specifically take into account, in a subjective sense, the superadded objective of inducing compliance.[14]

Burden of Proof

See the commentary to Articles 4.10 and 4.11 as well as *US – Upland Cotton (Arbitration under Articles 22.6 DSU and 7.10 ASCM)*.[15]

Further Issues

The following findings made in *US – Upland Cotton (Arbitration under Articles 22.6 DSU and 7.10 ASCM)* are also noteworthy. They deal with the expiry of the law which was the legal basis for the payments classified as subsidies as well as with the level of the countermeasures:

- The US argued that no countermeasures should be authorized because the 2002 Farm Bill, which was the legal basis for the contested payments, had expired. The arbitrator noted that a review under Article 22.6 of the DSU is not tasked to review whether compliance has been achieved or not (proceedings under Article 21.5 DSU would be the

[13] WT/DS267/ARB/2 of 31 August 2009, *United States – Subsidies on Upland Cotton (Arbitration under Article 22.6 DSU and 7.10 ASCM)*, paras 4.54–4.56.

[14] WT/DS267/ARB/2 of 31 August 2009, *United States – Subsidies on Upland Cotton (Arbitration under Article 22.6 DSU and 7.10 ASCM)*, paras 4.57–4.62.

[15] WT/DS267/ARB/2 of 31 August 2009, *United States – Subsidies on Upland Cotton (Arbitration under Article 22.6 DSU and 7.10 ASCM)*, para 4.116.

adequate forum). However, given (i) that the Panel found payments under the 2002 Farm Bill inconsistent with the ASCM (and not the Farm Bill as such) and (ii) that the US had subsequently enacted the 2008 Farm Bill which provided for similar payments, the arbitrator rejected the argument raised by the US.[16]

- There is no need to adjust the level of the countermeasures to take account of a threshold of 'significant' price suppression as opposed to all price suppression caused by the subsidies (i.e. no '*de minimis*' level to be deducted).[17]
- There was also some discussion on the selection of a particular reference period to determine the adverse effects.[18]
- Finally, the details of the calculation of the actual amount of countermeasures are interesting. Brazil's methodology entailed simulating a counterfactual scenario involving the permanent removal of the two subsidies in question (marketing loans and countercyclical payments). This simulation allowed estimating the world price and production levels of upland cotton if the subsidies had been removed. The arbitrator discussed *inter alia* the elasticities used in the model (supply elasticities of the US and rest of the world, demand elasticities) including their values, the coupling factor (degree of production incentive that a particular subsidy programme has on US upland cotton farmers) and price expectations.[19]
- As in the parallel arbitration proceeding concerning prohibited subsidies, the arbitrator limited Brazil's claims to the adverse effects on Brazil, and thus rejected Brazil's claim to take countermeasures at a level corresponding to the entirety of the adverse effects on non-US producers in other parts of the world.[20]

Care should be taken not to generalize the above findings as they are intimately linked to the particular circumstances of the case.[21]

[16] WT/DS267/ARB/2 of 31 August 2009, *United States – Subsidies on Upland Cotton (Arbitration under Article 22.6 DSU and 7.10 ASCM)*, paras 3.8–3.33.
[17] WT/DS267/ARB/2 of 31 August 2009, *United States – Subsidies on Upland Cotton (Arbitration under Article 22.6 DSU and 7.10 ASCM)*, paras 4.93–4.107.
[18] WT/DS267/ARB/2 of 31 August 2009, *United States – Subsidies on Upland Cotton (Arbitration under Article 22.6 DSU and 7.10 ASCM)*, paras 4.108–4.119.
[19] WT/DS267/ARB/2 of 31 August 2009, *United States – Subsidies on Upland Cotton (Arbitration under Article 22.6 DSU and 7.10 ASCM)*, paras 4.120–4.195. With regard to the calculation issues see also *Grossman/Sykes* (2011) p. 144.
[20] WT/DS267/ARB/2 of 31 August 2009, *United States – Subsidies on Upland Cotton (Arbitration under Article 22.6 DSU and 7.10 ASCM)*, para 4.92.
[21] See e.g. WT/DS267/ARB/2 of 31 August 2009, *United States – Subsidies on Upland Cotton (Arbitration under Article 22.6 DSU and 7.10 ASCM)*, para 4.73 *et passim*.

PART IV

NON-ACTIONABLE SUBSIDIES

Article 8

Identification of Non-Actionable Subsidies

According to Article 8, certain types of subsidies, essentially R&D subsidies, subsidies for disadvantaged regions and subsidies for environmental purposes, were non-actionable. Article 8 has expired by virtue of Article 31. For further details see *Rios Herran and Poretti* in *Wolfrum/Stoll/Koebele* (2008), commentary to Article 8, as well as the corresponding section of the WTO Analytical Index.[1]

Article 9

Consultations and Authorized Remedies

Article 9 has expired by virtue of Article 31. For further details see *Rios Herran and Poretti* in *Wolfrum/Stoll/Koebele* (2008), commentary to Article 9.

[1] www.wto.org/english/res_e/booksp_e/analytic_index_e/subsidies_e.htm (website visited on 1 August 2016).

PART V

COUNTERVAILING MEASURES

Article 10

Application of Article VI of GATT 1994

Introduction

Article 10 introduces Part V of the ASCM, i.e. the part dealing with countervailing investigations and countervailing measures. Three footnotes (footnotes 35 to 37) are attached to this provision. Article 10 clarifies essentially the following fundamental issues:

- the relationship between countervailing measures and Article VI of GATT 1994;
- the relationship between countervailing measures and the WTO dispute settlement track under Parts II and III of the ASCM;
- the definition of a countervailing duty;
- the need to carry out a pass-through analysis if a subsidy is bestowed on an input and this input is sold at arm's length to the producer of the product subject to investigation;
- countervailing measures can only be imposed after an investigation has been initiated and conducted in accordance with the provisions of the ASCM and the Agreement on Agriculture.

The next sections set out the relevant details for each of these issues.

Relationship between Countervailing Measures and Article VI of GATT 1994

It follows from Article 10 in conjunction with Article 32.1 that countervailing duties may only be imposed in accordance with the provisions of Part V of the ASCM and Article VI of the GATT 1994, taken together.[1]

[1] WT/DS22/AB/R of 21 February 1997, *Brazil – Measures Affecting Desiccated Coconut*, page 16.

The Panel in *Brazil – Desiccated Coconut* has qualified the two sets of rules as an 'inseparable whole'.[2]

If there is a conflict between the provisions of Article VI and those of the ASCM, the provisions of the ASCM would prevail as a result of the interpretative note to Annex 1A of the Marrakesh Agreement establishing the World Trade Organization.[3]

Relationship between Countervailing Measures and the WTO Dispute Settlement Track under Parts II and III of the ASCM

Footnote 35 permits that a Member initiates a countervailing investigation in parallel with dispute settlement procedures pursuant to Parts II and III of the ASCM. However, it requires WTO Members to choose between the two remedies available under both tracks,[4] i.e. between the remedies explicitly envisaged in Part V of the ASCM (provisional and definitive countervailing duties pursuant to Articles 17 and 19 as well as undertakings pursuant to Article 18) and countermeasures pursuant to Parts II and III (see Articles 4.10 and 7.9).

Footnote 35 also refers extensively to Article 8 which has lapsed in the meantime.

Definition of the Term 'Countervailing Duty' (Footnote 36)

Footnote 36 stipulates that the term 'countervailing duty' shall be understood as provided for in Article VI:3 of the GATT 1994. Therefore, a countervailing duty is 'a special duty levied for the purpose of offsetting any subsidy bestowed directly or indirectly upon the manufacture, production or export of any merchandise'. The term 'subsidy' is defined in Article 1 of the ASCM.

Based on the reference to 'manufacture, production or export of any merchandise' in footnote 36, the US in *US – Lead and Bismuth II* argued that the relevant benefit is a benefit to a company's productive operations, rather than, as the Panel held, a benefit to legal or natural persons. The US raised this argument because its Department of

[2] WT/DS22/R of 17 October 1996, *Brazil – Measures Affecting Desiccated Coconut*, para 241.

[3] WT/DS22/AB/R of 21 February 1997, *Brazil – Measures Affecting Desiccated Coconut*, page 16. The interpretative note is reproduced *supra* the introductory chapter, p. 27.

[4] WT/DS217/AB/R and WT/DS234/AB/R of 16 January 2003, *United States – Continued Dumping and Subsidy Offset Act of 2000*, para 270.

Commerce had not carried out a pass-through analysis in the privatization cases, arguing that the productive operation continued to exist, even if the new owner had received no benefit. The Appellate Body rejected this argument. It concluded that the benefit in Article 1.1(b) is a benefit to the recipient, and that such recipient must be a natural or legal person.[5]

Pass-through Analysis

The product subject to investigation may incorporate inputs that have benefitted from a financial contribution provided by the government. The question is whether and under what conditions can the subsidy on the input product be attributed to the product subject to investigation. Or, to put it differently, the question is when and to what amount did the subsidy bestowed on the input product flow through to the downstream product with the effect that it led to a decrease in the level of prices of the input product. *US – Softwood Lumber IV* and *Mexico – Olive Oil* are the leading cases in respect of this issue. These rulings have established that Article VI:3 of GATT 1994 as well as Footnote 36 of Article 10 of the ASCM (which repeats the second sentence of Article VI:3 of GATT 1994) require an investigating authority in a countervailing duty investigation to conduct a pass-through analysis in certain circumstances. The pre-WTO Panel *US – Canadian Pork* came to the same conclusion with regard to Article VI:3 of GATT.[6]

Article VI:3 of GATT 1994 clarifies that no countervailing duty shall be levied on any product in excess of an amount equal to the subsidy determined to have been granted, directly or indirectly, on the manufacture, production or export of such product in the country of origin or exportation. The reference to the word 'indirectly' implies that financial contributions by a government to the production of inputs that in turn are used in the manufacture of the product subject to investigation are not, in principle, excluded from the amount of subsidies that may be offset through the imposition of countervailing duties on such processed product. However, where the producer of the input is not the same entity as the producer of the processed product, and where the two of them operate at arm's length,

[5] WT/DS138/AB/R of 10 May 2000, *United States – Imposition of Countervailing Duties on Certain Hot-Rolled Lead and Bismuth Carbon Steel Products originating in the United Kingdom*, paras 56–58.

[6] For a general overview on pass-through see *Shadikhodjaev* (2012).

it cannot be presumed that the subsidy bestowed on the input passes automatically through to the downstream product.[7]

According to the Appellate Body, in such a case, it is necessary to analyse to what extent subsidies on inputs may be included in the determination of the total amount of subsidies bestowed upon the downstream product. As far as subsidies on inputs are concerned, only the amount of the subsidy on the input product that flowed through, or passed through, downstream, to the producer of the product that incorporates the input, can be countervailed. In short, there is no need that the recipient of a financial contribution and the recipient of the benefit are identical. However, it has to be demonstrated that there was a pass-through of the subsidy given to the input producer to the producer of the product under investigation.[8] The details are explained below.

In *US – Softwood Lumber IV*, the product subject to investigation was both primary and remanufactured lumber. Timber is an important input for lumber. Stumpage programmes of Canadian provinces provided subsidized standing timber to timber harvesters. The standing timber eventually becomes felled trees or logs, which are processed into primary softwood lumber. Part of the primary softwood lumber is subsequently transformed into remanufactured lumber products. The question was therefore whether the lumber producers benefitted from the subsidized stumpage programmes. Three types of actors functions had to be distinguished in the timber supply chain:

- tenured timber harvesters (i.e. enterprises holding a stumpage contract to fell trees and produce logs)
- sawmills (i.e. enterprises that process logs into softwood lumber and do not have a stumpage contract)
- and remanufacturers (i.e. enterprises that further process softwood lumber into remanufactured lumber products).

Two configurations were at issue in this case. The first configuration concerned sales of logs between tenured timber harvesters and sawmills on an arm's length basis. The question was whether a pass-through analysis was necessary in order to determine whether a subsidy received by independent harvesters was indirectly bestowed on the production of

[7] WT/DS257/R of 29 August 2003, *United States – Final Countervailing Duty Determination with Respect to Certain Softwood Lumber from Canada*, para 7.95.

[8] WT/DS257/AB/R of 19 January 2004, *United States – Final Countervailing Duty Determination with Respect to Certain Softwood Lumber from Canada*, paras 134–146.

softwood lumber. The Panel held that such a pass-through examination was indeed necessary in such circumstances.[9] This configuration was only examined by the Panel and not by the Appellate Body.

The second configuration covered arm's length sales of logs and lumber by companies that both were tenure-holding timber harvesters and also owned sawmills and thus produced lumber. In other words, these entities combined the first two abovementioned functions. They produced logs and either sold these logs directly or first transformed them into (primary) lumber. Here again the question was whether the unrelated purchasers of the logs or primary lumber received an indirect subsidy or, put differently, whether the subsidy bestowed on the timber passed through to these purchasers.

According to both the Panel and the Appellate Body, a pass-through analysis was required in case of arm's length sales of logs. The US argued unsuccessfully that no pass-through was necessary with regard to arm's length sales of logs by companies that produce and sell both logs and softwood lumber. The US claimed that benefits, initially attached to logs, but retained by a harvester/sawmill when the logs are sold in arm's length transactions to unrelated buyers, may be used by such a vendor to cross-subsidize its own production of softwood lumber processed in-house from other logs. The Appellate Body agreed that such cross-subsidization is possible, but whether this occurs depends on the particular case under examination. Moreover, the Appellate Body disagreed with the US proposition that, as long as an enterprise manufactures products subject to investigation, any benefits accruing to the same enterprise from subsidies conferred on any different products it produces (which are not subject to that investigation – logs in *US – Softwood Lumber IV*) could be included, without need of a pass-through analysis, in the total amount of subsidization found to exist for the investigated product.[10]

With regard to arm's length sales of primary lumber to remanufacturers of softwood lumber, the Panel found that a pass-through was also necessary. The Appellate Body reversed this finding. The Appellate Body noted that once it has been established that benefits received by input manufacturers (logs obtained from standing timber) have passed through to manufacturers of subject products (primary and remanufactured softwood

[9] WT/DS257/AB/R of 19 January 2004, *United States – Final Countervailing Duty Determination with Respect to Certain Softwood Lumber from Canada*, para 155 *et seq.*

[10] WT/DS257/AB/R of 19 January 2004, *United States – Final Countervailing Duty Determination with Respect to Certain Softwood Lumber from Canada*, para 155 *et seq.*

lumber) no further pass-through analysis is necessary between producers of subject products. Note that this conclusion seems to be limited to an investigation conducted on an aggregate basis pursuant to Article 19.3. According to the Appellate Body, in these circumstances it would be superfluous to calculate how precisely benefits are divided up between the producers of subject products (here primary lumber and remanufactured lumber) in order to calculate, on an aggregate basis, the total amount of subsidy and the country-wide countervailing duty rate for the subject imports. The Appellate Body hastened to add that the pass-through question would not be the same when determining, through the review procedure under Article 19.3, an individual countervailing duty rate for the exporter that requested that review. In such a review, it is likely that a pass–through analysis would be required to determine whether input subsidies on logs, having passed through to the production of softwood lumber inputs (primary lumber), have finally passed through to remanufactured lumber produced from primary lumber by a particular exporter.[11]

The Implementation Panel had to decide whether a pass-through analysis is always required with regard to sales between unrelated parties or whether in addition, the transaction must also have been made at arm's length. The Implementation Panel held that sales between unrelated parties necessitated a pass-through analysis, irrespective of any consideration as to whether or not such sales were arm's length. The Implementation Panel recognized that, contrary to its own ruling in the original investigation, the subsequent Appellate Body ruling referred on a number of occasions to arm's length transactions, but it did not consider this relevant. Finally, the Implementing Panel accepted that an investigating authority can request company-specific and/or transaction-specific data in order to determine whether or not the parties to the transaction were related.[12]

The Panel in *US – Anti-Dumping and Countervailing Duties (China)* has clarified how such a pass-through test can be conducted where the input was produced by a State-owned company, then sold to an unrelated trading company and subsequently resold to the producer of the product subject to investigation. The US took the position that a pass-through

[11] WT/DS257/AB/R of 19 January 2004, *United States – Final Countervailing Duty Determination with Respect to Certain Softwood Lumber from Canada*, para 160 *et seq*.

[12] WT/DS257/RW of 1 August 2005, *United States – Final Countervailing Duty Determination with Respect to Certain Softwood Lumber from Canada* (Article 21.5), paras 4.58–4.82, 4.88.

test was not necessary in the case of sales via a trading company. The USDOC simply compared the prices of inputs manufactured by State-owned enterprises and subsequently sold via a trading company to the producer of the good subject to investigation with the benchmark price, in the same way in fact as they compared the price a State-owned input supplier charged directly to the producer of the good in question. The US justified this approach by asserting that their methodology could never lead to inflated subsidy margins. The Panel had a more nuanced view on this. It held that no pass-through would be required in a situation where the producer of an investigated product nominally purchases from a trading company, but the trading company in turn places a specific order for that purchase with the producer of the input, and the merchandise is then shipped to the producer of the investigated product on the basis of that particular order. This is because in such a configuration, there is no possibility of an inflated calculation of the benefit obtained by the producer of the product concerned. The Panel went on to say that this is one particular role that a trading company might play, but that trading companies in fact operate in a range of different ways. For example, some trading companies act as distributors or stockists, taking ownership and physical possession of goods and selling out of their own inventories. Others might enter into contracts to purchase in bulk (even if they never take physical possession), and then make individual sales from their bulk purchases. Price fluctuations in the market between the time a trading company purchased inputs and the time it sold them to a producer of an investigated product would inevitably give rise to situations where the benchmark price applicable to the trading company's purchase of the inputs was different from the benchmark price applicable to the re-sale of those inputs to the producer of the investigated product.[13]

In *Japan – DRAMs (Korea)*, Korea claimed that Japan should have carried out a pass-through analysis because of the changes in the ownership of Hynix that resulted from the October 2001 and December 2002 restructurings. These restructurings included debt-to-equity swaps. The Panel did not agree. It pointed out that the jurisprudence to pass-through was in relation to pre-privatization subsidies. In the case at hand, the change in ownership took place as a result of the restructurings, and the countervailable subsidies at issue were also given in the context of these restructurings. The Panel also saw no reason to

[13] WT/DS379/R of 22 October 2010, *US – Definitive Anti-Dumping and Countervailing Duties on Certain Products from China*, paras 12.39–12.58.

examine the need for an extension of the pass-through jurisprudence. The principle underlying that jurisprudence is a presumption against pass-through when a market price is paid for the privatized entity. However, in the case at hand that question would already have been examined in the context of the benefit analysis. Had the restructuring been on market terms, Hynix would already not have received a benefit.[14]

Mexico – Olive Oil clarified that Article 1.1 and the transparency requirement in the last part of the first sentence of Article 14 do not contain any obligation to carry out a pass-through analysis.[15]

The pass-through analysis can also have a specificity dimension. If the subsidized input is widely available (e.g. natural gas), the downstream manufacturers using such natural gas will most likely not constitute 'certain enterprises' as defined by Article 2.[16]

See also *supra* the commentary to Article 1, pp. 149–150 with regard to export financing provided to the purchaser of the good and the pass-through to the seller of the merchandise.

Last but not least it should be noted that the Appellate Body in *US – Upland Cotton* held that a pass-through analysis was not critical for an assessment of significant price suppression under Article 6.3(c), i.e. a serious prejudice case, because no precise quantification of the subsidies is required. However, it added that if the challenged payments do not subsidize the product at issue in the serious prejudice claim, this may undermine the conclusion that the effect of the subsidy is significant price suppression of that product in the relevant market.[17] See also *supra* the commentary to Article 5, p. 268–269 and the commentary to Article 6, pp. 344–346.

[14] WT/DS336/R of 13 July 2007, *Japan – Countervailing Duties on Dynamic Random Access Memories from Korea*, paras 7.447–7.458. This aspect was not appealed.

[15] WT/DS341/R of 4 September 2008, *Mexico – Definitive Countervailing Measures on Olive Oil from the European Communities*, paras 7.145–7.169.

[16] WT/DS414/R of 15 June 2012, *China – Countervailing and Anti-Dumping Duties on Grain-Oriented Flat-Rolled Electrical Steel from the US*, para 7.135. For details see *infra* the commentary to Article 11, pp 382–386.

[17] WT/DS267/AB/R of 3 March 2005, *United States – Subsidies on Upland Cotton*, para 472. See also WT/DS353/R of 31 March 2011, *United States – Measures Affecting Trade in Large Civil Aircraft (Second Complaint)*, paras 7.284–7.287; WT/DS316/AB/R of 18 May 2011, *EC and certain Member States – Measures Affecting Trade in Large Civil Aircraft*, paras 773–776.

Countervailing Measures Can Only Be Imposed after an Investigation Has Been Initiated and Conducted in Accordance with the Provisions of the ASCM and the Agreement on Agriculture

The second sentence of Article 10 makes it clear that countervailing duties can only be imposed if all the procedural requirements set out in Part V of the ASCM have been met. Footnote 37 is attached to this sentence and sheds some light on the term 'initiated'. 'Initiated' means procedural action by which a Member formally commences an investigation as provided in Article 11. Footnote 37 corresponds to Footnote 1 of the WTO Anti-Dumping Agreement. Initiation constitutes the beginning of the 18-month period set in Article 11.11.

In *Mexico – Olive Oil*, the parties disagreed as to what act taken by Mexico constituted the initiation of the investigation. The Panel held this is based on the internal law of the importing Member. Consequently, it examined what constituted the procedural act by which an investigation is formally commenced in the Mexican system.[18]

[18] WT/DS341/R of 4 September 2008, *Mexico – Definitive Countervailing Measures on Olive Oil from the European Communities*, paras 7.24–7.28. See also *infra* the commentary to Article 13, pp. 425–426.

Article 11

Initiation and Subsequent Investigation

Introduction

Article 11 deals primarily with the initiation of a countervailing duty investigation but addresses also some issues relating to the subsequent investigation. Article 5 is the corresponding provision in the WTO Anti-Dumping Agreement.

The initiation of an investigation can already have a chilling effect on the imports which are made subject to such investigation. The purpose of the provisions on initiation in Article 11 is to avoid unjustified disruptions in international trade on the basis of allegations and claims that are manifestly incorrect.[1]

Article 11.1 sets out the principle that an investigation normally can only be initiated following the receipt of a properly documented application of the domestic industry in the importing country. Only in 'special circumstances' (see paragraph 6) can the investigating authority initiate *ex officio*. The evidentiary standards in the case of an *ex officio* initiation are the same as in the case of an investigation following an application by the domestic industry.

Paragraphs 1 to 5, 7 and 9 of Article 11 deal with the application by the domestic industry to initiate a countervailing duty investigation and the review of such application by the investigating authority. Paragraph 1 clarifies that the initiation can only be based upon a properly substantiated application by or on behalf of the domestic industry, except in the circumstances provided for in paragraph 6 (*ex officio* initiation). Paragraph 2 gives guidance as to what may constitute sufficient evidence for the purposes of an application. Paragraph 3 directs the authorities to review the accuracy and adequacy of the evidence provided in the application to determine whether the evidence is sufficient to justify the initiation of an

[1] WT/DS213/R of 3 July 2002, *United States – Countervailing Duties on Certain Corrosion-Resistant Carbon Steel Flat Products from Germany*, paras 8.35–8.37.

investigation. Paragraph 4 requires that the domestic industry has standing to lodge an application, i.e. that the application is supported by a sufficient number of domestic producers. Paragraph 6 applies the sufficient evidence standard in paragraph 2 to any self-initiation by an investigating authority. Paragraph 9 requires an authority to reject an application that does not contain sufficient evidence of subsidization and consequent injury.

Paragraphs 7 to 11 deal essentially with the subsequent investigation. Paragraph 7 requires that the evidence of subsidization and injury be considered simultaneously. Paragraph 9 sets out *de minimis* thresholds in terms of market share and level of subsidization. It also stipulates that applications shall be rejected and an investigation shall be terminated promptly if these *de minimis* levels are not met or if there is no injurious subsidization. Paragraph 10 clarifies that a countervailing duty investigation shall not hinder customs procedures and paragraph 11 sets a maximum duration of 18 months for such investigation. Last but not least, paragraph 8 addresses the consequences if the subject merchandise is not shipped directly from the subsidizing country of origin but via an intermediate country. It clarifies that the provisions of the ASCM shall be fully applicable and the transaction shall be regarded as having taken place between the country of origin and the importing Member.

The Appellate Body has explicitly ruled that Articles 11.6 and 11.9 do not apply to sunset reviews.[2]

The investigation is normally launched by the publication of a notice of initiation. The minimum content of such notice is defined in Article 22.2.

Application for the Initiation of a Countervailing Duty Investigation (Paragraphs 1 to 5 as well as Paragraphs 7 and 9 of Article 11)

Content of the Application (Article 11.2)

Article 11.2 sets out in detail the evidentiary standards which a written application by the domestic industry of the importing country must meet. Subparagraphs (i) to (iv) are essentially self-explanatory.

The wording of Article 11.2 of the ASCM contains some minor differences as compared to that of Article 5.2 of the WTO Anti-Dumping Agreement. These differences go beyond the different scopes of the two agreements. Article 11.2 of the ASCM requires 'sufficient evidence' of

[2] See *infra* the commentary to Article 21, pp. 539–543.

injurious subsidization while Article 5.2 of the WTO Anti-Dumping Agreement does not reproduce the adjective 'sufficient'.[3] However, both Article 5.3 and Article 11.3 task the investigating authority to determine 'whether the evidence is *sufficient* to justify the initiation of an investigation' (emphasis added). The terms 'evidence' and 'sufficient' have been discussed by the Panel in *China – GOES*.[4]

The chapeau of Article 11.2 highlights two potentially conflicting principles concerning the need to substantiate allegations in the application. On the one hand, it points out that '[s]imple assertion, unsubstantiated by relevant evidence, cannot be considered to meet the requirements by this paragraph'. On the other hand, it accepts that '[t]he application shall contain such information as is reasonably available to the applicant'. The practical implications of this are addressed in the next section.

Non-confidential Summary of the Application. In case the application contains confidential information, a non-confidential summary has to be provided or, if exceptionally the information is not susceptible to summary, the reasons have to be provided why summarization is not possible (see Article 12.4.1).[5]

Review of the Application by the Investigating Authority (Article 11.3)

Article 11.3 provides that the investigating authority shall review the accuracy and adequacy of the evidence provided in the application to determine whether the evidence is sufficient to initiate an investigation.

In relation to the analogous provision of the WTO Anti-Dumping Agreement, *US – Softwood Lumber V* has concluded that the quantity and quality of the evidence required to meet the threshold of sufficiency of the evidence is of a different standard for purposes of initiation of an investigation compared to that required for a preliminary or final determination.[6] At the stage of initiation, an investigating authority is not required to reach definitive conclusions regarding the existence of a subsidy, injury or a causal link between the two. Rather, an investigation is a process

[3] See also *Bourgeois and Wagner* in *Wolfrum/Stoll/Koebele* (2008), para 7 to Article 11.

[4] WT/DS414/R of 15 June 2012, *China – Countervailing and Anti-Dumping Duties on Grain-Oriented Flat-Rolled Electrical Steel from the US*, para 7.54.

[5] WT/DS414/R of 15 June 2012, *China – Countervailing and Anti-Dumping Duties on Grain-Oriented Flat-Rolled Electrical Steel from the US*, para 7.188.

[6] WT/DS264/R of 13 April 2004, *United States – Final Dumping Determination on Softwood Lumber from Canada*, para 7.84; WT/DS437/R of 14 July 2014, *United States – Countervailing Duty Measures on Certain Products from China*, para 7.151.

where certainty on the existence of all elements necessary in order to adopt a measure is reached gradually, as the investigation moves forward.[7] Therefore, the amount and quality of the evidence required at the time of initiation is less than that to reach a final determination.[8] However, for the purposes of Article 11.3, adequate evidence, tending to prove or indicating the existence of subsidization, injury and a causal link is required. In other words, in relation to subsidization, the evidence should provide an indication that a subsidy actually exists. For the Panel in *China – GOES*, it was clear from Article 11.2, that a simple assertion, unsubstantiated by relevant evidence, is not sufficient to justify the initiation, even if such evidence is not reasonably available by the applicant requesting the initiation.[9] The implications of this latter finding will have to be considered carefully, as a balance has to be struck between the interests of the domestic industry to secure the initiation of the case and the interest of potential respondents to avoid a frivolous investigation. A 'simple assertion' is clearly insufficient. However, countries that operate an intransparent system of subsidization and/or do not comply with their notification requirements pursuant to Article 25 should not be allowed to escape from legitimate countervailing duty investigations.

More generally, the obligation in Article 11.3 must be read together with Article 11.2. If an investigating authority were to initiate a case without sufficient evidence before it, this would be inconsistent with Article 11.3. Therefore, the Panel in *China – GOES* reached conclusions concerning the initiation of an investigation only in relation to Article 11.3, but by reference to the requirements for sufficient evidence set forth in Article 11.2. However, it did not consider it necessary to reach separate conclusions under Article 11.2.[10]

Concerning the sufficiency of evidence of subsidization at initiation, the Panel in *China – GOES* clarified this issue considerably. Pursuant to

[7] WT/DS414/R of 15 June 2012, *China – Countervailing and Anti-Dumping Duties on Grain-Oriented Flat-Rolled Electrical Steel from the US*, para 7.54; WT/DS156/R of 24 October 2000, *Guatemala – Definitive Anti-Dumping Measures on Grey Portland Cement from Mexico*, para 8.35.

[8] WT/DS414/R of 15 June 2012, *China – Countervailing and Anti-Dumping Duties on Grain-Oriented Flat-Rolled Electrical Steel from the US*, para 7.55.

[9] WT/DS414/R of 15 June 2012, *China – Countervailing and Anti-Dumping Duties on Grain-Oriented Flat-Rolled Electrical Steel from the US*, paras 7.55 and 7.56.

[10] WT/DS414/R of 15 June 2012, *China – Countervailing and Anti-Dumping Duties on Grain-Oriented Flat-Rolled Electrical Steel from the US*, paras 7.49 and 7.50; WT/DS437/R of 14 July 2014, *United States – Countervailing Duty Measures on Certain Products from China*, paras 7.143–7.145.

Article 1.1, a subsidy exists if there is (a) a financial contribution or any form of income or price support, (b) which confers a benefit. Therefore, evidence of the existence of a subsidy requires evidence of these two elements. The parties to the dispute disagreed what level of evidence was required with regard to specificity. China argued that the lack of any direct reference to specificity under Article 11.2 suggested a different and lower evidentiary standard in relation to specificity as compared to the aforementioned other two elements of a subsidy, i.e. financial contribution and benefit. The Panel disagreed. The reference in Article 11.2 to evidence regarding the nature of a subsidy includes evidence regarding whether the subsidy is specific. According to the Panel, any other interpretation could lead to a situation where the investigating authority accepts applications that could never result in the imposition of a duty in cases where it was known already at the initiation stage that the subsidy was broadly available. Rather, the same standard of sufficient evidence applies regardless of whether the evidence relates to the existence of a financial contribution, benefit or specificity.[11] The fact that an exporting producer is a user of a government programme is not in itself sufficient evidence that the subsidy is specific.[12]

China – GOES also addressed the issue of *de facto* specificity of a programme that covered a wide range of applications. The State of Pennsylvania operated an Economic Stimulus Plan that encouraged a broad range of different initiatives. In these circumstances it was not sufficient that the application simply contained evidence that the allegedly subsidized foreign manufacturers were eligible for a programme because they are located in the region covered (federal state of Pennsylvania) and were prominent manufacturers in that region. The complaint should have provided more information to demonstrate specificity.[13]

Moreover, the evidence must indicate the existence of a present subsidy. In case of non-recurring or expired subsidies, present subsidization

[11] WT/DS414/R of 15 June 2012, *China – Countervailing and Anti-Dumping Duties on Grain-Oriented Flat-Rolled Electrical Steel from the US*, paras 7.58–7.66. China also claimed that the information on specificity was not necessary because it is typically not reasonably available to an applicant. The Panel rejected this argument in para 7.67. See also para 7.130. As to the necessary evidence on a financial contribution see para 7.97.

[12] WT/DS414/R of 15 June 2012, *China – Countervailing and Anti-Dumping Duties on Grain-Oriented Flat-Rolled Electrical Steel from the US*, paras 7.63–7.68.

[13] WT/DS414/R of 15 June 2012, *China – Countervailing and Anti-Dumping Duties on Grain-Oriented Flat-Rolled Electrical Steel from the US*, paras 7.105–7.114. The Panel also discussed the issue of whether the applicants could have claimed that the Stimulus Plan consisted of individual programmes, see in particular paras 7.111 and 7.112.

requires the benefit of the subsidy to be allocated to the period of investigation and to the period of imposition of countervailing duties. The application has to contain evidence to this effect.[14]

More generally, as an investigating authority has to assess the adequacy and accuracy of information submitted in a complaint according to Article 11.3, such authority has also to weigh the evidence that was not in the application but that was relevant to the decision to initiate.[15] Put differently, Article 11.2 defines the kind of evidence that is required for an initiation while Article 11.3 sets out the standard by which the investigating authority has to review this evidence.[16]

In *China – GOES*, the US also challenged the initiation of the investigation concerning a particular programme. The application did not contain any evidence on the existence of a benefit. Moreover, the US also submitted in the pre-initiation consultations a list of companies that benefited from the programme in question. None of the companies listed was a producer of the subject product or indeed part of the steel industry. Therefore, the Panel held that when evidence is not in the application but relevant to the decision to initiate and it has been submitted to an investigating authority, for instance by an exporting Member, an unbiased and objective investigating authority should weigh this evidence in its consideration of whether initiation is justified.[17] The evidence on benefit includes also appropriate evidence on a market benchmark.[18]

If the initiation concerns a subsidy to the upstream industry, there should also be evidence that the subsidy passed through to the producers of the subject product and that any pass-through that occurs is specific to the industry of the subject product. In the case in question, the US government gave a subsidy to producers of natural gas. According to the Panel, there was no reason to assume that the benefit did not pass through to all purchasers of natural gas, rather than to the steel industry

[14] WT/DS414/R of 15 June 2012, *China – Countervailing and Anti-Dumping Duties on Grain-Oriented Flat-Rolled Electrical Steel from the US*, paras 7.69–7.74. See also paras 7.75–7.78 and 7.102–7.103 as well as infra the commentary to Article 19, pp. 526–531.

[15] WT/DS414/R of 15 June 2012, *China – Countervailing and Anti-Dumping Duties on Grain-Oriented Flat-Rolled Electrical Steel from the US*, para 7.52.

[16] *Prusa/Vermulst* (2014) p. 233.

[17] WT/DS414/R of 15 June 2012, *China – Countervailing and Anti-Dumping Duties on Grain-Oriented Flat-Rolled Electrical Steel from the US*, paras 7.115–7.119.

[18] WT/DS414/R of 15 June 2012, *China – Countervailing and Anti-Dumping Duties on Grain-Oriented Flat-Rolled Electrical Steel from the US*, paras 7.115–7.119.

specifically. While the gas industry operated differentiated gas prices, there was no basis to conclude that any price differentiation indicated that pass-through was specific to the steel industry. Rather, the price differentiation was due to market forces.[19]

US – Countervailing Measures (China) held that an initiation of a countervailing duty investigation in respect of certain export restraints was inconsistent with Article 11.3. The Panel based its finding on the particular facts of the case. It did not exclude the possibility that initiation of a countervailing duty investigation with respect to measures involving export restraints might be justified under other factual scenarios.[20]

Guatemala – Cement II has held that in relation to the initiation of an anti-dumping investigation, that if essential information is not reasonably available to the complainant, the investigating authority itself has to provide such missing information.[21] It would appear that this principle is also relevant with regard to Article 11.3.

Note finally that the ASCM does not require an investigating authority to make any findings or explain its understanding of a financial contribution or public body when initiating an investigation. This is in contrast with the requirements set out in Article 22.3 when making a preliminary or definitive determination.[22]

Standard of Review by a Panel. The standard of review by a panel of the obligations under Article 11.3 is whether an unbiased and objective investigating authority would have found that the application contained sufficient information to justify initiation of an investigation. The investigating authority's conclusions on the sufficiency of information must be reasonable in the light of this test.[23]

[19] WT/DS414/R of 15 June 2012, *China – Countervailing and Anti-Dumping Duties on Grain-Oriented Flat-Rolled Electrical Steel from the US*, para 7.135.

[20] WT/DS437/R 14 July 2014, *United States – Countervailing Duty Measures on Certain Products from China*, paras 7.404–7.406. This part of the ruling was not appealed. Whether export restraints can be classified as entrustment or direction, see *supra* the commentary to Article 1, pp. 111–112.

[21] WT/DS156/R of 24 October 2000, *Guatemala – Definitive Anti-Dumping Measures on Grey Portland Cement from Mexico*, para 8.62.

[22] WT/DS437/R of 14 July 2014, *United States – Countervailing Duty Measures on Certain Products from China*, para 7.154.

[23] WT/DS414/R of 15 June 2012, *China – Countervailing and Anti-Dumping Duties on Grain-Oriented Flat-Rolled Electrical Steel from the US*, para 7.51; WT/DS264/R of 13 April 2004, *United States – Final Dumping Determination on Softwood Lumber from Canada*, para 7.78; WT/DS156/R of 24 October 2000, *Guatemala – Definitive Anti-Dumping Measures on Grey Portland Cement from Mexico*, para 8.35.

Standing of the Complainant (Article 11.4)

Article 11.4 contains the so-called standing test. It defines the circumstances in which the domestic industry of the importing WTO Member has standing to lodge an application for the initiation of a countervailing duty investigation. The notion of 'domestic industry' is defined in Article 16.

Two footnotes are attached to Article 11.4. Footnote 38 refers to the use of statistically valid sampling techniques in case of applications by fragmented industries. Footnote 39 acknowledges that some WTO Members allow employees of domestic producers of the like product to make or support an application for the initiation of a countervailing duty investigation. Article 11.4 is identical with Article 5.4 of the WTO Anti-Dumping Agreement.

This somewhat long-winded provision essentially stipulates the following: producers in the importing country will often disagree amongst themselves whether they should launch a countervailing duty investigation, or many of them may have no opinion on such subject. Article 11.4 addresses this issue by setting the thresholds for the necessary support by domestic producers. If the domestic producers of the like product in favour of initiation represent more than 50 per cent of the output of such product, they have *ipso jure* standing. If they represent less than 25 per cent, they will have no standing. If they represent between 25 per cent and 50 per cent of the domestic output, the collective output represented by those in favour of the investigation and the collective output represented by those against the initiation will be determined. In this scenario, domestic producers in favour of the case will only have standing if they represent a larger output than those that are against initiation.

Article 11.4 does not contain a requirement that an investigating authority examine the motives of domestic producers that support an investigation. This provision requires an examination of the degree of support, but not the nature of the support. In other words, it is the 'quantity', rather than the 'quality' of support that is at issue.[24]

Article 11.4 does not permit an investigating authority to presume the existence of the necessary industry support for an application. *Mexico – Olive Oil* is an illustrative example as to an investigating authority's efforts

[24] WT/DS217/AB/R and WT/DS234/AB/R of 16 January 2003, *United States – Continued Dumping and Subsidy Offset Act of 2000*, paras 283 and 291. See also the discussion in paras 292–294 about the Byrd Amendment being an incentive for the US industry to file applications for the initiation of CVD investigations and what legal consequences this might have.

to determine whether the application has been lodged by or on behalf of the domestic industry, i.e. whether the complainant had standing. The question at issue was whether or not there existed producers other than the complainants?[25] This is obviously relevant for the above-mentioned 25 percent threshold but also for the determination whether the companies supporting the complaint represent a higher share of national production than producers opposing such complaint. Note also that *Mexico – Olive Oil* has held that neither Article 11.4, nor any other provision in the ASCM, prohibits an investigating authority from basing its standing determination solely on evidence provided by the applicant. However, the Panel also recalled in this respect that this does not exonerate an investigating authority from the obligations set out in the second sentence of Article 11.2 ('[s]imple assertion, unsubstantiated by relevant evidence, cannot be considered sufficient') and in Article 11.3 ('[t]he authorities shall review the accuracy and adequacy of the evidence provided').[26] In this regard, the Panel stated that the evidentiary standard for standing at the initiation stage is no higher than the standard applicable to subsidization, injury and causation. Whether the investigating authority needs to seek information beyond that contained in the complaint is a case-by-case decision.[27]

No Publicizing of the Existence of a Complaint (Article 11.5)

According to Article 11.5, the authorities shall avoid, unless a decision has been made to initiate an investigation, any publicizing of the application for the initiation of an investigation.[28] However, Article 13.1 requires that consultations are offered to the exporting country if an application has been accepted under Article 11.

Ex officio Initiation of a Countervailing Duty Investigation (Article 11.6)

An investigating authority cannot self-initiate a countervailing duty investigation unless the requirement of sufficient evidence of subsidization,

[25] WT/DS341/R of 4 September 2008, *Mexico – Definitive Countervailing Measures on Olive Oil from the European Communities*, paras 7.221–7.248.

[26] WT/DS341/R of 4 September 2008, *Mexico – Definitive Countervailing Measures on Olive Oil from the European Communities*, para 7.225.

[27] WT/DS341/R of 4 September 2008, *Mexico – Definitive Countervailing Measures on Olive Oil from the European Communities*, paras 7.227–7.228.

[28] See also *Bourgeois and Wagner* in *Wolfrum/Stoll/Koebele* (2008), para 12 to Article 11.

injury and causality is met.[29] Moreover, self-initiation is only possible in special circumstances although the ASCM does not define what such circumstances could be.

De minimis Thresholds; Rejection of Application or Termination of an Investigation if These Thresholds Are Not Met or if There Is No Injurious Subsidization (Article 11.9)

If the subsidization is *de minimis* or if the volume of subsidized imports or the injury is negligible, there shall be immediate termination.

According to Article 11.9, subsidization is *de minimis* if it is less than 1 per cent *ad valorem*. Higher thresholds apply for exporters in developing countries. Under Article 27.11, for least developed countries in Annex VII and other developing countries which eliminated export subsidies prior to the eight-year period provided for in Article 27.2(b), the *de minimis* level of subsidization was 3 per cent. However, this 3 per cent threshold expired at the end of 2002. For other developing countries the threshold has always been 2 per cent (see Article 27.10(a)) and now, after the expiry of the eight-year period, it would seem that all developing countries are subject to this 2 per cent threshold.

The ASCM defines negligible imports only for developing countries. According to Article 27.10(b) the negligible volume is set at 4 per cent of the total imports of the like product in the importing Member. If imports originate from several developing country they are negligible if each of them represents less than 4 per cent and if these imports collectively represent less than 9 per cent of all imports of the like product.

US – Carbon Steel examined the rationale underlying the *de minimis* margin of subsidization of 1 per cent. The Panel argued that the *de minimis* standard in Article 11.9 represented a threshold below which subsidization was always non-injurious. Consequently, it applied this standard also to sunset reviews. It relied on a note that was prepared in 1987 by the GATT Secretariat for the Uruguay Round negotiations. The note recognized two theoretical justifications for a *de minimis* standard: (1) no action should be taken where the effect of the subsidy on the industry in the importing country is not such as to cause material injury and (2) '*de minimis non curat lex*' (the law does not take notice of minimal matters). The Appellate Body did not agree. It criticized that the Panel did not

[29] See also WT/DS213/R of 3 July 2002, *United States – Countervailing Duties on Certain Corrosion-Resistant Carbon Steel Flat Products from Germany*, para 8.34.

explain why it thought that it was appropriate to rely on the aforementioned note. For the Appellate Body, there was nothing in Article 11.9 to suggest that its *de minimis* standard was intended to create a special category of non-injurious subsidization, or that it reflects a concept that subsidization at less than the *de minimis* threshold can never cause injury. Article 11.9 does no more than lay down an agreed rule that if *de minimis* subsidization is found in an initial investigation, the investigating authority is obliged to terminate this investigation without imposing a countervailing duty.[30]

Exporters for which no subsidization or a *de minimis* subsidy has been found in an investigation initiated pursuant to Article 11, cannot be made subject to subsequent changed circumstances and sunset reviews pursuant to Article 21.[31]

Maximum Duration of an Investigation (Article 11.11)

Article 11.11 stipulates that investigations shall, except in special circumstances, be concluded within one year and in no case more than 18 months after their initiation. In *Mexico – Olive Oil*, Mexico's investigation lasted 24 months. Mexico argued that the purpose of Article 11.11 is to protect interested parties from any unjustified delay or inaction but that in the case in question, the delays were caused by requests for extension of deadlines and by requests that the investigating authority consider additional information at late stages of the investigation. The Panel did not accept these arguments as Article 11.11 was unequivocal – it does not permit any prolongation beyond the 18-month period under any circumstances.[32]

[30] WT/DS213/AB/R of 28 November 2002 – *United States – Countervailing Duties on Certain Corrosion-Resistant Carbon Steel Flat Products from Germany*, paras 75–84. With regard to the implications of applying *de minimis* standards to sunset reviews see *infra* the commentary to Article 21, pp. 540–543.

[31] WT/DS295/AB/R of 29 November 2005, *Mexico – Definitive Anti-Dumping Measures on Beef and Rice / Complaint with Respect to Rice*, paras 300–307. The preceding Panel made it also clear that this does not apply to results of reviews which resulted in a *de minimis* finding, see WT/DS295/R of 6 June 2005, *Mexico – Definitive Anti-Dumping Measures on Beef and Rice / Complaint with Respect to Rice*, para 7.251.

[32] WT/DS341/R of 4 September 2008, *Mexico – Definitive Countervailing Measures on Olive Oil from the European Communities*, paras 7.120–7.123.

Article 12

Evidence

Introduction

Article 12 is one of the longest provisions of the ASCM. Article 12 sets out evidentiary rules that apply throughout the course of a countervailing duty investigation. It provides also for due process rights that are enjoyed by interested parties during such investigation.[1]

However, *Mexico – Olive Oil* noted that Article 12 (and some other provisions of the ASCM) leaves considerable discretion to Members to define their own procedures. The Panel believed that, in general, unless a specific procedure is set forth in the ASCM, the precise procedures for how investigating authorities will implement those obligations is left to the Members to decide.[2]

Chapeau of Article 12.1 as an Overarching Provision

The chapeau of Article 12.1 establishes two overarching requirements: (i) that the investigating authority must give notice to interested parties of the information required of them and (ii) that interested parties must be given ample opportunity to present in writing all evidence which they consider relevant. The Panel in *US – Anti-Dumping and Countervailing Duties (China)* acknowledged that neither of these requirements is circumscribed in any way, in terms of form or time period.[3]

The Appellate Body noted in relation to the chapeau of Article 6.1 of the WTO Anti-Dumping Agreement, i.e. the parallel provision to the chapeau of Article 12.1 ASCM, that the obligation deriving from that

1 WT/DS295/AB/R of 29 November 2005, *Mexico – Definitive Anti-Dumping Measures on Beef and Rice / Complaint with Respect to Rice*, para 292.

2 WT/DS341/R of 4 September 2008, *Mexico – Definitive Countervailing Measures on Olive Oil from the European Communities*, footnote 63 attached to para 7.26.

3 WT/DS379/R of 22 October 2010, *US – Definitive Anti-Dumping and Countervailing Duties on Certain Products from China*, para 15.23.

provision is not satisfied where the investigating authority did not take into account information submitted by an interested party. The Appellate Body made this statement when reviewing Mexican legislation that stipulated that the highest dumping or subsidy margin based on facts available should be used if, *inter alia*, an exporting producer failed to provide information requested in a proper and timely fashion.[4] This has implications for the use of facts available. If a party only submitted part of the information requested, this cannot be rejected categorically.

Questionnaires (Article 12.1.1)

Deadlines for Replying to Questionnaires

The first sentence of Article 12.1.1 stipulates that exporters, foreign producers or interested Members receiving questionnaires shall be given at least 30 days to reply. Footnote 40, which is attached to this sentence, clarifies how the 30 days are calculated. Notably, the period shall be counted from the date of receipt of the questionnaire. The date of receipt is deemed to take place one week after the investigating authority has sent the questionnaire. Given modern means of communication (fax, e-mail etc.), which provide for quasi-instantaneous transmission, exporters, foreign producers and interested Members have in reality 37 days to respond to the questionnaire, if the domestic law does not stipulate otherwise.

In *Mexico – Beef and Rice*, Mexico argued that the 30-day period in Article 12.1.1 applied only to exporters and foreign producers to whom the investigating authority sends a questionnaire at the outset of the investigation, i.e. the exporters and foreign producers that are known to the investigating authority at that point in time. According to Mexico, if an investigating authority were to provide 30 days to every respondent that makes itself known to the agency in the course of the investigation, investigations could not be completed within the time limit set in Article 11.11. The Appellate Body did not agree. It held that the period of at least 30 days to reply to questionnaires must be extended to all exporters and foreign producers, whether known to the investigating authority at the

[4] See WT/DS295/AB/R of 29 November 2005, *Mexico – Definitive Anti-Dumping Measures on Beef and Rice / Complaint with Respect to Rice*, footnote 350 to para 292, that refers to WT/DS268/AB/R of 29 November 2004, *United States – Sunset Reviews of Anti-Dumping Measures on Oil Country Tubular Goods from Argentina*, para 246. The Mexican law at issue is described in more detail *infra* this chapter pp. 408–411.

outset of the investigation or at some point thereafter. It pointed out that the ASCM contemplates, in a typical case, that exporters and foreign producers not identified in the petition will make themselves known to the investigating authority in the earlier stages of the proceeding – for example shortly after publication of the notice of initiation (see Article 22.2) – rather than at some later stage. But it also recognized that it is theoretically possible that the notification of interest by an exporter or producer is at such a late stage in the proceeding that an investigating authority, seeking to comply with the time limits provided for in Article 11.11, could not reasonably take into account information submitted by that respondent. The Appellate Body also recognized that the due process rights in Article 11 cannot extend indefinitely but, instead, are limited by the investigating authority's need to control the conduct of its inquiry and to carry out the multiple steps required to reach a timely completion of the proceeding. Note that Mexico's law, which was found inconsistent with Article 12.1.1, only provided for 28 days to reply to a questionnaire in respect of those exporters and foreign producers that did not get a questionnaire at the outset of the investigation. The Appellate Body also dismissed Mexico's argument that its investigating authority could grant extensions to meet the 30-day requirement because a party should not be forced to use the possibility of requesting extensions to obtain the 30-day period it is entitled to.[5]

Definition of Questionnaire

The Panel in *US – Anti-Dumping and Countervailing Duties (China)* had to decide as to what information request constituted a questionnaire pursuant to Article 12.1.1. The US claimed that only the initial questionnaire issued at the beginning of the investigation qualifies as a questionnaire in the sense of Article 12.1.1. In contrast, China argued that a supplemental questionnaire containing follow-up inquiries to questions posed in a prior questionnaire and any new allegation questionnaire in respect of each new subsidy allegation filed during the course of the investigation should also be regarded as a questionnaire falling under Article 12.1.1. If China's point of view had been accepted, it would have meant that addressees of each supplemental questionnaire or new allegation questionnaire would have had 30 days to respond. The Panel did not agree with China. It

[5] WT/DS295/AB/R of 29 November 2005, *Mexico – Definitive Anti-Dumping Measures on Beef and Rice / Complaint with Respect to Rice*, paras 276–283.

held that only the questionnaire issued at the initiation of the investigation falls under Article 12.1. It arrived at this view in particular on the basis of the chapeau of Article 12.1, footnote 40 and paragraphs 6 and 7 of Annex VI as well as interpretations by Panels of the corresponding provisions in the WTO Anti-Dumping Agreement. The Panel noted in relation to new allegation questionnaires that these did not include the full range of questions contained in the initial comprehensive questionnaire, i.e. their scope was considerably more limited than the initial questionnaire.[6]

Duty to Provide the Application Made by the Domestic Industry to Exporters and the Exporting Member Concerned (Article 12.1.3)

Article 12.1.3 including its footnote 41 is essentially self-explanatory. It would appear that no WTO jurisprudence exists in relation to this provision.

Non-confidential File (Articles 12.1.2 and 12.3)

It would seem that Article 12.1.2 has to be read together with Article 12.3 which also deals with the non-confidential file while the rules on confidentiality are set out under Article 12.4.

Article 12.1.2 obliges an investigating authority to make promptly available to other interested parties and Members any evidence presented in writing by one interested party or Member. This obligation is subject to the requirement to protect confidential information. The rules on the protection of confidentiality (including the obligation to present non-confidential summaries or, if the information is not susceptible to summary, a statement of reasons why such summarization is not possible) are explained *infra* this chapter, pp. 395–402.

According to Article 12.3, the authorities shall, whenever practicable, provide timely opportunities for all interested Members and interested parties to see all information that is relevant to the presentation of their cases, that is not confidential, and that is used by the authorities in a countervailing duty investigation, and to prepare presentations on the basis of this information.

In practice, this means that submissions by parties (or their non-confidential summaries) are processed into the so-called non-confidential

[6] WT/DS379/R of 22 October 2010, *US – Definitive Anti-Dumping and Countervailing Duties on Certain Products from China*, paras 15.16–15.49.

file which can then be consulted by all other interested parties and Members. The non-confidential file is an important vehicle in order to ensure transparency in countervailing duty investigations.

Article 12.3 has a somewhat different scope than Article 12.1.2 although there seems to be overlaps between the two provisions. In terms of information covered by the two provisions, Article 12.1.2 refers to 'evidence presented in writing by one interested Member or interested party' while Article 12.3 covers 'all information that is relevant to the presentation of [a party's] case … and that is used by the authorities in a countervailing duty investigation'. In terms of time, Article 12.1.2 requires that the evidence shall be made available 'promptly' while Article 12.3 requests that '[t]he authorities shall whenever practicable provide timely opportunities … to see all the information'.

There is an increasing tendency to make the non-confidential file available online. Some WTO Members do not limit access to interested parties and Members but allow also the interested public such access.

Hearings, Treatment of Information Received during Such Hearings, Evidence on the Record (Article 12.2)

Interested Members and interested parties shall have the right, upon justification, to present information orally. Contrary to Article 6.2 of the WTO Anti-Dumping Agreement, the ASCM does not contain any rules concerning 'confrontation hearings' with interested parties having adverse interests.

Article 12.2 prescribes to reproduce in writing any information that has been submitted orally. The written submissions shall be put in the record established pursuant to Article 12.3 so that other interested parties have the possibility to comment. Only information confirmed in writing and put into the record open for inspection by other parties can be used by the investigating authority in its decisions.[7]

Confidentiality (Article 12.4)

Principles

The chapeau of Article 12.4 stipulates that the investigating authority has to respect the confidentiality of such information if 'good cause' is shown.

[7] WT/DS296/AB/R of 27 June 2005, *United States – Countervailing Duty Investigation on Dynamic Random Access Memory Semiconductors (DRAMs) from Korea*, para 138.

Other parts of the ASCM also recall the need to respect confidentiality (e.g. Articles 12.1.2, 12.3, 22.4). In countervailing duty investigations, an investigating authority has to typically process an important amount of confidential information, e.g. tax declarations of exporters, turnover figures of cooperating companies, amounts and terms of loans taken out by companies, production figures etc. Such information is typically specific to the company furnishing such information, while a countervailing duty investigation concerns normally a multitude of parties with conflicting interests as to the outcome of such investigation. Therefore, the duty to respect confidentiality has to be counterbalanced with some mechanism ensuring the necessary transparency in these investigations. The two subparagraphs of Article 12.4 ensure the necessary level of transparency and due process by requesting parties that submit confidential information to furnish also non-confidential summaries thereof. Such summaries have to be sufficient in detail to permit a reasonable understanding of the substance of the information submitted in confidence. If such summarization is in exceptional circumstances not possible, a statement of the reasons has to be provided why this is so.[8] Information that is not confidential as well as the non-confidential summaries are integrated in the non-confidential file, see *supra* this chapter pp. 394–395.

Footnote 42 is attached to the chapeau of Article 12.4. It acknowledges that WTO Members are aware that in the territory of certain Members, disclosure pursuant to a narrowly drawn protective order may be required. This so-called APO system is currently operated by the US, Canada and Mexico. It essentially entails that legal counsel to interested parties has access to all information submitted by all parties including confidential information. But the counsel shall not disclose such information to his client or to any other person. The abbreviation 'APO' stands for 'administrative protective order'.

The chapeau of Article 12.4 distinguishes between two types of confidential information:

- information which is by nature confidential (for example, because its disclosure would be of significant competitive advantage to a competitor or because its disclosure would have a significantly adverse effect upon a person supplying the information or upon a person from whom the supplier acquired the information) or
- information which is provided on a confidential basis.

[8] WT/DS397/AB/R of 15 July 2011, *European Communities – Definitive Anti-Dumping Measures on Certain Iron or Steel Fasteners from China*, para 542 refers with regard to Articles 6.5 and 6.5.1, i.e. the mirror provisions in the WTO Anti-Dumping Agreement, to this trinity of confidentiality, transparency and due process.

According to the chapeau of Article 12.4 *in fine*, confidential information shall be treated as such if 'good cause' is shown. The requirement to show 'good cause' for confidential treatment applies to both information that is 'by nature' confidential and information which is provided to the authority on 'a confidential basis'. The good cause alleged must constitute a reason sufficient to justify the withholding of information from both the public and from the other parties interested in the investigation who would otherwise have a right to view this information. 'Good cause' must demonstrate the risk of a potential consequence, the avoidance of which is important enough to warrant the non-disclosure of the information. 'Good cause' must be assessed and determined objectively by the investigating authority, and cannot be determined merely based on the subjective concern of the submitting party.

As to what could constitute 'good cause', the Appellate Body referred to the examples in the Agreement which describe why information could be confidential 'by nature'. The Appellate Body pointed out that these examples are only illustrative and it considered that a wide range of other reasons could constitute 'good cause' justifying treatment of information as confidential.[9]

Article 12.4.2 describes the consequences if the request for confidentiality is not warranted and if the supplier of the information is either unwilling to make the information public or to authorize its disclosure in generalized or summary form. In such circumstances, the investigating authority may disregard such information unless it can be demonstrated to their satisfaction from appropriate sources that the information is correct. Footnote 43 is attached to Article 12.4.2. It states that Members agree

- that requests for confidentiality should not be arbitrarily rejected and
- that the investigating authority may request the waiving of confidentiality only regarding information that is relevant to the proceedings.

Non-confidential Summaries (Article 12.4.1)

Pursuant to Article 12.4.1, in case an interested Member or an interested party submits confidential information and shows good cause for

[9] WT/DS397/AB/R of 15 July 2011, *European Communities – Definitive Anti-Dumping Measures on Certain Iron or Steel Fasteners from China*, paras 537–544 with regard to Article 6.5, i.e. the mirror provision in the WTO Anti-Dumping Agreement. The Appellate Body also referred to pertinent Panel rulings.

confidential treatment, it has also to furnish a non-confidential summary of such information. The summary shall be sufficient in detail to permit a reasonable understanding of the substance of the information submitted in confidence. The obligations in Article 12.4.1 fall upon the investigating authorities, i.e. they have to require parties providing confidential information to furnish also meaningful non-confidential summaries or, in exceptional circumstances, to provide a statement of reasons why summarization is not possible.[10]

In *EC – Fasteners (China)*, the Appellate Body has stated that although the sufficiency of the summary will depend on the confidential information at issue, the summary must permit a reasonable understanding of the substance of the information submitted in confidence, and allow the other parties to the investigation a meaningful opportunity to respond and defend their interests.[11]

The obligation set out in Article 12.4.1 to furnish a non-confidential summary has to be respected even if a country operates an APO system.[12]

The summary needs to be provided before the investigating authority has reached its determination. An investigating authority cannot claim that the requirement of providing such summary is fulfilled because the authority itself summarized the information in its determination. Such summarization by the authority in its determination would not allow an interested party the opportunity to defend its interests. Information, summary or analysis provided by the investigating authority cannot remedy the absence of, or shortcomings in, a summary provided by the interested party submitting confidential information.[13]

[10] WT/DS397/AB/R of 15 July 2011, *European Communities – Definitive Anti-Dumping Measures on Certain Iron or Steel Fasteners from China*, para 542 with regard to Article 6.5.1, i.e. the mirror provision in the WTO Anti-Dumping Agreement. See also WT/DS414/R of 15 June 2012, *China – Countervailing and Anti-Dumping Duties on Grain-Oriented Flat-Rolled Electrical Steel from the US*, para 7.189; WT/DS427/R of 2 August 2013, *China – Anti-Dumping and Countervailing Duty Measures on Broiler Products from the United States*, para 7.53; WT/DS341/R of 4 September 2008, *Mexico – Definitive Countervailing Measures on Olive Oil from the European Communities*, paras 7.89 and 7.92.

[11] WT/DS397/AB/R of 15 July 2011, *European Communities – Definitive Anti-Dumping Measures on Certain Iron or Steel Fasteners from China*, para 542 with regard to Article 6.5.1, i.e. the mirror provision in the WTO Anti-Dumping Agreement; WT/DS427/R of 2 August 2013, *China – Anti-Dumping and Countervailing Duty Measures on Broiler Products from the United States*, para 7.50.

[12] WT/DS341/R of 4 September 2008, *Mexico – Definitive Countervailing Measures on Olive Oil from the European Communities*, paras 7.93–7.95.

[13] WT/DS414/R of 15 June 2012, *China – Countervailing and Anti-Dumping Duties on Grain-Oriented Flat-Rolled Electrical Steel from the US*, para 7.190; WT/DS427/R of 2 August

In *China – GOES*, China also argued that a non-confidential summary exists where an interested party is able to derive, or infer from the context, the possible nature of the confidential information. The Panel rejected this argument. According to the Panel, there is an explicit obligation under Article 12.4.1 for an interested party submitting confidential information to furnish a non-confidential summary of it permitting a reasonable understanding of the information submitted in confidence.[14]

Mexico – Olive Oil also clarified that where confidentiality is claimed, a provision of a public version of the document in question from which confidential information has simply been removed may not necessarily satisfy the requirements of Article 12.4.1. This is because what is required to be summarized according to Article 12.4.1 is the confidential information. The remaining non-confidential parts may not, by themselves, be sufficient to convey a reasonable understanding of the substance of the confidential information. Indeed, the circumstances where the remaining part is sufficient are likely to be limited.[15]

If the investigation is initiated as a result of an application made by the domestic industry, the obligations in Article 12.4.1 also apply with regard to the application which triggered the initiation pursuant to Article 11.2.[16] See also *infra* the description of *China – Broiler Products*.

China – Broiler Products gives some examples as to the standard of meaningful non-confidential summary. These examples[17] are taken from the domestic industry's petition for the initiation of a countervailing duty investigation.

With regard to standing, the non-confidential summary explained that production by petitioners accounted for more than 50 per cent of total production during the period 2006–2009, and consequently, that the petitioner had standing. The actual production figures were redacted. In the Panel's view, a range between 50 per cent and 100 per cent did not permit a reasonable understanding of the redacted information about standing, particularly

2013, *China – Anti-Dumping and Countervailing Duty Measures on Broiler Products from the United States*, para 7.53.

[14] WT/DS414/R of 15 June 2012, *China – Countervailing and Anti-Dumping Duties on Grain-Oriented Flat-Rolled Electrical Steel from the US*, paras 7.222 and 7.224; WT/DS427/R of 2 August 2013, *China – Anti-Dumping and Countervailing Duty Measures on Broiler Products from the United States*, para 7.60.

[15] WT/DS341/R of 4 September 2008, *Mexico – Definitive Countervailing Measures on Olive Oil from the European Communities*, paras 7.87 and 7.88.

[16] WT/DS414/R of 15 June 2012, *China – Countervailing and Anti-Dumping Duties on Grain-Oriented Flat-Rolled Electrical Steel from the US*, para 7.188.

[17] See also the summaries by *Prusa/Vermulst* (2015) pp. 292–295.

when the list of producers and the data concerning the total production in China were provided in confidence and not summarized. A conclusory statement that the information was sufficient to demonstrate standing cannot replace the summary of the confidential information, particularly if such a statement does not provide interested parties with the means to challenge whether the confidential information provided a basis for that conclusion.[18]

With regard to the development of production capacity, yield and capacity utilization of the Chinese domestic broiler industry during the period 2006–2009, the yearly figures were redacted in the non-confidential summary. Only the numerical figures for the year-to-year change in capacity utilization were provided. The tables were followed by graphs but the graphs did not give any figures or ranges of figures. The Panel did not consider this sufficient.[19]

Finally, with regard to inventories, wages, employment, cash flow and labour productivity, the petitioner provided year-on-year percentage changes only for some indicators but not for all of them. For some of the indicators, a graph was also provided showing the linear depiction of the yearly trends, but no scale. According to the Panel, providing year-over-year changes in percentage terms without a non-confidential summary of what constitutes the baseline does not allow a reasonable understanding of the magnitude of the change.[20]

Whether or not the respondent makes a substantive challenge regarding the subject matter that has been treated confidentially does not affect the standard for an adequate non-confidential summary under Article 12.4.1. Without an adequate non-confidential summary, the ability of an interested party to contest the relevant issue is compromised.[21]

If the exceptional circumstances exemption (see the next section) is not invoked, a Panel will assess the adequacy of the non-confidential summary by reference to whether it permits a reasonable understanding of the information submitted in confidence.[22] In the case in question, the

[18] WT/DS427/R of 2 August 2013, *China – Anti-Dumping and Countervailing Duty Measures on Broiler Products from the United States*, paras 7.54–7.57.

[19] WT/DS427/R of 2 August 2013, *China – Anti-Dumping and Countervailing Duty Measures on Broiler Products from the United States*, paras 7.58–7.61.

[20] WT/DS427/R of 2 August 2013, *China – Anti-Dumping and Countervailing Duty Measures on Broiler Products from the United States*, paras 7.62–7.64.

[21] WT/DS414/R of 15 June 2012, *China – Countervailing and Anti-Dumping Duties on Grain-Oriented Flat-Rolled Electrical Steel from the US*, para 7.191.

[22] WT/DS414/R of 15 June 2012, *China – Countervailing and Anti-Dumping Duties on Grain-Oriented Flat-Rolled Electrical Steel from the US*, para 7.193.

Panel held that the non-confidential summary provided minimal descriptions of the nature, rather than the substance, of the information treated as confidential. This was not considered adequate.[23]

Non-confidential Summarization Not Possible

The ASCM recognizes that not all confidential information can be summarized into a non-confidential summary. The last two sentences of Article 12.4.1 govern such a situation. They stipulate: 'In exceptional circumstances, such Members or parties may indicate that such information is not susceptible to summary. In such exceptional circumstances, a statement of the reasons why summarization is not possible must be provided.' According to the Appellate Body in *EC – Fasteners (China)* with regard to the parallel provision in the WTO Anti-Dumping Agreement, the party must identify the exceptional circumstances and provide a statement explaining why summarization is not possible. Furthermore, the investigating authority must scrutinize such statements to determine whether they establish exceptional circumstances and whether the reasons given appropriately explain why, under the circumstances, no summary that permits a reasonable understanding of the information's substance is possible.[24]

Mexico – Olive Oil made it clear that unsubstantiated assertions that summarization is not possible do not meet the standard established by the last sentence of Article 12.4.1.[25] The Panel also opined that a statement

[23] WT/DS414/R of 15 June 2012, *China – Countervailing and Anti-Dumping Duties on Grain-Oriented Flat-Rolled Electrical Steel from the US*, paras 7.198 and 7.199. The non-confidential summary pointed out that the confidential information consisted of sales prices of the subject merchandise between 2006 and 2009 and that this was business proprietary information. The party submitting the information in confidence probably should have claimed that summarization of this information was not possible, see next section. The same problem was encountered in WT/DS427/R of 2 August 2013, *China – Anti-Dumping and Countervailing Duty Measures on Broiler Products from the United States*, para 7.56.

[24] WT/DS397/AB/R of 15 July 2011, *European Communities – Definitive Anti-Dumping Measures on Certain Iron or Steel Fasteners from China*, para 544. The Appellate Body's examination of the two instances where it was claimed that summarization was not possible can be found in para 545 *et seq.* The Appellate Body also refers to Panel rulings that adopted the same approach. See also WT/DS414/R of 15 June 2012, *China – Countervailing and Anti-Dumping Duties on Grain-Oriented Flat-Rolled Electrical Steel from the US*, para 7.189; WT/DS341/R of 4 September 2008, *Mexico – Definitive Countervailing Measures on Olive Oil from the European Communities*, para 7.92.

[25] WT/DS341/R of 4 September 2008, *Mexico – Definitive Countervailing Measures on Olive Oil from the European Communities*, paras 7.100 and 7.101.

of reasons, that summarization is not possible, can substitute for a non-confidential summary only in exceptional circumstances. The use of the word 'exceptional' signifies that the drafters considered that confidential information should usually be capable of being summarized. Summarization of confidential information is expected to be the norm.[26] It could be argued that this statement might perhaps be too sweeping as the question of whether summarization is possible depends very much on the nature of the information.

Accuracy of Any Information Submitted and Used as a Basis of Findings (Article 12.5)

Article 12.5 requires investigating authorities to satisfy themselves in the course of an investigation as to the accuracy of the information supplied by interested Members or interested parties if findings are based on such information. This obligation does not apply in the circumstances provided for in Article 12.7, i.e. in case of non-cooperation by an interested Member or an interested party and the consequent use of 'facts available'.

A comparison of paragraphs 5 and 6 of Article 12 shows that an investigating authority is not required to base all its findings on information that has been verified at the premises of Members or firms. Rather, the benchmark for using any information submitted is whether the investigating authority is satisfied about the accuracy of such information.

Verification Visits (Article 12.6 and Annex VI)

Article 12.6 and Annex VI of the ASCM set out the rules for on-spot verifications at the premises of firms including the preparation of such visit. Annex VI of the ASCM is identical with Annex I of the WTO Anti-Dumping Agreement. These provisions are essentially self-explanatory.

Note that Article 12.6 refers to verification visits at the premises of a 'firm' and not to such visits at the premises of an 'interested party'.

Verification visits can only be carried out if the firm or Member has been notified in good time and if the other Member does not object and if the firm agrees to such visit. Failure by an interested party to accept such verification

[26] WT/DS341/R of 4 September 2008, *Mexico – Definitive Countervailing Measures on Olive Oil from the European Communities*, para 7.90.

visit or lack of cooperation during such visit can trigger the use of facts available pursuant to Article 12.7.[27]

The purpose of the visits envisaged in Article 12.6 is typically the verification of the questionnaire reply (see *supra* this chapter, pp. 392–394. However, the aim of such a visit can also be to obtain further details on issues relevant to the investigation.

The results of the verification shall be made available, either in the form of a verification report or in the disclosure provided pursuant to Article 12.8.

Panels examined issues related to verification visits in *US – Countervailing Duty Investigation on DRAMs*[28] and in *China – Broiler Products*.[29] There exists also WTO jurisprudence with regard to the mirror provisions in the WTO Anti-Dumping Agreement, notably about the mandatory nature of Annex I of the WTO Anti-Dumping Agreement although this Annex uses occasionally the present conditional tense.

Use of Facts Available (Article 12.7)

Introduction

Article 12.7 provides that in cases in which any interested WTO Member or interested party refuses access to, or otherwise does not provide, necessary information within a reasonable period or significantly impedes the investigation, preliminary and final determinations, affirmative or negative, may be made on the basis of the facts available.

Therefore, Article 12.7 permits an investigating authority, under certain circumstances, to fill in gaps in the information necessary to arrive at a conclusion as to subsidization and injury. Article 12.7 prescribes the information that may be used to fill in such gaps as 'facts available'. This provision is intended to ensure that the failure of an interested party to provide necessary information does not hinder the authority's investigation. The provision permits the use of facts on record solely for the

[27] WT/DS296/R/3 of 21 February 2005, *United States – Countervailing Duty Investigation on Dynamic Random Access Memory Semiconductors (DRAMs) from Korea*, paras 7.404–7.406. This aspect of the Panel's ruling was not appealed.

[28] WT/DS296/R/3 of 21 February 2005, *United States – Countervailing Duty Investigation on Dynamic Random Access Memory Semiconductors (DRAMs) from Korea*, para 7.399 *et seq.* The question at issue was whether the third country Member could link its acceptance of verification visits in its territory to one or more conditions. This aspect of the ruling was not appealed.

[29] WT/DS427/R of 2 August 2013, *China – Anti-Dumping and Countervailing Duty Measures on Broiler Products from the United States*, paras 7.261 and 7.263.

purpose of replacing information that may be missing because of a failure to cooperate, in order to arrive at an accurate subsidization or injury determination.[30] *EC – Countervailing Measures on DRAM Chips* has summarized the purpose of Article 12.7 very succinctly: 'Article 12.7 of the SCM Agreement is an essential part of the limited investigative powers of an investigating authority in obtaining the necessary information to make proper determinations.'[31]

DSB rulings given with regard to the mirror provision Article 6.8 of the WTO Anti-Dumping Agreement and its Annex II are also relevant in relation to Article 12.7 ASCM. Unlike the WTO Anti-Dumping Agreement, the ASCM does not expressly set out in an Annex the conditions for determining precisely which facts might be available. However, Annex II of the WTO Anti-Dumping Agreement can provide relevant context for the evaluation of claims under Article 12.7.[32] *Mexico – Beef and Rice* has also underlined that the absence of Annex II of the WTO Anti-Dumping Agreement in the ASCM does not mean that no conditions exist for determining which facts might be available.[33]

US – Carbon Steel (India) further clarified the obligations of an investigating authority under Article 12.7. The Appellate Body agreed with the Panel that the standard of Article 12.7 requires that all substantiated facts on the record be taken into account, that 'facts available' determinations have a factual foundation, and that 'facts available' be generally limited to those facts that may reasonably replace the missing information. However, in India's opinion, Article 12.7 required also, when selecting facts available, a comparative evaluation of all evidence with a view to identifying the best information, or in other words, the most fitting or appropriate information on the record. Note that India's opinion is in line with the standard articulated by the Appellate Body in the anti-dumping case concerning *Mexico – Beef and Rice* that in turn referred to Annex II of the

[30] WT/DS295/AB/R of 29 November 2005, *Mexico – Definitive Anti-Dumping Measures on Beef and Rice / Complaint with Respect to Rice*, paras 291 and 293. See also WT/DS437/AB/R of 18 December 2014, *United States – Countervailing Duty Measures on Certain Products from China*, para 4.178.

[31] WT/DS299/R of 17 June 2005, *European Communities – Countervailing Measures on Dynamic Random Access Memory Chips from Korea*, para 7.61. WT/DS336/R of 13 July 2007, *Japan – Countervailing Duties on Dynamic Random Access Memories from Korea*, para 7.392 took the same position.

[32] WT/DS414/R of 15 June 2012, *China – Countervailing and Anti-Dumping Duties on Grain-Oriented Flat-Rolled Electrical Steel from the US*, para 7.289.

[33] WT/DS295/AB/R of 29 November 2005, *Mexico – Definitive Anti-Dumping Measures on Beef and Rice / Complaint with Respect to Rice*, para 291.

Anti-Dumping Agreement. Annex II refers to '*best* information available'. The Panel's ruling in *US – Carbon Steel (India)* was somewhat ambiguous in this respect. The Appellate Body disagreed with the Panel's finding to the extent it could be read as ruling out entirely the standard proposed by India. The Appellate Body also held, thereby agreeing with the Panel, that Annex II of the Anti-Dumping Agreement should not be imported into the ASCM. However, the Appellate Body also recalled its previous ruling in *Mexico – Beef and Rice* that it would be anomalous if Article 12.7 of the ASCM were to permit the use of 'facts available' in countervailing duty investigations in a manner markedly different from that in anti-dumping investigations. It found India's approach, that Article 12.7 requires a comparative evaluation of all available evidence as a pre-requisite of making a determination under this provision, too rigid. Rather, the extent to which an evaluation of the facts available is required and the form it should take depend on the particular circumstances of a given case, including the quality and quantity of the available facts on the record, and the types of determinations to be made in any given investigation. The Appellate Body recognized that there may be circumstances where the kind of comparative evaluation proposed by India may not be practicable, for instance if there is only one set of reliable information on the record that is relevant to a particular issue. It also pointed out that ascertaining the reasonable replacements for the missing necessary information involves a process of reasoning and evaluation on the part of the investigating authority, although the degree and nature of that reasoning and evaluation required will depend on the circumstances of a particular case. If the investigating authority can choose from several facts available, it would seem natural that the process of reasoning and evaluation would involve a degree of comparison in order to arrive at an accurate determination.[34]

[34] WT/DS436/AB/R of 8 December 2014, *United States – Countervailing Measures on Certain Hot-Rolled Carbon Steel Flat Products from India*, paras 4.399–4.438. WT/DS437/AB/R of 18 December 2014, *United States – Countervailing Duty Measures on Certain Products from China*, paras 4.178 and 4.179 repeated some of the above statements including the reference to the connection between the necessary information that is missing and the facts available as well as the 'reasonable replace standard'. The statement in WT/DS299/R of 17 June 2005, *European Communities – Countervailing Measures on Dynamic Random Access Memory Chips from Korea*, para 7.249 that Article 12.7 is not about the weight that is given to the secondary sources of information and the interpretation of such documents and that the weighing of the information and the evidence before it is part of the discretionary power of the investigating authority, does not sit well with the above-mentioned findings of the Appellate Body in *US – Carbon Steel (India)*.

China – Broiler Products has also discussed the textual differences between Article 12.7 of the ASCM and the Anti-Dumping Agreement. It concluded that Article 6.8 and Annex II of the WTO Anti-Dumping Agreement, on the one hand, and Article 12.7 of the ASCM, on the other, impose similar disciplines concerning the circumstances under which an authority may resort to facts available. According to the Panel, the textual differences between these two provisions are not significant.[35] However, given *US – Carbon Steel (India)*, *China – Broiler Products* seems to be somewhat less pertinent.

Under What Conditions Can an Investigating Authority Resort to Facts Available?

The Panel in *EC – Countervailing Measures on DRAM Chips* held that Article 12.7 identifies the circumstances in which investigating authorities may overcome a lack of information, in the response of interested parties, by using 'facts' which are otherwise 'available' to the investigating authority.[36] In other words, Article 12.7 allows investigating authorities to use information or facts to fill gaps in the record resulting from non-cooperation on the part of interested parties.[37] According to the Panel, Article 12.7 deals with a situation in which information is not provided, or cannot be used, and other secondary source information is used instead.[38]

An investigating authority may invoke Article 12.7 not only in relation to a failure to reply to the original questionnaire but also in relation to follow-up questions (deficiency letters) as well as the verification during verification visits, since acceptance of such a visit by the party concerned gives rise to an obligation to cooperate during the visit.[39]

[35] WT/DS427/R of 2 August 2013, *China – Anti-Dumping and Countervailing Duty Measures on Broiler Products from the United States*, para 7.355.

[36] WT/DS299/R of 17 June 2005, *European Communities – Countervailing Measures on Dynamic Random Access Memory Chips from Korea*, para 7.245.

[37] WT/DS414/R of 15 June 2012, *China – Countervailing and Anti-Dumping Duties on Grain-Oriented Flat-Rolled Electrical Steel from the US*, paras 7.295 and 7.450. The latter paragraph states '[T]he provision permits the use of facts available only for the purposes of replacing information that may be missing, in order to arrive at an accurate subsidization or injury determination.'

[38] See WT/DS299/R of 17 June 2005, *European Communities – Countervailing Measures on Dynamic Random Access Memory Chips from Korea*, para 7.249.

[39] WT/DS414/R of 15 June 2012, *China – Countervailing and Anti-Dumping Duties on Grain-Oriented Flat-Rolled Electrical Steel from the US*, para 7.285; WT/DS299/R of 17 June 2005, *European Communities – Countervailing Measures on Dynamic Random Access Memory Chips from Korea*, para 7.249.

An investigating authority is required to notify interested parties of the necessary information before it may resort to facts available. This follows from Article 12.1 ('interested parties ... shall be given notice of the information which the authorities require'). According to the Panel in *China – GOES*, in the absence of being notified of the necessary information in the context of a particular investigation, it is difficult to conclude that unknown exporters refused access to or failed to provide necessary information or otherwise impeded the investigation. The Panel's conclusion seems to be appropriate with regard to the specific circumstances of the case, where the Chinese investigating authority set an 'all others rate' based on facts available and about twice as high as for the two cooperating US exporters. Given that it was undisputed that there were no other exporters than those two cooperating, a conclusion that non-existent exporters refused to provide information or impeded the investigation seemed understandably illogical to the Panel.[40]

The situation was different in *China – Broiler Products*. The Panel held that MOFCOM was entitled to base an 'all others rate' on facts available with regard to exporters that did not register with the investigation. MOFCOM had posted the Notice of Initiation (including a warning that facts available could be resorted to in the case of failure to register) and the Registration Form on its website. The Panel held that failure to register and to provide the requested information could be classified as failure 'to otherwise ... provide ... necessary information' within the meaning of Article 12.7.[41]

The questions posed by the investigating authority to an interested party must be specific enough so that the party that is requested to cooperate knows what is expected from it.[42] And the information requested must be relevant for the determination to be made.[43]

In *US – Anti-Dumping and Countervailing Duties (China)*, the USDOC relied on information submitted by China's legal counsel but which has never been asked for by the USDOC. At a late stage of the investigation, the USDOC decided that this information was not reliable and therefore resorted to facts available. The Panel did not accept this because

[40] WT/DS414/R of 15 June 2012, *China – Countervailing and Anti-Dumping Duties on Grain-Oriented Flat-Rolled Electrical Steel from the US*, para 7.446.

[41] WT/DS427/R of 2 August 2013, *China – Anti-Dumping and Countervailing Duty Measures on Broiler Products from the United States*, para 7.356.

[42] WT/DS299/R of 17 June 2005, *European Communities – Countervailing Measures on Dynamic Random Access Memory Chips from Korea*, paras 7.250–7.255.

[43] WT/DS299/R of 17 June 2005, *European Communities – Countervailing Measures on Dynamic Random Access Memory Chips from Korea*, para 7.255.

the conditions of Article 12.7 for applying 'facts available' were not met ('refuses access', 'significantly impedes' etc.).[44]

Article 12.7 also applies if requested information is only supplied partially. In *EC – Countervailing Measures on DRAM Chips*, the European Commission as the investigating authority requested a report prepared by an accounting firm that allegedly established the going concern and the liquidation value of the exporter concerned, Hynix. Hynix did not provide the report invoking confidentiality reasons but offered the Commission access to the report at the time of the verification visit. The Commission insisted in a deficiency letter on the submission of the report and offered to treat the report confidentially. In response to this letter Korea submitted an excerpt of one page setting forth the conclusions on the going concern and liquidation values. The Commission did not take into account this page and applied facts available instead. Korea argued that Hynix was under the impression that, by submitting the one page, the conclusion of the report, the Commission was satisfied. It argued that, by not informing Hynix that it would not be able to rely on the report unless the full report was submitted, the EU failed to respect the two-way communication that was essential to a proper application of Article 12.7. The Panel rejected Korea's argument. It was of the opinion that even assuming that Article 12.7 contained a basic due process requirement of informing a party concerned that certain information is considered not to have been properly provided, the EU complied with its procedural obligation.[45]

The fact that interested parties are prohibited under domestic law or contractual obligations to disclose requested information to the investigating authority does not prevent the application of Article 12.7.[46] Note that parties can request that information submitted to the investigating authority be treated confidential if the conditions of Article 12.4 are met.

What Constitutes 'Facts Available'?

See first *US – Carbon Steel (India)* described *supra* this chapter pp. 403–406. In other words, while there is no rigid requirement to make

[44] WT/DS379/R of 22 October 2010, *US – Definitive Anti-Dumping and Countervailing Duties on Certain Products from China*, paras 16.6–16.18.

[45] WT/DS299/R of 17 June 2005, *European Communities – Countervailing Measures on Dynamic Random Access Memory Chips from Korea*, paras 7.256–7.261.

[46] WT/DS299/R of 17 June 2005, *European Communities – Countervailing Measures on Dynamic Random Access Memory Chips from Korea*, paras 7.264 and 7.265.

a comparative evaluation of all available evidence on the record when selecting facts available, such an analysis may well be necessary depending on the circumstances of the case.

'Facts available' refers to those facts that are in the possession of the investigating authority and on its written record.[47] As determinations made under Article 12.7 are to be made on the basis of 'facts available', they cannot be made on the basis of non-factual assumptions or speculation.[48]

With respect to the facts that an investigating authority may use when faced with missing information as a result of non-cooperation, the authority's discretion is not unlimited. The determination must have a factual foundation or a factual support. *China – GOES* concerned the alleged subsidization by 'Buy America' legislation, on the basis that sales by US exporters to the US government were made for more than adequate remuneration. China determined that because of the non-cooperation of US exporters all their domestic sales were made to the US government and hence were subsidized. The Panel disagreed because the record was at odds with this conclusion. The use of facts available should be distinguished from the application of adverse inferences. According to paragraph 7 of Annex II of the WTO Anti-Dumping Agreement, non-cooperation could lead to a result which is less favourable to the party than if the party did cooperate. However, this is not a basis for the drawing of adverse inferences. The purpose of the facts available mechanism is not to punish non-cooperation by interested parties but to close the gap in the record. Nor does non-cooperation justify determinations that are devoid of any factual foundation.[49]

The above is in line with *Mexico – Beef and Rice*. Mexico's law contained a provision that stipulated, *inter alia*, that the authority should

[47] WT/DS437/AB/R of 18 December 2014, *United States – Countervailing Duty Measures on Certain Products from China*, para 4.178; WT/DS436/AB/R of 8 December 2014, *United States – Countervailing Measures on Certain Hot-Rolled Carbon Steel Flat Products from India*, para 4.417.

[48] WT/DS437/AB/R of 18 December 2014, *United States – Countervailing Duty Measures on Certain Products from China*, para 4.178; WT/DS436/AB/R of 8 December 2014, *United States – Countervailing Measures on Certain Hot-Rolled Carbon Steel Flat Products from India*, para 4.417.

[49] WT/DS414/R of 15 June 2012, *China – Countervailing and Anti-Dumping Duties on Grain-Oriented Flat-Rolled Electrical Steel from the US*, para 7.295 *et seq.* See also WT/DS436/AB/R of 8 December 2014, *United States – Countervailing Measures on Certain Hot-Rolled Carbon Steel Flat Products from India*, para 4.468; WT/DS437/AB/R of 18 December 2014, *United States – Countervailing Duty Measures on Certain Products from China*, para 4.179 (footnote 738).

calculate the highest possible margin on the basis of facts available and apply that margin

- when producers failed to appear in the investigation;
- when producers failed to provide the information in a proper and timely fashion, significantly impeded the investigation or supplied information that was incomplete, incorrect or did not derive from their accounts, thus preventing the determination of an individual margin of subsidization; or
- when producers did not export the subject product during the investigation period.

The Appellate Body held that this provision was not consistent with Article 12.7 for the following reasons:

- Mexico's law required the calculation of the highest possible margin on the basis of the facts available.
- This law did not permit the investigating authority to use any information that might have been provided by a foreign producer or exporter, even if incomplete, where the use of such information would result in a margin lower than the highest facts available margin.
- This law did not allow the investigating authority to engage in an evaluative, comparative assessment necessary in order to determine which facts are 'best' (see Annex II of the WTO Anti-Dumping Agreement) to fill in the necessary information.
- This law required the investigating authority to use those facts necessary to arrive at the highest margin that could be calculated, even if those facts, although substantiated, might be deemed unreliable by the authority after exercising special circumspection.
- The Appellate Body also highlighted that the recourse to facts available does not permit an investigating authority to use any information in whatever way it chooses. The recourse to facts available is not a licence to rely on only part of the evidence provided. To the extent possible, an investigating authority using facts available in a countervailing duty investigation must take into account all the substantiated facts provided by an interested party, even if those facts may not constitute the complete information requested from that party.[50]

[50] WT/DS295/AB/R of 29 November 2005, *Mexico – Definitive Anti-Dumping Measures on Beef and Rice / Complaint with Respect to Rice*, paras 290–298. In arriving at the above conclusion, the Appellate Body also referred to the purpose of Article 12.7 and it quoted the chapeau of Article 12.1 as relevant context, see *supra* this chapter, pp. 391–392.

- In short, Mexico's law prevented the authority from engaging in a reasoned and selective use of the facts available directed by Article 12.7.

China – Broiler Products is also consistent with the above. MOFCOM calculated a so-called 'all others rate' for exporters that did not register with the investigating authority nor otherwise cooperate. The 'all others rate' was set at 30.3 per cent while the highest individual rate stood at 12.5 per cent. MOFCOM's discussion of its calculation of the 'all others rate' in the disclosure and the determinations did not indicate precisely which subsidy programmes MOFCOM took into consideration. Moreover, the 'all others rate' did not appear to have any logical relation with the highest individual rate. Furthermore, MOFCOM used a different approach in calculating the benefit for the 'all others rate' as compared to individual rates, without explaining the reasons underlying this methodological choice. Therefore, the Panel concluded that it was not possible to establish that MOFCOM had determined the 'all others rate' consistently with the principles of Article 12.7.[51]

The circumstances in *China – GOES* were similar to those in *China – Broiler Products*. When calculating the 'all others rate', MOFCOM also included in this rate programmes that it found not to be countervailable.[52]

Degree of Non-cooperation May Influence the Selection of Facts Available

US – Carbon Steel (India) is the leading case. US law provided that when selecting facts available, the investigating authority was entitled (but not obliged) to use an inference that is adverse to the interests of the party if that party withheld information, failed to provide information or significantly impeded the investigation. The Appellate Body held that this provision was not necessarily inconsistent with Article 12.7. As part of the process of reasoning and evaluating which facts available constitute reasonable replacements for the missing necessary information, an investigating authority may use inferences. The procedural circumstances in which information is missing, including the non-cooperation of an interested party, may be taken into account in this process. But the Appellate Body also underlined that the determinations under Article 12.7 must be

[51] WT/DS427/R of 2 August 2013, *China – Anti-Dumping and Countervailing Duty Measures on Broiler Products from the United States*, paras 7.357–7.360.

[52] WT/DS414/R of 15 June 2012, *China – Countervailing and Anti-Dumping Duties on Grain-Oriented Flat-Rolled Electrical Steel from the US*, para 7.449 *et seq*.

based on facts and may not be made on the basis of non-factual assumptions or speculation.[53]

EC – Countervailing Measures on DRAM Chips is in line with the above. This ruling is very relevant for the understanding of the concept of non-cooperation and the use of facts available in countervailing duty investigations. The Panel stated that the extent to which the interested parties cooperated with the authority is also a relevant element to be taken into account. In those cases where certain essential information which was clearly requested by the investigating authority was not provided, such uncooperative behaviour may be taken into account by the authority when weighing the evidence and the facts before it. The fact that certain information was withheld from the authority may be the element that tilts the balance in a certain direction. Depending on the circumstances, an authority may be justified in drawing certain inferences, which may be adverse, from the failure to cooperate with the investigating authority. The Panel noted approvingly a statement made by the Appellate Body in *US – Hot Rolled Steel* that referred to Article 6.8 of the WTO Anti-Dumping Agreement, which is very similar both textually and contextually to Article 12.7 of the ASCM. On that occasion, the Appellate Body said that investigating authorities are entitled to expect a very significant degree of effort – to the best of their abilities – from the investigated exporters. But investigating authorities were not entitled to insist upon absolute standards or impose unreasonable burdens upon exporters. The Panel held that a similar significant degree of cooperation was to be expected in countervailing duty investigations, despite the fact that the ASCM did not contain provisions that were similar to Annex II of the WTO Anti-Dumping Agreement. In the absence of any *subpoena* or other evidence-gathering powers, the possibility to resort to facts available and, thus, also the possibility of drawing certain inferences from the failure to cooperate plays a crucial role in inducing parties to provide the necessary information. The Panel also added that non-cooperation does not provide a blank cheque for simply basing a determination on speculative assumptions or on the worst information available. It went on to say that in the absence of supporting facts, mere non-cooperation by itself did not suffice to justify a conclusion which is negative to the non-cooperating party.[54]

[53] WT/DS436/AB/R of 8 December 2014, *United States – Countervailing Measures on Certain Hot-Rolled Carbon Steel Flat Products from India*, para 4.463 *et seq.* (in particular paras 4.467 and 4.468).

[54] WT/DS299/R of 17 June 2005, *European Communities – Countervailing Measures on Dynamic Random Access Memory Chips from Korea*, paras 7.60, 7.61 and 7.76 *et seq.* See

The line established by the Panel is a thin one. This is illustrated by the Panel's review of the EU's determination of entrustment or direction in relation to the May 2001 Restructuring Programme and the Syndicated Loan. The Panel accepted the EU's determination with regard to the Syndicated Loan, but not with regard to the May 2001 Restructuring Programme.

Syndicated Loan

- The Syndicated Loan was developed during the second semester of 2000 as part of a financial plan to resolve Hynix's short term liquidity problems. The EU examined three out of ten banks that participated in this Syndicated Loan and considered that the participation of these three banks constituted a financial contribution by the government.
- The three banks could only participate in the Syndicated Loan because they received from the Korean Financial Supervisory Commission, a governmental body, a waiver to exceed credit ceilings that were stipulated by law. According to the law, the waiver could be granted 'when it is recognized that it is inevitable for industrial development … or the stability of national life'. The minutes of the meeting in which the waiver was granted, *inter alia*, pointed out that the semiconductor industry was considered a strategic industry and that its support via a syndicated loan would improve Korea's international competitiveness.
- Prior to the application for the waiver, the banks in question received a letter from the Ministry of Finance and Economy signed by the Minister himself. The letter transmitted the results of a discussion on alleviating the cash crunch of Hyundai Electronics that was on the agenda of the Economic Minister's meeting. It ordered the recipients to make sure that the measures decided in that meeting would be 'carried out perfectly'. One such measure was that an extension of the credit ceilings should be requested.
- A letter and other information concerning the Economic Ministers' meeting described above were originally withheld from the European Commission, i.e. the investigating authority. The Commission only

also para 7.143 where the Panel pointed out that Article 12.7 did not allow an authority to automatically reach a conclusion which is negative for the un-cooperative party in the absence of additional facts, simply because the information was not provided. However, if there were certain facts on the record which pointed in a certain direction, then it was not unreasonable for the investigating authority to read these facts in the light of the non-cooperation by the interested party concerned.

obtained it after it had adopted provisional CVD measures. The withholding of this information triggered the use of facts available.

- The Panel recognized that the letter could be read in more than one way. But it could accept that the failure to cooperate with the investigating authority was an important element in tilting the balance towards a reading of this information that was less favourable to the interested party that was withholding the information. The Panel also underlined that in the absence of any additional facts such as the withholding of information, the letter would not, in and of itself, necessarily imply that the government actually entrusted or directed the banks in question.
- The Panel also considered relevant that the waiver was approved for public interest reasons. It again underlined that this may not be, in and of itself, sufficient evidence of entrustment or direction of the banks in question. But it did strengthen the position of the EU that it was reasonable to read the letter as requiring the banks to participate in the Syndicated Loan.[55]

May 2001 Restructuring Programme

- The programme consisted of three measures, i.e. an injection of fresh capital into Hynix through the offering of global depositary receipts (GDR), an extension of the maturities of short and long-term debt and the purchase of Hynix convertible bonds (CB) by the creditor banks. The 18 creditors agreed to the last two measures on the condition that the sale of the GDR was successful, which was indeed the case.
- The EU concluded that the creditors were directed with regard to the purchase of CBs. In reaching this conclusion, the EU emphasized the importance of the fact that essential information was withheld concerning the presence of important officials of Korean Financial Supervisory Bodies at the Creditors' Council meeting that took place on 10 March 2001 – in spite of explicit requests to the Korean government to make known any government involvement in the restructuring and any government participation in the meetings of the creditor banks. This information was only discovered through press reports.
- It was also later revealed that officials of Korean Financial Supervisory Bodies had contacts with the creditor banks during the relevant period (March–May 2001).

[55] WT/DS299/R of 17 June 2005, *European Communities – Countervailing Measures on Dynamic Random Access Memory Chips from Korea*, para 7.64 *et seq.*

- The Panel considered that the information about the presence of the high-ranking officials at the 10 March meeting was not irrelevant but was not enough, in and of itself, to use facts available. The most one could conclude from the presence of the high-ranking officials was that the private bodies may have felt that the government was interested in seeing the creditor banks reach agreement to rescue Hynix.
- The following table lists a number of arguments that the EU has made in this context and the reasons why the Panel dismissed them:

Argument by EU	Response by the Panel
Totality of facts reveals that the government had been directing banks since November 2000 to take measures to alleviate Hynix's liquidity problem.	Most of the previous financial contributions relied on by the EU were provided by public bodies.
Creditor banks had no commercial reason to purchase CBs.	Correct that banks were aware that investment in Hynix was very risky. But: Some of the indicators invoked by the EU for Hynix's bad shape (decreasing share prices, wide-spread write off of loans) only happened after the purchase of CBs. There were also some positive prospects for the DRAM industry at the time of the purchase of the CBs. Hynix's credit rating was clearly not good (B- or B++) but not such as to make investment decisions automatically suspicious or extraordinary. Prior successful sale of GDRs.
Press allegations of government pressure exercised on one bank, i.e. the KorAmBank.	According to KorAmBank itself, the bank was simply waiting for a memorandum to be delivered by Hynix pledging to make its best efforts to reduce its debt. KorAmBank purchased CBs as soon as the memorandum was delivered. The Panel considered that allegations in a press article are insufficient in the absence of any additional supporting material.[56]

[56] WT/DS299/R of 17 June 2005, *European Communities – Countervailing Measures on Dynamic Random Access Memory Chips from Korea*, para 7.94 *et seq.*

With regard to the alleged burden of evidence requested and whether this bars the investigating authority to invoke Article 12.7, see *China – GOES*.[57]

Disclosure before Making a Final Determination (Article 12.8)

Article 12.8 stipulates that the authorities shall, before a final determination is made, inform all interested Members and interested parties of the essential facts under consideration which form the basis for the decision whether to apply definitive measures.

According to *China – Broiler Products*, the nature of the obligations under Article 12.8 ASCM is the same as under the mirror provision in the WTO Anti-Dumping Agreement, i.e. Article 6.9 of that Agreement.[58]

Article 12.8 only concerns the disclosure of facts and not, unlike Article 22.5, also the disclosure of legal considerations. Not all facts under consideration need to be disclosed but only the essential ones. Article 12.8 clarifies that essential facts are those that form the basis for the decision whether to apply definitive measures. The context provided by the last sentence of Article 12.8 ('Such disclosure shall take place in sufficient time for the parties to defend their interests.') also indicates that essential facts are those that ensure the ability of interested parties to defend their interests. On this basis, the Appellate Body concluded in *China – GOES*:

- Essential facts refer to those facts that are significant in the process of reaching a decision as to whether or not to apply definitive measures. This includes facts that are salient for a decision to apply definitive measures, as well as those that are salient for a contrary outcome.
- An authority must disclose such facts, in a coherent way, so as to permit an interested party to understand the basis for the decision whether or not to apply definitive measures.
- Disclosing the essential facts under consideration is paramount for ensuring the ability of the parties concerned to defend their interests.
- What constitutes essential facts must be understood in the light of the content of the findings needed to satisfy the substantive obligations under the ASCM, as well as the factual circumstances of each case.

[57] WT/DS414/R of 15 June 2012, *China – Countervailing and Anti-Dumping Duties on Grain-Oriented Flat-Rolled Electrical Steel from the US*, para 7.293.

[58] WT/DS427/R of 2 August 2013, *China – Anti-Dumping and Countervailing Duty Measures on Broiler Products from the United States*, para 7.361.

- In the context of the second sentence of Article 15.2 (price undercutting etc.), the essential facts that investigating authorities need to disclose are those that are required to understand the basis for their price effects examination.
- Similarly, if the investigating authority found that exporters pursued a 'low price strategy', a summary of the essential facts supporting that finding was required, rather than merely stating the conclusion that such a strategy existed.[59]

The preceding Panel ruling, although upheld by the Appellate Body, was based on the standard formulated in *Mexico – Olive Oil*, which was less elaborate. According to *Mexico – Olive Oil*, essential facts are those that underlie an investigating authority's final findings and conclusions in respect of the essential elements that must be present in the application of definitive measures. In the case of a countervailing duty investigation, these elements are subsidization, injury and causation.[60] According to the Panel in *China – GOES*, disclosure must also cover the amount of subsidization (because in case of *de minimis* subsidization the investigation must be terminated). Moreover, in the light of the particular circumstances of the case at issue (substantial increase of the 'all others rate' at definitive stage as compared to provisional findings; significant difference between the rates for known exporters representing the totality of exporters and 'all others') a more detailed disclosure of the essential facts leading to the 'all others rate' was equally required.[61] The same Panel also clarified that 'essential facts' are the facts that are actually under consideration by the investigating authority, and not those that should have been considered by a reasonable authority. Finally, the Panel seems to have been of the opinion that the scope of disclosure is not necessarily dependent on the issues parties raised.[62]

[59] WT/DS414/AB/R of 18 October 2012, *China – Countervailing and Anti-dumping Duties on Grain Oriented Flat-Rolled Electrical Steel from the United States*, paras 239–242, 249. The essential facts of this case in question are described in para 243 *et seq.*, in particular in para 247.

[60] See WT/DS341/R of 4 September 2008, *Mexico – Definitive Countervailing Measures on Olive Oil from the European Communities*, para 7.110.

[61] WT/DS414/R of 15 June 2012, *China – Countervailing and Anti-Dumping Duties on Grain-Oriented Flat-Rolled Electrical Steel from the US*, paras 7.461–7.463.

[62] WT/DS414/R of 15 June 2012, *China – Countervailing and Anti-Dumping Duties on Grain-Oriented Flat-Rolled Electrical Steel from the US*, paras 7.651 and 7.653. China did not disclose certain information concerning imports from sources not subject to investigation. China argued that there was no such need because (i) following the preliminary determination interested parties made no further arguments on this issue and (ii) interested

As can be inferred from the description above of *China – GOES*, the obligation to provide the essential facts also applies with regard to the 'all others rate'.[63]

Mexico – Olive Oil also noted that a preliminary determination is one possible means of making the required disclosure but that this will not necessarily be so in every case. In particular, if new essential facts, i.e. facts that bring about a change in the authority's findings relating to subsidization, injury or causation, are incorporated in the record after the issuance of the preliminary determination, then that preliminary determination by definition cannot satisfy the requirements set by Article 12.8.[64]

Interested Parties (Article 12.9)

Article 12.9 defines interested parties to an investigation. It first specifies that certain groups of parties are automatically qualified as interested parties, i.e. an exporter or foreign producer or the importer of a subject product as well as the producer of the like product in the importing country. Trade or business associations in which a majority of the aforementioned groups of parties (exporters, importers, domestic producers of the like product) are members equally qualify as interested parties. Note that industrial users of the subject product or consumer organizations in the importing country are not listed. Second, the last sentence of Article 12.9 says that WTO Members can also accept as interested parties other than those mentioned in the two preceding sentences.

In *Japan – DRAMs (Korea)*, Japan and Korea disagreed as to whether the Japanese investigating authority was entitled to classify creditors to Hynix as interested parties. The private creditors in question participated

parties could have consulted publicly available information. The Panel was not impressed by these arguments. It pointed out, *inter alia*, that Article 12.8 is not a means by which an investigating authority responds to arguments made by interested parties. Rather, this provision allows interested parties to defend their interests through review and response to the essential facts under consideration. This ability depends on adequate disclosure of the facts under consideration. Note, however, that the Panel found that it ultimately needed not to decide whether China respected its disclosure obligations concerning non-subject imports.

[63] WT/DS427/R of 2 August 2013, *China – Anti-Dumping and Countervailing Duty Measures on Broiler Products from the United States*, para 7.362.

[64] WT/DS341/R of 4 September 2008, *Mexico – Definitive Countervailing Measures on Olive Oil from the European Communities*, para 7.110 *et passim*. The Panel referred also to the ruling *Argentina – Ceramic Tiles*.

in debt restructurings of Hynix, and Japan examined whether they were entrusted or directed by the Korean government. The classification of these private creditors as interested parties had important consequences. If private creditors to Hynix could be considered interested parties, a questionnaire could be addressed to them and their failure to cooperate could legitimately entail the use of facts available pursuant to Article 12.7. Note that Article 12.7 conditions the use of facts available on an action (or relevant absence thereof) of an interested party. A number of private creditors indeed failed to reply to the questionnaire.

First, Korea argued that interested parties under Article 12.9 could only be such parties that had an interest in the outcome of the proceeding, which was not the case in relation to creditors of Hynix. Both the Panel and the Appellate Body rejected that argument. The Appellate Body agreed that the entities listed in subparagraphs (i) and (ii) of Article 12.9 were likely to have an interest in the outcome of the proceeding. It also acknowledged that the term 'interested parties' by definition suggests that the party must have an interest related to the investigation. However, the mere fact that the lists in subparagraphs (i) and (ii) comprise entities that may be directly interested in the outcome of the investigation did not imply that parties that may have other forms of interests pertinent to the investigation were excluded. The Appellate Body also dismissed Korea's argument related to the last sentence of Article 12.9. This last sentence stipulates that the lists in subparagraphs (i) and (ii) shall not preclude Members from 'allowing' other domestic or foreign parties to be included as interested parties. The term 'allowing' connotes the power or authority given to a WTO Member to include parties other than those listed in the two subparagraphs as interested parties, rather than a restriction on such power of inclusion to those parties that made a request. Finally, the Appellate Body also pointed out that investigating authorities did not enjoy unfettered discretion in designating entities as interested parties regardless of the relevance of such entities to the conduct of an objective investigation. As the term 'interested party' by definition suggests that the party must have some interest related to the investigation, a consideration of interest should also take account of the perspective of the investigating authority. An investigating authority needs some discretion to include as interested parties entities that are relevant to the investigation at hand but it must also be mindful of the burden that it entails for an entity to be designated an interested party. In view of the particular circumstances described at the beginning of this section, the Appellate Body considered it reasonable to seek information from Hynix's creditor institutions.[65] Note also that the preceding Panel highlighted that the scope of the right of investigating authorities to include parties as 'interested parties' must be interpreted with a view to ensuring that investigating authorities are able to obtain the necessary information.[66]

Information Provided by Industrial Users and Representative Consumer Organizations (Article 12.10)

According to Article 12.10, an investigating authority shall provide opportunities for industrial users of the product under investigation, and for representative consumer organizations in cases where the product is commonly sold at retail level, to provide information which is relevant regarding subsidization, injury and causality.

Given their knowledge of the market in the importing country, these two types of parties will normally focus their comments on issues of injury and causality.

Need to Take Due Account of Difficulties Experienced by Interested Parties (Article 12.11)

According to Article 12.11, an investigating authority shall take due account of any difficulties experienced by interested parties, in particular small companies, in supplying information requested, and shall provide any assistance practicable.

Cooperation in countervailing duty investigations represents a significant challenge of interested parties, in particular the mandatory respondents. The sheer amount of information to be provided within a comparatively short time frame in response to questionnaires, as well as language barriers, are often difficult to handle, in particular in the case of small and medium-sized enterprises. Article 12.11 acknowledges this, although it contains no concrete obligations over and above the procedural rules set out in the other paragraphs of Article 12.

[65] WT/DS336/AB/R of 28 November 2007, *Japan – Countervailing Duties on Dynamic Random Access Memories from Korea*, paras 230–245. Confirmed in WT/DS397/AB/R of 15 July 2011, *European Communities – Definitive Anti-Dumping Measures on Certain Iron or Steel Fasteners from China*, para 540 with regard to the parallel provision in the WTO Anti-Dumping Agreement.

[66] WT/DS336/R of 13 July 2007, *Japan – Countervailing Duties on Dynamic Random Access Memories from Korea*, para 7.392.

Expeditious Proceedings (Article 12.12)

Article 12 ASCM establishes numerous procedural requirements and safeguards. Compliance with these rules typically requires time as appropriate deadlines have to be given etc. Article 12.12 seems to frame somewhat these procedural rules including those set out in Article 12.1 by stipulating that the procedures set out in Article 12 are not intended to prevent an investigating authority from proceeding expeditiously with regard to the initiation of an investigation as well as with preliminary or final determinations, subject, however, to respecting the relevant rules set forth in the ASCM. See also the similar rule set out in Article 13.3 with regard to pre-initiation consultations.

Investigation Period

The Panel in *US – Anti-Dumping and Countervailing Duties (China)* concluded that countervailing duty investigations inherently have a temporal component, as alleged subsidies must be analysed in relation to a particular period. This in turn allows the calculation ultimately of an overall amount of subsidization for the investigated product. However, this does not mean that any benefits found, e.g. for a given subsidized input, have to be offset with negative benefits for the same input. There is also no obligation to offset negative benefits across different types of inputs for the product subject to investigation. The Panel made these statements on the basis of Article 14(d).[67] In relation to input subsidies, the Panel also pointed out that rather than viewing the period of investigation monolithically, an investigating authority in the context of an Article 14(d) determination should be seeking to match the transactions under examination to contemporaneous benchmarks, and that the existence or absence of a benefit in respect of one transaction or group of transactions is independent to the existence or absence of a benefit in other transactions.[68]

Mexico – Olive Oil was of the view that the selection of an investigation period by an investigating authority is a critical element in the

[67] WT/DS379/R of 22 October 2010, *US – Definitive Anti-Dumping and Countervailing Duties on Certain Products from China*, paras 11.45–11.47.

[68] WT/DS379/R of 22 October 2010, *US – Definitive Anti-Dumping and Countervailing Duties on Certain Products from China*, para 11.48. See infra the commentary to Article 14, p. 46.

countervailing duty investigative process. The investigation period determines the data that will form the basis for the assessment of subsidization, injury and causal link. The Panel agreed that the selection of a period is necessary to ensure the completeness and reliability of the data used as the basis for the injury determination. However, and although the ASCM does not set forth an express requirement regarding the selection of the investigation period for the purpose of conducting an injury analysis, this does not mean that the authority's discretion in this respect is unlimited. Rather, the requirements in Article 15.1 to base the determination of injury on positive evidence and an objective examination impose certain constraints on the investigating authority's discretion in selecting the investigation period.[69]

When applying these principles to the case in question, the Panel noted that according to *Mexico – Steel Pipes and Tubes*, to justify a truncated analysis based on discontinuous partial year-periods, an investigating authority needs to provide a sufficient explanation that takes into consideration whether the developments within the temporal subsets examined reflect developments throughout the entirety of the multi-year period, and whether and why those subsets are justified and not anomalous in the particular case at issue.[70] The Mexican investigating authority investigated injury based on data relating to April to December for the years 2000, 2001 and 2002. The period was suggested by the applicant domestic olive oil industry. It was also found that harvesting of olives typically begins in the autumn of a given year and continues into the first trimester of the following year. The exact duration of the harvesting period depends on the weather conditions. Olives have to be pressed within 24 hours after harvesting. The Panel found that it would not be impossible, as a legal matter, to justify a truncated injury analysis period. However, in the case in question, given the particular circumstances of the Mexican olive oil industry, it was evident that the investigating authority would have had more reliable data and a fuller picture of the state of the industry if it had not excluded from its analysis the periods in time when the industry was actually producing olive oil. The Panel also noted that Mexico did not

[69] WT/DS341/R of 4 September 2008, *Mexico – Definitive Countervailing Measures on Olive Oil from the European Communities*, para 7.267. The Panel referred in this context to WT/DS331/R of 8 June 2007, *Mexico – Anti-Dumping Duties on Steel Pipes and Tubes from Guatemala*, para 7.249.

[70] WT/DS341/R of 4 September 2008, *Mexico – Definitive Countervailing Measures on Olive Oil from the European Communities*, para 7.286; WT/DS331/R of 8 June 2007,

provide any substantive rationale for having chosen the nine-month periods, instead of simply selecting full calendar years.[71]

See also *EC – Countervailing Measures on DRAM Chips* concerning an investigation period that ended nearly seven months before the initiation.[72]

Mexico – Anti-Dumping Duties on Steel Pipes and Tubes from Guatemala, paras 7.252 and 7.253.

[71] WT/DS341/R of 4 September 2008, *Mexico – Definitive Countervailing Measures on Olive Oil from the European Communities*, paras 7.284–7.290.

[72] WT/DS299/R of 17 June 2005, *European Communities – Countervailing Measures on Dynamic Random Access Memory Chips from Korea*, para 7.341. A description of the relevant facts can be found *infra* the commentary to Article 15, pp. 476–477.

Article 13

Consultations

Introduction

Article 13 obliges a WTO Member that intends to conduct a countervailing duty investigation to offer consultations to the exporting WTO Member concerned before initiation of the investigation (see Article 13.1). Furthermore, throughout the investigation, the exporting WTO Member shall be afforded a reasonable opportunity to continue consultations, with a view to clarifying the factual situation and to arriving at a mutually agreed solution (see Article 13.2). Footnote 44 is attached to Article 13.2. It highlights that no affirmative preliminary or definitive determination shall be made without a reasonable opportunity for consultations to be given.

Article 13.4 stipulates that the exporting WTO Member shall, upon request, be granted access to the non-confidential file including the non-confidential version of the data used for initiating the investigation pursuant to Article 11. Finally, Article 13.3 clarifies that the provisions regarding consultations are not intended to prevent the importing Member from proceeding expeditiously to reach preliminary and final determinations.

The obligations arising out of Article 13.1 must be met before initiation. Hence, the precise date of initiation of an investigation can be of critical importance. Moreover, a Panel ruling has clarified that while there is an obligation to offer consultations prior to initiation, there is no obligation to have consultations prior to initiation (see for both issues *infra* this chapter, pp. 425–426).

The WTO Anti-Dumping Agreement does not contain such provisions on consultation while the WTO Safeguards Agreement provides for consultations with regard to some key steps in an investigation (see Articles 5.2(b), 8.1 and 12.3 of the WTO Safeguards Agreement).

Invitation to Consultation Prior to Initiation (Article 13.1)

According to Article 13.1, the WTO Member that intends to carry out a countervailing duty investigation has to invite the exporting WTO Member for consultations as soon as possible after an application under Article 11 is accepted and in any event before the initiation of any investigation. The aim of such consultations is to clarify the situation as to the matters referred to in Article 11.2, i.e. essentially the allegations of injurious subsidization, and to arrive at a mutually agreed solution. Such consultations allow the exporting Member to be briefed on the allegations. The exporting Member could also provide evidence disproving the allegation of injurious subsidization. The investigating authority has to weigh such information in the context of the review of the evidence pursuant to Article 11.3.[1]

Mexico – Olive Oil shed some light on the obligations of an investigating authority arising out of Article 13.1. Mexico issued its invitation for consultation on the 4 July 2003. The parties disagreed on the actual date of the initiation of the investigation. The EC contended that the investigation was initiated on 2 July 2003, the date on which the Mexican minister signed the Initiation Resolution. By contrast, Mexico countered that the investigation was only initiated on 16 July 2003, the day when the Initiation Resolution was published in the *Official Journal of Mexico*. The Panel sided with Mexico. It referred to footnote 37 of Article 10 of the ASCM ('The term "initiated" as used hereinafter means procedural action by which a Member formally commences an investigation as provided in Article 11') as well as Articles 22.2 (ii) (public notice shall specify the date of initiation of the investigation), 11.11 (deadline for completion of questionnaires), 12.1.3 (requirement to provide the application to known exporters and to the authorities of the third country concerned) and 17.3 (provisional measures may not be applied sooner than 60 days from the date of initiation). According to the Panel, these provisions leave the determination of the date of initiation to the internal law of the initiating WTO Member. The Panel found, as a matter of fact, that under Mexican law, the procedural act by which an investigation is formally commenced

[1] See *supra* the commentary to Article 11, pp. 382–386 and WT/DS414/R of 15 June 2012, *China – Countervailing and Anti-Dumping Duties on Grain-Oriented Flat-Rolled Electrical Steel from the US*, paras 7.115–7.119.

in the Mexican system is the publication of the Initiation Resolution, which takes legal effect the following day.[2]

The EC also claimed (i) that Article 13.1 contains an obligation to hold consultations prior to initiation and (ii) that this provision requires that a sufficient amount of time be allowed, between the invitation for consultations and the initiation, for consultations to be held. The Panel disagreed with regard to both claims. With regard to the first claim, the Panel did not see any requirement in the text of the ASCM for holding such consultations. It also found contextual support in Article 13.3. The Panel, however, emphasized that the invitation must be a *bona fide* one. By this it meant that assuming that the exporting Member accepts the invitation, the Member considering initiation of a case cannot then refuse to participate in the consultations. With regard to the second claim, the Panel referred to the text of the ASCM that did not contain a requirement that a sufficient interval must be allowed between issuance of the invitation and the initiation so that consultations could be held. The Panel found support of its position in Articles 11.9, 13.2 and 13.3 and also made an *a contrario* argument based on footnote 44 to Article 13. The Panel did not consider that consultations would be wholly devoid of purpose if they occurred only after initiation of the investigation. If it became clear that the factual basis of the initiation decision was erroneous (because, for example, the alleged subsidy programmes either were not subsidies or were not specific), then pursuant to Article 11.9, the investigating authority would be obligated to terminate the investigation immediately.[3]

Continued Consultations (Article 13.2)

Throughout the investigation, Members whose exported product is subject to an investigation shall be afforded a reasonable opportunity to continue consultations, with a view to clarifying the factual situation and to arriving at a mutually agreed solution. Article 19.1 authorizes the importing Member to impose a countervailing duty if, *inter alia*, reasonable efforts have been made to complete consultations. There is no jurisprudence in relation to Article 13.2. However, rulings with regard to Article 12.3 of the WTO Safeguards Agreement may be pertinent.[4]

[2] WT/DS341/R of 4 September 2008, *Mexico – Definitive Countervailing Measures on Olive Oil from the European Communities*, paras 7.21–7.31.

[3] WT/DS341/R of 4 September 2008, *Mexico – Definitive Countervailing Measures on Olive Oil from the European Communities*, paras 7.32–7.43.

[4] See *Dwyer* in Wolfrum/Stoll/Koebele (2008), para 12 to Article 13.

Article 13 Is Not Intended to Prevent the Expeditious Conclusion of a Countervailing Duty Investigation (Article 13.3)

Article 13.3 stipulates that without prejudice to the obligation to afford reasonable opportunity for consultations, the provisions regarding consultations are not intended to prevent the investigating authority from proceeding expeditiously with regard to the initiation and preliminary as well as definitive determinations, in accordance with the provisions of the ASCM. Article 12.12 contains similar language, but with regard to the procedural rules in that Article.

Access to Non-confidential Evidence (Article 13.4)

Article 13.4 entitles a Member whose exports might be or are already subject to investigation to have access to non-confidential evidence including non-confidential summaries of confidential information being used for initiating or conducting the investigation. The scope of Article 13.4 overlaps to some extent with that of Article 12.3. Exporting Members also have access to the non-confidential file pursuant to Article 12.3. The latter provision only applies once the investigation has been initiated. Moreover, pursuant to Article 13.4, a simple 'request' by the exporting Member to have access is sufficient while pursuant to Article 12.3, the investigating authority shall provide 'timely opportunities' to see the non-confidential file.

Article 14

Calculation of the Amount of a Subsidy in Terms of the Benefit to the Recipient

Introduction

Article 14 is concerned with the calculation of the amount of a subsidy in terms of the benefit to the recipient. In contrast, Article 1.1(b) is concerned with the existence of a benefit.[1] The ASCM itself does not define the notion of 'benefit' although pursuant to Article 1.1(b) the existence of a benefit is a constituent element of a subsidy. However, the notion of a benefit has been extensively discussed in various DSB rulings and these rulings are described in detail either in the commentary to Article 1.1(b) or, if the focus was on the calculation of the benefit, in the commentary to Article 14. Essentially, a benefit exists if the government contribution makes the recipient better off than it would have been had it obtained the same contribution, e.g. a loan, in the market place.

WTO Members have anticipated in Article 14 that investigating authorities will use different methods to calculate the benefit of the recipient when determining the amount of countervailing duties to offset a subsidy.[2] Article 14 essentially regulates two areas, one of a more procedural nature and one of a more substantive nature. First, the chapeau of Article 14 requires that the method used by an investigating authority to calculate the benefit shall be provided in the national legislation or implementing regulations of the WTO Member concerned and the application to each particular case shall be transparent and adequately explained. Second, it requires that any such method shall be consistent with the guidelines given in subparagraphs (a) to (d). The guidance given by these subparagraphs concerning the calculation of the benefit covers

[1] WT/DS412/AB/R and WT/DS426/AB/R of 6 May 2013, *Canada – Certain Measures Affecting the Renewable Energy Generation Sector; Canada – Measures Relating to Feed-In Tariff Program*, para 5.165.

[2] WT/DS212/AB/R of 9 December 2002, *United States – Countervailing Measures Concerning Certain Products from the European Communities*, para 128.

the provision of equity capital, loans and loan guarantees and, last but not least, the provision of goods or services as well as the purchase of goods by a government.

Pursuant to Article 19.2, the full amount of the subsidy is the maximum level of any countervailing duty. Hence, the calculation of the benefit to the recipient will determine this duty level while no precise calculation is necessary for an adverse effects claim (see *supra* the commentary to Article 1, p. 142).

Two issues stand out in relation to Article 14. First, privatization cases, or more specifically to what extent does the privatization of a company eliminate any benefit resulting from subsidies received by such company prior to its privatization (see *infra* this chapter, pp. 433–446)? Second, the use of out-of-country benchmarks under subparagraph (d). In other words, when and how can an investigating authority determine the amount of benefit e.g. resulting from the provision of goods by the government by comparing the price paid to the government to an international price instead of a price paid to private parties in the country in question (see *infra* this chapter, pp. 454–467)?

Article 14 Constitutes Relevant Context for Article 1

Article 14 is integrated in Part V of the ASCM, i.e. the chapter on countervailing measures. For an adverse effects claim pursuant to Part III or for any action against prohibited subsidies pursuant to Part II of the ASCM, a precise calculation of the level of benefit is not necessary. However, numerous dispute settlement rulings have recognized that Article 14 provides relevant context for the interpretation of the term 'benefit' in Article 1.1(b). See *supra* the commentary to Article 1, 142–143.

Chapeau of Article 14: Three Procedural Rules

The chapeau of Article 14 sets out three requirements. First, any method used by an investigating authority to calculate the amount of a subsidy in terms of benefit to the recipient shall be provided for in the national legislation or implementing regulations of the WTO Member concerned. Second, the application of that method in each particular case shall be transparent and adequately explained. Third, any such method to calculate the benefit shall be consistent with the guidelines contained in subparagraphs (a) to (d) of Article 14. These guidelines cover four basic government financial contributions: equity infusions, loans, loan guarantees and government provision of goods or services or government purchase of goods which are explained in detail *infra*.

The nature of the obligations contained in the chapeau has been examined by the Appellate Body on two occasions, i.e. in *US – Softwood Lumber IV* and *Japan – DRAMs (Korea)*. In *US – Softwood Lumber IV*, the Appellate Body first pointed out that the chapeau of Article 14 provides a WTO Member with some latitude as to the method it chooses to calculate the amount of benefit. The chapeau of Article 14 requires that 'any' method used by investigating authorities shall be provided for in the WTO Member's legislation or regulations. The reference to 'any' method clearly implies that more than one method consistent with Article 14 is available to investigating authorities for the purposes of calculating the benefit. Second, the Appellate Body held that the term 'shall' in the last sentence of the chapeau of Article 14 suggests that calculating benefit consistently with the guidelines set out in subparagraphs (a) to (d) is mandatory. Third, the use of the term 'guidelines' in relation to subparagraphs (a) to (d) suggests that Article 14 provides the framework within which this calculation is to be performed, although the precise detailed method is not determined. Thus, subparagraphs (a) to (d) establish parameters. They are not rigid rules that purport to contemplate every conceivable factual circumstance.[3]

EC – Countervailing Measures on DRAM Chips echoed *US – Softwood Lumber IV* by stating that an investigating authority is entitled to considerable leeway in adopting a reasonable (!) methodology for calculating the amount of benefit.[4]

[3] WT/DS257/AB/R of 19 January 2004, *United States – Final Countervailing Duty Determination with Respect to Certain Softwood Lumber from Canada*, para 92. See also WT/DS212/RW of 17 August 2005, *United States – Countervailing Measures Concerning Certain Products from the European Communities (Article 21.5)*, para 7.114 in relation to the notion of 'any method'; WT/DS341/R of 4 September 2008, *Mexico – Definitive Countervailing Measures on Olive Oil from the European Communities*, footnote 63 attached to para 7.26 states that Article 14 leaves considerable discretion to Members to define their own procedures. *Ditto* WT/DS299/R of 17 June 2005, *European Communities – Countervailing Measures on Dynamic Random Access Memory Chips from Korea*, para 7.211 in relation to Article 14(a).

[4] WT/DS299/R of 17 June 2005, *European Communities – Countervailing Measures on Dynamic Random Access Memory Chips from Korea*, para 7.213. See also WT/DS212/RW of 17 August 2005, *United States – Countervailing Measures Concerning Certain Products*

In *Japan – DRAMs (Korea)*, the Appellate Body held that Article 14 does not contemplate that the method be set out in detail by the WTO Member. The requirement of the chapeau would be met if the method used in a particular case can be derived from, or is discernible from, the national legislation or implementing regulations. The Appellate Body believed that this view struck an appropriate balance between the flexibility that is needed for adapting the benefit calculation to the particular factual situation of an investigation, and the need to ensure that other members and interested parties are made aware of the method that will be used by the Member concerned under Article 14.[5]

The Appellate Body also had to clarify the term 'method used' in the Japanese DRAMs case. This term appears twice in the chapeau of Article 14. The Panel concluded that Japan had used two formulae for the calculation of a benefit and that these constituted 'methods' that were not provided for in *Japan's Guidelines for Procedures Relating to Countervailing and Anti-Dumping Duties*. The first formula was used by Japan to calculate the benchmark interest rate for non-creditworthy companies for transactions involving loans. The second formula was used for the calculation of the benefit to be allocated to the year in which the subsidy was allegedly received for transactions involving debt forgiveness and equity infusions. The Appellate Body disagreed with the Panel. It held that the two formulae were not in and of themselves methods but rather constituted components or elements of the methods used by the Japanese investigating authority to calculate the benefit conferred to Hynix. Indeed, for instance with regard to loans, the Japanese investigating authority set out three steps it would follow, i.e.

first it would identify the appropriate benchmark for calculating the amount of subsidy;
second, it would determine the time of receipt of the subsidy; and
third it would determine the manner in which the subsidy would be allocated.

In the view of the Appellate Body, the three steps together constituted the method. The abovementioned first formula is a mathematical rule that only applied to the first step of the process of determining the benefit in

from the European Communities (Article 21.5), para 7.118 in relation to the requirement that the methodology be 'reasonable'.

5 WT/DS336/AB/R of 28 November 2007, *Japan – Countervailing Duties on Dynamic Random Access Memories from Korea*, paras 190–192.

relation to loans. Therefore, it was only a part, albeit an important part, of the method used by the Japanese investigating authority. According to the Appellate Body, the Panel should have gone further to determine the entire methodology used by the Japanese investigating authority in calculating the amount of benefit for each type of transaction. If it had done so, the Panel could then have properly proceeded to consider whether those methodologies applied in the case, in their entirety, were provided for under Japan's guidelines. The Appellate Body did not, however, decide itself on this latter question so that the issue ultimately remained unresolved.[6]

With regard to the transparency requirement set out *in fine* in the first sentence of the chapeau ('application [of the method] to each particular case shall be transparent and adequately explained'), *Mexico – Olive Oil* held that it saw nothing in this provision that requires a WTO Member to conduct a pass-through analysis.[7]

The requirement in the chapeau of Article 14 to provide an adequate explanation was discussed in the following cases:

- Adequate explanation: *Mexico – Olive Oil* (transparent and adequate explanation concerning the calculation of the benefit of the subsidy programme with regard to the pass-through issue).[8]
- Examples of an inadequate explanation: *US – Countervailing Measures Concerning Certain Products from the EC (Article 21.5)*[9] and *US – Carbon Steel (India).*[10]

[6] WT/DS336/AB/R of 28 November 2007, *Japan – Countervailing Duties on Dynamic Random Access Memories from Korea*, paras 193–202. The two formulae in question can be found in footnotes 382 and 383 of the Appellate Body report.

[7] WT/DS341/R of 4 September 2008, *Mexico – Definitive Countervailing Measures on Olive Oil from the European Communities*, para 7.159.

[8] WT/DS341/R of 4 September 2008, *Mexico – Definitive Countervailing Measures on Olive Oil from the European Communities*, paras 7.159–7.170.

[9] WT/DS212/RW of 17 August 2005, *United States – Countervailing Measures Concerning Certain Products from the European Communities (Article 21.5)*, para 7.137.

[10] WT/DS436/AB/R of 8 December 2014, *United States – Countervailing Measures on Certain Hot-Rolled Carbon Steel Flat Products from India*, paras 4.290–4.291. See also para 4.337 that summarized the Panel findings with regard to SDF loans. According to the Panel, the term 'transparent' conveys the sense that the application of the benefit methodology should be set out in such a fashion that it can be easily understood or discerned. 'Adequately explain' conveys the sense of making clear or intelligible, and giving details of how the methodology was explained. According to the Panel, the chapeau of Article 14 does not require an investigating authority to indicate the reasons why it chose to determine the benefit on a particular basis.

Benefit to the Recipient – Privatization Cases

Imports are only countervailable if the financial contribution confers a benefit on the entity producing the subject product. Therefore, it will be examined in the context of a countervailing duty investigation whether a manufacturer of the subject product obtained a benefit either directly or indirectly. A producer subject to an investigation can obtain a benefit indirectly if that benefit passed through to it from the recipient of the subsidy. One issue in this context is whether a subsidy provided to a State-owned enterprise extinguishes if such enterprise is subsequently fully privatized. Similar questions arise if a privately-owned enterprise that has received a subsidy subsequently changes ownership. Finally, it will have to be examined whether it makes a difference if the State-owned company receiving such subsidy has only partially been privatized. The pass-through issue also arises in the case of a partial change in ownership of a privately owned company that has received a subsidy. In legal terms, the question is about the notion of the 'recipient'. Can the legal entity receiving the subsidies and its shareholders be examined together for the purposes of the benefit analysis? Is it sufficient to demonstrate that the continuing productive operations (machinery etc.) benefit from the subsidy or should the legal entity be the focus of the benefit analysis? The next two sections describe relevant DSB rulings in this respect.

Impact of 'Full' Privatizations and Changes in Ownership

US – Lead and Bismuth II and *US – Countervailing Measures Concerning Certain Products from the EC* centred around the question whether a benefit (under Article 1.1(b)) which is derived from a non-recurring (but not fully amortized) financial contribution, continues to exist following a transfer of ownership of a State-owned enterprise to a new private owner at arm's length and for fair market value, where the government retains no controlling interest in the privatized producer and transfers all or substantially all the property. During the 1990s, the USDOC imposed a number of countervailing duties on imports from EU exporters which had been privatized following the granting of non-recurring subsidies. The EU criticized that the USDOC failed to adequately address the impact of these changes in ownership.

The first dispute to address this issue was *US – Lead and Bismuth II*. This case concerned countervailing duties imposed by USDOC on leaded bars from the UK in 1993. The duties related principally to non-recurring subsidies granted to the State-owned BSC (British Steel Corporation) between 1977 and 1986, which USDOC allocated over time. At the time of the CVD investigation, the leaded bars were produced by United Engineering Steels Limited (UES). UES was a joint venture between Guest, Keen and Nettlefolds (GKN) and British Steel. British Steel had been privatized in 1988. In 1995, it repurchased 100 per cent of UES, which became BSES (British Steel Engineering Steels). The EU's claim, which related to three annual reviews initiated in 1995, 1996 and 1997 (concerning imports into the US made in 1994, 1995 and 1996 respectively), was that since these transactions of shares were at arm's length and for fair market value, the benefit of the past subsidies had been extinguished and therefore no countervailing duties could be imposed in accordance with Article VI:3 of GATT 1994, in the absence of current subsidization. The US argued that, in accordance with its 'gamma' change-in-ownership methodology, the benefit of the past subsidies had 'travelled' from BSC to UES and BSES, since subsidies continue to benefit the productive operations of firms, while changes in ownership, even at fair market value, only affect the benefit to the owners.

The panel in *US – Lead and Bismuth II* found that the USDOC erred in not examining the impact of the changes in ownership from the point of view of UES and BSES (i.e. the firms producing leaded bars during the periods of review) and agreed with the EU that since fair market value was paid, there was no basis for finding that leaded bars imported into the US from the UK in 1994, 1995 and 1996 benefitted from prior subsidies to BSC.[11]

The Appellate Body upheld the findings of the panel. It concluded that the US could not simply assume that there was a continuing benefit from a previous financial contribution, since Article 1.1 does not address the time at which the financial contribution and the benefit may be conferred. Although an investigating authority, in an administrative review under Article 21.2, may initially presume that a benefit continues, this presumption cannot be 'irrebuttable'.[12] The Appellate Body also rejected the US argument that subsidies benefit productive operations, recalling its *Canada – Aircraft* finding that there must be a benefit to a

[11] WT/DS138/R of 23 December 1999, *United States – Imposition of Countervailing Duties on Certain Hot-Rolled Lead and Bismuth Carbon Steel Products originating in the United Kingdom*, paras 6.70 and 6.81.

[12] WT/DS138/AB/R of 10 May 2000, *United States – Imposition of Countervailing Duties on Certain Hot-Rolled Lead and Bismuth Carbon Steel Products originating in the United Kingdom*, paras 59–62.

legal person.[13] Finally, the Appellate Body found no fault with the Panel's finding that the payment of fair market value for the productive assets, goodwill etc. employed by UES and BSES in its production of leaded bars meant that none of the prior subsidies to BSC could have benefited these firms.[14] In short, *US – Lead and Bismuth II* established that investigating authorities could not simply assume that benefits continued during the period of allocation of non-recurring subsidies but had to address the impact of intervening events, such as changes in ownership. *US – Lead and Bismuth II* also showed that, in the cases in question, the payment of fair market value by the buyers of a firm served to eliminate the impact of prior subsidies.

The *US – Lead and Bismuth II* dispute was something of a test case and was limited to the countervailing measures in question. Since the USDOC maintained countervailing duties on a large number of privatized EU firms following the adoption of the Panel and Appellate Body reports in *US – Lead and Bismuth II*, in *US – Countervailing Measures Concerning Certain Products from the EC*, the EU challenged 12 US countervailing duty measures as well as the new US 'same person' test and the US legal provision on changes in ownership, Section 771(5)(F) of the United States Tariff Act of 1930 (which is codified in 19 U.S.C. § 1677(5)(F)). The US, by means of its so-called 'same person' test, argued that the benefit continued to exist if the recipient of the subsidy is the same legal person. Refining its argument made in *US – Lead and Bismuth II*, it argued that a distinction should be made between, on the one hand, the legal person producing the subject merchandise (and which received the subsidy) and, on the other, the new owner of the legal entity. Legal persons are distinct from their shareholders and the term recipient cannot include both a legal person and the shareholder of that legal person. According to the US, a change in ownership, irrespective of the price paid for the transaction, will never extinguish the benefit when the State-owned enterprise and the new privatized firm are the same legal person, i.e. they produce the same product with the same workforce and equipment. Subsidies shift the recipient's supply curve and subsequent privatization does not move the

[13] WT/DS138/AB/R of 10 May 2000, *United States – Imposition of Countervailing Duties on Certain Hot-Rolled Lead and Bismuth Carbon Steel Products originating in the United Kingdom*, paras 56–58.

[14] WT/DS138/AB/R of 10 May 2000, *United States – Imposition of Countervailing Duties on Certain Hot-Rolled Lead and Bismuth Carbon Steel Products originating in the United Kingdom*, para 68. *Grossman/Mavroidis* (2003) pp. 187–193 *et passim* and *Grossman/Mavroidis* (2005/2) disagree with the Appellate Body's findings.

supply curve back to where it had been, and thus does not affect the continued existence of the subsidy. The US noted that change in ownership of a subsidy recipient did not remove the new equipment or increase the previously lowered debt.

The Appellate Body did not agree with the US. It held in relation to the case at issue that

- for the purpose of determining whether a benefit exists under the ASCM, no distinction should be made between a company producing merchandise and its shareholders and
- there is a rebuttable presumption that a benefit that results from a financial contribution to a State-owned company producing merchandise ceases to exist if that company has been privatized at arm's length and for fair market value.

The following points of the Appellate Body's reasoning seem particularly noteworthy:

- The Appellate Body accepted the US's argument that the privatization did not remove the equipment that a State-owned enterprise may have acquired (or received) with the financial contribution and that, consequently the same firm may continue to make the same products on the same equipment. However, this observation served only to illustrate that, following privatization, the *utility* value of equipment acquired as a result of a financial contribution is not extinguished. But the utility value of such equipment was legally irrelevant for determining the continued existence of a benefit. Therefore, once a fair market price is paid for the equipment, its market value is redeemed, regardless of the utility the firm may derive from the equipment. Accordingly, it is the market value of the equipment that is the focal point of the analysis, and not the equipment's utility value to the privatized firm (para 102).
- The Appellate Body did not accept the US's argument that, irrespective of the price paid by the new private owner, the artificially enhanced competitiveness generated by the subsidies would not be eliminated, as the firm will continue to produce at the same costs and in the same volumes. According to the Appellate Body, the production costs include, as a necessary component, the cost of capital, which depends on the purchasing price for the enterprise.[15] The Appellate Body agreed with the

[15] The Panel also referred repeatedly to the link between the subsidy and the return on investment. The production and export of goods is done by a producer for the purpose of generating an economic benefit to its owners. When the existence of a subsidy improves the

Panel's statement that the US seemed to be attaching the benefit from a subsidy to the production activity and viewed countervailing duties as designed to counteract all market distortions (paras 103 and 104).

- The Appellate Body noted that the ASCM does not identify the recipient of a benefit by using any particular legal term of art. Rather, the ASCM uses several terms to describe the economic entity that receives a benefit, as evidenced by Articles 2, 6.1(b), 11.2(ii), 14, 19.3 as well as footnote 36 to Article 10 and Annex IV (para 112).
- The transfer of funds could be provided directly from the government to the legal person that is the producer of the subsidized product, or it could be provided indirectly, e.g. through an income tax concession to the natural persons that own the firm (inasmuch as they invest in the legal person's productive activities). In both cases, the cost of raising capital for the legal person that is the producer would be reduced. Article VI:3 of GATT 1994 and footnote 36 of Article 10 contemplate the possibility of providing a subsidy to the shareholder by providing that a subsidy may be bestowed *indirectly* upon the manufacture, production or export of merchandise (para 113).
- The approach advocated by the US could potentially undermine the ASCM by opening a wide door enabling subsidizing governments to circumvent the Agreement's provisions by bestowing benefits directly on the firms' owners rather than on the firms themselves (para 115).
- The Appellate Body, however, found that the Panel adopted too sweeping an interpretation of the ASCM by finding that for the purposes of a benefit determination, when the ASCM refers to the recipient of the benefit, it means the company and its shareholder together and that no distinction should be made between the two. The Panel examined only a narrow set of circumstances and some of the financial contribution provided to owners may not flow into the firm (paras 116–118).
- The Appellate Body also took issue with the Panel's finding that a benefit is necessarily extinguished following privatization at arm's length and for fair market value. According to the Appellate Body, there is only a rebuttable presumption that a benefit ceases to exist after such a privatization. The investigating authority has the burden of identifying evidence which establishes that the benefit from the previous financial contribution does

ability of a producer to produce and export a good, it necessarily impacts on its profitability and, therefore, on the rate of return to shareholders. See WT/DS212/R of 31 July 2002, *United States – Countervailing Measures Concerning Certain Products from the European Communities*, para 7.50 *et passim*.

indeed continue beyond privatization. With regard to this latter aspect, the Appellate Body pointed out that, for instance, privatizations involve complex and long-term investments in which the seller, namely the government, is not always a passive price taker and, consequently, the fair market price of a State-owned enterprise is not necessarily always unrelated to government action. In privatizations, governments have the ability, by designing economic and other policies, to influence the circumstances and the conditions of the sale so as to obtain a certain market valuation of the enterprise (paras 120–127). In other words, government policies to promote an industry may, for instance, lead to the creation of substantial over-capacity and severely distort the market, thus depressing 'market' prices to an unreasonably low level.

- The Appellate Body applied the above findings to the US's 'same person method'. This method provided that when the USDOC determined that no new legal person was created as a result of privatization, the USDOC would conclude from this determination, without any further analysis, and irrespective of the price paid by the new owners for the newly-privatized enterprise, that the newly-privatized enterprise continues to receive the benefit of a previous financial contribution. Not surprisingly, the Appellate Body concluded that this method is of itself inconsistent with Articles 19.1, 21.2 and 21.3 of the ACSM because it impedes the USDOC from complying with its obligation to examine whether a countervailable benefit continues to exist in a firm subsequent to that firm's change in ownership (paras 128–153).
- However, the Appellate Body did not find any inconsistency of Section 771(5)(F) of the United States Tariff Act of 1930 with WTO law 'as such' because the Tariff Act did not prescribe any specific methodology and therefore did not mandate the US to apply the 'same person' methodology and thus breach WTO law. This provision stipulated that a change in ownership 'does not by itself require a determination by the administering authority' that a past countervailable subsidy is no longer countervailable, even if the change in ownership is accomplished through an arm's-length transaction. The Appellate Body ruled that the Panel's finding that the provision was 'as such' inconsistent with WTO rules was premised on its incorrect finding that privatizations at fair market value necessarily removed prior subsidies. Therefore, it reversed the Panel's finding (paras 154–160).[16]

[16] WT/DS212/AB/R of 9 December 2002, *United States – Countervailing Measures Concerning Certain Products from the European Communities*, paras 85, 87–89, 95, 99, 102–160. See

The implementation of the above ruling was also subject to panel review. In the 21.5 Panel, the EU challenged the US implementation in three sunset reviews, including *Certain Corrosion-Resistant Carbon Steel Flat Products from France* (C-427–810) (Case No. 9).[17] This case concerned the USDOC's likelihood-of-subsidization determination in 1999, which the EU claimed was in breach of WTO rules because the privatization of Usinor during the period 1995–1998 removed the benefit of any prior subsidies. Therefore, in the view of the EU, there could be no continuation or recurrence of subsidy under Article 21.3. France incrementally privatized this company over a period of three years. Prior to the privatization, the Government of France wholly owned Usinor, holding 80 per cent directly and 20 per cent through a bank that at the time was government-controlled. The French government issued four types of share offerings to four different classes of purchasers. The USDOC found that the privatization of Usinor was at arm's length and fair market value with the exception of the employee/former employee offering, which constituted 5.16 per cent of the sale. According to the USDOC, the sale of shares to Usinor employees at prices below fair market value did not extinguish certain allocable, nonrecurring, pre-privatization subsidies that continued at an above *de minimis* rate beyond the original sunset review. Therefore, the USDOC reaffirmed its original likelihood-of-subsidization determination and renewed the countervailing duty rate of 15.13 per cent. The EU challenged this implementation.[18]

First, it claimed that USDOC wrongly applied a segmented analysis per class of purchasers instead of analysing the privatization as a whole. According to the EU, this should have been done by examining whether the actual share price exceeded the average share price recognized by the Privatization Commission as necessary to recoup the value of the company. Second, the EU claimed that the USDOC did not properly assess whether the sales of shares to employees and former employees were at arm's length and for fair market value. This group of buyers could purchase the shares either at a market price or – provided a buyer agreed to

also WT/DS138/AB/R of 10 May 2000, *United States – Imposition of Countervailing Duties on Certain Hot-Rolled Lead and Bismuth Carbon Steel Products originating in the United Kingdom*, paras 61 and 62. This jurisprudence was heavily criticized by *Grossman/Mavroidis* (2005/2) p. 83 *et seq.*

[17] The original countervailing duty determination was in 1993 and therefore not subject to WTO dispute settlement.

[18] WT/DS212/RW of 17 August 2005, *United States – Countervailing Measures Concerning Certain Products from the European Communities (Article 21.5)*, paras 7.88–7.93.

keep the shares for 24 months – with a 20 per cent discount. According to the EU, the 20 per cent discount reflected a risk premium because of the 24 months holding period of the shares given to (former) employees.

The Panel rejected both of the EU's claims. With regard to the EU's first claim, it noted that in the absence of a legally prescribed methodology, it is within a Member's discretion to develop a reasonable methodology which must be applied in a transparent manner and adequately explained. The Panel acknowledged that it would have difficulties formulating an arm's length analysis for Usinor's privatization as a whole given the diversity of buyers and purchasers. With regard to the EU's second claim, the Panel noted that the USDOC never actually analysed the effect of the different restrictions and instead merely asserted that the resale restrictions *per se* provide no explanation for the substantial discount offered to Usinor's employees. This is normally not enough. However, in a subsidy case such as the one at issue, the government that is privatizing its own company is best placed to provide specific information on privatization and it would therefore have been incumbent on the French government to provide a justification for the 20 per cent discount. No such information was provided by the EU.

Note that the USDOC also claimed that the sales transactions to (former) Usinor employees were not at arm's length because the former employees were related to the seller of Usinor's shares. The Panel did not agree with the USDOC's assessment. It held that one could be entitled to assume that an employee is related to his/her employer and that the same could be said in relation to a former employee (e.g. a retiree's pension may depend on the employer's performance). But a conclusion that the employees/former employees are related to another entity that owns the employer company requires at least some explanation. The arm's length analysis should focus on the relationship between the seller and the purchaser at the time of the transaction, since the purpose of the analysis is to determine whether the terms of that transaction are affected by the relation between those parties. In this context, the Panel also recalled that the chapeau of Article 14 requires that the method to determine the existence of a benefit be adequately explained. However, the fact that the USDOC did not demonstrate the existence of a relationship between the seller and the buyer of the shares did finally not invalidate the USDOC's finding. According to the Panel, an arm's length test, in the sense of whether or not a relationship exists, is an ancillary examination that provides the context for, or otherwise informs, the decision on fair market value. The arm's length test merely affects the level of scrutiny for the fair market value analysis. Where a relationship exists, a closer analysis of the actual terms is warranted to determine if the transaction at issue is consistent with market principles. Thus, regardless of whether the transaction occurred at arm's length, an investigating authority must analyse whether the privatization was for fair market value to ultimately determine whether a benefit passed through. As the USDOC found (and the Panel accepted this) that the transaction was not at fair market value, the inadequate application of the arm's length test did not have any further consequences.[19]

Scholars have been critical with the privatization jurisprudence.[20]

Partial Privatization and Private-to-Private Changes in Ownership

The findings in *US – Lead and Bismuth II* and in *US – Countervailing Measures Concerning Certain Products from the EC* as described in the preceding section concerned 'full' privatizations, i.e. where the government transfers all or substantially all the property and retains no controlling interest in the firm.[21] With regard to the impact of other changes in ownership, the Appellate Body stated in *US – Lead and Bismuth II* that '[t]he Panel's absolute rule of "no benefit" may be defensible in the context of transactions between two private parties taking place in reasonably competitive markets'.[22] The question is whether the Appellate Body's statement could be read that a 'full' private-to-private change in ownership could be presumed to remove the benefit of prior non-recurring subsidies and that such a presumption would be irrebuttable. The Panel in *EC and certain Member States – Large Civil Aircraft* explicitly disagreed with this reading[23] while the Appellate Body in this case was more nuanced. The latter stated that a private-to-private sale would be more likely to be at

[19] WT/DS212/RW of 17 August 2005, *United States – Countervailing Measures Concerning Certain Products from the European Communities (Article 21.5)*, paras 7.94–7.150. Paras 7.159–7.176 contain the considerations as to the amount of benefit that passes through in such a privatization where only 5.16 per cent of shares were not sold at fair market value.

[20] See e.g. *Sykes* (2010) pp. 510–511.

[21] WT/DS138/AB/R of 10 May 2000, *United States – Imposition of Countervailing Duties on Certain Hot-Rolled Lead and Bismuth Carbon Steel Products originating in the United Kingdom*, para 117.

[22] WT/DS138/AB/R of 10 May 2000, *United States – Imposition of Countervailing Duties on Certain Hot-Rolled Lead and Bismuth Carbon Steel Products originating in the United Kingdom*, para 124.

[23] WT/DS316/R of 30 June 2010, *EC and certain Member States – Measures Affecting Trade in Large Civil Aircraft*, paras 7.251–7.254.

market value and that a comprehensive assessment of change in ownership and control would have to take place for such transactions.[24]

Other types of changes in ownership, notably partial privatizations and partial private-to-private sales, were also discussed in the *EC and certain Member States – Large Civil Aircraft* case. This case did not concern countervailing duties under Part V of the ASCM Agreement but rather a serious prejudice case under Part III, i.e. the question was whether past subsidies were causing present adverse effects under Article 5. The EU alleged that the extinction of all or part of prior subsidies had an impact on whether subsidies were causing present adverse effects. Although the panel in this case found that there was no need to establish a 'continuing benefit' in a Part III case, it considered the European Union's claims of extinction of subsidies *in the alternative*.

On the substance, the Panel disagreed with the European Union's assertion that *Lead and Bismuth II* and *US – Countervailing Measures Concerning Certain Products from the EC* established a 'principle' that an arm's length, fair market value sale of all or part of a subsidized producer, whether by a government or a private owner, presumptively extinguishes all or part of the prior subsidies.[25] The Panel could find no distinction between the transactions identified by the European Union (e.g. the partial privatization of Aérospatiale) and the daily trading of shares in a public company. It considered that the recognition of a principle that changes in ownership presumptively remove prior subsidies would 'potentially eviscerate' the disciplines of the ASCM.[26] In its analysis, the Panel, while relying on the argument that the findings in *Lead and Bismuth II* and *US – Countervailing Measures Concerning Certain Products from the EC* were limited to full privatizations, explicitly rejected certain conclusions of the findings of the Panel in *US – Countervailing Measures Concerning Certain Products from the EC*.[27] Thus, it appeared to revisit certain elements of the Appellate Body's analysis. In particular, the Panel suggested that there was nothing in the Appellate Body's reports to support the conclusion that a firm and its owners must *necessarily* be considered the recipient. In

[24] WT/DS316/AB/R of 18 May 2011, *EC and certain Member States – Measures Affecting Trade in Large Civil Aircraft*, para 728.

[25] WT/DS316/R of 30 June 2010, *EC and certain Member States – Measures Affecting Trade in Large Civil Aircraft*, para 7.255.

[26] WT/DS316/R of 30 June 2010, *EC and certain Member States – Measures Affecting Trade in Large Civil Aircraft*, para 7.246.

[27] WT/DS316/R of 30 June 2010, *EC and certain Member States – Measures Affecting Trade in Large Civil Aircraft*, paras 7.240–7.247.

addition, it concluded that the argument that the payment of fair market value ensures that the buyer gets nothing for free (and therefore removes the subsidy) is misplaced. For the Panel, the payment of fair market value only ensures that the transaction is on a commercial basis and does not provide a *new* subsidy. The Panel also disputed that *US – Countervailing Measures Concerning Certain Products from the EC (21.5 Panel)* established a principle that partial privatizations could also remove prior subsidies.[28]

The European Union appealed. The Appellate Body recalled its previous findings with regard to full privatizations but noted its previous statement that there was no 'inflexible rule' that privatizations automatically extinguish subsidies and that such a conclusion 'depends on the facts of each case'.[29] The three members of the Appellate Body expressed different views on the extinction of subsidies by partial privatizations or private-to-private sales. The one Member who considered that the rationale underlying the Appellate Body's case law on full privatizations could equally apply to partial privatizations and private-to-private transactions, emphasized that an important question would be to what extent the transaction resulted in a transfer of control to the new owners who paid fair market value for the shares. Ultimately, the Appellate Body reversed the Panel's findings that the sales transactions did not extinguish a portion of past subsidies, on the basis that the panel had failed to correctly examine whether the transactions were at arm's length and for fair market value, and to what extent they involved a transfer of ownership and control to the new owners. It ruled also that there were insufficient factual findings by the panel to enable a completion of the analysis.[30]

The issue of the impact of partial privatizations and private-to-private sales remains unresolved and continues to be discussed in the ongoing Article 21.5 panel.

Equity Capital (Subparagraph (a))

Introduction

According to subparagraph (a) a government provision of equity capital shall not be considered as conferring a benefit, unless the investment

[28] WT/DS316/R of 30 June 2010, *EC and certain Member States – Measures Affecting Trade in Large Civil Aircraft*, para 7.250.

[29] WT/DS316/AB/R of 18 May 2011, *EC and certain Member States – Measures Affecting Trade in Large Civil Aircraft*, para. 723.

[30] WT/DS316/AB/R of 18 May 2011, *EC and certain Member States – Measures Affecting Trade in Large Civil Aircraft*, paras 730–736.

decision can be regarded as inconsistent with the usual investment practice (including for the provision of risk capital) of private investors in the territory of that Member. It is worth noting that subparagraph (a) does not refer to calculation of the benefit as such but only to the situation in which a benefit exists.

In *EC and certain Member States – Large Civil Aircraft*, the Appellate Body clarified the term 'usual investment practice':

> The words 'usual' and 'practice' [in Article 14(a)] are in a sense reinforcing, with the former signifying '{c}ommonly or customarily observed or practised' [footnote omitted] and the latter 'usual or customary action or performance'. [footnote omitted] Thus, we understand the term 'usual practice' to describe common or customary conduct of private investors in respect of equity investment. We also observe that Article 14(a) focuses the inquiry on the 'investment decision'. This reflects an *ex ante* approach to assessing the equity investment by comparing the decision, based on the costs and expected returns of the transaction, to the usual investment practice of private investors at the moment the decision to invest is undertaken. [footnote omitted] The focus in Article 14(a) on the 'investment decision' is thus critical, in our view, because it identifies *what* is to be compared to a market benchmark, and *when* that comparison is to be situated. (emphasis in original)[31]

Risk Capital As a Form of Equity Capital

In *EC – Countervailing Measures on DRAM Chips*, the question was how to calculate the benefit conferred on Hynix resulting from the numerous restructuring measures (provision of new loans and loan guarantees, extension of maturities, debt-to-equity swaps). As the chances of ever recovering the money invested in these restructurings were minimal, the EU considered all these financial contributions as grants. The Panel did not agree. It held that in such circumstances the funding provided, in whatever form, is equal to the provision of risk capital, and that Article 14(a) did not provide a precise method for calculating the benefit for this. The Panel then pointed out that all the aforementioned restructuring measures required the recipient to repay the money or to surrender an ownership share in the company. This was not the same as a grant. In other words, the restructuring measures that provided

[31] WT/DS316/AB/R of 18 May 2011, *EC and certain Member States – Measures Affecting Trade in Large Civil Aircraft*, para 999 (see also para 1019). The factual background is described in detail *supra* the commentary to Article 1, pp. 152–156.

for repayment could not reasonably be considered to have conferred the same benefit as the provision of funds without such obligation, i.e. a grant. The Panel finally added that it realized that it might be difficult to apply Article 14 in such a situation and that an investigating authority was entitled to considerable leeway in adopting a reasonable methodology.[32]

Debt-to-Equity Swap

In *Japan – DRAMs (Korea)*, Japan and Korea disagreed as to the proper amount of benefit that Hynix received as a result of a debt-to-equity swap by four of its creditors. Korea criticized the Japanese anti-subsidy measure on the grounds

(1) that Japan had applied the wrong benchmark for calculating the benefit;
(2) that Japan assigned a zero value to the equity that the four creditors received in Hynix; and
(3) that Japan wrongly did not take into account that the debt-to-equity swaps diluted the ownership of Hynix's existing shareholders.

With regard to the first issue, Korea claimed at the Panel stage, and the Panel agreed, that Japan wrongly calculated the benefit accruing to Hynix from the debt-to-equity swaps on the basis of an exclusively outside investor benchmark, i.e. from the perspective of an investor that previously had not given any loans to Hynix. The Appellate Body disagreed with the Panel. It took issue with the Panel's conclusion that since both parties agreed that the *inside* investor standard constituted a valid benchmark (something which Japan disputed before the Appellate Body), there was no need for the Panel to make any findings on this matter. The Appellate Body considered that the Panel should have identified the appropriate benchmark for calculating the amount of benefit during the investigation period. It did not consider the distinction between inside and outside investors to be helpful in order to determine the appropriate benchmark for calculating the amount of benefit under Articles 1.1(b) and 14. The terms of the financial transaction must be assessed against the terms that would result from unconstrained exchange in the relevant market. In this respect, the Appellate Body also referred to the existence of markets for

[32] WT/DS299/R of 17 June 2005, *European Communities – Countervailing Measures on Dynamic Random Access Memory Chips from Korea*, paras 7.211–7.215.

distressed debts that exist in many economies. It underlined that it did not consider that there were different standards applicable to inside and outside investors. There was but one standard – the market standard – according to which rational investors act. It also referred to Article 14(a) and (b) and that none of these provisions made a distinction between outside or inside investors.[33]

With regard to the second issue, the Appellate Body held that the Japanese investigating authority did not sufficiently explain, in its determination, how it reached the conclusion that the value of the shares received by the four creditors was zero from the perspective of Hynix, the recipient of the subsidy.[34]

Finally, with regard to the third point, Japan submitted that dilution was irrelevant to this case, not least because even if dilution had occurred, it would have taken place at the level of the shareholders, not at the level of Hynix, i.e. the recipient of the subsidy. The Appellate Body agreed with Japan that dilution of the rights of existing shareholders did not appear to be a relevant issue on the facts of the case – the Panel referred to the issue of dilution merely to support its finding that the Japanese investigating authority did not calculate the amount of the benefit from the perspective of the recipient. But the Appellate Body, referring to its report in *US – Countervailing Duties on Certain EC Products* (paras 116–118) did not wish to exclude the possibility that there might be circumstances in which the relationship between a company and its shareholders might be relevant for calculating the amount of benefit to the recipient.[35]

Loan (Subparagraph (b))

Article 14(b) stipulates as a benchmark 'a comparable commercial loan which the firm could actually obtain in the market'. Contrary to subparagraph (d), subparagraph (b) thus does not contain an express notion of territoriality. Therefore, the paradigm of an 'in-the-country' benchmark versus an 'out-of-the-country' benchmark does not arise. The amount of the benefit is the difference between the market benchmark and the

[33] WT/DS336/AB/R of 28 November 2007, *Japan – Countervailing Duties on Dynamic Random Access Memories from Korea*, paras 171–174.

[34] WT/DS336/AB/R of 28 November 2007, *Japan – Countervailing Duties on Dynamic Random Access Memories from Korea*, paras 175–178.

[35] WT/DS336/AB/R of 28 November 2007, *Japan – Countervailing Duties on Dynamic Random Access Memories from Korea*, paras 179–182.

amount that the firm has actually paid for the loan, if the latter is lower than the former.

The Appellate Body held that subparagraph (b) does not contain any inherent limitations that would prevent an investigating authority from using as benchmarks interest rates on loans denominated in currencies other than the currency of the investigated loan, or from using proxies instead of observed interest rates, in situations where the interest rates on loans in the currency of the investigated loan are distorted and thus cannot be used as a benchmark. Any other interpretation would be excessively formalistic and potentially frustrate the purpose of this provision in cases of distorted markets. For instance, there may be circumstances where all loans in the same currency are distorted by government intervention.

The Appellate Body arrived at this conclusion by interpreting the terms 'comparable', 'commercial' and a 'loan which the firm could actually obtain on the market'. In order to be 'comparable', a benchmark loan should have as many elements as possible in common with the investigated loan. Ideally, the investigating authority should use as a benchmark a loan to the same borrower that has been established around the same time, has the same structure as, and similar maturity to the government loan, is about the same size, and is denominated in the same currency. Both the Panel and the Appellate Body recognized, however, that such an ideal benchmark loan would be extremely rare and that a comparison should also be possible with other loans that present a lesser degree of similarity.

As to the term 'commercial', the Appellate Body observed that this term does not refer to the identity of the provider of the loan. Thus, the fact that the loan has been provided by a government does not render such a loan *ipso facto* as non-commercial. An investigating authority would have to establish that the government presence or influence in the market causes distortions that render interest rates unusable as benchmarks. The Appellate Body defined 'commercial' as 'interested in financial return rather than artistry; likely to make a profit; regarded as a mere matter of business'.

As to the last criterion ('loan which the firm could actually obtain on the market'), the Appellate Body observed that the use of the conditional language ('could') suggests that the benchmark loan need not in every case be a loan that exists or can in fact be obtained in the market. Rather, this criterion refers first and foremost to the borrower's risk profile.[36]

[36] WT/DS379/AB/R of 11 March 2011, *US – Definitive Anti-Dumping and Countervailing Duties on Certain Products from China*, paras 471–490; WT/DS436/AB/R of 8 December

The Appellate Body also indicated as to how an investigating authority should approach the selection of an appropriate benchmark. According to the Appellate Body, this involves a progressive search for a comparable loan, starting with the commercial loan that is closest to the investigated loan (a loan to the same borrower that is nearly identical to the investigated loan in terms of timing, structure, maturity, size and currency) and moving to less similar commercial loans while adjusting them to ensure comparability to the investigated loan. The further away an investigating authority moves from the ideal benchmark of the identical or nearly identical loan, the more adjustments will be necessary to ensure that the benchmark loan approximates the comparable commercial loan which the firm could actually obtain on the market. In line with *US – Softwood Lumber IV*, the Appellate Body also pointed out that in situations where an investigating authority does not use the private prices in the market of the country of provision, it should nevertheless select a method for calculating the benefit that relates or refers to, or is connected with the prevailing market conditions in the country of provision. Moreover, any method used, as well as how it approximates the loan in another currency or the proxy to a comparable commercial loan that the firm could actually obtain on the market, must be transparent and adequately explained.[37]

The Appellate Body also confirmed that the USDOC was entitled not to rely on Chinese interest rates as a benchmark for the purposes of the benefit analysis under Article 14(b). China argued that the USDOC should have evaluated how the government's predominant role as a commercial lender could have any effect on benchmark interest rates, let alone an effect that is clearly distinct from the implementation of monetary policy and that would cause benchmark interest rates to be lower than they otherwise would be. The Appellate Body did not accept this. There is no specific requirement that, in order to reject in-country prices, investigating authorities must show that government prices are artificially low, i.e. that interest rates are distorted. Rather, investigating authorities must

2014, *United States – Countervailing Measures on Certain Hot-Rolled Carbon Steel Flat Products from India*, para 4.345. Note, however, that WT/DS273/R of 7 March 2005, *Korea – Measures Affecting Trade in Commercial Vessels*, paras 7.172, 7.179 has concluded that a loan given by a public body does not constitute a convincing market benchmark.

[37] WT/DS379/AB/R of 11 March 2011, *US – Definitive Anti-Dumping and Countervailing Duties on Certain Products from China*, paras 486, 488 and 489; *United States – Countervailing Measures on Certain Hot-Rolled Carbon Steel Flat Products from India*, paras 4.345 and 4.346. See also *supra* this chapter, pp. 429–432.

show that government intervention as a whole distorts the market, not that each factor taken in isolation has that effect.[38]

Note that the conclusion that the Chinese loan market was distorted was based on the following findings:

- The Chinese government's role in the banking sector and influence on interest rates.
- The fact that interest rates were largely undifferentiated, with most loans being made at rates close to the government-set benchmark rate, which the USDOC considered to be evidence that market forces were not operating and that banks still lacked adequate risk management and analytical skills.
- Foreign banks in China were subject to the same government controls as domestic banks.
- Privately owned Chinese banks accounted for a very small percentage of total lending.

In sum, the role of the Chinese government in the banking sector went much beyond the implementation of monetary policy so that interest rates were distorted.[39]

The USDOC constructed a proxy based on a regression analysis of inflation-adjusted interest rates in 33 lower-middle-income countries. It justified this approach by referring to a broad inverse relationship between income levels and interest rates. The Panel uphold the US approach. The Appellate Body reversed the Panel's findings because the Panel did not test the reasonableness of the methodology employed by the USDOC. The Panel should also have looked at the proxy benchmark used in the light of alternative proxies as proposed by China. However, the Appellate Body could not complete the analysis because there were insufficient undisputed facts on the record.[40]

The benefit analysis is, as explained in more detail in the benefit section of the commentary to Article 1, an *ex ante* analysis. The benefit analysis in relation to loans illustrates this perfectly. The question is what loan could the recipient have obtained in the market at the time when he took out the subsidized loan. By contrast, it is irrelevant how the subsidized

[38] WT/DS379/AB/R of 11 March 2011, *US – Definitive Anti-Dumping and Countervailing Duties on Certain Products from China*, paras 496, 505–508.

[39] WT/DS379/AB/R of 11 March 2011, *US – Definitive Anti-Dumping and Countervailing Duties on Certain Products from China*, paras 491–501.

[40] WT/DS379/AB/R of 11 March 2011, *US – Definitive Anti-Dumping and Countervailing Duties on Certain Products from China*, para 510 *et seq.*

loan actually performed. See *supra* the commentary to Article 1, pp. 137, 144–148.

If the loan recipient has incurred costs in taking out the actual loan, such costs must be taken into consideration when comparing the conditions of the loan received with the undistorted benchmark. The Appellate Body reversed the previous Panel ruling. The Panel wrongly concluded that there was no need that a benefit analysis accounts for such costs as Article 14(b) does not make any reference to the amount of any cost incurred in obtaining the loans.[41]

The statements made by the Appellate Body in *Japan – DRAMs (Korea)* in relation to Article 14(a) on the question of inside/outside investor benchmarks also apply in relation to Article 14(b).[42]

Loan Guarantee (Subparagraph (c))

According to Article 14(c) a loan guarantee by a government shall not be considered as conferring a benefit, unless there is a difference between the following: (a) the amount that the firm receiving the guarantee pays on the loan guaranteed by the government and (b) the amount the firm would pay on a comparable commercial loan absent that guarantee. The benefit shall be the difference between these two amounts adjusted for any differences in fees.[43]

Indeed, a loan guarantee by a State or one of its emanations can result in the borrower's inferior credit rating being substituted by a superior governmental credit rating.[44]

The Panel in *Canada – Aircraft Credits and Guarantees* has held that Article 14(c) is also relevant for calculating the benefit in case of equity guarantees by a government programme. According to the Panel, there are sufficient similarities between loan guarantees and equity guarantees.[45]

[41] WT/DS436/AB/R of 8 December 2014, *United States – Countervailing Measures on Certain Hot-Rolled Carbon Steel Flat Products from India*, para 4.343 *et seq.*

[42] See *supra* this chapter, pp. 445–446.

[43] See also WT/DS299/R of 17 June 2005, *European Communities – Countervailing Measures on Dynamic Random Access Memory Chips from Korea*, paras 7.189 and 7.190. The export credit guarantee arrangement is described in para 7.85.

[44] WT/DS222/R of 28 January 2002, *Canada – Export Credits and Loan Guarantees for Regional Aircraft*, para 7.389 *et seq.*

[45] WT/DS222/R of 28 January 2002, *Canada – Export Credits and Loan Guarantees for Regional Aircraft*, para 7.345.

Provision of Goods or Services, Purchase of Goods (Subparagraph (d))

Overview

According to Article 14(d), the provision of goods and services or purchase of goods by a government shall not be considered as conferring a benefit unless the provision is made for less than adequate remuneration, or the purchase is made for more than adequate remuneration. This provision stipulates as well that the adequacy of remuneration shall be determined in relation to prevailing market conditions for the good or service in question in the country of provision or purchase (including price, quality, availability, marketability, transportation and other conditions of purchase or sale).

The most difficult issue in relation to Article 14(d) is when and how out-of-country benchmarks can be used in order to calculate the benefit instead of benchmarks from within the country of provision or purchase. *US – Softwood Lumber IV* has established the principle that the use of out-of-country benchmarks is possible in limited circumstances. Subsequent Appellate Body rulings have further clarified the matter.

The remainder of this overview section describes, based on *US – Carbon Steel (India)*, in more general terms the market benchmark envisaged by Article 14(d). The next section addresses more specifically the rationale underlying the use of out-of-country benchmarks and attempts to summarize the jurisprudence as to when and how an investigating authority can resort to such out-of-country benchmarks in order to calculate the benefit for the provision of goods or services and the purchase of goods.

US – Carbon Steel (India) discussed extensively the market benchmark to be used under Article 14(d). The Appellate Body elaborated both on the relevant substantive conditions and procedural requirements. The backdrop of this discussion was twofold. First, whether US law that provided for the possibility of the use of out-of-country benchmarks was consistent with Article 14(d). Second, whether the USDOC, when determining whether India provided subsidized iron ore, could use an out-of-country benchmark or whether it should have used Indian prices instead. In terms of substance, the Appellate Body considered it important to emphasize the market orientation of the inquiry under Article 14(d). 'Prevailing market conditions', in the context of Article 14(d), consist of generally accepted characteristics of an area of economic activity in which the forces of supply and demand interact to determine market prices. The benchmark against which the adequacy of the subsidized remuneration is to be measured must consist of market-determined prices for the same or similar goods that relate to, or are connected with, the prevailing market conditions for the good in question in the country of provision. Proper benchmark prices would normally emanate from the market for the good in question in the country of provision to the extent they are market-determined. Indeed, the Appellate Body has considered that the primary benchmark, and therefore the starting point for the analysis to determine the benchmark for the purposes of Article 14(d), is the prices at which the same or similar goods are sold by private suppliers in arm's length transactions in the country of provision.

In-country prices could come from a variety of potential sources, including government-related entities. In other words, whether a price may constitute a benchmark under Article 14(d) is not a function of the source but, rather, whether it is reflective of prevailing market conditions in the country of provision. For example, prices on record of government-related entities other than the entity providing the financial contribution at issue also need to be analysed in order to determine whether they are market-determined and could therefore form part of a proper benchmark. Article 14(d) establishes no legal presumption that in-country prices from any particular source can be discarded in a benchmark analysis. Moreover, Article 14(d) does not prescribe a preference for the use of particular alternative benchmarks over others.[46]

From a procedural point, investigating authorities bear the responsibility to conduct the necessary analysis to determine, on the basis of information supplied by petitioners and respondents, whether proposed benchmark prices are market-determined. The Appellate Body also referred to the obligation set out in the chapeau of Article 14 to adequately explain the method used to calculate the amount of the subsidy. Moreover, it recalled its finding in DS379 that Article VI:3 of GATT 1994 encompasses a requirement to conduct a sufficiently diligent investigation into, and solicitation of, relevant facts and to base any determination on positive evidence in the record. The Appellate Body found that Article 14 encompasses the same requirement when it comes to calculate the amount of the benefit. However, what an investigating authority must do in conducting the necessary analysis to identify a proper

[46] As to the use of out-of-the-country-of-provision benchmarks see the next section. See also WT/DS437/AB/R of 18 December 2014, *United States – Countervailing Duty Measures on Certain Products from China*, para 4.91 *et passim*.

benchmark will vary. Relevant factors are the circumstances of the case, the characteristics of the market being examined and the nature, quantity and quality of the information supplied by petitioners and respondents, including such additional information an investigating authority seeks so that it may base its determination on positive evidence on the record. The examination may involve an assessment of the structure of the relevant market, including the types of entities operating in that market, their respective market share, as well as the entry barriers. It could also require assessing the behaviour of the entities operating in the market in order to determine whether the government itself, or acting through government-related entities, exerts market power so as to distort in-country prices. In the case in question, the Appellate Body would have expected the USDOC to explain why it was excluding benchmarks that it had used in previous review investigations.[47]

In *US – Carbon Steel (India)*, India also argued that Article 14(d) required a two-step analysis. First, it should be examined whether the remuneration received is less than adequate from the perspective of the government provider. If this is answered in the positive, the investigating authority is then, in a second step, required to assess whether a benefit has been conferred on the recipient. The Appellate Body rejected India's claim essentially on the grounds that the two notions 'less than adequate remuneration' and 'benefit' in Article 14(d) are consonant. Nor does Article 14(d) require that the adequacy of remuneration be assessed from the perspective of the government provider. Note that India raised this argument in the context of an as-such claim against a provision of the US countervailing law. This provision stipulated that the investigating authority, when determining the adequacy of remuneration, will first seek a market-determined price in the exporting country, or, if such price is not available or usable, a world-market price that would be available to purchasers in the exporting country. Only if both tests fail would the USDOC normally measure the adequacy of remuneration by assessing whether the government price is consistent with market principles.[48]

[47] WT/DS436/AB/R of 8 December 2014, *United States – Countervailing Measures on Certain Hot-Rolled Carbon Steel Flat Products from India*, paras 4.150–4.159, 4.235–4.263, 4.283–4.291 *et passim*. WT/DS437/AB/R of 18 December 2014, *United States – Countervailing Duty Measures on Certain Products from China*, paras 4.45–4.52, paras 4.62, 4.86, 4.95, 4.96 and 4.101 repeated many of these considerations.

[48] WT/DS436/AB/R of 8 December 2014, *United States – Countervailing Measures on Certain Hot-Rolled Carbon Steel Flat Products from India*, paras 4.106, 4.117 *et seq*. *Ditto* WT/

Note finally that in *US – Carbon Steel (India)* the Government of India provided rights to mine iron ore. For the purposes of determining the amount of the benefit, the Appellate Body accepted that in respect of the granting of mining rights, it was proper for the USDOC to consider that the provided good consisted of the extracted minerals. Hence, it was permissible for the USDOC to construct the price of the iron ore by adding any fees and royalties paid for the mining rights plus the cost and profit of the extraction process.[49] This price was subsequently compared to the benchmark price as further explained in the remainder of this chapter.

Use of Out-of-Country Benchmarks for Input Prices

Rationale for Using Exceptionally Out-of-Country Benchmarks

Building on the preceding section which described the market benchmark envisaged by subparagraph (d), this section examines more closely the logic underlying the use of data relating to an external benchmark for establishing the benefit, instead of using data in the country of export. Subparagraph (d) requires that '[t]he adequacy of remuneration shall be determined *in relation to prevailing market conditions* for the good or service in question *in the country*[50] *of provision or purchase*' (emphasis added). A superficial reading of Article 14(d) might suggest that out-of-country benchmarks are not permitted. This provision as interpreted by various DSB rulings is, however, more complex. The Appellate Body discussed this issue extensively in *US – Softwood Lumber IV*, *US – Anti-Dumping and Countervailing Duties (China)*, *US – Carbon Steel (India)* and in *US – Countervailing Measures (China)*.

US – Softwood Lumber IV illustrates the underlying problem. The product subject to the USDOC's investigation was softwood lumber. The USDOC found that Canadian provinces provided a subsidy to their lumber producers because they were entitled to harvest trees on government-owned land at advantageous rates. In order to determine the benefit, the USDOC compared the fee paid to the Canadian authorities with a stumpage fee that US lumber producers paid to private American wood owners

DS437/AB/R of 18 December 2014, *United States – Countervailing Duty Measures on Certain Products from China*, para 4.47.

[49] WT/DS436/AB/R of 8 December 2014, *United States – Countervailing Measures on Certain Hot-Rolled Carbon Steel Flat Products from India*, para 4.332.

[50] For the negotiating history of the term 'in the country' see *Horlick* (2013/1) p. 299.

in certain US states bordering Canada. It did so because the Canadian provinces were the predominant suppliers of stumpage and private timber sales in Canada did not represent a commercial market because they were distorted by government intervention. The Panel rejected the use of out-of-country benchmarks if there are private suppliers in that country, even if prices of private suppliers may be artificially suppressed because of the prices charged for the same goods by the government. It did so although it acknowledged that such an interpretation would not necessarily be the most sensible one from the perspective of economic logic.[51]

The Appellate Body reversed the Panel's finding. It accepted that the use of out-of-country benchmarks may be necessary in certain circumstances and based this conclusion *inter alia* on the following considerations:

- The phrase 'in relation to' in Article 14(d) implies a comparative exercise, but, contrary to the opinion of the Panel, its meaning is not limited to 'in comparison with'. Rather, 'in relation to' has a meaning similar to the phrases 'as regards' and 'with respect to'. These phrases imply a broader sense of 'relation, connection, reference'. According to the Appellate Body, the use of the phrase 'in relation to' suggests that the drafters of the ASCM did not intend to exclude any possibility of using as a benchmark something other than private prices in the market of the country of provision.
- Private prices in the market of provision will generally represent an appropriate benchmark of the 'adequacy of remuneration' for the provision of goods. However, this may not always be the case. An investigating authority may use a benchmark other than private prices in the country of provision under Article 14(d) if it is established that private prices in that country are distorted because of the government's *predominant* role in providing those goods.
- The Panel's interpretation would not only have frustrated the purpose of Article 14, but also the object and purpose of the ASCM, which includes disciplining the use of subsidies and countervailing measures, while, at the same time, enabling WTO Members whose domestic industries are harmed by subsidized imports to use such remedies. Prices in the market of the country of provision are the primary, but not the exclusive, benchmark for calculating benefit.

[51] The Panel accepted that in certain circumstances it will not be possible to use in-country prices as a benchmark. It gave two examples: (1) where the government is the only supplier of the particular goods in the country; (2) where the government administratively controls all of the prices for those goods in the country.

- However, the Appellate Body rejected the interpretation advanced by the US which claimed that the term 'market conditions' necessarily implies a market undistorted by the government's financial contribution. This interpretation would have gone too far.[52]

After a succession of Appellate Body rulings on this issue, the contours of the principle allowing the use of out-of-country benchmarks are now more clearly drawn: the inquiry of an investigating authority for the purposes of finding the proper benchmark under Article 14(d) has to focus on whether or not in-country prices of the (subsidized) input are distorted.[53] The remainder of this section describes relevant jurisprudence as to when and how such out-of-country benchmarks can be used because of distorted in-country prices.[54]

What Are the Specific Circumstances in Which an Investigating Authority May Use a Benchmark Other Than Private Prices in the Country of Provision?

US – Carbon Steel (India) has recently given comprehensive guidance on the use of out-of-country benchmarks. Prior to *US – Carbon Steel (India)*, the debate for using out-of-country benchmarks centred essentially on the question whether the State was a 'predominant' or at least 'significant' supplier for the input product in question. India argued essentially that the use of an out-of-country benchmark is limited to situations where the government is a predominant supplier of the good in question. The Appellate Body rejected this interpretation. This does not come as a surprise given the Appellate Body's prior ruling in *US – Anti-Dumping and Countervailing Duties on Certain Products (China)*. The Appellate Body held that the rationale underpinning its findings in *US – Softwood Lumber IV* is that Article 14(d) does not prohibit the use of alternative benchmarks in situations where in-country prices cannot properly be used as a basis for determining a benchmark. There may be circumstances other than the configuration 'domestic prices are distorted as a result of government

[52] WT/DS257/AB/R of 19 January 2004, *United States – Final Countervailing Duty Determination with Respect to Certain Softwood Lumber from Canada*, paras 82–96.

[53] See e.g. WT/DS437/AB/R of 18 December 2014, *United States – Countervailing Duty Measures on Certain Products from China*, paras 4.59 and 4.105; WT/DS379/AB/R of 11 March 2011, *US – Definitive Anti-Dumping and Countervailing Duties on Certain Products from China*, para 446.

[54] See also *Horn/Mavroidis* (2005) p. 238 *et seq*. They point out that price differences between two countries may be the result of different policy preferences between these countries that are non-protectionist, such as environmental considerations.

intervention' where an investigating authority could use out-of-country-benchmarks. According to the Appellate Body, the need for an out-of-country benchmark could, for instance, arise if information pertaining to in-country prices cannot be verified so as to determine whether they are market-determined in accordance with the second sentence of Article 14(d). The Appellate Body pointed out that the 'predominant supplier situation' was the only one raised in the Softwood Lumber appeal. Therefore, that ruling could not be interpreted as limiting the use of out-of-country benchmarks only to this specific configuration. It hastened to add all this does not suggest that an investigating authority may easily have recourse to out-of-country prices. In this context, the Appellate Body also recalled the various procedural safeguards which had been described *supra* this chapter, pp. 451–454.[55]

The Appellate Body emphasized already in *US – Softwood Lumber IV* that circumstances where out-of-country benchmarks can be used are very limited. In that particular case it justified the use of an out-of-country benchmark instead of private in-country prices because 'those private prices are distorted, because of the predominant role of the government in the market as a provider of the same or similar goods'. The Appellate Body considered that, as far as market distortion and effect on prices are concerned, 'there may be little difference between situations where the government is the sole provider of certain goods and situations where the government has a predominant role in the market as a provider of those goods'. Whenever the government is the predominant provider of certain goods, even if not the sole provider, it is likely that it can affect through its own pricing strategy the prices of private providers for those goods. In other words, there is a situation where the government effectively acts as a price-setter and private suppliers are price-takers. However, an allegation that a government is a significant supplier would not, on its own, prove such distortion. A determination whether private prices are distorted has to be made on a case-by-case basis, according to the particular facts underlying each investigation.[56]

US – Anti-Dumping and Countervailing Duties on Certain Products (China) has further elaborated on the distinction made in *US – Softwood Lumber IV* between the government being a 'predominant' supplier as

[55] WT/DS436/AB/R of 8 December 2014, *United States – Countervailing Measures on Certain Hot-Rolled Carbon Steel Flat Products from India*, paras 4.184–4.191.

[56] WT/DS257/AB/R of 19 January 2004, *United States – Final Countervailing Duty Determination with Respect to Certain Softwood Lumber from Canada*, paras 99–103.

opposed to being a 'significant' supplier. In the former case, the Appellate Body pointed out that the terms 'predominant' and 'significant' as used in *US – Softwood Lumber IV* refer to two different sets of circumstances, and not to interchangeable concepts. If the government is a significant supplier, this fact alone cannot justify a finding that prices are distorted. Evidence pertaining to factors other than the government market share will be needed, as the government's role as a significant supplier cannot, on its own, prove distortion of private prices. By contrast, where the government is the predominant supplier, it is likely that prices are distorted, but a case-by-case analysis is still required. In sum, it is price distortion that would allow an investigating authority to reject in-country private prices, not the fact that the government is the predominant supplier *per se*. An investigating authority cannot, based simply on a finding that the government is the predominant supplier, refuse to consider evidence relating to factors other than government market share. The Appellate Body also clarified that it did not consider that, in cases in which the government is the predominant supplier, an investigating authority would be required to conduct the same type of analysis as in cases where the government is only a significant supplier. In both cases, the investigating authority would have to reach its conclusions based on all the evidence that is put on the record, including evidence regarding factors other than government market share. Finally, the concept of predominance does not exclusively refer to market shares, but may also refer to market power.[57] As to the type of market analysis that an investigating authority should conduct see *supra* this chapter, pp. 452–453.

The Appellate Body underlined in *US – Anti-Dumping and Countervailing Duties on Certain Products (China)* and in *US – Countervailing Measures (China)* that there is no threshold above which the fact that the government is a predominant supplier in the market alone becomes sufficient to establish price distortion, regardless of any other evidence. However, the more predominant a government's role in the market is, the more likely this role will result in the distortion of private prices. In any event, the Appellate Body has cautioned against equating the concept of government predominance with the concept of price distortion, and has highlighted that the link between the two concepts is an evidentiary one.[58]

[57] WT/DS379/AB/R of 11 March 2011, *US – Definitive Anti-Dumping and Countervailing Duties on Certain Products from China*, para 442 *et seq.*

[58] WT/DS437/AB/R of 18 December 2014, *United States – Countervailing Duty Measures on Certain Products from China*, paras 4.51, 4.52 and 4.86; WT/DS379/AB/R of 11 March

The standard established by the Appellate Body in *US – Anti-Dumping and Countervailing Duties on Certain Products (China)* is perhaps best illustrated by examining its application to the case at hand. The USDOC found, relying at least to some extent on facts available, that Chinese State-owned enterprises produced 96.1 per cent of all hot-rolled steel produced in China, i.e. the input to the subject product. All State-owned companies were majority government owned. Imports of hot-rolled steel represented 3 per cent of the total Chinese market. China did not contest these facts but pointed out:

- State-owned producers were profitable.
- Private investment in the Chinese hot-rolled steel industry has been growing.
- Many State-owned producers of hot-rolled steel are publicly listed corporations that operate under the same Chinese company law as companies with no State ownership.
- The hot-rolled steel market is heavily fragmented, with numerous State-owned and non-State-owned suppliers competing for sales.
- There is no uniform or government-set price for hot-rolled steel.
- Prices for hot-rolled steel fluctuate by producer, by time, and by region.

The USDOC rejected both prices of Chinese and imported hot-rolled steel as possible benchmarks. In doing so they relied essentially on the high market share of State-owned enterprises and the low volume of imports. The USDOC examined the evidence relating to other factors of the market in a somewhat cursory fashion. Before the Appellate Body, China claimed that the USDOC's approach amounted to a *per se* rejection of in-country input prices solely based on the government's predominant role as a supplier. The Appellate Body did not follow China but sided with the US. It observed that,

> with a 96.1% market share, the position of the government in the market is much closer to a situation where the government is the sole supplier of the goods than to a situation where it is merely a significant supplier of the goods. This made it likely that the government as the predominant supplier has the market power to affect through its own pricing strategy the pricing of private providers for the same goods, and to induce them to align with government prices. In such a situation, evidence of factors other than government market share will have less weight in the determination of price distortion than in a situation where the government has only a 'significant' presence in the market.

2011, *US – Definitive Anti-Dumping and Countervailing Duties on Certain Products from China*, paras 444–446.

The Appellate Body characterized the 96.1 per cent share as an 'overwhelming' involvement in the market that outweighed the USDOC's cursory analysis. It also noted that the USDOC had discussed the small role of imports.[59]

In the same case, only the Panel but not the Appellate Body dealt with the issue of the provision of Chinese land-use rights. The Panel accepted the USDOC's use of out-of-country benchmarks instead of land-use prices in China. The USDOC invoked the following main grounds in order to justify its conclusion that the Chinese government retained a predominant role in the land market:

- Chinese government authorities controlled, albeit on a decentralized basis, the supply and allocation of land that could be used by non-State enterprises for non-agricultural activities.
- Industrial land-use rights relate often to land that was previously held by farmers. However, farmers' agricultural land-use rights remained limited in scope, were poorly defined and weakly enforced.
- Land-use rights were still transferred via closed-door negotiations and not via public auctions, tenders or listings as required by law.[60]

Turning to the Appellate Body's ruling in *US – Countervailing Measures (China)*, this case could, however, be interpreted as establishing a more stringent standard than the one the Appellate Body established in *US – Anti-Dumping and Countervailing Duties on Certain Products (China).* In *US – Countervailing Measures (China)*, the Appellate Body *inter alia* reversed the Panel's finding that the USDOC was right in rejecting in four CVD investigations Chinese private prices as potential benchmarks under Article 14(d). The Appellate Body completed the legal analysis and found that in none of the four cases, the USDOC's justification for the use of out-of-country benchmarks was consistent with Article 14(d). The main arguments applied by the Appellate Body can be summarized as follows:

- Prices charged by a company are not 'as such' distorted (in the sense of not market-determined) by virtue of the fact that the company is government-owned or government-controlled.

[59] WT/DS379/AB/R of 11 March 2011, *US – Definitive Anti-Dumping and Countervailing Duties on Certain Products from China*, para 455 *et passim*.

[60] WT/DS379/R of 22 October 2010, *US – Definitive Anti-Dumping and Countervailing Duties on Certain Products from China*, paras 11.33–11.68. The examples where offsetting might be appropriate are listed in paras 10.76–10.82.

- In the solar panel CVD investigation, the question was whether the Chinese government provided a subsidy by providing polysilicon, an important input for solar panels, at less than adequate remuneration. The USDOC found that 37 out of 47 Chinese polysilicon producers were owned or controlled by the PRC government. The Chinese government did not provide the production volumes of any of these polysilicon producers, although the USDOC had requested such information. Therefore, the USDOC concluded that the government of China is the predominant supplier of polysilicon in the PRC and that its significant presence in the market distorts all transaction prices. Hence, an in-country benchmark could not be used. The Appellate Body accepted that the role of these 37 polysilicon producers in the Chinese market could in principle be considered as 'significant' or 'predominant'. However, according to the Appellate Body, the USDOC was not entitled to refuse to consider evidence relating to factors other than government market share. Moreover, the Appellate Body criticized that the USDOC did not explain whether and how the relevant 37 producers possessed and exerted market power such that other in-country prices were distorted. Nor did the USDOC explain whether the prices of the 37 government-related entities themselves were market-determined.
- The Appellate Body expressed the same type of criticism in relation to the US pressure pipe CVD investigation. The input in question was stainless steel coil. Chinese State-owned enterprises accounted for 82 per cent of the production of stainless steel coil in China and for 71 per cent of stainless steel coil consumption in that country. The USDOC concluded that stainless steel coil prices from private transactions within China could not be used because they were not sufficiently free from GOC action. Again, the Appellate Body accepted that the relevant market shares could in principle be considered as 'significant' or 'predominant'. But it criticized that the USDOC had simply assumed that prices charged by government-owned entities were automatically distorted due to their relationship with the government and that the USDOC did not explain how the market shares held by SOEs resulted in the government's possession and exercise of market power.[61]

[61] WT/DS437/AB/R of 18 December 2014, *United States – Countervailing Duty Measures on Certain Products from China*, paras 4.83–4.107. Footnote 244 *et seq.* of the preceding Panel report provide further information as to the type of evidence that was on record.

Note that it is not necessary for a finding of distortion of the prices in question (and the resulting use of out-of-country benchmarks) that the State-owned enterprises operating on the relevant market are classified as public bodies within the meaning of Article 1.1(a)(1). Rather, there is a need to conduct a proper market analysis in order to evaluate whether the proposed benchmark prices are market-determined so that they can be used to assess whether the remuneration is less than adequate.[62]

US – Carbon Steel (India) also sheds some light on the necessary level of evidence in relation to alternative in-country benchmarks. Indian exporters proposed prices charged by Indian private suppliers of iron ore (an input of the product subject to investigation) as an alternative to out-of-country benchmarks. The US rejected this information and the Appellate Body report contains a short summary of the relevant considerations.[63]

In *Japan – DRAMs (Korea)*, the question was whether *US – Softwood Lumber IV* also applied to cases of prior subsidization. Japan refused to use as a benchmark the terms and conditions of a restructuring of Hynix applied by a number of non-entrusted/non-directed creditors because that restructuring was based on prior subsidies given by Korea. The Panel found that this was not a sufficient reason to reject that possible benchmark. In the Panel's view, prior subsidization of an object does not necessarily mean that the market price for that object is distorted. A buyer may have paid a market price even though the object only exists because of prior subsidies. Thus, the Panel did not extend *US – Softwood Lumber IV* that was concerned with distortion caused by present or contemporaneous government involvement and intervention in markets, to cases of prior subsidization.[64]

Note finally that *Korea – Commercial Vessels* found (with express reference to *US – Softwood Lumber IV*) that 'there could be circumstances in which a government influences the market to such an extent that it becomes distorted, so that private parties no longer operate pursuant to purely commercial principles'. However, ultimately the Panel did not

[62] WT/DS437/AB/R of 18 December 2014, *United States – Countervailing Duty Measures on Certain Products from China*, para 4.39 *et seq.*, paras 4.60–4.65.

[63] WT/DS436/AB/R of 8 December 2014, *United States – Countervailing Measures on Certain Hot-Rolled Carbon Steel Flat Products from India*, para 4.270.

[64] WT/DS336/R of 13 July 2007, *Japan – Countervailing Duties on Dynamic Random Access Memories from Korea*, paras 7.296 and 7.297. This issue was not appealed.

apply any external benchmark because it did not see any evidence justifying this in the case in question.[65]

What Alternative to an In-Country Benchmark May an Investigating Authority Use?

In General According to the Appellate Body in *US – Softwood Lumber IV*, the alternative benchmark chosen must 'relate or refer to, or be connected with, the prevailing market conditions in that country, and must reflect price, quality, availability, marketability, transportation and other conditions of purchase or sale, as required by Article 14(d)'[66] It also pointed out alternative methods for determining the adequacy of remuneration that could include proxies that take into account prices for similar goods quoted on world markets, or proxies constructed on the basis of production costs if they conform to the conditions listed in the preceding sentence. More generally, any price that is used for the purpose of determining an alternative benchmark must approximate prevailing market conditions in the country of provision. If necessary, appropriate adjustments must be made to the out-of-country benchmark selected in order to ensure that the selected alternative benchmark reflects prevailing market conditions in the country of provision. Moreover, countervailing measures may not be used to offset differences in comparative advantages between countries. Finally, the Appellate Body also described the difficulties associated with choosing benchmarks in other countries including the need to make adjustments, but found itself unable to decide whether the US solution was appropriate because there were not enough facts on the record.[67]

[65] WT/DS273/R of 7 March 2005, *Korea – Measures Affecting Trade in Commercial Vessels*, para 7.434.

[66] WT/DS257/AB/R of 19 January 2004, *United States – Final Countervailing Duty Determination with Respect to Certain Softwood Lumber from Canada*, paras 103 and 106. Confirmed by WT/DS436/AB/R of 8 December 2014, *United States – Countervailing Measures on Certain Hot-Rolled Carbon Steel Flat Products from India*, para 4.208; WT/DS437/AB/R of 18 December 2014, *United States – Countervailing Duty Measures on Certain Products from China*, para 4.53; WT/DS412/AB/R and WT/DS426/AB/R of 6 May 2013, *Canada – Certain Measures Affecting the Renewable Energy Generation Sector; Canada – Measures Relating to Feed-In Tariff Program*, para 5.239.

[67] WT/DS257/AB/R of 19 January 2004, *United States – Final Countervailing Duty Determination with Respect to Certain Softwood Lumber from Canada*, para 106 *et seq.* (in particular paras 108 and 109). The notion of 'comparative advantage' was also at issue in WT/DS436/AB/R of 8 December 2014, *United States – Countervailing Measures on Certain Hot-Rolled Carbon Steel Flat Products from India*, paras 4.252–4.257, 4.284. The Appellate Body observed in the latter case that it did not consider that a country enjoys necessarily

As the discussion in *US – Carbon Steel (India)* in relation to making adjustments e.g. for transport costs has shown (see *infra*), the use of a out-of-country benchmark is not necessarily limited to simply replacing the distorted input prices.

Export Prices from the Country Subject to Investigation *US – Carbon Steel (India)* discussed the use of export prices as an alternative benchmark. The question at issue was whether the export prices of the provider of the financial contribution under investigation could be used in determining a world market price and assessing, by reference to that world market price, the adequacy of the remuneration. India argued that export prices of iron charged by an Indian government agency should have been used as a benchmark. The US rejected this request on the grounds that the export prices pertained to the very same government provider that was subject to investigation. The Panel upheld the USDOC's determination because a government may set prices on the basis of public policy considerations rather than market principles. In the view of the Panel, the same risks arise in respect of a government's export prices, for instance because the government might provide goods to export customers to promote domestic production and employment.

The Appellate Body disagreed. It pointed out that an export price from the country of provision to another country would normally relate to prevailing market conditions in the export market, rather than the market in the country of provision. Therefore, such a price is not *per se* an in-country price. The Appellate Body was not taking a position that the export prices of the Indian government agency should have been used in the case in question. But it was pointing out that there cannot be a presumption that export prices set by the government are inherently unreliable for the purposes of determining the world market price. The fact that governments may set prices in pursuit of public policy objectives does not permit a general inference that government-related prices other than the financial contribution at issue may be presumptively discarded in determining a benchmark. Rather, this must be proven on the basis of positive

a comparative advantage in every situation where local supply of a good in the country of provision is sufficient to cater for local demand. See also WT/DS379/AB/R of 11 March 2011, *US – Definitive Anti-Dumping and Countervailing Duties on Certain Products from China*, para 483, where the Appellate Body pointed out that the use of an out-of-country benchmark may be permissible in a given case, but that the investigating authority would nevertheless have to approximate the conditions specified in Article 14(d).

evidence on the record. The Appellate Body also noted that the USDOC had used these very export prices in previous reviews.[68]

Use of International Prices (Upward Adjustments for Delivery Costs to the Exporting Country Subject to Investigation) In *US – Carbon Steel (India)*, the Appellate Body also had to examine whether the relevant US law was compatible with the second sentence of Article 14(d). US law stipulated in relevant part that in measuring the adequacy of remuneration, the comparison or benchmark price will be adjusted to reflect the price that a firm actually paid or would pay if it imported the product. Such adjustment will include delivery charges and import duties. India was concerned with cases where the distorted (Indian) government price in question did not include delivery charges. Therefore, according to India, the US investigating authority was in such circumstances prevented from examining the prevailing market conditions because US law allegedly required it to use a delivered price while the examination should have been carried on an ex works basis. The Appellate Body rejected India's 'as such' claim but accepted the 'as applied' claim. According to the Appellate Body, the USDOC was wrong to compare in the case at hand Indian government prices of iron ore with corresponding Brazilian prices that included transportation costs from Brazil to India when calculating benefit.

Many of the Appellate Body's considerations turn around the particular articulation of India's claims. However, the following points of the Appellate Body's reasoning are of a more general nature and also elucidate the concept of 'prevailing market conditions' contained in the second sentence of Article 14(d):

- An assessment of prevailing market conditions within the meaning of Article 14(d) necessarily involves an analysis of the market generally, rather than isolated transactions in that market (paras 4.245 and 4.249).
- Prevailing market conditions cannot be assessed solely from the perspective of the providers of the relevant good in question, i.e. the government. Such a limitation would stand in tension with the notion of benefit, i.e. that the financial contribution makes the recipient better off than it would otherwise have been, absent that contribution. Therefore,

[68] WT/DS436/AB/R of 8 December 2014, *United States – Countervailing Measures on Certain Hot-Rolled Carbon Steel Flat Products from India*, para 4.283 *et seq.*

a determination of the adequacy of remuneration in relation to prevailing market conditions in the country of provision must capture the full cost to the recipient of receiving the government-provided good in question (para 4.245).

- The fact that delivery charges are not generally paid directly to the providers of the good in question in the country of provision does not mean that the benefit comparison must be conducted at an ex works level (para 4.248). Indeed, Article 14(d) explicitly refers to transportation when clarifying the term 'prevailing market conditions' (para 4.302). This confirms that the costs associated with the transportation of the good in question is a factor that must be accounted for in determining the adequacy of remuneration in relation to prevailing market conditions (para 4.246).
- Insofar as adjustments for delivery charges are necessary, any such adjustments must reflect the generally applicable delivery charges for the good in question in the country of provision. For example, in cases where the imports of the good into the country concerned (India in the case in question) are minimal in relation to the quantity supplied domestically of that good, it may not be appropriate to compare that benchmark price, adjusted to reflect international delivery charges, with the government price, adjusted to reflect local delivery charges. In such a case, international delivery charges might not be representative of the generally applicable delivery charges for the good in question in the country of provision (para 4.249).
- Note that the US law in question provided for sufficient flexibility in determining the amounts of such adjustments and hence the 'as such' claim failed (see para 4.251).
- However, the facts of the case underlying the USDOC's determination did not support the conclusion that delivered import prices should be used as a benchmark because, *inter alia*, the US only relied on a single isolated import transaction in which an Indian steel producer purchased iron ore from a Brazilian mine on a delivered basis. It cannot be inferred, without more, that such a single import transaction for a particular good reflects or relates to prevailing market conditions for that good in the country of provision, in this case India (paras 4.299–4.317).
- More generally, in order to assess the adequacy of remuneration in relation to prevailing market conditions in the country of provision, it may be necessary for an investigating authority to seek, and engage with,

evidence concerning the prevailing market conditions for the good in question (para 4.306).[69]

Land-Use Rights in China See the Panel in *US – Anti-Dumping and Countervailing Duties on Certain Products (China)* with regard to out-of-country benchmarks for Chinese prices of land-use rights.[70]

Should Negative Benefits Be Offset?

In *US – Anti-Dumping and Countervailing Duties (China)*, the US countervailed the provision of certain types of rubber that were subsequently used to produce the product subject to investigation, i.e. off-road tyres. The USDOC compared on a monthly basis the prices for each type of rubber paid by the tyre producers to State-owned rubber suppliers with the corresponding price that had been paid to private rubber suppliers. In each month during which the rubber price charged by State-owned enterprises was lower than the price paid to private rubber suppliers, the USDOC concluded that the tyre producers had received a benefit. During months for which the rubber price paid to the State-owned enterprises was higher than the price charged by private suppliers the USDOC simply found no benefit, without offsetting any such negative amount from the benefits already found. China claimed that this amounted to zeroing and that this was not permissible under Article 14. The Panel dismissed China's claims. It saw nothing in Article 14(d) mandating the approach suggested by China. It considered that the ASCM points more to a disaggregated analysis of the pricing of government provided goods for the purposes of the benefit calculation. However, it also recognized that there could be certain situations in which some sort of grouping or averaging of transactions relating to inputs (i.e. the rubber in the case in question) might be necessary in order to determine the benefit.[71]

[69] WT/DS436/AB/R of 8 December 2014, *United States – Countervailing Measures on Certain Hot-Rolled Carbon Steel Flat Products from India*, para 4.200 *et seq.*

[70] WT/DS379/R of 22 October 2010, *US – Definitive Anti-Dumping and Countervailing Duties on Certain Products from China*, paras 10.187–10.188.

[71] WT/DS379/R of 22 October 2010, *US – Definitive Anti-Dumping and Countervailing Duties on Certain Products from China*, paras 11.33–11.68. The examples where offsetting might be appropriate are listed in para 11.66.

China's and Vietnam's Accession Protocols to the WTO

The Protocols of Accession of China and Vietnam contain a special provision concerning the determination of benefit. Section 15(b) of the Chinese Accession Protocol reads:

> (b) In proceedings under Parts II, III and V of the SCM Agreement, when addressing subsidies described in Articles 14(a), 14(b), 14(c) and 14(d), relevant provisions of the SCM Agreement shall apply; however, if there are special difficulties in that application, the importing WTO Member may then use methodologies for identifying and measuring the subsidy benefit which take into account the possibility that prevailing terms and conditions in China may not always be available as appropriate benchmarks. In applying such methodologies, where practicable, the importing WTO Member should adjust such prevailing terms and conditions before considering the use of terms and conditions prevailing outside China.[72]

Contrary to Section 15(a)(ii) in conjunction with the second sentence of Section 15(d), there is no explicit stipulation that Section 15(b) is to expire. To date no jurisprudence exists with regard to Section 15(b).[73]

[72] WT/L/432 of 23 November 2001, Protocol on the Accession of the People's Republic of China. Vietnam's accession documents contain similar language, see WT/ACC/VNM/48 of 27 October 2006, Accession of Viet Nam – Report of the Working Party on the Accession of Viet Nam, Section 255(b). With regard to the Chinese Accession Protocol see also *Yamaoka* (2013) pp. 125–126.

[73] Note that Section 15 was not at issue in *US – Anti-Dumping and Countervailing Duties (China)*, see WT/DS379/AB/R of 11 March 2011, *US – Definitive Anti-Dumping and Countervailing Duties on Certain Products from China*, para 436.

Article 15

Determination of Injury

Introduction

Article 15 sets out the rules on injury, i.e. a central requirement for the imposition of countervailing measures. In order to impose such measures, subsidized imports must have caused injury to the domestic industry of the importing country producing the like product.

Footnote 45 is attached to the title of Article 15. It clarifies that under the ASCM, the term 'injury' shall, unless otherwise specified, be taken to mean material injury to a domestic industry, threat of material injury to a domestic industry or material retardation of the establishment of such an industry.[1] Moreover, this footnote stipulates that the term 'injury' shall be interpreted in accordance with the provisions of Article 15. This is for instance relevant with regard to an adverse effects claim pursuant to Article 5 based on the existence of material injury.[2]

Up to now, the meaning of the adjective 'material' has not been clarified by jurisprudence. In the area of trade remedies, there exist two further qualifiers to the noun 'injury'. First, Article 11.9 of the ASCM stipulates that there shall be immediate termination of a countervailing investigation where the injury is 'negligible'. Second, the WTO Agreement on Safeguards prescribes that safeguard measures can only be imposed if the industry has suffered 'serious' injury. It is generally believed that serious injury is a more demanding standard than material injury because the ASCM addresses unfairly traded imports (because they benefit from subsidies) while the safeguard instrument is a safety valve to provide temporary relief to the industry of the importing country. It is not necessary to demonstrate an element of unfairness with regard to the imports in order to impose safeguard measures.[3]

[1] For material retardation see *Narayanan* (2004).

[2] DSB rulings dealing with material injury in the context of an adverse effects claim are described *supra* Article 5.

[3] Explicitly confirmed in WT/DS177/AB/R and WT/DS178/AB/R of 1 May 2001, *United States – Safeguard Measures on Imports of Fresh, Chilled or Frozen Lamb Meat from New Zealand and Australia*, para 124.

Contrary to Article 1, which defines a subsidy, Article 15 does not define injury. Rather, it sets out a series of procedural instructions that an investigating authority must follow in order to make a determination as to whether or not the domestic industry is injured as a result of the subsidized imports.[4] Pursuant to Article 15.1, the injury analysis consists of a two-pronged approach. First, the volume and price effects of the subsidized imports are examined (see *infra* this chapter, pp. 479–493). Second, the consequent impact of these imports on the industry producing the like product in the importing country is examined (see *infra* this chapter, pp. 493–496). Finally, a causal link must be demonstrated between the imports and the injury of the industry in the importing country (see *infra* this chapter, pp. 497–506). According to Article 15.1, the demonstration of injury must be based on 'positive evidence' and must involve an 'objective examination' of the two aforementioned steps as well as the causation analysis.

The injurious effects of subsidized imports from several countries on the injury of the importing country can be examined collectively if the conditions for cumulation as set out in Article 15.3 are met (see *infra* this chapter, p. 478).

Whether or not there is injury will be normally examined on the basis of import and domestic industry data usually covering a timespan of three to four years. The period for which such data are collected is called the 'investigation period' (see *supra* the commentary to Article 12, pp. 421–423, *infra* this chapter, pp. 480–483 and *infra* this chapter, pp. 476–477).

Note finally that the ASCM does not define injury in relation to any specific level of subsidization or imports. However, if the subsidization of imports is below *de minimis* or if the volume of imports is negligible, no measures shall be imposed and the investigation shall be terminated immediately.[5]

DSB Rulings Concerning Article 3 WTO Anti-Dumping Agreement Are Relevant

In cases concerning claims under Article 15, panels and the Appellate Body are regularly guided by DSB rulings on Article 3 of the Anti-Dumping Agreement because the latter provision is very similar to

[4] See also *Durling* in *Wolfrum/Stoll/Koebele* (2008), para 41 to Article 15.

[5] See *supra* the commentary to Article 11, pp 389–390.

Article 15 of the ASCM. This guidance relates for instance to the notions of 'positive evidence', 'objective examination' and that Article 15.1 sets out the guiding principle underlying all aspects of an injury determination etc.

Like Product

The term 'like product' is of considerable practical and legal importance. It essentially refers to the products manufactured and sold in the importing country and that compete with the subsidized imports.

Footnote 46 to Article 15.1 defines the term 'like product':

> Throughout this Agreement the term 'like product' ('produit similaire') shall be interpreted to mean a product which is identical, i.e. alike in all respects to the product under consideration, or in the absence of such a product, another product which, although not alike in all respects, has characteristics closely resembling those of the product under consideration.

This definition is identical to the one in Article 2.6 of the WTO Anti-Dumping Agreement.

As this definition is applicable throughout the ASCM, it applies e.g. with regard to standing of the domestic industry (Article 11.4), the definition of the domestic industry (Article 16) and, in relevant part, in adverse effects cases (see subparagraphs (a) and (c) of Article 6.3). Like product was prominently at issue in *Indonesia – Autos*. The Panel had to define which EC and US cars sold in Indonesia could properly be considered to be like products to the Indonesian Timor car that benefitted from various subsidies granted by the Indonesian government. The EC took the view that all cars falling within the category of passenger cars constituted a single like product on the ground that there were virtually limitless variations with respect to passenger cars, and that any effort to divide them into two or more like products would produce arbitrary results. The Panel did not agree. First, it found that on its face, the term 'like product' is quite narrow because it is not sufficient that the products resemble each other. Rather, they must closely resemble each other. Second, the analysis whether the various cars closely resemble each other must include as an important element the physical characteristics of the cars in question. This follows from the other possible criteria identified by the parties in respect of like product such as brand loyalty, brand image/reputation, status and resale value. These criteria reflect, at least in part, an assessment by the purchasers of the physical characteristics. Third, according to the Panel, the ASCM does not preclude looking also at criteria other than physical characteristics such as differences in uses or prices[6] between the various products but, as mentioned before, these differences generally arise out of different physical characteristics. The Panel also pointed out that an analysis of tariff classification principles may be useful because it provides guidance as to which physical distinctions between products were considered important by customs experts. Finally, the Panel noted the Appellate Body's statement in *Alcoholic Beverages* that the issue of like product must be considered on a case-by-case basis and that a panel's analysis of this question will always involve an unavoidable element of individual, discretionary judgement.

The Panel accepted that there were innumerable differences among passenger cars and that the identification of appropriate dividing lines between them may not be a simple task. However, it found that a reasonable approach was to use as a starting point a market segmentation analysis that was widely used within the car industry. This was complemented by individual comparisons of the physical characteristics of the various models in question (e.g. weight, engine size, equipment, security features such as airbags and ABS), based on information on the record which tended to confirm the industry-wide market segmentation analysis.[7] Cars imported as CKD (completely knocked-down) kits and assembled in Indonesia were considered alike to the cars produced in Indonesia. These CKD kits had characteristics closely resembling the like Indonesian cars because the Indonesian content was very small and the CKD kits were effectively 'cars in a box'. The Panel referred in this context also to the General Rules of Interpretation of the Harmonized System.[8]

Note that the Panel rejected a claim made by Indonesia according to which complainants bear a heavier than usual burden of proof in the dispute or that the concept of like product should be interpreted more narrowly than usual because Indonesia is a developing country.[9]

[6] However, in the case at hand the Panel was very critical with regard to the use of the price as a criterion for classification purposes, see para 14.192.

[7] WT/DS54/R, WT/DS55/R, WT/DS59/R and WT/DS64/R of 2 July 1998, *Indonesia – Certain Measures Affecting the Automobile Industry*, para 14.163 *et seq*., in particular para 14.173.

[8] WT/DS54/R, WT/DS55/R, WT/DS59/R and WT/DS64/R of 2 July 1998, *Indonesia – Certain Measures Affecting the Automobile Industry*, paras 14.194–14.197.

[9] WT/DS54/R, WT/DS55/R, WT/DS59/R and WT/DS64/R of 2 July 1998, *Indonesia – Certain Measures Affecting the Automobile Industry*, paras 14.168 and 14.169.

In *US – Countervailing Duty Investigation on DRAMs*, an interesting problem arose a crossroads between the definition of the product concerned by the investigation, i.e. the imported product, and the definition of the industry producing the like product. The USITC defined the product concerned as (i) fabbed and (ii) cased/assembled DRAMs. Consequently, US companies fabbing and/or casing/assembling DRAMs were considered as US domestic producers manufacturing the like product. Korea complained that sales of DRAMs that had been assembled/cased in the US were counted as US sales of US producers even if the DRAMs had been fabbed in a third country. Therefore, Korea argued that if assembly/casing is sufficient to constitute a US domestic production activity when undertaken by a producer located in the US, assembling/casing by a third country producer should also have been sufficient to change the origin of a DRAM. As a consequence, a DRAM that was fabbed in the US but assembled/cased in a third country and subsequently imported into the US should not be treated as a US product but as an import from a country not concerned. This would have reduced the market share of the US producers and increased the market share of non-subsidized imports. Or, as Korea has alleged, the approach adopted by the USITC resulted in an artificially reduced volume of non-subject imports, and an increased volume of US domestic production, thereby rendering the USITC's considerations of the importance of subject imports relative to non-subject imports and domestic production inconsistent with Articles 15.2 and 15.4. The Panel did not agree. It held that the inconsistency alleged by Korea could only have been challenged under Article 16, i.e. the definition of the domestic industry, which, however, Korea had not done.[10]

Framework of the Injury and Causation Analysis

The Leading Case: China – GOES

The Appellate Body in *China – GOES* has summarized and further elaborated on the essential elements and the nature of an injury analysis under Article 15 of the ASCM (and under Article 3 of the Anti-Dumping Agreement). It recalled the Appellate Body's finding in *Thailand – H-Beams*, that Article 3.1 WTO Anti-Dumping Agreement (and by extension

[10] WT/DS296/R/3 of 21 February 2005, *United States – Countervailing Duty Investigation on Dynamic Random Access Memory Semiconductors (DRAMs) from Korea*, paras 7.382–7.386. This aspect of the ruling was not appealed.

Article 15.1 ASCM) is an overarching provision that sets forth a Member's fundamental, substantive obligation with respect to the injury determination and informs the more detailed obligations in subsequent paragraphs (para 126 of the Appellate Body report). It then recalled the definitions of 'positive evidence' and 'objective examination', which are reproduced in the next sections,[11] and that Article 3.1 of the Anti-Dumping Agreement and Article 15.1 of the ASCM outline the content of an injury determination. This determination consists of:

- volume of subject imports;
- the effect of such imports on the prices of like domestic products; and
- the consequent impact of such imports on domestic producers of the like products.

The Appellate Body then explained that the subsequent paragraphs of Article 3.1 of the Anti-Dumping Agreement and Article 15.1 of the ASCM further elaborate on these three essential elements. Articles 3.2 of the Anti-Dumping Agreement and 15.2 of the ASCM concern items (i) and (ii). They spell out the precise content of an investigating authority's consideration regarding the volume of subject imports and the effect of such imports on domestic prices in the importing country. Article 3.4 of the Anti-Dumping Agreement and 15.4 of the ASCM, together with Articles 3.5 and 15.5 respectively, concern item (iii), i.e. the consequent impact of subject imports on the domestic industry of the importing country. More specifically, Articles 3.4 of the Anti-Dumping Agreement and 15.4 of the ASCM set out the economic factors that must be evaluated regarding the impact of such imports on the state of the domestic industry, and Articles 3.5 and 15.5 respectively require an investigating authority to demonstrate that subject imports are causing injury to the domestic industry of the importing country.

The Appellate Body went on to state, and this is in fact the novelty in *China – GOES*, that the various paragraphs of Article 3 and Article 15 respectively contemplate a logical progression of inquiry leading to an investigating authority's ultimate injury and causation determination. The three elements listed above are then linked through a causation analysis between subject imports and the injury to the domestic industry. The inquiries set forth in Articles 3.2 of the Anti-Dumping Agreement and 15.2 of the ASCM as well as in Articles 3.4 and 15.4 respectively are

[11] See *infra* this chapter, pp. 475–477.

necessary in order to answer the ultimate question in Articles 3.5 and 15.5, i.e. whether subject imports are causing injury to the domestic industry. They form the basis for the overall causation analysis.[12]

Positive Evidence

Panels and the Appellate Body have repeatedly referred approvingly to the definition of the term 'positive evidence' given by the Appellate Body in *US – Hot-Rolled Steel* in relation to Article 3.1 of the Anti-Dumping Agreement.[13] According to *US – Hot-Rolled Steel* the term 'positive evidence' relates to the quality of the evidence that authorities may rely upon in making a determination. The word 'positive' means that the evidence must be of an affirmative, objective and verifiable character, and it must be credible (see para 192 of the Appellate Body report). Positive evidence focuses on the facts underpinning and justifying the injury determination (see para 193 of the Appellate Body report).[14]

Objective Examination

Panels and the Appellate Body also have repeatedly referred approvingly to the definition of 'objective examination' in AD cases given by the Appellate Body in *US – Hot-Rolled Steel*.[15]

[12] WT/DS414/AB/R of 18 October 2012, *China – Countervailing and Anti-dumping Duties on Grain Oriented Flat-Rolled Electrical Steel from the United States*, paras 125–128. The relationship between Article 15.1 and the subsequent paragraphs of this Article was also at issue in WT/DS277/R of 22 March 2004, *United States – Investigation of the International Trade Commission in Softwood Lumber from Canada*, para 7.24 *et seq.* However, in the absence of independent argument by Canada concerning its Article 15.1 claim, the Panel concluded that the resolution of Canada's Article 15.1 claim was substantively dependent on the resolution of Canada's specific claims.

[13] See e.g. WT/DS414/AB/R of 18 October 2012, *China – Countervailing and Anti-dumping Duties on Grain Oriented Flat-Rolled Electrical Steel from the United States*, para 126; WT/DS427/R of 2 August 2013, *China – Anti-Dumping and Countervailing Duty Measures on Broiler Products from the United States*, para 7.410; WT/DS299/R of 17 June 2005, *European Communities – Countervailing Measures on Dynamic Random Access Memory Chips from Korea*, para 7.271 *et seq.*

[14] WT/DS184/AB/R of 24 July 2001, *United States – Anti-Dumping Measures on Certain Hot-Rolled Steel Products from Japan*, paras 192 and 193.

[15] WT/DS414/AB/R of 18 October 2012, *China – Countervailing and Anti-dumping Duties on Grain Oriented Flat-Rolled Electrical Steel from the United States*, para 126; WT/DS427/R of 2 August 2013, *China – Anti-Dumping and Countervailing Duty Measures on Broiler Products from the United States*, para 7.410; WT/DS299/R of 17 June 2005, *European Communities – Countervailing Measures on Dynamic Random Access Memory Chips from Korea*, para 7.271 *et seq.*

The following points are noteworthy in *US – Hot-Rolled Steel*:

- The term 'objective examination' is concerned with the investigative process itself. The word 'examination' relates to the way in which the evidence is gathered, inquired into and, subsequently, evaluated. In other words, objective examination relates to the conduct of the investigation generally. The word 'objective', which qualifies the word 'examination', indicates essentially that the examination process must conform to the dictates of the basic principles of good faith and fundamental fairness (para 193).
- An 'objective examination' requires that the domestic industry, and the effects of the subsidized imports be investigated in an unbiased manner, without favouring the interests of any interested party, or group of parties, in the investigation. The duty of the investigating authorities to conduct an 'objective examination' will be influenced by the objectivity, or any lack thereof, of the investigation process (para 193).
- Thus, for an examination to be 'objective', the identification, investigation and evaluation of the relevant factors must be 'even-handed' and the investigating authorities are not entitled to conduct their investigation in such a way that it becomes more likely that, as a result of the fact-finding or evaluation process, they will reach a certain determination (para 196).[16]

China – Broiler Products is also relevant here. The Panel has held that the need of an objective assessment of the evidence may require the authority to place the relevant data in context in a manner that is informative of the injury, if any, suffered by the domestic industry rather than simply review evolution in yearly figures.[17]

Further Jurisprudence

Mexico – Olive Oil held, based on the Panel in *Mexico – Beef and Rice*, that the requirements of positive evidence and an objective examination impose certain obligations on investigating authorities with regard to the completeness of the data used as a basis for their injury determinations. An examination can only be objective if it is based on data which provide an accurate and unbiased picture of what it is that one is examining. This

[16] WT/DS184/AB/R of 24 July 2001, *United States – Anti-Dumping Measures on Certain Hot-Rolled Steel Products from Japan*, paras 193 and 196.

[17] WT/DS427/R of 2 August 2013, *China – Anti-Dumping and Countervailing Duty Measures on Broiler Products from the United States*, para 7.554.

statement was made in the context of the selection of the investigation period.[18]

In *EC – Countervailing Measures on DRAM Chips*, the EU initiated its investigation on 25 July 2002. The investigation period[19] ended on 31 December 2001. Korea claimed that the EU should have included in its pricing analysis data covering the most recent period prior to initiation, i.e. for the first semester of 2002, especially in the light that 2001 was generally considered the worst year for the industry in decades. The Panel did not agree. In its view, there was simply no basis for reading such a requirement into the text of Articles 15.1 and 15.2. It did not consider that it was unreasonable or not objective of the EU to refuse to extend the period of investigation for injury purposes beyond the period used to establish subsidization in the case in question. The EU gathered data which covered three years, including the last full year for accounting purposes prior to the initiation. Therefore, the EU's analysis was clearly based on the recent past.[20]

There is no jurisprudence yet as to whether an improper definition of the domestic industry pursuant to Article 16.1 could result in a violation of Article 15.1, in the sense that the examination was not objective.[21]

Panel rulings have repeatedly referred approvingly to the role of Article 3.1 of the Anti-Dumping Agreement as defined by *Thailand – H Beams*.[22] Moreover, and in line with Article 15.1, it has been held that an investigating authority must ensure that the determination of injury, and specifically the findings under Articles 15.2, 15.4 and 15.5, are made on the basis of 'positive evidence' and involve an 'objective examination'.[23]

[18] WT/DS341/R of 4 September 2008, *Mexico – Definitive Countervailing Measures on Olive Oil from the European Communities*, para 7.266 (see *supra* the commentary to Article 12, pp. 421–423).

[19] See *supra* the commentary to Article 12, pp. 421–423.

[20] WT/DS299/R of 17 June 2005, *European Communities – Countervailing Measures on Dynamic Random Access Memory Chips from Korea*, para 7.341.

[21] WT/DS427/R of 2 August 2013, *China – Anti-Dumping and Countervailing Duty Measures on Broiler Products from the United States*, paras 7.413 and 7.414; WT/DS397/AB/R of 15 July 2011, *European Communities – Definitive Anti-Dumping Measures on Certain Iron or Steel Fasteners from China*, paras 430 and 438.

[22] See e.g. WT/DS299/R of 17 June 2005, *European Communities – Countervailing Measures on Dynamic Random Access Memory Chips from Korea*, para 7.271 *et seq.*

[23] WT/DS299/R of 17 June 2005, *European Communities – Countervailing Measures on Dynamic Random Access Memory Chips from Korea*, para 7.272; WT/DS296/R/3 of 21 February 2005, *United States – Countervailing Duty Investigation on Dynamic Random Access Memory Semiconductors (DRAMs) from Korea*, para 7.214. This aspect was not appealed.

Cumulation (Article 15.3)

Imports from more than one country can be subsidized and injuring the industry of the importing country. Article 15.3 allows examining the cumulated effects of imports from several countries if the conditions for cumulation are met. These conditions are:

- imports of a product from more than one country are simultaneously subject to countervailing duty investigations;
- the amount of subsidization established in relation to the imports from each country is more than *de minimis* as defined in Article 11.9 (however, the special and differential treatment provisions in Article 27 contain higher *de minimis* thresholds, see Article 27.10);
- the volume of imports from each country is not negligible (but Article 15.3 does not refer to any particular numerical threshold);
- a cumulative assessment of the effects of imports is appropriate in light of the conditions of competition between the imported products and the conditions of competition between the imported products and the like domestic product.

EC – Tube or Pipe Fittings is the leading case in relation to cumulation.[24]

US – Carbon Steel (India) clarified that Article 15.3 does not permit cross cumulation, i.e. a cumulative assessment of the effects of imports that are subject to a countervailing duty investigation with the effects of imports that are not subject to a countervailing duty investigation, but are subject to a parallel anti-dumping investigation. The Appellate Body arrived at this conclusion, *inter alia*, on the basis of the text of paragraph 3 as well as the fact that paragraphs 1, 2, 4 and 5 of Article 15 consistently refer to 'subsidized imports'. At the same time it dismissed the US argument in favour of cross-cumulation that relied in particular on the phrase 'as the case may be' in Article VI:6(a) of GATT 1994.[25]

[24] WT/DS219/AB/R of 22 July 2003, *European Communities – Anti-Dumping Duties on Malleable Cast Iron Tube or Pipe Fittings from Brazil*, para 103 *et seq.* See also WT/DS405/R of 28 October 2011, *European Union – Anti-Dumping Measures on Certain Footwear from China*, para 7.400 *et seq.*

[25] WT/DS436/AB/R of 8 December 2014, *United States – Countervailing Measures on Certain Hot-Rolled Carbon Steel Flat Products from India*, paras 4.563–4.600. See also *Ramanujan* (2015) pp. 309–310 who addresses extensively the issue of cumulation.

Volume and Price Effects of the Subsidized Imports (Article 15.2)

Introduction

The injury and causal link analysis starts with the examination of the volume and the price effects of the subsidized imports. Article 15.2 sets out the details. The investigating authority must 'consider' these effects (see *infra* the subsequent section). With regard to the volume of subsidized imports, the investigating authority must consider whether there has been a significant increase of such imports. Such increase can be either in absolute terms or relative to production or consumption in the importing Member. The latter can be seen in the development of market shares (see *infra* this chapter, pp. 480–483).

With regard to the effect of the subsidized imports on prices, the investigating authority shall consider whether there has been significant price undercutting by the subsidized imports as compared to the prices of the like product in the importing country, or whether the subsidized imports have resulted in significant depression or suppression of the prices of the competing industry in the importing country as defined pursuant to Article 16 (see *infra* this chapter, pp. 484–493).

Article 15.2 has to be read in conjunction with Article 15.1, which stipulates, *inter alia*, that a determination of injury shall be based on positive evidence and involve an objective examination of the effect of the subsidized imports on prices in the domestic market for like products. Hence the importance of the notions of 'positive evidence' and 'objective examination' as discussed above.[26]

Article 15.2 *in fine* also highlights that no one or several of the factors listed in this provision can necessarily give decisive guidance. This last sentence of Article 15.2 is similar to the last sentence of Article 15.4.

To 'Consider'

China – GOES has clarified the task of the investigating authority arising from the obligation to 'consider' the volume and the price effects listed

[26] See WT/DS299/R of 17 June 2005, *European Communities – Countervailing Measures on Dynamic Random Access Memory Chips from Korea*, para 7.290 and *supra* this chapter, pp. 473–477.

in Article 15.2. The Appellate Body followed essentially two earlier Panel rulings rendered with regard to Article 3.2 Anti-Dumping Agreement, i.e. *Thailand – H-Beams* and *Korea – Certain Paper*. The Appellate Body held that the word 'consider', when cast as an obligation upon a decision maker, obliges it to take something into account in reaching its decision. Thus, the word 'consider' does not impose an obligation on an investigating authority to make a definitive determination on the subject matter. This is in contrast for example to the verb 'to demonstrate' in Article 3.5 of the Anti-Dumping Agreement and Article 15.5 ASCM. The investigating authority's consideration must be reflected in the relevant documentation, e.g. its final determination, so as to allow interested parties to verify whether the authority has indeed considered the matter. Note finally that while the consideration of a matter is to be distinguished from the definitive determination, this does not change or diminish the scope of what an investigating authority is required to consider.[27]

Volume of Subsidized Imports

Article 15.2 requires an investigating authority to consider (see *supra* the preceding section) whether there has been a significant increase in subsidized imports. This provision lists three possibilities as to how this can be done, i.e. to consider

- whether there has been a significant increase in the volume of subsidized imports in absolute terms;
- whether there has been a significant increase in the volume of subsidized imports relative to domestic production;
- whether there has been a significant increase in the volume of subsidized imports relative to domestic consumption.

This provision also specifies that no one or several of these factors can necessarily give decisive guidance. Therefore, the fact that an investigating authority finds a significant increase in subsidized imports for two out of the three possibilities listed in Article 15.2 is not *per se* inconsistent with Article 15.2.[28]

[27] WT/DS414/AB/R of 18 October 2012, *China – Countervailing and Anti-dumping Duties on Grain Oriented Flat-Rolled Electrical Steel from the United States*, paras 131 and 132, para 150.

[28] WT/DS296/R/3 of 21 February 2005, *United States – Countervailing Duty Investigation on Dynamic Random Access Memory Semiconductors (DRAMs) from Korea*, para 7.234. This aspect of the ruling was not appealed.

Imports from exporters that were found not to benefit from subsidies shall not be included in the analysis of the volume of subsidized imports.[29]

If an exporting producer acquires during the injury investigation period another producer in the exporting country, the question arises how the exports of this other producer should be treated throughout the injury investigation period. In *EC – Countervailing Measures on DRAM Chips*, the injury investigation period covered the calendar years 1998 to 2001. In July 1999, Hynix purchased LG Semicon. The EU combined the exports to the EU made by Hynix and LG Semicon from the date of the merger on. Hynix argued that exports made by LG Semicon prior to the merger should also have been combined with those from Hynix. In the opinion of Hynix, this would have shown that exports from Hynix in terms of market share in the EU had not increased during the injury examination period. The EU rejected this request because LG Semicon was a separate legal entity before the merger and the merger did not have any retroactive effects on the market. The Panel agreed with the EU. Article 15.2 does not set forth specific rules concerning the treatment of imports from companies which merged in the course of the period of injury investigation, thereby forming the company found to have been subsidized. Therefore, the question was whether the EU's approach was reasonable. The Panel considered it important to recall that the term 'subsidized imports' in Article 15.2 referred to imports from a source found to have been subsidized. In other words, Article 15.2 is about imports from a particular source. The EU determined that during the year 2001 Hynix received subsidies from Korea. In its injury analysis, the EU thus examined the volume of imports from this source as part of its consideration whether the imports from this source had increased significantly. The Panel also noted that even after rejecting Korea's request the EU calculated the combined volume of Hynix and LG Semicon through the period and found an increase of subsidized imports, in absolute terms.[30]

Part V of the ASCM is concerned with providing relief from injury caused by subsidized imports. In *US – Countervailing Duty Investigation on DRAMs*, exports from Korea produced by Hynix were subsidized. Hynix also produced DRAMs in the US, i.e. these goods were not imported at all in the US. Korea submitted that the US finding of a significant increase

[29] WT/DS299/R of 17 June 2005, *European Communities – Countervailing Measures on Dynamic Random Access Memory Chips from Korea*, paras 7.292–7.298.

[30] WT/DS299/R of 17 June 2005, *European Communities – Countervailing Measures on Dynamic Random Access Memory Chips from Korea*, paras 7.299–7.305.

in subsidized imports was not based on an objective examination of positive evidence, contrary to the first two paragraphs of Article 15, because the market share of sales of the Hynix brand (i.e. DRAMs produced by Hynix in Korea and the US) developed negatively (from 15.8 per cent in 1998 to 10.4 per cent in 2002). The Panel disagreed, noting that Article 15.2 requires a focus on subsidized imports and that consequently a brand analysis which includes production in the importing country has no basis in that provision.[31]

Korea also claimed that the increase in imports from Hynix was not significant. According to Korea, market shares developed as follows:

	1999	2000	2001	2002	1st quarter 2003
US shipments of US domestic producers	45.8%	43.4%	34.3%	30.7%	29.8%
Subsidized exports from Hynix Korea to the US	8.5%	6.7%	9.0%	8.9%	5.8%
Non-subsidized exports to the US from all other sources	45.7%	49.9%	56.7%	60.4%	64.4%

Korea invoked four reasons: first, Hynix's market share fell in both 2002 and the beginning of 2003. Second, non-subsidized imports consistently dwarfed subsidized imports from Hynix. Third, the small increase in subsidized imports could not be considered significant in light of the much larger increase in non-subsidized imports. Fourth, all of the increase in Hynix's market share of subsidized imports occurred from 2000 to 2001, i.e. prior to Hynix receiving the bulk of the alleged subsidies in the fourth quarter of 2001.

The Panel rejected all these arguments. In relation to the first argument, the Panel noted that the US did not accord much weight to the decrease during the first quarter of 2003 because this was related to the 'pendency' of the investigation and Korea did not challenge this finding. The Panel also pointed out that Hynix's exports to the US increased from 6.7 per cent in 2000 to 8.9 per cent in 2002.

[31] WT/DS296/R/3 of 21 February 2005, *United States – Countervailing Duty Investigation on Dynamic Random Access Memory Semiconductors (DRAMs) from Korea*, paras 7.237 and 7.320. This aspect was not appealed.

In relation to the second and third argument invoked by Korea, the Panel first noted that Article 15.2 requires in relevant part a consideration of whether there is a significant increase in the volume of subsidized imports relative to domestic consumption. Since non-subsidized imports are only one part of domestic consumption, the volume of subsidized imports relative to non-subsidized imports was not determinative. The Panel underlined that there was an increase of market share of 2.2 percentage points between 2000 and 2002 and that the market share of Korean subsidized imports had risen by 32.8 per cent. Korea has not established that an increase of this magnitude could not be considered as significant. Korea also argued that the increase in market share of subsidized imports was largely accounted for by a temporary closure of Hynix's US plant in order to upgrade this production facility. To this, the Panel replied, *inter alia*, that Article 15.2 is concerned with subsidized imports. The rest of the Panel's reasoning in this respect is largely based on business confidential information.

In relation to the fourth argument, the Panel pointed out that Article 15.2 does not require an investigating authority to demonstrate that all of the subject imports covered by the period of injury investigation are subsidized.[32]

In the parallel case *EC – Countervailing Measures on DRAM Chips*, the notion 'significant' in the first sentence of Article 15.2 was also at issue. The Panel observed that Article 15.2 permits a wide latitude for investigating authorities. It also pointed out that the ordinary meaning of 'significant' encompasses 'important', 'notable', 'major' as well as 'consequential', which all suggest something that is more than just a nominal or marginal movement. In the view of the Panel, the increase of subsidized DRAM imports from Korea (361 per cent in absolute terms and 20 per cent in market share) could be categorized as 'significant'. The fact that the DRAM market is highly transparent, and thus susceptible to rapid transmissions of price shocks, constituted a factor that also pleaded to the significance of the increases determined by the EU.[33]

[32] WT/DS296/R/3 of 21 February 2005, *United States – Countervailing Duty Investigation on Dynamic Random Access Memory Semiconductors (DRAMs) from Korea*, paras 7.238–7.245, 7.249. The table is taken from para 7.224. These aspects were not appealed.

[33] WT/DS299/R of 17 June 2005, *European Communities – Countervailing Measures on Dynamic Random Access Memory Chips from Korea*, paras 7.306–7.308.

Price Effects of Subsidized Imports

Introduction

The second sentence of Article 15.2 sets out how the investigating authority shall consider the effect of the subsidized imports on prices. There are three possibilities:

- Has there been a significant price undercutting by the subsidized imports as compared with the price of a like product of the importing Member? See *infra* this chapter, pp. 484–486.
- Was the effect of the subsidized imports to depress prices of the like product in the importing country to a significant degree? See *infra* this chapter, pp. 486–490.
- Was the effect of the subsidized imports price suppression, i.e. to prevent price increases of the like product in the importing country, which otherwise would have occurred, to a significant degree? See *infra* this chapter, pp. 486–490

Article 15.2 confers a wide latitude on the investigating authority because Article 15.2 does not impose a specific methodology on the investigating authority in performing its price effect analysis.[34] However, an investigating authority has to ensure comparability when it is comparing prices of subject imports to those of the like product manufactured by the industry in the importing country.[35]

Price Undercutting

In *EC – Countervailing Measures on DRAM Chips*, Korea argued that an exporter who is losing market share cannot have an effect on domestic prices in the importing country. The Panel was not impressed by this argument. In the view of the Panel, Article 15.2 requires an investigating authority to consider whether there has been significant price undercutting by the subsidized imports. But it does not require an investigating authority to establish what caused the price undercutting. Note also that

[34] WT/DS427/R of 2 August 2013, *China – Anti-Dumping and Countervailing Duty Measures on Broiler Products from the United States*, para 7.474 with further references; WT/DS299/R of 17 June 2005, *European Communities – Countervailing Measures on Dynamic Random Access Memory Chips from Korea*, para 7.328.

[35] See *infra* this chapter, 491–493.

Korea's argument, that the market share of subsidized imports from Korea decreased, was factually incorrect.[36]

Korea also argued that the EU's finding that there was no price leader in the DRAMs market called into serious doubt the EU's determination that Hynix's price undercutting was significant. The Panel held that there was nothing in the text of Article 15.2 precluding an investigating authority from finding significant price undercutting in the absence of a concurrent finding that the subsidized exporting producer was a price leader. The Panel failed to see why only a price leader could be engaged in price undercutting, thereby driving prices down. In a situation where there is no one price leader, all competitors on such a highly price sensitive market as the DRAMs market may cause prices to go down. Therefore, a finding of no price leader is not inconsistent with a finding of significant price undercutting.[37]

In *EC – Countervailing Measures on DRAM Chips*, Korea asserted that the particular methodology used by the EU made it more likely to find price undercutting. Therefore, it alleged that the EU methodology was biased and consequently did not represent an 'objective examination' of whether there was 'significant' price undercutting. The Panel did not agree. It pointed out that the EU examined price undercutting on the basis of three different methodologies (comparison on the basis of yearly, monthly and daily average prices per model). No undercutting was found by using the first methodology while significant price undercutting was found by using the two other methodologies. The EU also explained why it did not find the first methodology appropriate in the case in question. The Panel also noted that Article 15.2 did not set forth any particular methodology for examining price undercutting, as long as the methodology chosen was reasonable and objective. It also pointed out that each methodology has its strengths and weaknesses, but that, as long as the methodology is not unreasonable, a Panel cannot find against it.[38]

The Appellate Body in *China – GOES* considered that the existence of a pricing policy by importers to undercut the prices of domestic producers could, when successful, lead to actual price undercutting. However, even in the absence of price undercutting, a policy that aims

[36] WT/DS299/R of 17 June 2005, *European Communities – Countervailing Measures on Dynamic Random Access Memory Chips from Korea*, paras 7.327 and 7.328.

[37] WT/DS299/R of 17 June 2005, *European Communities – Countervailing Measures on Dynamic Random Access Memory Chips from Korea*, paras 7.329 and 7.330.

[38] WT/DS299/R of 17 June 2005, *European Communities – Countervailing Measures on Dynamic Random Access Memory Chips from Korea*, paras 7.331–7.336.

to undercut a competitor's prices may still be relevant in the context of an examination of the price depressive or suppressive effects of the subsidized imports. If an importer pursues a policy of undercutting a competitor but if that competitor anticipates or responds to that policy by lowering its price to win the sales, this may still reveal that subject imports have the effect of depressing, or preventing the increase of, domestic prices.[39]

Price Depression and Price Suppression of the Like Domestic Product

According to Article 15.2, price depression means that the subsidized imports depress prices of the like product in the importing country to a significant degree. Price suppression exists if the effect of the subsidized imports is to prevent price increases of the like product in the importing country, which otherwise would have occurred, to a significant degree. The concepts of price depression and price suppression are not only used in Article 15.2 but also in Article 6.3(c). The reader is referred to *supra* the commentary to Article 6, pp. 295–303 as well as to as well to *China – GOES*.[40]

According to the Appellate Body in *China – GOES*, the examination of price depression and price suppression requires consideration of the relationship between subject imports and prices of like domestic products. In that case, the parties disagreed as to the meaning of the latter part of the second sentence of Article 15.2, i.e. 'whether the effect of such imports is otherwise to depress prices to a significant degree or to prevent price increases, which otherwise would have occurred, to a significant degree'. China contended that Article 15.2 does not require establishment of a link between domestic prices and subject imports. The Appellate Body did not agree. It held, based on the text of the provision together with its context and objective, that 'specifically' with regard to price depression and suppression, an investigating authority is required to consider the relationship between subject imports and prices of like domestic products, so as to understand whether subject imports provide explanatory force for the occurrence of significant price depression or suppression. The outcome of such inquiry will enable the authority to advance its analysis, and to have

[39] WT/DS414/AB/R of 18 October 2012, *China – Countervailing and Anti-dumping Duties on Grain Oriented Flat-Rolled Electrical Steel from the United States*, paras 206, 207 and 226.

[40] WT/DS414/AB/R of 18 October 2012, *China – Countervailing and Anti-dumping Duties on Grain Oriented Flat-Rolled Electrical Steel from the United States*, para 141.

a meaningful basis for its determination as to whether subject imports, through such price effects, are causing injury to the domestic industry. The Appellate Body also added that this interpretation does not duplicate the different and broader examination regarding the causal relationship between subject imports and injury to the domestic industry pursuant to Article 15.5. Nor does Article 15.2 require the conduct of an exhaustive and full-fledged non-attribution analysis regarding all possible factors that may be causing injury. However, as the inquiry under Article 15.2 is focused on the relationship between subject imports and domestic prices, the investigating authority may not disregard evidence that calls into question the explanatory force of the former for significant price depression or suppression of the latter.[41]

The Appellate Body also explained how it understood the term 'relationship': the investigating authority should consider whether the dumped or subsidized imports do something to domestic prices, i.e. to depress prices or prevent price decreases, or to put it differently, whether certain price effects are the consequences of subject imports. The language of Article 15.2 expressly links significant price depression and suppression with subject imports, and contemplates an inquiry into the relationship between two variables, namely, subject imports and domestic prices. Furthermore, the Appellate Body pointed out that even if prices of subject imports do not significantly undercut those of like domestic products, subject imports could still have a price-depressing or price suppressing effect on domestic prices. However, it would not be sufficient to identify a downward trend in the price of like domestic products over the period of investigation when considering significant price depression, or to note that prices have not risen, even though they would normally be expected to have risen, when analysing price suppression. Rather, an investigating authority is required to examine domestic prices in conjunction with subject imports in order to understand whether subject imports have explanatory force for the occurrence of price depression or suppression of domestic prices.[42]

In the case in question, China based its finding of price suppression simply on a change in the cost/price ratio between the production cost of

[41] WT/DS414/AB/R of 18 October 2012, *China – Countervailing and Anti-dumping Duties on Grain Oriented Flat-Rolled Electrical Steel from the United States*, para 154 as well as paras 134–153.

[42] WT/DS414/AB/R of 18 October 2012, *China – Countervailing and Anti-dumping Duties on Grain Oriented Flat-Rolled Electrical Steel from the United States*, paras 135–139.

the domestic like product and the import price. The US argued that the changes in the cost/price ratio merely reflected changes in the underlying cost structure of the domestic Chinese industry, as a significant amount of new capacity was added by one of the two Chinese producers. Therefore, an objective and impartial investigating authority would have recognized the need to examine whether the change in the cost/price ratio was merely a function of the inclusion of the additional start-up costs incurred by one of the two Chinese producers, rather than an adverse effect of subject imports on price.[43]

The Appellate Body also noted that China referred in its price suppression analysis to both the volume and the prices of the subject imports. However, there was no explanation or reasoning as to whether or how the prices and volume of subject imports interacted to produce an effect on Chinese domestic prices. Nor did MOFCOM's determination indicate whether the effect of either prices or volume alone could have sustained MOFCOM's finding of significant price depression or suppression. In these circumstances, neither the Panel nor the Appellate Body was able to disentangle the relative contribution of price and volume effects without substituting their judgements with that of the investigating authority. To have done so, would have risked constituting a *de novo* review, which would have been inappropriate.[44] See also *infra* this chapter, pp. 490–491.

In short, an examination of price depression, by definition, calls for more than a simple observation of price decline. It also comprises an analysis of what is pushing down the prices.[45]

The Appellate Body ruling that price depression and price suppression do not require a full-fledged non-attribution analysis is in line with two previous DRAM cases. In respect of price depression, the USITC employed in *US – Countervailing Duty Investigation on DRAMs* two methodologies. First, it compared a weighted average import price to a weighted average US producer price. Prices for US produced DRAMs and subsidized imports from Korea followed the same general trends, i.e. declines of 70

[43] WT/DS414/AB/R of 18 October 2012, *China – Countervailing and Anti-dumping Duties on Grain Oriented Flat-Rolled Electrical Steel from the United States*, para 166 *et seq.*

[44] WT/DS414/AB/R of 18 October 2012, *China – Countervailing and Anti-dumping Duties on Grain Oriented Flat-Rolled Electrical Steel from the United States*, paras 213–221. Similar *China – Anti-Dumping and Countervailing Duty Measures on Broiler Products from the United States*, paras 7.510–7.511.

[45] WT/DS414/AB/R of 18 October 2012, *China – Countervailing and Anti-dumping Duties on Grain Oriented Flat-Rolled Electrical Steel from the United States*, para 141.

to 90 per cent from late 2000 through 2001, a modest rebound in early 2002, then a further decline over the course of 2002. There was agreement among parties that the price decline in 2001 was the most severe in DRAM history. The ITC also found that the increasing frequency of underselling of subsidized imports from 2000 to 2002 corresponded with the substantial decline in US prices over the same years. Korea took issue with this finding by arguing that the reason prices were depressed was not because of subsidized imports from Korea but because of a much larger volume of imports from other sources. The Panel rejected this argument. The fact that non-subsidized imports might have had negative price effects did not preclude a finding that subsidized imports also had negative effects on prices. Note also that the ITC did not identify a price leader in the US market. However, purchasers of DRAMs identified Hynix as a source of low-priced DRAM products and confirmed that the US domestic industry lost sales and/or revenue due to competition from Hynix.[46]

Second, the USITC performed a disaggregated lowest-price analysis. Korea also challenged the lowest-price analysis because it was not done on a combined, aggregated brand analysis, i.e. all imports not subject to investigation plus US domestic sources of the same brand combined together. The Panel rejected Korea's argument. It held that Article 15.2 requires the investigating authority only to examine the price effects of subsidized imports, but it does not require the examination of the price effects of non-subsidized imports, or pricing on a combined brand basis.[47]

In the parallel case *EC – Countervailing Measures on DRAM Chips*, the Panel also was of the opinion that Article 15.2 does not, as such, require an investigating authority to establish a causal link between the subsidized imports and the domestic prices. This in turn would require the examination of all other factors affecting prices. Korea claimed that it was known to the investigating authority that there were a number of other factors which affected DRAM prices, notably the general economic downturn and decrease in demand, excess capacities and imports from other suppliers. The Panel disagreed and pointed out that Article 15.2 did not, as such, require an investigating authority to establish a causal link between

[46] WT/DS296/R/3 of 21 February 2005, *United States – Countervailing Duty Investigation on Dynamic Random Access Memory Semiconductors (DRAMs) from Korea*, paras 7.270–7.274. This aspect was not appealed. See also the table on market shares above in this chapter on p. 482.

[47] WT/DS296/R/3 of 21 February 2005, *United States – Countervailing Duty Investigation on Dynamic Random Access Memory Semiconductors (DRAMs) from Korea*, paras 7.267–7.269. This aspect was not appealed.

the subsidized imports and the domestic prices which would require it to examine all other factors affecting domestic prices at the same time. Korea's arguments were therefore discussed under Article 15.5, i.e. in relation to the question of causation.[48]

Unitary or Two-Step Analysis?

The Appellate Body in *China – GOES* held that Article 15.2 ASCM and Article 3.2 Anti-Dumping Agreement appear to make a unitary analysis of the effect of subject imports on domestic prices more appropriate, rather than a two-step analysis that first seeks to identify the market phenomena and then, as a second step, examines whether such phenomena are the effect of subject imports. Thus, the Appellate Body promoted the same approach as in relation to the examination of the market phenomena under Article 6.3 ASCM. However, the Appellate Body also accepted that a two-step analysis is legally possible.[49]

Parallel Trends of Subject Import and Domestic Prices

An observation of parallel price trends might support a price depression or suppression analysis. For instance, the fact that prices of subject imports and domestic products move in tandem might indicate the nature of competition between the products, and may explain the extent to which factors relating to the pricing behaviour of importers have an effect on domestic prices. It follows from the above that it would appear to be also necessary that the investigating authority provide a reasoning or an explanation regarding the role of such parallel trends in the price effects analysis.[50]

Subject Import Volumes May Also Have an Effect on Domestic Prices

The effect of subject imports on domestic prices may be examined through the vector of subject import prices, subject import volumes, or both. Therefore, a finding of significant price depression or suppression

[48] WT/DS299/R of 17 June 2005, *European Communities – Countervailing Measures on Dynamic Random Access Memory Chips from Korea*, paras 7.337–7.339.

[49] WT/DS414/AB/R of 18 October 2012, *China – Countervailing and Anti-dumping Duties on Grain Oriented Flat-Rolled Electrical Steel from the United States*, para 142. See also *supra* the commentary to Article 6, pp. 284–285.

[50] WT/DS414/AB/R of 18 October 2012, *China – Countervailing and Anti-dumping Duties on Grain Oriented Flat-Rolled Electrical Steel from the United States*, para 210.

can rest on an examination of the effect of both the prices and the volume of subject imports on domestic prices. However, if an investigating authority relies on both the prices and volumes of subject imports, it would appear to be necessary that it explains whether or how the prices and volumes of subject imports interacted to produce an effect on domestic prices.[51]

Moreover, if the finding of price suppression made by an investigating authority relies on both price effects and volume effects of subject imports, and if the examination of price effects was legally flawed, a Panel could in principle examine whether the price suppression finding can stand independently on the basis of the investigating authority's findings on volume and market share effects. However, if the investigating authority has provided no explanation as to how the prices and volume of subject imports interacted to produce an effect on domestic prices, a Panel will find it impossible to perform such examination. Disentangling the respective contributions of prices and volume of subject imports in such circumstances would be tantamount to substituting the investigating authority's judgement by the Panel's judgement.[52]

Price Comparability

General Any comparison of prices under this provision must ensure price comparability, e.g. in terms of levels of trade, although there is no explicit requirement in Article 15.2 to this effect. If subject import and domestic prices were not comparable, this would defeat the explanatory force that subject import prices might have for the depression or suppression of domestic prices. The need to ensure price comparability also follows from the requirements under Article 15.1 that a determination of injury is based on 'positive evidence' and an 'objective examination'. Finally, the question of whether price adjustments are needed to ensure price comparability cannot be determined by whether a respondent objects to the

[51] WT/DS414/AB/R of 18 October 2012, *China – Countervailing and Anti-dumping Duties on Grain Oriented Flat-Rolled Electrical Steel from the United States*, paras 211–221. The ruling is not entirely clear as to what extent an investigating authority should also indicate in these circumstances whether the effect of either import prices or import volumes alone could sustain a finding of significant price depression or suppression. See also footnote 364 of the Appellate Body's report.

[52] WT/DS414/AB/R of 18 October 2012, *China – Countervailing and Anti-dumping Duties on Grain Oriented Flat-Rolled Electrical Steel from the United States*, paras 220–221; WT/DS427/R of 2 August 2013, *China – Anti-Dumping and Countervailing Duty Measures on Broiler Products from the United States*, paras 7.510–7.513.

use of unadjusted prices.[53] In sum, as *China – Broiler Products* has put it, there can be no question that the prices being compared must correspond to products and transactions that are comparable if they are to provide any reliable indication of the existence and extent of price undercutting by the dumped or subsidized imports as compared with the price of the domestic like product. This may then be relied upon in assessing causality. This Panel also examined two factors that play an important role in price comparisons, i.e. level of trade and physical characteristics – *see infra*.[54] It would appear that similar considerations apply with regard to the analysis of price depression and price suppression.

Level of Trade With regard to level of trade, *China – Broiler Products* noted that depending on the particular realities of the relevant market, additional pricing elements are added as the product gets traded further down the distribution chain, from producer to wholesaler, from wholesaler to retailer, and from retailer to end-user. The level of trade at which the transaction takes place is an important characteristic of the transaction in question. The comparison should be made at the same level of trade. Alternatively, appropriate adjustments must be made to render the transactions comparable in terms of the pricing components that they include. In the case at issue, the US argued that CIF import prices (which were adjusted for customs duties paid but not for handling or customs clearance fees) should have been adjusted by a mark-up corresponding to the importers' costs (e.g. transportation costs to the importer's warehouse) and profits in order to make them comparable to ex factory prices of Chinese domestic producers. According to the US, the imported merchandise only competed with Chinese merchandise at importer's level. The Panel was not convinced. It held that both prices used by MOFCOM were situated at the first point at which a purchaser may take delivery of the product in the country of importation. They contained both pricing elements that reflected the first point in the distribution chain where imported and like domestic products enter into competition. Expressed differently, they were

53 WT/DS414/AB/R of 18 October 2012, *China – Countervailing and Anti-dumping Duties on Grain Oriented Flat-Rolled Electrical Steel from the United States*, paras 200 and 201. Therefore, the Appellate Body upheld the Panel's statement that as soon as price comparisons are made, price comparability necessarily arises as an issue. See also WT/DS427/R of 2 August 2013, *China – Anti-Dumping and Countervailing Duty Measures on Broiler Products from the United States*, para 7.475 *et seq.*

54 See also WT/DS427/R of 2 August 2013, *China – Anti-Dumping and Countervailing Duty Measures on Broiler Products from the United States*, paras 7.475, 7.480–7.483.

at prices upon which the first purchaser in the country of import could base its purchasing decision either to import directly or to buy directly from domestic producers. In the Panel's view, the pricing elements that according to the US should have been added to the CIF price were not by definition contained in the domestic producer's ex works price.[55]

Physical Characteristics In *China – Broiler Products*, China took the view that it was sufficient to compare the weighted average price of all imports with the weighted average price of the sales of the domestic industry on the basis that all products fall under the same category, i.e. they were broiler products. The US pointed to evidence on the file according to which the product mix of imports was different from that of sales made by the domestic industry. Ninety-seven per cent of US imports consisted of lower-valued product types (paws, chicken cuts with bones, offal etc. as opposed, for instance, to breast meat). The Panel sided with the US. There was in fact no dispute about the differences in product mix between US imports and domestic sales. The information before MOFCOM (invoices etc.) revealed important price differences between the different broiler products. This meant that the differences in product mix risked affecting price comparability and distorting any price effects analysis.[56]

Period for Which the Effect of Imports on Prices Should Be Determined

See *supra* this chapter, pp. 476–477.

Examination of the Impact of the Subsidized Imports on the Domestic Industry (Article 15.4)

Examination of All Economic Factors and Indices

It follows from Article 15.1, which has the character of an overarching provision, that the examination under Article 15.4 must be an objective one and based on positive evidence.[57]

[55] See also WT/DS427/R of 2 August 2013, *China – Anti-Dumping and Countervailing Duty Measures on Broiler Products from the United States*, paras 7.480, 7.481, 7.485–7.489.

[56] See also WT/DS427/R of 2 August 2013, *China – Anti-Dumping and Countervailing Duty Measures on Broiler Products from the United States*, paras 7.480, 7.483 7.490–7.493.

[57] WT/DS341/R of 4 September 2008, *Mexico – Definitive Countervailing Measures on Olive Oil from the European Communities*, para 7.270; WT/DS299/R of 17 June 2005, *European*

An investigating authority must examine and evaluate all factors listed in Article 15.4.[58] The consideration of each of the factors must be apparent in the final determination of the investigating authority. However, an investigating authority may conclude that a particular factor is not probative in the circumstances of the domestic industry in a particular case, and therefore is not relevant in the actual determination.[59] Therefore, there is no requirement that each and every injury factor, individually, must be indicative of injury.[60] The last sentence of Article 15.4 also highlights this.

The list of factors in Article 15.4 is not exhaustive. Other factors can also be relevant (see *infra*).

In an *obiter dictum*, the Appellate Body in *China – GOES* held that Article 15.4 ASCM and Article 3.4 of the Anti-Dumping Agreement do not merely require an examination of the state of the domestic industry, but contemplate that an investigating authority must derive an understanding of the impact of the subject imports on the basis of such an examination. In other words, the investigating authority must examine the impact of subject imports on the domestic industry. Thus, these two provisions require an examination of the explanatory force of subject imports for the state of the domestic industry. According to the Appellate Body, this relationship is akin to the type of link contemplated by the term 'the effect of' in Articles 15.2 and 3.2 respectively. This analysis is not the same as demonstrating that subject imports are causing injury to the domestic industry, as set out in Articles 15.5 and 3.5 respectively. The outcomes of the inquiries under Articles 15.2 and 15.4 as well as 3.2 and 3.4 respectively form the basis for the overall causation analysis contemplated in Articles 15.5 ASCM and 3.5 of the

Communities – Countervailing Measures on Dynamic Random Access Memory Chips from Korea, para 7.356. See *supra* this chapter, pp. 473–477.

[58] WT/DS341/R of 4 September 2008, *Mexico – Definitive Countervailing Measures on Olive Oil from the European Communities*, para 7.270; WT/DS299/R of 17 June 2005, *European Communities – Countervailing Measures on Dynamic Random Access Memory Chips from Korea*, paras 7.340–7.344; WT/DS122/AB/R of 12 March 2001, *Thailand – Anti-Dumping Duties on Angles, Shapes and Sections of Iron or Non-Alloy Steel and H-Beams from Poland*, paras 121–128.

[59] WT/DS341/R of 4 September 2008, *Mexico – Definitive Countervailing Measures on Olive Oil from the European Communities*, para 7.270; WT/DS132/R of 28 January 2000, *Mexico – Anti-Dumping Investigation of High Fructose Corn Syrup (HFCS) from the United States*, para 7.128.

[60] WT/DS341/R of 4 September 2008, *Mexico – Definitive Countervailing Measures on Olive Oil from the European Communities*, para 7.270; WT/DS141/RW of 29 November 2002, *European Communities – Anti-Dumping Duties on Imports of Cotton-Type Bed Linen from India – Recourse to Article 21.5 of the DSU by India*, paras 6.163, 6.213.

Anti-Dumping Agreement and thus contribute to, rather than duplicate, the overall determination required under Articles 15.5 and 3.5 respectively.[61]

The Panel in *China – Broiler Products* has further developed the aforementioned principles:

> The United States' arguments raise the question of the manner in which an investigating authority should assess the situation of the domestic industry in the light of the relevant economic factors and indices. We recall in this respect that … an investigating authority's assessment of the evidence must be objective. This may require the authority to place the relevant data in context in a manner that is informative of the injury, if any, suffered by the domestic industry rather than simply review evolution in yearly figures. Furthermore, to comply with Articles 3.4 of the Anti-Dumping Agreement and 15.4 of the SCM Agreement, the authority must also evaluate the relevant factors and indices in a manner which allows it to determine whether relevant trends in these relevant factors and indices result from subject imports.[62]

Factors Other Than Those Enumerated in Article 15.4 Can Also Play a Role

The business cycle of the industry is not listed as a factor in Article 15.4. In *US – Countervailing Duty Investigation on DRAMs*, the parties agreed that the business cycle was a relevant economic factor. However, there was disagreement about the treatment of this factor in the USITC's injury determination. The Panel was satisfied with the ITC's treatment of this factor and did not attach any importance to the fact that the ITC dealt with this issue not in the section on the 'Impact of Subject Imports' (i.e. the section addressing issues falling under Article 15.4) but in the section on price effects (i.e. the section addressing issues falling under Article 15.2).[63]

In the parallel case *EC – Countervailing Measures on DRAM Chips*, Korea claimed that the EU should have examined under Article 15.4 as

[61] WT/DS414/AB/R of 18 October 2012, *China – Countervailing and Anti-Dumping Duties on Grain Oriented Flat-Rolled Electrical Steel from the United States*, paras 149 and 150. See also *supra* this chapter, pp. 479–493.

[62] WT/DS427/R of 2 August 2013, *China – Anti-Dumping and Countervailing Duty Measures on Broiler Products from the United States*, para 7.554.

[63] WT/DS296/R/3 of 21 February 2005, *United States – Countervailing Duty Investigation on Dynamic Random Access Memory Semiconductors (DRAMs) from Korea*, paras 7.288–7.294. This aspect was not appealed.

other factors the economic downturn in the market (i.e. the 'boom/bust cycle') and the export performance of the EU industry. The Panel rejected this claim. The Panel first clarified what a party had to demonstrate in front of a panel if it claims that a factor not explicitly listed in Article 15.4 should have been examined by the investigating authority: it must demonstrate (i) that a certain factor which was relevant in assessing the impact of the subsidized imports on the state of the domestic industry was not examined; and (ii) that the question of evaluation was raised during the investigation. Ultimately, the Panel seems to indicate that 'other factors' are typically considered in the causation analysis pursuant to Article 15.5 and not so much under the Article 15.4 examination. According to the Panel, the factors listed in Article 15.4 clarify that what is required under this provision is that the investigating authority examines and evaluates those factors and indices that provide it with a full and objective picture of the state of the domestic industry. However, forces that may have caused certain negative or positive developments are to be considered as part of the causation analysis under Article 15.5. In the view of the Panel, the economic downturn in the market and the export performance of the EU industry were precisely the kind of causal factors that should be addressed in the causation analysis.[64]

Domestic Industry Normally Defined by Production of the 'Like Product' (Article 15.6)

Article 15.6 clarifies that injury is normally established in relation to the like product as defined by footnote 46. However, this applies only if available data permit the separate identification of that production on the basis of such criteria as the production process, producers' sales and profits. If this is not possible, the effects of subsidized imports shall be assessed by the examination of the production of the narrowest group or range of products, which includes the like product, and for which the necessary information can be provided.

If the industry in the importing country sells the like product both on the open market but also consumes it internally, the situation relating to the captive market has also to be analysed.[65]

[64] WT/DS299/R of 17 June 2005, *European Communities – Countervailing Measures on Dynamic Random Access Memory Chips from Korea*, paras 7.363–7.366.

[65] WT/DS184/AB/R of 24 July 2001, *United States – Anti-Dumping Measures on Certain Hot-Rolled Steel Products from Japan*, para 181 *et seq.*

Overall Conclusion on the Impact of the Subsidized Imports on the Domestic Industry Pursuant to Article 15.4

Based on *EC – Countervailing Measures on DRAM Chips*, a rough summary of what an investigating authority has to do in order to comply with the requirements arising out of Article 15.4 could be:

- It is necessary to examine and evaluate all factors listed in Article 15.4 both individually and in an overall context.
- An adequate explanation has to be given as to how the facts support the determination made.
- An injury determination cannot just be based on those factors that showed a negative development. If some factors show positive developments it has to be explained how this supports the overall determination of injury to the domestic industry.[66]

EC and certain Member States – Large Civil Aircraft is also relevant here. The Panel concluded that the question whether or not there is injury is fact-specific in each case, depending on the nature of the product and the industry in question. Developments in various factors, such as a particular decline in production, sales or profit levels, that in one industry may support a finding of material injury, may not in another industry. Material injury can only be present if the industry's overall performance, or some relevant factors, deteriorated over the reference period. However, it is not necessary that all relevant factors, or even most or a majority of them, must show declines in order to make a finding of injury. Injury might even be found in the case of an industry whose performance is improved or improving. An overall evaluation of the information, in context, is necessary as well as an explanation of how the facts support the determination.[67]

Causal Link

Introduction

The problem with identifying a causal link between the subsidized subject imports and the injury of the domestic industry in the importing

[66] WT/DS299/R of 17 June 2005, *European Communities – Countervailing Measures on Dynamic Random Access Memory Chips from Korea*, paras 7.369–7.373.

[67] WT/DS316/R of 30 June 2010, *EC and certain Member States – Measures Affecting Trade in Large Civil Aircraft*, paras 7.2083 and 7.2084.

country is the following. Typically, not only the subsidized imports will have a negative effect on the situation of the domestic industry. Rather, it will usually be claimed that there are (also) other factors that impact negatively on the situation of the domestic industry. This raises the question whether subsidized imports have caused the injury found. The ASCM does not require that subsidized imports be the sole cause of injury. But countervailing duties can only be imposed if, pursuant to Article 15.5, the injury caused by the subsidized imports is material. The effect of other factors also injuring the domestic industry in the importing country may not be attributed to the subsidized imports.

The causal link analysis under Article 15.5 is a two-step analysis. First, it requires a demonstration that the subsidized imports are, through the effects of the subsidies as set forth in Articles 15.2 and 15.4, causing injury within the meaning of the ASCM ('causal link test I' – see *infra*). Second, Article 15.5 mandates investigating authorities to examine any known factors other than the subsidized imports, which at the same time are injuring the domestic industry, and requires that the injuries caused by these other factors not be attributed to the subsidized imports ('causal link test II' – see *infra*).[68] But see also *supra* this chapter, p. 490.

The second sentence of Article 15.5 also highlights that the causal link analysis is an 'examination of all relevant evidence before the authorities'.

Causal Link Test I

This is typically demonstrated by a correlation or coincidence in time between, on the one hand, rising subsidized and low-priced imports and, on the other, declining fortunes (in particular, profitability is a highly relevant Article 15.4 factor) of the industry in the importing country. Imports can rise in market share and/or also in absolute terms.[69] However, there

[68] This was the summary used by WT/DS299/R of 17 June 2005, *European Communities – Countervailing Measures on Dynamic Random Access Memory Chips from Korea*, para 7.397. See also WT/DS121/AB/R of 14 December 1999, *Argentina – Safeguard Measures on Imports of Footwear*, paras 144 and 145 in relation to a safeguard case. *Miranda* (2010) provides an excellent overview of WTO dispute settlement rulings concerning causation not only in the area of countervailing duty cases but also with regard to the two other remedy instruments, i.e. anti-dumping and safeguards.

[69] See e.g. WT/DS299/R of 17 June 2005, *European Communities – Countervailing Measures on Dynamic Random Access Memory Chips from Korea*, paras 7.398–7.403.

is no need to establish both a volume effect and a price effect of the subsidized imports to conclude that there is injury and causation. Contrary to the standard under the WTO Safeguard Agreement, a finding of price effect could be sufficient. In other words, there may be causation even in the absence of a significant increase in the volume of subsidized imports, provided that the requisite price effects exist.[70]

Causal link test I is not necessarily conclusive. It only provides a preliminary assessment that will have to be cross-checked and confirmed by applying the causal link text II.

Causal Link Test II

Causal link test II is essentially concerned with the effect of factors other than the subsidized imports. Its purpose is to ensure that other factors injuring the domestic industry are not wrongly attributed to the subsidized imports. The legal basis for this test can be found in the third and fourth sentence of Article 15.5. The fourth sentence sets forth specific examples of other factors but this list is not exhaustive. When interpreting Article 15.5, panels have been guided by DSB rulings concerning the non-attribution requirement set forth in Article 3.5 of the Anti-Dumping Agreement.[71] The leading case here is the Appellate Body ruling in *US – Hot-Rolled Steel*:

> [T]o comply with the non-attribution language in [Article 3.5 of the WTO Anti-Dumping Agreement], investigating authorities must make an appropriate assessment of the injury caused to the domestic industry by the other known factors, and they must separate and distinguish the injurious effects of the dumped imports from the injurious effects of those other factors. This requires a satisfactory explanation of the nature and the

[70] See e.g. WT/DS299/R of 17 June 2005, *European Communities – Countervailing Measures on Dynamic Random Access Memory Chips from Korea*, footnote 277 attached to para 7.399. It would appear that the Appellate Body arrived at a similar conclusion in the context of examining the cumulation of dumped imports from several countries, see WT/DS219/AB/R of 22 July 2003, *European Communities – Anti-Dumping Duties on Malleable Cast Iron Tube or Pipe Fittings from Brazil*, footnote 114 attached to para 111.

[71] See e.g. WT/DS341/R of 4 September 2008, *Mexico – Definitive Countervailing Measures on Olive Oil from the European Communities*, para 7.298 *et seq.*; WT/DS299/R of 17 June 2005, *European Communities – Countervailing Measures on Dynamic Random Access Memory Chips from Korea*, para 7.404; WT/DS296/R/3 of 21 February 2005, *United States – Countervailing Duty Investigation on Dynamic Random Access Memory Semiconductors (DRAMs) from Korea*, para 7.353. This aspect was not appealed.

> extent of the injurious effects of the other factors, as distinguished from the injurious effects of the dumped imports.[72]

In *EC – Tube or Pipe Fittings*, the Appellate Body referred to its ruling in *US – Hot-Rolled Steel* and reiterated that non-attribution requires separation and distinguishing of the effects of other causal factors from those of the dumped imports so that injuries caused by the dumped imports and those caused by other factors are not lumped together and made indistinguishable. It equally reiterated that the non-attribution obligation does not require an investigating authority to use any particular methodology.[73]

EC – Countervailing Measures on DRAM Chips has held that it does not suffice for an investigating authority merely to check the box with regard to other known factors. An investigating authority must do more than simply list other known factors, and then dismiss their role with bare qualitative assertions such as 'the factor did not contribute in any significant way to injury' or 'the factor did not break the causal link between subsidized imports and material injury'. At the very least, the non-attribution language of Article 15.5 requires from an investigating authority a satisfactory explanation of the nature and the extent of the injurious effects of the other factors, as distinguished from the injurious effects of the subsidized imports. The panel would have even preferred a certain effort to quantify the impact of the other known factors, relative to the subsidized imports, preferably using elementary economic constructs or models.[74] By contrast, the Panel in *US – Countervailing Duty Investigation on DRAMs* made it clear that there is no obligation under Article 15.5 to quantify the amount of injury caused by alleged subsidized and non-subsidized imports.[75]

EC – Countervailing Measures on DRAM Chips provides an example where an investigating authority did not sufficiently separate and

72 WT/DS184/AB/R of 24 July 2001, *United States – Anti-Dumping Measures on Certain Hot-Rolled Steel Products from Japan*, para 226.

73 WT/DS219/AB/R of 22 July 2003, *European Communities – Anti-Dumping Duties on Malleable Cast Iron Tube or Pipe Fittings from Brazil*, paras 188 and 189; WT/DS184/AB/R of 24 July 2001, *United States – Anti-Dumping Measures on Certain Hot-Rolled Steel Products from Japan*, para 224. With regard to an examination of causation based on statistical analysis see *Fetzer* (2008).

74 WT/DS299/R of 17 June 2005, *European Communities – Countervailing Measures on Dynamic Random Access Memory Chips from Korea*, para 7.405. See also *Fetzer* (2008).

75 WT/DS296/R/3 of 21 February 2005, *United States – Countervailing Duty Investigation on Dynamic Random Access Memory Semiconductors (DRAMs) from Korea*, para 7.360. This aspect was not appealed.

distinguish the injury caused by the subsidized imports from the injury caused by other known factors. The investigation period for subsidization was the calendar year 2002. Hynix and the Government of Korea argued that the impact of the cyclicality or rather the economic downturn should have been taken into account. They further argued that worldwide demand for DRAMs grew in 2001, i.e. the investigation period for subsidization, only by 59 per cent whilst the average year on year rate was 75 per cent. The EU replied that

- the worldwide growth rates quoted by Korea were highly subjective and contradicted by record evidence;
- it was recognized that the general economic downturn of personal computer and telecommunications market in 2001 might have had some downward effect on prices;
- however, DRAM consumption in the EU market continued its upward trend – the increase between 2000 and the bad year 2001 was almost the same as the increase between 1999 and the good year 2000, i.e. 51 per cent versus 57 per cent;
- therefore, it could be concluded that, whilst the economic downturn may have had some downward effect on prices, it can be assumed that, with consumption rising, this effect was not substantial.

The Panel was not impressed:

- It recalled that the development of prices constituted one of the main factors on which the EU based its finding of material injury.
- It criticized that the record was devoid of even elementary quantitative analysis of the importance of the economic downturn, or a thorough qualitative analysis of the nature and extent of this factor.
- It failed to see to what extent the EU's analysis of domestic consumption was sufficient for separating and distinguishing the effects of the economic downturn and the injurious effects of the subsidized imports.
- As the EU had acknowledged that the downturn in the market had a negative effect on prices, it should have examined the extent of this negative effect.[76]

[76] WT/DS299/R of 17 June 2005, *European Communities – Countervailing Measures on Dynamic Random Access Memory Chips from Korea*, paras 7.411–7.414. Moreover, the Panel held that the EU also did not separate and distinguish the effects of overcapacity and of non-subsidized imports, see paras 7.418–7.422 and paras 7.423–7.435 respectively. The parallel Panel in WT/DS296/R/3 of 21 February 2005, *United States – Countervailing Duty Investigation on Dynamic Random Access Memory Semiconductors (DRAMs) from Korea*,

The 'order of magnitude' test can often be a useful analytical tool when examining the effect of 'other factors'. In other words, what is the order of magnitude of the effects of other factors impacting on the domestic industry of the importing country as compared to the price and/or volume effects of the subsidized imports? If the former are small when compared to the latter, a causal link is normally met. However, the order of magnitude test will be less suitable if the injurious effect of the subsidized imports and the effect of other factors have a comparable weight.[77]

What Constitutes Any 'Other Factor' in a Particular Investigation?

A question preceding the non-attribution analysis is what constitutes any 'other factor'. The Appellate Body in *EC – Tube or Pipe Fittings* held that the non-attribution analysis is triggered where the factor concerned

- is known to the investigating authority,
- is a factor other than the subject imports and
- causes injury to the domestic industry concurrently with the subject imports.

This means that it is not necessary that an interested party identifies such 'other factor' e.g. by making a submission to the investigation file. Rather, it is sufficient if such 'other factor' is known to the investigating authority.[78] The Panel in *China – GOES* took a similar position. It did not consider that a respondent is required to provide evidence regarding 'other factors'. Article 15.5 of the ASCM and Article 3.5 of the Anti-Dumping Agreement provide that '[t]he authorities shall examine any known factors other than the [subject] imports which at the same time are injuring the domestic industry'. Accordingly, once a factor becomes known to the investigating authority, it is for the investigating authority to investigate.[79] In contrast to the aforementioned rulings, the Panel in *Thailand – H-Beams* seems to

para 7.368 also failed the USITC for not conducting a proper non-attribution analysis with regard to the negative impact of slowing demand. This aspect was not appealed.

77 *Miranda* (2010) pp. 756–758.

78 WT/DS219/AB/R of 22 July 2003, *European Communities – Anti-Dumping Duties on Malleable Cast Iron Tube or Pipe Fittings from Brazil*, paras 172, 175, 176 and 178. See also WT/DS122/R of 28 September 2000, *Thailand – Anti-Dumping Duties on Angles, Shapes and Sections of Iron or Non-Alloy Steel and H-Beams from Poland*, para 7.273.

79 WT/DS414/R of 15 June 2012, *China – Countervailing and Anti-Dumping Duties on Grain-Oriented Flat-Rolled Electrical Steel from the US*, para 7.636. See also WT/DS219/AB/R of 22 July 2003, *European Communities – Anti-Dumping Duties on Malleable Cast Iron Tube or Pipe Fittings from Brazil*, paras 176–178.

have somewhat shifted the onus of identifying any 'other factor' on to the parties. It held that other known factors would include causal factors that are clearly raised before the investigating authorities by interested parties in the course of the investigation. According to the Panel, there is no express requirement in Article 3.5 of the Anti-Dumping Agreement that investigating authorities seek out and examine in each case on their own initiative the effects of all possible factors other than imports that may be causing injury.[80]

For all practical intents and purposes, a non-attribution analysis is clearly necessary if such 'other factor' was raised before an investigating authority (and properly documented in the file) and if such factor could have caused injury to the domestic industry concurrently with the subject imports.[81]

Note finally that the Appellate Body in *EC – Tube or Pipe Fittings* left open the question whether or not such 'other factor' can be intrinsic to the subject imports, e.g. exchange rate fluctuations or the removal of an import quota, or whether such factor must be extrinsic.[82]

Non-subsidized Imports of the Product Concerned

In *US – Countervailing Duty Investigation on DRAMs*, non-subsidized imports had a much larger market share than the subsidized imports from Korea. According to Korea, non-subsidized imports were six to seven times higher than the subsidized imports. Therefore, Korea claimed that the USITC had not properly separated and distinguished the effects of these other imports. The Panel disagreed. According to the Panel, the USITC acknowledged that non-subsidized imports were responsible for the bulk of market share lost by US domestic producers during the period of investigation. However, the USITC found nevertheless a causal link between the subsidized imports and the material injury of the US industry. This conclusion was based on considerations relating to the product mix of the imports from the various sources and price considerations.

[80] WT/DS341/R of 4 September 2008, *Mexico – Definitive Countervailing Measures on Olive Oil from the European Communities*, para 7.300; WT/DS122/R of 28 September 2000, *Thailand – Anti-Dumping Duties on Angles, Shapes and Sections of Iron or Non-Alloy Steel and H-Beams from Poland*, para 7.273.

[81] *Miranda* (2010) p. 751.

[82] WT/DS219/AB/R of 22 July 2003, *European Communities – Anti-Dumping Duties on Malleable Cast Iron Tube or Pipe Fittings from Brazil*, para 176. If exports are invoiced in the currency of the importing country while the currency of the exporting country depreciates, the subject imports can heavily undercut the like product.

Non-subsidized imports had less impact than their absolute and relative volumes might otherwise have indicated. Approximately 20 per cent consisted of product types for which US domestic producers had no significant production while the imports from Hynix were equivalent to US merchandise. Moreover, the USITC found that the primary negative impact of Korean subsidized imports on the US domestic industry resulted from lower prices. Subsidized imports undersold non-subsidized imports in a majority of instances. According to the Panel, and based on the foregoing, the USITC demonstrated that alleged subsidized imports had injurious price effects independent of those of the larger volume non-subsidized imports.[83]

Situation of Other Domestic Producers

An investigating authority might need to assess the situation of other domestic producers, i.e. those not falling under the definition of domestic industry pursuant to Article 16.1, in its evaluation of a causal link and whether the strength of other domestic producers could be a possible separate cause of injury to the defined 'domestic industry'.[84]

Domestic Industry's Increase of Capacity and Production as Another Known Factor

In *China – GOES*, the US argued the Chinese industry's increase of capacity and production was a cause of the injury. China rejected this argument. In this respect, China relied on the correlation between inventory levels and subject imports as well as a lack of correlation between inventory levels and changes in production capacity. The Panel dismissed this argument. It established that domestic capacity and domestic production increased by more than the increase in the volume of subject imports. For one part of the injury investigation period, it was even found that there would have been a substantial increase in inventories even if there had not been any subject imports. In short, the increase of subject imports only accounted for a minor part of the increase of inventories.[85]

[83] WT/DS296/R/3 of 21 February 2005, *United States – Countervailing Duty Investigation on Dynamic Random Access Memory Semiconductors (DRAMs) from Korea*, paras 7.356–7.360. This aspect was not appealed.

[84] WT/DS427/R of 2 August 2013, *China – Anti-Dumping and Countervailing Duty Measures on Broiler Products from the United States*, para 7.419.

[85] WT/DS414/R of 15 June 2012, *China – Countervailing and Anti-Dumping Duties on Grain-Oriented Flat-Rolled Electrical Steel from the US*, paras 7.627–7.637. Capacity increase was also at issue in WT/DS296/R/3 of 21 February 2005, *United States – Countervailing Duty*

Examples of Other Known Factors Reviewed in DSB Rulings

- Decline in demand[86]
- Technological and production difficulties[87]
- Loss of a previous distribution network, loss of ability to use a leading brand name, high level of costs of domestic producer etc.[88]

Does an Investigating Authority Have to Examine the Collective Effects of Other Known Factors?

In *EC – Tube or Pipe Fittings*, the question was whether Article 3.5 of the Anti-Dumping Agreement, i.e. the mirror provision to Article 15.5 ASCM, obliges an investigating authority to examine the collective effects of other known factors, or whether it is sufficient to look at the individual effects of several different other known factors. The Appellate Body held that Article 3.5 does not compel, in every case, an assessment of the collective effects of causal factors other than the dumped imports. At the same time, the Appellate Body recognized that there may be cases where, because of the specific factual circumstances, a failure to undertake an examination of the collective impact of other causal factors would result in an improper attribution of the effects of such other factors to dumped imports.[89]

Investigation on Dynamic Random Access Memory Semiconductors (DRAMs) from Korea, paras 7.361–7.363 (this aspect of the ruling was not appealed) and WT/DS248/R, WT/DS249/R, WT/DS251/R, WT/DS252/R, WT/DS253/R, WT/DS254/R, WT/DS258/R and WT/DS259/R of 11 July 2003, *United States – Definitive Safeguard Measures on Imports of Certain Steel Products*, paras 10.480 and 10.482. See also *Miranda* (2010) p. 747.

[86] WT/DS296/R/3 of 21 February 2005, *United States – Countervailing Duty Investigation on Dynamic Random Access Memory Semiconductors (DRAMs) from Korea*, paras 7.364–7.368. This aspect of the ruling was not appealed. The Panel held that the US did not sufficiently separate and distinguish the injury caused by slowing demand and the injury caused by the subsidized imports.

[87] WT/DS296/R/3 of 21 February 2005, *United States – Countervailing Duty Investigation on Dynamic Random Access Memory Semiconductors (DRAMs) from Korea*, paras 7.369–7.371. This aspect of the ruling was not appealed.

[88] WT/DS341/R of 4 September 2008, *Mexico – Definitive Countervailing Measures on Olive Oil from the European Communities*, para 7.307 *et seq.*

[89] WT/DS219/AB/R of 22 July 2003, *European Communities – Anti-Dumping Duties on Malleable Cast Iron Tube or Pipe Fittings from Brazil*, para 192. See also WT/DS277/AB/RW of 13 April 2006, *United States – Investigation of the International Trade Commission in Softwood Lumber from Canada – Recourse to Article 21.5 of the DSU by Canada*, paras 153–155; WT/DS341/R of 4 September 2008, *Mexico – Definitive Countervailing Measures on Olive Oil from the European Communities*, paras 7.304 and 7.318.

Injury Caused 'through the Effect of Subsidies' (Article 15.5)?

In *Japan – DRAMs (Korea)*, Korea argued that according to Articles 15.5 and 19.1, an investigating authority not only has to demonstrate that the volume and price effects of the subsidized imports (see Article 15.2) caused injury to the industry of the importing country (see Article 15.4) but also that there was a separate step, namely an examination of the effects of the subsidies as distinguished from the effects of the subsidized imports. Korea based itself on the text of Article 15.5 that stipulates that it 'must be demonstrated that the subsidized imports are, through the effects of subsidies, causing injury within the meaning of [the ASCM]'. The Panel and the Appellate Body rejected Korea's proposition. In the view of the Appellate Body, Korea's point of view would have meant that an investigating authority would first have to examine the use of the subsidies by the exporting company and second, whether absent the subsidies, the product would have been exported in the same volumes or at the same prices. Such additional examinations were not contemplated by Articles 15.2 and 15.4. The Appellate Body referred notably to footnote 47 of the ASCM in support of its conclusion.[90]

Threat of Material Injury (Article 15.7)

General

Article 15.7 deals with the concept of a threat of material injury as opposed to actual material injury. It imposes on an investigating authority which has recourse to this provision a very demanding standard as evidenced by the following text. Its first sentence stipulates that 'a threat of material injury shall be based on facts and not merely on allegation, conjecture or remote possibility'. And the second sentence reads: 'The change of circumstances which would create a situation in which the subsidy would cause injury must be clearly foreseen and imminent.' Finally, the last sentence provides that 'the totality of the factors considered must lead to the conclusion that further subsidized exports are imminent and that, unless protective action is taken, material injury would occur'.[91] Moreover, the investigating authority should consider

[90] WT/DS336/AB/R of 28 November 2007, *Japan – Countervailing Duties on Dynamic Random Access Memories from Korea*, paras 257–278. See also *Miranda* (2010) pp. 732–735.

[91] Moreover, Article 15.8 requires with respect to threat of injury cases that the 'application of countervailing measures shall be considered and decided with special care'. See *infra*.

the following five specific threat of injury factors, that are set out in subparagraphs (i)–(v) of Article 15.7:

- nature of the subsidies in question and the trade effects likely to arise therefrom;
- significant rate of increase of subsidized imports indicating the likelihood of substantially increased importation;[92]
- sufficient freely disposable, or an imminent, substantial increase in, capacity of the exporter indicating the likelihood of substantially increased subsidized imports, taking into account the availability of other export markets to absorb any additional exports;
- whether imports are entering at prices that will have a significant depressing or supressing effect on domestic prices, and would likely increase demand for further imports;[93]
- inventories of the product being investigated.

Article 15.7 is largely identical to the mirror provision in the Anti-Dumping Agreement, i.e. Article 3.7 of that agreement. Two differences are noteworthy. First, there is no equivalent to the first threat of injury factor ('nature of the subsidy or subsidies in question and the trade effects likely to arise therefrom') in Article 3.7. Second, Article 15.7 does not contain an equivalent to footnote 10 of the Anti-Dumping Agreement. This footnote stipulates that one example in relation to the second sentence of Article 3.7, i.e. the changed circumstances provision, is 'that there is convincing reason to believe that there will be, in the near future, substantially increased importation of the product at dumped prices'. However, the likelihood of substantially increased imports is also a specific factor listed in subparagraph (ii).

Article 15.7 was extensively discussed in *US – Softwood Lumber VI*. The Panel held that the second sentence of this provision ('[t]he change of circumstances which would create a situation in which the subsidy would cause injury must be clearly foreseen and imminent') is not a model of clarity. According to Article 15.7, both the change of circumstances and further subsidized imports must be clearly foreseen and imminent. The Panel was of the opinion that the likelihood of increased imports is both a relevant change

[92] See also WT/DS277/AB/RW of 13 April 2006, *United States – Investigation of the International Trade Commission in Softwood Lumber from Canada – Recourse to Article 21.5 of the DSU by Canada*, paras 145–148.

[93] See also WT/DS277/AB/RW of 13 April 2006, *United States – Investigation of the International Trade Commission in Softwood Lumber from Canada – Recourse to Article 21.5 of the DSU by Canada*, paras 149–152.

of circumstances and a factor to be considered in determining the existence of threat. In the view of the Panel, it was not clear whether the various elements of Article 15.7 need necessarily be distinct factual circumstances.

US – Softwood Lumber VI also pointed out that the three concepts of injury, i.e. material injury, threat of injury and material retardation of the establishment of such industry, are different. In relation to threat of injury, the investigating authority must evaluate how the future will be different from the immediate past, such that the situation of no present injury will change in the imminent future to a situation of material injury, in the absence of measures. It must be clear from the determination of the investigating authority that this was actually evaluated. Thus, the Panel followed the GATT Panel on *Korea – Anti-Dumping Duties on Imports of Polyacetal Resins from the United States* that stated that a finding of injury cannot be based simultaneously on all three forms of injury, as such a finding would be internally inconsistent.

The change in circumstances that would give rise to a situation in which injury would occur can encompass a single event, a series of events, or developments in the situation of the industry, and/or concerning the subsidized imports which would lead to a conclusion that injury which has not yet occurred can be predicted to occur imminently.[94]

Article 15.7 stipulates that an investigating authority 'should consider' the five factors listed in this provision. *US – Softwood Lumber VI* interpreted the term 'to consider' in the same way as *Thailand – H Beams* in relation to Article 3.2 of the Anti-Dumping Agreement. Thus, in order to conclude that an investigating authority has 'considered' the factors set out in Article 15.7, it must be apparent from the determination that the investigating authority has given attention to and taken into account those factors. Consideration must go beyond a mere recitation of the facts in question, and must put them in context. However, an investigating authority is not required by Article 15.7 to make an explicit finding or determination with respect to the factors considered.[95]

Because the text of Article 15.7 uses the term 'should consider' in relation to the five factors, consideration of each of the factors listed in this provision is not mandatory. A failure to consider a factor at all, or

[94] WT/DS277/R of 22 March 2004, *United States – Investigation of the International Trade Commission in Softwood Lumber from Canada*, paras 7.53–7.60.

[95] WT/DS277/R of 22 March 2004, *United States – Investigation of the International Trade Commission in Softwood Lumber from Canada*, paras 7.66–7.67 *et passim*. The distinction between 'consideration' and 'conclusion' is very apparent in para 7.71 *et seq.*

a failure to address a particular factor adequately would not necessarily violate Article 15.7. Whether a violation exists based on an individual factor depends on the particular facts of the case, in the light of the totality of the factors considered and the explanations given.[96] The Panel also held that a failure to make an explicit finding with regard to the nature of the subsidies did not amount to a violation of the ASCM if the nature of the subsidies is not an element of the affirmative determination of threat of injury by the investigating authority.[97] See also *supra* this chapter, pp. 479–480.

US – Softwood Lumber VI also clarified the relationship between, on the one hand, Articles 15.2 and 15.4 and, on the other, Article 15.7. Canada argued that paragraphs 2 and 4 also have to be applied in a threat of injury case in the sense that the various factors listed in these provisions have to be assessed and, moreover, that such assessment should also comprise an assessment of the likely impact of future imports on projections of these factors. In other words, under paragraphs 2 and 4, a second analysis would be necessary in that the threat of injury examination should look for instance at the impact of the future imports on the projected productivity, projected return on investment, projected cash flow etc. The Panel agreed that the factors listed in paragraphs 2 and 4 need to be assessed. It thus followed the Panel in *Mexico – Corn Syrup*. Consideration of these factors is necessary in order to establish a background against which the investigating authority can evaluate whether imminent further subsidized imports will affect the industry's condition in such a manner that material injury would occur in the absence of protective action. However, according to the Panel, it is not necessary to engage in the projections requested by Canada. This might result in a degree of speculation in the decision-making process which is not consistent with the requirements of the ASCM (and the Anti-Dumping Agreement).[98]

Note that the legality of the proper examination of five individual factors listed in Article 15.7 has to be distinguished from the legality of the overall threat of injury determination. This follows from the last sentence

[96] WT/DS277/R of 22 March 2004, *United States – Investigation of the International Trade Commission in Softwood Lumber from Canada*, para 7.68.

[97] WT/DS277/R of 22 March 2004, *United States – Investigation of the International Trade Commission in Softwood Lumber from Canada*, para 7.68. See also paras 7.76–7.78 and paras 7.84–7.86.

[98] WT/DS277/R of 22 March 2004, *United States – Investigation of the International Trade Commission in Softwood Lumber from Canada*, para 7.68. See also paras 7.104–7.112. Note that *Mexico – Corn Syrup* only examined the relationship between paragraphs 4 and 7.

of Article 15.7 that stipulates that no one of the five factors by itself can necessarily give decisive guidance but the totality of the factors considered must lead to the conclusion that further subsidized exports are imminent and that, unless protective action is taken, material injury would occur.[99] An example of an overall inadequate threat of injury determination can be found in *US – Softwood Lumber VI*, where the USITC wrongly concluded that dumped and subsidized imports were likely to increase substantially. Nor was there a rational explanation in the USITC's determination that this increase was imminent.[100]

According to *US – Softwood Lumber VI*, the 'special care' requirement in Article 15.8 provides important context for the understanding of the obligations of an investigating authority in making a determination of threat of material injury.[101]

Causal Link Analysis

A causal link analysis including the non-attribution of other factors is also necessary in threat of injury cases. Thus, factors other than the subsidized imports that might at the same time potentially injure the domestic industry need to be considered as well. This means that, if necessary, the future impact of imports from countries not concerned, predicted demand, future domestic supplies of the product concerned etc. have to be examined.[102]

Investigating Authorities to Apply 'Special Care' in Cases of Threat of Material Injury (Article 15.8)

Article 15.8 requires with regard to threat of injury cases that the application of countervailing measures be considered and decided

[99] WT/DS277/R of 22 March 2004, *United States – Investigation of the International Trade Commission in Softwood Lumber from Canada*, paras 7.75 and 7.87; WT/DS277/AB/RW of 13 April 2006, *United States – Investigation of the International Trade Commission in Softwood Lumber from Canada – Recourse to Article 21.5 of the DSU by Canada*, para 137.

[100] WT/DS277/R of 22 March 2004, *United States – Investigation of the International Trade Commission in Softwood Lumber from Canada*, paras 7.87–7.96.

[101] WT/DS277/R of 22 March 2004, *United States – Investigation of the International Trade Commission in Softwood Lumber from Canada*, paras 7.33–7.37.

[102] WT/DS277/R of 22 March 2004, *United States – Investigation of the International Trade Commission in Softwood Lumber from Canada*, para 7.68. See also paras 7.129–7.137. A more detailed description of the causal link analysis can be found in the report of the preceding Panel, see WT/DS277/RW of 15 November 2005, *United States – Investigation of the International Trade Commission in Softwood Lumber from Canada – Recourse to Article 21.5 of the DSU by Canada*, para 7.58 *et seq.*

with special care. *US – Softwood Lumber VI* examined this special care requirement. It held that this provision requires an investigating authority to apply in threat of material injury cases a degree of attention over and above that which is required in cases of actual material injury. It also held that Article 15.8 applies, contrary to what the wording might suggest, not only after the investigation and consideration of all factors, but also during the process of investigation and determination of threat of material injury. In other words, the special care requirement shall be respected in the establishment of whether the prerequisites for application of a measure exist, and not merely afterwards when final decisions are taken whether to apply a measure. The Panel also examined the relationship of Article 15.8 with the other provisions of Article 15, notably its paragraph 7. According to the Panel, it would be appropriate to consider alleged violations of Article 15.8 only after consideration of the specific provisions of Article 15. The Panel opined that a violation of the special care obligation could be demonstrated in the absence of the more specific provisions governing the threat of injury determination. But such a demonstration would require additional or independent arguments concerning the alleged violation of the special care requirement beyond the arguments of a violation of a specific obligation of Article 15.7. Note that the Panel finally did not make any findings with respect to Article 15.8 but stated that this obligation provided important context for the understanding of the obligations of an investigating authority in making a determination of threat of material injury.[103]

Standard of Review by a WTO Panel

US – Softwood Lumber VI (Article 21.5) is interesting because it summarizes and clarifies the standard of review to be applied by the WTO dispute settlement system when reviewing the factual basis for a threat of injury determination. According to the Appellate Body, a panel must determine whether the investigating authority has provided a reasoned and adequate explanation of

- how individual pieces of evidence can be reasonably relied on in support of particular inferences and how the evidence on the record supports its factual findings;

[103] WT/DS277/R of 22 March 2004, *United States – Investigation of the International Trade Commission in Softwood Lumber from Canada*, paras 7.33–7.37.

- how the facts on the record, rather than allegation, conjecture or remote possibility, support and provide a basis for the overall threat of injury determination;
- how its projections and assumptions show a high degree of likelihood that the anticipated injury will materialize in the near future; and
- how it examined alternative explanations and interpretations of the evidence and why it chose to reject or discount such alternatives in coming to its conclusions.

It is not sufficient if a panel only considers whether the findings of an investigating authority appear to be reasonable or plausible in the abstract. To the contrary, a panel can assess whether the investigating authority's findings or conclusions are reasoned and adequate only if the panel critically examines that explanation in the light of the facts and the alternative explanations that were before the investigating authority. The Appellate Body found that the preceding Panel did not meet the aforementioned standard for the following reasons:

- The Panel repeatedly relied on the test that Canada has not demonstrated that an objective and unbiased investigating authority could not have reached the conclusion that the USITC did. This is different from the proper standard, i.e. to determine whether the conclusions reached by the investigating authority, in the light of the explanations given, were such as could have been reached by an unbiased and objective decision maker based on the facts.
- The Panel's reliance on references to the USITC's conclusions as 'not unreasonable' suggested that the Panel applied an insufficient degree of scrutiny.
- The Panel did not conduct a critical and searching analysis of the USITC's findings in order to test whether they were properly supported by evidence on the record and were reasoned and adequate in the light of alternative explanations of evidence.
- The Panel failed to conduct an analysis of whether the totality of the factors and evidence considered by the USITC supported the ultimate finding of a threat of material injury.[104]

[104] WT/DS277/AB/RW of 13 April 2006, *United States – Investigation of the International Trade Commission in Softwood Lumber from Canada – Recourse to Article 21.5 of the DSU by Canada*, paras 98 and 138 *et passim*.

Article 16

Definition of Domestic Industry

Introduction

Article 16 contains the definition of the domestic industry for purposes of the ASCM. The domestic industry as defined pursuant to Article 16 forms the basis of an injury determination under Article 15. Thus, Articles 16 and 15 are inextricably linked.[1] The notion of 'domestic industry' is also relevant for the initiation of a countervailing duty investigation in accordance with Article 11.

Only producers manufacturing the 'like product' as defined by footnote 45 are eligible to constitute the domestic industry, unless the conditions set out in Article 16.5 are met. Article 16.1 recognizes the possibility of diverging opinions and interests between domestic producers. Producers in the importing country likely benefit from the subsidized imports if they are related to the exporters of the subsidized imports or if they import themselves the subsidized merchandise. Such producers therefore do not necessarily share the same interests as those domestic producers who do not have such links. Article 16.1 gives an investigating authority the right to exclude such parties from the notion of 'domestic producers' (see *infra* this chapter pp. 514–516).

Article 16.1 contains the definition of the 'domestic industry' for a normal CVD case, i.e. with a focus on the territory of the WTO Member (or the free trade area or customs union in the case of Article 16.5) as a whole. By contrast, Articles 16.2 and 16.3 deal with so-called 'regional' CVD cases, i.e. where exceptionally the territory of a Member is, for the production in question, divided into two or more competitive markets and the producers in each market may be regarded as a separate domestic industry. Article 16.4 deals with the definition of the domestic industry in

[1] WT/DS427/R of 2 August 2013, *China – Anti-Dumping and Countervailing Duty Measures on Broiler Products from the United States*, para 7.408.

free trade areas and customs unions. Finally Article 16.5 in conjunction with Article 15.6 stipulates that the industry can also be defined as consisting of producers of the narrowest group or range of products, which includes the like product, if a separate identification of the production of the like product is not possible.

What Constitutes a Domestic Producer?

Whether or not a company qualifies as a 'domestic producer' is normally not a matter of dispute. However, there may be occasionally unusual configurations and *Mexico – Olive Oil*, the only DSB ruling which so far has addressed this issue, is certainly such a case. The Mexican olive oil industry consisted of only one company. At the time it launched the application pursuant to Article 11 and during the investigation period it did not, however, produce any olive oil. But it possessed the necessary production equipment and it had produced olive oil both before and after the aforementioned periods. The EU argued that in order to qualify as a domestic producer, an enterprise must actually produce output of the domestic like product at the two aforementioned periods. The Panel rejected the EU's view based on the ordinary meaning of Article 16.1 read in the light of its context and object and purpose.[2]

Domestic Industry As Defined Pursuant to Article 16.1 Is a Hybrid Notion

In a normal CVD case (as opposed to regional cases pursuant to Articles 16.2 and 16.3), the domestic industry pursuant to Article 16.1 is either the domestic producers as a whole or those of them whose collective output represents a major proportion of total domestic production. Article 16.1 also entitles an investigating authority to exclude the following types of producers that might otherwise fall within the aforementioned definition:

(i) producers that are related to the exporters or importers of the alleged subsidized product or a like product from other countries; footnote 48 contains a definition as to when a producer is deemed to be related to an exporter or importer;

[2] WT/DS341/R of 4 September 2008, *Mexico – Definitive Countervailing Measures on Olive Oil from the European Communities*, paras 7.188–7.205. It appears that the Panel's bottom line for recognizing a company as a producer was whether under certain circumstances it would be viable for that company to resume production, see para 7.211.

(ii) producers that are themselves importers of the alleged subsidized product or a like product from other countries.

If an investigating authority excludes a producer falling under (i) or (ii), the remaining producers or a major proportion thereof constitute the domestic industry. Note that Article 4 Anti-Dumping Agreement, that is the mirror provision of Article 16, does not contain a reference to a 'like product from other countries'.

The ASCM does not define what constitutes a 'major proportion'. *EC – Fasteners (China)*, which concerns an anti-dumping case, sheds some light on the issue. The collective output of producers that constituted the 'domestic industry' accounted for 27 per cent of total EU production. The Appellate Body did not agree with the EU's approach because the EU applied a minimum threshold of 25 per cent that was as such not relevant for determining 'a major proportion of total domestic production' and because the selection process applied by the EU Commission introduced a material risk of distorting the injury determination. Notwithstanding this, the Appellate Body noted that while 27 per cent represented a low proportion in relation to total production, the fragmented nature of the fasteners industry might have permitted such a low proportion due to the impracticability of obtaining more information.[3]

In *China – Broiler Products*, the US argued that an investigating authority first has to make an attempt to define the domestic producers as a whole and only if that proves impossible it may define the domestic industry as those producers representing a major proportion of the total domestic production. The Panel rejected this claim, *inter alia*, for the following reasons:

- The text of Article 16.1 does not explicitly indicate a hierarchy or sequencing between 'the domestic producers as a whole of the like products' and 'those of them whose collective output of the products constitute a major proportion'.
- The Appellate Body has confirmed that the use of a 'major proportion' within the mirror provision Article 4.1 Anti-Dumping Agreement

[3] WT/DS397/AB/R of 15 July 2011, *European Communities – Definitive Anti-Dumping Measures on Certain Iron or Steel Fasteners from China*, para 460. The Commission contacted 316 known producers requesting certain basic information. Seventy companies came forward and provided the information in question within the 15-day deadline set.

provides an investigating authority with flexibility to define the domestic industry in the light of what is reasonable and practically possible.

However, the Panel also pointed out:

- The determination that a group of domestic producers represents a 'major proportion' of total domestic output must necessarily be made in relation to the production of the domestic producers as a whole.
- An investigating authority must establish total domestic production in the same manner it would conduct any other aspect of the investigation, by actively seeking out pertinent information, and not remaining passive in the face of possible shortcomings in the evidence submitted e.g. by petitioners.
- An investigating authority may rely on information provided by the petitioner, particularly if it was gathered from independent sources. However, an investigating authority must take reasonable and practicable efforts to assure itself that the information it is relying on, whether obtained from the petitioner or from other sources, is accurate.[4]

Note also that *China – Broiler Products* examined whether MOFCOM's process for defining the domestic industry was structured in a way that it favoured a self-selection process in the sense that those companies that supported the petition would be likely to be included in the domestic industry definition, thus introducing a material risk of distortion of the injury analysis. The Panel rejected the allegations made by the US in this respect.[5] *EC – Fasteners (China)* examined a similar claim. The EU determination of the domestic industry was inconsistent with Article 4.1 of the Anti-Dumping Agreement because the EU only considered those domestic producers in the definition of domestic industry that were willing to be included in the sample.[6]

[4] WT/DS427/R of 2 August 2013, *China – Anti-Dumping and Countervailing Duty Measures on Broiler Products from the United States*, paras 7.415–7.424.

[5] WT/DS427/R of 2 August 2013, *China – Anti-Dumping and Countervailing Duty Measures on Broiler Products from the United States*, paras 7.425–7.437.

[6] WT/DS397/AB/R of 15 July 2011, *European Communities – Definitive Anti-Dumping Measures on Certain Iron or Steel Fasteners from China*, paras 422, 427, 429. See also para 460 where the Appellate Body concluded that nothing in Article 4.1 precludes an investigating authority from establishing deadlines for companies to come forward in order to be considered for inclusion in the domestic industry.

Regional Domestic Industry (Articles 16.2 and 16.3)

The provisions for regional countervailing duty cases are essentially self-explanatory. If the investigation is based on a regional domestic industry, countervailing measures must be limited to the region in question unless the constitutional law of the importing Member does not allow such limitation. If the constitutional law does not permit such limitation, the importing Member may levy a country-wide countervailing duty only if the conditions set out in Article 16.3 are met.

Article 17

Provisional Measures

Article 17 governs the imposition of provisional countervailing duties. This provision allows investigating authorities to impose expeditiously countervailing measures although the investigation has not yet been concluded. The text of Article 17 is essentially self-explanatory. The term 'countervailing duty' is defined in footnote 36 attached to Article 10.

The following points are noteworthy. First, the provisions as to the nature of the provisional countervailing measure are different to those of the Anti-Dumping Agreement. Article 17.2 stipulates that provisional measures may take the form of provisional countervailing duties guaranteed by cash deposits or bonds equal to the amount of the provisionally calculated amount of subsidization. The corresponding provision in the Anti-Dumping Agreement, i.e. its Article 7.2, gives more options. Under the Anti-Dumping Agreement, provisional measures are not limited to a cash deposit or security. While Article 7.2 classifies cash deposit and security as the preferred form of measures, it also provides for the possibility of a provisional anti-dumping measure in the form of a collection of the duty or of withholding of appraisement.

Second, according to Article 17.3, a provisional measure cannot be applied sooner than 60 days from the date of initiation of the investigation. However, in case of critical circumstances as defined in Article 20.6, the definitive countervailing duties may be assessed on imports which were entered for consumption up to 90 days prior to the date of application of provisional measures. This retroactive application of definitive measure might indeed cover at least part of the 60-day period. However, *Softwood Lumber III* has made it very clear that provisional measures may not be applied during the 60-day period and that a retroactive application of provisional countervailing measures, as opposed to the retroactive application of definitive measures, is not compatible with the ASCM.[1]

[1] WT/DS236/R of 27 September 2002, *United States – Preliminary Determinations with Respect to Certain Softwood Lumber from Canada*, paras 7.99–7.103.

Third, the provisions on the definitive collection of provisional measures can be found in paragraphs 2 to 5 of Article 20.

Fourth, according to Article 20.1, provisional measures shall only be applied to products that enter for consumption after the time when the decision under Article 17.1 enters into force, subject to the exceptions set out in Article 20.

Fifth, Article 17.6 provides that the relevant provisions of Article 19 (definitive measures) shall be followed in the application of provisional measures. It would appear that Article 17.6 refers essentially to paragraphs 2 to 4 of Article 19 (see *Bellis* in *Wolfrum/Stoll/Koebele* (2008) para 12 to Article 17 and *infra*).

Finally, the provisions on public notice and determinations set out in Article 22, notably Article 22.4, are also relevant for provisional measures.

Article 18

Undertakings

The investigating authority may accept an undertaking from exporters or the government of the exporting country as an alternative to the imposition of provisional or definitive countervailing duties. An undertaking provided by the government of the exporting country will provide that the government eliminates or limits the subsidy or takes other measures concerning the effect of the subsidy (Article 18.1(a)). By contrast, an exporter can undertake to revise its prices so that the injurious effect of the subsidy is eliminated. The last sentence of Article 18.1(b) defines as the upper limit of the price increase the amount of the subsidy but also encourages WTO Members to apply the lesser-duty rule, i.e. to settle for a smaller amount than the subsidy margin if such lower amount would be adequate to remove the injury to the domestic industry.

If the subsidy is a recurring subsidy (e.g. interest support for a loan), a government can comparatively easily eliminate or limit the subsidy. Matters are more complicated if the subsidy is a non-recurring one, e.g. a grant. A non-recurring subsidy will continue to have an effect, usually for the period of the normal lifetime of production assets of the industry in question. Article 18.1(a) takes account of this circumstance by allowing the government to 'take other measures concerning [the] effects [of the subsidy]'. There have been cases in the past where investigating authorities have allowed the government of the exporting country to 'collect' the countervailing duty in the form of an export tax to offset the subsidy.

Exporters may have an interest in accepting undertakings instead of having their exports be subject to a countervailing duty because the higher price goes into their own pockets while any price increase in the market of the importing country as a result of countervailing duties is pocketed by the authorities of the importing country. While the effect of this choice between either undertaking or a countervailing duty should in principle be neutral from the perspective of consumers in the importing country, such choice will likely have welfare effects if subject imports continue to be made in significant quantities.

An investigating authority has considerable discretion when it decides whether or not an undertaking should be accepted. The first sentence of Article 18.3 makes this plainly clear: 'Undertakings offered need not be accepted if the authorities of the importing Member consider their acceptance impractical, for example if the number of actual or potential exporters is too great, or for other reasons, including reasons of general policy.' Based on this text, the Panel in *US – Offset Act (Byrd Amendment)* has held that an investigating authority is under no obligation to make an objective examination of the appropriateness of accepting an undertaking.[1] However, the second sentence of Article 18.3 aims at improving due process by stipulating that the authorities shall provide, where practicable, to the exporter the reasons which have led them to consider acceptance of an undertaking as inappropriate, and shall, to the extent possible, give the exporter an opportunity to make comments thereon.

Article 18 ASCM and Article 8 of the Anti-Dumping Agreement are largely identical. The differences between the texts of these two provisions result essentially from the fact that the provider of the subsidy, and hence the origin of the trade distortion, is the government of the exporting country. Therefore, the government has been assigned a role similar to that of an exporter of the subject product. The following differences should be noted:

- Article 8 only mentions exporters as parties that can offer an undertaking while Article 18 refers to both exporters and the government of the exporting country.[2]
- According to Article 18.2, undertakings provided by exporters need the consent of the exporting Member. Article 8.2 does not contain such a requirement.
- If an undertaking is accepted prior to the final determination, the exporting Member can request that the importing Member completes the investigation of subsidization and injury. In anti-dumping investigations, exporters have such a right. In both types of investigations, the importing Member can also on its own initiative complete the investigation. See Articles 8.4 and 18.4 respectively.

The provisions of Article 18 are essentially self-explanatory.

Article 22.6, which contains the rules on 'Public Notice and Explanation of Determinations', is also relevant for undertakings.

[1] WT/DS217/R and WT/DS234/R of 16 September 2002 – *United States – Continued Dumping and Subsidy Offset Act of 2000*, para 7.81.

[2] WT/DS397/R of 3 December 2010, *European Communities – Definitive Anti-Dumping Measures on Certain Iron or Steel Fasteners from China*, footnote 279 to para 7.103.

Article 19

Imposition and Collection of Countervailing Duties

Imposition of a Countervailing Duty (Article 19.1)

A countervailing duty can be levied against a specific product from a specific country without regard to Article I of GATT 1994, i.e. the provision that embodies most-favoured nation treatment, if the relevant conditions set out in the ASCM and in Article VI of GATT 1994 are met. This follows from Article 10 ASCM. The term 'countervailing duty' is defined in footnote 36 attached to Article 10. Article 19.1 refers to the imposition of countervailing duties in an original investigation (as opposed to reviews pursuant to Article 21). In such original investigation, the investigating authority must establish all conditions set out in the ASCM for the imposition of countervailing duties. This includes a determination of the existence of a benefit[1] but also

- the other conditions for a subsidy finding such as financial contribution and specificity;
- a finding of injury including a causal link between the subsidized imports and the injury;[2]
- the subsidy or the subsidies were not withdrawn;
- reasonable efforts have been made to complete consultations.[3]

The provisions on public notice and determinations set out in Article 22, notably Article 22.5, are also relevant for definitive measures.

Note that Article 19.1 reads, *inter alia*, that it is demonstrated that 'through the effects of the subsidy, the subsidized imports are causing injury'. Article 15.5 uses a nearly identical term, i.e. 'through the effects

[1] See in relation to the privatization cases WT/DS212/AB/R of 9 December 2002, *United States – Countervailing Measures Concerning Certain Products from the European Communities*, para 146. See also WT/DS138/AB/R of 10 May 2000, *United States – Imposition of Countervailing Duties on Certain Hot-Rolled Lead and Bismuth Carbon Steel Products originating in the United Kingdom*, para 63.

[2] With regard to injury and causal link see Article 15.

[3] With regard to consultations see Article 13.

[footnote 47] of the subsidies'. Footnote 47 refers to paragraphs 2 and 4 of Article 15. *Japan – DRAMs (Korea)* interpreted both terms in Article 15.5 and 19.1 in the same way, i.e. it is sufficient that the volume and price effects of the subsidized imports cause the injury to the industry of the importing country. It is not necessary that a separate demonstration be made that injury is caused through the effects of the subsidy.[4]

Reference to a withdrawal of subsidies is also made in Articles 4.7 and 7.8. *Australia – Automotive Leather II (Article 21.5)* that had to interpret Article 4.7, found relevant context in Articles 7.8 and 19.1 and held that withdrawal under these provisions can also mean repayment of the subsidies by the recipient.[5]

The notion of 'duty' was at issue in *US – Customs Bond Directive*. The US, which operates a retrospective system of CVD and anti-dumping duty collection, adopted a law that provided for the possibility of requesting from importers a so-called 'enhanced continuous bond requirement' (EBR). This EBR was equivalent to 100 per cent of the anti-dumping/countervailing duty rate established in the original investigation or the most recent administrative review, multiplied by the value of imports made by the importer during the previous 12 months. The enhanced bond could be required in addition to the entry cash deposits that are mandatory under the US retrospective system and in addition to the basic bond amount equivalent to the greater of USD 50,000 or 10 per cent of the duties paid during the preceding year. The US introduced the possibility of requesting EBR in order to secure payment of anti-dumping/countervailing duties in any subsequent review as defaults on anti-dumping duty bills had increased. Both the Panel and the Appellate Body found that the EBR did not violate Article 19.1. A bond secures the payment of a duty. However, the bond is not a duty as it does not, by itself, entail any transfer of money from the importer to the government. Hence the bond did not fall within the scope of Article 19. Note that the EBR, as applied to subject shrimp imports, was found to be inconsistent with the *ad* Note to Article VI:2 and 3 of GATT 1994.[6]

4 WT/DS336/AB/R of 28 November 2007, *Japan – Countervailing Duties on Dynamic Random Access Memories from Korea*, para 277. See *supra* the commentary to Article 25, p. 506.

5 WT/DS126/RW of 21 January 2000, *Australia – Subsidies Provided to Producers and Exporters of Automotive Leather (Article 21.5)*, para 6.28.

6 WT/DS343/AB/R and WT/DS345/AB/R of 16 July 2008, *United States – Measures Relating to Shrimp from Thailand* and *United States – Customs Bond Directive for Merchandise Subject to Anti-Dumping/Countervailing Duties*, para 280.

Additional Points That Should Be Reflected in the Domestic Law Concerning the Application of Countervailing Measures (Article 19.2)

Article 19.2 lists a number of points that do not amount to legally binding obligations of WTO Members but that the domestic law of a WTO Member should ideally respect. According to Article 19.2, 'it is desirable'

- that the imposition of countervailing measures should be permissive and not mandatory;
- to apply the lesser-duty rule, i.e. that the amount of the countervailing duty to be imposed should be less than the amount of the subsidy if such lesser amount would be adequate to remove the injury to the domestic industry;
- that procedures should be established that would allow the authorities concerned to take due account of representations made by domestic interested parties whose interests might be adversely affected by the imposition of a countervailing duty. Footnote 50, which is attached, enlarges the list of domestic interested parties contained in Article 12.9 by adding, for the purposes of Article 19.2, consumers and industrial users of the imported product subject to investigation.

Imposition of a Countervailing Duty (Including on an Aggregate Basis), Individual Examination (Article 19.3)

According to the first sentence of Article 19.3, countervailing duties shall be levied 'in the appropriate amounts' in each case. The Appellate Body in *US – Anti-Dumping and Countervailing Duties (China)* took this to mean that double remedies, i.e. the concurrent imposition of anti-dumping and countervailing duties to address the same situation, are prohibited.[7] The first sentence also requires that the duty be levied on a non-discriminatory basis on imports from all sources found to be subsidized and causing injury, except as to imports from those sources which have renounced any subsidies in question or from which undertakings pursuant to Article 18 have been accepted.

The Appellate Body has recognized that countervailing duties can be imposed on an aggregate, i.e. country-wide, basis. In other words, it is

[7] See *supra* the introductory chapter, 48–52.

not necessary that each and every exporter of the subject merchandise is investigated with a view to determine whether its exports were subsidized. This follows from the last sentence of Article 19.3 which, *inter alia*, stipulates that '[a]ny exporter whose exports are subject to a definitive countervailing duty but who was not actually investigated ... shall be entitled to an expedited review in order that the investigating authorities promptly establish an individual countervailing duty rate for that exporter'. This implies that countervailing duties may be imposed on imports subject to investigation, even though specific shipments from exporters that were not investigated individually might not at all be subsidized, or not subsidized to an extent equal to a countervailing duty rate calculated on an aggregate (country-wide) basis. The Appellate Body found support for its position by Article 19.4 that requires the calculation of countervailing duty rates on a per-unit-basis.[8]

With regard to expedited reviews the following should be noted. First, according to the Appellate Body, it is not consistent with Article 19.3 to require a respondent to show a representative volume of exports to the importing country in order to request successfully an expedited review. By requiring such representative volume, a condition not provided for in Article 19.3 would be imposed.[9]

Second, the expedited review under Article 19.3 of the ASCM is similar to the so-called 'newcomer review' provided for in Article 9.5 of the Anti-Dumping Agreement. The only significant difference is that, unlike the Anti-Dumping Agreement, the ASCM contains no explicit provisions on sampling of exporters.

Note that in *US – Softwood Lumber III*, Canada claimed that US law prevented the USDOC from carrying out expedited reviews for all exporters, as envisaged by Article 19.3. The Panel found that US regulations were silent as to whether US authorities could conduct expedited reviews pursuant to Article 19.3 *in fine* if an investigation had been conducted on an aggregated basis. The US asserted that it was a long-established principle of US law that administrative agencies have the discretion to promulgate formal procedures or to proceed on a case-by-case basis, especially when the agency had not sufficient experience with a particular issue of

[8] WT/DS257/AB/R of 19 January 2004, *United States – Final Countervailing Duty Determination with Respect to Certain Softwood Lumber from Canada*, paras 148–154, 161, 164.

[9] WT/DS295/AB/R of 29 November 2005, *Mexico – Definitive Anti-Dumping Measures on Beef and Rice / Complaint with Respect to Rice*, paras 317–324.

formulating regulations. Investigations on an aggregate basis were apparently a rare feature in US law. On this basis, the Panel found that US law did not mandate the USDOC to deny any request for an expedited review. Consequently, US law did not violate Article 19.3 of the ASCM.[10]

No Countervailing Duty in Excess of the Subsidy Found to Exist (Article 19.4)

Article 19.4 prohibits the levying of a countervailing duty on any imported product in excess of the amount of the subsidy found to exist. The subsidy is to be calculated in terms of subsidization per unit of the subsidized and exported product. Footnote 51 attached to Article 19.4 defines the term 'levy': as used in the ASCM, 'levy' shall mean the definitive or final legal assessment or collection of a duty or tax.

Article VI:3 of GATT 1994 addresses the same issue.[11] Its first sentence sets the maximum level of a countervailing duty at 'an amount equal to the estimated bounty or subsidy determined to have been granted, directly or indirectly, on the manufacture, production or export of such product ... including any special subsidy to the transportation of a particular product'. Article VI:3 is linked with Article 19.4 by virtue of Article 10 which, *inter alia*, sets out that Members shall take all necessary steps to ensure that the imposition of a countervailable duty is in accordance with Article VI of GATT 1994.[12]

The Appellate Body has recently clarified Article 19.4 considerably in *US – Washing Machines*. The question was whether the subsidies received were tied to the investigated product or, conversely, may be attributed also to non-investigated products. The reply to this question has direct consequences on the calculation of the subsidy. The facts which triggered this discussion were as follows. Korea bestowed tax credits on Samsung for R&D expenditure that constituted a subsidy. Samsung is organized in different business units. The tax credits were granted for R&D expenditure in several of these business units, including the digital appliance business unit which manufactured the subject product, i.e. large residential washing machines. The US determined the *ad valorem* subsidization of these

[10] WT/DS236/R of 27 September 2002, *United States – Preliminary Determinations with Respect to Certain Softwood Lumber from Canada*, paras 7.135–7.142.

[11] See *supra* the introductory chapter, pp. 30–31.

[12] WT/DS464/AB/R of 7 September 2016, *United States – Anti-Dumping and Countervailing Measures on Large Residential Washers from Korea*, para 5.268.

washing machines by dividing all tax credits obtained by all business units (and not only those of the digital appliance business unit) and by the total value of all of Samsung's production in Korea during the period of investigation. The US approach was based on two considerations. First, the determination of whether a subsidy is tied to a product should focus on the purpose of the subsidy and not on the use or the effects of a subsidy (that is how the benefits are used by the company). A subsidy is tied to a product only if the intended use of the subsidy is known to or acknowledged by the provider of the subsidy prior to a, or concurrent with the bestowal of, the subsidy. However, the Korean government had no possibility to know if and how Samsung would spend the tax savings. Second, the US argued that the subsidies received by Samsung in the form of these tax credits simply reduced its overall tax burden. The Panel accepted the US approach but the Appellate Body reversed the ruling. The Appellate Body held:

- The ASCM does not dictate any particular methodology for calculating subsidy ratios, and does not specify explicitly which elements should be taken into account in the numerator and the denominator. Thus, an investigating authority has the discretion to choose the most appropriate methodology, provided that such methodology allows for a sufficiently precise determination of the amount of subsidization of the subject product. In particular, no provision in the ASCM expressly sets forth a specific method for assessing whether a subsidy is, or is not, tied to a specific product (para 5.269).
- A subsidy is 'tied' to a particular product if the bestowal is connected to, or conditioned upon, the production or sale of that product. An assessment of whether this connection or conditional relationship exists will inevitably depend on the specific circumstances of each case. In conducting such an assessment, an investigating authority must examine the design, structure and operation of the measure granting the subsidy at issue and take into account all the relevant facts surrounding the granting of that subsidy. A proper assessment of the existence of a product-specific tie is not necessarily based on whether the subsidy actually results in increased production or sale of the product in question, but rather on whether the subsidy operates in a manner that can be expected to foster or incentivize production or sale of the product concerned (para 5.270).
- The fact that the recipient obtains the proceeds of a subsidy before, at the same time as, or after conducting the eligible activities is not, in and

of itself, dispositive of whether that subsidy is tied to a particular product. Grants and loans are typically provided before the subsidy recipient undertakes a certain activity while tax credits and other forms of revenue foregone are usually after the recipient has carried out the eligible activity. Excluding the existence of a product specific tie whenever the recipient obtains the proceeds of the subsidy after it has carried out the eligible activities could result in an unwarranted distinction between different types of financial contributions (para 5.272).
- A subsidy that does not restrict the recipient's use of the proceeds of the financial contribution may, nonetheless, be found to be tied to a particular product if it induces the recipient to engage in activities connected to that product (para 5.273).[13]

The parties also argued whether the tax credits obtained by Samsung should be allocated only to the sales of washing machines of Korean origin or also to the sales of washing machines produced outside Korea by Samsung's overseas subsidiaries. The Panel held that the USDOC was entitled to presume (based on a rebuttable assumption) that the tax credits Samsung received did not benefit Samsung's overseas production. The Appellate Body did not agree. It pointed out:

- When calculating the per unit amount of subsidization, the authority must properly match the elements taken into account in the numerator (the subsidy) with the elements taken into account in the denominator (the relevant turnover). The ASCM does not expressly specify whether, in order to ensure the matching, the investigating authority should limit the denominator to the sales value of the recipient's production within the jurisdiction of the subsidizing Member or may also include in the denominator the sales value of the recipient's production in the jurisdiction of other Members (para 5.295).
- Read together, Article VI:3 of GATT 1994 and Articles 1 and 19.4 of the ASCM, indicate that subsidized products for the purposes of calculating the per unit subsidization are limited to those manufactured, produced or exported by the recipient. As these provisions do not indicate that the subsidized products should be limited to those produced by the recipient within the jurisdiction of the subsidizing Member, the Appellate Body considered that a subsidy may indeed be bestowed on the recipient's production outside that jurisdiction subsidized. The

[13] WT/DS464/AB/R of 7 September 2016, *United States – Anti-Dumping and Countervailing Measures on Large Residential Washers from Korea*, paras 5.261–5.274.

Appellate Body referred in this context to multinational corporations that produce in multiple countries (paras 5.296 and 5.297).

- In calculating the amount of the *ad valorem* subsidization, the investigating authority has the task of identifying the specific products for whose manufacturing, production or export a subsidy has been granted. This examination should be conducted on a case-by-case basis, based on the arguments and evidence submitted by interested parties and the specific facts surrounding the bestowal of the subsidy. Those facts may include the text, design, structure and operation of the measure under which the subsidy is granted, as well as the structure and location of the recipient's production operations. Sometimes, such examination may reveal that the subsidy is only bestowed on the recipient's domestic production, and sometimes it may also include the overseas production (para 5.298).

On this basis, the Appellate Body reversed the Panel's findings. It criticized the Panel for conflating the concepts of 'recipient of the subsidy' under Article 1.1(b) with the concept of 'subsidized product' under Article 19.4 of the ASCM and Article VI:3 of GATT 1994. It also took issue with the fact that the Panel accepted the USDOC's rebuttable presumption that attributed the tax credits received by Samsung to its domestic production while not addressing arguments and evidence submitted by interested parties. Note that according to the USDOC the only way for Samsung to rebut this presumption was to show that the GOK explicitly stated in the application and/or approval documents that the subsidy was being provided for more than domestic production.[14]

The Panel in *US – Lead and Bismuth II* stated, based on Article 19.4, that no countervailing duty may be imposed on an imported product if no countervailable subsidy is found to exist with respect to such product, since the amount of the subsidy would be zero in such cases. According to the Panel, Article 19.4 establishes, like Article 19.1, a clear nexus between the imposition of a countervailing duty and the existence of a countervailable subsidy.[15] The prohibition to levy a duty in excess of the subsidy found is without prejudice to the possibility to impose a duty on an aggregate basis as described in the preceding section.

[14] WT/DS464/AB/R of 7 September 2016, *United States – Anti-Dumping and Countervailing Measures on Large Residential Washers from Korea*, paras 5.287–5.306.

[15] WT/DS138/R of 23 December 1999, *United States – Imposition of Countervailing Duties on Certain Hot-Rolled Lead and Bismuth Carbon Steel Products originating in the United Kingdom*, para 6.52.

Present subsidization: in *Japan – DRAMs (Korea)*, the question was if countervailing duties can be imposed, in the case of non-recurring subsidies, when the determination made by the investigating authority indicates that the subsidy will no longer exist at the time of imposition, even though there was subsidization during the investigation period.[16] The Appellate Body answered this question to the negative. In the case in question, Japan allocated the benefit of the October 2001 restructurings to the years 2001 through 2005. No benefit was conferred in 2006, i.e. the year during which Japan imposed the countervailing duty measure because that year was outside the five-year life of the subsidy, as established by Japan's own allocation methodology. Japan nevertheless countervailed the October 2001 restructuring because in Japan's view, a finding of subsidization in respect of a past period of investigation (in the case in question this was the calendar year 2003) sufficed for the imposition of a countervailing duty. The Appellate Body found that such countervailing duty would be in excess of the amount of the subsidy found to exist and, therefore, contrary to the provisions of Article 19.4. However, it also highlighted that Article 19.4 did not contain any requirement for an investigating authority to conduct a new investigation or to update the determination at the time of imposition of a countervailing duty in order to confirm the continued existence of the subsidy.[17] In short, the imposition of a countervailing duty requires 'present subsidization'. If the product were not currently subsidized, there would be no subsidy to offset and, therefore, no basis for the imposition of a countervailing duty.[18]

Article 19.4 obligates an investigating authority to ascertain the precise amount of subsidy attributed to the imported product under investigation. According to *China – Broiler Products*, this requires more effort on the part of an investigating authority than simply accepting data and using it. The Panel held: 'Thus, MOFCOM needed to ensure that it had calculated the correct subsidy amount, rather than simply accept the information submitted by respondents, particularly as the respondents

[16] The term 'investigation period' is explained *supra* the commentary to Article 12, pp. 421–423.

[17] WT/DS336/AB/R of 28 November 2007, *Japan – Countervailing Duties on Dynamic Random Access Memories from Korea*, paras 205–215.

[18] WT/DS414/R of 15 June 2012, *China – Countervailing and Anti-Dumping Duties on Grain-Oriented Flat-Rolled Electrical Steel from the US*, para 7.71. See also para 7.103 in relation to a subsidy that was given more than 20 years prior to the application for the initiation of a case.

had alerted MOFCOM that they may have misunderstood the question and provided incorrect data.'[19]

In the aforementioned case, there was considerable disagreement between MOFCOM and the respondent exporters about the correct per unit subsidization rate. MOFCOM allocated all subsidies bestowed on an input product to the subject merchandise. The exporters argued in their response to the disclosure of the preliminary findings that the input in question was also used for the production of non-subject products and that the corresponding subsidies should be allocated accordingly. MOFCOM did not address this issue in the subsequent on-spot verification nor in the final disclosure. The Panel held that MOFCOM should have taken sufficient account of conflicting evidence and responded to competing plausible explanations of that evidence, in order to ensure that its calculation was correct. The Panel also noted that MOFCOM did not provide a reasoned and adequate explanation as to why the facts supported the conclusions it reached with respect to the precise amount of the subsidy attributed to the subject merchandise. During the investigation, MOFCOM confined itself to conclusory statements. Consequently, China acted inconsistently with Article 19.4.[20]

[19] WT/DS427/R of 2 August 2013, *China – Anti-Dumping and Countervailing Duty Measures on Broiler Products from the United States*, para 7.261.

[20] WT/DS427/R of 2 August 2013, *China – Anti-Dumping and Countervailing Duty Measures on Broiler Products from the United States*, paras 7.255–7.266.

Article 20

Retroactivity

Article 20.1 establishes the rule that provisional and definitive countervailing duties shall only be applied to imports which enter for consumption after the time when the decision to impose such duties enters into force. Exceptions to this rule of non-retroactivity are limited to those that can be found in the remainder of Article 20. According to *US – Softwood Lumber III*, the text of Article 20 provides for two exceptions in respect of definitive countervailing measures:

Article 20.2 allows investigating authorities to levy definitive countervailing duties retroactively for the period of application of provisional measures. However, in cases where the definitive countervailing duty is based on a finding of material retardation of injury, no retroactivity is possible for the period of application of provisional measures. Cash deposits and bonds must be released in such circumstances. If the definitive countervailing duty is based on a finding of threat of injury, retroactivity for the period of application of provisional measures is only possible where the effect of the subsidized imports would, in the absence of provisional measures, have led to a determination of injury.

Article 20.6 allows for the levying of definitive countervailing duties retroactively in case of critical circumstances. The period of such retroactive application of definitive duties is not more than 90 days prior to the date of application of provisional measures. Article 20.6 defines critical circumstances where for the subsidized product the authorities find that

- injury that is difficult to repair,
- such injury is caused by massive imports in a relatively short period of a product benefiting from subsidies that are inconsistent with GATT 1994 or the ASCM and

- retroactive application is deemed necessary in order to preclude the recurrence of such injury.[1]

However, the retroactive application of provisional measures is inconsistent with Article 20.6, as this provision allows for the retroactive application of definitive duties only.[2]

Paragraphs 3 to 5 of Article 20 deal with the release of provisional duties if and to the extent the definitive duties are lower than the provisional duties. The first sentence of Article 20.3 also stipulates that if the definitive countervailing duty is higher than the amount guaranteed by a cash deposit or bond, the difference shall not be collected.

In *US – Softwood Lumber III*, the Panel agreed with the US that a Member is allowed to take measures that are necessary to preserve the right to later apply definitive measures retroactively. What kind of measures may thus be taken by the Member will have to be determined on a case-by-case basis.[3]

Article 22 which contains the rules on public notice and explanation of determinations applies *mutatis mutandis* to decisions under Article 20 to apply duties retroactively.

[1] WT/DS236/R of 27 September 2002, *United States – Preliminary Determinations with Respect to Certain Softwood Lumber from Canada*, para 7.93. See also WT/DS184/R of 28 February 2001, *United States – Anti-Dumping Measures on Certain Hot-Rolled Steel Products from Japan*, paras 7.133–7.168.

[2] WT/DS236/R of 27 September 2002, *United States – Preliminary Determinations with Respect to Certain Softwood Lumber from Canada*, paras 7.93 and 7.94.

[3] WT/DS236/R of 27 September 2002, *United States – Preliminary Determinations with Respect to Certain Softwood Lumber from Canada*, paras 7.95–7.98.

Article 21

Duration and Review of Countervailing Duties and Undertakings

Introduction and General Rule (Article 21.1)

Article 21.1 sets out a general rule that '[a] countervailing duty shall remain in force only as long as and to the extent necessary to counteract subsidization which is causing injury'. *US – Carbon Steel* held that this provision is the expression of a general rule that, after the imposition of a countervailing duty, the continued application of that duty is subject to certain disciplines. These disciplines relate to the duration of the countervailing duty (only as long as necessary), its magnitude (only to the extent necessary) and to its purpose (to counteract subsidization which is causing injury).[1]

Articles 21.2 and 21.3 are further articulations, in respect of specific scenarios, of the obligations set out in Article 21.1. Article 21.2, which govern essentially changed circumstances reviews, sets out the conditions in order to comply with the general obligation during the five-year period of application of a countervailing duty (see *infra* this chapter, pp. 535–543). Article 21.3 sets out the conditions upon expiry of that period, i.e. if and under what circumstances the measures can be renewed for another five-year period (see *infra* this chapter, pp. 535–543).[2]

The term 'is causing injury' in Article 21.1 cannot be read literally. Otherwise it would not be compatible with Article 21.3, which stipulates that a CVD duty can be maintained not only in case of a likelihood of a

[1] WT/DS213/AB/R of 28 November 2002, *United States – Countervailing Duties on Certain Corrosion-Resistant Carbon Steel Flat Products from Germany*, para 70 (see also para 88); WT/DS436/AB/R of 8 December 2014, *United States – Countervailing Measures on Certain Hot-Rolled Carbon Steel Flat Products from India*, para 4.524. See also WT/DS212/R of 31 July 2002, *United States – Countervailing Measures Concerning Certain Products from the European Communities*, para 7.107.

[2] WT/DS213/R of 3 July 2002, *United States – Countervailing Duties on Certain Corrosion-Resistant Carbon Steel Flat Products from Germany*, para 8.33.

continuation of injurious subsidization, but also in case of a likelihood of recurrence of injurious subsidization. Therefore, the notion of recurrence contained in Article 21.3 has to be implied in Article 21.1, or it would be rendered meaningless.[3]

Changed Circumstances Reviews (Article 21.2)

Scope

Article 21.2 provides for a review mechanism during the five-year lifetime of a countervailing duty. Its purpose is to ensure that WTO Members comply with the rule set out in Article 21.1.[4] This type of review is commonly referred to as 'changed circumstances review'.

Changed circumstances reviews examine the need for the continued imposition of the duty. The second sentence of Article 21.2 clarifies further the concept of a 'need for a continued imposition of the duty'. Thus, an interested party has the right to request the authorities to examine:

- whether the continued imposition of the duty is necessary to offset subsidization;
- whether the injury would be likely to continue or recur if the duty were removed or varied;
- or both.

US – Softwood Lumber III pointed out that a changed circumstances review has nothing to do with finalizing the rate of a countervailing duty during a particular period for which estimated duties have been collected, for instance the yearly administrative reviews under the US's retrospective duty collection system.[5] See however *US – Carbon Steel (India)* that examined a US administrative review in the light of Article 21.2.

In an original investigation, the investigating authority must establish that all conditions set out in the ASCM for the imposition of countervailing duties are fulfilled. By contrast, the investigating authority must assess in a review pursuant to Article 21.2 those issues which have been

[3] WT/DS213/R of 3 July 2002, *United States – Countervailing Duties on Certain Corrosion-Resistant Carbon Steel Flat Products from Germany*, para 8.29.

[4] WT/DS138/AB/R of 10 May 2000, *United States – Imposition of Countervailing Duties on Certain Hot-Rolled Lead and Bismuth Carbon Steel Products originating in the United Kingdom*, paras 53 and 61.

[5] WT/DS236/R of 27 September 2002, *United States – Preliminary Determinations with Respect to Certain Softwood Lumber from Canada*, para 7.151.

raised before it by the interested parties or, in the case of an investigation conducted on its own initiative, those issues which warranted such review. Based on the foregoing, the Appellate Body rejected the Panel's implied view that, in the context of a review under Article 21.2, an investigating authority must always establish the existence of a benefit during the period of review in the same way as an investigating authority must establish a benefit in an original investigation. However, based on the evidence on the record, such determination was warranted in the circumstances of the case.[6] The Appellate Body made these statements in the context of whether the privatization of a company for fair market value and at arm's length that was subject to a countervailing duty warranted a determination that there was a continued benefit. Both the Panel and the Appellate Body agreed in this case that while an investigating authority may presume, in the context of a review under Article 21.2, that a benefit continues to flow from an untied, non-recurring financial contribution, this presumption can never be irrebuttable.[7]

According to the Appellate Body, the determination made in a review under Article 21.2 must be a meaningful one. It also found that this provision sets out the requirements for a rigorous review.[8] *US – Carbon Steel (India)* has further clarified that Article 21.2 calls for both a present and retrospective analysis (as it relates to the necessity and impact of the duty prior to and during the changed circumstances review) as well as a prospective analysis (with a focus on the likely future consequences of maintaining, changing or removing the duty).[9]

As far as the investigation of new subsidy schemes is concerned, *US – Carbon Steel (India)* has clarified this issue. The Appellate Body concluded that because the focus of Article 21.2 is on whether the injury resulting from subsidization is likely to continue or recur if the duty were removed or varied, this suggests that the scope of an administrative review may go

[6] WT/DS138/AB/R of 10 May 2000, *United States – Imposition of Countervailing Duties on Certain Hot-Rolled Lead and Bismuth Carbon Steel Products originating in the United Kingdom*, para 63.

[7] WT/DS138/AB/R of 10 May 2000, *United States – Imposition of Countervailing Duties on Certain Hot-Rolled Lead and Bismuth Carbon Steel Products originating in the United Kingdom*, para 62.

[8] WT/DS213/AB/R of 28 November 2002, *United States – Countervailing Duties on Certain Corrosion-Resistant Carbon Steel Flat Products from Germany*, para 71; WT/DS436/AB/R of 8 December 2014, *United States – Countervailing Measures on Certain Hot-Rolled Carbon Steel Flat Products from India*, para 4.525.

[9] WT/DS436/AB/R of 8 December 2014, *United States – Countervailing Measures on Certain Hot-Rolled Carbon Steel Flat Products from India*, para 4.530.

beyond the particular subsidies that were examined in the original investigation, provided that the requirements of Article 22 were met. However, this is subject to one important proviso. An investigating authority can only examine a new subsidy allegation if there is a sufficiently close nexus between the subsidies that were subject to the original investigation and the new subsidy allegation. Moreover, because Article 21.2 requires the investigating authority to assess whether the injury would be likely to continue or recur if the duty were removed or varied or both, only new subsidies that inform this inquiry may properly be considered by an investigating authority in the conduct of an administrative review. There are several factors that could potentially be taken into consideration on a case-by-case basis in determining whether there is a sufficiently close link between subsidies at issue in the original investigation or in previous changed circumstances reviews and a new subsidy allegation, e.g. whether they relate to the same product, the same beneficiary companies, the nature of the subsidy and whether a subsidy has been replaced by another subsidy.[10]

The Appellate Body has held that Articles 19.1 and 19.4 are provisions dealing with the imposition of countervailing duties as a result of a final determination (as opposed to a provisional determination pursuant to Article 17) but that they can provide useful context in interpreting the obligations regarding reviews carried out pursuant to Article 21.2.[11]

Initiation

Changed circumstances reviews can be initiated where warranted on the investigating authority's own initiative or upon request by any interested party. An initiation following a request by an interested party is subject to two conditions: (1) A reasonable period of time has elapsed since the imposition of the duty. (2) The interested party must submit positive information substantiating the need for a review.

The Appellate Body held that the conditions listed in Article 21.2 are exhaustive. Therefore, it would be inconsistent with Article 21.2 if an investigating authority seeks to impose additional conditions on a

[10] WT/DS436/AB/R of 8 December 2014, *United States – Countervailing Measures on Certain Hot-Rolled Carbon Steel Flat Products from India*, paras 4.527, 4.530, 4.532–4.543.

[11] WT/DS138/AB/R of 10 May 2000, *United States – Imposition of Countervailing Duties on Certain Hot-Rolled Lead and Bismuth Carbon Steel Products originating in the United Kingdom*, para 53.

respondent's right to a review. Consequently, the Appellate Body declared a provision in Mexico's law that stipulated that a party requesting a review should satisfy the minister that the volume of exports to Mexico during the review period is representative, as inconsistent with Article 21.2.[12]

Only a definitive countervailing duty or an undertaking can be subject to a changed circumstances review. In *US – Countervailing Measures Concerning Certain Products from the EC*, the Appellate Body held that the term 'definitive countervailing duty' refers to duties imposed on a product in the sense that a final determination has been made, following an original investigation initiated pursuant to Article 11, with respect to the countervailing duty liability for entries of such product.[13] The Appellate Body has also pointed out that the fact that the definitive determination of a countervailing duty is still subject to judicial proceedings does not render that determination not final. In short, the right to request a review pursuant to Article 21.2 is not affected by ongoing judicial proceedings concerning the final countervailing measure determination.[14]

The requirements of Article 11 (initiation) do not apply to changed circumstances reviews.

Evidence

In terms of evidence, Article 21.2 imposes on an investigating authority an obligation to take into account in a review 'positive information substantiating the need for a review'. According to *US – Lead and Bismuth II*, such information could relate to developments with respect to the subsidy, privatization at arm's length and for fair market value, or some other information. This in turn will be the basis to determine for instance whether a benefit continues to exist from a financial contribution given prior to privatization and whether there is a continuing need for the application of countervailing duties.[15]

[12] WT/DS295/AB/R of 29 November 2005, *Mexico – Definitive Anti-Dumping Measures on Beef and Rice / Complaint with Respect to Rice*, paras 308–316.

[13] WT/DS295/AB/R of 29 November 2005, *Mexico – Definitive Anti-Dumping Measures on Beef and Rice / Complaint with Respect to Rice*, paras 348 and 349.

[14] WT/DS295/AB/R of 29 November 2005, *Mexico – Definitive Anti-Dumping Measures on Beef and Rice / Complaint with Respect to Rice*, paras 348–349.

[15] WT/DS212/AB/R of 9 December 2002, *United States – Countervailing Measures Concerning Certain Products from the European Communities*, paras 146, 149; WT/DS138/AB/R of 10 May 2000, *United States – Imposition of Countervailing Duties on Certain Hot-Rolled Lead and Bismuth Carbon Steel Products originating in the United Kingdom*, paras 61 and 62; and *supra* the commentary to Article 14, pp. 433–441.

Conclusion of a Changed Circumstances Review

According to the last sentence of Article 21.2, if as a result of the review under this paragraph the authorities determine that the countervailing duty is no longer warranted, it shall be terminated immediately. Otherwise, the duty (or the undertaking) can be varied or maintained.

Sunset Reviews (Article 21.3)

Article 21.3 imposes an explicit temporal limit on the maintenance of countervailing duties. For countervailing duties that have been in place for five years, Article 21.3 requires their termination unless the conditions specified in this provision are met. These conditions are that a review had been conducted in which it is determined that the expiry of the countervailing duty would be likely to lead to a continuation or recurrence of subsidization and injury. If an affirmative determination has been made that the aforementioned conditions are met, the countervailing duty may be maintained for another five years. If no such review has been conducted or if there is no likelihood of the continuation or recurrence of injurious subsidization, the countervailing duty must be terminated.[16]

Initiation

According to Article 21.3, a sunset review can be initiated by an investigating authority on its own initiative or upon a duly substantiated request made by or on behalf of the domestic industry.

In *US – Carbon Steel*, the question arose whether the evidentiary standards in Article 11 apply also to a self-initiation by the investigating authority. The Appellate Body answered this question in the negative. A WTO Member can decide to automatically self-initiate sunset reviews. In other words, the evidentiary standards set forth in Article 11 that apply in case of an initiation based on an application by or on behalf of the domestic industry, or in the case of self-initiation of an initial investigation do not apply to self-initiation of a sunset review. Nor is there any other evidentiary standard prescribed for a self-initiation of a sunset review under Article 21.3. The Appellate Body

[16] See also WT/DS213/AB/R of 28 November 2002, *United States – Countervailing Duties on Certain Corrosion-Resistant Carbon Steel Flat Products from Germany*, para 63.

noted that the fact that the rules in Article 11 on initiation and subsequent investigation are not incorporated by reference into Article 21.3 suggests that they are not, *ipso facto*, applicable to sunset reviews.[17]

The sunset review must be initiated before the end of the five-year period (see first sentence of Article 21.3). The countervailing duty may remain in force pending the outcome of the sunset review (see second sentence of Article 21.3).

Investigation and Determination

Nature of the Investigation and Role of the Investigating Authority

The general rule of Article 21.1, i.e. that a countervailing duty shall remain in force only as long as and to the extent necessary to counteract subsidization which is causing injury, highlights the factors that must inform sunset reviews.[18]

A countervailing duty measure can only be maintained for another five-year period if the investigating authority has 'determined' that the expiry of the measure is likely to lead to continuation or recurrence of injurious subsidization. Two WTO dispute rulings have held that the notion 'to determine' imposes certain obligations on the investigating authority. *US – Countervailing Measures Concerning Certain Products from the ECs (Article 21.5)* found that 'to determine' requires in the context of a countervailing duty sunset review that the investigating authority acts with an appropriate degree of diligence and arrives at an adequately reasoned conclusion on the basis of information in the record of the proceedings, rather than simply making an assumption.[19] This Panel has also

[17] WT/DS213/AB/R of 28 November 2002, *United States – Countervailing Duties on Certain Corrosion-Resistant Carbon Steel Flat Products from Germany*, paras 98–118. See also *Grossman/Mavroidis* (2005/1) pp. 73–74 who agree with the Appellate Body decision but offer an additional rationale. While Article 11.6 restricts self-initiations to 'special circumstances', Article 21.3 does not contain such a limitation. In other words, when it comes to the initiation of an original case, such investigation should normally be linked to an interest of the domestic industry in the importing country. By contrast, Article 21.3 does not spell out such a link between initiation and the interest of the domestic industry.

[18] See *supra* this chapter, pp. 534–535 and WT/DS213/AB/R of 28 November 2002, *United States – Countervailing Duties on Certain Corrosion-Resistant Carbon Steel Flat Products from Germany*, para 70.

[19] WT/DS212/RW of 17 August 2005, *United States – Countervailing Measures Concerning Certain Products from the European Communities (Article 21.5)*, paras 7.213, 7.215, 7.216 and 7.275.

confirmed that the investigating authority is assigned an active rather than a passive decision-making role when performing a sunset review. It thus transposed to the ASCM a finding of the Appellate Body in relation to anti-dumping sunset reviews[20]

The Panel in *US Carbon Steel* found that 'determine' is defined, *inter alia*, as settle or decide as a judge or arbiter. The determination of likelihood under Article 21.3 must rest on a sufficient factual basis and should be based on the evaluation of evidence that the investigating authority has gathered during the initial investigation, the intervening reviews and in the sunset review.[21]

> In our view, one of the components of the likelihood analysis in a sunset review under Article 21.3 is an assessment of the likely rate of subsidisation. We do not consider, however, that an investigating authority must, in a sunset review, use the same calculation of the rate of subsidisation as in an original investigation. What the investigating authority must do under Article 21.3 is to assess whether subsidisation is likely to continue or recur should the CVD be revoked. This is, obviously, an inherently prospective analysis. Nonetheless, it must itself have an adequate basis in fact. The facts necessary to assess the likelihood of subsidisation in the event of revocation may well be different from those which must be taken into account in an original investigation. Thus, in assessing the likelihood of subsidisation in the event of revocation of the CVD, an investigating authority in a sunset review may well consider, *inter alia*, the original level of subsidisation, any changes in the original subsidy programmes, any new subsidy programmes introduced after the imposition of the original CVD, any changes in government policy, and any changes in relevant socio-economic and political circumstances.[22]

On this basis, the Panel found that the relevant US law on sunset reviews was as such not inconsistent with Article 21.3. However, the Panel was highly critical about a provision in the US law that stipulated that 'only under the most extraordinary circumstances will the Secretary rely on a

[20] WT/DS212/RW of 17 August 2005, *United States – Countervailing Measures Concerning Certain Products from the European Communities (Article 21.5)*, para 7.154.

[21] WT/DS213/R of 3 July 2002, *United States – Countervailing Duties on Certain Corrosion-Resistant Carbon Steel Flat Products from Germany*, paras 8.90, 8.94 and 8.95.

[22] WT/DS213/R of 3 July 2002, *United States – Countervailing Duties on Certain Corrosion-Resistant Carbon Steel Flat Products from Germany*, para 8.96. See also para 8.115. The subsequent Appellate Body ruling took a similar position, see WT/DS213/AB/R of 28 November 2002, *United States – Countervailing Duties on Certain Corrosion-Resistant Carbon Steel Flat Products from Germany*, paras 63 and 88 *et passim*.

countervailing duty rate … other than those it calculated and published in its prior determinations'.[23]

The investigating authority is obliged to consider evidence before it relating to subsidization, and to determine whether a benefit continues to exist following privatization of the investigated firm, before concluding whether subsidization exists and is likely to continue or to recur.[24] Therefore, the US's claim was rejected that when there have been no administrative reviews of a countervailing duty order, the only evidence of subsidization which an investigating authority need take into account in a sunset review is evidence from the original investigation. For instance, upon receiving information of a privatization resulting in a change in ownership, an investigating authority has to examine such information in order to determine whether a benefit resulting from subsidies previously bestowed to the State-owned producers continues to exist.[25] The subsequent implementation panel held more generally that Article 21.3 imposes an obligation on the investigating authority during a sunset review to take into account all the evidence placed on its record in making its determination of likelihood of continuation or recurrence of subsidization. The implementation panel is also interesting with regard to the extent to which an investigating authority has to examine evidence in making a redetermination in a sunset review in order to make the measure WTO-compliant.[26]

Moreover, an investigating authority is required to consider factual evidence already in its possession that is relevant to the assessment of the likelihood of continuation or recurrence of subsidization, particularly where that information may be relevant to the assessment of the rate at which subsidization is likely to continue or recur. On this basis, the Panel in *US – Carbon Steel* found that the USDOC breached Article 21.3 when it refused a request by a German exporter to place on the record of the sunset review investigation a calculation memorandum that was drawn

[23] WT/DS213/R of 3 July 2002, *United States – Countervailing Duties on Certain Corrosion-Resistant Carbon Steel Flat Products from Germany*, paras 8.97–8.107.

[24] WT/DS212/AB/R of 9 December 2002, *United States – Countervailing Measures Concerning Certain Products from the European Communities*, paras 148–150 and *supra* the commentary to Article 14, pp. 433–441.

[25] WT/DS212/R of 31 July 2002, *United States – Countervailing Measures Concerning Certain Products from the European Communities*, para 7.111.

[26] WT/DS212/RW of 17 August 2005, *United States – Countervailing Measures Concerning Certain Products from the European Communities (Article 21.5)*, paras 7.238, 7.253 and 7.288.

up by the USDOC in the original investigation and that was relevant for the sunset review at issue.[27]

Zero and *de minimis* Subsidization

US –Carbon Steel clarified that the 1 per cent *de minimis* subsidization standard that must be applied pursuant to Article 11.9 in an initial countervailing duty investigation, is not applicable in a sunset review carried out under Article 21.3. The Appellate Body arrived at this conclusion on the basis of a number of considerations, e.g. that Article 21.3 did not contain a cross-reference to Article 11.8 while in other parts of the ASCM (see for instance Article 21.4) the technique of cross-referencing was very well developed, the object and purpose of the ASCM and, more importantly, the differences in purpose between an initial investigation and a sunset review investigation. The former inquiry is directed to establish injurious subsidization while the latter should determine whether revocation of the duty is likely to lead to a continuation or recurrence of injurious subsidization. The Appellate Body also pointed out that where the level of subsidization at the time of the review is very low, there must be persuasive evidence that revocation of the duty would nevertheless lead to injury to the domestic industry. Mere reliance by the authorities on the injury determination made in the original investigation will not be sufficient.[28]

Footnote 52 is attached to Article 21.3. It clarifies that when the amount of the countervailing duty is assessed on a retrospective basis (like under the US system but unlike under the EU system), a finding in the most recent assessment proceeding that no duty is to be levied for the review investigation period shall not by itself require termination of the definitive duty.

Procedure, Duration and Conclusion of Reviews

According to Article 21.4, the provisions of Article 12 regarding evidence and procedure apply to any sunset review. And pursuant to Article 21.5, the provisions on sunset reviews also apply to undertakings accepted under Article 18.

[27] WT/DS213/R of 3 July 2002, *United States – Countervailing Duties on Certain Corrosion-Resistant Carbon Steel Flat Products from Germany*, paras 8.117 and 8.118.

[28] WT/DS213/AB/R of 28 November 2002, *United States – Countervailing Duties on Certain Corrosion-Resistant Carbon Steel Flat Products from Germany*, paras 58–92. Approving *Grossman/Mavroidis* (2005/1) pp. 69–72.

Article 21.4 provides that the review shall be carried out expeditiously and shall normally be concluded within 12 months of the date of initiation. This is not a mandatory deadline.

If, following a sunset review, there is an affirmative determination of the likelihood of continuation or recurrence of injurious subsidization, the countervailing measure can be maintained for another five-year period. The conclusion of a changed circumstances review can trigger another five-year period of application of the countervailing measures if such review has covered both subsidization and injury. Maintaining the duty during the new five-year period is subject to the provisions of Article 21.1 and 21.2.

Article 22, which contains the rules on public notice and explanation of determinations, applies *mutatis mutandis* to reviews under Article 21. This follows from Article 22.7.

Article 22

Public Notice and Explanation of Determinations

Introduction

Article 22 requires an investigating authority to give public notice at all major milestones of a countervailing duty investigation, i.e.

- initiation (paragraphs 1 and 2)
- preliminary determination (paragraph 3)
- provisional measures (paragraph 4)
- final determination (paragraph 3)
- affirmative determination providing for acceptance of undertaking or imposition of definitive duties (paragraph 5).

Article 22.1 also contains a requirement to notify the exporting Member and other interested parties at initiation stage (see *infra* this chapter, pp. 546–547)

Article 22 provides that the information and explanations to be given under this Article can also be provided in a separate report. Footnote 53 stipulates that in such instance, the authorities shall ensure that such report is readily available to the public. With regard to the separate report see also *infra* this chapter, pp. 547–548.

The provisions of Article 22 apply *mutatis mutandis* to review investigations pursuant to Article 21 and to decisions pursuant to Article 20 to apply duties retroactively (see Article 22.7).[1]

On the basis of the rulings described *infra*, the relevant standard in order to determine whether an investigating authority has complied with Articles 22.3 to 22.5 would appear to be:

Is the argument in question an issue of fact or law that is considered material by the investigating authority from the perspective of the determination at issue? If so:

[1] WT/DS138/AB/R of 10 May 2000, *United States – Imposition of Countervailing Duties on Certain Hot-Rolled Lead and Bismuth Carbon Steel Products originating in the United Kingdom*, paras 111–112.

Did the investigating authority in its determinations set forth the reasons for accepting or rejecting the argument in sufficient detail to allow to understand why the argument was treated as it was, and to assess compliance with domestic and/or WTO law?

In relation to the parallel provision of Article 12 of the Anti-Dumping Agreement, *Thailand – H Beams* has held that this provision provides important context for Article 3 (the equivalent to Article 15 of the ASCM) in indicating the significance attached by Members to allowing interested parties access to information on fact and law relevant to the final determination. Among other things, such access allows them (through interested Members) to assess the fruitfulness of bringing a WTO dispute settlement complaint.[2]

Initiation (Articles 22.1 and 22.2)

Notification

According to Article 22.1, when the authorities are satisfied that there is sufficient evidence to justify the initiation of an investigation pursuant to Article 11, the Member or Members whose products are subject to such an investigation and other interested parties known to the investigating authorities shall be notified.

In relation to the third country Member(s) concerned, Article 13.1 already provides for an obligation to invite such Member(s) for consultations prior to the initiation of the investigation.

As to the timing of the notification, *Guatemala – Cement II* provides guidance. This ruling is based on the parallel provision in the Anti-Dumping Agreement, i.e. its Article 12.1. According to the Panel, this provision requires notification (and public notice) once a Member has decided to initiate an investigation. Thus, the Panel rejected Mexico's request that the obligations arising out of Article 12.1 were already triggered once the Economic Integration Directorate recommended in a report to the competent minister to initiate the case. Mexico based its request on a literal reading of Article 12.1 ('When the authorities are satisfied that there is sufficient evidence … ').[3]

[2] WT/DS122/R of 28 September 2000, *Thailand – Anti-Dumping Duties on Angles, Shapes and Sections of Iron or Non-Alloy Steel and H-Beams from Poland*, para 7.151.

[3] WT/DS156/R of 24 October 2000, *Guatemala – Definitive Anti-Dumping Measures on Grey Portland Cement from Mexico*, paras 8.84–8.88.

In *Argentina – Poultry Anti-Dumping Duties*, the Panel has defined interested parties under Article 12.1 of the Anti-Dumping Agreement on the basis of Article 6.11 of the Anti-Dumping Agreement, i.e. the parallel provision to Article 12.9 of the ASCM. Hence, exporters or foreign producers of the subject merchandise are interested parties.[4]

If contact details of interested parties are not known, the investigating authority must make reasonable efforts to identify them. *Argentina – Poultry Anti-Dumping Duties* had to determine whether Argentina's efforts to notify exporters and foreign producers were sufficient. The application lodged by the Argentine domestic industry contained names of exporters but not their contact details. Argentina simply sent a letter to the Brazilian embassy in Buenos Aires requesting Brazil's cooperation in identifying the interested producers/exporters and providing them with the attached requests for information so that these parties cooperate. The letter did not, however, list the names of the potential exporters/producers. The Panel accepted that an exporter is known to the investigating authority but that the investigating authority may not have sufficient information to contact that exporter. However, in such circumstances, the nature of the Article 21.1 notification obligation is such that the investigating authority should make all reasonable efforts to obtain the requisite contact details. Sending a letter containing only a very general request for assistance without specifying the exporters for which contact details are required does not satisfy the need to make all reasonable efforts.[5]

Notice of Initiation

Article 22.1 *in fine* requires that public notice be given of the initiation of a countervailing duty investigation. Article 22.2 sets out in six subparagraphs the issues that such notice must cover. According to footnote 53, the issues can also be covered in a separate report if that report is readily available. In relation to the parallel provision in the Anti-Dumping Agreement, the Panel in *Guatemala – Cement II* held that if a WTO Member opts for a separate report, it is only in compliance with Article 12.1.1 of that Agreement if the public notice contains a reference to such separate report. Indeed, it cannot be said that a separate report is readily

[4] WT/DS241/R of 22 April 2003, *Argentina – Definitive Anti-Dumping Duties on Poultry from Brazil*, para 7.131.

[5] WT/DS241/R of 22 April 2003, *Argentina – Definitive Anti-Dumping Duties on Poultry from Brazil*, para 7.132.

available to the public, as required by the footnote, if the public is not informed about where, when and how to have access to the report, leave alone if they are not even publicly informed about its existence.[6]

The third subparagraph of Article 22.2 requires a description of the subsidy practice or practices to be investigated. This description should not only cover the legal basis as to the existence of subsidization but also the factual basis of subsidization alleged in the application.[7] However, according to *Mexico – Corn Syrup*, the parallel Article 12.1.1 of the Anti-Dumping Agreement does not require that the investigating authority sets out the conclusions it has drawn in relation to the evidence submitted in the application.[8]

Guatemala – Cement II did not accept arguments by defending WTO Members that errors in relation to Article 12.1.1 of the Anti-Dumping Agreement were harmless or without any negative consequences to exporting producers. Nor did it accept an invocation of acquiescence, estoppel or lack of nullification of benefits as a defence.[9]

Preliminary and Final Determinations etc. (Article 22.3)

This provision requires a public notice or a separate report of

- any preliminary and final determination (whether affirmative or negative)
- any decision to accept an undertaking pursuant to Article 18[10]
- the termination of such undertaking
- the termination of a definitive countervailing duty.

The notice or the separate report concerning the items covered by Article 22.3 have to include 'in sufficient detail the findings and conclusions reached on all issues of fact and law considered material by the investigating authorities'. By contrast, Article 22.5, which governs transparency

[6] WT/DS156/R of 24 October 2000, *Guatemala – Definitive Anti-Dumping Measures on Grey Portland Cement from Mexico*, paras 8.95–8.96.

[7] WT/DS156/R of 24 October 2000, *Guatemala – Definitive Anti-Dumping Measures on Grey Portland Cement from Mexico*, para 8.93 in relation to the parallel provision in the Anti-Dumping Agreement.

[8] WT/DS132/R of 28 January 2000, *Mexico – Anti-Dumping Investigation into High Fructose Corn Syrup (HFCS) from the United States*, paras 7.86–7.87.

[9] WT/DS156/R of 24 October 2000, *Guatemala – Definitive Anti-Dumping Measures on Grey Portland Cement from Mexico*, paras 8.22, 8.24, 8.111.

[10] See also Article 22.6.

in relation to definitive measures, requires that public notice be given of 'all relevant information on the matters of fact and law and reasons which have led to the imposition of final measures or the acceptance of an undertaking ... as well as the reasons for the acceptance or rejection of relevant arguments or claims made'. Accordingly, *China – Broiler Products* concluded not surprisingly that Articles 22.3, 22.4 and 22.5 are interrelated such that compliance with Article 22.3 is in part determined by compliance with Articles 22.4 or 22.5.[11]

The notice and the report have to be forwarded to interested parties.

According to the Panel in *China – GOES*, the obligation in Article 22.3 is procedural in character. It relates to the findings and conclusions actually made by an investigating authority and not to those which should have been reached under an objective standard. As the text of Article 22.3 refers to 'issues of fact and law considered material by the investigating authorities', the obligation relates to only those issues which the investigating authority subjectively considers material. In short, Article 22.3 does not discipline the substantive adequacy of an investigating authority's reasoning.[12]

The obligation to set forth in sufficient detail the findings and conclusions also covers the factual bases underlying the determination of the 'all others rate'.[13]

The Panel in *China – Broiler Products* adopted the standard established by *China – X-Ray Equipment* in relation to Article 12.2.2 of the Anti-Dumping Agreement:

> Since this provision concerns the arguments and claims made by exporters and importers, whose interests will be adversely affected by an affirmative determination, it is particularly important that the 'reasons' for rejecting or accepting such arguments should be set forth in sufficient detail to allow those exporters and importers to understand why their arguments or claims were treated as they were, and to assess whether or not the investigating authority's treatment of the relevant issue was consistent with domestic law and/or the WTO Agreement.[14]

[11] WT/DS427/R of 2 August 2013, *China – Anti-Dumping and Countervailing Duty Measures on Broiler Products from the United States*, para 7.521.

[12] WT/DS414/R of 15 June 2012, *China – Countervailing and Anti-Dumping Duties on Grain-Oriented Flat-Rolled Electrical Steel from the US*, para 7.356; WT/DS427/R of 2 August 2013, *China – Anti-Dumping and Countervailing Duty Measures on Broiler Products from the United States*, para 7.529.

[13] WT/DS427/R of 2 August 2013, *China – Anti-Dumping and Countervailing Duty Measures on Broiler Products from the United States*, para 7.366.

[14] WT/DS427/R of 2 August 2013, *China – Anti-Dumping and Countervailing Duty Measures on Broiler Products from the United States*, para 7.528 *et passim*; WT/DS425/R of 26

Jurisprudence in relation to Article 12.2 of the Anti-Dumping Agreement has tried to define the term 'material'. An issue is material if it has arisen in the course of an investigation and must be resolved in order for an investigating authority to reach their determination.[15] The fact that the investigating authority has disclosed a finding to an exporter does not render such finding automatically 'material'.[16]

In *China – Broiler Products*, the dispute was whether a request for a level of trade adjustment in the context of the price undercutting/price suppression analysis pursuant to Article 15.2 was an issue 'considered material' and whether MOFCOM set out in its report in sufficient detail the findings and conclusions reached and stated the underlying reasons.[17] In the anti-dumping case *EC – Tube or Pipe Fittings*, the Panel held that Article 3.4 of the Anti-Dumping Agreement (i.e. the provision similar to Article 15.4 of the ASCM) requires that an investigating authority must assess the role, relevance and relative weight of each injury factor in a particular investigation, and must explain its conclusions as to the lack of relevance or significance of factors determined not to be relevant or of significant weight. The Panel therefore considered that Article 12.2 and the textual link to Article 12.2.1 of the Anti-Dumping Agreement (i.e. the provisions similar to Article 22.2 and 22.3 of the ASCM) require that it must be discernible from the published determination that an investigating authority reflected this explanation as to the lack of relevance or significance of the injury factor(s) in question.[18]

Provisional Measures (Article 22.4)

Article 22.4 sets forth what explanations have to be given in relation to provisional countervailing duty measures. The provision is largely self-explanatory. The explanations have to be in sufficient detail. The obligation to provide sufficiently detailed explanations for the preliminary

February 2013, *China – Definitive Anti-Dumping Duties on X-Ray Security Inspection Equipment from the European Union*, para 7.472.

[15] WT/DS219/R of 7 March 2003, *European Communities – Anti-Dumping Duties on Malleable Cast Iron Tube or Pipe Fittings from Brazil*, para 7.424.

[16] WT/DS219/R of 7 March 2003, *European Communities – Anti-Dumping Duties on Malleable Cast Iron Tube or Pipe Fittings from Brazil*, para 7.441. See also paras 7.442–7.443.

[17] WT/DS427/R of 2 August 2013, *China – Anti-Dumping and Countervailing Duty Measures on Broiler Products from the United States*, paras 7.530–7.532. See also paras 7.601–7.607.

[18] WT/DS219/R of 7 March 2003, *European Communities – Anti-Dumping Duties on Malleable Cast Iron Tube or Pipe Fittings from Brazil*, para 7.432.

determination of the amount of subsidies comprises also the factual basis underlying the 'all others rate'.[19] See also *supra* the commentary to Article 22.3 and *infra* the commentary to Article 22.5.

Definitive Measures (Articles 22.5 and 22.6)

This provision describes the information to be given in a public notice or separate report with regard to affirmative determinations providing for a definitive countervailing duty or acceptance of an undertaking.

The Appellate Body examined Article 22.5 more extensively in *China – GOES*. According to the Appellate Body, this provision captures the principle that those parties whose interests are affected by the imposition of final countervailing duties are entitled to know, as a matter of fairness and due process, the facts, law and reasons that have led to the imposition of such duties. By requiring the disclosure of all relevant information, Article 22.5 seeks to guarantee that interested parties are able to pursue judicial review of a final determination as provided in Article 23.[20]

With regard to matters of fact, Article 22.5 does not require authorities to disclose all the factual information that is before them, but rather those facts that allow an understanding of the factual basis that led to the imposition of final measures. The inclusion of this information should therefore give a reasoned account of the factual support for an authority's decision to impose final measures.[21] In the same vein, the Appellate Body had held earlier that Article 22.5 does not require the investigating authority to cite or discuss every piece of supporting record evidence for each fact in the final determination as long as reliance on such evidence in a subsequent dispute settlement proceeding does not amount to a new reasoning or rationale.[22]

What constitutes relevant information on the matters of fact is to be understood in the light of the content of the findings needed to satisfy the

[19] WT/DS427/R of 2 August 2013, *China – Anti-Dumping and Countervailing Duty Measures on Broiler Products from the United States*, para 7.366.

[20] WT/DS414/AB/R of 18 October 2012, *China – Countervailing and Anti-dumping Duties on Grain Oriented Flat-Rolled Electrical Steel from the United States*, para 258.

[21] WT/DS414/AB/R of 18 October 2012, *China – Countervailing and Anti-dumping Duties on Grain Oriented Flat-Rolled Electrical Steel from the United States*, para 256; WT/DS427/R of 2 August 2013, *China – Anti-Dumping and Countervailing Duty Measures on Broiler Products from the United States*, para 7.328.

[22] WT/DS296/AB/R of 27 June 2005, *United States – Countervailing Duty Investigation on Dynamic Random Access Memory Semiconductors (DRAMs) from Korea*, para 159 *et seq.*

substantive requirements with respect to the imposition of final measures, as well as the factual circumstances of each case. For instance, with regard to the second sentence of Article 15.2, 'all relevant information on the matters of fact' consists of those facts that are required to understand an investigating authority's price effects examination leading to the imposition of final measures.[23] Thus, the Appellate Body used under Article 22.5 the same criterion as with regard to Article 12.8, i.e. the provision on disclosure.[24]

With respect to the form in which the relevant information must be disclosed, Article 22.5 allows authorities to decide whether to include the information in the public notice itself or otherwise make it available through a separate report. Article 22.5 provides that the notice or report shall pay due regard to the requirement for the protection of confidential information. According to the Appellate Body, when confidential information is part of the relevant information on matters of fact within the meaning of Article 22.5, the disclosure obligation under this provision should be met by disclosing non-confidential summaries of that information.[25] See also the commentary to Article 12.4.

The obligation to give public notice is triggered once there is an affirmative determination providing for the imposition of definitive duties.[26]

Further examples where Article 22.5 was reviewed by a panel or the Appellate Body:

- *China – GOES*: Non-inclusion of dumping calculations in public notice does not constitute a violation of Article 12.2.2 of the Anti-Dumping Agreement.[27]
- *China – GOES*: 'All others rate', use of facts available pursuant to Article 12.7.[28]

[23] WT/DS414/AB/R of 18 October 2012, *China – Countervailing and Anti-dumping Duties on Grain Oriented Flat-Rolled Electrical Steel from the United States*, paras 257 and 260.

[24] See *supra* the commentary to Article 12, pp. 416–418.

[25] WT/DS414/AB/R of 18 October 2012, *China – Countervailing and Anti-dumping Duties on Grain Oriented Flat-Rolled Electrical Steel from the United States*, para 259.

[26] WT/DS414/AB/R of 18 October 2012, *China – Countervailing and Anti-dumping Duties on Grain Oriented Flat-Rolled Electrical Steel from the United States*, para 256.

[27] WT/DS414/R of 15 June 2012, *China – Countervailing and Anti-Dumping Duties on Grain-Oriented Flat-Rolled Electrical Steel from the US*, paras 7.330–7.339.

[28] WT/DS414/R of 15 June 2012, *China – Countervailing and Anti-Dumping Duties on Grain-Oriented Flat-Rolled Electrical Steel from the US*, para 7.474. The obligation to provide relevant information concerning the final determination of the amount of subsidies comprises also the factual basis underlying the 'all others rate', see para 7.366.

- *China – GOES*: No disclosure of information underlying China's conclusion regarding low subject import prices.[29]
- *China – GOES*: Volume of imports from countries not subject to investigation.[30]
- *China – Broiler Products*: Gain of market shares by subject imports but not to the detriment of domestic industry.[31]
- *China – Broiler Products*: Inability of domestic industry to supply product concerned.[32]
- *US – Softwood Lumber VI*: Relationship of claims under Article 22.5 with those under Article 15.[33]
- *EC – Bed Linen*: Article 12.2.2 of the Anti-Dumping Agreement (i.e. the parallel provision to Article 22.5 of the ASCM) does not require explanations relating to initiation.[34]
- *Mexico – Corn Syrup*: Explanations concerning retroactivity.[35]
- *China – X-Ray Equipment*: Price effects analysis and other points concerning causation, factual basis of the residual or 'all others rate', calculations and underlying data regarding the dumping margin.[36]

See also *supra* the commentary to Article 22.3 and to Article 22.4. With regard to the acceptance of an undertaking pursuant to Article 18, see also Article 22.6.

[29] WT/DS414/R of 15 June 2012, *China – Countervailing and Anti-Dumping Duties on Grain-Oriented Flat-Rolled Electrical Steel from the US*, paras 7.587–7.592. Upheld by the Appellate Body, see WT/DS414/AB/R of 18 October 2012, *China – Countervailing and Anti-Dumping Duties on Grain-Oriented Flat-Rolled Electrical Steel from the United States*, paras 252–267.

[30] WT/DS414/R of 15 June 2012, *China – Countervailing and Anti-Dumping Duties on Grain-Oriented Flat-Rolled Electrical Steel from the US*, para 7.669 *et seq.*

[31] WT/DS427/R of 2 August 2013, *China – Anti-Dumping and Countervailing Duty Measures on Broiler Products from the United States*, paras 7.601–7.607.

[32] WT/DS427/R of 2 August 2013, *China – Anti-Dumping and Countervailing Duty Measures on Broiler Products from the United States*, paras 7.601–7.607.

[33] WT/DS277/R of 22 March 2004, *United States – Investigation of the International Trade Commission in Softwood Lumber from Canada*, paras 7.38–7.42.

[34] WT/DS141/R of 30 October 2000, *European Communities – Anti-Dumping Duties on Imports of Cotton-Type Bed Linen from India*, para 6.260.

[35] WT/DS132/R of 28 January 2000, *Mexico – Anti-Dumping Investigation into High Fructose Corn Syrup (HFCS) from the United States*, para 7.191.

[36] WT/DS425/R of 26 February 2013, *China – Definitive Anti-Dumping Duties on X-Ray Security Inspection Equipment from the European Union*, para 7.456 *et seq.*

Article 22 Applies *mutatis mutandis* to Reviews under Article 21 and Decisions to Apply Duties Retroactively (Article 22.7)

Article 22 applies *mutatis mutandis* to reviews under Article 21 and to a decision to apply duties retroactively. Moreover, *US – Carbon Steel (India)* clarified that Articles 22.1 and 22.2 also apply to administrative reviews, i.e. reviews that set retroactively the duty rate.[37]

Article 23

Judicial Review

The provisions of Article 23 are essentially self-explanatory. Article X:3b of GATT 1994 contains a similar obligation. Article 13 of the Anti-Dumping Agreement is identical with Article 23 of the ASCM with one exception. The last part of the second sentence of Article 23 of the ASCM ('and shall provide all interested parties who participated in the administrative proceeding … ') is not reproduced in Article 13.

[37] WT/DS436/AB/R of 8 December 2014, *United States – Countervailing Measures on Certain Hot-Rolled Carbon Steel Flat Products from India*, paras 4.535, 4.540.

PART VI

INSTITUTIONS

Article 24

Committee on Subsidies and Countervailing Measures and Subsidiary Bodies

The WTO has essentially three basic functions, i.e. rule making through negotiations, dispute settlement and surveillance of the application of the various WTO agreements. The provisions in Parts VI and VII of the ASCM are designed to implement this third function.

The Committee on Subsidies and Countervailing Measures is a subsidiary body of the Council for Trade in Goods.[1] It is composed of representatives from each WTO Member.

The ASCM refers in a number of provisions to the Committee, i.e. Articles 8.3, 8.4, 9.3, 9.4, 25.9–25.12, 26, 27.4, 27.6, 27.11–27.15, 28.2, 29.3, 29.4, 31, 32.6, 32.7 and footnote 25. On this basis, the purpose and the functions of the Committee are:

- receipt and review of notifications
- supervision of the application and implementation of the ASCM
- forum for consultations and discussions on subsidy issues.[2]

Article 24.4 provides for the establishment of a Permanent group of experts. This provision constitutes special and additional rules or procedures identified in Appendix 2 to the DSU. The tasks of the Permanent group of experts are described in Articles 24.4 and 24.3. Up to now, the Permanent group of experts did not play any significant role.

[1] See the second sentence of Article 32.7 of the ASCM and Article IV:5 of the Marrakesh Agreement Establishing the World Trade Organization.

[2] See *Wolfrum* in *Wolfrum/Stoll/Koebele* (2008), para 3 to Article 24.

PART VII

NOTIFICATION AND SURVEILLANCE

Article 25

Notifications

Article 25 imposes on Members three different sets of notification requirements:

- notification of subsidies granted that are covered by Articles 1 and 2 of the ASCM (paragraphs 1 to 10)
- notification of preliminary and final actions taken with regard to countervailing duties (paragraph 11) and
- notification of the competent authorities as well as the domestic procedures governing the initiation and conduct of countervailing duty investigations (paragraph 12).

Members have to notify the list of subsidies granted every two years.

The Committee has adopted standard formats for all types of notifications.[1]

According to *Brazil – Aircraft*, Article 25 aims to promote transparency by requiring Members to notify their subsidies, without prejudging the legal status of these subsidies.[2] *Canada – Aircraft* has held that Article 25.7 effectively precludes a finding of a *prima facie* case of an actionable, prohibited or countervailable subsidy simply on the basis of a country's notification of the programme in question.[3]

[1] *Kazeki* (2010) p. 194 *et seq.* describes the development of the notification format but also points to the unchanged poor record of notifications by WTO Members.

[2] WT/DS46/AB/R of 2 August 1999, *Brazil – Export Financing Programme for Aircraft*, para 149.

[3] WT/DS70/R of 14 April 1999, *Canada – Measures Affecting the Export of Civilian Aircraft*, para 9.256.

Article 26

Surveillance

There is no jurisprudence with regard to Article 26. This provision is essentially self-explanatory and requires the Committee to examine notifications that Members have provided pursuant to Article 25 of the ASCM and Article XVI of GATT 1994 concerning the subsidies they have provided and their countervailing duty actions.

PART VIII

DEVELOPING COUNTRY MEMBERS

Article 27

Special and Differential Treatment of Developing Country Members

Introduction

The preamble of the WTO Agreement recognizes 'that there is a need for positive efforts designed to ensure that developing countries, and especially the least-developed among them, secure a share in the growth in international trade commensurate with the needs of their economic development'. This overarching concern finds ample reflection in the ASCM. The first paragraph of Article 27 echoes this need by stating that Members recognize that subsidies may play an important role in economic development programmes of developing country Members.[1]

According to the Panel in *Brazil – Aircraft (1st Article 21.5)*, the ASCM should not be interpreted in such a manner that the rules themselves place developing country Members at a disadvantage *vis-à-vis* developed country Members. However, the ASCM cannot remove competitive disadvantages arising from structural differences between WTO Members.[2]

Article 27 broadly covers the following areas:

- exemption from the prohibition of granting export subsidies (paragraphs 2, 4, 5, 6, 7 and 14);
- exemption from the prohibition of granting import substitution subsidies (paragraph 3);
- non-application of the presumption of serious prejudice as contained in Article 6.1 (paragraph 8);
- remedies under Article 7 against actionable subsidies granted by a developing country Member are only available under more limited

[1] WT/DS46/RW of 9 May 2000, *Brazil – Export Financing Programme for Aircraft (Article 21.5, first recourse)*, para 6.47. *Avgoustidi and Ballschmiede* in *Wolfrum/Stoll/Koebele* (2008), para 11 to Article 27 have characterized Article 27.1 as 'a programmatic provision rather than a compulsory one providing precise obligations for the developed country Members'. Note also the use of the word 'may' in Article 27.1.

[2] WT/DS46/RW of 9 May 2000, *Brazil – Export Financing Programme for Aircraft (Article 21.5, first recourse)*, para 6.47.

circumstances than against non-developing Members (paragraphs 9 and 13);
- developing country Members benefit from higher *de minimis* thresholds in terms of subsidization and import shares (paragraphs 10, 11, 12 and 15).

Article 27 with its 15 paragraphs is one of the longest provisions of the ASCM. In particular provisions concerning the (temporary) exemption of developing countries from the prohibition of granting export subsidies are not easily understandable because of the numerous cross-references within Article 27 and to Annex VII.

Indonesia – Autos rejected a claim made by Indonesia according to which complainants bear a heavier than usual burden of proof in the dispute in question or that the concept of like product should be interpreted more narrowly than usual because Indonesia is a developing country.[3]

The special and differential (S&D) treatment of developing countries provided for in the Anti-Dumping Agreement is different to that of the ASCM. Article 15 of the Anti-Dumping Agreement stipulates that special regard must be given by developed country Members to the special situation of developing country Members when considering the application of anti-dumping measures. Furthermore, possibilities of constructive remedies provided for by the Anti-Dumping Agreement should be explored before applying anti-dumping duties.

Article 27 distinguishes between least developed countries as defined by the United Nations (see subparagraph (a) of Annex VII), developing countries on the list of subparagraph (b) of Annex VII and all other developing countries. Unless a country falls under Annex VII, the label 'developing country' is a self-selected status that could be challenged by other Members. To date, no such challenge has occurred.[4] China has renounced being treated as a developing country for the purposes of claims under Part II and Part III of the ASCM,[5] but requests S&D treatment in respect of CVD investigations.

[3] WT/DS54/R, WT/DS55/R, WT/DS59/R and WT/DS64/R of 2 July 1998, *Indonesia – Certain Measures Affecting the Automobile Industry*, paras 14.168 and 14.169.

[4] *Coppens* (2014) p. 267.

[5] China will not invoke Articles 27.8, 27.9 and 27.13, see para 171 of the Report of the Working Party of 10 November 2001, WT/MIN(01)/3.

Non-application of the Prohibition of Export Subsidies to Certain Developing Country Members (Paragraphs 2, 4, 5, 6, 7 and 14 of Article 27)

Introduction

The essence of the provisions listed in the title of this section is that developing countries are temporarily exempted from the prohibition to grant export subsidies. Moreover, once the exemption has expired, developing countries do not immediately need to abolish the export subsidies. Rather, they benefit from a transition period during which they have to phase out such subsidies.

These provisions provide for a *géométrie variable* in the sense that the duration of this exemption varies depending on the category to which the developing country in question belongs. The same is true for the duration of the phasing out period.

Article 27.4 has to be read together with Article 27.2(b) and Article 3.1(a). The Appellate Body in *Brazil – Aircraft* has held that these provisions contain a carefully negotiated balance of rights and obligations for developing country Members.[6] Article 27.4 constitutes special and additional rules or procedures identified in Appendix 2 to the DSU.

The following table gives an overview of how Article 27 exempts developing countries from the prohibition to grant export subsidies by establishing different categories of such countries and by differentiating the duration of the exemption.

A developing country Member falling under Article 27.2(b) is only exempt from the prohibition to grant export subsidies if it meets certain conditions set out in the first and second sentences of Article 27.4, i.e.

- it shall not increase the level of its export subsidies;
- it shall eliminate them within an eight-year period (preferably in a progressive manner) or any extension thereof;
- it shall eliminate the export subsidies within a shorter period than eight years when the use of such subsidies is inconsistent with its developing needs.

[6] WT/DS46/AB/R of 2 August 1999, *Brazil – Export Financing Programme for Aircraft*, para 139.

Category of developing country Member	Duration of exemption	Period during which export subsidies have to be gradually phased out in case export competitiveness has been reached
Least-developed countries designated as such by the United Nations (Article 27.2(a) in conjunction with Annex VII (a))[7]	Indefinite, unless export competitiveness has been reached pursuant to Article 27.6	Eight years (second sentence of Article 27.5 in conjunction with Article 27.6)
Annex VII(b) countries: they are treated like least-developed countries until their GNP *per capita* has reached USD 1,000 *per annum*.[8] Once this threshold has been reached they are treated as other developing country Members (see line below)		Eight years (second sentence of Article 27.5 in conjunction with Article 27.6). However, if GNP *per capita* has reached USD 1,000 *per annum*, these countries are treated like Article 27.2(b) countries, see line below
Other developing country Members (Article 27.2(b))[9]	Eight years (but progressive phasing out during that period is preferable) if following conditions are met: - no increase of the level of export subsidies (second sentence of Article 27.4); - elimination within a shorter period than eight years when use of export subsidies is inconsistent with its development needs (second sentence of Article 27.4) - country did not reach export competitiveness (Article 27.5) Possibility to receive extensions of the eight-year period pursuant to Article 27.4	Two years (first sentence of Article 27.5 in conjunction with Article 27.6)

[7] See also WT/MIN(01)/17, Decision adopted at the Doha WTO Ministerial Conference on 14 November 2001 on Implementation-related issues and concerns, para 10.5, G/SCM/110 and various addendums thereto.

[8] See also WT/MIN(01)/17, Decision adopted at the Doha WTO Ministerial Conference on 14 November 2001 on Implementation-related issues and concerns, paras 10.1 and 10.4, G/SCM/110 and various addendums thereto.

[9] See also WT/MIN(01)/17, Decision adopted at the Doha WTO Ministerial Conference on 14 November 2001 on Implementation-related issues and concerns, para 10.5, G/SCM/110 and various addendums thereto.

In other words, if such developing country Member does not comply with one of these conditions, the prohibition of granting export subsidies as contained in Article 3.1(a) applies to this developing country Member.[10]

Finally, it has to be noted that Members can apply for an extension of the period set in Article 27.4.

According to Article 27.7, export subsidies which are in conformity with paragraphs 2 through 5, are not subject to the provisions of Article 4. The relevant provisions in such a case shall be those of Article 7 (see also *infra* this chapter, pp. 573–574). Export subsidies can also be countervailed.

The relevant details are explained in the next sections.

Prohibition to Increase the Level of Export Subsidies

In order to be exempt from the prohibition of giving export subsidies, according to the second sentence of Article 27.4, a developing country Member *inter alia* must not increase the level of export subsidies. Footnote 55 of the ASCM stipulates that for a developing country Member not granting export subsidies at the date of entry into force of the WTO Agreement, Article 27.4 shall apply on the basis of the level of export subsidies granted in 1986.

For the purposes of determining whether or not the level of export subsidies has increased, the level of subsidies actually provided is relevant, not the level of subsidies which a Member planned or authorized its government to provide through its budgetary process. In short, not the budgeted amounts are decisive but the actual expenditures. Both Panel and Appellate Body arrived at this conclusion *inter alia* on the basis of the aforementioned footnote 55 that uses the verb 'granted' and the meaning of this verb, i.e. 'something actually provided'.[11]

When calculating whether or not the level of export subsidies has increased, the precise point in time as to when such subsidy was granted may also become disputed. The Appellate Body saw for the purposes of Article 27.4 the issue of the existence of a subsidy and the issue of the point in time at which the subsidy is granted as two legally distinct issues. It held that the subsidy was granted when the beneficiary obtained the

[10] WT/DS46/AB/R of 2 August 1999, *Brazil – Export Financing Programme for Aircraft*, para 165 *et passim*.

[11] WT/DS46/AB/R of 2 August 1999, *Brazil – Export Financing Programme for Aircraft*, paras 146–149.

unconditional legal right to receive the payments, even if the payments themselves have not yet occurred. In other words, the subsidy is granted if all the legal conditions have been fulfilled that entitle the beneficiary to receive the subsidy. The Appellate Body also underlined that, contrary to the Panel, it did not find it relevant for the purposes of calculating the level of export subsidies under Article 27.4 whether the financial contribution involved a 'direct transfer of funds' or a 'potential transfer of funds'.[12]

In *Brazil – Aircraft*, the parties disagreed as to the benchmark period, against which it had to be judged whether there was an increase in the level of the export subsidies. This issue is addressed in footnote 55. Thus, the ceiling for such subsidies is either the period immediately preceding the entry into force of the WTO Agreement (i.e. 1994) or, if the developing country Member did not provide such export subsidies during that period, the year 1986 (i.e. the year during which the Uruguay Round launched).[13]

Up to now, there is no ruling whether the determination has to be based on constant or nominal currency units. In *Brazil – Aircraft*, Canada argued that it was appropriate in the case in question to use constant dollars rather than nominal dollars to assess whether Brazil has increased the level of export subsidies. Both the Panel and the Appellate Body made no legal finding as to how the increase should be measured because the conclusion would have been the same whether constant or nominal dollars were used, i.e. Brazil had increased the level of export subsidies. However, both also noted that the use of constant dollars was more appropriate in the case because using nominal dollars would not take account of inflation and would therefore render meaningless the special and differential treatment provisions in Article 27.[14]

Article 27.2(b) Countries Shall Phase Out Export Subsidies

The first sentence of Article 27.4 stipulates that a developing country Member as defined in paragraph 2 shall phase out its export subsidies

[12] WT/DS46/AB/R of 2 August 1999, *Brazil – Export Financing Programme for Aircraft*, paras 151–159.

[13] WT/DS46/R of 14 April 1999, *Brazil – Export Financing Programme for Aircraft*, paras 7.61–7.62.

[14] WT/DS46/AB/R of 2 August 1999, *Brazil – Export Financing Programme for Aircraft*, paras 160–164.

within the eight-year period or any extension thereof (see *infra*), preferably in a progressive manner.

The Panel in *Brazil – Aircraft* concluded that Brazil did not meet the requirement to phase out its export subsidies within the eight-year-period. In the case in question, it was found that Brazilian export subsidies came into existence once certain bonds under the export credit programme PROEX were issued. These bonds were only issued once it was confirmed that an export transaction would occur, essentially the delivery of the airplane. Before the actual issuance of bonds, Brazil entered into legally binding commitments to issue such bonds if all conditions (including delivery of the airplane) were met. As these commitments to issue bonds were given in relation to transactions where the delivery of the airplane and hence the issuance of a bond was well after the expiry of the eight-year period, i.e. after 31 December 2002, provided for in Article 27.4, Brazil was found not to have phased out its export subsidies within the eight-year period.[15] Note that the Panel handed down its ruling in April 1999, that is nearly three years before the expiry of the eight-year period. The Panel also examined the relationship between the main clause and the subordinate clause of the first sentence of Article 27.4. The latter provision stipulates that the developing country Member shall phase out its export subsidies 'preferably in a progressive manner'. The Panel did not need to make a finding in this respect.[16]

'[I]nconsistent with Its Development Needs'

See the Panel in *Brazil – Aircraft*.[17] Pursuant to Article 27.14, the Committee on Subsidies and Countervailing Measures can, upon request by an interested Member, examine whether a specific export subsidy practice of a developing country Member is in conformity with its development needs.

[15] WT/DS46/R of 14 April 1999, *Brazil – Export Financing Programme for Aircraft*, paras 7.77–7.86.

[16] WT/DS46/R of 14 April 1999, *Brazil – Export Financing Programme for Aircraft*, paras 7.79–7.81.

[17] WT/DS46/R of 14 April 1999, *Brazil – Export Financing Programme for Aircraft*, paras 7.87–7.93.

Burden of Proof

According to the Appellate Body in *Brazil – Aircraft*, the conditions set forth in paragraph 4 are positive obligations for developing country Members, not affirmative defences. If a developing country Member complies with the conditions set forth in Article 27.4, a claim of violation of Article 3.1(a) cannot be entertained during the eight-year period, and any extension thereof, because the export subsidy prohibition simply does not apply to that developing country Member. However, if the developing country Member does not comply with those obligations, Article 3.1(a) does apply. The burden is on the complaining party (which in the case in question was Canada) to demonstrate that the developing country Member is not in compliance with at least one of the elements set forth in Article 27.4.[18]

Extension Procedure (Article 27.4)

The eight-year transition period set out in Article 27.2(b) expired on 31 December 2002. However, the second part of Article 27.4 provides for the possibility to extent the non-application of the prohibition to grant export subsidies. Such extension can be granted by the Committee on Subsidies and Countervailing Measures (see Article 24).

The following WTO documents contain relevant rules in relation to extensions:

- G/SCM/39 of 20 November 2001, *Procedures for Extension under Article 27.4 for Certain Developing Country Members*, adopted by the Doha Ministerial Conference
- Articles 10.5 and 10.6 of WT/MIN(01)/17 of 20 November 2001, *Implementation-Related Issues and Concerns*, adopted by the Doha Ministerial Conference
- WT/L/691 of 31 July 2007, Procedures for continuation of extensions pursuant to Article 27.4 of the SCM Agreement of the transition period under Article 27.2(b) of the SCM Agreement for certain developing country Members.

The extension package was not prolonged beyond 2015.

[18] WT/DS46/AB/R of 2 August 1999, *Brazil – Export Financing Programme for Aircraft*, paras 140–141.

Exemption from the Prohibition of Granting Import Substitution Subsidies (Article 27.3)

Article 27.3 stipulates that it only applies for a transition period that already expired.

Actions against Subsidies under Part III (Paragraphs 8, 9 and 13 of Article 27)

Pursuant to Article 27.9, actionable subsidies given by a developing WTO Member can be challenged under the dispute settlement track pursuant to Article 7 if nullification or impairment of tariff concessions or other obligations under GATT 1994 is found to exist as a result of such subsidy, in such a way as to displace or impede imports of the like product into the market of the subsidizing developing country Member or if injury to a domestic industry in the market of an importing Member occurs.[19]

The question is to what extent a Member can bring claims against a developing country under Article 5(c) in conjunction with Article 6. The issue is not clear. Article 27.8 stipulates:

- there shall be no presumption in terms of Article 6.1 that a subsidy granted by a developing country Member results in serious prejudice, as defined by the ASCM; and
- that such serious prejudice, where applicable under Article 27.9, shall be demonstrated by positive evidence, in accordance with the provisions of paragraphs 3 through 8 of Article 6.

Article 6.1 expired by virtue of Article 31. Some have taken the view that because of the expiry of Article 6.1, actions under Article 6.1 cannot be brought against a developing country Member. Others have argued that serious prejudice claims can be brought against a developing country Member if the complaining Member demonstrates that one of the four situations listed in Article 6.1 is present (as opposed to deemed serious prejudice).[20]

[19] Article 27.9 was examined by WT/DS54/R, WT/DS55/R, WT/DS59/R and WT/DS64/R of 2 July 1998, *Indonesia – Certain Measures Affecting the Automobile Industry*, paras 14.156 *et seq*. The ruling was handed down before the expiry of Article 6.1.

[20] See *Coppens* (2014) p. 267 *et seq*.

Finally, pursuant to Article 27.13, no action against developing country Members is possible under Part III of the ASCM against certain subsidies granted within and directly linked to a privatization programme of a developing country Member if such subsidies are

- notified to the Committee on Subsidies and Countervailing measures;
- the programme and the subsidies involved are granted for a limited period; and
- the programme results in eventual privatization of the enterprise concerned.

Uncertainties exist with regard to the relationship between Article 27.7 and Article 27.13. This former provision stipulates that Article 4, i.e. the dispute settlement provisions for prohibited subsidies, does not apply to a developing country Member with regard to export subsidies if such subsidies are in conformity with the provisions of paragraphs 2 to 5. Instead, Article 7, i.e. the dispute settlement provisions with regard to actionable subsidies, applies. The unresolved question is whether Article 6.3 applies fully or whether Article 6.3 can only be applied subject to the limitations spelled out in Article 27.13, i.e. that it cannot be used against certain privatization subsidies.[21]

Higher *de minimis* thresholds for Developing Countries in Countervailing Duty Investigations (Paragraphs 10, 11, 12 and 15 of Article 27)

For developing country Members, higher *de minimis* thresholds apply than to other Members. These higher thresholds are set out in Article 27.10 and are derogations to the normally applicable thresholds as set out in Article 11.9.

[21] See *Coppens* (2014) p. 267 *et seq.*

Category of Member	*De minimis* subsidization	*De minimis* imports
Developing country Members (Article 27.10)	2%	< 4% of total imports, unless imports from developing country Members whose import share represents < 4% collectively account for > 9% of the total imports
Other Members (Article 11.9)	1%	Volume of subsidized imports is negligible but ASCM does not define thresholds

Article 27.12 makes it clear that the thresholds in Article 27.10 apply also for the purposes of deciding whether or not to cumulate in a countervailing investigation imports from various origins pursuant to Article 15.3. Article 27.11 expired by the end of 2002.

Pursuant to Article 27.15, an interested developing country Member can request the Committee on Subsidies and Countervailing Measures to review the consistency of a countervailing measure with paragraph 10 of Article 27.

PART IX

TRANSITIONAL ARRANGEMENTS

Article 28

Existing Programmes

Article 28 is essentially self-explanatory. It exempts for a transition period of three years subsidy programmes that have been established before the date of accession in the territory of a WTO Member and that are inconsistent with the ASCM, from the disciplines of Part II of the ASCM, i.e. the section dealing with prohibited subsidies. This exemption only applies if certain conditions are met that are listed in Article 28. However, Part III ('Actionable Subsidies') and Part V ('Countervailing Measures') of the ASCM do not contain a similar exemption.

The exemption contained in Article 28 of a Member from the disciplines of Part II of the ASCM is not relevant if these disciplines do not apply to such WTO Member by virtue of Article 27.[1]

For the notion of 'programme', see commentary to Article 1 pp. 62–65.

Article 29

Transformation into a Market Economy

Article 29 is essentially self-explanatory. The exemptions from the disciplines of the ASCM provided for in Article 29.2 were only applicable within a period of seven years from the date of entry into force of the WTO Agreement, i.e. until 31 December 2001.[1]

[1] WT/DS54/R, WT/DS55/R, WT/DS59/R and WT/DS64/R of 2 July 1998, *Indonesia – Certain Measures Affecting the Automobile Industry*, para 14.261.

[1] *Rios Herran* and *Poretto* in Wolfrum/Stoll/Koebele (2008), paragraph 2 to Article 29.

PART X

DISPUTE SETTLEMENT

Article 30

Article 30 is the sole provision in Part X of the ASCM. While Article 30 does not have any title, Part X is entitled 'Dispute Settlement'. Article 30 stipulates that the provisions of Articles XXII and XXIII of GATT 1994 as elaborated and applied by the DSU shall apply to consultations and the settlement of disputes under the ASCM, except as otherwise specifically provided.

Contrary to Article 17.6 of the Anti-Dumping Agreement, the ASCM does not specify any special standard of review for disputes.

In *US – Lead and Bismuth II*, the US claimed that the standard of review set out in Article 17.6 of the WTO Anti-Dumping Agreement also applied to disputes concerning countervailing duty measures. Article 17.6 requires a panel to exercise a higher decree of deference to the findings of an investigating authority than Article 11 of the DSU.[1] The US invoked the Ministerial *Declaration on Dispute Settlement Pursuant to the Agreement on Implementation of Article VI of the General Agreement on Tariffs and Trade 1994 or Part V of the Agreement on Subsidies and Countervailing Measures*. That Declaration recognizes the need for a consistent resolution of disputes arising from anti-dumping and countervailing duty measures.[2]

Both the Panel and the Appellate Body did not accept this claim. The Appellate Body noted in relation to the aforementioned Ministerial Declaration that it is couched in hortatory language and does not specify any particular action to be taken or any particular standards of review to be applied. The Appellate Body also referred to the *Decision on Review of Article 17.6 of the Agreement in Implementation of Article VI of the General*

[1] See, for instance, WT/DS184/AB/R of 24 July 2001, *United States – Anti-Dumping Measures on Certain Hot-Rolled Steel Products from Japan*, para 53 *et seq.*

[2] The Declaration is reproduced *supra* the introductory chapter, pp. 52–53.

Agreement on Tariffs and Trade 1994. And it pointed out that the ASCM did not contain any special or additional rules and procedures with regard to the standard of review. Appendix 2 of the DSU does not refer to Article 30 of the ASCM. Consequently, the standard of review set forth in Article 11 of the DSU applies also to disputes arising under Part V of the ASCM.[3]

Note that the Panel in *US – Softwood Lumber VI* found that there might well be cases in which the application of the Vienna Convention principles together with the additional provisions of Article 17.6 of the Anti-Dumping Agreement could result in a different conclusion being reached in a dispute under the Anti-Dumping Agreement than under the ASCM.[4] This possibility exists for instance in relation to rules concerning the initiation and the conduct of parallel anti-dumping and countervailing duty investigations as well as with regard to injury determinations. However, there was finally no need to address this issue in *US – Softwood Lumber VI*.

The Appellate Body in *US – Countervailing Duty Investigation on DRAMs* gives a good overview as to the standard of review to be applied by a Panel when examining a countervailing measure. The relevant parts of the Appellate Body's decision are reproduced hereafter:[5]

Basic Approach

> 182. Article 11 of the DSU sets out the proper standard of review to be applied by panels when examining Members' subsidy determinations. [footnote omitted] That provision states, in relevant part: [A] panel should make an objective assessment of the matter before it, including an objective assessment of the facts of the case and the applicability of and conformity with the relevant covered agreements.
>
> 184. … we recall that an 'objective assessment' under Article 11 of the DSU must be understood in the light of the obligations of the particular covered agreement at issue in order to derive the more specific contours of the appropriate standard of review. [footnote omitted] In this respect, we are especially mindful, in this appeal, of Articles 12, 19, and 22 of the *SCM Agreement*.

[3] WT/DS138/AB/R of 10 May 2000, *United States – Imposition of Countervailing Duties on Certain Hot-Rolled Lead and Bismuth Carbon Steel Products originating in the United Kingdom*, paras 44–51.

[4] WT/DS277/R of 22 March 2004, *United States – Investigation of the International Trade Commission in Softwood Lumber from Canada*, para 7.22.

[5] WT/DS296/AB/R of 27 June 2005, *United States – Countervailing Duty Investigation on Dynamic Random Access Memory Semiconductors (DRAMs) from Korea*.

186. In the light of the above, we are of the view that the 'objective assessment' to be made by a panel reviewing an investigating authority's subsidy determination will be informed by an examination of whether the agency provided a reasoned and adequate explanation as to: (i) how the evidence on the record supported its factual findings; and (ii) how those factual findings supported the overall subsidy determination. [footnote omitted] Such explanation should be discernible from the published determination itself. The explanation provided by the investigating authority – with respect to its factual findings as well as its ultimate subsidy determination – should also address alternative explanations that could reasonably be drawn from the evidence, as well as the reasons why the agency chose to discount such alternatives in coming to its conclusions. [footnote omitted]

187. A panel may not reject an agency's conclusions simply because the panel would have arrived at a different outcome if it were making the determination itself. In addition, in the absence of an allegation that the agency failed to investigate sufficiently or to collect certain information [footnote omitted], a panel must limit its examination to the evidence that was before the agency during the course of the investigation, and must take into account all such evidence submitted by the parties to the dispute. In other words, a panel may not conduct a *de novo* review of the evidence or substitute its judgement for that of the investigating authority. A failure to apply the proper standard of review constitutes legal error under Article 11 of the DSU. [footnote omitted]

188. These general principles reflect the fact that a panel examining a subsidy determination should bear in mind its role as *reviewer* of agency action, rather than as *initial trier of fact*. Thus, a panel examining the evidentiary basis for a subsidy determination should, on the basis of the record evidence before the panel, inquire whether the evidence and explanation relied on by the investigating authority reasonably supports its conclusions. In the context of reviewing individual pieces of evidence, for example, a panel should focus on issues such as the accuracy of a piece of evidence, or whether that piece of evidence may reasonably be relied on in support of the particular inference drawn by the investigating authority. As we observed above [footnote omitted], however, the Panel in this case examined whether certain pieces of evidence were sufficient to establish certain conclusions that the USDOC did not seek to draw, at least solely on the basis of those pieces of evidence. Moreover, it failed to examine the evidence in its *totality*. [footnote omitted] The Panel thus failed to assess the agency's determination. Instead, the Panel's examination reflected its own view of whether entrustment or direction existed in this case; the Panel thereby engaged, improperly, in a *de novo* review of the evidence before the agency. [footnote omitted]

Panel Review of an Investigating Authority's Decision Based on the Totality of Evidence

150. In our view, having accepted an investigating authority's approach, a panel normally should examine the probative value of a piece of evidence in a similar manner to that followed by the investigating authority. Moreover, if, as here, an investigating authority relies on individual pieces of circumstantial evidence viewed together as support for a finding of entrustment or direction, a panel reviewing such a determination normally should consider that evidence in its totality, rather than individually, in order to assess its probative value with respect to the agency's determination …

154. … In other words, a piece of evidence that may initially appear to be of little or no probative value, when viewed in isolation, *could*, when placed beside another piece of evidence of the same nature, form part of an overall picture that gives rise to a reasonable inference of entrustment or direction …

157. … In our view, when an investigating authority relies on the totality of circumstantial evidence, this imposes upon a panel the obligation to consider, in the context of the *totality* of the evidence, how the *interaction* of certain pieces of evidence may justify certain inferences that could not have been justified by a review of the individual pieces of evidence in isolation.

Admissibility of Evidence

161. There is no doubt that a Member may not seek to defend its agency's decision on the basis of evidence not contained in the record of the investigation. Indeed, neither participant seeks to argue otherwise …

165. … we find no basis for the Panel's exclusion of the United States evidence in question. That evidence was on the record of the investigation and it was not put before the Panel in support of a new reasoning or rationale. We therefore *find* that the Panel *erred*, … , in declining to consider certain record evidence not cited by the USDOC in its published determination.

Non-record Evidence

175. The United States brings its challenge under Article 11 of the DSU, which requires that a panel 'make an objective assessment of the matter before it'. The Appellate Body has stated previously that, when assessing an investigating authority's determination, a panel may not fault the agency for failing to take into account facts that it could not reasonably

> have known. [footnote omitted] A panel must therefore limit its examination to the facts that the agency should have discerned from the evidence on record. Where a panel reads evidence with the 'benefit of hindsight', it fails to consider how the evidence should have fairly been understood at the time of the investigation, and thereby fails to make an 'objective assessment' in accordance with Article 11 of the DSU. [footnote omitted]

The Panel in *Japan – DRAMs (Korea)* should also be mentioned here:

> In light of the above guidance afforded by the Appellate Body in *US – Countervailing Duty Investigation on DRAMs*, we shall not be requiring JIA's finding of entrustment or direction to have been based on a 'probative and compelling' standard of evidence. Rather, we shall consider whether or not JIA's evidence could support its conclusion.[6]

[6] WT/DS336/R of 13 July 2007, *Japan – Countervailing Duties on Dynamic Random Access Memories from Korea*, para 7.78.

PART XI

FINAL PROVISIONS

Article 31

Provisional Application

Article 31 stipulates that Articles 6.1, 8 and 9 shall apply for a period of five years, beginning with the date of entry into force of the WTO Agreement. The Committee on Subsidies and Countervailing Measures established pursuant to Article 24 was entrusted to determine whether to extend the application of these provisions. No consensus was reached within the Committee. Hence, Articles 6.1, 8 and 9 lapsed by the end of 1999.

In *US – FSC (Arbitration)*, it was held that Articles 8 and 9, although expired, could nevertheless be helpful in understanding the overall architecture of the ASCM with respect to different types of subsidies it sought and seeks to address.[1]

[1] WT/DS108/ARB of 30 August 2002, *United States – Tax Treatment for 'Foreign Sales Corporations' (Arbitration under Articles 22.6 DSU and 4.11 ASCM)*, footnote 56 to para 5.32.

Article 32

Other Final Provisions

Introduction

Article 32 contains transitional and other final provisions. Most of these provisions are self-explanatory. The first paragraph not only clarifies the conditions that specific actions against subsidization must fulfill, but also the relationship between the ASCM and GATT 1994. Paragraph 2 makes it clear that a WTO Member may not enter a reservation against the provisions of the ASCM without the consent of other WTO Members. Paragraphs 3 to 5 contain transitional provisions with regard to laws, countervailing investigations and measures. Paragraph 6 requires Members to notify to the Committee on Subsidies and Countervailing Measures changes in their laws and regulations relevant to the ASCM, as well as changes in the administration of such laws and regulations. Paragraph 7 entrusts the aforementioned Committee to review annually the implementation and operation of the ASCM. Finally, paragraph 8 stipulates that the seven annexes to the ASCM constitute an integral part thereof.

Specific Action against Subsidies Must Be in Conformity with GATT 1994, as Interpreted by the ASCM (Article 32.1)

Introduction

Article 32.1 sets out that no specific action against a subsidy of another WTO Member can be taken except in accordance with the provisions of GATT 1994, as interpreted by the ASCM. The terms 'specific action', 'against' and 'in accordance with the provisions of GATT 1994' are further discussed *infra*. Footnote 56 to Article 32.1 clarifies that this paragraph is not intended to preclude action under the other relevant provisions of GATT 1994, where appropriate. Article 32.1 fulfils a function of limiting the range of actions that a Member may take unilaterally to counter subsidization.[1]

It follows from Article 32.1 in conjunction with Article 10 that countervailing duties may only be imposed in accordance with the provisions of Part V of the ASCM and Article VI of GATT 1994, taken together. If there is a conflict between the provisions of Article VI and those of the ASCM, the provisions of the ASCM would prevail as a result of the interpretative note to Annex 1A of the Marrakesh Agreement establishing the World Trade Organization.[2]

The leading case with regard to the interpretation of Article 32.1 is *US – Offset Act (Byrd Amendment)*. In this case, the Appellate Body followed closely the reasoning that it developed in *US – 1916 Act*, where the parallel provision in the Anti-Dumping Agreement (Article 18.1) was at issue.

In *US – Offset Act (Byrd Amendment)*, the US adopted in 2000 the so-called Continued Dumping and Subsidy Offset Act (also referred to as the Byrd Amendment). This Act, *inter alia*, provided that the US customs authorities shall distribute, on an annual basis, countervailing duties collected to affected domestic producers for qualifying expenditures. An affected producer was defined, *inter alia*, as a US domestic producer that was a petitioner or interested party in support of a petition which resulted finally in a countervailing duty order, and that remained in operation. The term 'qualifying expenses' referred, amongst others, to certain expenditure that was related to the same product that was subject to the countervailing duty order and that was incurred after the issuance of that order.[3] Both the Panel and the Appellate Body found, although for slightly different reasons and as described *infra*, that this Act was in violation of Article 32.1.

The Term 'Specific Action' in Article 32.1

According to the Appellate Body, a 'specific action' against a subsidy is an action taken in response to subsidization, if such measure may be taken

[1] WT/DS217/AB/R and WT/DS234/AB/R of 16 January 2003, *United States – Continued Dumping and Subsidy Offset Act of 2000*, para 252.

[2] WT/DS22/AB/R of 21 February 1997, *Brazil – Measures Affecting Desiccated Coconut*, page 16. The interpretative note is reproduced *supra* in the introductory chapter, p. 27.

[3] The relevant facts are summarized in WT/DS217/AB/R and WT/DS234/AB/R of 16 January 2003, *United States – Continued Dumping and Subsidy Offset Act of 2000*, paras 11–14.

only when the constituent elements of a subsidy are present. In other words, the measure must be inextricably linked to, or have a strong correlation with, the constituent elements of a subsidy. Such a link or correlation may be derived from the text of the measure itself. The constituent elements of a subsidy are set out in the definition of a subsidy found in Article 1 of the ASCM.

The US argued that the Byrd Amendment did not fall under the subsidy definition because the constituent elements of a subsidy did not form part of the essential components of the Act. The Appellate Body rejected this argument. The criterion was not whether the constituent elements of a subsidy were explicitly referred to in the measure at issue, nor whether subsidization triggered the application of the action, nor whether the constituent elements of a subsidy formed part of the essential components of the measure at issue. The test is already met if the constituent elements of a subsidy are implicit in the express conditions for taking such action. Both Panel and Appellate Body found that there was a clear, direct and unavoidable connection between the determination of a subsidy and the payments under the Byrd Amendment.[4]

EC – Commercial Vessels concluded that the EU's Temporary Defence Mechanism for Shipbuilding (TDM) Regulation was a specific action within the meaning of Article 32.1. The Panel applied the standard established by the Appellate Body in *US – 1916 Act* and *US – Offset Act (Byrd Amendment)*. On this basis, the Panel carried out a two-step test. First, it examined whether the TDM Regulation was in fact related to subsidies. Second, it examined the closeness of this relationship, i.e. whether the TDM Regulation was inextricably linked to, or had a strong relation to the constituent elements of the subsidy.[5]

With regard to the first test, the Panel noted that the TDM Regulation was adopted by the Council of the European Union in response to a certain conduct of the Korean government and practices of Korean shipyards. The Panel recognized that the TDM Regulation did not refer explicitly to subsidies given by Korea. Nevertheless, it concluded that the

[4] WT/DS217/AB/R and WT/DS234/AB/R of 16 January 2003, *United States – Continued Dumping and Subsidy Offset Act of 2000*, paras 239–245. Note that in *US – 1916 Act*, the Appellate Body dismissed the US argument, that the 1916 Act targeted predatory pricing, as opposed to dumping, on the grounds that the constituent elements of dumping were built into the civil and criminal liability under the 1916 Act. Action under the 1916 Act could be taken only with respect to a conduct that constituted dumping.

[5] WT/DS301/R of 22 April 2005, *EC – Measures Affecting Trade in Commercial Vessels*, para 7.138.

TDM Regulation was linked to alleged subsidies given by Korea, based on the following considerations:

- The TDM Regulation used a terminology that was intimately linked to the ASCM, i.e. 'adverse effects', 'material injury', 'serious prejudice'. These terms denote the effects of actionable subsidies.
- The relationship of the TDM Regulation with the findings made in an investigation under the EU's Trade Barriers Regulation: in that investigation the European Commission established that subsidies within Article 1 of the ASCM to Korean shipyards had adverse effects on EU shipyards. While this investigation was not formally concluded at the time of the adoption of the TDM Regulation, it had already resulted in a report sent by the Commission to EU Member States. The Panel also noted that the sectorial scope of the TDM Regulation corresponded to that of the Trade Barrier Regulation.
- The relationship between the temporal application of the TDM Regulation, the WTO dispute settlement case *Korea – Commercial Vessels* and the 'effective' implementation (or rather lack thereof) of the Agreed Minutes between the Korean Government and the European Commission dating from June 2000. Indeed, aid under the TDM Regulation could only be granted for the period starting with the request for consultations with Korea under the DSU until the end of such dispute.[6]

The Panel found further confirmation of the aforementioned conclusion in public statements of the European Commission.[7]

With regard to the second test, the Panel concluded that there was a close relationship between the TDM Regulation and the alleged subsidies given by Korea:

- A European shipyard was only eligible for aid where there had been competition from a Korean shipyard offering a lower price. Thus, there was a correlation between the Korean subsidies found in the Trade Barriers investigation and the scope of the TDM Regulation.
- The scope of the TDM Regulation, i.e. the type of ships at issue, corresponded closely to the sectors of the Korean shipbuilding industry that in the Trade Barriers investigation were found to be subsidized and having consequent adverse effects on the European industry.

[6] WT/DS301/R of 22 April 2005, *EC – Measures Affecting Trade in Commercial Vessels*, paras 7.113–7.137.

[7] WT/DS301/R of 22 April 2005, *EC – Measures Affecting Trade in Commercial Vessels*, para 7.136.

- The temporal application of the TDM Regulation was linked to the WTO dispute *Korea – Commercial Vessels*.[8]

See also *Mexico – Beef and Rice*.[9]

The Term 'Against' in Article 32.1

Both Panel and Appellate Body held in *US – Offset Act (Byrd Amendment)* that an action is 'against' a subsidy within the meaning of Article 32.1 if it has an adverse bearing on subsidization. The US argued that the proper interpretation of the term 'against' implied that the action applies directly to the imported good or entity responsible for it. According to the US, the definition of the term 'against' therefore should be one of the following: (1) 'of motion or action in opposition', (2) 'in hostility or active opposition to' and (3) 'in contact with'. The Appellate Body found that the first two definitions could arguably be of some relevance but that the third one could not be used to ascertain the meaning of 'against'. Article 32.1 contains no express requirement that the measure must be against the imported subsidized good, or the entity responsible for that product. Recalling the two other definitions invoked by the US, the Appellate Body believed it was necessary to assess whether the design and structure of a measure is such that the measure is opposed to, has an adverse bearing on or, more specifically, has the effect of dissuading the practice of subsidization, or creates an incentive to terminate such practices. The Byrd Amendment met these conditions. The countervailing duties paid on imported merchandise were used to finance US producers of the like product and thus bolstered their competitive position *vis-à-vis* their overseas competitors. Thus, the Act created an incentive to terminate such practices.[10]

The Appellate Body also clarified that it was neither necessary nor relevant in this context to examine the conditions of competition under which domestic products and subsidized imports compete, and to assess the impact of the measure on the competitive relationship between them. Finally, the Appellate Body took issue with the finding of the Panel that

[8] WT/DS301/R of 22 April 2005, *EC – Measures Affecting Trade in Commercial Vessels*, paras 7.139–7.142.

[9] WT/DS295/R of 6 June 2005, *Mexico – Definitive Anti-Dumping Measures on Beef and Rice / Complaint with Respect to Rice*, paras 7.227–7.229.

[10] WT/DS217/AB/R and WT/DS234/AB/R of 16 January 2003, *United States – Continued Dumping and Subsidy Offset Act of 2000*, paras 246–256.

the Act, *inter alia*, was a measure 'against' a subsidy because it provided a financial incentive for domestic producers to file or support application for the initiation of a CVD proceeding and that such an incentive would likely result in a greater number of applications, initiations and CVD orders. According to the Appellate Body, a measure cannot be 'against' a subsidy because it facilitates or induces the exercise of rights that are WTO-consistent.[11] The Appellate Body also ruled that a finding that a measure is 'against' a subsidy, cannot simply be based on the intent of the legislator.[12]

EC – Commercial Vessels followed closely the test established by the Appellate Body in *US – Offset Act (Byrd Amendment)*. The Panel concluded that the EU's TDM Regulation did not meet the criterion of being against a subsidy. It held that the parameters established by the Appellate Body amount to a high standard. The US measure had the effect that exporters shipping dumped or subsidized products to the US were financing their US competitors, through the transfer of the AD or CVD duties collected on those exports. In contrast, the TDM Regulation only allowed EU Member States to provide support to European shipyards in order to mitigate the competitive impact of a subsidy granted by Korea to its own shipyards. The Panel recognized that there was a linkage between the TDM Regulation, the failed implementation of a bilateral agreement previously agreed between Korea and the EU and a parallel dispute settlement case *Korea – Commercial Vessels*. However, should this type of support granted by EU Member States be considered as being directed against a subsidy, this would be tantamount to a new subsidy discipline under the SCM Agreement. Indeed, such support could be challenged by other WTO Members independently of whether the subsidy was inconsistent with Parts II or III of the SCM Agreement. This would also create an incentive for WTO Members to make the first move, i.e. to give the subsidy before other countries give one. In sum, the fact that a counter-subsidy granted by a WTO Member diminishes or even eliminates the competitive advantages that another Member may be seeking by granting a subsidy is not sufficient to consider such counter-subsidy is directed 'against' the other subsidy. Rather, there must be some additional element, inherent to the design and structure of the measure that serves to dissuade

[11] WT/DS217/AB/R and WT/DS234/AB/R of 16 January 2003, *United States – Continued Dumping and Subsidy Offset Act of 2000*, paras 257 and 258.

[12] WT/DS217/AB/R and WT/DS234/AB/R of 16 January 2003, *United States – Continued Dumping and Subsidy Offset Act of 2000*, para 259.

the practice of subsidization or to encourage its termination, such as the transfer of duties collected from foreign exporters to their US competitors in *US – Offset Act (Byrd Amendment)*.[13]

Action 'in Accordance with the Provisions of GATT 1994, as Interpreted by [the ASCM]'

GATT 1994 and the ASCM provide four responses to a countervailable subsidy:

- definitive countervailing duties
- provisional countervailing duties
- price undertakings
- multilaterally sanctioned countermeasures under the WTO dispute settlement system.[14]

Other actions are not provided for in GATT 1994 and the ASCM. Hence, they would not be in compliance with Article 32.1.

Footnote 56

According to the Appellate Body, footnote 56 is a clarification of the main provision, i.e. Article 32.1, that was added to avoid ambiguity. It confirms what is implicit in Article 32.1, namely that an action that is not 'specific' within the meaning of Article 32.1, but is nevertheless related to dumping or subsidization, is not prohibited by the aforementioned provision.[15]

Transitional Rules (Articles 32.3 and 32.5)

The provisions of paragraphs 3 to 5 of Article 32 contain transitional rules and are essentially self-explanatory. Today, these provisions are relevant in the context of WTO accessions as they define the date from which anti-subsidy laws as well as initiations and investigations of countervailing cases and measures resulting therefrom have to be in conformity with the ASCM.

[13] WT/DS301/R of 22 April 2005, *EC – Measures Affecting Trade in Commercial Vessels*, paras 7.154–7.173.

[14] WT/DS217/AB/R and WT/DS234/AB/R of 16 January 2003, *United States – Continued Dumping and Subsidy Offset Act of 2000*, para 269.

[15] WT/DS217/AB/R and WT/DS234/AB/R of 16 January 2003, *United States – Continued Dumping and Subsidy Offset Act of 2000*, paras 260–262.

According to Article 32.3, countervailing duty investigations which were ongoing or with respect to which an initiation decision was pending (but an application had already been filed) at the date of entry into force of the Marrakesh Agreement are not subject to Article VI of GATT 1994 in conjunction with the ASCM. *Brazil – Desiccated Coconut* is the leading case as to when the applicability of the Tokyo Round Subsidies Code ended and when the ASCM started to be applicable. The term 'this Agreement' in Article 32.3 means the ASCM and Article VI of GATT 1994. This follows from Article 32.3 read in conjunction with Articles 10 and 32.1.[16]

Article 32.3 if read literally would apply only to investigations and reviews initiated pursuant to applications from the domestic industry, but not to those initiated on an *ex officio* basis. The Panel in *US – Carbon Steel* held in an *obiter dictum* that this provision cannot be construed so narrowly.[17]

Article 32.4 ensures that countervailing duty measures to which the Marrakesh Agreement was not immediately applicable will nevertheless be brought under WTO disciplines. This will be achieved via sunset reviews which have to be initiated at the latest five years after the Marrakesh Agreement has entered into force with regard to a WTO Member.[18]

Notification of Any Changes of Laws and Regulations to the Committee on Subsidies and Countervailing Measures (Article 32.6)

Article 32.6 stipulates that each Member shall inform the Committee of any changes in its laws and regulations relevant to the ASCM and in the administration of such laws and regulations.

US – Customs Bond Directive noted that Article 32.6 does not contain any specific deadline in order for any notification to be effective. It held that in the absence of such deadline, the notification must be made within

[16] WT/DS22/AB/R of 21 February 1997, *Brazil – Measures Affecting Desiccated Coconut*, page 17. See also the report of the Panel, WT/DS22/R of 17 October 1996, *Brazil – Measures Affecting Desiccated Coconut*, para 241 *et seq.*

[17] WT/DS213/R of 3 July 2002, *United States – Countervailing Duties on Certain Corrosion-Resistant Carbon Steel Flat Products from Germany*, para 8.29.

[18] See also WT/DS22/R of 17 October 1996, *Brazil – Measures Affecting Desiccated Coconut*, paras 276 and 277.

a reasonable time.[19] The Panel also found that the US Customs Bond Directive had to be notified pursuant to Article 32.6 because, *inter alia*, it constituted specific action against subsidization pursuant to Article 32.1 and it amended the procedure for collecting security from importers who may be liable for countervailing duties.[20]

[19] WT/DS345/R of 29 February 2008, *United States – Customs Bond Directive for Merchandise Subject to Anti-Dumping/Countervailing Duties*, para 7.283.

[20] WT/DS345/R of 29 February 2008, *United States – Customs Bond Directive for Merchandise Subject to Anti-Dumping/Countervailing Duties*, para 7.282.

Annex I

Illustrative List of Export Subsidies

Introduction

Annex I contains mostly examples of government support that constitute export subsidies. As its title indicates, it is purely illustrative, i.e. it does not purport to be an exhaustive list of export subsidies. According to the Panel in *Brazil – Aircraft (1st Article 21.5)*, it is legally possible – and as a matter of fact, highly likely – that there are prohibited export subsidies within the meaning of Article 3.1(a) that do not fall within the scope of Annex I.[1] Annex I is, like all other six annexes, an integral part of the ASCM (see Article 32.8).

Article 3.1(a) as well as footnotes 1 and 5 of the ASCM refer to Annex I.

A measure that falls within the scope of the illustrative list of Annex I is deemed to be a prohibited export subsidy. In other words, it can be established that a measure is a prohibited export subsidy by going directly to the illustrative list, without first demonstrating that a measure falls within the scope of Article 3.1(a). This follows directly from the text of Article 3.1(a) ('subsidies contingent ... upon export performance, including those illustrated in Annex I').[2]

Moreover, Annex I contains a number of so-called affirmative defences, i.e. where the respondent can prove that there is no export subsidy, e.g. the second paragraph of item (k). This provision stipulates in essence that an export credit given in conformity with the OECD Arrangement on Officially Supported Export Credits, shall not be considered an export subsidy

[1] WT/DS46/RW of 9 May 2000, *Brazil – Export Financing Programme for Aircraft (Article 21.5, first recourse)*, para 6.30.

[2] WT/DS46/RW of 9 May 2000, *Brazil – Export Financing Programme for Aircraft (Article 21.5, first recourse)*, para 6.31. Note, however, that in para 6.42 the Panel declared that 'it would be possible to demonstrate that a measure falls within the scope of an item of the Illustrative List and was thus prohibited without being required to demonstrate that Article 3, and thus Article 1, was satisfied'. The implications of the reference to Article 1 are not clear.

prohibited by the ASCM. This example clearly falls under the scope of footnote 5 of the ASCM, which stipulates: 'Measures referred to in Annex I as not constituting export subsidies shall not be prohibited under this [Article 3.1(a)] or any other provision of this Agreement.' However, such subsidies could still be actionable under Articles 5 and 6 as well as being subject to a countervailing duty.[3] There is, however, some doubt whether the aforementioned principle, i.e. that such subsidies remain actionable and countervailable, also applies to the fifth sentence of footnote 59.[4]

In some DSB proceedings, the question arose as to what extent an *a contrario* interpretation in relation to footnote 5 is permissible. In other words, would an export subsidy that simply does not fall under any of the items in Annex I (without being explicitly classified as 'not constituting export subsidies') also benefit from footnote 5, i.e. not being prohibited but at best be actionable or countervailable? For instance, item (j) of Annex I stipulates that there is an export subsidy if the export credit is given 'at premium rates which are inadequate to cover the long-term operating costs and losses of the programmes'. If the *a contrario* argument is accepted, an export credit at a premium rate which is adequate to cover the long-term costs and losses would automatically not constitute an export subsidy. DSB rulings up to now did not accept this *a contrario* argument. The primary role of Annex I is not to provide guidance as to when measures are not prohibited export subsidies, but rather to provide clarity that measures are prohibited export subsidies. It is a list of *per se* violations of Article 3.1(a).[5] The Panel in *Brazil – Aircraft (1st Article 21.5)*

[3] WT/DS108/AB/R of 24 February 2000, *United States – Tax Treatment for 'Foreign Sales Corporations'*, para 93.

[4] See *infra* this chapter, pp. 606–607.

[5] In relation to item (j): WT/DS273/R of 7 March 2005, *Korea – Measures Affecting Trade in Commercial Vessels*, para 7.195 *et seq*. In relation to item (k): WT/DS273/R of 7 March 2005, *Korea – Measures Affecting Trade in Commercial Vessels*, para 7.310 *et seq*.; WT/DS46/RW of 9 May 2000, *Brazil – Export Financing Programme for Aircraft (Article 21.5, first recourse)*, para 6.32 *et passim*; confirmed in WT/DS46/RW/2 of 26 July 2001, *Brazil – Export Financing Programme for Aircraft (Article 21.5, second recourse)*, paras 5.271–5.275. The Appellate Body did not consider it necessary to rule on this issue, see WT/DS46/AB/RW of 21 July 2000, *Brazil – Export Financing Programme for Aircraft (Article 21.5, first recourse)*, paras 79 and 81. The issue was also left open in WT/DS46/AB/R of 2 August 1999, *Brazil – Export Financing Programme for Aircraft*, para 187. In relation to item (e): the US raised unsuccessfully the *a contrario* argument with regard to item (e) in conjunction with footnote 59, see WT/DS108/R of 8 October 1999, *United States – Tax Treatment for 'Foreign Sales Corporations'*, paras 7.113–7.120 and WT/DS108/AB/R of 24 February 2000, *United States – Tax Treatment for 'Foreign Sales Corporations'*, para 93. See also the more general

also pointed out that an *a contrario* reading of the first paragraph of item (k) would have as a consequence that a WTO Member benefited from a safe harbour and could grant a permitted export subsidy whenever it provided an export credit at above its own cost of funds. Such a broad interpretation would place developing countries at a disadvantage to developed country Members because the former generally incur a higher cost of financing because of their higher risk of default. Similar considerations apply with regard to item (j).[6]

The relationship between Annex I, on the one hand, and Articles 3.1(a) and 1.1, on the other, also was at issue in *US – Upland Cotton*. The Panel found that the US operated an export credit guarantee programme that was not respecting item (j). In other words, the premiums charged were not adequate to cover long-term operating costs and losses and hence the export credit guarantee programme constituted a *per se* export subsidy. Brazil requested that the Panel should also find that the US violated the requirements under Articles 3.1(a) and 1.1 not to confer a benefit. Brazil's claim was premised on the assumption that item (j) is a distinct obligation from that contained in Article 3.1(a), read together with Article 1.1. Brazil claimed that because of the different benchmarks that apply under item (j) and Articles 3.1(a) and 1.1 respectively, a measure that no longer constitutes an export subsidy under item (j) may still constitute an export subsidy under Articles 1.1 and 3.1(a). The US rejected this claim arguing that Annex I, and more specifically item (j), does not establish a separate obligation from that of Article 3.1(a). According to the Panel, neither item (j) nor the rest of Annex I imposes obligations *per se*. The Panel exercised judicial economy and the Appellate Body upheld the Panel's ruling.[7] The issue was again touched upon in the arbitration procedure. The arbitrator noted that subsidies consistent with item (j), i.e. that the premium rates of export credit guarantees etc. are adequate to cover the long-term operating costs and losses of the programme, will not necessarily ensure full withdrawal of the prohibited export subsidy pursuant to Article 4.7. The mere fact that the programme is consistent with item (j) does not exclude that it might nevertheless continue to confer a benefit on the basis of the standard set out in Article 14(c), and as a consequence Brazil would be

statement of the Appellate Body in WT/DS108/AB/R of 24 February 2000, *United States – Tax Treatment for 'Foreign Sales Corporations'*, para 93 and *Coppens* (2014) p. 136 *et seq.*

6 WT/DS46/RW of 9 May 2000, *Brazil – Export Financing Programme for Aircraft (Article 21.5, first recourse)*, paras 6.46–6.66.

7 WT/DS267/AB/R of 3 March 2005, *United States – Subsidies on Upland Cotton*, paras 730 and 731.

entitled to apply countermeasures.[8] In relation to export credit guarantees and other programmes falling under item (j), the rejection of an *a contrario* reading means that a guarantee is still considered a subsidy under Articles 1 and 3 of the ASCM if it confers a benefit to an importer, i.e. it is provided at better terms than the market would offer.

Annex I was imported into the ASCM from the Tokyo Round Subsidies Code with only minor differences. This also explains why some of the items listed in Annex I, notably items (a), (b) and (l), do not add anything to the disciplines spelled out in the ASCM or have today hardly any practical relevance.[9]

The remainder of the commentary on Annex I focuses on the jurisprudence rendered in relation to the various items of this Annex.

Provision of Goods or Services (Items (c) and (d))

Item (d) was touched upon in *Canada – Dairy (2nd Article 21.5)*. Both items cover the provision of goods and services not only directly by the government, but also via a third party, that is somehow 'mandated' by the government. The Appellate Body observed that in these provisions, as well as in items (j) and (k) and Article 1.1(a)(iv), some kind of government mandate, direction or control is an element of a subsidy provided through a third party. It did not, however, embark on exploring the contours of such a mandate, neither as such nor in relation to the direction and entrustment provisions in Article 1.1(a)(iv).[10]

Exemption or Remission of Direct Taxes or Social Welfare Charges (Item (e))

Exemption or remission of direct taxes upon export is treated in a markedly different way than indirect taxes and duty drawback. While the

[8] WT/DS267/ARB/1 of 31 August 2009, *United States – Subsidies on Upland Cotton (Arbitration under Article 22.6 DSU and 4.11 ASCM)*, para 4.162.

[9] *Coppens* (2014) pp. 124–125. See also *Luengo* (2007) pp. 150–151. He also points out that item (l), which refers to any other` charge on the public account that constitutes an export subsidy in the sense of Article XVI GATT 1994, does not make sense in the system established by the ASCM. This is *inter alia* because the ASCM and Article XVI regulate export subsidies differently and because the ASCM contains a definition of the term 'subsidy' contrary to its predecessor.

[10] WT/DS103/AB/RW2 and WT/DS113/AB/RW2 of 20 December 2002, *Canada – Measures Affecting the Importation of Milk and the Exportation of Dairy Products (2nd Article 21.5)*, footnote 113 to para 128. See also the preceding panel report, para 5.149 *et seq.*

exemption/remission of indirect taxes and duty drawback does not necessarily constitute an export subsidy (see items (g) to (i) for details), the exemption or remission of direct taxes does. According to item (e), the full or partial exemption, remission or deferral specifically related to exports, of direct taxes or social welfare charges paid or payable by industrial or commercial enterprises constitutes an export subsidy. The underlying logic between this different treatment of, on the one hand, direct taxes and welfare charges and, on the other, indirect taxes and duty drawback, is that the latter are considered to be imposed directly or indirectly on the product while the former are imposed on the producer.[11]

Footnotes 58 and 59 are attached to item (e). Footnote 58 contains a number of definitions of terms used, *inter alia*, in item (e) such as 'direct taxes', 'import charges' or 'indirect taxes'. Footnote 59 essentially contains some mechanisms that are designed to avoid export prices being misused to transfer profits, i.e. are not on an arm's length basis. It also clarifies that item (e) is not intended to limit a WTO Member from taking measures to avoid double taxation.

Item (e) and in particular its footnote 59 were extensively discussed in *US – FSC* and *US – FSC (1st Article 21.5)*. The Panel in *US – FSC* found that the FSC exemptions amounted to an export subsidy falling under item (e) because they constituted a full or partial remission, or deferral of direct taxes paid or payable by industrial or commercial enterprises and that these exemptions were specifically related to exports.[12]

Footnote 59 does not purport to establish an exception to the general definition of a subsidy as contained in Article 1.1.[13] The second sentence of footnote 59 'reaffirms' that in allocating export sales revenues, for tax purposes, between exporting enterprises and controlled foreign buyers, the price for the goods shall be determined according to the arm's length principle.[14] With regard to this second sentence, the US argued in *US – FSC* that it is implicit in the requirement to use the arm's length principle that WTO Members are not obliged to tax foreign-source income, and

[11] *Coppens* (2014) p. 128 *et passim*.

[12] WT/DS108/R of 8 October 1999, *United States – Tax Treatment for 'Foreign Sales Corporations'*, paras 7.109–7.112.

[13] WT/DS108/AB/R of 24 February 2000, *United States – Tax Treatment for 'Foreign Sales Corporations'*, paras 89, 92–94; WT/DS108/AB/RW of 14 January 2002, *United States – Tax Treatment for 'Foreign Sales Corporations' (Article 21.5, first recourse)*, para 131 (in relation to the fifth sentence).

[14] WT/DS108/AB/R of 24 February 2000, *United States – Tax Treatment for 'Foreign Sales Corporations'*, para 98.

also that Members may tax such foreign-source income less than they tax domestic-source income. For the US, it followed from this that it was entitled to operate the particular tax treatment of foreign sales corporations. The Appellate Body agreed for the sake of argument with the US's first premise and added that, even in the absence of footnote 59, WTO Members are not obliged, by WTO rules, to tax any categories of income, whether foreign- or domestic-source. However, according to the Appellate Body, the use of the arm's length principle did not resolve the question at issue. The second sentence of footnote 59 does not address the question as to whether a country is allowed under the ASCM to carve out an export-contingent exemption from the category of foreign-source income that is taxed under its other rules of taxation. The operation of the arm's length principle in the second sentence of footnote 59 is unaffected by the choice a Member makes as to which categories of foreign-source income, if any, it will not tax, or will tax less. Nor does the arm's length principle affect a Member's choice to grant exemptions from the generally applicable rules of taxation of foreign-source income. The logical conclusion of the US argument would have been that there could never be a foregoing of revenue 'otherwise' due (see Article 1.1(a)(1)(ii)) because, in principle, under WTO law generally, no revenues are ever due and no revenue would, in this view, ever be 'foregone'.[15]

With regard to the question whether the fourth sentence of footnote 59 requires a Member to first resort to alternative tax fora before resorting to WTO dispute settlement, see the Panel in *US – FSC*.[16]

The fifth sentence clarifies that item (e) is not intended to limit a Member from taking measures to avoid the double taxation of foreign-source income earned by its enterprises or the enterprises of another Member. Thus, it applies to measures taken by a WTO Member to avoid the double taxation of income earned by a taxpayer of that Member in a foreign State.[17] This sentence of footnote 59 constitutes an exception to the legal regime applicable to export subsidies under Article 3.1(a). The fifth sentence provides explicitly that when a measure is taken to avoid double taxation of foreign-source income, a WTO Member is entitled to adopt it,

[15] WT/DS108/AB/R of 24 February 2000, *United States – Tax Treatment for 'Foreign Sales Corporations'*, paras 89, 98 and 99.

[16] WT/DS108/R of 8 October 1999, *United States – Tax Treatment for 'Foreign Sales Corporations'*, paras 7.12–7.22. There was no need for the Appellate Body to decide this issue.

[17] WT/DS108/AB/RW of 14 January 2002, *United States – Tax Treatment for 'Foreign Sales Corporations' (Article 21.5, first recourse)*, para 137 *et passim*.

notwithstanding that the measure constitutes an export subsidy.[18] As the fifth sentence constitutes an affirmative defence that justifies a prohibited export subsidy, the burden of proving the fulfilment of the conditions of this sentence rests upon the responding party.[19]

The term 'foreign-source income' in the fifth sentence refers to income which is susceptible of being taxed in two States. Otherwise, there would be no justification for permitting an exception to the prohibition of export subsidies. Members enjoy a certain scope of discretion when it comes to the decision if, how and to what extent double taxation should be avoided. Indeed, the Appellate Body conceded that it is no easy matter to determine in every situation when income is susceptible of being taxed in two different States. In this context, the Appellate Body recalled previous statements that Members have the sovereign authority to determine their own rules of taxation, provided they respect WTO obligations. Subject to this proviso, each Member is free to determine the rules it will use to identify the source of income and the fiscal consequences. Therefore, footnote 59 does not oblige WTO Members to adopt any particular legal standard to determine whether income is foreign-source for the purposes of double-taxation-avoidance measures. At the same time, footnote 59 does not give WTO Members an unfettered discretion to avoid double taxation of foreign-source income through the grant of export subsidies. As the fifth sentence is an exception to the prohibition of granting export subsidies, great care must be taken in defining its scope. The term 'foreign-source income' as used in footnote 59 cannot be interpreted by reference solely to the rules of the Member taking the measure to avoid double taxation.[20] On this basis, the Appellate Body concluded:

> The avoidance of double taxation is not an exact science. Indeed, the income exempted from taxation in the State of residence of the taxpayer might not be subject to a corresponding, or any, tax in a 'foreign' State. Yet, this does not necessarily mean that the measure is not taken to avoid double taxation of foreign-source income ... measures falling under footnote

[18] WT/DS108/AB/RW of 14 January 2002, *United States – Tax Treatment for 'Foreign Sales Corporations' (Article 21.5, first recourse)*, para 132. The meaning of this statement made by the Appellate Body is not clear. *Luengo* (2007) p. 152 wonders whether this means that such measure would not even be actionable.

[19] WT/DS108/AB/RW of 14 January 2002, *United States – Tax Treatment for 'Foreign Sales Corporations' (Article 21.5, first recourse)*, para 133.

[20] WT/DS108/AB/RW of 14 January 2002, *United States – Tax Treatment for 'Foreign Sales Corporations' (Article 21.5, first recourse)*, paras 138–140.

> 59 are not required to be perfectly tailored to the actual double income tax burden. (para 146)
>
> However, the fact that measures falling under footnote 59 … may grant a tax exemption even for income that is not taxed in another jurisdiction does not mean that such tax exemptions may be granted, under the fifth sentence of footnote 59, for *any* income. Footnote 59 prescribes that the income benefitting from a double-taxation avoidance measure must be 'foreign-source' and … that means that the income must have links with a 'foreign' State such that it could properly be subjected to tax in that State, as well as in the Member taking the double taxation-avoidance measure. (para 147)
>
> … [W]e do not believe that measures falling under footnote 59 must grant relief from *all* double tax burdens. Rather, Members retain the sovereign authority to determine for themselves whether, and to what extent, they will grant such relief. (para 148)

For more information on the notion of 'foreign-source income' see also paragraphs 145, 154, 156, 165.[21]

The Appellate Body then examined the design, structure and architecture of the contested US measure in order to determine whether it falls within the fifth sentence of footnote 59. It concluded that the contested measure did not fall under this provision. According to the Appellate Body, the measure was a complex instrument. In some situations, it exempted foreign-source income while in other situations, the exemption covered income that was not foreign-source. The measure also covered situations where a combination of both domestic- and foreign-source income was exempt. In fact, some of the allocation rules under the measure systematically resulted in a tax exemption for income that had no link with a 'foreign' State and that could not be regarded as foreign-source under any of the widely accepted principles of taxation. For instance, taxpayers benefitted automatically from tax exemptions if their declared foreign trading gross receipts did not exceed USD 5 million. In other words, the simple sale of merchandise to a buyer outside the US triggered already the tax

[21] WT/DS108/AB/RW of 14 January 2002, *United States – Tax Treatment for 'Foreign Sales Corporations' (Article 21.5, first recourse)*. See also the preceding Panel that did not view footnote 59 as requiring a measure to avoid double taxation entirely, exclusively or precisely. However, according to the Panel, the relationship between the measure and the asserted purpose, i.e. to avoid double taxation, must be reasonably discernible. The fact that a measure may incidentally prevent certain income from being subject to double taxation in a particular set of circumstances would not, in and of itself, be sufficient to bring the measure within the scope of footnote 59. See WT/DS108/RW of 20 August 2001, *United States – Tax Treatment for 'Foreign Sales Corporations' (Article 21.5, first recourse)*, paras 8.94 and 8.95. The question whether the full amount of drawback or only the excess amount can be countervailed if there is no verification system is subject to dispute, see *infra* p. 611 and DS 486.

exemption although that did not mean that the seller undertook activities in a foreign State generating income there. Thus, the US measure, if accepted, would have rendered 'foreign-source' any income derived from exportation, provided it was below the aforementioned threshold.[22]

According to the Appellate Body, there was no order of priority of examination between footnote 59 and the provisions governing the general definition of a subsidy, i.e. Article 1.1, as in the case in question the outcome would always have been the same. In other words, irrespective of whether the examination of the EU's claim under Article 3.1(a) had begun with Article 1.1 or footnote 59, there would always have been a finding of an export subsidy.[23]

Exemption, Remission or Drawback of Indirect Taxes and Import Charges (Items (g), (h) and (i))

An export subsidy exists if a WTO Member exempts or remits indirect taxes (see item (g)) and prior-stage cumulative indirect taxes (see item (h)) in excess of the amounts that would be payable if the product were sold on the domestic market. The same is true with regard to the remission or drawback of import charges in excess of those levied on imported products that are consumed in the production of the exported product (see item (i)).[24] Footnote 58 contains a number of relevant definitions. Note, however, that according to footnote 1 to the ASCM, the exemption of an exported product from duties or taxes borne by the like product when destined for domestic consumption, or the remission of such duties or taxes in amounts not in excess of those which have accrued, shall not be deemed to be a subsidy.

The Panel in *Brazil – Aircraft (1st Article 21.5)* detected in both items (h) and (i) affirmative statements in the sense of footnote 5 of the ASCM.[25]

The concept of 'excessive' remission or drawback of (prior-stage cumulative) indirect taxes or import charges involves a comparison between the

[22] A detailed account of the Appellate Body's description of the system can be found in WT/DS108/AB/RW of 14 January 2002, *United States – Tax Treatment for 'Foreign Sales Corporations' (Article 21.5, first recourse)*, paras 149–186.

[23] WT/DS108/AB/R of 24 February 2000, *United States – Tax Treatment for 'Foreign Sales Corporations'*, para 89.

[24] WT/DS139/R and WT/DS142/R of 11 February 2000, *Canada – Certain Measures Affecting the Automotive Industry*, para 10.169.

[25] WT/DS46/RW of 9 May 2000, *Brazil – Export Financing Programme for Aircraft (Article 21.5, first recourse)*, para 6.36.

indirect taxes, import duties or charged levies on inputs consumed in the production of an exported product, on the one hand, and the amount of remission or drawback granted on the other.[26] The term 'input' is defined in footnote 61 of the ASCM, i.e. inputs physically incorporated, energy, fuels and oil used in the production process and catalysts which are consumed in the course of their use to obtain the exported product.

Note that there is no export subsidy pursuant to item (i) if a firm uses a quantity of home market inputs equal to, and having the same quality and characteristics as the imported inputs as a substitute for them. However, in order to benefit from this possibility the import and the corresponding export operations must both occur within a reasonable period of time, not to exceed two years.

Annexes II and III further clarify items (h) and (i) Annex II deals with the consumption of inputs in the production process while Annex III deals with Substitution Drawback schemes as export subsidies. Both items (h) and (i) refer to Annex II while obviously only item (i) refers to Annex III.

Some developing countries consider the carve-outs from the export subsidies as defined in items (h) and (i) as too restrictive and consequently sought in the Doha Round a renegotiation of certain aspects of these carve-outs. The following issues have been raised in relation to items (h) and (i) as well as Annexes II and III:

- According to Annex II the exporting Member should set up a reasonable verification system so as to ensure that there is no excess remission of prior-stage indirect taxes or import charges levied on inputs that are consumed in the production of the exported product. Annex II also stipulates that the importing Member should effectively apply such a system. Some WTO Members took the view that the conditions as to what constitutes a reasonable verification system and as to what constitutes an effective application of such a system should be relaxed.
- They also argue that the scope of items that qualify as inputs should be enlarged to notably capital goods and consumables, i.e. items that are not physically incorporated in the product subject to investigation. In other words, the scope of footnote 61 should be broadened.
- If there is no reasonable verification system or if it is not effectively applied, the amount of the subsidy should be limited to the excess

[26] WT/DS139/R and WT/DS142/R of 11 February 2000, *Canada – Certain Measures Affecting the Automotive Industry*, para 10.169.

remission (as opposed to the total amount of remitted prior stage indirect input taxes or import charges).

- Moreover, an exporter should be entitled to sell to another party its entitlement for importing duty-free inputs having the same quality and characteristics as the domestic substitute.[27]

Official Export Credit Support (Items (j) and (k))

Item (k) covers export credits while item (j) covers export credit guarantee programmes, export credit insurance programmes, insurance or guarantee programmes against increases in the cost of exported products as well as exchange risk programmes provided by the government or by private financial institutions acting on behalf of the government.

According to *Korea – Commercial Vessels*, only credits provided to a foreign buyer qualify as export credits under the ASCM. Thus, a credit given to a seller of the export transaction is not covered by item (k).[28]

Guarantees and insurances of export credits are also called 'pure cover support' while export credits are also labelled as 'official financing support'. Export credits are a necessary instrument in international trade. Conceptually, official export credit support is useful if and to the extent it addresses market failures. Thus, if private banks or credit insurance companies are for instance not able to cover certain country risks or transactions above a certain value, the government can step in. At the same time, official financing support and pure cover support can have, as the Panel in *Canada – Aircraft (Article 21.5)* has put it, the most immediate and thus greatest potential to distort trade flows.[29] Hence, the need for a carefully crafted balance between an adequate official export credit support and stringent disciplines in this area.

Items (j) and (k) have two particular features. First, an export credit guarantee or insurance programme or any other support falling under item (j) only constitutes an export subsidy if the premium rates are inadequate to cover the long-term costs and losses. In other words, while for

[27] See also the submissions and proposals in TN/RL/W/120 and TN/RL/W/153 Rev. 1 made by India to the Negotiation Group on Rules in the context of the DDA negotiations. See also *supra* the introductory chapter, pp. 25–26.

[28] See *infra* this chapter, pp. 621–622.

[29] WT/DS70/RW of 9 May 2000, *Canada – Measures Affecting the Export of Civilian Aircraft (Article 21.5 – Brazil)*, para 5.137.

a subsidy to exist the benefit-to-the-recipient standard is relevant, item (j) focuses on the cost-to-government standard. Similar rules apply with regard to item (k). For an export credit to fall under item (k) it has *inter alia* to be demonstrated that rates charged by the government are below those which they actually have to pay for the funds so employed (or would have to pay if they borrowed on international capital markets in order to obtain funds of the same maturity and other credit terms and denominated in the same currency as the export credit). With regard to the application of the cost-to-government standard, the difference between items (j) and (k) is that under item (j) the analysis is done on an aggregate overall level, while under item (k) it is also possible to carry out the analysis at the level of the individual transaction.

Second, the safe haven provided for in item (k) for export credits is only available if the export credit practice is in conformity with an international undertaking on official export credits to which at least 12 original Members to the ASCM have subscribed. There is only one such undertaking, i.e. the OECD Arrangement on Officially Supported Export Credits. Thus, the ASCM accepts as a defence against its own disciplines the demonstration that the contested practice complies with the rules set by another organization. This construction has its origin in the fact that work on export credits was undertaken both by a GATT Working Party, on the one hand, and the Berne Union (a group of export credit agencies) and subsequently by the OECD, on the other. When the Tokyo Round Subsidies Code was negotiated, many countries were unwilling to condemn as export subsidies practices they accepted under the OECD Arrangement. Hence, the solution to establish the OECD Arrangement as a safe haven.[30]

Export Credit Guarantees or Insurance (Item (j))

Item (j) classifies as an export subsidy the provision by governments (or special institutions controlled by the government) of export credit guarantee or insurance programmes at premium rates which are inadequate to cover the long-term operating costs and losses of programmes. The provision of insurance and guarantee programmes against increases in the cost of exported products or of exchange risk programmes at such inadequate premium rates constitute also export subsidies.

30 *Hufbauer/Erb* (1984) pp. 68–70 with further references.

Relationship with Other Provisions of the ASCM

The Panel in *US – Upland Cotton (Article 21.5)* held that item (j) does not, in itself, provide that certain measures are prohibited. It merely indicates that certain measures are export contingent under Article 3.1(a).[31] According to *EC – Countervailing Measures on DRAM Chips*, item (j) is relevant in determining whether a prohibited export subsidy existed, but not whether a benefit existed. Item (j) applies a cost-to-government standard rather than a benefit-to-recipient standard, and as such, the test set forth in item (j) is irrelevant in determining whether a benefit in terms of Article 1.1 exists.[32]

These two rulings are an expression of the function of Annex I, i.e. measures that fall under one of the items are deemed export contingent, but they are not necessarily a subsidy. The latter issue is governed by Article 1 of the ASCM.

What Is an Export Credit Guarantee?

The Panel in *Korea – Commercial Vessels* had to examine as to what falls under the term 'export credit guarantee'. According to the Panel, an instrument is an export credit guarantee if it guarantees an export credit. An instrument will guarantee an export credit if it covers default by a borrower in respect of an export credit provided to that borrower. In the case in question Korea had guaranteed advance payments made by buyers of a ship to Korean shipyards against the default of the latter (so-called APRGs). Korea did not argue that the advance payments constitute an export credit but claimed that there is a sufficiently close connection between advance payments made by the buyers of ships to exporters and guarantees of the advance payments given by KEXIM (a Korean public body) for the latter to be treated as export guarantees. The Panel rejected this.[33] It also rejected Korea's claim that the advance payments constitute guarantees against increases in the cost of the exported product.[34] Korea argued that the guarantees given by KEXIM constituted an export guarantee or a guarantee against the increase in the cost of the exported

[31] WT/DS267/RW of 18 December 2007, *United States – Subsidies on Upland Cotton (Article 21.5)*, para 14.51.

[32] WT/DS299/R of 17 June 2005, *European Communities – Countervailing Measures on Dynamic Random Access Memory Chips from Korea*, para 7.191.

[33] WT/DS273/R of 7 March 2005, *Korea – Measures Affecting Trade in Commercial Vessels*, para 7.213 *et seq*.

[34] WT/DS273/R of 7 March 2005, *Korea – Measures Affecting Trade in Commercial Vessels*, paras 7.218–7.220.

product because it claimed that an *a contrario* interpretation of item (j) is permissible. It is recalled that the Panel rejected this interpretation.

Adequacy of Premium Rates to Cover the Long-term Operating Costs and Losses of the Programme

Item (j) establishes a cost-to-government standard, i.e. the government activities listed do not constitute export subsidies by virtue of item (j) if the premium rates are adequate to cover the long-term operating costs and losses of the programme. As the Appellate Body in *Canada – Dairy (1st Article 21.5)* has put it, the measure of value under item (j) is the overall cost to the government.[35]

US – Upland Cotton has shown that the examination of the adequacy of the premium rates is a very complex task. In the original case, the US claimed that the Panel erred when it concluded that the premium rates charged by the US were inadequate to cover long-term costs and losses. According to the US this required some determination as to what the operating costs and losses are. By contrast, Brazil took the view that neither item (j), nor Articles 3.1(a) and 3.2 required the Panel to make specific factual findings on the monetary extent to which premium rates are inadequate to cover the long-term operating costs and losses of the US's export credit programmes.

The Appellate Body sided with Brazil as the various methods put forward by the parties led to the same conclusion, namely, that the premiums for the US export credit guarantee programme were inadequate to cover the programme's long-term operating expenses and losses. Note that the US treated rescheduled debt not as an outstanding claim but rather as a new direct loan. However, this treatment of rescheduled debt was rejected by the Appellate Body for the purposes of determining the adequacy of the premium.[36]

More generally, the Appellate Body agreed with the Panel's view that item (j) does not set forth, or require the use of, any particular methodological approach or accounting philosophy in conducting the examination of the adequacy of the premiums.[37] It does also not require a finding

[35] WT/DS103/AB/RW and WT/DS113/AB/RW of 3 December 2001, *Canada – Measures Affecting the Importation of Milk and the Exportation of Dairy Products (1st Article 21.5)*, para 93.

[36] WT/DS267/AB/R of 3 March 2005, *United States – Subsidies on Upland Cotton*, paras 658–674, in particular paras 666, 670 and 672.

[37] WT/DS267/AB/R of 3 March 2005, *United States – Subsidies on Upland Cotton*, para 665. Confirmed in WT/DS267/AB/RW of 16 May 2008, *United States – Subsidies on Upland Cotton (Article 21.5)*, para 277.

of the precise difference between premiums and long-term operating costs and losses.[38]

The Appellate Body also approved that the Panel carried out a two-step analysis. That is the Panel examined not only the past financial performances of the US's export credit guarantee programmes, i.e. a purely retrospective analysis, but also the structure, design and operation of the programmes.[39] By this second step, the Panel meant to inquire whether the programme, including in terms of premiums charged, was set up in such a way that the total of all premiums would be likely to cover all operating costs and losses under the programme. The Panel found several elements which led it to believe that the programme was not designed to avoid a net cost to the government, in particular,

- there was a fee cap for two out of the three sub programmes;
- premiums were not risk-based (neither with respect to country-risk nor the creditworthiness of the borrower);
- fees were not raised adequately although the US government recognized itself in a report that they might not be reflecting current costs.

The Panel concluded that the premiums charged by the US may have served to offset long-term operating costs and losses to a certain degree, but they were by no means proportionate to covering long-term operating costs and losses.[40]

Other elements of the Panel ruling that are of interest:

- The US requested the Panel to follow a 'cohort'-specific approach, i.e. to look at all loan guarantees for a given fiscal year and to track the performance

[38] WT/DS267/AB/R of 3 March 2005, *United States – Subsidies on Upland Cotton*, para 666. Confirmed in WT/DS267/AB/RW of 16 May 2008, *United States – Subsidies on Upland Cotton (Article 21.5)*, para 277.

[39] WT/DS267/AB/R of 3 March 2005, *United States – Subsidies on Upland Cotton*, para 671. Confirmed in WT/DS267/AB/RW of 16 May 2008, *United States – Subsidies on Upland Cotton (Article 21.5)*, para 278 where the Appellate Body also explained that the examination of the structure, design and operation of the programmes may be relevant in situations where financial data about the past performance is not available. And even if such data is available, such examination may serve as a supplementary means for assessing the adequacy of premiums. In this context, the Panel concluded that the programmes were not designed to avoid a net cost to government and that premiums were not geared toward ensuring adequacy to cover long-term operating costs and losses for the purpose of item (j).

[40] WT/DS267/R of 8 September 2004, *United States – Subsidies on Upland Cotton*, paras 7.805, 7.857–7.869. The US programme provided, however, that sales to certain countries were not eligible. These countries were excluded on a risk-based analysis.

of the credits within each cohort over their lifetime, that is until the credit period has expired or lapsed. According to the US, not until a cohort is closed can one make an assessment as to whether or not that particular cohort represents a cost to the government. At the time when the Panel had to review the US export credit guarantee programme in question, all cohorts provided subsequent to a credit reform were still open. The Panel rejected the US request on the following grounds: (1) There is a duty to examine Brazil's claims within the periods specified under the Agreements. (2) There is no need to use the accounting or regulatory principles of the WTO Member concerned in examining the claim. (3) Item (k) does not contain a requirement to await the closure of any or all export credit guarantee cohorts before making an assessment.[41]

- 'Premium' is the amount to be paid for a contract of insurance.[42] And premiums, rather than any other source of revenue, have to cover the long-term operating costs and losses.[43]
- The Panel understood 'long-term' in item (j) to refer to a period of sufficient duration so as to ensure an objective examination which allows a thorough appraisal of the programme and which avoids attributing overdue significance to any unique or atypical experiences on a given day, month, trimester, half-year, year or other specific time period. In the case in question, the Panel chose a period of ten years (1992–2002). One of the reasons for selecting the start date of 1992 was that it coincided with the entry into force of the US Credit Reform Act which introduced a reformed accounting methodology to measure the performance, *inter alia*, of the export credit guarantee programmes. The Panel also underlined that the item (j) analysis need not be a purely retrospective one but that, as pointed out above and approved by the Appellate Body, the analysis should also take account of the structure, design and operation of the programme.[44]
- The meaning of 'operating costs and losses' is not necessarily to be determined purely by reference to the domestic laws of the WTO Member whose measures are subject to examination. Administrative expenses are part of the operating costs.[45]

[41] WT/DS267/R of 8 September 2004, *United States – Subsidies on Upland Cotton*, paras 7.812–7.816.

[42] WT/DS267/R of 8 September 2004, *United States – Subsidies on Upland Cotton*, para 7.817.

[43] WT/DS267/R of 8 September 2004, *United States – Subsidies on Upland Cotton*, para 7.826.

[44] WT/DS267/R of 8 September 2004, *United States – Subsidies on Upland Cotton*, paras 7.827–7.835.

[45] WT/DS267/R of 8 September 2004, *United States – Subsidies on Upland Cotton*, paras 7.838 and 7.840.

One of the three export credit guarantee programmes, i.e. GSM 102, was again at issue in the Article 21.5 implementation proceedings. This programme applied to guarantees of export credits with credit terms between 90 days and three years. In order to implement the DSB rulings, the US applied a new fee structure. Under the new fee structure, fees were increased (by 46 per cent on average and by 23 per cent on a weighted average basis) and different fees were applicable depending on country risk, repayment term and repayment frequency. Countries were classified into eight risk categories, according to the extent of risk. Credit guarantees for exports to countries in a higher risk category were subject to higher fees, and exports to countries in the highest risk category were not eligible for credit guarantee. However, the 1 per cent statutory fee cap was maintained.[46] As the Article 21.5 dispute concerned a new fee structure, by definition no past performance data existed and only projections of the long-term net cost of the programme to the US government were available.[47]

The Implementation Panel concluded, based on the totality of the evidence submitted by Brazil, that premium rates were also under the revised scheme inadequate to cover the long-term operating costs and losses. The Appellate Body concurred with the Implementation Panel's overall conclusion but differed in the assessment of certain pieces of evidence. The following points are noteworthy:

- The Implementation Panel, like the original Panel, conducted a two-step analysis. It first reviewed evidence of a quantitative nature submitted by the parties. Then, it examined evidence pertaining to elements of the structure, design and operation of the GSM 102 Programme.
- Under the first step, i.e. the quantitative analysis, the Panel *inter alia* examined a comparison submitted by Brazil of the premiums charged under the revised GSM 102 Programme and the Minimum Premium Rates provided in the OECD Arrangement on Officially Supported Export Credits. The Implementation Panel observed that, contrary to item (k), the OECD Minimum Premium Rates did not provide a legally binding benchmark for determining whether a programme constitutes an export subsidy within the scope of item (j). But it considered them relevant from an evidentiary point of view because of the magnitude of the difference between the fees under the OECD Minimum Premium

[46] WT/DS267/AB/RW of 16 May 2008, *United States – Subsidies on Upland Cotton (Article 21.5)*, para 258.

[47] WT/DS267/RW of 18 December 2007, *United States – Subsidies on Upland Cotton (Article 21.5)*, para 14.107.

Rates and those under the GSM 102 Programme. The former were on average 106 per cent above the fees of the GSM 102 Programme. According to the Implementation Panel, the Minimum Premium Rates may provide an 'indication' that GSM 102 fees were set at a level which was insufficient to cover the long-term operating costs and losses. But it also cautioned that it was not suggesting that *any* difference with the OECD Rates could be relied upon as an indication that an export guarantee programme meets the criteria of item (j). The Implementation Panel also noted that the OECD Minimum Premium Rates did not cover exports of agricultural commodities and applied only for government support for credit terms of two years and more. It added that if anything, the Minimum Premium Rates would increase if they extended to agricultural products because agricultural products are perishable and therefore can serve less as a security. The Appellate Body upheld this part of the Implementation Panel's analysis.

- However, the Appellate Body reversed the Panel's assessment of certain pieces of evidence on file. Based on this reversal, the Appellate Body concluded that the quantitative evidence submitted by Brazil and the US supported two plausible and equally probable, but conflicting, conclusions regarding the profitability of the revised GSM 102 Programme: (i) the financial statements of the export credit guarantee agency indicated that the programme is making losses; and (ii) the re-estimates of the Programme's profitability prepared by the US government indicated that the programme was making profits. In other words, the conditions of item (j) were either met or not met. Therefore, the Appellate Body proceeded to review the second step of the Panel's analysis.[48]
- Under the second step, i.e. the analysis of the structure, design and operation of the revised GSM 102 Programme, the Panel noted:
  - the premiums charged were not risk based with regard to the creditworthiness of the borrower in an individual transaction because they did not reflect the risk of default of the foreign obligor;
  - there was still a 1 per cent fee cap and that this was an indication that the premiums charged were not based on the country risk;
  - there was insufficient scaling (namely, the rate of increase) in relation to the country risk and the length of tenor when compared to other US export guarantee programmes; and

[48] WT/DS267/AB/RW of 16 May 2008, *United States – Subsidies on Upland Cotton (Article 21.5)*, paras 264, 302–307.

    - the US export credit guarantee agency had access to funds from the US Treasury and benefited from the full faith and credit of the US government;
    - moreover, the Panel noted Brazil's argument that prudent fiscal management compels commercial banks to take varying borrower risk into account via exposure limits (which the US Programme indeed stipulated) but also through different fees (which the Programme did not).

- On this basis, the Panel concluded that the GSM 102 programme was not designed to cover long-term operating losses and costs. Again the Appellate Body rejected the US arguments against the Panel's analysis for the following reasons:

    - The Panel did not focus on the difference of the fees under the two programmes but on the fact that the fee increases for higher risk countries were much slower under the GSM 102 Programme than under the other programme.
    - The Panel did not say that because of the fee cap, premium rates could not cover long-term operating costs and losses but rather that the fee cap affected the adequacy of the fees in relation to the risks.
    - The Appellate Body rejected the US argument that item (j) does not impose a condition that fees need be risk-based. It pointed out that an export credit guarantee programme exposed to risk of default is more likely to incur costs and losses if its design and structure do not adequately safeguard against such. Therefore, risk is a relevant factor in the assessment of the programme's structure, design and operation under item (j).
    - As far as the access to government funds was concerned, the Appellate Body held that this alone is not a significant factor in order to determine profitability under item (j) but that the Implementation Panel did not seem to have placed much emphasis on this factor.

- In sum, the Appellate Body concluded that the Implementation Panel's finding on the structure, design and operation, in the light of the two possible outcomes with similar probabilities that emerged from the quantitative evidence, provided a sufficient evidentiary basis for the conclusion that it is more likely than not that the revised GSM 102 Programme operates at a loss.[49]

[49] WT/DS267/AB/RW of 16 May 2008, *United States – Subsidies on Upland Cotton (Article 21.5)*, paras 265–267, 308–321.

- Note also the Appellate Body's more general description of the nature of the analysis under item (j): to the extent relevant data is available, an analysis under item (j) will primarily involve a quantitative evaluation of the financial performance of the programme. Such an analysis will focus on the difference, if any, between the revenues derived from the premiums charged under the programme and the long-term operating costs and losses. The analysis may examine both retrospective data relating to the programme's historical performance and projections of its future performance. As described above, evidence concerning the programme's structure, design and operation may also be relevant.[50]

Direct Export Credits (Item (k))

General

The first paragraph of item (k) identifies measures in the field of export credits that are prohibited export subsidies. These measures are that (1) governments offer direct export credits at rates below those the government have to pay or would have to pay for the funds so used or that (2) governments pay all or part of the costs incurred by exporters (or financial institutions) in obtaining the credits. Any of these items only falls under the first paragraph if the export credits are used to secure a material advantage in the field of export credit terms. However, if a measure meets all the requirements of the second paragraph of item (k), i.e. essentially if it is in conformity with the OECD Arrangement, it follows from footnote 5 that it is not prohibited under the ASCM.

Subsidized export credits arguably have the most immediate and thus the greatest potential to distort trade flows. Therefore, according to the Panel in *Canada – Aircraft (Article 21.5)*, an interpretation of item (k) that would create a very broad exemption from the prohibition in respect of export credits would not be consistent with the purpose of item (k). In particular, the broad reading would significantly weaken any actual disciplines on export credits and related practices.[51] The Panel made this statement in the context of interpreting the safe haven rule in the second paragraph of item (k).[52]

[50] WT/DS267/AB/RW of 16 May 2008, *United States – Subsidies on Upland Cotton (Article 21.5)*, para 278.

[51] WT/DS70/RW of 9 May 2000, *Canada – Measures Affecting the Export of Civilian Aircraft (Article 21.5 – Brazil)*, para 5.137.

[52] WT/DS70/R of 14 April 1999, *Canada – Measures Affecting the Export of Civilian Aircraft*, paras 9.220–9.224. In this dispute, Canada admitted to provide prohibited export credits

Note that an *a contrario* argument has not been accepted with regard to item (k). Thus, an export credit that does not fall under paragraph 1 of item (k) e.g. because it is not used to secure a material advantage in the field of export credit terms, is not *per se* permitted under the ASCM. In other words, it does not benefit from footnote 5. For details see *supra* this chapter, pp. 602–603.

A panel or an investigating authority should consider a defence based in item (k) of Annex I before determining whether Article 3.1(a) even applied.[53]

Scope of the First Paragraph of Item (k)

The first paragraph of item (k) refers to two forms of government activity that fall under its scope, i.e.:

- grant of export credits at rates below those which the government actually has to pay for the funds so employed (or would have to pay if they borrowed on international capital markets);
- payment of all or part of the costs incurred by exporters or financial institutions in obtaining credits.

These activities fall under item (k) if they are carried out either by governments or special institutions controlled by governments and if they are used to secure a material advantage in the field of export credit terms. The remainder of the commentary on the first paragraph of item (k) addresses the following key notions:

- What are export credits in the sense of item (k)?
- What is a payment of the costs incurred by exporters or financial institutions in obtaining credits?
- When are these export credits and payments '*used to secure a material advantage in the field of export credit terms*'?

What Are Export Credits in the Sense of Item (k)? The Panel in *Korea – Commercial Vessels* noted that the reference to export credits in the first paragraph of item (k) should necessarily be defined in the same way as the reference to 'official export credits' in the second paragraph thereof.[54]

because it recognized that the terms and conditions of the export credits provided were 'close to commercial'.

[53] WT/DS46/AB/R of 2 August 1999, *Brazil – Export Financing Programme for Aircraft*, para 14.

[54] WT/DS273/R of 7 March 2005, *Korea – Measures Affecting Trade in Commercial Vessels*, para 7.671. By contrast, the Panel in WT/DS70/RW of 9 May 2000, *Canada – Measures*

The Panel then had to decide whether so-called pre-shipment loans given by Korea to her shipyards could be considered as an export credit that could benefit from the safe haven in the second paragraph of item (k). The loans were given in connection with export contracts for the purpose of assisting Korean exporters to finance production. The Panel answered this question in the negative. It held that the notion of an 'export credit' relates to credits provided to a foreign buyer. However, an agreement between a shipyard and a foreign buyer according to which certain money should only be paid upon execution of the contract (delivery of the ship) could not be considered as a loan or credit, to the buyer, since nothing is lent or credited to the foreign buyer in the period leading up to the completion of the contract. The Panel relied in this respect also on material prepared by the OECD and submitted by the parties, *inter alia* the OECD Handbook on Export Credits that states:

> Broadly defined, an export credit is an insurance, guarantee or financing arrangement which enables a foreign buyer of exported goods and/or services to defer payment over a period of time … Export credits may take the form of 'supplier credits' extended by the exporter or of 'buyer credits' where the exporter's bank or other financial institution lends to the buyer (or his bank).[55]

Consequently, a stand-alone pre-export financing to an exporter does not qualify as an export credit under the first paragraph of item (k). There must be a link to a credit (in the sense of a deferral of the payment post delivery) given to a foreign buyer.[56]

What Is a Payment of the Costs Incurred by Exporters or Financial Institutions in Obtaining Credits? In *Brazil – Aircraft (1st Article 21.5)*, Brazil made payments under its PROEX scheme to a lender (i.e. a financial institution) that amounted to interest support. In fact, under Brazil's scheme the borrower negotiated the best interest rate it could obtain in international financial markets, and then benefited from a buy-down of that interest rate of 2.5 percentage points (or 3.8 percentage points at the time of the original Panel Report). The Brazilian aircraft manufacturer

Affecting the Export of Civilian Aircraft (Article 21.5 – Brazil), para 5.80 held that the term 'export credit practices' in the second paragraph of item (k) is broader than the term 'export credits' in the first paragraph of item (k).

55 See quote in WT/DS273/R of 7 March 2005, *Korea – Measures Affecting Trade in Commercial Vessels*, para 7.316.

56 WT/DS273/R of 7 March 2005, *Korea – Measures Affecting Trade in Commercial Vessels*, para 7.315 *et seq.*

Embraer did not itself provide export credit financing and the financial institutions receiving PROEX payments were not necessarily Brazilian financial institutions. The Panel had to determine whether the PROEX interest rate support constituted a 'payment by governments … of the costs incurred by exporters or financial institutions in obtaining credits'. The Panel answered this question in the negative. It first pointed out that the word 'credits' refers to 'export credits'. Second, the costs involved under item (k) are those relating to obtaining export credits, and not costs relating to providing them. While the financial institutions involved in financing PROEX-supported transactions provide export credits, they cannot be seen as obtaining such credit. Note that the PROEX scheme did not fall under the first alternative ('grant by governments … '), as the issue of providing export credits at below the costs of funds of financial institutions did not arise.[57]

'[U]sed to Secure a Material Advantage in the Field of Export Credit Terms' The Panel in *Brazil – Aircraft (1st Article 21.5)* tried to describe the purpose of the material advantage clause in relation to the other conditions of the first paragraph of item (k). According to the Panel, this clause serves an important role by narrowing the range of measures that would otherwise be subject to the *per se* violation of paragraph 1.[58]

The meaning of the term 'used to secure a material advantage in the field of export credit terms' was clarified in *Brazil – Aircraft*, in *Brazil – Aircraft (1st Article 21.5)* and in *Brazil – Aircraft (2nd Article 21.5)*. In short, Brazil argued that export credits are used to secure a material advantage if the export credit terms are better than those provided to competing products, e.g. the competing Canadian Bombardier aircraft. Both the Panel and the Appellate Body disagreed, but for different reasons. The Panel equated this criterion with the notion of benefit. This ruling was overturned by the Appellate Body that held that normally the export credit was used to secure a material advantage if it was not in conformity with the OECD Export

[57] WT/DS46/RW of 9 May 2000, *Brazil – Export Financing Programme for Aircraft (Article 21.5, first recourse)*, paras 6.69–6.73, 6.89. See also WT/DS46/RW/2 of 26 July 2001, *Brazil – Export Financing Programme for Aircraft (Article 21.5, second recourse)*, paras 5.215–5.228. In relation to the first of these two Panel rulings, the Appellate Body stated in the context of examining the *a contrario* argument that these findings were moot and, thus, of no legal effect, see WT/DS46/AB/RW of 21 July 2000, *Brazil – Export Financing Programme for Aircraft (Article 21.5, first recourse)*, paras 78 and 81.

[58] WT/DS46/RW of 9 May 2000, *Brazil – Export Financing Programme for Aircraft (Article 21.5, first recourse)*, paras 6.43 and 6.44.

Credit Arrangement. In the Article 21.5 proceeding, the Appellate Body, however, seemed to have made a step towards a benefit-based approach in case the OECD benchmark was exceptionally not appropriate.

The relevant details are as follows. In the original case, Brazil argued that the proper benchmark for determining whether its export credit subsidies to Embraer are used to secure a material advantage in the field of export credit terms is to compare the export credit terms of transactions supported by its PROEX payments with the export credit terms available to the competing Canadian Bombardier regional aircraft. In other words, an export credit subsidy should not be deemed to be prohibited if it can be demonstrated merely to offset some advantage available to the competing product of another Member. Both the Panel and the Appellate Body dismissed this interpretation, albeit for different reasons.

The Panel equated the term 'material advantage in the field of export credit terms' with the concept of benefit. According to the Panel, an item (k) payment is used to secure a material advantage where the payment has resulted in the availability of export credit on terms which are more favourable than the terms that would otherwise be available in the marketplace to the purchaser with respect to the transaction in question (see paras 7.33 and 7.37 of the Panel report). It also pointed to a number of practical problems that Brazil's interpretation would entail (see para 7.27 of the Panel report). It finally rejected Brazil's claim that its interpretation was warranted because it was necessary to protect the rights of developing country Members (see paras 7.29 to 7.32 of the Panel report).[59]

The Appellate Body overturned this ruling *inter alia* because if the material advantage clause in item (k) is to have any meaning, it must mean something different from benefit in Article 1.1(b). The Appellate Body went on to state that the second paragraph of item (k) provides a useful context for interpreting the material advantage clause of the first paragraph. It also said that in order to determine whether the payment is used to secure such material advantage, it is appropriate to make a comparison between the actual interest rate applicable to a particular export sales transaction after deduction of the government payment (i.e. the net interest rate) and the relevant CIRR. The fact that a particular net interest rate is below the relevant CIRR is a positive indication that the government payment in that case has been used to secure a material advantage in the field of export credit terms. The Appellate Body added that the

[59] WT/DS46/R of 14 April 1999, *Brazil – Export Financing Programme for Aircraft*, para 7.19 *et seq.*

OECD Arrangement is one example providing a specific benchmark to determine that a payment was used to secure a material advantage. As it was for Brazil to establish a *prima facie* case that the export subsidies for its regional Embraer aircraft did not result in net interest rates below the relevant CIRR (Brazil conceded that it had the burden of proving this alleged affirmative defence under item (k)) and as Brazil did not provide any information on the net interest rates paid by purchasers of Embraer aircraft in actual export sales transactions, it rejected Brazil's appeal in this respect.[60]

The Appellate Body further clarified this condition in the subsequent first Article 21.5 proceeding. It recognized that the CIRR is a constructed interest rate for a particular currency, at a particular time, that does not always reflect the state of the credit markets. According to the Appellate Body, where the CIRR does not reflect the rates available in the market place, a WTO Member should be able, in principle, to rely on evidence from the market place itself in order to establish an alternative market benchmark which it might use in one or more transactions. The CIRR is not, necessarily, the sole market benchmark that may be used to determine whether a payment is used to secure a material advantage in the field of export credit terms. However, Brazil was not able to demonstrate that its interest rates under the revised PROEX were at or above the relevant CIRR or an appropriate alternative market benchmark other than the CIRR. Brazil advanced two alternatives that were both rejected. First, it referred to one export financing transaction, at a floating interest rate, for large civil aircraft supported by an export credit guarantee from the Export-Import Bank of the US. In the Appellate Body's view, the evidence relating to a single export credit transaction was not sufficient, on its own, to justify the generalized market benchmark as, *inter alia*, the terms and conditions of export credit transactions in the marketplace vary considerably. The Appellate Body also noted some differences between the revised Brazilian export credit financing and the alternative US transaction proposed as a benchmark. For instance, the US transaction referred to large aircraft while the Brazil supported regional aircraft. Second, Brazil asserted that Canada had provided financing for its regional aircraft at below the relevant CIRR (which Canada admitted at least partially). The

[60] WT/DS46/AB/R of 2 August 1999, *Brazil – Export Financing Programme for Aircraft*, paras 165–187. See also WT/DS222/R of 28 January 2002, *Canada – Export Credits and Loan Guarantees for Regional Aircraft*, para 7.234.

Appellate Body did not consider this as an alternative generalized market benchmark below the CIRR.[61]

The Appellate Body in *Brazil – Aircraft* also noted that the OECD Arrangement allows a government to match, under certain conditions, officially supported export credit terms provided by another government which could result in interest rates below the relevant CIRR. However, it was persuaded that matching in the sense of the OECD Arrangement was not applicable in the case in question, not least because Brazil gave subsidies amounting to 3.8 per cent for all export sales transactions.[62]

Brazil also argued that the notion 'export credit term' included the price at which the product was sold and that Brazil was therefore entitled to offset all the subsidies provided by Canada to Bombardier aircraft, i.e. the product competing with Brazil's Embraer aircraft. Both the Panel and the Appellate Body rejected this claim. Even if the matching provisions of the OECD Arrangement applied in the case in question, they clearly did not allow a comparison to be made between the net interest rates applied as a consequence of subsidies granted by a particular Member and the total amount of subsidies provided by another Member.[63]

In *Brazil – Aircraft (2nd Article 21.5)*, Brazil *inter alia* argued that the CIRR only would be the appropriate benchmark to conclude that no material advantage was sought. The Panel rejected this view. According to the Panel, in order to demonstrate that Brazil's interest rate equalization payments under PROEX are not used to secure a material advantage, Brazil should have established, in addition to respecting the CIRR itself, that it also respected the applicable rules of the OECD Arrangement which relate to the application of the CIRR and which operate to support or reinforce the CIRR as a minimum interest rate.[64]

Last but not least, the Panel in *Brazil – Aircraft (2nd Article 21.5)* also rejected the following arguments made by Canada in relation to the CIRR and the material advantage clause. Canada argued that whenever the

[61] WT/DS46/AB/RW of 21 July 2000, *Brazil – Export Financing Programme for Aircraft (Article 21.5, first recourse)*, paras 59–77.

[62] WT/DS46/AB/R of 2 August 1999, *Brazil – Export Financing Programme for Aircraft*, para 185.

[63] WT/DS46/AB/R of 2 August 1999, *Brazil – Export Financing Programme for Aircraft*, para 185.

[64] WT/DS46/RW/2 of 26 July 2001, *Brazil – Export Financing Programme for Aircraft (Article 21.5, second recourse)*, paras 5.234–5.252. See *infra* this chapter, pp. 630–633.

CIRR was not an adequate proxy for market rates, a benchmark other than the CIRR must be used. Specifically, Canada asserted that the CIRR was not an appropriate benchmark with respect to transactions involving regional aircraft because the CIRR is usually significantly different from the rates available for comparable market transactions involving regional aircraft. Canada also invoked an example where the CIRR was significantly different from the rates available to an airline with the best credit rating. Canada also argued that account should be taken of the creditworthiness of the borrower in question. In the opinion of the Panel, the CIRR is an absolute benchmark, i.e. one that could be used even where the borrower in question could not have obtained a rate at the CIRR level in the commercial market. The Panel accepted that the Brazilian legislation *per se* did not require Brazil to provide interest rate support contrary to the terms of the OECD Arrangement. The analysis applied by the Panel was the same as the one applied when examining whether Brazil could rely on the safe haven clause.[65]

Safe Haven (Second Paragraph of Item (k))

Introduction The second paragraph of item (k) means in essence that an export credit which is in conformity with the interest rate provisions of the OECD Arrangement shall not be considered as an export subsidy prohibited by the ASCM. In other words, such export credit practices would be prohibited export subsidies absent the second paragraph of item (k).[66] Note that item (k) does not explicitly refer to the OECD Arrangement but to an 'international undertaking on official export credits to which at least twelve original Members to the [ASCM] are parties as of 1 January 1979'. But the OECD Arrangement is the only undertaking which meets these conditions (see below).

What matters is that the interest rate provisions of the OECD Arrangement are in practice applied. By contrast, it does not matter whether or not a WTO Member is a party to the OECD Arrangement.

The second paragraph of item (k) is unique in the sense that it creates an exemption from a prohibition in a WTO Agreement while the scope of this exemption is left in the hands of a subgroup of WTO Members. Therefore, it was held that the second paragraph must be interpreted in a

[65] WT/DS46/RW/2 of 26 July 2001, *Brazil – Export Financing Programme for Aircraft (Article 21.5, second recourse)*, paras 5.253–5.268.

[66] WT/DS46/RW/2 of 26 July 2001, *Brazil – Export Financing Programme for Aircraft (Article 21.5, second recourse)*, paras 5.60 and 5.61.

manner that does not allow that subgroup of Members to create for itself *de facto* a more favourable treatment under the ASCM than is available to all other Members. Moreover, the interpretation of this second paragraph needs to provide clarity and certainty concerning what the ASCM rules are and how to comply with them.[67]

Note that the design of the second paragraph of item (k) puts all WTO Members, including those that have not subscribed to the OECD Arrangement, at the same level. Because the existence of a subsidy is based on the existence of a benefit to the recipient, and without regard to whether there is a cost to the government, all Members compete on a level playing field.[68]

Burden of Proof The second paragraph of item (k) makes available an exception. Therefore, it must be possible to invoke it as an affirmative defence to a claim of violation. The burden of establishing an affirmative defence rests with the party raising it.[69]

'[I]nternational Undertaking on Official Export Credits to Which At Least Twelve Original Members to This Agreement Are Parties as of 1 January 1979 (or a Successor Undertaking Which Has Been Adopted by Those Original Members)' The OECD Arrangement is an international undertaking on official export credits. At present, it is the only existing international undertaking qualifying for the safe haven under item (k).[70] The current 'Arrangement on Officially Supported Export Credits' dates from 15 October 2015, carries the document number TAD/PG(2015)7 and can be found on the website of the OECD.

The Arrangement is a 'Gentleman's Agreement' among the participant countries and seeks to foster a level playing field for official support in order to encourage competition among exporters based on quality and price of the goods and services rather than on the most favourable

[67] WT/DS46/AB/R of 2 August 1999, *Brazil – Export Financing Programme for Aircraft*, para 180; WT/DS70/RW of 9 May 2000, *Canada – Measures Affecting the Export of Civilian Aircraft (Article 21.5 – Brazil)*, para 5.78. See also WT/DS46/RW/2 of 26 July 2001, *Brazil – Export Financing Programme for Aircraft (Article 21.5, second recourse)*, paras 5.86–5.87.

[68] WT/DS46/RW of 9 May 2000, *Brazil – Export Financing Programme for Aircraft (Article 21.5, first recourse)*, para 6.60.

[69] WT/DS46/RW/2 of 26 July 2001, *Brazil – Export Financing Programme for Aircraft (Article 21.5, second recourse)*, para 5.63.

[70] WT/DS70/RW of 9 May 2000, *Canada – Measures Affecting the Export of Civilian Aircraft (Article 21.5 – Brazil)*, paras 5.132 and 5.133.

officially supported financial terms and conditions (see Articles 1 and 2 of the current Arrangement). The Arrangement sets out limitations on terms and conditions that may be officially supported including minimum premium benchmarks, minimum down payments to be made at or before the starting point of the credit, maximum repayment terms, minimum fixed interest rates (i.e. the CIRR) etc. (see chapeau of Chapter II of the current Arrangement as well as its Articles 10, 12, 19). Moreover, if one country wants to derogate below the floor terms or if it wants to match the non-conforming export credit terms given by another country, it must first notify the other members (Article 18 and Annex VII). There are also Sector Understandings on export credits for ships, nuclear power plants, civil aircraft and projects concerning renewable energies, climate change mitigations and water.[71]

In *Brazil – Aircraft (2nd Article 21.5)*, the question arose what was meant by the term 'successor undertaking'. Is it the OECD Arrangement that had been adopted at the date of entry into force of the ASCM or is it the most recent version of the OECD Arrangement that has been adopted? The Panel held that it is the latter one.[72]

What Types of Export Credit Practices Benefit from the Safe Haven? The term 'export credit practice' in the second paragraph of item (k) is a broad one which on its face encompasses any practice relating to export credits.[73]

The OECD Arrangement does not apply to exports of military equipment and agricultural commodities (see Article 5). It only covers a limited number of export credit practices and only those contained in the OECD Arrangement potentially qualify as a safe haven.[74] The OECD Arrangement covers financing with repayment terms of two years but not

[71] A description of the Arrangement applicable to the disputes concerning aircraft financing by Canada and Brazil can, for instance, be found in WT/DS70/RW of 9 May 2000, *Canada – Measures Affecting the Export of Civilian Aircraft (Article 21.5 – Brazil)*, para 5.82.

[72] WT/DS46/RW/2 of 26 July 2001, *Brazil – Export Financing Programme for Aircraft (Article 21.5, second recourse)*, paras 5.67–5.91. See also WT/DS70/RW of 9 May 2000, *Canada – Measures Affecting the Export of Civilian Aircraft (Article 21.5 – Brazil)*, footnote 69 to para 5.78 which concluded that the sectorial understandings contained in Annexes to the OECD Arrangement are successor undertakings.

[73] WT/DS46/RW/2 of 26 July 2001, *Brazil – Export Financing Programme for Aircraft (Article 21.5, second recourse)*, para 5.66; WT/DS70/RW of 9 May 2000, *Canada – Measures Affecting the Export of Civilian Aircraft (Article 21.5 – Brazil)*, para 5.80.

[74] WT/DS70/RW of 9 May 2000, *Canada – Measures Affecting the Export of Civilian Aircraft (Article 21.5 – Brazil)*, paras 5.80 and 5.81. As to the term 'export credit practices' in the

more than 12 years and with fixed interest rates. Moreover, it is limited to 'official financing support'. This term is defined as direct credits/financing, refinancing and interest rate support. Only the aforementioned items can be potentially in conformity with the interest rate provisions of the OECD Arrangement.

Brazil – Aircraft (2nd Article 21.5) had to define the term 'interest rate support' as used in the OECD Arrangement. According to the Panel, 'interest rate support' relates broadly to official support for one particular export credit term, namely the interest rate to be applied in connection with export credits. Official interest rate support is distinct from direct credits/financing, refinancing, export credit insurance and guarantees. Therefore, official interest rate support will normally involve government payments to providers of export credits. Finally, for such payments to amount to support, they need to be made with the aim or effect of securing net borrowing rates for the recipients of export credits which are lower than they would have been in the absence of official financing support.[75] The Panel also found that the Brazilian programme constituted 'interest rate support' and was therefore an export credit practice subject to the interest rate provisions of the OECD Arrangement because it involved payments by the government to commercial providers of export credits, and was designed to lower the net interest rates charged by a commercial lender so that these levels were compatible with those prevailing in the international market.[76]

'[I]n Conformity' with the Interest Rate Provisions

What Are the OECD Arrangement's Interest Rates Provisions?

The Arrangement's interest rates provisions, i.e. the provisions with which the export credit must be in conformity in order to benefit from the safe haven, comprise the provisions that specifically address interest rates as such (the so-called 'Commercial Interest Reference Rates', abbreviated 'CIRRs', and certain sector-specific minimum interest rates) as well as the other rules of the Arrangement that operate to support or reinforce

second paragraph of item (k) and 'export credits' in the first paragraph of item (k), see *supra* this chapter, pp. 621–622.

75 WT/DS46/RW/2 of 26 July 2001, *Brazil – Export Financing Programme for Aircraft (Article 21.5, second recourse)*, paras 5.132 and 5.133. See also the definition in Annex XI lit. h of the current Arrangement.

76 WT/DS46/RW/2 of 26 July 2001, *Brazil – Export Financing Programme for Aircraft (Article 21.5, second recourse)*, paras 5.133 and 5.134.

the minimum interest rate rule by limiting the generosity of the terms of official financial support. Therefore, the application of the CIRR (or the relevant sector-specific minimum interest rate) by itself, while a necessary condition for conformity with the interest rates provisions, is not in itself sufficient. The other provisions supporting the minimum interest rate also would need to be fully respected for a transaction to be 'in conformity' with the interest rates provisions.[77]

According to *Canada – Aircraft (Article 21.5)*, the safe haven does not cover export guarantee and insurance, i.e. the so-called pure cover, because in relation to pure cover the OECD Arrangement only contains disciplines for credit risk and the duration of the cover, but no provisions on interest rates.[78]

The OECD Arrangement refers to a number of situations in which certain variations, exceptions and derogations from the Arrangement's terms are possible. The question is whether official financing support provided under those exceptions and derogations could be viewed as being 'in conformity' with the OECD Arrangement's interest rate provisions. In other words, would such financing benefit from the safe haven of the second paragraph of item (k)? The Panel in *Canada – Aircraft (Article 21.5)* noted that the Arrangement, by its terms, drew a distinction between 'permitted exceptions' and 'derogations'. According to the Panel, permitted exceptions were in conformity with the rules of the OECD Arrangement and thus qualify for the safe haven.[79] By contrast, derogations from the OECD Arrangement are not in conformity with the Arrangement and thus do not benefit from the safe haven. Such derogations involve a departure from relevant provisions of the OECD Arrangement in a way which is not foreseen and not permitted and affect the minimum interest rate provisions.[80] These derogations also include the so-called matching provisions.

[77] WT/DS70/RW of 9 May 2000, *Canada – Measures Affecting the Export of Civilian Aircraft (Article 21.5 – Brazil)*, paras 5.82–5.119, 5.128; WT/DS46/RW/2 of 26 July 2001, *Brazil – Export Financing Programme for Aircraft (Article 21.5, second recourse)*, para 5.92 *et seq.* See notably Article 24 (Minimum Premium Rates for Risk) of the OECD Arrangement.

[78] WT/DS70/RW of 9 May 2000, *Canada – Measures Affecting the Export of Civilian Aircraft (Article 21.5 – Brazil)*, para 5.98.

[79] WT/DS46/RW/2 of 26 July 2001, *Brazil – Export Financing Programme for Aircraft (Article 21.5, second recourse)*, see para 5.167 and footnote 110. Articles 13(a) (with the exception of the first repayment instalment after six months) and (b), 14(a), 27(b), 48 and 49 of the Arrangement applicable at the time of the disputes that opposed Brazil and Canada were considered as permitted exceptions.

[80] WT/DS46/RW/2 of 26 July 2001, *Brazil – Export Financing Programme for Aircraft (Article 21.5, second recourse)*, footnote 112. Articles 28, 29 and 47(b) of the Arrangement

According to the Panel, such derogations and the matching thereof are only 'tolerated' by the Arrangement, but are not in conformity with it. To consider such derogations to be in conformity with the ASCM would directly undercut real disciplines on official support for export credits. Matching is a practice whereby a participant to the Arrangement matches an initiating offer by another participant or a non-participant that does not comply with the Arrangement. The Arrangement also contains notification procedures that need to be followed in these situations. At the time of the dispute, the notified information was only shared with Members of the Arrangement.[81]

The issue of whether the interest rate provisions included matching was again raised in *Brazil – Aircraft (2nd Article 21.5)*. The US (which was a third party) argued that the term 'interest rate provisions' in the second paragraph of item (k) should be understood as a shorthand for all of the terms and conditions of the Arrangement. This would have included the matching provisions. The US considered that it would be unfortunate if participants to the OECD Arrangement were dissuaded from using its matching provisions for fear that doing so might be contrary to the provisions of the ASCM. In other words, the US seemed to have argued that participants would somehow be left defenceless in the face of non-conforming practices by others. The Panel rejected this claim by pointing out that practices that were not in conformity with the OECD Arrangement could be countered through the WTO dispute settlement mechanism.[82] Matching was again not found to be part of the relevant OECD Arrangement's interest rate provisions in *Canada – Export Credits and Loan Guarantees*.[83]

Note that subsequent to these disputes, the OECD Arrangement was changed. Matching is now not only 'tolerated', but also in conformity with the Arrangement. Its current Article 18 reads:

> 18. Matching
>
> Taking into account a Participant's international obligations and consistent with the purpose of the Arrangement, a Participant may match,

applicable at the time of the disputes that opposed Brazil and Canada were considered as derogations.

[81] WT/DS70/RW of 9 May 2000, *Canada – Measures Affecting the Export of Civilian Aircraft (Article 21.5 – Brazil)*, paras 5.120–5.127, 5.131, 5.134.

[82] WT/DS46/RW/2 of 26 July 2001, *Brazil – Export Financing Programme for Aircraft (Article 21.5, second recourse)*, paras 5.99 and 5.114–5.117.

[83] WT/DS222/R of 28 January 2002, *Canada – Export Credits and Loan Guarantees for Regional Aircraft*, para 7.158 *et seq*.

> according to the procedures set out in Article 45, financial terms and conditions offered by a Participant or a non-Participant. Financial terms and conditions provided in accordance with this Article are considered to be *in conformity* with the provisions of Chapters I, II and, when applicable, Annexes I, II, III, IV, V and VI. (emphasis added)

In addition, the rules on the provision of information to non-Participants to the Arrangement have been improved (see Article 4). These changes can be considered as a direct response by the Participants to the OECD Arrangement to the above-mentioned rulings in order to extend the safe haven of item (k) also to export credit practices that include 'matching'. When this book went into print, there was no DSB ruling available yet that examined these new provisions of the OECD Arrangement.

An example of a successful safe haven claim can be found in *Brazil – Aircraft (2nd Article 21.5)*.[84]

Minimum Standards for Domestic Law to Ensure Compliance with the OECD Arrangement?

In *Canada – Aircraft (Article 21.5)*, the question was whether the following reference in Canada's Policy Guideline concerning the 'Canada Account' programme was sufficient to be considered as a withdrawal of an export subsidy in the form of export credits: any transaction or class of transactions that 'does not comply with the OECD Arrangement on Guidelines for Officially Supported Export Credits would not be in the national interest'. While this meant that under the governing Canadian legislation such transaction could not be authorized, the Panel held that this did not amount to an effective withdrawal of the export subsidy. The Panel noted that in order to fall under the exemption in the second paragraph of item (k) the following would have to be determined:

- First, the transaction has to be in the form of direct credits/financing, refinancing or interest rate support with repayment terms of at least two years, at fixed interest rates (at the time, the OECD Arrangement only covered this type of support).
- Second, the interest rates would need to at least correspond to the CIRRs or the sector-specific interest rates if applicable.

[84] WT/DS46/RW/2 of 26 July 2001, *Brazil – Export Financing Programme for Aircraft (Article 21.5, second recourse)*, paras 5.137–5.208.

- Third, the other provisions of the OECD Arrangement that operate to reinforce the minimum interest rate rule to the extent they are relevant for the transaction in question, need to be respected. Such other provisions cover for instance maximum repayment, down payments, and treatment of country risk.
- Fourth, the transaction must not involve any derogation or matching of derogations which is possible under the OECD Arrangement.

Thus, according to the Panel, a great deal more detail would have been needed than the above summary statement contained in Canada's Policy Guideline in order that Canada could reasonably ensure that future Canada Account transactions in the regional aircraft sector will qualify for the safe haven of the second paragraph of item (k) and therefore will not be prohibited export subsidies. In short, Canada should have provided an explanation how the Policy Guideline ensured conformity with the OECD Arrangement.[85] The Panel in *Brazil – Aircraft (2nd Article 21.5)* took a different approach. When examining whether Brazil's PROEX III legislation was *per se* in compliance with the interest rate provisions of the OECD Arrangement, it applied the GATT/WTO distinction between mandatory and discretionary legislation. The Panel found that Brazil's programme was not, as such, inconsistent with Article 3.1(a) of the ASCM and was in any event justified under the safe haven of the second paragraph of item (k).[86]

[85] WT/DS70/RW of 9 May 2000, *Canada – Measures Affecting the Export of Civilian Aircraft (Article 21.5 – Brazil)*, paras 5.141–5.148 and para 5.153. Contrary to Brazil's request, the Panel did not, however, make a separate finding concerning the sufficiency of the legal form of the guideline, see paras 5.149–5.152. See also WT/DS46/RW of 9 May 2000, *Brazil – Export Financing Programme for Aircraft (Article 21.5, first recourse)*, footnote 67 to para 6.65, where the Panel stated that also those provisions have to be respected that affect interest rates.

[86] WT/DS46/RW/2 of 26 July 2001, *Brazil – Export Financing Programme for Aircraft (Article 21.5, second recourse)*, paras 5.119–5.126, para 5.137 *et seq.*, notably para 5.188.

Annex II

Guidelines on Consumption of Inputs in the Production Process

Annex III

Guidelines in the Determination of Substitution Drawback Systems as Export Subsidies

Annexes II and III are essentially related to items (h) and (i) of Annex I. They provide 'Guidelines on Consumption of Inputs in the Production Process' and 'Guidelines in the Determination of Substitution Drawback Systems as Export Subsidies'.

So far, there are no rulings under the WTO dispute settlement system in relation to these two annexes.

Annex IV

Calculation of the Total *Ad Valorem* Subsidization (Paragraph 1(a) of Article 6)

Annex IV is linked to Article 6.1. Article 6.1 ceased to apply at the end of 1999 pursuant to Article 31. Hence, Annex IV as well no longer applies since this date.[1]

[1] WT/DS464/AB/R of 7 September 2016, *United States – Anti-Dumping and Countervailing Measures on Large Residential Washers from Korea*, footnote 601 to para 5.270. With regard to the purpose of Annex IV and its function in the system of the relief provided by Article 6, see WT/DS267/R of 8 September 2004, *United States – Subsidies on Upland Cotton*, para 7.1183 *et seq*.

Annex V

Procedures for Developing Information Concerning Serious Prejudice

Introduction

The nine paragraphs of Annex V contain an information-gathering procedure that can be used in WTO disputes where the complaining party alleges that another WTO Member's subsidization has caused serious prejudice to its interests pursuant to Article 7 of the ASCM. By contrast, Annex V is not available for claims under Articles 3 and 4 in respect of prohibited subsidies.[1]

Annex V, together with Articles 4.2 through 4.12, 6.6, 7.2 through 7.10, Articles 24.4, 27.7 and footnote 35 of the ASCM are listed in Appendix 2 of the DSU ('Special or Additional Rules and Procedures Contained in the Covered Agreements').

Annex V sets out a comprehensive scheme designed to collect the kind of information that will need to be relied upon by the parties involved in a serious prejudice dispute. It provides for an early and targeted collection of information that is pertinent to a Member's subsequent presentation of their case to the panel.[2] The Annex V procedure is somewhat of a mirror in WTO law of a common-law type 'discovery' procedure.[3] Annex V contains provisions on the initiation of the procedure, its mandatory nature (including the possibility to draw adverse inferences in case of non-cooperation by the subsidizing Member or a third-country Member in whose market the effects of the subsidy occur), the time line for the information collection and the nomination of a facilitator. Thus, Annex V seeks to ensure that a complaining party is afforded access to information

[1] WT/DS273/R of 7 March 2005, *Korea – Measures Affecting Trade in Commercial Vessels*, para 7.5 (subparas 4–7) has found that the same information that had been obtained for a claim under Part III of the ASCM could also be used for a claim under Part II against prohibited subsidies.

[2] WT/DS353/AB/R of 12 March 2012, *United States – Measures Affecting Trade in Large Civil Aircraft(Second Complaint)*, paras 517, 520.

[3] *Bohanes/Rueda Garcia* (2012/2) p. 441.

critical to its claims, and that such Member is not hampered in the subsequent panel proceeding, in case of a responding party's non-cooperation in an Annex V procedure.[4] Annex V is recognition of the fact that information relevant for a serious prejudice claim may be within the sole control of the subsidizing Member or a third country.[5]

At the same time, Annex V limits the scope for a complainant to abuse an information-gathering procedure or transform it into an open-ended and unduly burdensome fishing expedition. See in this respect paragraph 2, which stipulates that only information can be sought that is necessary for a limited number of purposes, and paragraph 8, that *inter alia* assigns to the facilitator appointed pursuant to paragraph 4 the role of giving advice as to whether or not a request for information was reasonable.[6]

The origin of Annex V can be traced back to a proposal made by the US in the course of the Uruguay Round negotiations with the title 'Proposal for Improvement in Procedures for Dealing with Adverse Effects in the Home Market of the Subsidizing Country and in Third-Country Markets'.[7]

To date, the most extensive discussion on Annex V can be found in *US – Large Civil Aircraft (2nd complaint)*. In this case, no Annex V procedure was carried out despite a request made by the EU. However, the Appellate Body could not resolve all the issues that had arisen in that dispute because of the relationship of this case with an earlier DSB case (DS317) concerning the same product and in which an Annex V procedure was carried out.[8]

The first sentence of paragraph 2, the last two sentences of paragraph 5 as well as paragraph 3 describe what type of information could be developed under the Annex V procedure (amount of subsidies in question, prices of the subsidized product as well as prices of the non-subsidized product, changes in the market shares, rebuttal evidence etc.).

[4] WT/DS353/AB/R of 12 March 2012, *United States – Measures Affecting Trade in Large Civil Aircraft (Second Complaint)*, para 518.

[5] WT/DS353/AB/R of 12 March 2012, *United States – Measures Affecting Trade in Large Civil Aircraft (Second Complaint)*, para 513.

[6] WT/DS353/AB/R of 12 March 2012, *United States – Measures Affecting Trade in Large Civil Aircraft (Second Complaint)*, para 519.

[7] WT/DS353/AB/R of 12 March 2012, *United States – Measures Affecting Trade in Large Civil Aircraft (Second Complaint)*, para 525 *et seq.* and MTN.GNG/NG10/W/40 of 5 October 1990.

[8] WT/DS353/AB/R of 12 March 2012, *United States – Measures Affecting Trade in Large Civil Aircraft (Second Complaint)*, para 534 *et seq.* See also the detailed account given by *Bohanes/Rueda Garcia* (2012/2) of the factual circumstances underlying this case as well as DS317, i.e. the EU's first complaint on Boeing subsidies.

Annex C to the report of the Panel in *EC and certain Member States – Large Civil Aircraft* contains a recent example of the working procedures under Annex V including the treatment of business confidential information as well as the report of the facilitator to the Panel.[9]

Initiation of an Annex V Procedure (Paragraph 2)

The first sentence of paragraph 2 of Annex V stipulates that

> [i]n cases where matters are referred to the DSB under paragraph 4 of Article 7, the DSB shall, upon request, initiate a procedure to obtain such information from the government of the subsidizing Member as necessary to establish the existence and amount of subsidization, the value of total sales of the subsidized firms, as well as the information necessary to analyze the adverse effects caused by the subsidized product.

Paragraph 2 of Annex V is the only direct reference to the initiation of an Annex V procedure. In *US – Large Civil Aircraft (2nd complaint)*, the question arose as to how an Annex V procedure is initiated. The EU submitted that such procedure is initiated, upon request, automatically while the US claimed that such initiation was conditional upon a DSB decision taken by consensus. The Appellate Body sided with the EU. According to the Appellate Body, the first sentence of paragraph 2 of Annex V sets two conditions that must be met: first, there must be a request by a WTO Member for initiation of an Annex V procedure. Second, the relevant matter must be referred to the DSB under Article 7.4, i.e. a Panel to resolve a serious prejudice claim must have been requested and established. The DSB does not have any margin of appreciation in respect of the initiation of an Annex V procedure when establishing a panel.[10] *Bohanes/Rueda Garcia* have pointed out that the Appellate Body ruling does not, however, address the procedure if the request for establishing a Panel did not contain a request for an Annex V procedure but if such request was made only subsequently.[11]

[9] WT/DS316/R of 30 June 2010, *EC and certain Member States – Measures Affecting Trade in Large Civil Aircraft*, pages C-1 – C-20. *Kang* (2006) p. 193 *et seq.* examines Annex V also de *lege ferenda*.

[10] WT/DS353/AB/R of 12 March 2012, *United States – Measures Affecting Trade in Large Civil Aircraft (Second Complaint)*, paras 504–524, 531.

[11] *Bohanes/Rueda Garcia* (2012/2) p. 444.

Information-Gathering from a Third-Country Member (Paragraph 3)

Serious prejudice claims can also cover negative effects of a subsidy in a third country market, as evidenced for instance by Article 6.3(b). Paragraph 3 of Annex V provides for the possibility to use the Annex V procedure also in relation to obtaining information from the third-country Member. This paragraph also underlines that such requests should be administered in such a way as not to impose an unreasonable burden in the third-country Member. See also the commentary to Article 6.6.

Facilitator (Paragraph 4)

In an *obiter dictum, US – Large Civil Aircraft (2nd complaint)* also addressed the process to be followed by the DSB in appointing an Annex V facilitator. It seemed to the Appellate Body that, as the representative of the DSB, the DSB chairman is in principle responsible for discharging the function of facilitating an Annex V procedure until such time as that function is delegated through the DSB's designation of another individual as a facilitator pursuant to paragraph 4 of Annex V.[12] Note that paragraph 4 does not explicitly refer to the Chairman of the DSB but stipulates that '[t]he *DSB* shall designate a representative to serve the function of facilitating the information gathering process' (emphasis added).[13]

Time Lines for the Information-Gathering and Submission of Information Obtained to the Panel (Paragraph 5)

The time lines prescribed by paragraph 5 are rather short, i.e. 60 days. The facilitator will therefore set up a timetable for a round of questions and responses, and then a round of follow-up questions and responses. Note that in *Korea – Commercial Vessels* the parties agreed to modify the procedure to give additional time to translate voluminous documentation into one of the three WTO working languages.[14]

[12] WT/DS353/AB/R of 12 March 2012, *United States – Measures Affecting Trade in Large Civil Aircraft (Second Complaint)*, para 521.

[13] See also *Bohanes/Rueda Garcia* (2012/2) p. 445.

[14] See *Kang* (2006) p. 187.

Paragraph 5 also provides for the transmission of the information obtained to the panel.

Obligation to Cooperate and Adverse Inferences in Case of Non-cooperation (Paragraphs 1, 6–9)

According to *US – Large Civil Aircraft (2nd complaint)*, Annex V and Article 6.6

> prominently and unambiguously require cooperation from all WTO Members that may be involved in a serious prejudice dispute. The first paragraph of Annex V imposes mandatory duties of cooperation on the parties to such dispute, as well as upon all WTO Members whose markets may be relevant to the issues in dispute.[15]

This obligation to cooperate is a cornerstone of the scheme and is given teeth through paragraphs 6 through 9 of Annex V which set out the potential consequences of non-cooperation.[16] In particular the possibility to draw adverse inferences should be mentioned here. Paragraphs 6 through 9 are essentially self-explanatory.

The following rulings with regard to adverse inferences are noteworthy:

- Adverse inferences in relation to a certain market benchmark are only possible if the party claiming the use of adverse inferences has in fact established that the market benchmark exists in reality.[17]
- It is up to the parties to bring to the Panel's attention that material that each party considers relevant for its case. If the Panel conducted its own review of all the material produced in a procedure under Annex V, it would run the risk of making a party's case which it must not do.[18]
- See also *Korea – Commercial Vessels*, paras 7.445–7.451.[19]
- In *EC and certain Member States – Large Civil Aircraft*, the US claimed that the Panel should draw adverse inferences because the EU failed to

[15] WT/DS353/AB/R of 12 March 2012, *United States – Measures Affecting Trade in Large Civil Aircraft (Second Complaint)*, para 514.

[16] WT/DS353/AB/R of 12 March 2012, *United States – Measures Affecting Trade in Large Civil Aircraft (Second Complaint)*, para 517.

[17] WT/DS273/R of 7 March 2005, *Korea – Measures Affecting Trade in Commercial Vessels*, para 7.162.

[18] WT/DS273/R of 7 March 2005, *Korea – Measures Affecting Trade in Commercial Vessels*, para 7.516.

[19] WT/DS273/R of 7 March 2005, *Korea – Measures Affecting Trade in Commercial Vessels*, paras 7.445–7.451.

provide all the information requested on the Mühlenburger Loch project during the Annex V process. The Panel did not agree. It pointed out that the EU had during the course of the panel proceeding submitted additional information and therefore, the Panel was not faced with a situation where a party has failed to supply any part of the information. As a consequence, the Panel did not simply accept, as the US suggested, that the failure to provide the requested information during the Annex V process warranted drawing on adverse inference against the European Union. Rather, it considered it appropriate to address the evidence that has been put before it on the issue of benefit.[20]

- In *EC and certain Member States – Large Civil Aircraft*, in relation to ZAC Aéroconstellation, the EU failed to provide any of the requested information during the Annex V process. Subsequently, in the course of the Panel proceeding, the EU submitted some information while it did not dispute the remaining facts alleged by the US and that were publicly available. Thus, the Panel found that it was not faced with a situation where a party has failed to supply requested information. The Panel pointed out that to the extent reliance on the information alleged by the US may be adverse to the EU, it considered that such reliance, which is not in itself an adverse inference, was entirely justified.[21]
- In the same case, the Spanish PROFIT research programme was found to be specific pursuant to Article 2.1(c) because the EU did not furnish sufficient information neither in the Annex V process nor in response to a question posed by the Panel.[22]

Confidentiality (Footnote 67)

According to footnote 67, the information-gathering process shall take into account the need to protect information which is by nature confidential or which is provided on a confidential basis by any Member involved

[20] WT/DS316/R of 30 June 2010, *EC and certain Member States – Measures Affecting Trade in Large Civil Aircraft*, paras 7.1087, 7.1089. This aspect was not appealed. See also paras 7.1125 *et seq.* and 7.1216.

[21] WT/DS316/R of 30 June 2010, *EC and certain Member States – Measures Affecting Trade in Large Civil Aircraft*, para 7.1184. This aspect was not appealed.

[22] WT/DS316/R of 30 June 2010, *EC and certain Member States – Measures Affecting Trade in Large Civil Aircraft*, paras 7.1578–5.1580. This aspect was not appealed.

in this process. The two types of confidential information mentioned in footnote 67 correspond exactly to those listed in Article 12.4.[23]

Annex V Procedure Does Not Circumscribe a Panel's Fact-Finding Authority in the Related Panel Proceeding (Paragraph 9)

The information-gathering process does not limit a panel's ability to seek additional information it deems essential to a proper resolution to the dispute, and which was not adequately sought or developed during the Annex V process. The last sentence of paragraph 9, however, sets out one exception to this rule:

> [O]rdinarily the panel should not request additional information to complete the record where the information would support a particular party's position and the absence of that information in the record is the result of unreasonable non-cooperation by that party in the information-gathering process.

WTO dispute settlement panels retain a residual authority to draw adverse inferences outside of the circumstances set forth in Annex V.[24]

[23] An example of the working procedures for the treatment of confidential information can be found in Attachment 2 to Annex C of WT/DS316/R of 30 June 2010, *EC and certain Member States – Measures Affecting Trade in Large Civil Aircraft*, pp. C-13 – C-20.

[24] WT/DS273/R of 7 March 2005, *Korea – Measures Affecting Trade in Commercial Vessels*, para 7.162. With regard to adverse inferences outside Annex V, see also WT/DS70/AB/R of 2 August 1999, *Canada – Measures Affecting the Export of Civilian Aircraft*, para 198.

Annex VI

Procedures for On-the-Spot Investigations Pursuant to Paragraph 6 of Article 12

Annex VI is essentially self-explanatory. Reference is also made to the commentary on Article 12.6.

Annex VII

Developing Country Members Referred to in Paragraph 2(a) of Article 27

Issues related to Annex VII are dealt with in the commentary on Article 27.

III

APPENDICES

Appendix 1

Text of the Agreement on Subsidies and Countervailing Measures

Members hereby *agree* as follows:

PART I: GENERAL PROVISIONS

Article 1 Definition of a Subsidy

1.1 For the purpose of this Agreement, a subsidy shall be deemed to exist if:

(a)(1) there is a financial contribution by a government or any public body within the territory of a Member (referred to in this Agreement as 'government'), i.e. where:

(i) a government practice involves a direct transfer of funds (e.g. grants, loans, and equity infusion), potential direct transfers of funds or liabilities (e.g. loan guarantees);
(ii) government revenue that is otherwise due is foregone or not collected (e.g. fiscal incentives such as tax credits)[1];
(iii) a government provides goods or services other than general infrastructure, or purchases goods;
(iv) a government makes payments to a funding mechanism, or entrusts or directs a private body to carry out one or more of the type of functions illustrated in (i) to (iii) above

[1] In accordance with the provisions of Article XVI of GATT 1994 (Note to Article XVI) and the provisions of Annexes I through III of this Agreement, the exemption of an exported product from duties or taxes borne by the like product when destined for domestic consumption, or the remission of such duties or taxes in amounts not in excess of those which have accrued, shall not be deemed to be a subsidy.

which would normally be vested in the government and the practice, in no real sense, differs from practices normally followed by governments;

or

(a)(2) there is any form of income or price support in the sense of Article XVI of GATT 1994;

and

(b) a benefit is thereby conferred.

1.2 A subsidy as defined in paragraph 1 shall be subject to the provisions of Part II or shall be subject to the provisions of Part III or V only if such a subsidy is specific in accordance with the provisions of Article 2.

Article 2 Specificity

2.1 In order to determine whether a subsidy, as defined in paragraph 1 of Article 1, is specific to an enterprise or industry or group of enterprises or industries (referred to in this Agreement as 'certain enterprises') within the jurisdiction of the granting authority, the following principles shall apply:

(a) Where the granting authority, or the legislation pursuant to which the granting authority operates, explicitly limits access to a subsidy to certain enterprises, such subsidy shall be specific.

(b) Where the granting authority, or the legislation pursuant to which the granting authority operates, establishes objective criteria or conditions[2] governing the eligibility for, and the amount of, a subsidy, specificity shall not exist, provided that the eligibility is automatic and that such criteria and conditions are strictly adhered to. The criteria or conditions must be clearly spelled out in law, regulation, or other official document, so as to be capable of verification.

(c) If, notwithstanding any appearance of non-specificity resulting from the application of the principles laid down in subparagraphs (a) and (b), there are reasons to believe that the subsidy may in

[2] Objective criteria or conditions, as used herein, mean criteria or conditions which are neutral, which do not favour certain enterprises over others, and which are economic in nature and horizontal in application, such as number of employees or size of enterprise.

fact be specific, other factors may be considered. Such factors are: use of a subsidy programme by a limited number of certain enterprises, predominant use by certain enterprises, the granting of disproportionately large amounts of subsidy to certain enterprises, and the manner in which discretion has been exercised by the granting authority in the decision to grant a subsidy.[3] In applying this subparagraph, account shall be taken of the extent of diversification of economic activities within the jurisdiction of the granting authority, as well as of the length of time during which the subsidy programme has been in operation.

2.2 A subsidy which is limited to certain enterprises located within a designated geographical region within the jurisdiction of the granting authority shall be specific. It is understood that the setting or change of generally applicable tax rates by all levels of government entitled to do so shall not be deemed to be a specific subsidy for the purposes of this Agreement.

2.3 Any subsidy falling under the provisions of Article 3 shall be deemed to be specific.

2.4 Any determination of specificity under the provisions of this Article shall be clearly substantiated on the basis of positive evidence.

PART II: PROHIBITED SUBSIDIES

Article 3 Prohibition

3.1 Except as provided in the Agreement on Agriculture, the following subsidies, within the meaning of Article 1, shall be prohibited:

(a) subsidies contingent, in law or in fact[4], whether solely or as one of several other conditions, upon export performance, including those illustrated in Annex I[5];

[3] In this regard, in particular, information on the frequency with which applications for a subsidy are refused or approved and the reasons for such decisions shall be considered.

[4] This standard is met when the facts demonstrate that the granting of a subsidy, without having been made legally contingent upon export performance, is in fact tied to actual or anticipated exportation or export earnings. The mere fact that a subsidy is granted to enterprises which export shall not for that reason alone be considered to be an export subsidy within the meaning of this provision.

[5] Measures referred to in Annex I as not constituting export subsidies shall not be prohibited under this or any other provision of this Agreement.

(b) subsidies contingent, whether solely or as one of several other conditions, upon the use of domestic over imported goods.

3.2 A Member shall neither grant nor maintain subsidies referred to in paragraph 1.

Article 4 Remedies

4.1 Whenever a Member has reason to believe that a prohibited subsidy is being granted or maintained by another Member, such Member may request consultations with such other Member.

4.2 A request for consultations under paragraph 1 shall include a statement of available evidence with regard to the existence and nature of the subsidy in question.

4.3 Upon request for consultations under paragraph 1, the Member believed to be granting or maintaining the subsidy in question shall enter into such consultations as quickly as possible. The purpose of the consultations shall be to clarify the facts of the situation and to arrive at a mutually agreed solution.

4.4 If no mutually agreed solution has been reached within 30 days[6] of the request for consultations, any Member party to such consultations may refer the matter to the Dispute Settlement Body ('DSB') for the immediate establishment of a panel, unless the DSB decides by consensus not to establish a panel.

4.5 Upon its establishment, the panel may request the assistance of the Permanent Group of Experts[7] (referred to in this Agreement as the 'PGE') with regard to whether the measure in question is a prohibited subsidy. If so requested, the PGE shall immediately review the evidence with regard to the existence and nature of the measure in question and shall provide an opportunity for the Member applying or maintaining the measure to demonstrate that the measure in question is not a prohibited subsidy. The PGE shall report its conclusions to the panel within a time-limit determined by the panel. The PGE's conclusions on the issue of whether or not the measure in question is a prohibited subsidy shall be accepted by the panel without modification.

[6] Any time-periods mentioned in this Article may be extended by mutual agreement.

[7] As established in Article 24.

4.6 The panel shall submit its final report to the parties to the dispute. The report shall be circulated to all Members within 90 days of the date of the composition and the establishment of the panel's terms of reference.

4.7 If the measure in question is found to be a prohibited subsidy, the panel shall recommend that the subsidizing Member withdraw the subsidy without delay. In this regard, the panel shall specify in its recommendation the time-period within which the measure must be withdrawn.

4.8 Within 30 days of the issuance of the panel's report to all Members, the report shall be adopted by the DSB unless one of the parties to the dispute formally notifies the DSB of its decision to appeal or the DSB decides by consensus not to adopt the report.

4.9 Where a panel report is appealed, the Appellate Body shall issue its decision within 30 days from the date when the party to the dispute formally notifies its intention to appeal. When the Appellate Body considers that it cannot provide its report within 30 days, it shall inform the DSB in writing of the reasons for the delay together with an estimate of the period within which it will submit its report. In no case shall the proceedings exceed 60 days. The appellate report shall be adopted by the DSB and unconditionally accepted by the parties to the dispute unless the DSB decides by consensus not to adopt the appellate report within 20 days following its issuance to the Members.[8]

4.10 In the event the recommendation of the DSB is not followed within the time-period specified by the panel, which shall commence from the date of adoption of the panel's report or the Appellate Body's report, the DSB shall grant authorization to the complaining Member to take appropriate[9] countermeasures, unless the DSB decides by consensus to reject the request.

4.11 In the event a party to the dispute requests arbitration under paragraph 6 of Article 22 of the Dispute Settlement Understanding ('DSU'), the arbitrator shall determine whether the countermeasures are appropriate.[10]

[8] If a meeting of the DSB is not scheduled during this period, such a meeting shall be held for this purpose.

[9] This expression is not meant to allow countermeasures that are disproportionate in light of the fact that the subsidies dealt with under these provisions are prohibited.

[10] This expression is not meant to allow countermeasures that are disproportionate in light of the fact that the subsidies dealt with under these provisions are prohibited.

4.12 For purposes of disputes conducted pursuant to this Article, except for time-periods specifically prescribed in this Article, time-periods applicable under the DSU for the conduct of such disputes shall be half the time prescribed therein.

PART III: ACTIONABLE SUBSIDIES

Article 5 Adverse Effects

No Member should cause, through the use of any subsidy referred to in paragraphs 1 and 2 of Article 1, adverse effects to the interests of other Members, i.e.:

(a) injury to the domestic industry of another Member[11];
(b) nullification or impairment of benefits accruing directly or indirectly to other Members under GATT 1994 in particular the benefits of concessions bound under Article II of GATT 1994[12];
(c) serious prejudice to the interests of another Member.[13]

This Article does not apply to subsidies maintained on agricultural products as provided in Article 13 of the Agreement on Agriculture.

Article 6 Serious Prejudice

6.1 Serious prejudice in the sense of paragraph (c) of Article 5 shall be deemed to exist in the case of:
  (a) the total *ad valorem* subsidization[14] of a product exceeding 5 per cent[15];
  (b) subsidies to cover operating losses sustained by an industry;

[11] The term 'injury to the domestic industry' is used here in the same sense as it is used in Part V.

[12] The term 'nullification or impairment' is used in this Agreement in the same sense as it is used in the relevant provisions of GATT 1994, and the existence of such nullification or impairment shall be established in accordance with the practice of application of these provisions.

[13] The term 'serious prejudice to the interests of another Member' is used in this Agreement in the same sense as it is used in paragraph 1 of Article XVI of GATT 1994, and includes threat of serious prejudice.

[14] The total *ad valorem* subsidization shall be calculated in accordance with the provisions of Annex IV.

[15] Since it is anticipated that civil aircraft will be subject to specific multilateral rules, the threshold in this subparagraph does not apply to civil aircraft.

(c) subsidies to cover operating losses sustained by an enterprise, other than one-time measures which are non-recurrent and cannot be repeated for that enterprise and which are given merely to provide time for the development of long-term solutions and to avoid acute social problems;
(d) direct forgiveness of debt, i.e. forgiveness of government-held debt, and grants to cover debt repayment.[16]

6.2 Notwithstanding the provisions of paragraph 1, serious prejudice shall not be found if the subsidizing Member demonstrates that the subsidy in question has not resulted in any of the effects enumerated in paragraph 3.

6.3 Serious prejudice in the sense of paragraph (c) of Article 5 may arise in any case where one or several of the following apply:
(a) the effect of the subsidy is to displace or impede the imports of a like product of another Member into the market of the subsidizing Member;
(b) the effect of the subsidy is to displace or impede the exports of a like product of another Member from a third country market;
(c) the effect of the subsidy is a significant price undercutting by the subsidized product as compared with the price of a like product of another Member in the same market or significant price suppression, price depression or lost sales in the same market;
(d) the effect of the subsidy is an increase in the world market share of the subsidizing Member in a particular subsidized primary product or commodity[17] as compared to the average share it had during the previous period of three years and this increase follows a consistent trend over a period when subsidies have been granted.

6.4 For the purpose of paragraph 3(b), the displacement or impeding of exports shall include any case in which, subject to the provisions of paragraph 7, it has been demonstrated that there has been a change in relative shares of the market to the disadvantage of the non-subsidized like product (over an appropriately representative period sufficient to demonstrate clear trends in the development of the market for the

[16] Members recognize that where royalty-based financing for a civil aircraft programme is not being fully repaid due to the level of actual sales falling below the level of forecast sales, this does not in itself constitute serious prejudice for the purposes of this subparagraph.

[17] Unless other multilaterally agreed specific rules apply to the trade in the product or commodity in question.

product concerned, which, in normal circumstances, shall be at least one year). 'Change in relative shares of the market' shall include any of the following situations: *(a)* there is an increase in the market share of the subsidized product; *(b)* the market share of the subsidized product remains constant in circumstances in which, in the absence of the subsidy, it would have declined; *(c)* the market share of the subsidized product declines, but at a slower rate than would have been the case in the absence of the subsidy.

6.5 For the purpose of paragraph 3(c), price undercutting shall include any case in which such price undercutting has been demonstrated through a comparison of prices of the subsidized product with prices of a non-subsidized like product supplied to the same market. The comparison shall be made at the same level of trade and at comparable times, due account being taken of any other factor affecting price comparability. However, if such a direct comparison is not possible, the existence of price undercutting may be demonstrated on the basis of export unit values.

6.6 Each Member in the market of which serious prejudice is alleged to have arisen shall, subject to the provisions of paragraph 3 of Annex V, make available to the parties to a dispute arising under Article 7, and to the panel established pursuant to paragraph 4 of Article 7, all relevant information that can be obtained as to the changes in market shares of the parties to the dispute as well as concerning prices of the products involved.

6.7 Displacement or impediment resulting in serious prejudice shall not arise under paragraph 3 where any of the following circumstances exist[18] during the relevant period:

(a) prohibition or restriction on exports of the like product from the complaining Member or on imports from the complaining Member into the third country market concerned;

(b) decision by an importing government operating a monopoly of trade or state trading in the product concerned to shift, for non-commercial reasons, imports from the complaining Member to another country or countries;

(c) natural disasters, strikes, transport disruptions or other *force majeure* substantially affecting production, qualities, quantities

[18] The fact that certain circumstances are referred to in this paragraph does not, in itself, confer upon them any legal status in terms of either GATT 1994 or this Agreement. These circumstances must not be isolated, sporadic or otherwise insignificant.

or prices of the product available for export from the complaining Member;

(d) existence of arrangements limiting exports from the complaining Member;

(e) voluntary decrease in the availability for export of the product concerned from the complaining Member (including, *inter alia*, a situation where firms in the complaining Member have been autonomously reallocating exports of this product to new markets);

(f) failure to conform to standards and other regulatory requirements in the importing country.

6.8 In the absence of circumstances referred to in paragraph 7, the existence of serious prejudice should be determined on the basis of the information submitted to or obtained by the panel, including information submitted in accordance with the provisions of Annex V.

6.9 This Article does not apply to subsidies maintained on agricultural products as provided in Article 13 of the Agreement on Agriculture.

Article 7 Remedies

7.1 Except as provided in Article 13 of the Agreement on Agriculture, whenever a Member has reason to believe that any subsidy referred to in Article 1, granted or maintained by another Member, results in injury to its domestic industry, nullification or impairment or serious prejudice, such Member may request consultations with such other Member.

7.2 A request for consultations under paragraph 1 shall include a statement of available evidence with regard to *(a)* the existence and nature of the subsidy in question, and *(b)* the injury caused to the domestic industry, or the nullification or impairment, or serious prejudice[19] caused to the interests of the Member requesting consultations.

7.3 Upon request for consultations under paragraph 1, the Member believed to be granting or maintaining the subsidy practice in question shall enter into such consultations as quickly as possible. The

[19] In the event that the request relates to a subsidy deemed to result in serious prejudice in terms of paragraph 1 of Article 6, the available evidence of serious prejudice may be limited to the available evidence as to whether the conditions of paragraph 1 of Article 6 have been met or not.

purpose of the consultations shall be to clarify the facts of the situation and to arrive at a mutually agreed solution.

7.4 If consultations do not result in a mutually agreed solution within 60 days[20], any Member party to such consultations may refer the matter to the DSB for the establishment of a panel, unless the DSB decides by consensus not to establish a panel. The composition of the panel and its terms of reference shall be established within 15 days from the date when it is established.

7.5 The panel shall review the matter and shall submit its final report to the parties to the dispute. The report shall be circulated to all Members within 120 days of the date of the composition and establishment of the panel's terms of reference.

7.6 Within 30 days of the issuance of the panel's report to all Members, the report shall be adopted by the DSB[21] unless one of the parties to the dispute formally notifies the DSB of its decision to appeal or the DSB decides by consensus not to adopt the report.

7.7 Where a panel report is appealed, the Appellate Body shall issue its decision within 60 days from the date when the party to the dispute formally notifies its intention to appeal. When the Appellate Body considers that it cannot provide its report within 60 days, it shall inform the DSB in writing of the reasons for the delay together with an estimate of the period within which it will submit its report. In no case shall the proceedings exceed 90 days. The appellate report shall be adopted by the DSB and unconditionally accepted by the parties to the dispute unless the DSB decides by consensus not to adopt the appellate report within 20 days following its issuance to the Members.[22]

7.8 Where a panel report or an Appellate Body report is adopted in which it is determined that any subsidy has resulted in adverse effects to the interests of another Member within the meaning of Article 5, the Member granting or maintaining such subsidy shall take appropriate steps to remove the adverse effects or shall withdraw the subsidy.

7.9 In the event the Member has not taken appropriate steps to remove the adverse effects of the subsidy or withdraw the subsidy within six

[20] Any time-periods mentioned in this Article may be extended by mutual agreement.

[21] If a meeting of the DSB is not scheduled during this period, such a meeting shall be held for this purpose.

[22] If a meeting of the DSB is not scheduled during this period, such a meeting shall be held for this purpose.

months from the date when the DSB adopts the panel report or the Appellate Body report, and in the absence of agreement on compensation, the DSB shall grant authorization to the complaining Member to take countermeasures, commensurate with the degree and nature of the adverse effects determined to exist, unless the DSB decides by consensus to reject the request.

7.10 In the event that a party to the dispute requests arbitration under paragraph 6 of Article 22 of the DSU, the arbitrator shall determine whether the countermeasures are commensurate with the degree and nature of the adverse effects determined to exist.

PART IV: NON-ACTIONABLE SUBSIDIES

Article 8 Identification of Non-Actionable Subsidies

8.1 The following subsidies shall be considered as non-actionable[23]:
- (a) subsidies which are not specific within the meaning of Article 2;
- (b) subsidies which are specific within the meaning of Article 2 but which meet all of the conditions provided for in paragraphs 2(a), 2(b) or 2(c) below.

8.2 Notwithstanding the provisions of Parts III and V, the following subsidies shall be non-actionable:
- (a) assistance for research activities conducted by firms or by higher education or research establishments on a contract basis with firms if:[24,25,26]

[23] It is recognized that government assistance for various purposes is widely provided by Members and that the mere fact that such assistance may not qualify for non-actionable treatment under the provisions of this Article does not in itself restrict the ability of Members to provide such assistance.

[24] Since it is anticipated that civil aircraft will be subject to specific multilateral rules, the provisions of this subparagraph do not apply to that product.

[25] Not later than 18 months after the date of entry into force of the WTO Agreement, the Committee on Subsidies and Countervailing Measures provided for in Article 24 (referred to in this Agreement as 'the Committee') shall review the operation of the provisions of subparagraph 2(a) with a view to making all necessary modifications to improve the operation of these provisions. In its consideration of possible modifications, the Committee shall carefully review the definitions of the categories set forth in this subparagraph in the light of the experience of Members in the operation of research programmes and the work in other relevant international institutions.

[26] The provisions of this Agreement do not apply to fundamental research activities independently conducted by higher education or research establishments. The term 'fundamental

the assistance covers[27] not more than 75 per cent of the costs of industrial research[28] or 50 per cent of the costs of pre-competitive development activity[29,30]; and provided that such assistance is limited exclusively to:

(i) costs of personnel (researchers, technicians and other supporting staff employed exclusively in the research activity);
(ii) costs of instruments, equipment, land and buildings used exclusively and permanently (except when disposed of on a commercial basis) for the research activity;
(iii) costs of consultancy and equivalent services used exclusively for the research activity, including bought-in research, technical knowledge, patents, etc.;
(iv) additional overhead costs incurred directly as a result of the research activity;
(v) other running costs (such as those of materials, supplies and the like), incurred directly as a result of the research activity.

research' means an enlargement of general scientific and technical knowledge not linked to industrial or commercial objectives.

[27] The allowable levels of non-actionable assistance referred to in this subparagraph shall be established by reference to the total eligible costs incurred over the duration of an individual project.

[28] The term 'industrial research' means planned search or critical investigation aimed at discovery of new knowledge, with the objective that such knowledge may be useful in developing new products, processes or services, or in bringing about a significant improvement to existing products, processes or services.

[29] The term 'pre-competitive development activity' means the translation of industrial research findings into a plan, blueprint or design for new, modified or improved products, processes or services whether intended for sale or use, including the creation of a first prototype which would not be capable of commercial use. It may further include the conceptual formulation and design of products, processes or services alternatives and initial demonstration or pilot projects, provided that these same projects cannot be converted or used for industrial application or commercial exploitation. It does not include routine or periodic alterations to existing products, production lines, manufacturing processes, services, and other on-going operations even though those alterations may represent improvements.

[30] In the case of programmes which span industrial research and pre-competitive development activity, the allowable level of non-actionable assistance shall not exceed the simple average of the allowable levels of non-actionable assistance applicable to the above two categories, calculated on the basis of all eligible costs as set forth in items (i) to (v) of this subparagraph.

(b) assistance to disadvantaged regions within the territory of a Member given pursuant to a general framework of regional development[31] and non-specific (within the meaning of Article 2) within eligible regions provided that:

(i) each disadvantaged region must be a clearly designated contiguous geographical area with a definable economic and administrative identity;
(ii) the region is considered as disadvantaged on the basis of neutral and objective criteria[32], indicating that the region's difficulties arise out of more than temporary circumstances; such criteria must be clearly spelled out in law, regulation, or other official document, so as to be capable of verification;
(iii) the criteria shall include a measurement of economic development which shall be based on at least one of the following factors:
- one of either income per capita or household income per capita, or GDP per capita, which must not be above 85 per cent of the average for the territory concerned;
- unemployment rate, which must be at least 110 per cent of the average for the territory concerned;

as measured over a three-year period; such measurement, however, may be a composite one and may include other factors.

(c) assistance to promote adaptation of existing facilities[33] to new environmental requirements imposed by law and/or regulations which result in greater constraints and financial burden on firms, provided that the assistance:

[31] A 'general framework of regional development' means that regional subsidy programmes are part of an internally consistent and generally applicable regional development policy and that regional development subsidies are not granted in isolated geographical points having no, or virtually no, influence on the development of a region.

[32] 'Neutral and objective criteria' means criteria which do not favour certain regions beyond what is appropriate for the elimination or reduction of regional disparities within the framework of the regional development policy. In this regard, regional subsidy programmes shall include ceilings on the amount of assistance which can be granted to each subsidized project. Such ceilings must be differentiated according to the different levels of development of assisted regions and must be expressed in terms of investment costs or cost of job creation. Within such ceilings, the distribution of assistance shall be sufficiently broad and even to avoid the predominant use of a subsidy by, or the granting of disproportionately large amounts of subsidy to, certain enterprises as provided for in Article 2.

[33] The term 'existing facilities' means facilities which have been in operation for at least two years at the time when new environmental requirements are imposed.

(i) is a one-time non-recurring measure; and
(ii) is limited to 20 per cent of the cost of adaptation; and
(iii) does not cover the cost of replacing and operating the assisted investment, which must be fully borne by firms; and
(iv) is directly linked to and proportionate to a firm's planned reduction of nuisances and pollution, and does not cover any manufacturing cost savings which may be achieved; and
(v) is available to all firms which can adopt the new equipment and/or production processes.

8.3 A subsidy programme for which the provisions of paragraph 2 are invoked shall be notified in advance of its implementation to the Committee in accordance with the provisions of Part VII. Any such notification shall be sufficiently precise to enable other Members to evaluate the consistency of the programme with the conditions and criteria provided for in the relevant provisions of paragraph 2. Members shall also provide the Committee with yearly updates of such notifications, in particular by supplying information on global expenditure for each programme, and on any modification of the programme. Other Members shall have the right to request information about individual cases of subsidization under a notified programme.[34]

8.4 Upon request of a Member, the Secretariat shall review a notification made pursuant to paragraph 3 and, where necessary, may require additional information from the subsidizing Member concerning the notified programme under review. The Secretariat shall report its findings to the Committee. The Committee shall, upon request, promptly review the findings of the Secretariat (or, if a review by the Secretariat has not been requested, the notification itself), with a view to determining whether the conditions and criteria laid down in paragraph 2 have not been met. The procedure provided for in this paragraph shall be completed at the latest at the first regular meeting of the Committee following the notification of a subsidy programme, provided that at least two months have elapsed between such notification and the regular meeting of the Committee. The review procedure described in this paragraph shall also apply, upon request, to substantial modifications of a programme notified in the yearly updates referred to in paragraph 3.

[34] It is recognized that nothing in this notification provision requires the provision of confidential information, including confidential business information.

8.5 Upon the request of a Member, the determination by the Committee referred to in paragraph 4, or a failure by the Committee to make such a determination, as well as the violation, in individual cases, of the conditions set out in a notified programme, shall be submitted to binding arbitration. The arbitration body shall present its conclusions to the Members within 120 days from the date when the matter was referred to the arbitration body. Except as otherwise provided in this paragraph, the DSU shall apply to arbitrations conducted under this paragraph.

Article 9 Consultations and Authorized Remedies

9.1 If, in the course of implementation of a programme referred to in paragraph 2 of Article 8, notwithstanding the fact that the programme is consistent with the criteria laid down in that paragraph, a Member has reasons to believe that this programme has resulted in serious adverse effects to the domestic industry of that Member, such as to cause damage which would be difficult to repair, such Member may request consultations with the Member granting or maintaining the subsidy.

9.2 Upon request for consultations under paragraph 1, the Member granting or maintaining the subsidy programme in question shall enter into such consultations as quickly as possible. The purpose of the consultations shall be to clarify the facts of the situation and to arrive at a mutually acceptable solution.

9.3 If no mutually acceptable solution has been reached in consultations under paragraph 2 within 60 days of the request for such consultations, the requesting Member may refer the matter to the Committee.

9.4 Where a matter is referred to the Committee, the Committee shall immediately review the facts involved and the evidence of the effects referred to in paragraph 1. If the Committee determines that such effects exist, it may recommend to the subsidizing Member to modify this programme in such a way as to remove these effects. The Committee shall present its conclusions within 120 days from the date when the matter is referred to it under paragraph 3. In the event the recommendation is not followed within six months, the Committee shall authorize the requesting Member to take appropriate countermeasures commensurate with the nature and degree of the effects determined to exist.

PART V: COUNTERVAILING MEASURES

Article 10 Application of Article VI of GATT 1994[35]

Members shall take all necessary steps to ensure that the imposition of a countervailing duty[36] on any product of the territory of any Member imported into the territory of another Member is in accordance with the provisions of Article VI of GATT 1994 and the terms of this Agreement. Countervailing duties may only be imposed pursuant to investigations initiated[37] and conducted in accordance with the provisions of this Agreement and the Agreement on Agriculture.

Article 11 Initiation and Subsequent Investigation

11.1 Except as provided in paragraph 6, an investigation to determine the existence, degree and effect of any alleged subsidy shall be initiated upon a written application by or on behalf of the domestic industry.

11.2 An application under paragraph 1 shall include sufficient evidence of the existence of *(a)* a subsidy and, if possible, its amount, *(b)* injury within the meaning of Article VI of GATT 1994 as interpreted by this Agreement, and *(c)* a causal link between the subsidized imports and the alleged injury. Simple assertion, unsubstantiated by relevant evidence, cannot be considered sufficient to meet the requirements of this paragraph. The application shall contain such information as is reasonably available to the applicant on the following:

[35] The provisions of Part II or III may be invoked in parallel with the provisions of Part V; however, with regard to the effects of a particular subsidy in the domestic market of the importing Member, only one form of relief (either a countervailing duty, if the requirements of Part V are met, or a countermeasure under Articles 4 or 7) shall be available. The provisions of Parts III and V shall not be invoked regarding measures considered non-actionable in accordance with the provisions of Part IV. However, measures referred to in paragraph 1(a) of Article 8 may be investigated in order to determine whether or not they are specific within the meaning of Article 2. In addition, in the case of a subsidy referred to in paragraph 2 of Article 8 conferred pursuant to a programme which has not been notified in accordance with paragraph 3 of Article 8, the provisions of Part III or V may be invoked, but such subsidy shall be treated as non-actionable if it is found to conform to the standards set forth in paragraph 2 of Article 8.

[36] The term 'countervailing duty' shall be understood to mean a special duty levied for the purpose of offsetting any subsidy bestowed directly or indirectly upon the manufacture, production or export of any merchandise, as provided for in paragraph 3 of Article VI of GATT 1994.

[37] The term 'initiated' as used hereinafter means procedural action by which a Member formally commences an investigation as provided in Article 11.

(i) the identity of the applicant and a description of the volume and value of the domestic production of the like product by the applicant. Where a written application is made on behalf of the domestic industry, the application shall identify the industry on behalf of which the application is made by a list of all known domestic producers of the like product (or associations of domestic producers of the like product) and, to the extent possible, a description of the volume and value of domestic production of the like product accounted for by such producers;

(ii) a complete description of the allegedly subsidized product, the names of the country or countries of origin or export in question, the identity of each known exporter or foreign producer and a list of known persons importing the product in question;

(iii) evidence with regard to the existence, amount and nature of the subsidy in question;

(iv) evidence that alleged injury to a domestic industry is caused by subsidized imports through the effects of the subsidies; this evidence includes information on the evolution of the volume of the allegedly subsidized imports, the effect of these imports on prices of the like product in the domestic market and the consequent impact of the imports on the domestic industry, as demonstrated by relevant factors and indices having a bearing on the state of the domestic industry, such as those listed in paragraphs 2 and 4 of Article 15.

11.3 The authorities shall review the accuracy and adequacy of the evidence provided in the application to determine whether the evidence is sufficient to justify the initiation of an investigation.

11.4 An investigation shall not be initiated pursuant to paragraph 1 unless the authorities have determined, on the basis of an examination of the degree of support for, or opposition to, the application expressed[38] by domestic producers of the like product, that the application has been made by or on behalf of the domestic industry.[39] The application shall be considered to have been made 'by

[38] In the case of fragmented industries involving an exceptionally large number of producers, authorities may determine support and opposition by using statistically valid sampling techniques.

[39] Members are aware that in the territory of certain Members employees of domestic producers of the like product or representatives of those employees may make or support an application for an investigation under paragraph 1.

or on behalf of the domestic industry' if it is supported by those domestic producers whose collective output constitutes more than 50 per cent of the total production of the like product produced by that portion of the domestic industry expressing either support for or opposition to the application. However, no investigation shall be initiated when domestic producers expressly supporting the application account for less than 25 per cent of total production of the like product produced by the domestic industry.

11.5 The authorities shall avoid, unless a decision has been made to initiate an investigation, any publicizing of the application for the initiation of an investigation.

11.6 If, in special circumstances, the authorities concerned decide to initiate an investigation without having received a written application by or on behalf of a domestic industry for the initiation of such investigation, they shall proceed only if they have sufficient evidence of the existence of a subsidy, injury and causal link, as described in paragraph 2, to justify the initiation of an investigation.

11.7 The evidence of both subsidy and injury shall be considered simultaneously *(a)* in the decision whether or not to initiate an investigation and *(b)* thereafter, during the course of the investigation, starting on a date not later than the earliest date on which in accordance with the provisions of this Agreement provisional measures may be applied.

11.8 In cases where products are not imported directly from the country of origin but are exported to the importing Member from an intermediate country, the provisions of this Agreement shall be fully applicable and the transaction or transactions shall, for the purposes of this Agreement, be regarded as having taken place between the country of origin and the importing Member.

11.9 An application under paragraph 1 shall be rejected and an investigation shall be terminated promptly as soon as the authorities concerned are satisfied that there is not sufficient evidence of either subsidization or of injury to justify proceeding with the case. There shall be immediate termination in cases where the amount of a subsidy is *de minimis*, or where the volume of subsidized imports, actual or potential, or the injury, is negligible. For the purpose of this paragraph, the amount of the subsidy shall be considered to be *de minimis* if the subsidy is less than 1 per cent *ad valorem*.

11.10 An investigation shall not hinder the procedures of customs clearance.

11.11 Investigations shall, except in special circumstances, be concluded within one year, and in no case more than 18 months, after their initiation.

Article 12 Evidence

12.1 Interested Members and all interested parties in a countervailing duty investigation shall be given notice of the information which the authorities require and ample opportunity to present in writing all evidence which they consider relevant in respect of the investigation in question.

12.1.1 Exporters, foreign producers or interested Members receiving questionnaires used in a countervailing duty investigation shall be given at least 30 days for reply.[40] Due consideration should be given to any request for an extension of the 30-day period and, upon cause shown, such an extension should be granted whenever practicable.

12.1.2 Subject to the requirement to protect confidential information, evidence presented in writing by one interested Member or interested party shall be made available promptly to other interested Members or interested parties participating in the investigation.

12.1.3 As soon as an investigation has been initiated, the authorities shall provide the full text of the written application received under paragraph 1 of Article 11 to the known exporters[41] and to the authorities of the exporting Member and shall make it available, upon request, to other interested

[40] As a general rule, the time-limit for exporters shall be counted from the date of receipt of the questionnaire, which for this purpose shall be deemed to have been received one week from the date on which it was sent to the respondent or transmitted to the appropriate diplomatic representatives of the exporting Member or, in the case of a separate customs territory Member of the WTO, an official representative of the exporting territory.

[41] It being understood that where the number of exporters involved is particularly high, the full text of the application should instead be provided only to the authorities of the exporting Member or to the relevant trade association who then should forward copies to the exporters concerned.

parties involved. Due regard shall be paid to the protection of confidential information, as provided for in paragraph 4.

12.2 Interested Members and interested parties also shall have the right, upon justification, to present information orally. Where such information is provided orally, the interested Members and interested parties subsequently shall be required to reduce such submissions to writing. Any decision of the investigating authorities can only be based on such information and arguments as were on the written record of this authority and which were available to interested Members and interested parties participating in the investigation, due account having been given to the need to protect confidential information.

12.3 The authorities shall whenever practicable provide timely opportunities for all interested Members and interested parties to see all information that is relevant to the presentation of their cases, that is not confidential as defined in paragraph 4, and that is used by the authorities in a countervailing duty investigation, and to prepare presentations on the basis of this information.

12.4 Any information which is by nature confidential (for example, because its disclosure would be of significant competitive advantage to a competitor or because its disclosure would have a significantly adverse effect upon a person supplying the information or upon a person from whom the supplier acquired the information), or which is provided on a confidential basis by parties to an investigation shall, upon good cause shown, be treated as such by the authorities. Such information shall not be disclosed without specific permission of the party submitting it.[42]

12.4.1 The authorities shall require interested Members or interested parties providing confidential information to furnish non-confidential summaries thereof. These summaries shall be in sufficient detail to permit a reasonable understanding of the substance of the information submitted in confidence. In exceptional circumstances, such Members or parties may indicate that such information is not susceptible of summary. In such exceptional circumstances, a

[42] Members are aware that in the territory of certain Members disclosure pursuant to a narrowly-drawn protective order may be required.

statement of the reasons why summarization is not possible must be provided.

12.4.2 If the authorities find that a request for confidentiality is not warranted and if the supplier of the information is either unwilling to make the information public or to authorize its disclosure in generalized or summary form, the authorities may disregard such information unless it can be demonstrated to their satisfaction from appropriate sources that the information is correct.[43]

12.5 Except in circumstances provided for in paragraph 7, the authorities shall during the course of an investigation satisfy themselves as to the accuracy of the information supplied by interested Members or interested parties upon which their findings are based.

12.6 The investigating authorities may carry out investigations in the territory of other Members as required, provided that they have notified in good time the Member in question and unless that Member objects to the investigation. Further, the investigating authorities may carry out investigations on the premises of a firm and may examine the records of a firm if *(a)* the firm so agrees and *(b)* the Member in question is notified and does not object. The procedures set forth in Annex VI shall apply to investigations on the premises of a firm. Subject to the requirement to protect confidential information, the authorities shall make the results of any such investigations available, or shall provide disclosure thereof pursuant to paragraph 8, to the firms to which they pertain and may make such results available to the applicants.

12.7 In cases in which any interested Member or interested party refuses access to, or otherwise does not provide, necessary information within a reasonable period or significantly impedes the investigation, preliminary and final determinations, affirmative or negative, may be made on the basis of the facts available.

12.8 The authorities shall, before a final determination is made, inform all interested Members and interested parties of the essential facts under consideration which form the basis for the decision whether

[43] Members agree that requests for confidentiality should not be arbitrarily rejected. Members further agree that the investigating authority may request the waiving of confidentiality only regarding information relevant to the proceedings.

to apply definitive measures. Such disclosure should take place in sufficient time for the parties to defend their interests.

12.9 For the purposes of this Agreement, 'interested parties' shall include:

(i) an exporter or foreign producer or the importer of a product subject to investigation, or a trade or business association a majority of the members of which are producers, exporters or importers of such product; and
(ii) a producer of the like product in the importing Member or a trade and business association a majority of the members of which produce the like product in the territory of the importing Member.

This list shall not preclude Members from allowing domestic or foreign parties other than those mentioned above to be included as interested parties.

12.10 The authorities shall provide opportunities for industrial users of the product under investigation, and for representative consumer organizations in cases where the product is commonly sold at the retail level, to provide information which is relevant to the investigation regarding subsidization, injury and causality.

12.11 The authorities shall take due account of any difficulties experienced by interested parties, in particular small companies, in supplying information requested, and shall provide any assistance practicable.

12.12 The procedures set out above are not intended to prevent the authorities of a Member from proceeding expeditiously with regard to initiating an investigation, reaching preliminary or final determinations, whether affirmative or negative, or from applying provisional or final measures, in accordance with relevant provisions of this Agreement.

Article 13 Consultations

13.1 As soon as possible after an application under Article 11 is accepted, and in any event before the initiation of any investigation, Members the products of which may be subject to such investigation shall be invited for consultations with the aim of clarifying the situation as to the matters referred to in paragraph 2 of Article 11 and arriving at a mutually agreed solution.

13.2 Furthermore, throughout the period of investigation, Members the products of which are the subject of the investigation shall be afforded a reasonable opportunity to continue consultations, with a view to clarifying the factual situation and to arriving at a mutually agreed solution.[44]

13.3 Without prejudice to the obligation to afford reasonable opportunity for consultation, these provisions regarding consultations are not intended to prevent the authorities of a Member from proceeding expeditiously with regard to initiating the investigation, reaching preliminary or final determinations, whether affirmative or negative, or from applying provisional or final measures, in accordance with the provisions of this Agreement.

13.4 The Member which intends to initiate any investigation or is conducting such an investigation shall permit, upon request, the Member or Members the products of which are subject to such investigation access to non-confidential evidence, including the non-confidential summary of confidential data being used for initiating or conducting the investigation.

Article 14 Calculation of the Amount of a Subsidy in Terms of the Benefit to the Recipient

For the purpose of Part V, any method used by the investigating authority to calculate the benefit to the recipient conferred pursuant to paragraph 1 of Article 1 shall be provided for in the national legislation or implementing regulations of the Member concerned and its application to each particular case shall be transparent and adequately explained. Furthermore, any such method shall be consistent with the following guidelines:

(a) government provision of equity capital shall not be considered as conferring a benefit, unless the investment decision can be regarded as inconsistent with the usual investment practice (including for the provision of risk capital) of private investors in the territory of that Member;

(b) a loan by a government shall not be considered as conferring a benefit, unless there is a difference between the amount that the firm receiving the loan pays on the government loan and the amount the

[44] It is particularly important, in accordance with the provisions of this paragraph, that no affirmative determination whether preliminary or final be made without reasonable opportunity for consultations having been given. Such consultations may establish the basis for proceeding under the provisions of Part II, III or X.

firm would pay on a comparable commercial loan which the firm could actually obtain on the market. In this case the benefit shall be the difference between these two amounts;

(c) a loan guarantee by a government shall not be considered as conferring a benefit, unless there is a difference between the amount that the firm receiving the guarantee pays on a loan guaranteed by the government and the amount that the firm would pay on a comparable commercial loan absent the government guarantee. In this case the benefit shall be the difference between these two amounts adjusted for any differences in fees;

(d) the provision of goods or services or purchase of goods by a government shall not be considered as conferring a benefit unless the provision is made for less than adequate remuneration, or the purchase is made for more than adequate remuneration. The adequacy of remuneration shall be determined in relation to prevailing market conditions for the good or service in question in the country of provision or purchase (including price, quality, availability, marketability, transportation and other conditions of purchase or sale).

Article 15 Determination of Injury[45]

15.1 A determination of injury for purposes of Article VI of GATT 1994 shall be based on positive evidence and involve an objective examination of both *(a)* the volume of the subsidized imports and the effect of the subsidized imports on prices in the domestic market for like products[46] and *(b)* the consequent impact of these imports on the domestic producers of such products.

15.2 With regard to the volume of the subsidized imports, the investigating authorities shall consider whether there has been a significant increase in subsidized imports, either in absolute terms or relative to

[45] Under this Agreement the term 'injury' shall, unless otherwise specified, be taken to mean material injury to a domestic industry, threat of material injury to a domestic industry or material retardation of the establishment of such an industry and shall be interpreted in accordance with the provisions of this Article.

[46] Throughout this Agreement the term 'like product' ('produit similaire') shall be interpreted to mean a product which is identical, i.e. alike in all respects to the product under consideration, or in the absence of such a product, another product which, although not alike in all respects, has characteristics closely resembling those of the product under consideration.

production or consumption in the importing Member. With regard to the effect of the subsidized imports on prices, the investigating authorities shall consider whether there has been a significant price undercutting by the subsidized imports as compared with the price of a like product of the importing Member, or whether the effect of such imports is otherwise to depress prices to a significant degree or to prevent price increases, which otherwise would have occurred, to a significant degree. No one or several of these factors can necessarily give decisive guidance.

15.3 Where imports of a product from more than one country are simultaneously subject to countervailing duty investigations, the investigating authorities may cumulatively assess the effects of such imports only if they determine that *(a)* the amount of subsidization established in relation to the imports from each country is more than *de minimis* as defined in paragraph 9 of Article 11 and the volume of imports from each country is not negligible and *(b)* a cumulative assessment of the effects of the imports is appropriate in light of the conditions of competition between the imported products and the conditions of competition between the imported products and the like domestic product.

15.4 The examination of the impact of the subsidized imports on the domestic industry shall include an evaluation of all relevant economic factors and indices having a bearing on the state of the industry, including actual and potential decline in output, sales, market share, profits, productivity, return on investments, or utilization of capacity; factors affecting domestic prices; actual and potential negative effects on cash flow, inventories, employment, wages, growth, ability to raise capital or investments and, in the case of agriculture, whether there has been an increased burden on government support programmes. This list is not exhaustive, nor can one or several of these factors necessarily give decisive guidance.

15.5 It must be demonstrated that the subsidized imports are, through the effects[47] of subsidies, causing injury within the meaning of this Agreement. The demonstration of a causal relationship between the subsidized imports and the injury to the domestic industry shall be based on an examination of all relevant evidence before the authorities. The authorities shall also examine any known factors other

[47] As set forth in paragraphs 2 and 4.

than the subsidized imports which at the same time are injuring the domestic industry, and the injuries caused by these other factors must not be attributed to the subsidized imports. Factors which may be relevant in this respect include, *inter alia*, the volumes and prices of non-subsidized imports of the product in question, contraction in demand or changes in the patterns of consumption, trade restrictive practices of and competition between the foreign and domestic producers, developments in technology and the export performance and productivity of the domestic industry.

15.6 The effect of the subsidized imports shall be assessed in relation to the domestic production of the like product when available data permit the separate identification of that production on the basis of such criteria as the production process, producers' sales and profits. If such separate identification of that production is not possible, the effects of the subsidized imports shall be assessed by the examination of the production of the narrowest group or range of products, which includes the like product, for which the necessary information can be provided.

15.7 A determination of a threat of material injury shall be based on facts and not merely on allegation, conjecture or remote possibility. The change in circumstances which would create a situation in which the subsidy would cause injury must be clearly foreseen and imminent. In making a determination regarding the existence of a threat of material injury, the investigating authorities should consider, *inter alia*, such factors as:

(i) nature of the subsidy or subsidies in question and the trade effects likely to arise therefrom;
(ii) a significant rate of increase of subsidized imports into the domestic market indicating the likelihood of substantially increased importation;
(iii) sufficient freely disposable, or an imminent, substantial increase in, capacity of the exporter indicating the likelihood of substantially increased subsidized exports to the importing Member's market, taking into account the availability of other export markets to absorb any additional exports;
(iv) whether imports are entering at prices that will have a significant depressing or suppressing effect on domestic prices, and would likely increase demand for further imports; and
(v) inventories of the product being investigated.

No one of these factors by itself can necessarily give decisive guidance but the totality of the factors considered must lead to the conclusion that further subsidized exports are imminent and that, unless protective action is taken, material injury would occur.

15.8 With respect to cases where injury is threatened by subsidized imports, the application of countervailing measures shall be considered and decided with special care.

Article 16 Definition of Domestic Industry

16.1 For the purposes of this Agreement, the term 'domestic industry' shall, except as provided in paragraph 2, be interpreted as referring to the domestic producers as a whole of the like products or to those of them whose collective output of the products constitutes a major proportion of the total domestic production of those products, except that when producers are related[48] to the exporters or importers or are themselves importers of the allegedly subsidized product or a like product from other countries, the term 'domestic industry' may be interpreted as referring to the rest of the producers.

16.2 In exceptional circumstances, the territory of a Member may, for the production in question, be divided into two or more competitive markets and the producers within each market may be regarded as a separate industry if *(a)* the producers within such market sell all or almost all of their production of the product in question in that market, and *(b)* the demand in that market is not to any substantial degree supplied by producers of the product in question located elsewhere in the territory. In such circumstances, injury may be found to exist even where a major portion of the total domestic industry is not injured, provided there is a concentration of subsidized imports into such an isolated market and provided further

[48] For the purpose of this paragraph, producers shall be deemed to be related to exporters or importers only if *(a)* one of them directly or indirectly controls the other; or *(b)* both of them are directly or indirectly controlled by a third person; or *(c)* together they directly or indirectly control a third person, provided that there are grounds for believing or suspecting that the effect of the relationship is such as to cause the producer concerned to behave differently from non-related producers. For the purpose of this paragraph, one shall be deemed to control another when the former is legally or operationally in a position to exercise restraint or direction over the latter.

that the subsidized imports are causing injury to the producers of all or almost all of the production within such market.

16.3 When the domestic industry has been interpreted as referring to the producers in a certain area, i.e. a market as defined in paragraph 2, countervailing duties shall be levied only on the products in question consigned for final consumption to that area. When the constitutional law of the importing Member does not permit the levying of countervailing duties on such a basis, the importing Member may levy the countervailing duties without limitation only if *(a)* the exporters shall have been given an opportunity to cease exporting at subsidized prices to the area concerned or otherwise give assurances pursuant to Article 18, and adequate assurances in this regard have not been promptly given, and *(b)* such duties cannot be levied only on products of specific producers which supply the area in question.

16.4 Where two or more countries have reached under the provisions of paragraph 8(a) of Article XXIV of GATT 1994 such a level of integration that they have the characteristics of a single, unified market, the industry in the entire area of integration shall be taken to be the domestic industry referred to in paragraphs 1 and 2.

16.5 The provisions of paragraph 6 of Article 15 shall be applicable to this Article.

Article 17 Provisional Measures

17.1 Provisional measures may be applied only if:

(a) an investigation has been initiated in accordance with the provisions of Article 11, a public notice has been given to that effect and interested Members and interested parties have been given adequate opportunities to submit information and make comments;

(b) a preliminary affirmative determination has been made that a subsidy exists and that there is injury to a domestic industry caused by subsidized imports; and

(c) the authorities concerned judge such measures necessary to prevent injury being caused during the investigation.

17.2 Provisional measures may take the form of provisional countervailing duties guaranteed by cash deposits or bonds equal to the amount of the provisionally calculated amount of subsidization.

17.3 Provisional measures shall not be applied sooner than 60 days from the date of initiation of the investigation.

17.4 The application of provisional measures shall be limited to as short a period as possible, not exceeding four months.

17.5 The relevant provisions of Article 19 shall be followed in the application of provisional measures.

Article 18 Undertakings

18.1 Proceedings may[49] be suspended or terminated without the imposition of provisional measures or countervailing duties upon receipt of satisfactory voluntary undertakings under which:

(a) the government of the exporting Member agrees to eliminate or limit the subsidy or take other measures concerning its effects; or

(b) the exporter agrees to revise its prices so that the investigating authorities are satisfied that the injurious effect of the subsidy is eliminated. Price increases under such undertakings shall not be higher than necessary to eliminate the amount of the subsidy. It is desirable that the price increases be less than the amount of the subsidy if such increases would be adequate to remove the injury to the domestic industry.

18.2 Undertakings shall not be sought or accepted unless the authorities of the importing Member have made a preliminary affirmative determination of subsidization and injury caused by such subsidization and, in case of undertakings from exporters, have obtained the consent of the exporting Member.

18.3 Undertakings offered need not be accepted if the authorities of the importing Member consider their acceptance impractical, for example if the number of actual or potential exporters is too great, or for other reasons, including reasons of general policy. Should the case arise and where practicable, the authorities shall provide to the exporter the reasons which have led them to consider acceptance of an undertaking as inappropriate, and shall, to the extent possible, give the exporter an opportunity to make comments thereon.

[49] The word 'may' shall not be interpreted to allow the simultaneous continuation of proceedings with the implementation of undertakings, except as provided in paragraph 4.

18.4 If an undertaking is accepted, the investigation of subsidization and injury shall nevertheless be completed if the exporting Member so desires or the importing Member so decides. In such a case, if a negative determination of subsidization or injury is made, the undertaking shall automatically lapse, except in cases where such a determination is due in large part to the existence of an undertaking. In such cases, the authorities concerned may require that an undertaking be maintained for a reasonable period consistent with the provisions of this Agreement. In the event that an affirmative determination of subsidization and injury is made, the undertaking shall continue consistent with its terms and the provisions of this Agreement.

18.5 Price undertakings may be suggested by the authorities of the importing Member, but no exporter shall be forced to enter into such undertakings. The fact that governments or exporters do not offer such undertakings, or do not accept an invitation to do so, shall in no way prejudice the consideration of the case. However, the authorities are free to determine that a threat of injury is more likely to be realized if the subsidized imports continue.

18.6 Authorities of an importing Member may require any government or exporter from whom an undertaking has been accepted to provide periodically information relevant to the fulfilment of such an undertaking, and to permit verification of pertinent data. In case of violation of an undertaking, the authorities of the importing Member may take, under this Agreement in conformity with its provisions, expeditious actions which may constitute immediate application of provisional measures using the best information available. In such cases, definitive duties may be levied in accordance with this Agreement on products entered for consumption not more than 90 days before the application of such provisional measures, except that any such retroactive assessment shall not apply to imports entered before the violation of the undertaking.

Article 19 Imposition and Collection of Countervailing Duties

19.1 If, after reasonable efforts have been made to complete consultations, a Member makes a final determination of the existence and amount of the subsidy and that, through the effects of the subsidy, the subsidized imports are causing injury, it may impose a countervailing duty in accordance with the provisions of this Article unless the subsidy or subsidies are withdrawn.

19.2 The decision whether or not to impose a countervailing duty in cases where all requirements for the imposition have been fulfilled, and the decision whether the amount of the countervailing duty to be imposed shall be the full amount of the subsidy or less, are decisions to be made by the authorities of the importing Member. It is desirable that the imposition should be permissive in the territory of all Members, that the duty should be less than the total amount of the subsidy if such lesser duty would be adequate to remove the injury to the domestic industry, and that procedures should be established which would allow the authorities concerned to take due account of representations made by domestic interested parties[50] whose interests might be adversely affected by the imposition of a countervailing duty.

19.3 When a countervailing duty is imposed in respect of any product, such countervailing duty shall be levied, in the appropriate amounts in each case, on a non-discriminatory basis on imports of such product from all sources found to be subsidized and causing injury, except as to imports from those sources which have renounced any subsidies in question or from which undertakings under the terms of this Agreement have been accepted. Any exporter whose exports are subject to a definitive countervailing duty but who was not actually investigated for reasons other than a refusal to cooperate, shall be entitled to an expedited review in order that the investigating authorities promptly establish an individual countervailing duty rate for that exporter.

19.4 No countervailing duty shall be levied[51] on any imported product in excess of the amount of the subsidy found to exist, calculated in terms of subsidization per unit of the subsidized and exported product.

Article 20 Retroactivity

20.1 Provisional measures and countervailing duties shall only be applied to products which enter for consumption after the time when the decision under paragraph 1 of Article 17 and paragraph 1 of Article

[50] For the purpose of this paragraph, the term 'domestic interested parties' shall include consumers and industrial users of the imported product subject to investigation.

[51] As used in this Agreement 'levy' shall mean the definitive or final legal assessment or collection of a duty or tax.

19, respectively, enters into force, subject to the exceptions set out in this Article.

20.2 Where a final determination of injury (but not of a threat thereof or of a material retardation of the establishment of an industry) is made or, in the case of a final determination of a threat of injury, where the effect of the subsidized imports would, in the absence of the provisional measures, have led to a determination of injury, countervailing duties may be levied retroactively for the period for which provisional measures, if any, have been applied.

20.3 If the definitive countervailing duty is higher than the amount guaranteed by the cash deposit or bond, the difference shall not be collected. If the definitive duty is less than the amount guaranteed by the cash deposit or bond, the excess amount shall be reimbursed or the bond released in an expeditious manner.

20.4 Except as provided in paragraph 2, where a determination of threat of injury or material retardation is made (but no injury has yet occurred) a definitive countervailing duty may be imposed only from the date of the determination of threat of injury or material retardation, and any cash deposit made during the period of the application of provisional measures shall be refunded and any bonds released in an expeditious manner.

20.5 Where a final determination is negative, any cash deposit made during the period of the application of provisional measures shall be refunded and any bonds released in an expeditious manner.

20.6 In critical circumstances where for the subsidized product in question the authorities find that injury which is difficult to repair is caused by massive imports in a relatively short period of a product benefiting from subsidies paid or bestowed inconsistently with the provisions of GATT 1994 and of this Agreement and where it is deemed necessary, in order to preclude the recurrence of such injury, to assess countervailing duties retroactively on those imports, the definitive countervailing duties may be assessed on imports which were entered for consumption not more than 90 days prior to the date of application of provisional measures.

Article 21 Duration and Review of Countervailing Duties and Undertakings

21.1 A countervailing duty shall remain in force only as long as and to the extent necessary to counteract subsidization which is causing injury.

21.2 The authorities shall review the need for the continued imposition of the duty, where warranted, on their own initiative or, provided that a reasonable period of time has elapsed since the imposition of the definitive countervailing duty, upon request by any interested party which submits positive information substantiating the need for a review. Interested parties shall have the right to request the authorities to examine whether the continued imposition of the duty is necessary to offset subsidization, whether the injury would be likely to continue or recur if the duty were removed or varied, or both. If, as a result of the review under this paragraph, the authorities determine that the countervailing duty is no longer warranted, it shall be terminated immediately.

21.3 Notwithstanding the provisions of paragraphs 1 and 2, any definitive countervailing duty shall be terminated on a date not later than five years from its imposition (or from the date of the most recent review under paragraph 2 if that review has covered both subsidization and injury, or under this paragraph), unless the authorities determine, in a review initiated before that date on their own initiative or upon a duly substantiated request made by or on behalf of the domestic industry within a reasonable period of time prior to that date, that the expiry of the duty would be likely to lead to continuation or recurrence of subsidization and injury.[52] The duty may remain in force pending the outcome of such a review.

21.4 The provisions of Article 12 regarding evidence and procedure shall apply to any review carried out under this Article. Any such review shall be carried out expeditiously and shall normally be concluded within 12 months of the date of initiation of the review.

21.5 The provisions of this Article shall apply *mutatis mutandis* to undertakings accepted under Article 18.

Article 22 Public Notice and Explanation of Determinations

22.1 When the authorities are satisfied that there is sufficient evidence to justify the initiation of an investigation pursuant to Article 11, the Member or Members the products of which are subject to such investigation and other interested parties known to the investigating

[52] When the amount of the countervailing duty is assessed on a retrospective basis, a finding in the most recent assessment proceeding that no duty is to be levied shall not by itself require the authorities to terminate the definitive duty.

authorities to have an interest therein shall be notified and a public notice shall be given.

22.2 A public notice of the initiation of an investigation shall contain, or otherwise make available through a separate report[53], adequate information on the following:

(i) the name of the exporting country or countries and the product involved;
(ii) the date of initiation of the investigation;
(iii) a description of the subsidy practice or practices to be investigated;
(iv) a summary of the factors on which the allegation of injury is based;
(v) the address to which representations by interested Members and interested parties should be directed; and
(vi) the time-limits allowed to interested Members and interested parties for making their views known.

22.3 Public notice shall be given of any preliminary or final determination, whether affirmative or negative, of any decision to accept an undertaking pursuant to Article 18, of the termination of such an undertaking, and of the termination of a definitive countervailing duty. Each such notice shall set forth, or otherwise make available through a separate report, in sufficient detail the findings and conclusions reached on all issues of fact and law considered material by the investigating authorities. All such notices and reports shall be forwarded to the Member or Members the products of which are subject to such determination or undertaking and to other interested parties known to have an interest therein.

22.4 A public notice of the imposition of provisional measures shall set forth, or otherwise make available through a separate report, sufficiently detailed explanations for the preliminary determinations on the existence of a subsidy and injury and shall refer to the matters of fact and law which have led to arguments being accepted or rejected. Such a notice or report shall, due regard being paid to the requirement for the protection of confidential information, contain in particular:

[53] Where authorities provide information and explanations under the provisions of this Article in a separate report, they shall ensure that such report is readily available to the public.

(i) the names of the suppliers or, when this is impracticable, the supplying countries involved;
(ii) a description of the product which is sufficient for customs purposes;
(iii) the amount of subsidy established and the basis on which the existence of a subsidy has been determined;
(iv) considerations relevant to the injury determination as set out in Article 15;
(v) the main reasons leading to the determination.

22.5 A public notice of conclusion or suspension of an investigation in the case of an affirmative determination providing for the imposition of a definitive duty or the acceptance of an undertaking shall contain, or otherwise make available through a separate report, all relevant information on the matters of fact and law and reasons which have led to the imposition of final measures or the acceptance of an undertaking, due regard being paid to the requirement for the protection of confidential information. In particular, the notice or report shall contain the information described in paragraph 4, as well as the reasons for the acceptance or rejection of relevant arguments or claims made by interested Members and by the exporters and importers.
22.6 A public notice of the termination or suspension of an investigation following the acceptance of an undertaking pursuant to Article 18 shall include, or otherwise make available through a separate report, the non-confidential part of this undertaking.
22.7 The provisions of this Article shall apply *mutatis mutandis* to the initiation and completion of reviews pursuant to Article 21 and to decisions under Article 20 to apply duties retroactively.

Article 23 Judicial Review

Each Member whose national legislation contains provisions on countervailing duty measures shall maintain judicial, arbitral or administrative tribunals or procedures for the purpose, *inter alia*, of the prompt review of administrative actions relating to final determinations and reviews of determinations within the meaning of Article 21. Such tribunals or procedures shall be independent of the authorities responsible for the determination or review in question, and shall provide all interested parties who participated in the administrative proceeding and are directly and individually affected by the administrative actions with access to review.

PART VI: INSTITUTIONS

Article 24 Committee on Subsidies and Countervailing Measures and Subsidiary Bodies

24.1 There is hereby established a Committee on Subsidies and Countervailing Measures composed of representatives from each of the Members. The Committee shall elect its own Chairman and shall meet not less than twice a year and otherwise as envisaged by relevant provisions of this Agreement at the request of any Member. The Committee shall carry out responsibilities as assigned to it under this Agreement or by the Members and it shall afford Members the opportunity of consulting on any matter relating to the operation of the Agreement or the furtherance of its objectives. The WTO Secretariat shall act as the secretariat to the Committee.

24.2 The Committee may set up subsidiary bodies as appropriate.

24.3 The Committee shall establish a Permanent Group of Experts composed of five independent persons, highly qualified in the fields of subsidies and trade relations. The experts will be elected by the Committee and one of them will be replaced every year. The PGE may be requested to assist a panel, as provided for in paragraph 5 of Article 4. The Committee may also seek an advisory opinion on the existence and nature of any subsidy.

24.4 The PGE may be consulted by any Member and may give advisory opinions on the nature of any subsidy proposed to be introduced or currently maintained by that Member. Such advisory opinions will be confidential and may not be invoked in proceedings under Article 7.

24.5 In carrying out their functions, the Committee and any subsidiary bodies may consult with and seek information from any source they deem appropriate. However, before the Committee or a subsidiary body seeks such information from a source within the jurisdiction of a Member, it shall inform the Member involved.

PART VII: NOTIFICATION AND SURVEILLANCE

Article 25 Notifications

25.1 Members agree that, without prejudice to the provisions of paragraph 1 of Article XVI of GATT 1994, their notifications of subsidies shall be submitted not later than 30 June of each year and shall conform to the provisions of paragraphs 2 through 6.

25.2 Members shall notify any subsidy as defined in paragraph 1 of Article 1, which is specific within the meaning of Article 2, granted or maintained within their territories.

25.3 The content of notifications should be sufficiently specific to enable other Members to evaluate the trade effects and to understand the operation of notified subsidy programmes. In this connection, and without prejudice to the contents and form of the questionnaire on subsidies[54], Members shall ensure that their notifications contain the following information:

(i) form of a subsidy (i.e. grant, loan, tax concession, etc.);
(ii) subsidy per unit or, in cases where this is not possible, the total amount or the annual amount budgeted for that subsidy (indicating, if possible, the average subsidy per unit in the previous year);
(iii) policy objective and/or purpose of a subsidy;
(iv) duration of a subsidy and/or any other time-limits attached to it;
(v) statistical data permitting an assessment of the trade effects of a subsidy.

25.4 Where specific points in paragraph 3 have not been addressed in a notification, an explanation shall be provided in the notification itself.

25.5 If subsidies are granted to specific products or sectors, the notifications should be organized by product or sector.

25.6 Members which consider that there are no measures in their territories requiring notification under paragraph 1 of Article XVI of GATT 1994 and this Agreement shall so inform the Secretariat in writing.

25.7 Members recognize that notification of a measure does not prejudge either its legal status under GATT 1994 and this Agreement, the effects under this Agreement, or the nature of the measure itself.

25.8 Any Member may, at any time, make a written request for information on the nature and extent of any subsidy granted or maintained by another Member (including any subsidy referred to in Part IV), or for an explanation of the reasons for which a specific measure has been considered as not subject to the requirement of notification.

[54] The Committee shall establish a Working Party to review the contents and form of the questionnaire as contained in BISD 9S/193–194.

25.9 Members so requested shall provide such information as quickly as possible and in a comprehensive manner, and shall be ready, upon request, to provide additional information to the requesting Member. In particular, they shall provide sufficient details to enable the other Member to assess their compliance with the terms of this Agreement. Any Member which considers that such information has not been provided may bring the matter to the attention of the Committee.

25.10 Any Member which considers that any measure of another Member having the effects of a subsidy has not been notified in accordance with the provisions of paragraph 1 of Article XVI of GATT 1994 and this Article may bring the matter to the attention of such other Member. If the alleged subsidy is not thereafter notified promptly, such Member may itself bring the alleged subsidy in question to the notice of the Committee.

25.11 Members shall report without delay to the Committee all preliminary or final actions taken with respect to countervailing duties. Such reports shall be available in the Secretariat for inspection by other Members. Members shall also submit, on a semi-annual basis, reports on any countervailing duty actions taken within the preceding six months. The semi-annual reports shall be submitted on an agreed standard form.

25.12 Each Member shall notify the Committee *(a)* which of its authorities are competent to initiate and conduct investigations referred to in Article 11 and *(b)* its domestic procedures governing the initiation and conduct of such investigations.

Article 26 Surveillance

26.1 The Committee shall examine new and full notifications submitted under paragraph 1 of Article XVI of GATT 1994 and paragraph 1 of Article 25 of this Agreement at special sessions held every third year. Notifications submitted in the intervening years (updating notifications) shall be examined at each regular meeting of the Committee.

26.2 The Committee shall examine reports submitted under paragraph 11 of Article 25 at each regular meeting of the Committee.

PART VIII: DEVELOPING COUNTRY MEMBERS

Article 27 Special and Differential Treatment of Developing Country Members

27.1 Members recognize that subsidies may play an important role in economic development programmes of developing country Members.

27.2 The prohibition of paragraph 1(a) of Article 3 shall not apply to:

(a) developing country Members referred to in Annex VII.

(b) other developing country Members for a period of eight years from the date of entry into force of the WTO Agreement, subject to compliance with the provisions in paragraph 4.

27.3 The prohibition of paragraph 1(b) of Article 3 shall not apply to developing country Members for a period of five years, and shall not apply to least developed country Members for a period of eight years, from the date of entry into force of the WTO Agreement.

27.4 Any developing country Member referred to in paragraph 2(b) shall phase out its export subsidies within the eight-year period, preferably in a progressive manner. However, a developing country Member shall not increase the level of its export subsidies[55], and shall eliminate them within a period shorter than that provided for in this paragraph when the use of such export subsidies is inconsistent with its development needs. If a developing country Member deems it necessary to apply such subsidies beyond the 8-year period, it shall not later than one year before the expiry of this period enter into consultation with the Committee, which will determine whether an extension of this period is justified, after examining all the relevant economic, financial and development needs of the developing country Member in question. If the Committee determines that the extension is justified, the developing country Member concerned shall hold annual consultations with the Committee to determine the necessity of maintaining the subsidies. If no such determination is made by the Committee, the developing country Member shall phase out the remaining export subsidies within two years from the end of the last authorized period.

[55] For a developing country Member not granting export subsidies as of the date of entry into force of the WTO Agreement, this paragraph shall apply on the basis of the level of export subsidies granted in 1986.

27.5 A developing country Member which has reached export competitiveness in any given product shall phase out its export subsidies for such product(s) over a period of two years. However, for a developing country Member which is referred to in Annex VII and which has reached export competitiveness in one or more products, export subsidies on such products shall be gradually phased out over a period of eight years.

27.6 Export competitiveness in a product exists if a developing country Member's exports of that product have reached a share of at least 3.25 per cent in world trade of that product for two consecutive calendar years. Export competitiveness shall exist either *(a)* on the basis of notification by the developing country Member having reached export competitiveness, or *(b)* on the basis of a computation undertaken by the Secretariat at the request of any Member. For the purpose of this paragraph, a product is defined as a section heading of the Harmonized System Nomenclature. The Committee shall review the operation of this provision five years from the date of the entry into force of the WTO Agreement.

27.7 The provisions of Article 4 shall not apply to a developing country Member in the case of export subsidies which are in conformity with the provisions of paragraphs 2 through 5. The relevant provisions in such a case shall be those of Article 7.

27.8 There shall be no presumption in terms of paragraph 1 of Article 6 that a subsidy granted by a developing country Member results in serious prejudice, as defined in this Agreement. Such serious prejudice, where applicable under the terms of paragraph 9, shall be demonstrated by positive evidence, in accordance with the provisions of paragraphs 3 through 8 of Article 6.

27.9 Regarding actionable subsidies granted or maintained by a developing country Member other than those referred to in paragraph 1 of Article 6, action may not be authorized or taken under Article 7 unless nullification or impairment of tariff concessions or other obligations under GATT 1994 is found to exist as a result of such a subsidy, in such a way as to displace or impede imports of a like product of another Member into the market of the subsidizing developing country Member or unless injury to a domestic industry in the market of an importing Member occurs.

27.10 Any countervailing duty investigation of a product originating in a developing country Member shall be terminated as soon as the authorities concerned determine that:

(a) the overall level of subsidies granted upon the product in question does not exceed 2 per cent of its value calculated on a per unit basis; or
(b) the volume of the subsidized imports represents less than 4 per cent of the total imports of the like product in the importing Member, unless imports from developing country Members whose individual shares of total imports represent less than 4 per cent collectively account for more than 9 per cent of the total imports of the like product in the importing Member.

27.11 For those developing country Members within the scope of paragraph 2(b) which have eliminated export subsidies prior to the expiry of the period of eight years from the date of entry into force of the WTO Agreement, and for those developing country Members referred to in Annex VII, the number in paragraph 10(a) shall be 3 per cent rather than 2 per cent. This provision shall apply from the date that the elimination of export subsidies is notified to the Committee, and for so long as export subsidies are not granted by the notifying developing country Member. This provision shall expire eight years from the date of entry into force of the WTO Agreement.

27.12 The provisions of paragraphs 10 and 11 shall govern any determination of *de minimis* under paragraph 3 of Article 15.

27.13 The provisions of Part III shall not apply to direct forgiveness of debts, subsidies to cover social costs, in whatever form, including relinquishment of government revenue and other transfer of liabilities when such subsidies are granted within and directly linked to a privatization programme of a developing country Member, provided that both such programme and the subsidies involved are granted for a limited period and notified to the Committee and that the programme results in eventual privatization of the enterprise concerned.

27.14 The Committee shall, upon request by an interested Member, undertake a review of a specific export subsidy practice of a developing country Member to examine whether the practice is in conformity with its development needs.

27.15 The Committee shall, upon request by an interested developing country Member, undertake a review of a specific countervailing measure to examine whether it is consistent with the provisions of paragraphs 10 and 11 as applicable to the developing country Member in question.

PART IX: TRANSITIONAL ARRANGEMENTS

Article 28 Existing Programmes

28.1 Subsidy programmes which have been established within the territory of any Member before the date on which such a Member signed the WTO Agreement and which are inconsistent with the provisions of this Agreement shall be:

(a) notified to the Committee not later than 90 days after the date of entry into force of the WTO Agreement for such Member; and

(b) brought into conformity with the provisions of this Agreement within three years of the date of entry into force of the WTO Agreement for such Member and until then shall not be subject to Part II.

28.2 No Member shall extend the scope of any such programme, nor shall such a programme be renewed upon its expiry.

Article 29 Transformation into a Market Economy

29.1 Members in the process of transformation from a centrally-planned into a market, free-enterprise economy may apply programmes and measures necessary for such a transformation.

29.2 For such Members, subsidy programmes falling within the scope of Article 3, and notified according to paragraph 3, shall be phased out or brought into conformity with Article 3 within a period of seven years from the date of entry into force of the WTO Agreement. In such a case, Article 4 shall not apply. In addition during the same period:

(a) Subsidy programmes falling within the scope of paragraph 1(d) of Article 6 shall not be actionable under Article 7;

(b) With respect to other actionable subsidies, the provisions of paragraph 9 of Article 27 shall apply.

29.3 Subsidy programmes falling within the scope of Article 3 shall be notified to the Committee by the earliest practicable date after the date of entry into force of the WTO Agreement. Further notifications of such subsidies may be made up to two years after the date of entry into force of the WTO Agreement.

29.4 In exceptional circumstances Members referred to in paragraph 1 may be given departures from their notified programmes and measures and their time-frame by the Committee if such departures are deemed necessary for the process of transformation.

PART X: DISPUTE SETTLEMENT

Article 30

The provisions of Articles XXII and XXIII of GATT 1994 as elaborated and applied by the Dispute Settlement Understanding shall apply to consultations and the settlement of disputes under this Agreement, except as otherwise specifically provided herein.

PART XI: FINAL PROVISIONS

Article 31 Provisional Application

The provisions of paragraph 1 of Article 6 and the provisions of Article 8 and Article 9 shall apply for a period of five years, beginning with the date of entry into force of the WTO Agreement. Not later than 180 days before the end of this period, the Committee shall review the operation of those provisions, with a view to determining whether to extend their application, either as presently drafted or in a modified form, for a further period.

Article 32 Other Final Provisions

32.1 No specific action against a subsidy of another Member can be taken except in accordance with the provisions of GATT 1994, as interpreted by this Agreement.[56]

[56] This paragraph is not intended to preclude action under other relevant provisions of GATT 1994, where appropriate.

32.2 Reservations may not be entered in respect of any of the provisions of this Agreement without the consent of the other Members.

32.3 Subject to paragraph 4, the provisions of this Agreement shall apply to investigations, and reviews of existing measures, initiated pursuant to applications which have been made on or after the date of entry into force for a Member of the WTO Agreement.

32.4 For the purposes of paragraph 3 of Article 21, existing countervailing measures shall be deemed to be imposed on a date not later than the date of entry into force for a Member of the WTO Agreement, except in cases in which the domestic legislation of a Member in force at that date already included a clause of the type provided for in that paragraph.

32.5 Each Member shall take all necessary steps, of a general or particular character, to ensure, not later than the date of entry into force of the WTO Agreement for it, the conformity of its laws, regulations and administrative procedures with the provisions of this Agreement as they may apply to the Member in question.

32.6 Each Member shall inform the Committee of any changes in its laws and regulations relevant to this Agreement and in the administration of such laws and regulations.

32.7 The Committee shall review annually the implementation and operation of this Agreement, taking into account the objectives thereof. The Committee shall inform annually the Council for Trade in Goods of developments during the period covered by such reviews.

32.8 The Annexes to this Agreement constitute an integral part thereof.

ANNEX I ILLUSTRATIVE LIST OF EXPORT SUBSIDIES

(a) The provision by governments of direct subsidies to a firm or an industry contingent upon export performance.

(b) Currency retention schemes or any similar practices which involve a bonus on exports.

(c) Internal transport and freight charges on export shipments, provided or mandated by governments, on terms more favourable than for domestic shipments.

(d) The provision by governments or their agencies either directly or indirectly through government-mandated schemes, of imported or domestic products or services for use in the production of exported goods, on terms or conditions more favourable than for provision of like or directly competitive products or services for use in the production of goods for domestic consumption, if (in the case of products) such terms or conditions are more favourable than those commercially available[57] on world markets to their exporters.

(e) The full or partial exemption remission, or deferral specifically related to exports, of direct taxes[58] or social welfare charges paid or payable by industrial or commercial enterprises.[59]

(f) The allowance of special deductions directly related to exports or export performance, over and above those granted in respect to production for domestic consumption, in the calculation of the base on which direct taxes are charged.

(g) The exemption or remission, in respect of the production and distribution of exported products, of indirect taxes[58] in excess of those levied in respect of the production and distribution of like products when sold for domestic consumption.

(h) The exemption, remission or deferral of prior-stage cumulative indirect taxes[58] on goods or services used in the production of exported

[57] The term 'commercially available' means that the choice between domestic and imported products is unrestricted and depends only on commercial considerations.

[58] For the purpose of this Agreement: The term 'direct taxes' shall mean taxes on wages, profits, interests, rents, royalties, and all other forms of income, and taxes on the ownership of real property; The term 'import charges' shall mean tariffs, duties, and other fiscal charges not elsewhere enumerated in this note that are levied on imports; The term 'indirect taxes' shall mean sales, excise, turnover, value added, franchise, stamp, transfer, inventory and equipment taxes, border taxes and all taxes other than direct taxes and import charges; 'Prior-stage' indirect taxes are those levied on goods or services used directly or indirectly in making the product; 'Cumulative' indirect taxes are multi-staged taxes levied where there is no mechanism for subsequent crediting of the tax if the goods or services subject to tax at one stage of production are used in a succeeding stage of production; 'Remission' of taxes includes the refund or rebate of taxes; 'Remission or drawback' includes the full or partial exemption or deferral of import charges.

[59] The Members recognize that deferral need not amount to an export subsidy where, for example, appropriate interest charges are collected. The Members reaffirm the principle that prices for goods in transactions between exporting enterprises and foreign buyers under their or under the same control should for tax purposes be the prices which would be charged between independent enterprises acting at arm's length. Any Member may draw the attention of another Member to administrative or other practices which may contravene this principle and which result in a significant saving of direct taxes in export transactions. In such circumstances the Members shall normally attempt to resolve their differences using the facilities of existing bilateral tax treaties or other specific international mechanisms, without prejudice to the rights and obligations of Members under GATT 1994, including the right of consultation created in the preceding sentence. Paragraph (e) is not intended to limit a Member from taking measures to avoid the double taxation of foreign-source income earned by its enterprises or the enterprises of another Member.

products in excess of the exemption, remission or deferral of like prior-stage cumulative indirect taxes on goods or services used in the production of like products when sold for domestic consumption; provided, however, that prior-stage cumulative indirect taxes may be exempted, remitted or deferred on exported products even when not exempted, remitted or deferred on like products when sold for domestic consumption, if the prior-stage cumulative indirect taxes are levied on inputs that are consumed in the production of the exported product (making normal allowance for waste).[60] This item shall be interpreted in accordance with the guidelines on consumption of inputs in the production process contained in Annex II.

(i) The remission or drawback of import charges[58] in excess of those levied on imported inputs that are consumed in the production of the exported product (making normal allowance for waste); provided, however, that in particular cases a firm may use a quantity of home market inputs equal to, and having the same quality and characteristics as, the imported inputs as a substitute for them in order to benefit from this provision if the import and the corresponding export operations both occur within a reasonable time period, not to exceed two years. This item shall be interpreted in accordance with the guidelines on consumption of inputs in the production process contained in Annex II and the guidelines in the determination of substitution drawback systems as export subsidies contained in Annex III.

(j) The provision by governments (or special institutions controlled by governments) of export credit guarantee or insurance programmes, of insurance or guarantee programmes against increases in the cost of exported products or of exchange risk programmes, at premium rates which are inadequate to cover the long-term operating costs and losses of the programmes.

(k) The grant by governments (or special institutions controlled by and/or acting under the authority of governments) of export credits at rates below those which they actually have to pay for the funds so employed (or would have to pay if they borrowed on international capital markets in order to obtain funds of the same maturity and other credit terms and denominated in the same currency as the export credit), or the payment by them of all or part of the costs

[60] Paragraph (h) does not apply to value-added tax systems and border-tax adjustment in lieu thereof; the problem of the excessive remission of value-added taxes is exclusively covered by paragraph (g).

incurred by exporters or financial institutions in obtaining credits, in so far as they are used to secure a material advantage in the field of export credit terms.

Provided, however, that if a Member is a party to an international undertaking on official export credits to which at least twelve original Members to this Agreement are parties as of 1 January 1979 (or a successor undertaking which has been adopted by those original Members), or if in practice a Member applies the interest rates provisions of the relevant undertaking, an export credit practice which is in conformity with those provisions shall not be considered an export subsidy prohibited by this Agreement.

(l) Any other charge on the public account constituting an export subsidy in the sense of Article XVI of GATT 1994.

ANNEX II GUIDELINES ON CONSUMPTION OF INPUTS IN THE PRODUCTION PROCESS[61]

I

1. Indirect tax rebate schemes can allow for exemption, remission or deferral of prior-stage cumulative indirect taxes levied on inputs that are consumed in the production of the exported product (making normal allowance for waste). Similarly, drawback schemes can allow for the remission or drawback of import charges levied on inputs that are consumed in the production of the exported product (making normal allowance for waste).
2. The Illustrative List of Export Subsidies in Annex I of this Agreement makes reference to the term 'inputs that are consumed in the production of the exported product' in paragraphs (h) and (i). Pursuant to paragraph (h), indirect tax rebate schemes can constitute an export subsidy to the extent that they result in exemption, remission or deferral of prior-stage cumulative indirect taxes in excess of the amount of such taxes actually levied on inputs that are consumed in the production of the exported product. Pursuant to paragraph (i), drawback schemes can constitute an export subsidy to the extent that

[61] Inputs consumed in the production process are inputs physically incorporated, energy, fuels and oil used in the production process and catalysts which are consumed in the course of their use to obtain the exported product.

they result in a remission or drawback of import charges in excess of those actually levied on inputs that are consumed in the production of the exported product. Both paragraphs stipulate that normal allowance for waste must be made in findings regarding consumption of inputs in the production of the exported product. Paragraph (i) also provides for substitution, where appropriate.

II

In examining whether inputs are consumed in the production of the exported product, as part of a countervailing duty investigation pursuant to this Agreement, investigating authorities should proceed on the following basis:

1. Where it is alleged that an indirect tax rebate scheme, or a drawback scheme, conveys a subsidy by reason of over-rebate or excess drawback of indirect taxes or import charges on inputs consumed in the production of the exported product, the investigating authorities should first determine whether the government of the exporting Member has in place and applies a system or procedure to confirm which inputs are consumed in the production of the exported product and in what amounts. Where such a system or procedure is determined to be applied, the investigating authorities should then examine the system or procedure to see whether it is reasonable, effective for the purpose intended, and based on generally accepted commercial practices in the country of export. The investigating authorities may deem it necessary to carry out, in accordance with paragraph 6 of Article 12, certain practical tests in order to verify information or to satisfy themselves that the system or procedure is being effectively applied.
2. Where there is no such system or procedure, where it is not reasonable, or where it is instituted and considered reasonable but is found not to be applied or not to be applied effectively, a further examination by the exporting Member based on the actual inputs involved would need to be carried out in the context of determining whether an excess payment occurred. If the investigating authorities deemed it necessary, a further examination would be carried out in accordance with paragraph 1.
3. Investigating authorities should treat inputs as physically incorporated if such inputs are used in the production process and are physically present in the product exported. The Members note that an input need not be present in the final product in the same form in which it entered the production process.

4. In determining the amount of a particular input that is consumed in the production of the exported product, a 'normal allowance for waste' should be taken into account, and such waste should be treated as consumed in the production of the exported product. The term 'waste' refers to that portion of a given input which does not serve an independent function in the production process, is not consumed in the production of the exported product (for reasons such as inefficiencies) and is not recovered, used or sold by the same manufacturer.
5. The investigating authority's determination of whether the claimed allowance for waste is 'normal' should take into account the production process, the average experience of the industry in the country of export, and other technical factors, as appropriate. The investigating authority should bear in mind that an important question is whether the authorities in the exporting Member have reasonably calculated the amount of waste, when such an amount is intended to be included in the tax or duty rebate or remission.

ANNEX III GUIDELINES IN THE DETERMINATION OF SUBSTITUTION DRAWBACK SYSTEMS AS EXPORT SUBSIDIES

I

Drawback systems can allow for the refund or drawback of import charges on inputs which are consumed in the production process of another product and where the export of this latter product contains domestic inputs having the same quality and characteristics as those substituted for the imported inputs. Pursuant to paragraph (i) of the Illustrative List of Export Subsidies in Annex I, substitution drawback systems can constitute an export subsidy to the extent that they result in an excess drawback of the import charges levied initially on the imported inputs for which drawback is being claimed.

II

In examining any substitution drawback system as part of a countervailing duty investigation pursuant to this Agreement, investigating authorities should proceed on the following basis:

1. Paragraph (i) of the Illustrative List stipulates that home market inputs may be substituted for imported inputs in the production of a product for export provided such inputs are equal in quantity to, and have the same quality and characteristics as, the imported inputs

being substituted. The existence of a verification system or procedure is important because it enables the government of the exporting Member to ensure and demonstrate that the quantity of inputs for which drawback is claimed does not exceed the quantity of similar products exported, in whatever form, and that there is not drawback of import charges in excess of those originally levied on the imported inputs in question.

2. Where it is alleged that a substitution drawback system conveys a subsidy, the investigating authorities should first proceed to determine whether the government of the exporting Member has in place and applies a verification system or procedure. Where such a system or procedure is determined to be applied, the investigating authorities should then examine the verification procedures to see whether they are reasonable, effective for the purpose intended, and based on generally accepted commercial practices in the country of export. To the extent that the procedures are determined to meet this test and are effectively applied, no subsidy should be presumed to exist. It may be deemed necessary by the investigating authorities to carry out, in accordance with paragraph 6 of Article 12, certain practical tests in order to verify information or to satisfy themselves that the verification procedures are being effectively applied.
3. Where there are no verification procedures, where they are not reasonable, or where such procedures are instituted and considered reasonable but are found not to be actually applied or not applied effectively, there may be a subsidy. In such cases a further examination by the exporting Member based on the actual transactions involved would need to be carried out to determine whether an excess payment occurred. If the investigating authorities deemed it necessary, a further examination would be carried out in accordance with paragraph 2.
4. The existence of a substitution drawback provision under which exporters are allowed to select particular import shipments on which drawback is claimed should not of itself be considered to convey a subsidy.
5. An excess drawback of import charges in the sense of paragraph (i) would be deemed to exist where governments paid interest on any monies refunded under their drawback schemes, to the extent of the interest actually paid or payable.

ANNEX IV CALCULATION OF THE TOTAL *AD VALOREM* SUBSIDIZATION (PARAGRAPH 1(A) OF ARTICLE 6)[62]

1. Any calculation of the amount of a subsidy for the purpose of paragraph 1(a) of Article 6 shall be done in terms of the cost to the granting government.
2. Except as provided in paragraphs 3 through 5, in determining whether the overall rate of subsidization exceeds 5 per cent of the value of the product, the value of the product shall be calculated as the total value of the recipient firm's[63] sales in the most recent 12-month period, for which sales data is available, preceding the period in which the subsidy is granted.[64]
3. Where the subsidy is tied to the production or sale of a given product, the value of the product shall be calculated as the total value of the recipient firm's sales of that product in the most recent 12-month period, for which sales data is available, preceding the period in which the subsidy is granted.
4. Where the recipient firm is in a start-up situation, serious prejudice shall be deemed to exist if the overall rate of subsidization exceeds 15 per cent of the total funds invested. For purposes of this paragraph, a start-up period will not extend beyond the first year of production.[65]
5. Where the recipient firm is located in an inflationary economy country, the value of the product shall be calculated as the recipient firm's total sales (or sales of the relevant product, if the subsidy is tied) in the preceding calendar year indexed by the rate of inflation experienced in the 12 months preceding the month in which the subsidy is to be given.

[62] An understanding among Members should be developed, as necessary, on matters which are not specified in this Annex or which need further clarification for the purposes of paragraph 1(a) of Article 6.

[63] The recipient firm is a firm in the territory of the subsidizing Member.

[64] In the case of tax-related subsidies the value of the product shall be calculated as the total value of the recipient firm's sales in the fiscal year in which the tax-related measure was earned.

[65] Start-up situations include instances where financial commitments for product development or construction of facilities to manufacture products benefiting from the subsidy have been made, even though production has not begun.

6. In determining the overall rate of subsidization in a given year, subsidies given under different programmes and by different authorities in the territory of a Member shall be aggregated.
7. Subsidies granted prior to the date of entry into force of the WTO Agreement, the benefits of which are allocated to future production, shall be included in the overall rate of subsidization.
8. Subsidies which are non-actionable under relevant provisions of this Agreement shall not be included in the calculation of the amount of a subsidy for the purpose of paragraph 1(a) of Article 6.

ANNEX V PROCEDURES FOR DEVELOPING INFORMATION CONCERNING SERIOUS PREJUDICE

1. Every Member shall cooperate in the development of evidence to be examined by a panel in procedures under paragraphs 4 through 6 of Article 7. The parties to the dispute and any third-country Member concerned shall notify to the DSB, as soon as the provisions of paragraph 4 of Article 7 have been invoked, the organization responsible for administration of this provision within its territory and the procedures to be used to comply with requests for information.
2. In cases where matters are referred to the DSB under paragraph 4 of Article 7, the DSB shall, upon request, initiate the procedure to obtain such information from the government of the subsidizing Member as necessary to establish the existence and amount of subsidization, the value of total sales of the subsidized firms, as well as information necessary to analyse the adverse effects caused by the subsidized product.[66] This process may include, where appropriate, presentation of questions to the government of the subsidizing Member and of the complaining Member to collect information, as well as to clarify and obtain elaboration of information available to the parties to a dispute through the notification procedures set forth in Part VII.[67]
3. In the case of effects in third-country markets, a party to a dispute may collect information, including through the use of questions to the government of the third-country Member, necessary to analyse

[66] In cases where the existence of serious prejudice has to be demonstrated.

[67] The information-gathering process by the DSB shall take into account the need to protect information which is by nature confidential or which is provided on a confidential basis by any Member involved in this process.

adverse effects, which is not otherwise reasonably available from the complaining Member or the subsidizing Member. This requirement should be administered in such a way as not to impose an unreasonable burden on the third-country Member. In particular, such a Member is not expected to make a market or price analysis specially for that purpose. The information to be supplied is that which is already available or can be readily obtained by this Member (e.g. most recent statistics which have already been gathered by relevant statistical services but which have not yet been published, customs data concerning imports and declared values of the products concerned, etc.). However, if a party to a dispute undertakes a detailed market analysis at its own expense, the task of the person or firm conducting such an analysis shall be facilitated by the authorities of the third-country Member and such a person or firm shall be given access to all information which is not normally maintained confidential by the government.

4. The DSB shall designate a representative to serve the function of facilitating the information-gathering process. The sole purpose of the representative shall be to ensure the timely development of the information necessary to facilitate expeditious subsequent multilateral review of the dispute. In particular, the representative may suggest ways to most efficiently solicit necessary information as well as encourage the cooperation of the parties.
5. The information-gathering process outlined in paragraphs 2 through 4 shall be completed within 60 days of the date on which the matter has been referred to the DSB under paragraph 4 of Article 7. The information obtained during this process shall be submitted to the panel established by the DSB in accordance with the provisions of Part X. This information should include, *inter alia*, data concerning the amount of the subsidy in question (and, where appropriate, the value of total sales of the subsidized firms), prices of the subsidized product, prices of the non-subsidized product, prices of other suppliers to the market, changes in the supply of the subsidized product to the market in question and changes in market shares. It should also include rebuttal evidence, as well as such supplemental information as the panel deems relevant in the course of reaching its conclusions.
6. If the subsidizing and/or third-country Member fail to cooperate in the information-gathering process, the complaining Member will present its case of serious prejudice, based on evidence available to

it, together with facts and circumstances of the non-cooperation of the subsidizing and/or third-country Member. Where information is unavailable due to non-cooperation by the subsidizing and/or third-country Member, the panel may complete the record as necessary relying on best information otherwise available.

7. In making its determination, the panel should draw adverse inferences from instances of non- cooperation by any party involved in the information-gathering process.
8. In making a determination to use either best information available or adverse inferences, the panel shall consider the advice of the DSB representative nominated under paragraph 4 as to the reasonableness of any requests for information and the efforts made by parties to comply with these requests in a cooperative and timely manner.
9. Nothing in the information-gathering process shall limit the ability of the panel to seek such additional information it deems essential to a proper resolution to the dispute, and which was not adequately sought or developed during that process. However, ordinarily the panel should not request additional information to complete the record where the information would support a particular party's position and the absence of that information in the record is the result of unreasonable non-cooperation by that party in the information-gathering process.

ANNEX VI PROCEDURES FOR ON-THE-SPOT INVESTIGATIONS PURSUANT TO PARAGRAPH 6 OF ARTICLE 12

1. Upon initiation of an investigation, the authorities of the exporting Member and the firms known to be concerned should be informed of the intention to carry out on-the-spot investigations.
2. If in exceptional circumstances it is intended to include non-governmental experts in the investigating team, the firms and the authorities of the exporting Member should be so informed. Such non-governmental experts should be subject to effective sanctions for breach of confidentiality requirements.
3. It should be standard practice to obtain explicit agreement of the firms concerned in the exporting Member before the visit is finally scheduled.

4. As soon as the agreement of the firms concerned has been obtained, the investigating authorities should notify the authorities of the exporting Member of the names and addresses of the firms to be visited and the dates agreed.
5. Sufficient advance notice should be given to the firms in question before the visit is made.
6. Visits to explain the questionnaire should only be made at the request of an exporting firm. In case of such a request the investigating authorities may place themselves at the disposal of the firm; such a visit may only be made if *(a)* the authorities of the importing Member notify the representatives of the government of the Member in question and *(b)* the latter do not object to the visit.
7. As the main purpose of the on-the-spot investigation is to verify information provided or to obtain further details, it should be carried out after the response to the questionnaire has been received unless the firm agrees to the contrary and the government of the exporting Member is informed by the investigating authorities of the anticipated visit and does not object to it; further, it should be standard practice prior to the visit to advise the firms concerned of the general nature of the information to be verified and of any further information which needs to be provided, though this should not preclude requests to be made on the spot for further details to be provided in the light of information obtained.
8. Enquiries or questions put by the authorities or firms of the exporting Members and essential to a successful on-the-spot investigation should, whenever possible, be answered before the visit is made.

ANNEX VII DEVELOPING COUNTRY MEMBERS REFERRED TO IN PARAGRAPH 2(A) OF ARTICLE 27

The developing country Members not subject to the provisions of paragraph 1(a) of Article 3 under the terms of paragraph 2(a) of Article 27 are:

(a) Least-developed countries designated as such by the United Nations which are Members of the WTO.
(b) Each of the following developing countries which are Members of the WTO shall be subject to the provisions which are applicable to other developing country Members according to paragraph 2(b) of Article 27 when GNP per capita has reached $1,000 per

annum[68]: Bolivia, Cameroon, Congo, Côte d'Ivoire, Dominican Republic, Egypt, Ghana, Guatemala, Guyana, India, Indonesia, Kenya, Morocco, Nicaragua, Nigeria, Pakistan, Philippines, Senegal, Sri Lanka and Zimbabwe.

[68] The inclusion of developing country Members in the list in paragraph (b) is based on the most recent data from the World Bank on GNP per capita.

Appendix 2

Text of Article VI of the General Agreement on Tariffs and Trade as well as the Notes and Supplementary Provisions to Article VI

Article VI

Anti-dumping and Countervailing Duties

1. The contracting parties recognize that dumping, by which products of one country are introduced into the commerce of another country at less than the normal value of the products, is to be condemned if it causes or threatens material injury to an established industry in the territory of a contracting party or materially retards the establishment of a domestic industry. For the purposes of this Article, a product is to be considered as being introduced into the commerce of an importing country at less than its normal value, if the price of the product exported from one country to another

   (a) is less than the comparable price, in the ordinary course of trade, for the like product when destined for consumption in the exporting country, or,
   (b) in the absence of such domestic price, is less than either

      (i) the highest comparable price for the like product for export to any third country in the ordinary course of trade, or
      (ii) the cost of production of the product in the country of origin plus a reasonable addition for selling cost and profit.

   Due allowance shall be made in each case for differences in conditions and terms of sale, for differences in taxation, and for other differences affecting price comparability.*
2. In order to offset or prevent dumping, a contracting party may levy on any dumped product an anti-dumping duty not greater in amount than the margin of dumping in respect of such product. For the purposes of this Article, the margin of dumping is the price difference determined in accordance with the provisions of paragraph 1.*

3. No countervailing duty shall be levied on any product of the territory of any contracting party imported into the territory of another contracting party in excess of an amount equal to the estimated bounty or subsidy determined to have been granted, directly or indirectly, on the manufacture, production or export of such product in the country of origin or exportation, including any special subsidy to the transportation of a particular product. The term 'countervailing duty' shall be understood to mean a special duty levied for the purpose of offsetting any bounty or subsidy bestowed, directly, or indirectly, upon the manufacture, production or export of any merchandise.*
4. No product of the territory of any contracting party imported into the territory of any other contracting party shall be subject to anti-dumping or countervailing duty by reason of the exemption of such product from duties or taxes borne by the like product when destined for consumption in the country of origin or exportation, or by reason of the refund of such duties or taxes.
5. No product of the territory of any contracting party imported into the territory of any other contracting party shall be subject to both anti-dumping and countervailing duties to compensate for the same situation of dumping or export subsidization.
6. (a) No contracting party shall levy any anti-dumping or countervailing duty on the importation of any product of the territory of another contracting party unless it determines that the effect of the dumping or subsidization, as the case may be, is such as to cause or threaten material injury to an established domestic industry, or is such as to retard materially the establishment of a domestic industry.

   (b) The CONTRACTING PARTIES may waive the requirement of subparagraph (*a*) of this paragraph so as to permit a contracting party to levy an anti-dumping or countervailing duty on the importation of any product for the purpose of offsetting dumping or subsidization which causes or threatens material injury to an industry in the territory of another contracting party exporting the product concerned to the territory of the importing contracting party. The CONTRACTING PARTIES shall waive the requirements of subparagraph (*a*) of this paragraph, so as to permit the levying of a countervailing duty, in cases in which they find that a subsidy is causing or threatening material injury to an industry in the territory of another contracting party exporting the product concerned to the territory of the importing contracting party.*

(c) In exceptional circumstances, however, where delay might cause damage which would be difficult to repair, a contracting party may levy a countervailing duty for the purpose referred to in subparagraph (*b*) of this paragraph without the prior approval of the CONTRACTING PARTIES; *Provided* that such action shall be reported immediately to the CONTRACTING PARTIES and that the countervailing duty shall be withdrawn promptly if the CONTRACTING PARTIES disapprove.

7. A system for the stabilization of the domestic price or of the return to domestic producers of a primary commodity, independently of the movements of export prices, which results at times in the sale of the commodity for export at a price lower than the comparable price charged for the like commodity to buyers in the domestic market, shall be presumed not to result in material injury within the meaning of paragraph 6 if it is determined by consultation among the contracting parties substantially interested in the commodity concerned that:

(a) the system has also resulted in the sale of the commodity for export at a price higher than the comparable price charged for the like commodity to buyers in the domestic market, and
(b) the system is so operated, either because of the effective regulation of production, or otherwise, as not to stimulate exports unduly or otherwise seriously prejudice the interests of other contracting parties.

Ad Article VI

Paragraph 1

1. …
2. …

Paragraphs 2 and 3

1. As in many other cases in customs administration, a contracting party may require reasonable security (bond or cash deposit) for the payment of anti-dumping or countervailing duty pending final determination of the facts in any case of suspected dumping or subsidization.

2. Multiple currency practices can in certain circumstances constitute a subsidy to exports which may be met by countervailing duties under paragraph 3 or can constitute a form of dumping by means of a partial depreciation of a country's currency which may be met by action under paragraph 2. By 'multiple currency practices' is meant practices by governments or sanctioned by governments.

Paragraph 6(b)

Waivers under the provisions of this subparagraph shall be granted only on application by the contracting party proposing to levy an anti-dumping or countervailing duty, as the case may be.

BIBLIOGRAPHY

Adamantopoulos, K.; Pereyra, M. J. (2007). *EU Anti-Subsidy Law and Practice*, 2nd edition, London.

Ahn, D. (2011). *United States – Definitive Anti-Dumping and Countervailing Duties on Certain Products from China*, WT/DS379/AB/R, 105:4 *American Journal of International Law*, available at papers.ssrn.com/sol/3/papers.cfm?abstract=1864025.

Anderson, M.; Husisian, G. (1996). The Subsidies Agreement, in Stewart, T. (ed.): *The World Trade Organization: The Multilateral Framework for the 21st Century and U.S. Implementing Legislation*, Chicago, IL, pp. 299–358.

Bagwell, K. W.; Mavroidis, P. C. (2010). Too Much, Too Little … Too Late?, in Bagwell, K. W.; Bermann, G. A.; Mavroidis, P. C. (eds.): *Law and Economics of Contingent Protection in International Trade*, Cambridge, pp. 168–171.

Staiger, R. (2004). *The Economics of the World Trading System*, Cambridge, MA.

Bhagwati, J. (1988). *Protectionism*, Cambridge, MA.

Bohanes, J; Rueda Garcia, D. (2012/1). Case Note Part One: Appellate Body Report in *United States – Measures Affecting Trade in Large Civil Aircraft (Second Complaint)* (DS353) *(US – Boeing)*, 7:9 *Global Trade and Customs Journal* 365–378.

Rueda Garcia, D. (2012/2). 'Automatic' Discovery Procedures in the WTO: The Treatment of Annex V to the SCM Agreement by Appellate Body Report in *United States Measures Affecting Trade in Large Civil Aircraft (Second Complaint)* (DS353) *(US – Boeing)*, 7:10 *Global Trade and Customs Journal* 441–446.

Rueda Garcia, D. (2012/3). Case Note Part One: Appellate Body Report in *United States – Measures Affecting Trade in Large Civil Aircraft (Second Complaint)* (DS353) *(US – Boeing)*, Part II – Serious Prejudice, 7:10 *Global Trade and Customs Journal* 396–405.

Brink, T. (2011). What Is a 'Public Body' for the Purposes of Determining a Subsidy after the Appellate Body Ruling in *US – AD/CVD*, 6:6 *Global Trade and Customs Journal* 313–315.

Cartland, M.; Depayre, G.; Woznowski, J. (2012). Is Something Going Wrong in the WTO Dispute Settlement? 46:5 *Journal of World Trade* 979–1016.

Caryl, B. B. (2011). Is China's Currency Regime a Countervailable Subsidy? A Legal Analysis under the World Trade Organization's SCM Agreement, 45:1 *Journal of World Trade* 187–219.

Charnovitz, S.; Fischer, C. (2015). *Canada – Renewable Energy*: Implications for WTO Law on Green and Not-So-Green Subsidies, 14:2 *World Trade Review* 177–210.

Coppens, D. (2013). How Special Is the Special and Differential Treatment under the SCM Agreement? A Legal and Normative Analysis of WTO Subsidy Disciplines on Developing Countries, 12:1 *World Trade Review* 79–109.

(2014). *WTO Disciplines on Subsidies and Countervailing Measures: Balancing Policy Space and Legal Constraints*, Cambridge.

Cosbey, A. (2013). *Green Industrial Policy and the World Trading System*, ENTWINED Issue Brief 17, Stockholm.

Mavroidis, P. (2014). A Turquoise Mess: Green Subsidies, Blue Industrial Policy and Renewable Energy: The Case for Redrafting the Subsidies Agreement of the WTO, 17:1 *Journal of International Economic Law* 11–47.

Depayre, G. (1995). Subsidies and Countervailing Measures after the Uruguay Round: An Overview, in Bourgois, J.; Berrod, F.; Gippini Fournier, E. (eds.): *The Uruguay Round Results: A European Lawyers' Perspective*, Brussels, pp. 247–254.

Ding, R. (2014). 'Public Body' or Not: Chinese State-Owned Enterprise, 48:1 *Journal of World Trade* 167–190.

Evaluation Study (2012). BKP Development Research & Consulting, *Evaluation of the European Union's Trade Defence Instruments, Volume 1: Main Report*. Published on the website of the European Commission, DG Trade.

Farah, P. D.; Cima, E. (2015). WTO and Renewable Energy: Lessons from the Case Law, 49:6 *Journal of World Trade* 1103–1116.

Fetzer, J. J. (2008). Inference for Econometric Modelling in Antidumping, Countervailing Duty and Safeguard Investigations, 8:4 *World Trade Review* 545–557.

Flett, J. (2012). From Political Pre-occupation to Legitimate Rule against Market Partitioning: Export Subsidies in WTO Law after the Appellate Body Ruling in the *Airbus* Case, 7:2 *Global Trade and Customs Journal* 50–58.

François, J. (2010). Subsidies and Countervailing Measures: Determining the Benefit of Subsidies, in Bagwell, K. W.; Bermann, G. A.; Mavroidis, P. C. (eds.): *Law and Economics of Contingent Protection in International Trade*, Cambridge, pp. 103–115.

Goh, G.; Ziegler, A. R. (2003). Retrospective Remedies in the WTO after *Automobile Leather*, 6:3 *Journal of International Economic Law* 545–564.

Grané, P. (2001). Remedies under WTO Law, 4:4 *Journal of International Economic Law* 755–772.

Green, A; Trebilcock, M. (2010). The Enduring Problem of World Trade Organization Export Subsidies Rules, in Bagwell, K. W.; Bermann, G. A.; Mavroidis, P. C. (eds.): *Law and Economics of Contingent Protection in International Trade*, Cambridge, pp. 116–167.

Grossman, G. M.; Mavroidis, P. C. (2003). *US – Lead and Bismuth II: United States – Imposition of Countervailing Duties on Certain Hot-Rolled Lead and Bismuth Carbon Steel Products Originating in the United Kingdom*: Here Today, Gone Tomorrow? Privatisation and the Injury Caused by Non-Recurring Subsidies?, 2:1 *World Trade Review* 170–200.

Mavroidis, P. C. (2005/1). *United States – Countervailing Duties on Certain Corrosion-Resistant Carbon Steel Flat Products from Germany* (WTO Doc. WT/DS213/AB/R): The Sounds of Silence, 4:1 *World Trade Review* 64–77.

Mavroidis, P. C. (2005/2). *United States – Countervailing Measures Concerning Certain Products from the European Communities* (WTO Doc. WT/DS212/AB/R): Recurring Misunderstanding of Non-Recurring Subsidies, 4:1 *World Trade Review* 78–87.

Grossman, G.; Sykes, A. (2011). 'Optimal' Retaliation in the WTO: A Commentary on the *Upland Cotton* Arbitration, 10:1 *World Trade Review* 133–164.

Guan, S. (2014). WTO Retaliation Rules in Subsidy-Related Cases: What Can We Learn from the *US – Upland Cotton* Arbitration?, 48:4 *Journal of World Trade* 815–842.

Hagemeyer, T. H. (2014). Tied Aid: Immunization for Export Subsidies against the Law of the WTO?, 48:2 *Journal of World Trade* 259–294.

Hahn, M.; Mehta, K. (2013). It's a Bird, It's a Plane: Some Remarks on the *Airbus* Appellate Body Report (*EC and Certain Member States – Large Civil Aircraft*, WT/DS316/AB/R), 12:2 *World Trade Review* 139–161.

Henschke, L. (2012). Going It Alone on Climate Change. A New Challenge to WTO Subsidies Disciplines: Are Subsidies in Support of Emissions Reductions Schemes Permissible under the WTO, 11:1 *World Trade Review* 27–52.

Hestermeyer, H. P.; Nielsen, L. (2014). The Legality of Local Content Measures under WTO Law, 48:3 *Journal of World Trade* 553–592.

Horlick, G. N. (2013/1). An Annotated Explanation of Articles 1 and 2 of the WTO Agreement on Subsidies and Countervailing Measures, 8:9 *Global Trade and Customs Journal* 297–299.

(2013/2). A Personal History of the WTO Subsidies Agreement, 47:2 *Journal of World Trade* 447–452.

Horn, H.; Mavroidis, P. C. (2005). *United States – Preliminary Determination with Respect to Certain Softwood Lumber from Canada*: What Is a Subsidy? 4:1 *World Trade Review* 220–247.

Howse, R. (2010). Do the World Trade Organization Disciplines on Domestic Subsidies Make Sense? The Case for Legalizing Some Subsidies, in Bagwell, K.

W.; Bermann, G. A.; Mavroidis, P. C. (eds.): *Law and Economics of Contingent Protection in International Trade*, Cambridge, pp. 85–102.

Hufbauer, G. C. (2010). Tax Discipline in the WTO, 44:4 *Journal of World Trade* 763–777.

Hufbauer, G. C.; Charnovitz, S.; Kim, J. (2009). *Global Warming and the World Trading System*, Washington, DC.

Shelton-Erb, J. (1984). *Subsidies in International Trade*, Washington, DC.

Jackson, J. H. (2000). *The World Trading System: Law and Policy of International Economic Relations*, 2nd edition, Cambridge (MA).

Janow, M.; Staiger, R. (2003). *US – Export Restraints – Measures Treating Export Restraints as Subsidies*, 2:1 *World Trade Review* 201–235.

Staiger, R. (2004). *Canada – Dairy; Canada – Measures Affecting the Importation of Dairy Products and the Exportation of Milk*, 3:2 *World Trade Review* 277–315; reproduced from: *The WTO Case Law of 2001*, The American Law Institute Reporters' Studies, Cambridge 2003.

Kang, S. (2006). Comment on Annex V of the WTO SCM Agreement Procedures in the Context of *Korea – Shipbuilding* Dispute, 33:2 *Legal Issues of Economic Integration* 183–197.

Kazeki, J. (2010). The 'Middle Pillar': Transparency and Surveillance of Subsidies in the SCM Committee: Reflections after the Global Economic Crisis, 5:5 *Global Trade and Customs Journal* 191–198.

Kelly, B. D. (2014/1). Market Economies and Concurrent Antidumping and Countervailing Duty Remedies, 17:1 *Journal of International Economic Law* 105–123.

(2014/2). The Pass-Through of Subsidies to Price, 48:2 *Journal of World Trade* 295–322.

Krugman, P. R.; Obstfeld, M.; Melitz, M. J. (2015). *International Economics: Theory and Policy*, 10th edition, Harlow.

Lima, A. de; Gaviria, J. A. (2012). A Case for Misaligned Currencies as Countervailable Subsidies, 46:5 *Journal of World Trade* 1017–1044.

Low, P.; Marceau, G.; Reinaud, J. (2012). The Interface between the Trade and Climate Change Regimes: Scoping the Issues, 46:3 *Journal of World Trade* 485–544.

Luengo, E. G. (2007). *Regulation of Subsidies and State Aids and WTO and EC Law*, Alphen aan den Rijn.

McDonough, P. J. (1999). Subsidies and Countervailing Measures, in Stewart, T. P. (ed.): *The GATT Uruguay Round: A Negotiating History (1986–1994), Volume IV: The End Game (Part I)*, The Hague; London; Boston, MA, pp. 221–421.

Maruyama, W. H. (2011). Climate Change and the WTO: Cap and Trade versus Carbon Tax?, 45:4 *Journal of World Trade* 679–726.

Miranda, J. (2010). Causal Link and Non-attribution as Interpreted in WTO Trade Remedy Disputes, 44:4 *Journal of World Trade* 729–762.

Moulis, D.; O'Donnell, B. (2000). Case Comment: Does 'Withdraw the Subsidy' Mean 'Repay the Subsidy'? The Implications of the *Howe Leather* Case for Firms in Receipt of Government Subsidies, 6:5 *International Trade Law and Regulation*.

Narayanan, P. (2004). Injury Investigations in 'Material Retardation' Antidumping Cases, 25:1 *Northwest Journal of International Law & Business* 37–68.

Neven, D.; Sykes, A. (2014). *United States – Measures Affecting Trade in Large Civil Aircraft (Second complaint)*: Some Comments, 13:2 *World Trade Review* 281–298.

Paemen, H.; Bensch, A. (1995). *From the GATT to the WTO: The European Community in the Uruguay Round*, Leuven.

Pal, R. (2014). Has the Appellate Body's Decision in *Canada – Renewable Energy / Canada – Feed-in Tariff Program* Opened the Door for Production Subsidies?, 17:1 *Journal of International Economic Law* 125–134.

Pauwelyn, J. (2013). Treaty Interpretation or Activism? Comment on the AB Report on *United States – ADs and CVDs on Certain Products from China*, 12:2 *World Trade Review* 235–241.

Piérola, F. (2013). The Question of the 'Benefit', 8:9 *Global Trade and Customs Journal* 293–296.

Poretti, P. (2009). *The Regulation of Subsidies within the General Agreement on Trade in Services of the WTO: Problems and Prospects*, Alphen aan den Rijn.

Prusa, T.; Vermulst, E. (2013). *United States – Definitive Anti-Dumping and Countervailing Duties on Certain Products from China*: Passing the Buck on Pass-Through, 12:2 *World Trade Review* 197–234.

Vermulst, E. (2014). *China – Definitive Countervailing Duties and Anti-Dumping Duties on Grain Oriented Flat-rolled Electrical Steel from the United States*: Exporting US AD/CVD Methodologies through WTO Dispute Settlement?, 13:2 *World Trade Review* 229–266.

Vermulst, E. (2015). *China – Definitive Anti-Dumping and Countervailing Measures on Broiler Products from the United States*: How the Chickens Came Home to Roost, 14:2 *World Trade Review* 287–335.

Ramanujan, A. (2015). To Cumulate or Not to Cumulate: That Is the Question, 10:9 *Global Trade and Customs Journal* 308–322.

Ramanujan, A.; Sampath, S. (2015). 'Double Counting': Is There Light at the End of the Tunnel?, 49:2 *Journal of World Trade* 223–252.

Rivers, R.; Greenwald, J. (1979). The Negotiation of a Code on Subsidies and Countervailing Measures: Bridging Fundamental Policy Differences, 11:3 *Law and Policy in International Business* 1447–1495.

Rosenstock, M. (1995). *Die Kontrolle und Harmonisierung nationaler Beihilfen durch die Kommission der Europäischen Gemeinschaften*, Frankfurt am Main.

Rubini, L. (2009). *The Definition of Subsidy and State Aid*, Oxford; New York.

(2012). *Ain't Waistin' Time No More*: Subsidies for Renewable Energy, the SCM Agreement, Policy Space, and Law Reform, 15:2 *Journal of International Economic Law* 525–579.

(2014). 'The Good, the Bad, and the Ugly': Lessons on Methodology in Legal Analysis from the Recent WTO Litigation on Renewable Energy Subsidies, 48:5 *Journal of World Trade* 895–938.

(2015). 'The Wide and the Narrow Gate': Benchmarking in the SCM Agreement after the *Canada-Renewable Energy/FIT* Ruling, 14:2 *World Trade Review* 211–237.

Shadikhodjaev, S. (2012). How to Pass a Pass-Through Test: The Case of Input Subsidies, 15:2 *Journal of International Economic Law* 621–646.

Staiger, R.; Sykes, A. (2010). 'Currency Manipulation' and World Trade, 9:4 *World Trade Review* 583–627.

Steger, D. P. (2010). The Subsidies and Countervailing Measures Agreement: Ahead of Its Time or Time for Reform, 44:4 *Journal of World Trade* 779–796.

Stoler, A. L. (2010). The Evolution of Subsidies Disciplines in GATT and the WTO, 44:4 *Journal of World Trade* 797–808.

Sun, Zesheng; Wang, Shuyun (2013). Revisiting the Economic Effect of Export Subsidy: An Expansion of the Traditional Analysis, 6:1 *Journal of Chinese Economic and Foreign Trade Studies* 35–45.

Sykes, A. O. (2005). Subsidies and Countervailing Measures, in Macrory, P. F. J.; Appleton, A. E.; Plummer, M. G. (eds.): *The World Trade Organization: Legal, Economic and Political Analysis, Volume 2*, Heidelberg, pp. 83–107.

Sykes, A.O. (2010). The Questionable Case for Subsidies Regulation: A Comparative Perspective, 2:2 *Journal of Comparative Legal Analysis* 473–523.

Thorstensen, V.; Müller, C.; Ramos, D. (2015). Exchange Rate Measures: Who Judges the Issue – IMF or WTO?, 18:1 *Journal of International Economic Law* 117–135.

Weber, R. H.; Koch, R. (2015). International Trade Law Challenges by Subsidies for Renewable Energy, 49:5 *Journal of World Trade* 757–780.

Wolfrum, R.; Stoll, P.-W.; Koebele, M. (2008). *WTO: Trade Remedies*, Leiden; Boston, MA.

Wouters, J.; Coppens, C. (2010). An Overview of the Agreement on Subsidies and Countervailing Measures: Including a Discussion of the Agreement on Agriculture, in Bagwell, K. W.; Bermann, G. A.; Mavroidis, P. C.: *Law and Economics of Contingent Protection in International Trade*, Cambridge, pp. 7–84.

Yamaoka, T. (2013). Analysis of China's Accession Commitments in the WTO: New Taxonomy of More and Less Stringent Commitments, and the Struggle for Mitigation by China, 47:1 *Journal of World Trade* 105–158.

INDEX